T0329826

Globalization and Sustainable Development in Africa

Rochester Studies in
African History and the Diaspora

Toyin Falola, Series Editor
The Frances Higginbotham Nalle Centennial Professor in History
University of Texas at Austin

(ISSN: 1092-5228)

A complete list of titles in the Rochester Studies in African History and the Diaspora series, in order of publication, may be found at the end of this book.

Globalization and Sustainable Development in Africa

Edited by Bessie House-Soremekun and
Toyin Falola

UNIVERSITY OF ROCHESTER PRESS

First published 2011
Reprinted in paperback and transferred to digital printing 2016

University of Rochester Press
668 Mt. Hope Avenue, Rochester, NY 14620, USA
www.urpress.com
and Boydell & Brewer Limited
PO Box 9, Woodbridge, Suffolk IP12 3DF, UK
www.boydellandbrewer.com

hardcover ISBN-13: 978-1-58046-392-8
paperback ISBN-13: 978-1-58046-550-2
ISSN: 1092-5228

Library of Congress Cataloging-in-Publication Data

Globalization and sustainable development in Africa / edited by Bessie House-Soremekun and Toyin Falola.
p. cm. — (Rochester studies in African history and the diaspora, ISSN 1092-5228 ; v. 51)
Includes bibliographical references and index.
ISBN 978-1-58046-392-8 (hardcover : alk. paper) 1. Sustainable development—Africa. 2. Globalization—Africa. 3. Africa—Economic policy. 4. Africa—Economic conditions—1960– I. House-Soremekun, Bessie, 1956– II. Falola, Toyin. III. Series: Rochester studies in African history and the diaspora ; v. 51.
HC800.Z9E5447 2011
338.96'07—dc23

2011019571

A catalogue record for this title is available from the British Library.

This publication is printed on acid-free paper.
Printed in the United States of America.

Cover image: *Yo*, 2006 oil painting by dele jegede. Cover design: Frank Gutbrod.

This book is dedicated to Chief Dr. Maurice Adekunle Ebun Soremekun.
Thanks for your unswerving support and encouragement.
We are very grateful.

Contents

Part Three: Industrial and Financial Networking

Part Four: Insecurity and Conflicts

Preface

As the processes of globalization have accelerated in recent decades, virtually all countries of the world have experienced its multifaceted impacts, most particularly as we move further into the twenty-first century. Economic restructuring processes, which have been underway for several decades, have posed new challenges for nation-states and the international citizenry within the changing contours of the global economy. These challenges are likely to persist in the coming decades as a result of technological changes, an increase in international-trade activities, the widening digital divide, global warming, and the increasing levels of complexity that characterize contemporary political and economic relationships.

This edited volume is the outgrowth of the First Public Scholars in Africana Studies International Conference on Globalization which was held at Indiana University–Purdue University Indianapolis (IUPUI) from October 29–31, 2009. The theme of the conference was "Rethinking Economic Development in the Context of Globalization: Entrepreneurship, the Knowledge Economy, and Sustainable Development." The purpose of the conference was to examine the impacts of globalization on various countries of the world, with a particular emphasis on Africa and the African Diaspora. Scholars were asked to rethink and reconceptualize globalization within the broader context of the twenty-first century knowledge economy and efforts put forward by nation-states of the world to achieve sustainable development. A second goal of the conference was to develop public policy recommendations that could be implemented by nation-states, political leaders, NGOs, and members of the public at large to enhance the attainment of economic and sustainable development. Although not all the presenters are represented here, we would like to acknowledge the contributions of all of them.

We have numerous people to thank for their support in helping us to organize the conference. We are grateful to Dr. Charles Bantz, chancellor at Indiana University–Purdue University Indianapolis for his strong support of the event as well as Dr. Uday Sukhatme, executive vice chancellor and dean of the faculties, Dr. William Blomquist, dean of the School of Liberal Arts, and Dr. Monroe Little, former director of the Africana Studies Program. We are especially grateful to His Royal Majesty, Oba Michael Adedotun Gbadebo, the Alake and Paramount Ruler of Egbaland and Her Royal Majesty, Olori, Dr. Tokunbo Gbadebo for being our special guests for four days during the week of the conference and for the wonderful keynote address provided by His Royal Majesty at the Awards Dinner. We want to thank all of the members of the organizing committee as well as our conference sponsors, which include The Public Scholars in Africana Studies, the Olaniyan Scholars, the IUPUI School of Liberal Arts, the Africana Studies Program, the Office of the Chancellor, the IUPUI Fortieth Anniversary Fund Grant, the New Perspectives in the Humanities Grant, the IU Conference and Workshop Grant, the Academic Affairs Conference Grant, the Office of the Assistant Chancellor for Diversity, Equity and Inclusion, the Office of the Vice-Chancellor for Research, the Office of the Indiana University Foundation, the Office of the Associate Vice Chancellor for International Programs, the Office of the Dean of Health and Rehabilitation Sciences, the Committee on African and African American Studies (CAAS), the Solution Center Venture Fund Grant, the Egba National Association and New York Chapter, the University Place Hotel and Conference Center, the Above and Beyond Limousine Services, Inc., the Circle City Chapter of the Links, Inc., Mr. and Mrs. Kayode Akiwowo and Chiefs Drs. Maurice and Bessie Soremekun. We are grateful to our community partners that include Mr. Shola Ajiboye, Mrs. Cynthia Bates, Mr. Dave Rozzell, and Mr. Peter Kirkwood.

We also acknowledge the wonderful keynote presentations made by Dr. Keenan Grenell, Dr. Toyin Falola, and Chief Jimmy Gboyega Delano, as well as the numerous scholars who presented papers at the conference, some of whom also made significant contributions to this book. These scholars represented North America, South America, Africa, and Europe. We are grateful to the panel chairs, college student presenters, as well as student participants from the Crispus Attucks Medical Magnet High School in Indianapolis who presented a wonderful roundtable discussion on strategies that can be used to improve relations between Africans and African Americans.

We would also like to thank Ms. Suzanne Guiod, editorial director for the University of Rochester Press, members of the editorial board, as well as the reviewers of this manuscript who provided insightful comments on ways to strengthen our work. Last, we acknowledge the wonderful support we have received from our respective spouses, Chief Dr. Maurice A. E. Soremekun and Mrs. Bisi Falola, and our children.

Bessie House-Soremekun
Indiana University–Purdue University Indianapolis

Toyin Falola
University of Texas at Austin

Some of the attendees at the First Public Scholars in Africana Studies International Conference on Globalization, October 29–31, 2009, Indiana University–Purdue University Indianapolis.

His Royal Majesty Oba Michael Adedotun Gbadebo receives the key to the city from Honorable Greg Ballard, mayor of Indianapolis, Indiana, October 29, 2009.

His Royal Majesty Oba Michael Adedotun Gbadebo, Her Royal Majesty Olori Dr. (Mrs.) Tokunbo Gbadebo, Honorable Mayor Greg Ballard, officials from the Mayor's Office, IUPUI officials, conference attendees, and members of the community.

Teachers and student participants from Crispus Attucks Medical Magnet High School participate in the conference.

His Royal Majesty Oba Gbadebo receives the Africana Studies Appreciation Award from Dr. Charles Bantz, Chancellor of Indiana University–Purdue University Indianapolis.

Dr. Toyin Falola receives the Africana Studies Distinguished Global Scholar Lifetime Achievement Award from Chancellor Charles Bantz and Chief Dr. Mrs. Bessie House-Soremekun, conference convener.

Mr. Dave Rozzell; Chief Dr. Mrs. Bessie House-Soremekun; her daughter, Miss Adrianna Midamba; and her husband, Chief Dr. Maurice A. E. Soremekun.

Abbreviations

ACM	African Common Market
ADB	African Development Bank
AEC	African Economic Community
AKDN	Aga Khan Development Network
AMU	Arab Maghreb Union
AU	African Union
CEMAC	Communaute Economique et Monetaire de l'Afrique Centrale (Economic and Monetary Community of Central Africa)
CENSAD	Community of Sahel-Saharan States
CEPGL	Economic Community of Great Lake Countries
CMA	Common Monetary Area
COMESA	Common Market for Eastern and Southern Africa
CSR	corporate social responsibility
EAC	East African Community
EBID	Ecowas Bank for Investment and Development
Ecobank	Ecowas Bank Group
ECOWAS	Economic Community of West African States
EFCCD	Ecowas Fund for Cooperation, Compensation, and Development
EGI	economic globalization index
ERDB	Ecowas Regional Development Bank
ERDF	Ecowas Regional Development Fund
EU	European Union
FDI	foreign direct investment
FTA	free trade area
GATS	General Agreement on Trade in Services

ICT	information and communication technology
IGAD	Inter-Governmental Authority on Development
ILO	International Labor Organization
IMF	International Monetary Fund
IOC	Indian Ocean Commission
MNCs	multinational corporations
NEPAD	New Partnership for African Development
OCA	optimum currency area
RDPs	regional development poles
RECs	regional economic communities
SADC	Southern African Development Community
SAPs	structural adjustment programs
SROI	social return on investment
SSA	sub-Saharan Africa
SMEs	small and medium enterprises
UDEAC	Customs and Economic Union of Central Africa
UEMOA	Union E'conomique et Monetaire-Ouest Africaine (West African Economic and Monetary Union)
UNDP	United Nations Development Programme
VAT	value-added tax
WAMZ	West African Monetary Zone
WAMI	West African Monetary Institute
WB	World Bank
WTO	World Trade Organization

Introduction

Africana in the Margins

Toyin Falola and Bessie House-Soremekun

This particular moment in history is perfectly easy to interpret. Globalization presents Africa and black people as marginal: globalizing economies seek resources from every corner of the world, and globalized economies reap considerable benefits from their economic and political dominance. The "wealth of nations," to borrow the title of Adam Smith's famous book, is used not only to develop the resources within the boundaries of nation-states but also to tap into the resources of other countries. Africa has given to the outside world more than it has received in return, creating the basis to talk about the *poverty* of nations. Defenders of globalization insist that it represents progress for all nations, the ultimate peak of human progress. Globalization's critics point to the devastation of the environment, climate change, depletion of natural and mineral resources, labor exploitation, expropriation or control of land belonging to the poor, and indigenous profiting from food production as significant negative consequences.[1]

Africa is a case study of both positions, providing examples of the benefits and problems of globalization. Africa experiences globalization "from above," that is, a situation where powerful nations and companies with more resources are able to control the major actions and policies that determine the characteristics of global encounters.[2] If Africa is part of the equation of globalization "from below," any discussion of its place in the global system will draw us into issues of nationalism and resistance—how Africans can mobilize themselves to win power and privileges, and how international institutions must be reformed. The actors who control globalization from above often call on African countries to practice democracy, but the same democratic principles do not apply to the United Nations Security Council, where a handful of countries have veto power. Enormously powerful international financial institutions are not always accountable and transparent, and they have the capacity to enforce unpopular neoliberal policies, thus ensuring that the autocratic organization of globalization hurts Africa in such aspects as currency value, commodity pricing, and debt servicing. The challenge that Africans face is to seek the means to extend the benefits of globalization while curtailing the negative impacts on their worldview, culture, and values that hold together families, communities, and clans.

The encounters of Africa in particular and black people in general with the forces of globalization since the fifteenth century have been devastating for the most part. The evidence of domination and exploitation is clear to see, largely the result of a gradual process of incorporation of a periphery into the network of emerging global capitalism. The worth of Africa, indeed of black people, is the monetary value of their labor and their products when they are converted into cash. Global interactions can produce goods and services such that the rewards are not equal: powerful and dominant countries have far more resources from which to benefit than weaker ones. Consequently, we must focus on the pitfalls and drawbacks of this encounter before we can contextualize globalization's future possibilities.

To those who are ever impatient about change and the future, the past can appear irrelevant. To the contrary, the past is relevant, as it explains the emergence of contemporary structures and institutions. The imagination of a better future rests in part on the assumption that the limitations and weaknesses of contemporary arrangements can be corrected and transcended. The potential of people to effect change depends on necessary resources and capabilities. Dreams are one thing; turning them into realities is another thing altogether.

Just as globalization cannot be understood without the exploitation of black people, Africa and the African diaspora are not new to the phenomenon of globalization. Indeed, the history of black people cannot be fully understood without understanding their encounters with other races as structured by global economic and political forces underlying interactions and exchanges.[3] Migrations and transborder movements are common features of African history.[4] North Africa was part of the globalized empires of the Greco-Roman and Islamic worlds. The gold produced in the Mali Empire during the thirteenth century reached Europe. The leather of Kano, renamed in some literature as Moroccan leather, reached North Africa and the Middle East. The palm oil and palm kernels of the Niger Delta also found their way north. These facts point to the extensive long-distance trade between Africa and the rest of the world, within Africa, and among black people in various locations. Indeed, the examples supply evidence for the view that the present phenomenon of globalization has a "global heritage" made up of contributions from all parts of the world. The evidence of contacts shows the elements of history and time—how global forces have deep historical roots—and of space—how various places are connected. Whether in the trade of palm oil from the Niger Delta to Europe or of crude oil from the Niger Delta to the United States, we encounter the globalized past and the globalized present, and the role of commodities whose transactions are facilitated by global finance, communications, and technologies. We also encounter power, as in the ability of past colonial governments to take palm oil to Europe and of contemporary Western states to consume crude oil extracted elsewhere. The features and scale of globalization vary from time to time, depending on how economies, cultures, and places are linked. Even today, Lagos in Nigeria and Johannesburg in South Africa are far more connected to the non-African world than to many smaller African cities.

The colonial era extended the reach of globalization. Remarkable improvements in the technology of violence—for example, the Gatling and Maxim guns—delivered Africa to the Europeans. The economic practices of the time, in particular international commerce facilitated by the movement of companies and capital, favored the purchase of African products. Foreign companies established networks to extract minerals, buy crops, and exploit labor. Labor became mobile, as workers were moved from one area to another to ensure production. Commercial and political networks of empire linked Africa to other parts of the world.[5] Migrations outside the continent continued in various forms. As Africans were drawn into the two world wars, recruited as soldiers, thousands were enabled to visit other places. Many migrated within Africa to work in areas with minerals, and some went to Europe or the United States in pursuit of higher education.

If history is important, so too is ideology. Economic systems shape the institutions of nation-states, but they also shape the relationships between nations. Globalization, as far as Africa is involved, is dominated by capitalism and capitalist expansion. Even though a few postcolonial African countries tried the socialist alternative, the dominant ideology of their engagement with other nations was still structured by capitalism. The constant features of capitalist ideology have not necessarily benefited Africa. The assumption of a free market where productive labor will earn good incomes, and where producers will reap good profits, did not work within colonial regimes because profits went to foreign firms and governments while workers were forced to produce for survival wages. The assumption that market forces will regulate prices and the quantity of surpluses released for trade has not always panned out. African countries do not control the prices they receive for their exports nor what they pay for imports. Not only do they produce for external markets at the expense of food production, there is no "market arena" where the millions of local producers can negotiate over prices with their external buyers. The mediators—the firms that buy locally and sell abroad—do not necessarily face competition. Governments regulate the economy in ways that favor the accumulation of resources to be distributed not to advance domestic economic expansion but to maintain a hold on power. The politics of prebendalism—the use of state resources for personal political agendas—affect how public policies are formulated and implemented. Corruption and wasteful public spending ensure that the gains and promises of capitalism are already compromised.

Throughout the twentieth century, Africa had to wrestle with the challenges of modernization, Westernization, and globalization, all of which are synonymous to many. Christianity spread along with Western education, producing a new set of Africans with ideas and skills connected to the West's values and its formal economic system. Nation-states were created to replace older indigenous nations. Africans were connected with the outside world mainly as suppliers of raw materials and consumers of finished products. Africans became converted to what Karl Polanyi characterized as "fictitious commodities," objects who existed so that the market could function.[6] In the last few decades, capitalism has been extended to Africa in its most conservative forms, sold in a warfare mode by the World Bank and the International Monetary Fund (IMF) as a package of structural adjustment programs (SAPs) that insisted on devaluation of currencies, reduction in the size of bureaucracies, and privatization of business enterprises. Peasant products were to be obtained for cheap, and foreign companies were granted easier access to them. Market forces were extended even to villages accustomed to subsistence livelihoods. People were called upon to think globally, which meant to think about cash to purchase imported items. As social services were cut back, and jobs became harder to find, many people took to the streets in protest. Politics became highly unstable, and the neoliberal form of globalization became, for many, a deadly poison.

Over the last few decades, the world community has witnessed a tremendous intensification of globalization's processes and their attendant impacts on politics, economics, culture, and society. There has been an economic restructuring of many economies in the global North from a previous overreliance on manufacturing and agriculture as the basis for their development to an orientation now characterized by a proliferation of service-related enterprises. Moreover, the economic gap between countries of the North and the South has widened considerably, even as new economic superpowers such as China and India are playing more important roles. These effects are expected to intensify further in the coming years as a result of increased international trade, further reliance on the outsourcing of jobs from the North to the South, technological advances, climate change, and the widening digital divide.

Although a large literature has emerged that examines the phenomenon of globalization in its various modalities, few studies have provided a comprehensive analysis of the impact of globalization on African societies within the much broader context of sustainable development initiatives. It is in this area that the present volume makes an important contribution. Although some of the chapters presented here are situated within an analysis of broader historical processes, the majority focus primary attention on the postcolonial period. This collection enhances the state of knowledge on globalization with regard to sub-Saharan African countries in several important ways: First, the individual chapters interrogate both the theoretical and the empirical aspects of African economic and sustainable development initiatives in the era of globalization. While providing comprehensive analyses of theoretical issues that revolve around the complex processes of globalization, they also present detailed examinations of innovative and creative models of economic development that can be implemented in sub-Saharan Africa to drive economic growth, improve self-sufficiency, and promote sustainable development. In this way, we contextualize the issues in a framework that can be easily accessed by politicians, public policy analysts, scholars, students, international organizations, nongovernmental actors, and members of the public at large. Some of these models utilize the tremendous knowledge and capabilities of diasporic Africans, as well as new strategies of sustainability entrepreneurship.

Second, while many of the scholarly studies performed thus far have examined the impacts of globalization at the international level, this volume focuses on three levels: international, national, and local. Third, we provide insightful case studies of African countries that demonstrate creative and indigenous-based models of entrepreneurship and discuss efforts to achieve sustainable development and economic independence at the grassroots level of society. Another unique feature of this volume is its interdisciplinary nature. Contributors represent the disciplines of law, history, political science, economics, sociology, anthropology, business and management, African studies, art history, and education. They also reflect gender diversity and a sampling of scholarship from four continents: Africa, Europe, North America, and South America.

The essays are presented here in four parts. In part 1, we examine the multifaceted impacts of globalization on development prospects in African societies, with a particular emphasis on economic and sustainable development. While the contributors to this volume acknowledge that Africa has been besieged by the forces of globalization for a very long time, a general consensus is emerging that in more recent decades (e.g., the 1980s), the introduction of SAPs, implemented by the World Bank and IMF, had particularly dire impacts on Africa's economic prospects. To quote Baiyee-Mbi Agbor-Baiyee:

> According to the requirements of these SAPs, SSA nations, like other developing countries, were forced to adopt neoliberal concepts of market reform, currency devaluation, trade liberalization, and divestment or privatization of state-owned and state-run institutions. . . . The structural adjustment programs were abandoned in the mid-1990s because of the significant hardship they imposed on the poor in the region. Whether stated explicitly or not, the design of SAPs conceived SSA governments as constraints to socioeconomic

development. . . . The unanticipated consequence of SAPs was that without a vibrant private sector to provide employment and to absorb some of the responsibilities of the government, there was a general decrease in levels of public investment and social services provided by the governments. . . . The situation was worsened by high rates of inflation caused by the devaluation of SSA currencies—resulting in a significant rise in the prices of basic goods and services and the overall cost of living.[7]

In chapter 1, Martin Spechler examines globalization with a broad brush to explicate why more than a billion global citizens have not yet experienced its positive benefits. He argues that although most countries of the world have been affected by the processes of globalization to date, some countries have clearly benefited more than others. He notes that over the last twenty years in particular both the volume of world trade and net private investment have drastically increased. Multinational corporations have proliferated across the world, and the level of foreign direct investment has risen. He posits that most of the countries that opened their economies to the new imperatives of free trade experienced positive benefits. However, by itself openness to world trade, although important, is not a sufficient factor to accelerate economic growth and prosperity. Other variables that are also important include the provision of public education and health care, good governance structures, and equitable distributions of wealth and resources. In spite of these factors, one-fifth of the world's population of 6.6 billion still live in countries whose national incomes are only $935 per capita. Spechler emphasizes that globalization has had both positive and negative impacts on the poor countries of the world. Sub-Saharan African countries, similar to Caribbean and Latin American states, experienced sluggish economic growth during the last three decades. Per capita GDP declined by 1 percent each year in 32 countries in SSA from 1980 through the 1990s. Since 2005, roughly half of Africa's people (380 million) have been living on less than $1.25 each day. He attributes the declining economic growth rates during some of the periods he discusses to a number of factors such as Africans' inability to take advantage of global economic opportunities, loss of their former share of world markets, and failure to effectively diversify their economies.

In chapter 2, Baiyee-Mbi Agbor-Baiyee further expands the analysis of globalization's impact on development in Africa by providing an assessment of how well sub-Saharan African countries are faring in the era of globalization. To accomplish his goal, he compares and contrasts Africa's competitiveness with that of three other developing regions of the world—Southeast Asia, Latin America, and the Caribbean. He also identifies the five best-performing countries in sub-Saharan Africa based on the 2007 global competitiveness rankings (e.g., South Africa, Mauritius, Botswana, Namibia, and Kenya), as well as the sources of their competitive edge, in order to explain the best practices utilized by these countries in attaining a degree of economic success. He argues that these best practices can in turn be utilized by other countries in the region that share similar socioeconomic challenges. He makes use of the World Economic Forum's Global Competitiveness Index, the UN's Millennium Development Goals, and the World Bank's Global Development Indicators. Based on his statistical analyses, sub-Saharan African countries ranked in last place in all four of the basic competitiveness factors, which include effectiveness of institutions, infrastructural development, achievements in health and primary education, and effectiveness of the macroeconomic environment. When comparing the regions on the basis of performance as measured by the efficiency enhancers index, which influences factors that drive what Agbor-Baiyee calls the "efficiency-driven stage of development," sub-Saharan Africa was again in last place. The SSA region, however, ranked first in the area of business sophistication but was again in last place in terms of technological innovation. All of the developing regions were able to ameliorate their citizens' access to universal primary education except East Asia and the Pacific, while childhood mortality rates also declined in all of the developing regions. SSA also made the largest increase in the rate of contraceptive prevalence, and all of the developing regions achieved improvements in the area of gender equality and access to improved sanitation.

Chapters 3, 4, and 5 each offer prescriptive solutions and strategies that African countries can use to achieve genuine sustainable development. Benaiah Yongo-Bure shifts the focus of attention in chapter 3 to the importance of revisiting and implementing workable strategies such as creating "regional development poles," utilizing principles of self-reliance, and improving existing regional organizations and groupings on the continent that he believes are currently beset with problems of inconvertible currencies, the inability of member countries to produce diversified manufactured goods to trade within the groupings, and numerous nontariff barriers. According to Yongo-Bure, the rationale behind creating "regional development poles" is that these configurations will allow for African countries that are of sufficient size to industrialize relying on their own capacities while utilizing their significant human and natural resource endowments. These countries can develop into diversified industrialized economies that will in turn diffuse economic development to neighboring African states. Yongo-Bure argues that enhancing transportation and communication networks will greatly facilitate the economic development process. Overall, development that is sustained will greatly enhance Africa's standing and competitiveness in the context of globalization.

In chapter 4, Stephen Kpinpuo examines the critical role that Africans can play in enhancing development prospects through a renewed emphasis on improving the quality of education—both what is taught to Africans on the continent and what Americans learn about Africa and Africans in the US school system; incorporating sound governance structures in democratic African societies; and utilizing African cultural values of collective self-reliance and self-help initiatives to foster greater economic independence. While positing that African countries should emulate China and other East Asian nations with regard to the implementation of self-help projects to stimulate the attainment of sustainable development and economic growth, he points to many positive cultural values of African societies that if reasserted would give African countries a greater impact internationally. One of these cultural values is the African virtue of emphasizing the "we" over the "I," collective achievement and collective development over individual success. Within this context, he supports the continuous elevation of group pursuits including Pan-Africanism, patriotism, sound governance, cultural sharing as well as commitments to peace and security, and self-reliance. He emphasizes that globalization and interdependence are ultimately concerned with sharing and fostering collaborative activities and networking among members within the same communities or members of global communities. Consequently, reasserting the African cultural belief that "we are our brother's keeper" is in perfect alignment with the increasing demands that Africa find ways to successfully interact in a "globalizing world."

Chapter 5, by Rubin Patterson, introduces other innovative and creative strategies to assist Africa in attaining its sustainable development goals in the twenty-first-century global economy. While drawing on his previous research in this area as well as interviews and fieldwork recently performed in India and South Africa, he examines in some detail the important and ongoing relationship between developing viable sources of renewable energy, utilizing the migration-development model to enhance Africa's economic prospects, and practicing principles of sustainability entrepreneurship. Patterson emphasizes the urgent need of African countries to use innovative approaches to commercialize renewable energy sources that will protect their environments while simultaneously jumpstarting their economies. Patterson asserts that African countries can not only pioneer the development of green technologies, rather than competing with advanced countries in such areas as steel and computers, but also possibly emerge as early adopters of technologies that would help immeasurably to rejuvenate their economies and enhance the quality of life of their citizenry, if they move aggressively in this direction. The adoption of the migration-development model, which Patterson supports, was earlier used by European countries in the early 1900s and Asian countries later in the same century. The use of this model could greatly assist African countries because the requisite educational training is not readily available on the continent to spearhead the green innovations that are needed. Therefore, Patterson asserts the need to draw from the knowledge base of diasporic Africans whose tremendous human capital can help not only in the research phase but also in the commercialization phase of ecoindustrial technologies. Some African citizens can also migrate to countries that are utilizing cutting-edge techniques so that they can learn this information and make it available to African leaders. Patterson also discusses how African leaders can provide environments that are conducive to the development of sustainability entrepreneurship activities in Africa. Although some sustainability entrepreneurs focus on maximization of profit in their businesses, others aim to have a social impact.

In part 2 of this volume, we analyze the impacts of globalization on nation-states as well as on the local actors at the grassroots. Karen Bravo discusses in chapter 6 some of the inherent contradictions between the operation of trade liberalization and the imperatives of free trade in the post–World War II period with regard to activities of nation-states in contradistinction to the constraints that state actions place on the immobility of the transnational labor market. Chapters 7, 8, and 9 look at another part of this equation, the role of entrepreneurs in creating wealth and jobs for labor (workers) at the local level. According to Bravo, the crux of the matter is the virtual incompatibility between domestic immigration laws created by individual nation-states to curtail the free movement of labor from one country to another that often run counter to international trade laws that facilitate the free movement of goods, capital, services, and ideas across nation-state borders. The unresolved conflicts described above often lead to an increased incidence of illegal movement of workers across national boundaries and other exploitative activities. Bravo points out how these factors militate against the attainment of a truly globalized world, arguing in favor of the development and implementation of a global social contract that would protect labor and liberalize it from the stringent constraints currently imposed by nation-states in the global economy.

Chapters 7 and 8 introduce gender into our discourse by highlighting the role of women microentrepreneurs in African societies. In chapter 7, Gracia Clark draws on her extensive research performed since 1978 on the Asante ethnic group in Ghana to examine the tremendous contributions of African women market traders in Kumasi Central Market in enhancing economic development and creating sustainable economies. Clark argues that these women, through their involvement in trade and commercial activities, acquired a unique point of view of globalization's cultural and economic processes. Assessing women's entrepreneurial activities also provides significant insights with regard to predicting and assessing various trends in the globalization process. For example, these traders often observe conditions that influence the ongoing dynamics between supply and demand in a variety of areas that connect rural communities with urban neighborhoods in various business enterprises across the globe. They also see firsthand the manner in which producers and consumers interact on a number of important levels that involve internal and external factors. They must also maintain successful businesses through periods of instability in their country. They are also affected by economic and political changes at the global level that trigger impacts all the way down to the local level of African societies. Her research on Ghanaian market women demonstrates that there is a strong connection between the local and the global and that gender is also interwoven in a significant way into these important linkages.

Mary Johnson Osirim in chapter 8 provides an insightful analysis of the role of Zimbabwean women microentrepreneurs to explain how they carried a disproportionate share of the impacts of globalization when economic structural adjustment programs were imposed by the World Bank and IMF in 1990–91 and the Enhanced Structural Adjustment Facility a few years later in 1995. While drawing on tenets of feminist political economy theory as well as fieldwork carried out during the 1990s in Harare and Bulawayo, the two largest cities in Zimbabwe, she skillfully demonstrates how the women dealt with higher user fees for many social services, increased levels of competition and costs, and rising levels of unemployment and underemployment in their family units and in the country as a whole. Osirim provides a nuanced and informative historical analysis of Zimbabwe's transition from a colonial to a postcolonial state as well as the impacts of race and gender in developing an inequitable status quo; she then discusses how women entrepreneurs who were involved in sewing, crocheting, hairdressing, and market trade in the era of SAPs were able to maintain successful businesses and create jobs for members of their communities. They also learned how to reinvest their profits back into their businesses. They used innovative strategies to diversify both the production and the sales of their products as well as to utilize subcontracting opportunities to make their businesses more profitable.

While presenting the findings of fieldwork that was conducted at the International University of Grand-Bassam in Côte d'Ivoire in chapter 9, Ulf Richter makes a compelling assessment of ways local entrepreneurial activities can be stimulated to optimize the chances for developing more inclusive, pro-poor markets and to emphasize local cultures. He analyzes the extent to which an interactive e-commerce website that focuses on local artisanal products from West Africa can generate employment, foster entrepreneurship, and decrease poverty. He also identifies some of the major barriers that will need to be eliminated to attain these goals. His major argument is that the creation of employment opportunities for the citizenry at the local level through the promotion of artisanal work can make a positive contribution to enhancing Africans' attainment of business and technological skills and to successfully integrating African businesses into the global economy. Moreover, if steps can be taken to successfully decrease the political instability that currently exists in Côte d'Ivoire as well as the high level of corruption, it will be possible to use e-commerce to create positive economic change.

While the chapters in part 2 of this volume focus primary attention on the microlevel of analysis by highlighting links between local business activities and the global economy through the pivotal role of microentrepreneurs, the chapters in part 3 focus on "industrial and financial networking." Here, analysis is used to examine (a) regional prospects for creating an independent currency union, (b) the effects of SAPs on industrial development in Africa, (c) the growing imperative for countries in the global South to attract international capital, (d) the changing nexus of countries providing aid and loans to African states in the era of globalization, and (e) a variety of foreign direct investment activities conducted mostly under the auspices of multinational corporations.

In chapter 10, Christopher Warburton explores the possibility of developing an independent currency union for West African states. While drawing on World Bank time series data for the period 2000–2006, he asserts that French-speaking countries that are more globalized exhibit fairly low rates of inflation, albeit some of them taken collectively experience higher inflation rates. He found that countries that are "aspiring" to develop a monetary union demonstrated a lack of beta and sigma convergence when intragroup comparisons and extragroup comparisons were examined. More important, some West African countries were more *dollarized*, and this factor increased their potential for becoming economically integrated in the global economy more than did the presence of an independent currency union per se. The process of globalization, therefore, tends to favor the discarding of inconvertible currencies for convertible ones. According to Warburton, the inability of viable African states to establish a currency union will lead to further negative experiences of inconvertible currencies and instances of monetary nationalism. He further points out that member countries of the West African Economic and Monetary Union (WAEMU)—namely, Nigeria, Sierra Leone, Guinea, and Gambia (Gambia he argues is an exception)— experience higher rates of inflation in comparison to the de facto dollarized optimum currency area of the former French colonies and the de jure dollarized countries of Latin America. When discussing the inability of some countries to attain convergence for the creation of an optimum currency area (OCA), he argues that such a condition will continue significantly to hamper their ability to integrate successfully into global markets to acquire the desired resources that are so vital in providing economic stability, while increasing their production output and reducing unemployment.

Ulf Richter presents an interesting case study of Côte d'Ivoire in chapter 11 in which he examines the effects of globalization on its emerging markets. While pointing to the relative paucity of studies since 2002 that examine changes in Côte d'Ivoire, particularly developmental and industrialization polices in a time when China and India are also increasing their ties and levels of investment in Africa, Richter presents findings on this topic drawn from his field research in 2009. He briefly sketches the history of Ivorian development, explaining how the country, once considered a model of political stability and peaceful relations, subsequently became a high-risk area for investment activities primarily because of political destabilization. Richter recounts the successful military coup in 1999 that led to civil conflict and political instability, the failed military coup in 2002 that catapulted the country into full civil war, and the continual conflict and economic and political decline that occurred in the war's aftermath. He argues that a number of potential investors were waiting for the first postconflict elections to take place, which finally occurred in two rounds on October 31, 2010, and November 28, 2010. He discusses the importance of conflict diamonds, the impact of the discovery of oil reserves on generating economic wealth, the activities of multinational corporations, the prospects of achieving economic success through the use of joint ventures, and the changing investment patterns of Côte d'Ivoire's trading partners.

Chapters 12, 13, and 14, written by Kola Subair, Iyiola Ajayi and Adeyemi Babalola, and Charles Mambula, respectively, present insightful case studies of different aspects of Nigeria's challenges with regard to globalization. Subair uses time series analysis to examine the condition of the Nigerian industrial sector both prior to the onset of globalization and during the globalization process. He concludes that globalization led to deindustrialization in Nigeria. In particular, he argues that industrial policy in the country was defined by high costs of production, low levels of foreign investment, low capacity utilization, a high concentration of industries in particular geographic areas, and high levels of industrial imports even before SAPs were introduced. The impact of all of these variables, in conjunction with other factors, led to declining industrial capacity. Thus, Nigeria already had a weakened economic position when structural adjustment programs were first imposed, with the end result being that manufacturing's share of GDP continued to decline. Subair argues that the processes of liberalization, privatization, and deregulation, all fundamental components of globalization, led to an environment in which MNCs proliferated in the global South and invested heavily in extractive industries rather than in manufacturing. Countries such as Nigeria got short shrift in these economic relationships.

In "Interest Rates, Fiscal Policy, and Foreign Private Investment in Nigeria," Ajayi and Babalola discuss Nigeria's inability to garner sufficient foreign domestic investment to significantly enhance its economy. A number of studies have demonstrated that FDI is an important catalyst for economic growth and development as it affects balance of payments, technology transfer, and the ability to diversify an economy. The authors argue that Nigeria has not attracted sufficient FDI despite steps to embrace various types of structural reforms in the country. The FDI that has been received thus far has been invested disproportionately in the oil sector of the economy, which generates more than 90 percent of export earnings. While Subair in chapter 12 points out that Nigeria has not fared better in the post-SAP period in comparison to the pre-SAP period with regard to growth in its manufacturing sector, Ajayi and Babalola find similar results with regard to gross domestic investment, which they argue declined precipitously in the 1980s. The important role of multinational corporations in private direct foreign investment activities in developing countries makes these firms "the major force in the rapid globalization of world trade." The authors offer recommendations that Nigeria and other countries could implement to attract more foreign direct investment.

Charles Mambula's chapter complements Ajayi and Babalola's by adding a different perspective with regard to conditions that need to be in place in Nigeria in order to attract the needed foreign direct investment from MNCs. Mambula provides a comprehensive assessment of a host of political, economic, and social variables that continue to impede both the further development of large-scale entrepreneurship in Nigeria and higher levels of foreign direct investment. Mambula points out that multinational corporations seek countries with stable and supportive conditions before investing in order to maximize their profit-making opportunities. He argues that a number of problems continue to beset Nigeria and militate against its ability to achieve its development goals. Some of these include the fact that Nigeria is ranked the fifteenth "most failed nation" in the world out a total of 177 countries measured; a lack of transparency in the governance process; corruption and political instability, including terrorist activities fueled by religious and ethnic strife; an unfair and intrusive regulatory environment for foreign companies; unscrupulous and dishonest behavior of governmental officials; instability of the national currency and exchange rate volatility, among other factors. Mambula concludes by providing recommendations to improve the economic conditions in the country and make it a more attractive investment climate.

Part 4, "Insecurity and Conflicts," presents both theoretical and empirical analyses of various manifestations of conflictual behavior both within and between countries within the broader context of globalization. Here, we assess how globalization has affected the area of international security as well as to what extent the forces of globalization have helped to fuel political or religious unrest and violence. John Babatunde Bamidele Ojo opens this section by looking at the relationship between globalization and international security, with a particular emphasis on Africa and the European Union. He points out that, historically, security was defined primarily from the perspective of military issues. This has changed in recent decades as the concept has been broadened considerably to encompass a wide range of political, social, environmental, technological, and economic factors. First, he provides a definition of globalization that is interdisciplinary in nature.

Then, he provides a comprehensive assessment of various aspects of security in the contemporary world. In the area of military security, he argues that the development of globalization has coincided with the decline in the efficacy of "military adventurism" as nation-states have been forced to redirect their resources toward enhancing their domestic infrastructures and other concerns. Globalization has also created an environment conducive to "constructive dialogue" between states and individuals that has challenged many of the assumptions of both the realist and Western conflict models that were popularized in earlier decades. Consequently, more idealistic, transnational perspectives have gained currency and are challenging realist assumptions that states "must clash in a zero-sum game of unending war." These views argue that "global citizens" can work cooperatively together for mutual benefit. While in past decades political instability and security issues were given a high priority by nation-states, in the present, for most countries economic and social development issues have assumed a higher priority. Ojo argues that while organizations such as the United Nations still reflect a static Westphalian model that is outdated, the European Union exemplifies the weakening or erosion of this model. With regard to the continuous proliferation of intrastate conflicts in the post–Cold War era, he notes that twenty-seven major armed conflicts took place during this period and that with the exception of two wars of international scope, all of the rest consisted of intrastate conflicts that occurred in Asia and Africa, with five being in the Middle East. While arguing that single-state interventions in these conflicts have not been successful thus far, he stresses that the possibilities for success in this area lie in the utilization of multilateral intervention strategies that can only be implemented under the auspices of globalization through a "workable" United Nations or other such organizations that can lend a sense of legitimacy to the endeavor. Hence, Ojo believes that globalization provides a suitable environment to develop international institutions, expectations, and the skills that are vital for handling internal conflicts over time. Moreover, because globalization legitimizes the further development of democratic norms and values, it also militates against the development of intrastate hostilities.

Ojo's contribution connects quite well with that of Ricardo Real Pedrosa de Sousa (chapter 16), who focuses primarily on explicating the set of factors and variables that have been known to precipitate conflict in various societies of the world in the context of globalization. De Sousa reviews the literature closely associated with the phenomenon of the "resource curse"; that is, the idea that resource-endowed countries do not always capitalize on their natural wealth but instead suffer because of it, as well as the "greed and grievance model." He then discusses important additional factors that have contributed to the development of conflict, including economic factors, social and external variables, the process of governance, the role of history, and geography. For example, he notes that scholars have identified relationships between conflict and a country's dependence on various natural resource exports. The presence of oil in a country can increase the possibility of conflict developing, and this risk level will increase as the country becomes more dependent on oil. With regard to Africa, he points in particular to the conflicts raging in Sierra Leone and the Democratic Republic of the Congo because of the presence of lootable gemstones and argues that drugs and timber in Liberia and the Democratic Republic of the Congo have increased the risk of ethnic conflict and well as its longevity.

Ricardo de Sousa's interesting analysis in chapter 16 of factors that lead to conflict provides a perfect segue into chapter 17, in which Aderonke Adesanya presents an analysis of "The Politics of Oil and Development and Visual Metaphors of the Crisis in Nigeria's Niger Delta." She posits that although the Niger Delta is one of the wealthiest regions of the country in terms of its possession of large deposits of petroleum, in reality it is one of the poorest areas in terms of the living conditions experienced by its citizens. She provides a brief historical discussion about factors that precipitated the present-day crises, which are often characterized by high levels of violence and increasing poverty, corruption, and political instability that persist in the region. She anchors her analysis within the broader context of the greed and grievance theory first introduced by Paul Collier and Anke Hoeffler, which is also discussed by Ricardo de Sousa in the present volume.

She discusses the important role of multinational corporations as agents of capitalism and amplifies how certain companies have caused severe environmental damage in the region through frequent oil spills, pollution, gas flaring, and creation of toxic waste dumps. According to Adesanya, two MNCs that have perpetrated these practices are Chevron and Royal Dutch Shell, two of the world's largest corporations. She also examines the precarious situation of poor women in the Niger Delta region and discusses how art can be a mirror in society to expose the various manifestations of persistent inequality. She argues that women in the Niger Delta who experience these hardships respond to them in a fundamentally different way than their male counterparts; for example, environmental damage often leads to a situation of disadvantage and scarcity of many basic amenities that in turn causes psychological and physical problems for women. Some women who face these conditions respond by moving to other regions or other countries. In some cases, mothers must raise children that are born with birth defects caused by environmental pollutants. In other instances, women are forced to sell their bodies as prostitutes to survive, or they are victimized by soldiers.

Finally, in chapter 18, Abdoulaye Saine offers a nuanced examination of the relationship between development, globalization, and the "War on Terror" in West African countries. His major contention is that in West African societies, Islamist movements have developed as an outgrowth of local political and socioeconomic circumstances that have been heightened by the impacts of globalization as well as by stresses of increasing urbanization in predominantly Muslim states. Saine presents a brief historical outline of Africa's peripheralization in the world capitalist economy and argues that globalization has attenuated Africa's marginal role in the global arena. Although in the nineteenth century it was European powers that colonized Africa, in the contemporary era, he argues, it is China that now vies for access to Africa's precious resources, particularly oil. He discusses the creation of the United States Africa Command (AFRICOM) in 2007 to strengthen the borders of West African states in an attempt to decrease the number of terrorists in the region and help stabilize conditions in Africa for the promotion of political and economic development. Although some scholars and policymakers have asserted that a relationship exists between poverty as experienced by citizens in West Africa and engagement in "terrorist activities," and believe Africans in the region are therefore perhaps more likely to engage in terrorist acts, Saine endeavors to refute this argument. To the contrary, he points out, Muslims located in West Africa are not monolithic and are in actuality far less likely than either Arabs or other religious groups to be involved in anti-Western violence. Although he acknowledges that in the northern region of the country, which is now under sharia law, the violence that occurs is often oppositional violence of a political nature, rather than terrorist attacks per se. According to Saine, not only has radical political behavior in the Middle East not affected the relationships between West Africa and the United States, on the contrary, a number of countries such as Senegal, Niger, Nigeria, Mali, and Mauritania have actually worked to improve their relationships with the West. In addition, he notes that al-Qaeda has been unable to incite terrorism in the region, but has used its resources there primarily to exacerbate the conflict and political instability in Liberia and Sierra Leone.

Altogether, the essays collected herein provide insightful and thought-provoking analyses of the multivarious impacts of globalization on African countries as we move further into the twenty-first century. Taken as a whole, the chapters encourage us to be more proactive in developing workable strategies to help African countries implement far-ranging initiatives on a broad scale to achieve sustainable development both in the present and in the future.

Notes

1. See, among others, Vandana Shiva, *Stolen Harvest: The Hijacking of the Global Food Supply* (Cambridge: South End Press, 2000).

2. An official of the World Bank admits the fact of power inequality between rich and poor countries, and the implications of this disparity for outcomes of

globalization. See Branko Milanovic, "The Two Faces of Globalization: Against Globalization as We Know It," *World Development Journal* 31, no. 4 (2003): 667–83.

3. For quick access to this history, see Erik Gilbert and Jonathan T. Reynolds, *Africa in World History: From Prehistory to the Present* (Upper Saddle River, NJ: Pearson Prentice Hall, 2004).

4. Toyin Falola and Aribidesi Usman, eds., *Movements, Borders, and Identities in Africa* (Rochester, NY: University of Rochester Press, 2009).

5. Kerry Ward, *Networks of Empire: Forced Migration in the Dutch East India Company* (Cambridge: Cambridge University Press, 2009).

6. Karl Polanyi, *The Great Transformation: The Political and Economic Origins of Our Time* (1944; repr., Boston: Beacon Press, 1957).

7. Baiyee-Mbi Agbor-Baiyee, chapter 2 of this volume.

Part One

Globalization and Development

1

The Trouble with Globalization

It Isn't Global Enough!

MARTIN C. SPECHLER

Despite the current world economic slump, the most important international process of the last decades has been globalization—growth of international trade and the spread of the most advanced technology, of world cultures both secular and religious, and the proliferation of nongovernmental organizations. Increasing international cooperation is managed by such organizations as the United Nations, World Bank, and the International Monetary Fund. Hardly any society on earth is untouched by globalization, although the present world recession has stalled and even temporarily reversed some aspects of it. But the process is too diverse and deeply entrenched to be turned back. According to IMF figures, the share of emerging and developing countries in the world's output of goods and services jumped from about a third at the beginning of the twenty-first century to 47 percent in 2010. But some countries have benefited more than others from globalization since 1960, and that diversity is our subject.

Anyone who traveled abroad around the turn of the century has seen the signs of globalization, from the Far East to the Far South. Coca-Cola and Marlboros are sold on the streets of Budapest, Tashkent, Mexico City, and Beijing. McDonald's or Pizza Hut is quite often the cheapest and cleanest restaurant around, even in cosmopolitan Prague. In Asia, many families celebrate their children's birthdays with "Uncle" Ronald McDonald, something their parents never did. To avoid Ricky Martin or Mariah Carey is impossible. American-style Pentecostalism, which pushes "self-improvement" with emotion and lively music, is surging in Brazil, South Korea, and even in Muslim-majority Indonesia.[1] When I was in Urumqi, capital of the Xinjiang Uighur Autonomous Region of China—the farthest inland major city in the world—I stayed at the Holiday Inn and was greeted in excellent English. The staff at the Ibis Hotel in Dakar, Senegal, spoke English, as well as French. But globalization is not all Americanization. The beach at Ipanema has umbrellas advertising Belgian beers. CNN or the BBC World Service are available at all the better hotels. Latin telenovelas are a major source of entertainment for many outside Latin America, and Bollywood's *Slumdog Millionaire* captured more Academy Awards than Hollywood's best in 2009. Singapore Airlines is probably the world's finest.

Dollars, euros, or VISA credit cards are accepted everywhere, but the newest international currency is "miles." Cosmocrats, as the new global class has been dubbed, accumulate them incessantly by traveling the globe on Star Alliance or SkyTeam, partnerships among member airlines from Thailand to Australia to Brazil. Cosmocrats won't leave home without them. With enough miles, you can meet them in Lufthansa's Senator Lounge at the Frankfurt International Airport and have a shower while you wait for your connection. Dollars alone won't get you in. The universal equipment of the cosmocrat is his or her cell phone with global positioning (GPS)—there will soon be more than a billion of them. Or keep in touch with your colleagues by Skype, free of charge.

Historical trends toward internationalization have not gone unnoticed by the keenest observers in the past. To quote one of them:

> In place of the old local and national seclusion and self-sufficiency, we have intercourse in every direction, universal inter-dependence of nations. . . . The intellectual creations of individual nations become common property. . . . The bourgeoisie, by the rapid improvement of all instruments of production, by the immensely facilitated means of communication, draws all . . . nations into civilization.[2]

This, of course, is from the *Communist Manifesto*, authored by Karl Marx and Friedrich Engels over 160 years ago.

Economic Benefits of Globalization

For economists, the benefits of globalization through trade, migration, and finance are obvious, even axiomatic. Adam Smith's famous invisible hand guides investible capital and labor to their most profitable and socially most useful destinations. "Division of labor [which generates productivity growth, the ultimate source of "the wealth of nations," as Smith taught] is limited by the extent of the market."[3] The wider the market, the more specialization, the more learning by doing, the more room for mechanization—and thus more wealth will be created. When countries specialize in goods they produce relatively cheaply—that is, in which they have a comparative advantage—export proceeds allow them to import those goods and services that are produced more inexpensively elsewhere. As David Ricardo taught long ago, both sides benefit from the exchange, though not necessarily equally.

In confirmation of Smith's insight, the fifty years after World War II were the best half century ever for developing countries. Growth rates of over 2 percent a year were achieved, much better than the 0.5 percent growth Nobel laureate Sir Arthur Lewis once predicted. Much of this surprising success can be attributed to avoidance of another world war, macroeconomic management of developed economies, and the work of such international organizations as the World Bank, IMF, and the General Agreement on Tariffs and Trade (GATT) that reduced obstacles to international commerce. Over the last two decades, world trade has more than tripled, rising faster than output, and net private investment soared from $50 billion in 1985 to more than $1 trillion in 2007.[4] There are more than one hundred thousand transnational companies, whose sales exceed the total of the entire world's exports. Foreign direct investment (FDI), a common means for transferring skills and technology to poorer countries, was $1.8 trillion in 2007, and was still about $1.2 trillion in 2009.[5] Flows to South America and India have been especially strong. Domestic investment has grown too.

What is the connection between participation in the global economy and domestic prosperity? During the last half of the twentieth century, those countries that opened themselves to world trade and investment mostly prospered. One example is Singapore, a swampy fishing village after World War II that is now a world entrepôt filled with sparkling buildings and enjoying a GDP per capita of more than $48,000. South Korea recovered from a destructive war in the early 1950s by encouraging its export industries. That country's financial crisis of 1997–98 was temporary, and its national income, adjusted for inflation, now exceeds $25,000 per capita. By contrast, prison-like North Korea has an estimated household income of just $935 because the regime there devotes much of its attention and the lion's share of government spending to its military, leaving many of its citizens near starvation.[6] After decades of poverty and emigration, Ireland began specializing in assembling high-tech products designed abroad and accepted tens of thousands of immigrants from Poland and elsewhere. Consequently, it became one of the fastest-growing members of the European Union. Democratic India, having abandoned its bureaucratic protectionism for the most part, is now experiencing economic growth rates of 8 to 9 percent yearly, just short of the rate achieved by China for the last twenty-five years.[7] The same prescription of opening to foreign technology, investments, and competition has accelerated the growth of Angola, the Slovak Republic, and Liberia, among others. On every continent, open economies have prospered: Taiwan, the Netherlands, Uganda, Botswana, Vietnam, Israel, New Zealand, Chile, Mexico. Those countries that closed themselves off—Burma, Republic of the

Congo, Saddam's Iraq, Belarus, Zimbabwe, and Cuba—have fallen behind. As Ernesto Zedillo, the former socialist president of Mexico, said: "In every case where a poor country has significantly overcome its poverty, this has been achieved while engaging in production for export and opening itself to the influx of foreign goods, investment, and technology; that is by participating in globalization."[8]

Of course, openness to the global economy alone is not sufficient to guarantee prosperity, particularly for large and remote countries, such as Brazil or Kazakhstan. Honest administration, broad-based public health and education, social cohesion, and a fair distribution of national wealth are also important. Very possibly, growth engendered by these elements allows more openness, so that simply reducing tariffs would have little independent effect. China did not liberalize its trade regime until rather recently; it joined the World Trade Organization (WTO) only in 2002. South Korea and Taiwan practiced several forms of protectionism during the first decades of their rapid growth. Indeed, openness is consistent with independent policy choices—for example, on tax rates and expenditures. Fixed exchange rates are not necessary either. Flexible exchange rates allow open economies to have different monetary policies, and hence different inflation rates.[9]

For these reasons, nearly all economists favor free trade in goods, although many have doubts about some types of unregulated capital transactions. Direct investment transfers know-how and commercial opportunities, but portfolio investments, particularly the purchase of stocks and short-term bonds, are riskier for host countries. Most emerging market countries do not have the accounting and reporting standards of the developed countries. Their financial markets are thin and subject to wide fluctuations caused by the "herd mentality" of speculators or international contagions of pessimism. Arguably, opening up and deregulating the financial markets of developing countries in the 1980s was a mistake, or at least premature.[10] The Latin American debt crisis of the 1970s, its collapse in the 1990s, and worldwide crises of 1997–98 and 2008 are evidence of such vulnerability. If a country tries to guarantee stability by pegging its currency to the dollar or euro, as Argentina's experience showed, it could be placed under unbearable pressure. Even where the exchange rate is flexible, repaying debt denominated in dollars becomes far more expensive when a country is forced to depreciate its own currency. For this reason, Chile and some other countries have tried to limit the short-term inflow of funds. Rather than act unilaterally, some countries have joined together to stabilize their financial markets through currency swaps, as in the Chiang Mai Initiative. As recent IMF research indicates, steps toward trade and domestic financial liberalization should precede the opening up of the capital account of the balance of payments.[11]

Criticisms of the Economists' Consensus

A few "progressive" economists have challenged the value of globalization. For instance, Arthur MacEwan has written: "The current wave of globalization is bringing severe problems: greater inequality, new threats to our physical environment, and even greater concentration of power in the hands of a few very large corporations."[12] Because these views are so widely shared among the intelligent lay public, we must examine them and determine their degree of validity, even if no coherent alternative strategy is always presented.

First, does globalization increase inequality between wage earners and owners of capital in high-income countries, like the United States? Accepted economic theory posits that openness to goods from low-wage countries or immigration of low-skilled laborers could reduce wages of unskilled workers in developed countries. Inequality of incomes has been increasing in the United States since 1976.[13] The global labor supply has risen fourfold since 1980, as more countries have opened up.[14] Average weekly earnings in private nonagricultural industries, in constant 1983 prices, declined 12 percent from its peak in 1969 through 2004.[15] So in view of these facts there could be a connection. Careful empirical studies, however, show that imports from less developed countries are at most a minor factor in the widening gap between skilled and unskilled workers' incomes in the United States.[16] Because of American protectionism against agricultural imports, textiles, toys, and other goods that developing countries can produce at acceptable quality, these goods do not sell much on the American market. Americans import far more from western Europe, Canada, and Japan than from the low-income world. Significantly, the relative price of labor-intensive goods has actually risen in the United States, because technological progress and investments have cut the price of capital-intensive goods even more. As a result, American workers in the labor-intensive tradable goods sectors have done better than those in services not subject to foreign competition. Immigrants, who now constitute about 15 percent of the American labor force, find low-wage employment in services and construction but usually earn more than they could at home; as a result, they are able to send billions of dollars in remittances each year back to their families. Even so, over a generation when the share of imports to the US economy has doubled, average unemployment rates have not increased.

Openness to global business can promote competitive markets, but some people worry that giant multinationals will establish so much monopoly power that they can dictate prices. Microsoft, Coca-Cola, Ford, the Dutch combine Unilever, and Switzerland's food giant Nestlé might be mentioned in this connection. However, size alone does not seem to provide a permanent advantage, aside from a few markets where economies of scale are decisive—for example, large civilian aircraft. True monopolies are disappearing everywhere. The share of the largest companies in the manufacturing output of the United States, Germany, and France peaked in 1970. Microsoft, though the largest, is just one of thousands of software companies. Yesterday's high-tech standouts, such as AT&T and IBM, could not defend their dominant positions, even by swallowing up smaller companies. Even Boeing has to contend with Airbus, not to mention Embraer of Brazil.[17] Japanese competition has pushed General Motors and Ford to make more reliable cars.

Economic theory likewise predicts that capital will flow to places where total costs are relatively low, including wages, taxes, and the burden of regulations and other costs of doing business. Capital taxation has been reduced in the United States and western Europe, in part for fear of such mobility—a "race to the bottom," as it has been called. But capital does not go to Mississippi or Africa just because wages and benefits are lowest there. Most American FDI goes to other developed countries.[18] Though low wages relative to productivity—that is, wage costs per unit—are an attraction, without adequate transportation and communications infrastructure, honest officials, and easy access to markets, investors will be hesitant. There is no significant "race to the bottom" because of low wages alone.

Environmental pollution has become a worldwide problem because of spillovers from untreated effluents in industrializing countries, not to mention carbon dioxide emissions from high-income countries. The willingness of poor countries to build or accept plants that contaminate their own and others' air and water for the sake of employment seems to implicate globalization. But effective local government, reinforced by environmentalists from outside organizations, can ameliorate the situation. Cubatao, a petrochemical region between São Paulo and the Atlantic Ocean, was once called "the most polluted city on earth." It was cleaned up through pressure from local residents and overseas environmentalists. Where democracy gets stronger, as it has in Brazil, local people react to threats to their health and safety. Communist Poland had indescribably bad air pollution from a steel complex near the magnificent and historic city of Krakow. Now, under democratic rule, things are much better. Open economies, like Brazil's and Poland's, are more likely to be democratic and respect human rights, as well as the environment. A World Bank study found that economic growth yields environmental benefits: with greater incomes, CO_2 emissions fall, water pollution decreases, and deforestation is combated.[19] Ozone pollution has succumbed to international cooperation.

Critics say that globalization destroys the human diversity that we should value. While it is true that languages are disappearing all the time, the choice to speak Spanish rather than an indigenous Indian language, for example, is a family's free choice; often Spanish is chosen as a means of expanding opportunities for a family's children. "Western" business dress has replaced the Nehru jackets and pajamas of India and Maoist China. Many Arab oil ministers appear at OPEC meetings in suits and ties, rather than flowing white *thawbs*. But global companies do make allowances for strong local customs. McDonald's offers "veggie burgers" in India, kosher ones in Israel, and allows Asian customers to linger over their "fast food."

World poverty remains the greatest challenge for humankind. One-fifth of the world's 6.6 billion people live in about fifty nations with national incomes averaging $935 per capita.[20] The world's Gini coefficient, the most common measure of inequality, is at or above 0.63, higher than that for almost any individual country.[21] Looking at the issue in another way, about one-fifth of the world's people live on consumption of less than $1.25 per day, the lowest international poverty line. This proportion has come down somewhat, thanks to progress in China, Taiwan, South Korea, post-Pinochet Chile, and some other countries. Yet almost all of the two billion people to be added to the world's population during the next few decades will be found in fifty low-income countries. Does globalization help the neediest?

In fact, globalization in the poorest parts of the world has had mixed effects. The opening of a country's economy seems to raise the wages in the exporting sectors because of increased demand for skilled workers resulting from the upgrading of plants. Without significant reallocation of productive resources, however, workers in import-competing sectors may lose, resulting in an overall increase in inequality.[22] For example, when grain imports into Mexico in the 1980s replaced peasant production, meat and vegetable growers did not absorb all the labor that was released.[23] Many migrated to Mexico's already overpopulated cities.

Abundant foreign aid has been successful at times, when local leaders have made good choices in its use.[24] But notorious cases abound. The late Congolese dictator Mobutu Sese Seko, one of the biggest thieves in world history, kept power in his own hands for years thanks to foreign aid and investments in his resource-rich country. On a smaller scale but on far more numerous occasions, wealthy capitalists and officials in poor countries take money from donors and transfer "brokerage fees" to Swiss and Miami banks.

Corruption is not the only malady afflicting poor countries that may be related to globalization. The rapid spread of AIDS, fire ants, and Asian eels can also be traced to global connections. The critical health problems of sub-Saharan Africa—malaria, TB, and HIV/AIDS—require international assistance, but also effective local action and cooperation. Despite efforts of the United Nations, every year international narco-traffickers are leaving more addicts and victims of violent crime behind in transit countries such as Tajikistan and Uzbekistan. Another grim aspect of globalization is the worldwide arms bazaar. Many of the world's poorest countries are afflicted by civil wars, using small arms produced in the United States, Europe, or Russia.

Thanks to the acceleration and spread of communications worldwide, jihadists in Indonesia, the Philippines, and elsewhere can share their plans with like-minded extremists elsewhere. There were twenty-five thousand victims of terrorism in 2006, more than three times the number of casualties ten years before.[25] Almost all are innocent civilians. Social networking via the Internet allows even small and poorly financed groups to gather supporters no matter where they live.

On the positive side, some global companies have found effective ways of doing business in the poorer parts of the world. Sylvan Learning Centers, based in Baltimore, Maryland, is testing fifteen thousand Africans yearly in English for management jobs. The Nigerian civil service depends on Sylvan's test, which is objective, secure, and incorruptible. In sub-Saharan Africa only one household in two hundred has a landline telephone, so mobile phones are making a big difference. For example, farmers in Côte d'Ivoire can learn about coffee prices, thus circumventing local merchants who may exploit them. In Soweto, South Africa, "phone ladies" set up small businesses renting cell phones to their neighbors.

Although former colonial ties may facilitate a brain drain, developing countries with many returned emigrants, such as India, China, and Mexico, have the advantage of networks and familiarity with the most advanced technology. English-speaking Indians now work for American insurance companies servicing claims. Other Indians returning from sojourns in the United States have transformed that country's information technology industry. Sam Bahour, owner of the newest mall in the West Bank, is a Palestinian-American who has returned home after living in Youngstown, Ohio.

With the help of both returnees and the staff of multinational corporations, Taiwan, Hong Kong, Malaysia, and mainland China have become offshore platforms for assembling electronics for the US, European, and Japanese markets. True, much assembly-line work is monotonous, uncomfortable, and sometimes dangerous. Where child labor is permitted, children are often kept out of school. For many child laborers, it is a choice they or their parents have freely made in preference to rural serfdom or prostitution. By contrast, Volkswagen produces Jettas and Beetle automobiles in Puebla, Mexico, an enterprise that has created perhaps seventy-five thousand jobs in conditions equal to similar factories in Germany. Even if a plant begins by assembling imported parts, as does Ford Hermosillo, these become the stars of the *maquiladora* system, producing complete Fusions and Mercury Milans. In time, furthermore, such assembly zones increase the demand for local inputs, particularly if the government requires it, as has happened in South Korea. No wonder public opinion in developing countries mostly approves the activities of foreign investors, if properly regulated.[26]

The Latin American Conundrum

Economists agree that economic *growth* is the most effective way to reduce poverty, if not necessarily inequality.[27] But does globalization invariably promote growth? We have already cited individual globalizing successes and failures on every continent. But what about the whole region of Latin America and the Caribbean, which has now embraced globalization in preference to the failed protectionism of the 1950s and 1960s?[28]

For a while just after World War II, according to Alice Amsden, import-substitution policies and government ownership of industry may have worked for Latin American states. But these policies became inflexible and corrupt by the 1970s, which discouraged competition and technology transfer.[29] The "lost decade" of the 1980s was characterized there by heavy foreign debt and oil costs. Combined with attempts to fix exchange rates, inflation inevitably led to unsustainable import surpluses and balance of payments crises. Inflation remained quite high into the 1990s, during which time these two dozen economies grew at about 3.2 percent per year—half the rate of the 1960s, when they were more protectionist. The seven largest Latin American countries, which have 90 percent of the region's population, have done only a little better since. Brazil, Mexico, and Chile grew less rapidly in the first decade of the 2000s than in the 1990s.[30]

Considering the fact that Brazil, Chile, and Mexico have adopted macroeconomic reforms, therefore, the Latin American record so far is disappointing. With a young population growing at about 1.5 percent per year, the ranks of the jobless in this region increased, and some eleven million more people were living in poverty in 2000 than ten years earlier.[31] According to United Nations estimates, the unemployment rate on this continent was around 8.5 percent in 2009, but double that among young people. Why? Weak educational and health provision for the poor and high inequality are partly to blame.[32] As development expert Nancy Birdsall says, "Economic technicalities are not addressing the fundamental question of why countries are not growing or the constraint that all these people are being left out. Economists are way too allergic to the wishy-washy concept of fairness."[33] Higher food prices recently have hurt the poor and threatened stability in several low-income countries when food producers imposed restrictions on exports to shelter their own populations. Unstable countries cannot prosper.

Measured by their level of economic freedom, the business environment in several countries in Latin America has deteriorated in recent years. There is a clear and significant relationship between business freedom and prosperity in the Americas.[34] Previously high-ranked countries such as Uruguay, oil-rich Trinidad and Tobago, and El Salvador have lost some economic freedom from 2007 to 2008. Argentina has been a poor performer on this measure ever since its crisis of the early 2000s. Like populists in other

Latin American countries, Argentina "continues to blame the free market for its ills," which include price controls, political interference, weak capital markets, and an unresolved foreign debt problem.[35] The worst abusers of economic freedoms have become even worse—Castro's Cuba, Chávez's Venezuela, Bolivia, Guyana, Suriname, and Haiti. Rated as extremely open to trade owing to its low tariffs, Haiti's economy contracted during the 1990s by 1.5 percent per year and now has average incomes of less than $1,000. When food prices rose there in 2008, riots brought down the prime minister. Evidently, a long-misgoverned country cannot solve its problems simply by importing goods and collecting remittances from emigrants.

Well-regarded economies such as those of Chile, Barbados, and Peru have improved their business climates significantly, though, so the record is not all discouraging. Colombia has continued modest rates of GDP advance, despite ongoing internal conflicts. Most Latin American countries have small governments and considerable labor freedom, as well as moderate trade and financial restrictions, but corruption and inflation continue to plague much of the region. Unfortunately, weak rule of law and unstable money, which handicap normal private business, are legacies difficult to overcome without radical structural reform.

The Case of Africa

As in Latin America and the Caribbean, the last three decades have been marked by disappointingly slow growth throughout much of sub-Saharan Africa. As is sometimes forgotten, Africa's GDP per capita grew faster than that of Asian countries during the first half of the twentieth century, despite Africa's tropical climate, leached soils, and unreliable rainfall.[36] Then after 1960, with the waning of European colonialism on the continent, African economic growth accelerated along with that of South Asia. So popular theories about the negative effects of previous political arrangements in Africa, including artificial borders and neocolonial relations with local elites, lose their persuasiveness. But during the 1970s, African growth declined. From 1980 through the 1990s, per capita GDP in thirty-two sub-Saharan African countries dropped by almost 1 percent per year. Falling food production per capita was a major part of this economic decline through the 1970s and 1980s, despite considerable foreign assistance to this sector. As of 2005, half of Africa's population of 380 million was living below the lowest poverty line of $1.25 per day. Average consumption of these 200 million was barely 73 cents per day.[37] Many African states were run by urban cliques uninterested in the needs of their agricultural or private commercial classes for reliable transportation, power, and communication infrastructure—not to mention honest police and unbiased courts to enforce the rule of law. As a result, investment, even from profits, was sluggish, and locals began to take their wealth to more promising and less risky places, often to the European country that was once the colonial power there. Ethnic rivalries and the temptation to seize valuable resources such as diamonds led to civil wars, with disastrous economic consequences.

During the three decades from 1970 to 2000, Africa did not take advantage of its international opportunities to the same degree as other developing countries.[38] Efforts to create market power and raise prices failed with respect to coffee, cocoa, and oil. Other countries did exploit their export possibilities; consequently Africans lost their former share of overseas markets.[39] As exchange rates became more and more overvalued, exports were less profitable. As a result, many countries had to rely on loans and grants instead of export earnings. Several leaders in sub-Saharan Africa argued that export prospects were unfavorable because of (somewhat) more volatile terms of trade for their narrow range of products. Indeed, price shocks do occur and persist from year to year, though eventually they tend to revert to their long-term lack of any real trend. This means that without productivity improvement, real incomes of commodity producers could not increase.[40] Many regimes raised tariffs and quotas to protect their internal markets and raise money for an expanding public sector.

African countries endured the bitter lessons of their relative failure. The World Bank's *Development Report* for 1991 predicted that aid projects would be unsuccessful with trade restrictions, overvalued exchange rates (or black market premiums on hard currencies), and deficit spending.[41] But these necessary conditions did not suggest what policies *would* work in African (or Latin American) conditions, as the World Bank's Growth Commission has now recognized.

Major policy reforms occurred in the 1990s and after. Education, neglected by the colonial regimes and only slowly developed after independence, was now recognized as crucial.[42] But the related problem in West African cities became finding employment for educated workers in the private sector. Reforms (and critical exports) did pay off. Uganda has been growing at more than 7 percent per annum since 1990; Mozambique has accelerated to an 8 percent rate; Ethiopia, to 7.5 percent; Tanzania, to 6.7 percent; Zambia, to 5.1 percent; and Angola, to more than 12 percent! Since 2000 Sierra Leone has recovered from its previous war-torn decade, and Liberia has done so more recently.[43] In contrast, Côte d'Ivoire and Zimbabwe, despite earlier promise, have failed to provide their growing workforces with productive jobs.[44] Several of the weakest states are under severe demographic pressure too. A continent of fifty-five countries including the independent Republic of South Sudan, Africa has become economically more diverse than ever. Quite a few are in danger of another debt crisis, according to a 2008 UN report. But several low-income countries, such as Rwanda and Ethiopia, have continued to grow, albeit at slower rates.[45]

Many countries in Africa are dependent on exports of commodities such as petroleum, coffee, and metals, in which they have a worldwide comparative advantage. On account of rising demand for these resources, net foreign direct investment to Africa rose from less than $9 billion in 2000 to $45–53 billion in 2006–7. With African nations taken together receiving the highest rates of return of all developing countries, FDI to Africa began to outpace foreign aid, which usually target humanitarian issues like emergency food, shelter, and medical supplies.[46] Owing to the worldwide slump, however, Africa's petroleum exporters probably experienced negative growth rates in 2009, while the continent as a whole had advances in 2008–9 barely enough to keep up with population growth.[47]

Evidently, export of raw materials is not sufficient for broad-based and sustainable economic development. Putting minerals on a ship does not always help the entire population. Infrastructure and manufacturing is preferable. Millions of people in Nigeria and Angola have not benefited from the huge FDI received by these countries, and they resent it. Africans' low wages would seem to be an advantage in such labor-intensive industries as textiles and clothing, but transaction costs and financing are still expensive. Africans might learn from the experience of South Korea, where the government offered its industries some temporary protection from international competition to allow them to learn, while observing their ability to compete in export markets as a measure of their efficiency. "Learning by doing" is often location specific, and countries that build "growth nodes," perhaps in cooperation with foreign firms, develop the human capital necessary to achieve autonomous growth. Personal ties with developed countries help a lot in the effective transfer of ideas.

Several African countries are succeeding in turning globalization to their benefit. The Aga Khan Group is building a huge hydroelectric dam at Jinja, Uganda, at a cost of $860 million to help that country ease its electricity shortage. Some efforts to increase African market access have also had successes. The African Growth and Opportunity Act, passed by the Clinton administration and extended by the Bush administration, created forty thousand jobs in Lesotho alone, chiefly for women working in that country's textile industry.[48] Botswana (which exports diamonds, copper, and other minerals) and the sugar island of Mauritius have been successful for decades.

Landlocked Rwanda has been trying to make itself the services, transportation, and information hub of East Africa, and since 2000, its economy has been growing at around 6 percent per year. To help reunite his genocide-torn country, Paul Kagame, the austere and energetic president of Rwanda, is avidly courting private investors for real estate, construction, methane development, and even a Starbucks for Kigali. The country's anticorruption and security policies are zealous, even ruthless.[49]

After dark decades of autocracy symbolized by Idi Amin and Mobutu, more and more African countries have become democratic and more economically liberal (free) than before. Mauritius, Botswana, Uganda, Madagascar, and Namibia are in the top half of the *2008 Index of Economic Freedom* rankings of 157 countries.[50] By contrast, Zimbabwe, Libya, Guinea-Bissau, the Republic of the Congo, and Burundi were near the bottom.

The "Oil Curse" in the Arab World

Like many sub-Saharan African countries, the economies and financial institutions of most of the Arab-speaking world "are weakly integrated into the global economy," but with several notable exceptions.[51] Of course, the nine Arab countries that are well endowed with reserves of fossil fuels (one-third of the total Arab population of 325 million) benefited handsomely from high oil prices from 2000 to 2007, so much so that their problems have been attributed to an "oil curse."[52] The manufacturing exports of all twenty-two Arab countries together have recently been less than those of the Philippines or Israel, countries with much smaller populations and fewer natural resources. One reason is that technology and scientific education have been neglected in the Arab world. A recent study of math and science education revealed that out of forty-eight countries surveyed, the twelve Arab countries in the sample were all below average.[53] The number of books translated into Arabic is one-fifth the number translated into Modern Greek. Of the world's top five hundred universities, as judged by the Jiao Tong University of Shanghai, three are South African and six are Israeli, but no Arab institution of higher education made the list, despite an increase in enrollment.[54] Although Arab girls are now educated better, female labor force participation is exceedingly low. As one consequence of all this, "between 1980 and 2000 Saudi Arabia, Egypt, Kuwait, the United Arab Emirates, Syria, and Jordan between them registered 367 patents in the United States. Over the same period South Korea alone registered 16,328."[55]

In examining the effects of globalization on the Arab world, the most interesting are the six Mediterranean countries (excluding Israel and the Palestinian territories), which have 45 percent of the total population. Among them is Egypt, the largest Arab country, with more than seventy-five million citizens. All of these have Euro-Mediterranean agreements with the European Union, intended to spur their development.[56] The per capita growth rate of the six nations averaged 2.7 percent from 1970 to 2007. Nonetheless, the non-Arab countries of the Mediterranean littoral are much richer than these six, engendering frustration and emigration northward.

There are signs of progress, however. Both the fossil-fuel-endowed and Mediterranean Arab countries have become somewhat more democratic.[57]

Tunisia and Morocco have relatively effective governments and have begun to diversify their economies toward manufacturing. Egypt, too, has made progress lately by improving its business and trade freedoms and by privatizing several enterprises.[58] Its banking system, however, has been afflicted by nonperforming loans; in addition, commercial cases are often protracted and subject to political pressure. Bribery and corruption are perceived as common from top to bottom in Egyptian society, partly as a result of low tax collections. Both unemployment and inflation are quite high; expensive subsidies on food, energy, pharmaceuticals, and transportation are carryovers from Arab socialism. Elsewhere in the region, years of high oil prices, accumulation of wealth, and unresolved conflicts have weakened such reform efforts.

What Could Be Done?

With a constructive domestic response—which may differ in content and timing from country to country—globalization can promote economic growth, income equality, and environmental recovery. That requires, first of all, that the remaining autocrats and elites permit the openness that threatens their power and privileges. The World Bank and IMF, the WTO, the World Health Organization, and NGOs like Oxfam, Human Rights Watch, the Aga Khan Foundation, and Médecins sans Frontières are all ready to help. The World Bank has urged several African nations to reduce their subsidies to agriculture and to privatize farming, so that growers will compete to export to the world market. Abiding by the rules of the WTO, to which 153 countries belong, does not require completely free trade. As already noted, South Korea began to grow a decade or more before it adopted trade reforms. Targeted incentives for viable industries, which require a skilled and honest bureaucracy, made a difference there.

Ever since the famous speech by World Bank president James Wolfensohn in 1996, more public attention has been given to corruption as an obstacle to economic growth. On various international corruption comparisons, Africa comes out a little worse than the world average.[59] One reason for its poor showing is the natural desire of politicians in Africa's many ethnically diverse countries to direct funds and public employment to their kinsmen. But efforts at audits and publicity do seem to help.[60] Regrettably, the World Bank was not willing to make its grants conditional on improvements in this matter, or on more democratic governance generally.[61]

Globalization would be even more positive if the poor countries of the world were allowed to share its full benefits. The current Doha Round was supposed to lead to agreement on tariff and quota reductions for low-income agricultural producers. At its inception in 2001, WTO director general Pascal Lamy of France promised that by reforming the rules of world trade, the developed countries could help the poorer ones: "gains would accrue to the developing countries . . . especially the least-developed countries among them."[62] Regrettably, the Doha Round has failed so far, partly due to the unwillingness of the United States and the EU to reduce agricultural and textile protectionism.

The EU and the United States should open their doors to the agricultural and manufactured items that poor countries can produce efficiently. Agricultural protection—primarily in the form of subsidies to farmers of cotton, sugar, and other crops—costs American taxpayers $50 billion per year, of which some 70 percent goes to the largest agricultural corporations. Cotton grown with scarce irrigation water in the Imperial Valley of California reduces prices for cotton farmers in Mali, Uzbekistan, and Tajikistan. The EU bill for support of their farmers is $130 billion, and new export subsidies on dairy products have been passed lately. European farmers get more than one-third of their income from subsidies.[63]

During the previous period of globalization, from 1870 to 1914, intercontinental immigration and capital flows helped bring the wages of Eastern Hemisphere laborers closer to their Western Hemisphere counterparts.[64] Similarly massive flows of migrants seem unrealistic these days because of fears of unemployment and cultural conflict. But even temporary immigration could help the able-bodied poor directly.[65] If workers from Africa, Bangladesh, or the poorer countries of Central America were given three-year permits to work in US agriculture, where they are needed, the experience would also familiarize them with how a developed Western economy works. Part of their salaries might be paid only after they return to their home country, vacating their places to be taken up by others. Research suggests that this system would have little negative effect on workers in the United States or Europe, once the current economic slump ends.

At a meeting in Dakar, Senegal, in 2005, a representative of Britain's government promised a vast increase of aid. The subsequent G8 summit, he said, would arrange to give Africa $50 billion designed to integrate the continent into the world economy. In fact, official aid to all low-income countries has not been scarce; in 2007, it amounted to about $100 billion. From 1990 to 2006, the median African country received enough funds to finance 37 percent of its government expenditures.[66] The effects, however, have been disappointing because of waste and corruption. Perhaps to avoid appearing too paternalistic, donors have not insisted on proper accounting for use of the funds granted, so that recipient governments would have incentives to invest in sensible infrastructure, public health, education, and measures to strengthen the rule of law.

Direct and portfolio investments by private investors have been even larger than official aid flows, but they are less dependable. Lacking complete information about accounting results and being subject to "home bias" in choosing where to invest, foreign investors sometimes display "herd" behavior. Thus, when one country in a region seems to be in trouble, for-eign investors may withdraw funds from the entire region. The International Monetary Fund and the World Bank are supposed to serve as a kind of world central bank, compensating for the unreliable private capital flows. Over the last fifty years, the IMF has been called on to deal with many developing countries in financial distress. By requiring higher real interest rates to deal with the distress, however, IMF adjustment lending reduces growth some-what.[67] Nobel laureate Joseph Stiglitz has pointed out that higher interest rates put pressure on banks. But otherwise a country's exchange rate may fall even farther and make repayment of dollar-denominated debts impossi-ble—thus causing a default and long-lasting harm to its credit rating. Recap-italizing a competitive financial sector may be necessary, but so is objective regulation, which requires professionalism insulated from politics.

To engender more confidence among recipients of painful advice, more representation on the governing board of the IMF for emerging economies—recently instituted—and more transparency should help. With this reform, the IMF's former leader, French finance minister Domi-nique Strauss-Kahn, did much to increase its responsiveness and lending capacity too.

The WTO is another worldwide organization dominated by represen-tatives from high-income countries. It regularly makes complicated rules that require expert lawyers and staff to penetrate, thus putting low-income countries at a disadvantage. For example, the very poorest countries can still import drugs under patent until 2016, but Washington inserted some obstacles to the distribution of cheap AIDS drugs desperately needed in Africa. Of course, someone must pay for research on diseases common in poor tropical countries. Without royalties or subsidies, there would be no pharmaceuticals. As Jeffrey Sachs has argued, however, there is no solution to the AIDS pandemic or malaria in places like the Central African Republic other than to donate the necessary drugs, mosquito netting, and personnel to prevent deaths. Regrettably, too few in the United States or Europe—even those proud to call Africa their spiritual home—seem sufficiently interested in saving African lives.[68]

Conclusion

Globalization is not perfect, only better than any alternative development path ever tried. Countries on every continent have benefited from it, and those that have not have mostly their own leaders to blame. Our own time has been better than the interwar period (1919–39), but the global com-munity could falter if the real or imagined losers from globalization resort to terrorism, the most obvious threat to national security everywhere. If reactionaries inspired by false religious doctrines or resurgent nationalism were to win over more converts from among the losers from worldwide economic development, most of us would be deprived of what globalization has meant to our way of life.

To some extent, the current worldwide slump has led to deglobalization. Yet, we should not confuse cyclical downturns with a major counterrevolution. One can hope that the financial slump, in Asia and western Europe, will be temporary. Already commodity and energy prices are rising, in large part owing to the robust recovery in China, triggered by huge government stimulus spending there. This resumption of the price rises experienced in 2000–2007 offers many African countries opportunities to grow by expanding their exports, rather than by receiving aid or borrowing.

Coordinated national stimulus programs may make 2008–9 a bad memory. Unfortunately, the global financial institutions established just before and during the Cold War—especially the GATT/WTO and the IMF, but also the United Nations—have proved unable to deal with the challenges of the many globalizing threats we have touched on here, in part because the United States, the EU, Russia, and China are not prepared to cede enough of their national influence within these supranational organizations so they might deal with the threats directly.

In his recent encyclical, *Caritas in Veritate*, in which he justly condemned crude and loveless materialism in our world, Pope Benedict XVI wrote:

> Blind opposition [to globalization] would be a mistaken and prejudiced attitude, incapable of recognizing the positive aspects of the process, with the consequent risk of missing the chance to take advantage of its many opportunities for development. . . . The worldwide diffusions of prosperity should not . . . be held up by projects that are protectionist. . . . The principal form of assistance needed by developing countries is that of allowing and encouraging the gradual penetration of their products into international markets. . . . Human costs always include economic costs, and economic dysfunctions always involve human costs.

Indeed, globalization offers opportunities for leaders who wish to grasp them, but it also opens up threats of social conflict, which always accompanies change in incomes, status, and culture. Conflicts have become more deadly because of the arms trade. Especially in the poorest third of the world, humankind's challenge will be dealing with the unavoidable consequences of globalization: communicable diseases, environmental degradation, intrusion of foreign ideas, secularization, and the unpredictable risks of world markets. Our greatest asset is the increased consciousness that all members of the human race are now more closely connected and have much in common. Joint action, therefore, is both possible and desirable.

Notes

1. John Micklethwait and Adrian Woodridge, *God Is Back: How the Global Revival of Faith Is Changing the World* (New York: Penguin Press, 2009).

2. Robert C. Tucker, ed., *The Marx-Engels Reader* (New York: W. W. Norton & Company, 1972), 338–39, translated by Friedrich Engels in the 1888 edition.

3. Adam Smith, *An Inquiry into the Nature and Causes of the Wealth of Nations*, ed. Edwin Cannan (1776; repr., Chicago: University of Chicago Press, 1976), book 1, chap. 3, 21–25. Smith's "invisible hand" is mentioned just once, at book 4, chap. 2, 477.

4. World Bank and Institute for International Finance, cited in *Economist*, February 21, 2009.

5. United Nations Conference on Trade and Development (UNCTAD) and World Association of Investment Promotion Agencies.

6. World Bank, *World Development Indicators 2009* (Washington, DC, 2009), 14–16. Estimates are for 2007.

7. Ibid., 205.

8. Quoted in Dani Rodrik, "Trading in Illusions," *Foreign Policy* 123 (March–April 2001): 55–62. In a cross-sectional study by Jeffrey Frankel and Andrew Rose, a 10 percent increase in merchandise trade led to a 0.8 percent improvement in the GDP growth rate. A 1.0 percent gain in the cumulative share of FDI in GDP was associated with 0.6 percent more in national income. Gary C. Hufbauer, "Globalization Facts and Consequences," *Petersen Institute of International Economics* (March 13, 2001).

9. Dani Rodrik, "Symposium on Globalization in Perspective: An Introduction," *Journal of Economic Perspectives* 12 (Fall 1998): 3–8.

10. Alice Amsden, *Escape from Empire: The Developing World's Journey through Heaven and Hell* (Cambridge: MIT Press, 2007). Amsden believes that import-substitution industrialization of the 1950s and 1960s worked in several Latin American countries, but deregulation undermined them. "The Tyranny of Empire," *Challenge* 50, no. 5 (September–October 2007): 24–25.

11. Jonathan D. Ostry, Alessandro Prati, and Antonio Spilimbergo, "Structural Reforms and Economic Performance in Advanced and Developing Countries," *Occasional Paper No. 268* (Washington, DC: IMF, 2009), 43.

12. Arthur MacEwan, "Markets Unbound: The Heavy Price of Globalization," *Dollars & Sense* (September–October 1994), reprinted in Marc Breslow, David Levy, and Abby Sher, eds., *Real World International*, 5th ed. (Somerville, MA: Dollars & Sense, 1999), 16.

13. The share of the top 1.0 percent of family income recipients increased to 23.5 percent of personal incomes by 2007, according to Emmanuel Saez and Thomas Piketty in the *Wall Street Journal*, September 11, 2009, 1. Between 1980 and 2007 real income of the median American family rose only 22.0 percent, while the top 0.1 percent (top thousandth) of households increased their incomes seven times! Paul Krugman, "All the President's Zombies," *New York Times*, August 24, 2009, A17.

14. Market opening has occurred notably in India, China, and the former Communist countries. IMF, *World Economic Outlook*, cited in *Economist*, April 7, 2007, 76.

15. A major part of this fall came from a 10 percent decline in weekly hours. *Economic Report of the President 2005* (Washington, DC: USGPO, 2005), 266.

16. Foreign outsourcing accounted for 15–20 percent of the demand for skilled, relative to unskilled, labor in the United States. Technological upgrading was twice as potent. Gordon Hanson, "The Globalizing of Production," *NBER Reporter* (Spring 2001). Diminished unionization also accounts for a greater part of the stagnant wages and benefits of low-skilled males in the US labor force.

17. "Boeing and Airbus fight like rats in a sack for every sale, with the consequence that airlines have been able to buy cheaper and better aircraft than if one firm had been dominant." *Economist*, August 15, 2009, 12. Both firms now employ global supply chains, in part to promote sales to participating countries.

18. In 2000 81 percent of US FDI went to developed countries. US direct investment in Mexico is rising, but it still represents less than 1 percent of all American placements.

19. Vinod Thomas et al., *Quality of Growth* (New York: Oxford University Press for the World Bank, 2000), 3–4.

20. World Bank, *World Development Indicators 2009*, 16. The figures for 2007 are $1,489 per capita, when adjusted for the lower dollar cost of living in the low-income countries.

21. Sudhir Anand and Paul Segal, "What Do We Know about Global Income Inequality?" ms., October 2006, 54, 73, reprinted in Sudhir Anand, Paul Segal, and Joseph Stiglitz, *Debates on the Measurement of Global Poverty* (New York: Oxford University Press, 2010).

22. Pinelopi K. Goldberg and Nina Pavcnik, "Distributional Effects of Globalization in Developing Countries," *Journal of Economic Literature 45* (March 2007): 77.

23. Arthur MacEwan, *Neo-Liberalism or Democracy? Economic Strategy, Markets, and Alternatives for the 21st Century* (New York: St. Martin's Press, 2000), chap. 2.

24. William Easterly, *The Elusive Quest for Growth* (Cambridge: MIT Press, 2001), 103–4. Easterly credits modest aid projects with eradicating smallpox and river blindness.

25. Moisés Naim, "Think Again: Globalization," *Foreign Policy* 171 (February 16, 2009): 32.

26. According to a Pew Global Attitudes Project poll, majorities in nearly all the forty-seven countries surveyed approved of international trade; forty-one approved of multinational firms. *Economist*, February 21, 2009, 60. But there is now more support for state regulation of business than there was in 2007. The Edelman Trust found that more than 60 percent of respondents in twenty countries (including the United States) wanted there to be more governmental control over business activity.

27. A number of recent professional surveys have failed to find a clear causal relationship between globalization and overall interpersonal inequality or any trend in the best available data over the last thirty years. This is partly owing to incomparable and defective household budget studies. Anand and Segal, "What Do We Know?" 54. Within-country inequality, however, has risen in most countries since the 1970s. *Economist*, February 21, 2009, 59.

28. Between 1985 and 1987 Mexico unilaterally liberalized trade, FDI, and immigration and approved the North American Free Trade Agreement in 1994. Argentina and Colombia liberalized trade and devalued their currencies in the 1990s. Brazil undertook unilateral trade liberalization in the early 1990s and joined the

customs union Mercosur in 1991, along with Argentina. Goldberg and Pavcnik, "Distributional Effects of Globalization," 48–49.

29. Arminio Fraga, "Latin America since the 1990s: Rising from the Sickbed?" *Journal of Economic Perspectives* 18 (Spring 2004): 95. Fraga was president of the Central Bank of Brazil; see also Amsden, *Escape from Empire.*

30. World Bank, *World Development Indicators 2009*, 204–5.

31. Tina Rosenberg, "Globalization," *New York Times Magazine*, August 18, 2002, 31, quoting Nancy Birdsall.

32. Fraga, "Latin America since the 1990s," 105; see also UN News Centre, October 2, 2009, "Unemployment Rate Inches Higher in Latin America and Caribbean," http://www.un.org/apps/news/story.asp?NewsID=32400&Cr=unemployment &Cr1=.

33. Rosenberg, "Globalization," 74.

34. Kim R. Holmes, Edwin J. Feulner, and Mary A. O'Grady, *2008 Index of Economic Freedom* (Washington, DC, and New York: Heritage Foundation and Wall Street Journal, 2008), 64.

35. Gerald P. O'Driscoll Jr., Edwin J. Feulner, and Mary A. O'Grady, *2003 Index of Economic Freedom* (Washington, DC, and New York: Heritage Foundation and Wall Street Journal), 4; Holmes, Feulner, and O'Grady, *2008 Index of Economic Freedom*, 83.

36. Angus Maddison, *Monitoring the World Economy* (Paris: OECD, 1995). Maddison's conclusion was based on a sample of countries.

37. Shaohua Chen and Martin Ravallion, "The Developing World Is Poorer than We Thought, but No Less Successful in the Fight against Poverty," *World Bank Policy Research Working Paper 4703* (2008).

38. As compared with other developing countries, African producers are more "landlocked": only about one-fifth of the population lives fewer than 100 km from the sea or a navigable river. John Bloom and Jeffrey Sachs, "Geography, Demography, and Economic Growth in Africa," *Brookings Papers in Economic Activity* 2 (1998): 207–95.

39. Paul Collier and Jan Willem Gunning, "Why Has Africa Grown Slowly?" *Journal of Economic Perspectives* 13 (Summer 1999), table 2.

40. Angus Deaton, "Commodity Prices and Growth in Africa," *Journal of Economic Perspectives* 13 (Summer 1999): 27–28.

41. World Bank, *World Development Report 1991: The Challenge of Development* (New York: Oxford University Press, 1991).

42. The gross primary enrollment rate has gone from about 33 percent at independence to more than 90 percent now. Mathias Kuepie, C. J. Nordman, and F. Roubaud, "Education and Earnings in Urban West Africa," *Journal of Comparative Economics* 37 (2009): 492.

43. World Bank, *World Development Indicators 2009*, 204–5. Real GDP growth accelerated in 2000–2007 over the rates of the last decade of the twentieth century.

44. Côte d'Ivoire received twenty-six structural adjustment loans in 1980–99 to help them rectify price distortions related to international trade and finance. William Easterly, "Can the West Save Africa?" *Journal of Economic Literature* 47 (2009): 421. The conditions attached to such loans were usually violated, and many ended up having to be forgiven under the Heavily Indebted Poor Countries (HIPC) initiative. According to Daniel Chirot, France has overlooked a situation of "immense corruption, growing ethno-religious competition, and grossly incompetent government" in

this "favorite client government." "The Debacle in Côte d'Ivoire," *Journal of Democracy* 17 (2006): 63–77, and private communication, October 2009. But a major (if sorely delayed) devaluation of the CFA currency in 1994 did contribute to making real exchange rates more reasonable, even if it made Ivorians' trips to Paris more expensive. Overvaluations in Africa declined from about 80 percent in 1980 to adjusted purchasing power parity (PPP) by 1996. See Easterly, "Can the West Save Africa?" fig. 12.

45. International Monetary Fund, "Regional Economic Outlook: Sub-Saharan Africa," *World Economic and Financial Surveys* (April 2008), http://www.imf.org/external/pubs/ft/reo/2008/AFR/eng/sreo0408.htm; see also United Nations Economic Commission for Africa, *Economic Report on Africa 2008: Africa and the Monterrey Consensus: Tracking Performance and Progress* (Addis Ababa, Ethiopia, 2008), http://www.uneca.org/era2008/ERA2008Full.pdf.

46. The IMF estimates that sub-Saharan Africa suffered a drop of 18 percent in FDI in 2008. See International Monetary Fund, *Regional Economic Outlook, Sub-Saharan Africa* (April 2009), table SA3.

47. Ibid.

48. Jendayi E. Frazer, "Four Ways to Help Africa," *Wall Street Journal*, August 26, 2009, A15.

49. William Wallis, "Social Engineering in Pursuit of Peace," *Financial Times*, September 22, 2009, 3–4. The Mo Ibrahim Foundation, founded by the successful African telecommunications magnate, has recently criticized Rwanda for failing to uphold civil rights. *Economist*, October 3, 2009, 62.

50. Holmes, Feulner, and O'Grady, *2008 Index of Economic Freedom*, 9–13. This neoliberal ranking reflects trade and business freedom, low taxes and inflation rates, defense of property rights, and labor market flexibility, rather than political democracy. Alternatively, the Mo Ibrahim Foundation rates Mauritius, Cape Verde Islands, the Seychelles, Botswana, and South Africa as the best five of fifty-three African countries for overall progress, including rule of law, political participation and human rights, sustainable economic opportunity, and human development. Liberia, Angola, Burundi, and Sierra Leone have improved; Nigeria and Kenya have declined. *Economist*, October 3, 2009, 62.

51. *Economist*, July 25, 2009, 8.

52. Like non-Arab fossil-fuel-endowed economies, the Arab ones grew at less than 1 percent per year per capita in international dollars from 1970 to 2007. James E. Rauch and Scott Kostyshak, "The Three Arab Worlds," *Journal of Economic Perspectives* 23 (Summer 2009): table 2. Saudi Arabia is the prime case of oil dependency; hydrocarbons account for half its nominal GDP. The kingdom stagnated through the 1980s and 1990s and remains one of the poorest countries of the Persian Gulf, relatively speaking; it has a shrinking indigenous middle class and has postponed reforms. The oil boom allowed the octogenarian King Abdullah to pay off 80 percent of the kingdom's huge foreign debt by 2008, but the global crisis and lower oil prices have led to a small contraction in 2009. *Financial Times*, September 23, 2009, 5.

53. The Trends in International Mathematics and Science Study, *Economist*, October 19, 2009, 60.

54. Ibid.

55. *Financial Times*, September 23, 2009, 9.

56. Rauch and Kostyshak, "Three Arab Worlds," 169.

57. The Polity IV index, which measures participation, competitiveness of executive selection, and constraints on the chief executive, rates only Lebanon (and tiny Comoros) as "democratic." Rauch and Kostyshak, "Three Arab Worlds," table 6.

58. Holmes, Feulner, and O'Grady, *2008 Index of Economic Freedom*, 165–66.

59. Daniel Kaufmann, Aart Kraay, and Massimo Mastruzzi, "Governance Matters VI: Aggregate and Individual Governance Indicators, 1996–2006," *World Bank Policy Research Working Paper 4280* (2007).

60. Easterly, "Can the West Save Africa?" 428; Easterly relies on studies by Ritva Reinikka and Jakob Svensson in Uganda and similar studies elsewhere.

61. William Easterly, "Are Aid Agencies Improving?" *Economic Policy* 52 (September 2007): 633–68, esp. 675–78.

62. Quoted in Joshua Kurlantzick, "The World Is Bumpy: Deglobalization and Its Dangers," *New Republic* 240, nos. 12–13 (July 15, 2009): 19–21.

63. Rosenberg, "Globalization," 33.

64. Peter H. Lindert and Jeffrey Williamson, "Does Globalization Make the World More Unequal?" in National Bureau of Economic Research, *Globalization in Historical Perspective* (Cambridge, MA, 2001), 227–76.

65. International Organization for Migration, *World Migration 2005: Costs and Benefits of International Migration* (Geneva, 2005).

66. Easterly, "Can the West Save Africa?" 431.

67. Adam Przeworski and James Raymond Vreeland, "The Effect of IMF Programs on Economic Growth," *Journal of Development Economics* 62 (2000): 385–421. Some of the positive effect of these IMF policies may reflect favorable connections with the United States or France, however. Easterly, "Can the West Save Africa?" 424.

68. Jeffrey Sachs, *The End of Poverty* (New York: Penguin, 2005).

2

Can Africa Compete in a Global Economy?

BAIYEE-MBI AGBOR-BAIYEE

Introduction

Since their independence, the countries of sub-Saharan Africa (SSA) continue to face severe social, political, and economic developmental problems, notwithstanding the abundance of natural resources in the region. While some SSA countries are making significant progress toward socioeconomic development, the antecedents of underdevelopment are widespread even in the successful ones. It is not a stretch to characterize any of these nations as a microcosm of regionwide experiences, opportunities, and challenges. Accordingly, postindependence sub-Saharan Africa can best be described as a region overburdened with multifaceted, causally related precursors of underdevelopment. These factors include but are not limited to the following:

1. ethnic, civic, and social discontent, as manifested in political instability, conflicts, and wars;
2. susceptibility and vulnerability to preventable diseases, lack of basic medical care, low quality of life, and short life expectancy;
3. widespread civil service corruption, lack of accountability, ineffective governance, poor management skills, and inept leadership;
4. lack of physical capital stock, low-quality human capital stock, widespread brain drain, and high dependence on expatriates;
5. unstable macroeconomic and legal environments, weak private sector, weak property rights, balance-of-payments problems, high foreign investment risks, and low levels of foreign direct investment;
6. economic inefficiency, low levels of productivity and economic growth, high unemployment rates, lack of technological innovation, widespread poverty, low standards of living; and

7. environmental degradation and rapid depletion of highly valued and endangered flora and fauna.

As a result of the prevalence and pervasiveness of these manifold problem areas, SSA has proved incapable of fostering sustainable socioeconomic development through the ingenuity of its own peoples. In other words, there is a shortage of effective or visionary socioeconomic development initiatives, whether conceptualized, implemented, or driven by local leaders and governments. The situation has worsened in the past few decades, a period marked by the major structural transformation of the global business environment, what we call globalization. The concept of globalization can best be viewed as the emergence of a complex and dynamic set of forces that are fast changing, interdependent, and yet confounded with risks and uncertainties. Those forces have culminated in a new global business environment that is information driven and knowledge based. This new environment is changing the way institutional actors and stakeholders think and operate.[1]

As Martin Spechler has argued in chapter 1, globalization has had multifaceted impacts on Africa. This chapter expands the discussion of this theme, with the following objectives in mind: first, to assess how well the SSA region is globalizing—that is, whether the region is benefiting from the globalization process; and second, to determine and analyze the sources of competitiveness among the best-performing sub-Saharan African countries in order to delineate the practices that are inherent in or responsible for their success in achieving socioeconomic development. These objectives will be accomplished by analyzing the competitiveness of SSA and comparing the region with other developing regions of the world, while attempting to identify how the best practices might be adopted by other countries in the region that face similar socioeconomic challenges and opportunities.

The chapter is organized into three main sections. The first attempts to place SSA within a comprehensive context of the globalization process. Specifically, a formal explanation of globalization is presented, followed by a brief history of how SSA was forced to globalize and a cursory discussion of the factors affecting the region's competitiveness. The second section analyzes competiveness further, comparing SSA and other developing regions on the basis of the World Economic Forum's Global Competitiveness Index, the United Nations' Millennium Development Goals, and the World Bank's Global Development Indicators. It also examines the level of competitiveness among SSA countries. The third, concluding section provides a summary of the main findings and offers some recommendations on how to improve the competitiveness in SSA.

What Is Globalization and How Does Sub-Saharan Africa Fit in the Globalization Process?

Globalization Described

An attempt is made here to describe rather than define the globalization process because globalization is conceived as an ongoing (dynamic) process not a static concept whose transformation is complete and whose ramifications are fully understood. The globalization process is facilitated by two conflicting yet complementary structural changes; that is, the global economic environment is integrating while at the same time national economic environments are disintegrating.

On the one hand, globalization is aided by the integration of global economic activities, which involves (1) harmonization of dissimilar national and regional economic, financial, legal, political, and social systems, and (2) rules of engagement in the interaction between diverse global economic agents, institutions, and countries. The harmonization process requires that global agents and national and regional systems conform to the provisions of international financial, trade, labor, and legal institutions. In other words, the terms and management of the globalization process are defined and controlled by those international institutions.

On the other hand, the globalization process is reinforced by the disintegration of national economies. This involves the assimilation and conformation of national and regional economic, financial, legal, political, and social systems to international institutional policies governing the globalization process. Those policies are placing more emphasis on the importance of markets such that constraints associated with the procurement, mobilization, and distribution of factors of production, goods and services, and the flow of information across regional markets and national boundaries are lowered. For example, Philip Cerny argued that the increasing transnationalization of financial markets constrains policymakers and circumscribes the policy capacity of the state.[2] This has resulted in increased global competition between SSA countries and multinational interest groups for resources, markets, and investment capital. Competitive advantage in the emerging global economy is conferred on competitors who can develop distinct competencies that transcend national boundaries and that are able strategically to capture the benefits from complementarities and positive externalities that emanate or spill out from the interdependence of the global economic system.

The convergence of the conflicting yet complementary forces of integration and disintegration is facilitated by the advancement and adoption of modern information technologies. The ongoing technological revolutions in data collection, processing, and dissemination are contributing to globalization in three ways: First, information and communication technologies are facilitating real-time coordination of financial and capital markets, goods markets, labor markets, manufacturing activities, and global supply chains.[3] Secondly, information technologies are providing opportunities for multinational corporations (MNCs) and global economic agents to discover heterogeneous niche markets and untapped global markets. Success in reaching new markets and in capturing increased global market shares is facilitated by advancements in modern manufacturing technologies that are more flexible and thus can easily be adapted to produce differentiated products that meet the targeted needs of new consumers.[4] John Dunning credits South Africa's best performance in SSA to its business environment that is conducive to foreign investment and encourages the adoption of flexible manufacturing technology.[5] Finally, information and communication technologies are enabling real-time monitoring of the political, legal, social, and economic developments within national and regional boundaries, and this monitoring allows MNCs to formulate strategic responses to global events in a timely manner.

The emerging knowledge-based and information-driven global economic environment confers competitive advantage on countries and companies that are able to:

1. extract tangible and intangible knowledge that is embedded in human and physical resources, transforming them into value, and influence future consumption of goods and services whose immediate use is not yet apparent;
2. conceive value and define quality in terms of intangible assets such as trust, ideas, and business or national culture that are embedded in the product development process of the goods and services designed specifically to meet the idiosyncratic needs of heterogeneous global niche markets;
3. create new tacit knowledge from which economic rents can be appropriated across global economic markets with weak intellectual property rights;[6] and
4. coordinate and manage information flows effectively and establish strategic linkages and partnerships within and between interdependent global agents and environments.

Sub-Saharan Africa and the Globalization Process

The potential benefits of globalization as a panacea for rapid economic development were overstated by the IMF and the World Bank to SSA and other developing regions. They argued that SSA would benefit from globalization in that the infusion of foreign direct investment would be accompanied by in-flows of productive resources such as information, skills, knowledge, financial capital, raw materials, labor, and commodity and manufacturing systems, which in turn would improve the overall quantity and quality of human and physical capital, create employment opportunities, and increase the tax revenue base for the governments in the region. Those overstated benefits have been characterized as the economic myths of globalization.[7] Instead of realizing those benefits, SSA was marginalized in the globalization process as evidenced by the general decline in the region's share of international trade, decline in international development assistance, in FDI, and in the comparative advantage edge in its supply of raw materials.[8]

Those overoptimistic expectations of the potential benefits of globalization assumed that foreign investors would out of goodwill strive to maximize benefits to shareholders (profits) as well as the local community development (social welfare) in the SSA countries where they operate. Furthermore and what is more important, the rosy expectations of the outcomes of globalization did not take into account the fact that SSA economies lacked the necessary human, infrastructural, financial, technological, and industrial capacities, and that those economies are confounded by unstable macroeconomic environments. All those conditions are required to attract foreign investment and to respond effectively to changes in global economic events in a fashion that is consistent with features inherent in industrial or developed economies. For example, Gill Hammand, Revi Kanbur, and Eswar Prasad argued that SSA lacked attractive macroeconomic policy options because of constraints that are inherent in the system.[9] Central banks in the region—which are charged with the responsibility of achieving productivity and growth to keep inflation under control, and to maintain financial stability—continue to face weak banking environments as well as institutional independence constraints. Those constraints are confounded by questionable interest rate, exchange rate, and inflation policies that are directed at price stabilization and effective management of budget deficits and public debt.

As a consequence, SSA has not benefited from globalization at levels comparable to other developing regions of the world, and thus the globalization process marginalizes SSA. The immediate victims are the rural and urban poor who constitute the majority of the populations in SSA. They lack the purchasing power, employment skills, and necessary levels of education to participate and benefit from the globalization process.

Instead of building the badly needed capacities and competencies, SSA was forced to globalize through the infamous structural adjustment programs (SAPs) that were instituted by the IMF and World Bank in the 1980s. According to the requirements of these SAPs, SSA nations, like other developing countries, were forced to adopt neoliberal concepts of market reform, currency devaluation, trade liberalization, and divestment or privatization of state-owned and state-run institutions. The SAP concept by itself was not a bad idea because for the first time it forced countries in sub-Saharan Africa to realign their politics and economies by shifting their focus from reliance on cronyism and corruption to political support for economic development.[10] A related argument was made by Fantu Cheru that SSA countries could exploit the benefits of globalization and improve their competitive position through enhanced institutional effectiveness and the alignment of governance and effective economic management.[11]

Considering that the industrial base and private sector in SSA is very weak, that the region suffers from a lack of visionary leadership, and that national policies and institutional missions are ineffective, the implementation of SAP stipulations required that SSA nations promote economic development through continued emphasis on primary production instead of on value-added secondary or tertiary products, which would be required to foster export-oriented industrialization. In the process, the SAP regime forced SSA to remain a region for cheap and unskilled labor that primarily produced raw agricultural products to feed Western manufacturing industries.

The structural adjustment programs were abandoned in the mid-1990s because of the significant hardship they imposed on the poor in the region. Whether stated explicitly or not, the design of SAPs conceived SSA governments as constraints to socioeconomic development. This is inferred from the fact that SAPs placed more emphasis on the role of markets and the private sector to achieve socioeconomic development. The unanticipated consequence of SAPs was that without a vibrant private sector to provide employment and to absorb some of the responsibilities of the government, there was a general decrease in levels of public investment and social services provided by the governments. This was evident in the decline in resources directed to health care, housing, education, and agricultural development, which had direct implications for poverty alleviation and for improving the quality of life for the rural and urban poor in sub-Saharan Africa. The situation was worsened by high rates of inflation caused by the devaluation of SSA currencies—resulting in a significant rise in the prices of basic goods and services and the overall cost of living. This led to widespread criticism of SAPs in particular and the globalization process as a whole. Critics were emboldened to question the motives of the globalization stakeholders such as multinational corporations and investors from developed countries. It was argued that MNCs benefit more and are favored in the globalization process because their home countries are the headquarters and the major policymakers of the multinational institutions (IMF, ILO, World Bank, FAO, etc.) that set the terms of the globalization process.[12]

The ugly features of imperialism and neocolonialism that were used to describe the postindependent SSA have been invoked to characterize globalization. First, Yash Tandon argued that globalization is covert neocolonialism because it infringes on the social, cultural, economic, legal, and political autonomy and self-determination of developing nations.[13] Second, L. Banjo argued that because the terms of globalization are dictated to poorer nations by international labor, economic, trade, and financial institutions that are also based in the home countries of the MNCs, the policies of the international institutions are designed to protect the foreign investments, capital and portfolio flows, and new markets of the MNCs across the globe.[14] Finally, it has been argued that globalization exports cultural imperialism and institutionalizes the domination and exploitation of weaker SSA countries.[15] In spite of those criticisms, SSA countries that focused on building the necessary capacities have made measured progress toward socioeconomic development.

Implications of Globalization on the Competitiveness of Sub-Saharan Africa

The new realities of globalization require a change in the view that contextualized the geopolitical and socioeconomic situations of SSA as being isolated, unique, and to be neglected. In this regard, the old economic development paradigm in which there is a high dependence on foreign assistance to substitute for ineffective and inept leadership, poor governance, and misguided institutional missions is becoming unsustainable. It cannot be overstated that sustainable development in the region should be based on the ingenuity of SSA countries to improve their competitive positions and success should be measured in terms of improvement in the standard of living and the quality of life for the people of the region. Achieving this goal is contingent upon the following:

1. a macroeconomic environment based on sound fiscal and monetary policies that is conducive to private and foreign investments, that facilitates an effective legal system protective of property rights, and that fosters cooperative relationships between the public and the private sectors;
2. a regional shift in attitude and culture from lesser reliance on foreign aid to national policies that seek cooperative relationships with international development organizations, nongovernmental organizations, and multinational corporations to effectively identify and efficiently allocate development resources, so that a culture of advancing long-term socioeconomic development through self-reliant built-in capacities will become the norm in the region;

3. a strategic regional change in economic-development emphasis from a primarily raw-materials-supplying region, and thus a captive region for cheap labor supply, to a region that advances economic development through export-oriented industrialization, such that the food sector in SSA is transitioned from smallholder crop-production systems to vibrant agribusiness systems; and

4. finally, a higher call for MNCs, which have the potential to make exorbitant profits in SSA, to exercise some corporate social responsibility (CSR)—that is, in addition to maximizing their profits, MNCs should serve as agents of social development through sustainable investments in social, economic, education, and environmental development initiatives in the countries where they operate.

In other words, each MNC should conceive its community of operation in SSA as a legitimate stakeholder of the firm's mission. Similar calls for CSR were made during the imperial, colonial, and postindependence periods but were not taken seriously because MNCs conceived foreign development and their profit maximization objectives as mutually exclusive options. Recent calls for CSR in the ongoing globalization period have gained traction for two reasons. First, and ironically, the information and communication technologies that are enabling MNCs effectively to globalize are also used by environmental groups, labor unions, advocates for poor nations, and other self-appointed social activists and public interest groups to monitor the behavior and practices of MNCs worldwide. These groups use communication technologies such as conference calls, video conferencing, the Internet, especially social-networking sites (Facebook and Twitter), to organize massive real-time protests and public awareness campaigns against MNCs' practices or policies that are deemed harmful. Those public awareness campaigns could tarnish the image and reputation of MNCs. In these ways, contemporary interest groups are forcing global corporations to respond sensitively to the environmental, health, and poverty concerns in the developing countries where they operate.

Second, MNCs are now embracing CSR because empirical findings demonstrate that practicing CSR is not antithetical to profit maximization and does not adversely impact firm performance and competitiveness. A study that examined the linkages between financial performance and CSR found a positive relationship between CSR and prior financial performance and that CSR is positively related to the future financial performance of a firm.[16] In a related study by Jean McGuire, Allison Sungren, and Thomas Schneeweis, it was argued that a firm's prior performance, assessed by both stock market returns and accounting-based measures, are positively related to CSR.[17] These findings support the proposition that good management and CSR are positively related.

Relative Competitiveness Measures, Analyses, and Discussion of Results

Competitiveness Measures

As indicated earlier, analysis of the level of competiveness of SSA is based on three measures: the Global Competitiveness Index developed by the World Economic Forum, the UN's Millennium Development Goals, and the World Development Indicators developed by the World Bank.

Global Competitiveness Index

The Global Competitiveness Index (GCI) is a set of factors that drive and facilitate productivity, growth, efficiency, development, prosperity, and competitiveness among nations.[18] These factors are grouped into the following nine pillars: (1) institutions (effectiveness of public and private institutions); (2) infrastructure (quality of roads, railroads, ports, and airports, quality of electricity supply and telephone lines); (3) macroeconomic environment (savings rate, inflation, interest rates, government debt, and exchange rate); (4) health and primary education (primary school completion rate, business impact of malaria, tuberculosis, HIV/AIDS, infant mortality, and life expectancy); (5) higher education and training (secondary and postsecondary enrollment ratio, quality of education system, quality of math and science education, and quality of management training schools); (6) market efficiency (goods, labor, and financial markets); labor market flexibility and efficiency; and financial market sophistication and openness); (7) technological readiness (firm-level technological absorption, FDI and technology transfer, mobile phone subscribers, Internet users, and number of personal computers); (8) business sophistication (local supply chain quantity and quality and sophistication of firms' operations and strategies); and (9) innovation (quality of scientific research institutions, company spending on R&D, university-industry collaboration, intellectual property protection, and utility of patents).

The nine pillars are further organized under three indexes: basic requirements, efficiency enhancers, and innovation and business sophistication. These indexes represent the different stages of economic development in different countries.

The developing regions that are compared are grouped under North Africa, sub-Saharan Africa, Latin America and the Caribbean, and Southeast Asia. The data used for the analysis are based on the 2007 global competitiveness report.[19] The data contained therein are summarized in figures 2.1, 2.2, and 2.3.[20] Figure 2.1 shows the comparison in terms of the basic requirements pillars, figure 2.2 depicts the comparison in terms of the efficiency enhancers pillars, and figure 2.3 summarizes the comparison in terms of the innovation and business sophistication pillars. The three graphs contain the data on the annual average regional scores.

Basic Requirements Index

The basic requirements index focuses on factors that influence the production-driven stage of development. The countries here have a per capita GDP of less than $2,000. The pillars that drive this stage of development are institutions, infrastructure, macroeconomic environment, and health and primary education.

Figure 2.1 shows that compared to three other developing regions in the world, sub-Saharan Africa ranks last in all four 2007 basic requirements pillars. In terms of achievement of health and primary education, the highest score of 6.5 is reported in Latin America and the Caribbean, followed by 6.4 and 6.3 for North Africa and Southeast Asia, respectively. Sub-Saharan Africa scored 4.0, which is 62 percent of Latin America and the Caribbean's score. In terms of effectiveness of the macroeconomic environment, North Africa and Southeast Asia had the highest score of 4.6, followed by Latin America and the Caribbean with a score of 4.4; SSA had the lowest score of 4.0. With respect to infrastructural development, North Africa had the highest score of 3.5, followed by Latin America and the Caribbean with 3.3 and Southeast Asia with 3.1, and SSA in last place with 2.5. The final basic requirements pillar that is analyzed is the effectiveness of institutions. Figure 2.1 shows that the best-performing regions are Southeast Asia and North Africa with scores of 4.6, followed by Latin America and the Caribbean with a score of 4.2, and SSA last at 3.7.

Efficiency Enhancers Index

The efficiency enhancers index focuses on the factors that influence the efficiency-driven stage of development. It involves countries with per capita GDP of between $3,000 and $9,000. The pillars that drive this stage of development are higher education and training, market efficiency, and technological readiness.

The results that are summarized in figure 2.2 show that Southeast Asia was the leading developing region in market efficiency and higher education and training with scores of 4.6 and 4.1, respectively, followed by Latin America and the Caribbean (4.1 and 3.9) and North Africa (4.0 and 3.7). In terms of technological readiness, Latin America and the Caribbean lead

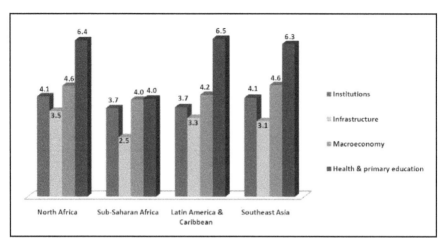

Figure 2.1. Comparison of developing regions on the basis of 2007 basic requirements index. World Economic Forum, *The African Competitiveness Report, 2007* (Geneva, 2007), 3–28.

the developing regions with a score of 3.4, followed by Southeast Asia (3.3) and North Africa (3.0). SSA scored 3.9 for market efficiency, 2.8 for higher education and training, and 2.7 for technological readiness.

Innovation and Business Sophistication Index

The innovation and business sophistication index focuses on factors that facilitate the innovation-driven stage of development, and it involves countries with per capita GDP of over $17,000. Figure 2.3 shows that compared to the other three developing regions, SSA ranked the highest in 2007 level of business sophistication, scoring 5.6, or about 30 percent higher than the performances of Southeast Asia and of Latin America and the Caribbean and 40 percent above the performance of North Africa. In terms of technological innovation, SSA scored the lowest in 2007 at 3.1, not significantly behind the performances of the other developing regions.

Comparison in Terms of Selected Millennium Development Goals

The comparison in terms of Millennium Development Goals (MDGs) is summarized in table 2.1 and figure 2.4. The six MDGs that are analyzed are: (a) the level of poverty, measured in terms of the proportion of people living on less than purchasing power parity of $1.25 per day; (b) access to

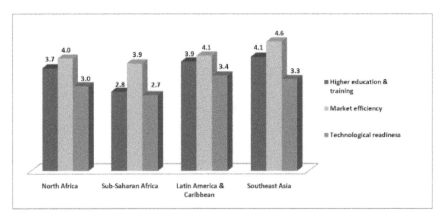

Figure 2.2. Comparison of developing regions on the basis of 2007 efficiency enhancers. World Economic Forum, *The African Competitiveness Report, 2007* (Geneva, 2007), 3–28.

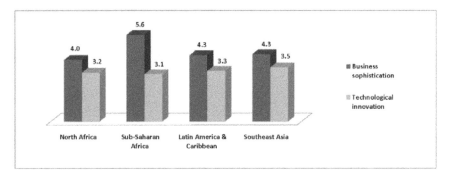

Figure 2.3. Comparison of developing regions on the basis of 2007 innovative factors. World Economic Forum, *The African Competitiveness Report, 2007* (Geneva, 2007), 3–28.

universal primary education, measured in terms of primary school completion; (c) reduction in child mortality rate, measured in under-five mortality per one thousand; (d) contraceptive prevalence rate, measured in percent of married women ages fifteen to forty-nine who have access to contraceptives; (e) promotion of gender equality, measured in terms of the ratio of girls' to boys' enrollment in primary and secondary school; and (f) access to improved sanitation facilities, measured in percent of total population. The developing regions are grouped thus: East Asia and the Pacific, Latin America and the Caribbean, the Middle East and North Africa, South Asia, and sub-Saharan Africa. The analysis is based on 2009 World Development Indicators for 1991–2007 MDGs.[21]

Table 2.1. Comparison of selected millennium development goals in developing regions, 1991 to 2007

	1. Poverty (pop. living on < US$1.25/day)			2. Universal primary education (%)		
	1991	2007	Progress (% change 1991–2007)	1991	2007	Progress (% change 1991–2007)
East Asia & Pacific	54.7	16.8	−106.0	100	98	−2.0
Latin America & Caribbean	11.3	8.2	−31.8	84	100	17.4
Middle East & North Africa	4.3	3.6	−17.7	78	90	14.3
South Asia	51.7	40.3	−24.8	62	80	25.4
Sub-Saharan Africa	57.6	50.9	−12.4	51	60	16.2

	3. Reduce child mortality rate per 1,000			4. Contraceptive prevalence rate (%)		
	1991	2007	Progress (% change 1991–2007)	1991	2007	Progress (% change 1991–2007)
East Asia & Pacific	56	27	−69.9	75	78	3.9
Latin America & Caribbean	55	26	−71.6	56	57	1.8
Middle East & North Africa	77	38	−67.8	42	62	38.5
South Asia	125	78	−46.3	40	53	28.0
Sub-Saharan Africa	183	146	−22.5	15	23	42.1

	5. Promote gender equality (%)			6. Access to improved sanitation (%)		
	1991	2007	Progress (% change 1991–2007)	1991	2007	Progress (% change 1991–2007)
East Asia & Pacific	89	99	10.6	48	66	31.6
Latin America & Caribbean	98	100	2.0	68	78	13.7
Middle East & North Africa	78	96	20.7	67	77	13.9
South Asia	70	89	23.9	18	33	58.8
Sub-Saharan Africa	79	86	8.5	26	31	17.5

Source: World Development Indicators Report 2009 (Washington, DC: World Bank, 2010).

The regions are compared on the basis of progress made in achieving MDGs, which is defined in terms of percentage changes of the targets over the analyzed period and are summarized in figure 2.4. The results indicate that the poverty rate decreased in all of the developing regions of the world but that the largest decrease in the poverty rate (106 percent) was recorded in East Asia and the Pacific, while SSA experienced the lowest decrease (12.4 percent) over the 1991–2007 period.

In terms of improvement in access to universal primary education, with the exception of East Asia and the Pacific, which experienced a 2 percent decline, there was an increase in all other developing regions. The highest percentage increase in access to primary education (25.4 percent) occurred in South Asia, followed by Latin America and the Caribbean (17.4 percent), SSA (16.2 percent), and the Middle East and North Africa (14.4 percent).

The childhood mortality rate decreased in all developing regions of the world, with Latin America and the Caribbean outperforming all other regions with a 71.6 percent drops, followed by declines of 69.9 percent in East Asia and the Pacific, 67.8 percent in the Middle East and North Africa, 46.3 percent in South Asia, and 22.5 percent—the lowest reduction in childhood mortality—in SSA.

All developing regions made progress in contraceptive prevalence rate, with the largest rate increase, of 42.1 percent, recorded in SSA, compared to increases of 38.5 percent in the Middle East and North Africa and 28 percent in South Asia In East Asia and the Pacific the rate increased by 3.9 percent, and the least progress in contraceptive prevalence (1.3 percent) occurred in Latin America and the Caribbean.

In terms of the promotion of gender equality, progress was made in all developing regions. The highest increase in gender equality rate, or the percentage of girls' to boys' enrollment in primary and secondary schools, of 23.8 percent occurred in South Asia; and the smallest progress among the developing regions of 2 percent occurred in Latin America and the Caribbean. The Middle East and North Africa, East Asia and the Pacific, and SSA recorded respective increases of 20.7 percent, 10.6 percent, and 8.5 percent in the gender equality rate.

Finally, the percentage of population in developing regions that had access to improved sanitation increased in all developing regions over the 1991–2007 period. South Asia had the highest increase in access to improved sanitation of 58.8 percent, followed by a 31.6 percent increase in East Asia and the Pacific; SSA was in the third position with an increase of 17.5 percent. The Middle East and North Africa and Latin America and the Caribbean had the lowest increases: 13.9 and 13.7 percent, respectively.

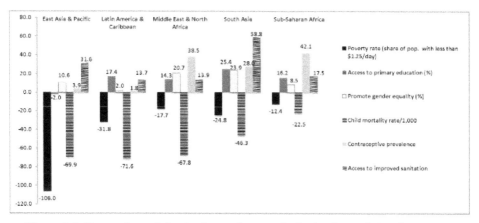

Figure 2.4. Comparison of developing regions on the basis of growth in selected millennium development goals from 1991 to 2007. *World Development Indicators Report 2009* (Washington, DC: World Bank, 2010).

Comparison in Terms of World Development Indicators

The World Development Indicators (WDIs) analyzed here focus on the structure of the economies of the developing regions. As with the MDGs, the regions are grouped thus: East Asia and the Pacific, Latin America and the Caribbean, the Middle East and North Africa, South Asia, and sub-Saharan Africa. The developing regions are analyzed and compared in terms of percentage changes (growth) in selected WDIs: structures of production, demand, and merchandise trade over the period 1995–2007 contained in the 2009 *World Development Indicators* report.[22] The data on the structures of production, demand, and merchandise trade are summarized in tables 2.2, 2.3, and 2.4, respectively, and also represented graphically in figures 2.5, 2.6, and 2.7.

Structure of Production

The summarized data on the structure of production in table 2.2 include the levels of (a) gross domestic product, defined as the sum of all value added by domestic producers plus any product taxes not included in output; (b) agricultural production, defined as the sum of gross output less the value of intermediate inputs used in production in agricultural industries including forestry and fishing (measured as a percentage of GDP); (c) industry, defined as the sum of gross output less the value of intermediate inputs used in production by companies involved in mining, manufacturing, construction, electricity, water, and gas and (d) manufacturing, defined as the sum of

Table 2.2. Comparison of the structure of production in developing regions, 1995 to 2007

	1. GDP (millions US$)			2. Agriculture growth (% GDP)		
	1995	2007	Growth (% change 1995–2007)	1995	2007	Growth (% change 1995–2007)
East Asia & Pacific	1,312,340	4,365,487	107.5	3.5	4	13.3
Latin America & Caribbean	1,751,109	3,615,910	69.5	2.1	3.5	50.0
Middle East & North Africa	315,655	850,182	91.7	2.9	4.4	41.1
South Asia	476,196	1,443,539	100.8	3.3	3.1	-6.2
Sub-Saharan Africa	327,582	847,438	88.5	3.2	3	-6.5

	3. Industry (% GDP)			4. Manufacturing (% GDP)		
	1995	2007	Growth (% change 1995–2007)	1995	2007	Growth (% change 1995–2007)
East Asia & Pacific	11	10.1	-8.5	10.9	9.7	-11.7
Latin America & Caribbean	3.1	3.3	6.2	2.9	3.3	12.9
Middle East & North Africa	4.1	3.6	-13.0	4.2	6	35.3
South Asia	6	8.3	32.2	6.4	8.1	23.4
Sub-Saharan Africa	2	5.2	88.9	2.1	3.2	41.5

Source: World Development Indicators Report 2009 (Washington, DC: World Bank, 2010).

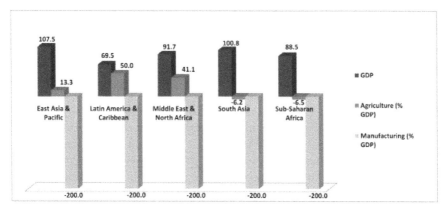

Figure 2.5. Comparison of developing regions on the basis of growth in structures of production from 1995 to 2007. *World Development Indicators Report 2009* (Washington, DC: World Bank, 2010).

gross output less the value of intermediate inputs used in selected industries not included in the industrial category.

The results for the growth in production in figure 2.5 show that East Asia experienced the highest percentage increase in GDP (107.5 percent), followed by South Asia (100.8 percent), the Middle East and North Africa (91.7 percent), SSA (88.5 percent), and Latin America and the Caribbean (69.5 percent).

Over the 1995–2007 period, the highest percentage increase in agricultural production occurred in Latin America and the Caribbean (50 percent), followed by the Middle East and North Africa (41.1 percent), and East Asia and the Pacific (13.3 percent) Agricultural production declined by 6.2 percent in South Asia, and SSA made the least progress with a decline of 6.5 percent.

East Asia and the Pacific also experienced the highest growth rate of 10.1 percent in industrial production from 1995 to 2007. The second-highest growth rate occurred in South Asia (8.3 percent), followed by SSA (5.2 percent) in the third position. The lowest levels of industrial production growth occurred in the Middle East and North Africa and in Latin America and the Caribbean (3.6 and 3.3 percent, respectively).

SSA outpaced all other developing regions in the rate of growth in manufacturing output with 41.5 percent, followed by the Middle East and North Africa (33.5 percent), South Asia (23.4 percent), and Latin America and the Caribbean (12.9 percent). East Asia and the Pacific saw a significant 11.5 percent decline, the only region not to experience growth in manufacturing output.

Structure of Demand

Table 2.3 contains the data on the structure of demand, including the levels of (a) household consumption expenditure, defined as the market value of all the goods and services purchased by households (measured as a percentage share of GDP); (b) government consumption expenditure, defined as the market value of total government current expenditures on all goods and services including spending on national defense and security but excluding military expenditures with potentially wider public use that are part of government capital formation; (c) gross capital formation, defined as the outlays on additions to fixed economic assets, net changes in inventories, and net acquisitions of valuables; and (d) gross savings, defined as gross national income less total consumption plus net transfers.

The results on the growth in household consumption in figure 2.6 show that over the period 1995–2007, all the developing regions experienced a decline in consumption. The largest decline in household consumption of 23.7 percent occurred in Latin America and the Caribbean, followed by decreases of 20.8 percent in sub-Saharan Africa, 13.6 percent in East Asia and the Pacific, 12.7 percent in South Asia, and 8.3 percent in the Middle East and North Africa.

The level of government purchases either decreased or remained constant in all the developing regions with the exception of SSA, where government purchases increased by 6.5 percent. Government purchases did not increase in East Asia and the Pacific and in South Asia, while in the Middle East and North Africa and in Latin America and the Caribbean government purchases decreased by 14.3 and 6.9 percent, respectively.

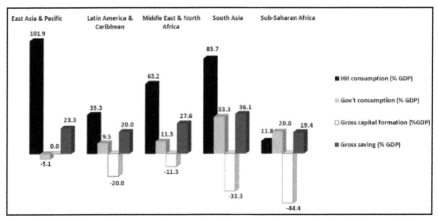

Figure 2.6. Comparison of developing-region economies on the basis of growth in structure of demand from 1995 to 2007. *World Development Indicators Report 2009* (Washington, DC: World Bank, 2010).

Table 2.3. Comparison of the structure of demand in developing regions, 1995 to 2007

	Household consumption (% of GDP)			Government consumption (% of GDP)		
	1995	2007	Growth (% change 1995–2007)	1995	2007	Growth (% change 1995–2007)
East Asia & Pacific	47	41	-13.6	13	13	0.0
Latin America & Caribbean	66	52	-23.7	15	14	-6.9
Middle East & North Africa	63	58	-8.3	15	13	-14.3
South Asia	67	59	-12.7	10	10	0.0
Sub-Saharan Africa	69	56	-20.8	15	16	6.5

	Gross capital formation (% of GDP)			Gross savings (% of GDP)		
	1995	2007	Growth (% change 1995–2007)	1995	2007	Growth (% change 1995–2007)
East Asia & Pacific	40	38	-5.1	38	48	23.3
Latin America & Caribbean	20	22	9.5	18	22	20.0
Middle East & North Africa	25	28	11.3	25	33	27.6
South Asia	25	35	33.3	25	36	36.1
Sub-Saharan Africa	18	22	20.0	14	17	19.4

Source: World Development Indicators Report 2009 (Washington, DC: World Bank, 2010).

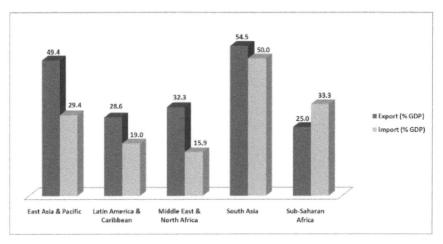

Figure 2.7. Comparison of developing-region economies on the basis of growth in exports and imports from 1995 to 2007. *World Development Indicators Report 2009* (Washington, DC: World Bank, 2010).

Structure of Merchandise Trade

The structure of merchandise trade is defined as the value of all goods and services provided to other countries (exports) or received from other countries (imports). This includes the value of merchandise, freight, insurance, transport, travel, royalties, and license fees. The data on merchandise trade are summarized in table 2.4.

The results on merchandise trade displayed in figure 2.7 show that over the period 1995–2007, the level of exports increased in all the developing regions. SSA experienced the smallest amount of increase (25 percent). The highest increase in exports occurred in South Asia (54.5 percent), followed by the Middle East and North Africa (32.3 percent), and Latin America and the Caribbean (28.6 percent).

Merchandise imports into SSA increased by 33.3 percent from 1995 to 2007, which was the second highest behind South Asia, where imports increased by 50 percent. The third-highest percentage increase in imports for this period was in East Asia and the Pacific (29.4 percent), followed by Latin America and the Caribbean (19 percent) and the Middle East and North Africa (15.9 percent).

Competitiveness among Sub-Saharan African Countries

Having analyzed sub-Saharan Africa's competitive position relative to other developing regions, it is important to delineate the sources of competitiveness

Table 2.4. Comparison of merchandise trade in developing regions, 1995 to 2007

	Merchandise trade—exports (% GDP)			Merchandise trade—imports (% GDP)		
	1995	2007	Growth (% change 1995–2007)	1995	2007	Growth (% change 1995–2007)
East Asia & Pacific	29	48	49.4	29	39	29.4
Latin America & Caribbean	18	24	28.6	19	23	19.0
Middle East & North Africa	26	36	32.3	29	34	15.9
South Asia	12	21	54.5	15	25	50.0
Sub-Saharan Africa	21	27	25.0	20	28	33.3

Source: *World Development Indicators Report 2009* (Washington, DC: World Bank, 2010).

within the region and the strategies that characterize the best practices of the top-performing countries. The best-performing SSA countries are selected on the basis of their world rankings. The top five SSA countries in the overall 2007 global competitiveness rankings are South Africa (forty-sixth), Mauritius (fifty-eighth), Botswana (eighty-third), Namibia (eighty-eighth), and Kenya (ninety-seventh). The nine pillars of competitiveness that are grouped under basic requirements, efficiency enhancers, and the innovation and business sophistication indexes are used to analyze and compare the competitiveness of the SSA countries.

Basic Requirements Index

Figure 2.8 summarizes the 2007 basic requirements index that deals with factors that drive the production stage of development. In terms of the effectiveness of its institutions, South Africa ranked top among all SSA countries with a score of 4.8. It was followed by Botswana (4.5), Mauritius (4.4), Namibia (4.2), and Gambia (4.1).

The infrastructure of Namibia and Mauritius were equally ranked as the best in SSA with a score of 4.2 in 2007. The next best infrastructure was that of South Africa (4.0), followed by Botswana (3.4) and Gambia (2.6).

In terms of macroeconomic environment, Botswana's was the best in SSA in 2007 with a score of 4.9, followed by Namibia (4.8), South Africa (4.7), and Gambia and Mauritius (both at 3.8).

Mauritius had the best health and primary education in SSA with a score of 6.6, followed by South Africa (5.1), Gambia (4.9), and Namibia (4.6); Botswana was in fifth position with a score of 4.4.

Efficiency Enhancers Index

Figure 2.9 summarizes the 2007 efficiency enhancers index, which focuses on how three factors—education and trading, market efficiency, and technological readiness—enhance the efficiency-driven stage of development. It shows that in 2007, South Africa led all SSA countries in market efficiency, education and training, and technological readiness with respective scores of 4.7, 4.2, and 3.9. Mauritius ranked second in education and training with 3.9, followed by Botswana and Kenya, which both scored 3.4, and Nigeria at 3.0. In terms of market efficiency in 2007, ranking behind South Africa were Botswana, with a score of 4.2, and Kenya, Mauritius, and Nigeria, all at 4.1. Finally, Mauritius ranked second in technological innovation with a score of 3.6, followed by Botswana (3.0) and Kenya and Nigeria (both at 2.9).

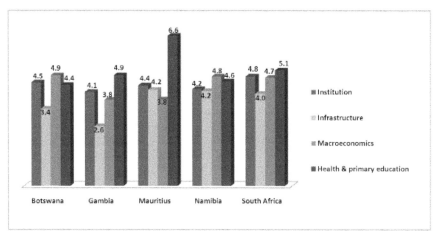

Figure 2.8. Comparison of top-performing sub-Saharan African countries on the basis of 2007 basic competitiveness factors. World Economic Forum, *The African Competitiveness Report, 2007* (Geneva, 2007), 3–28; World Economic Forum, *Global Competitiveness Report, 2007* (Geneva, 2008).

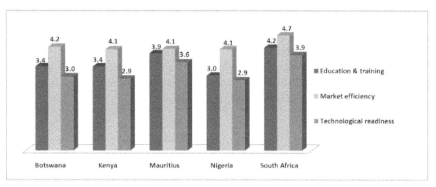

Figure 2.9. Comparison of top-performing sub-Saharan African countries on the basis of 2007 efficiency enhancers. World Economic Forum, *The African Competitiveness Report, 2007* (Geneva, 2007), 3–28; World Economic Forum, *Global Competitiveness Report, 2007* (Geneva, 2008).

Innovation and Business Sophistication Index

Figure 2.10 summarizes the 2007 business innovative factors (technological innovation and business sophistication) and drive the innovation stage of development. The analysis in figure 2.10 shows that South Africa led all SSA countries in business sophistication and technological innovation with respective scores of 4.8 and 3.9. Kenya ranked second in technological

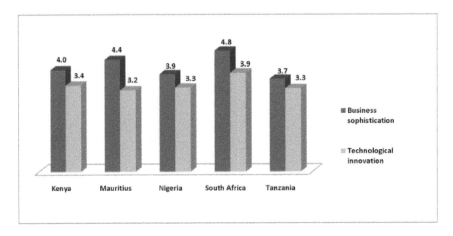

Figure 2.10. Comparison of top-performing sub-Saharan African countries on the basis of 2007 innovative factors. World Economic Forum, *The African Competitiveness Report, 2007* (Geneva, 2007), 3–28; World Economic Forum, *Global Competitiveness Report, 2007* (Geneva, 2008).

innovation (3.4) and third in business sophistication (4.0). Mauritius ranked second in business sophistication and fourth in technological innovation (4.4 and 3.2, respectively). When business sophistication was measured, Nigeria's score (3.9) ranked fourth, and Tanzania's (3.7) fifth; both countries scored 3.3 in technological innovation.

Summary of the Findings and Conclusion

The results of this study are summarized in this section in terms of the findings of the analyses conducted on the GCIs, MDGs, and WDIs. The initial main finding of this study is that all developing regions made socioeconomic progress as defined by Millennium Development Goals and World Development Indicators. In terms of progress in achieving MDGs, all developing regions experienced decreases in extreme poverty, reductions in childhood mortality, increases in contraceptive prevalence, increases in gender equality, and improvements in sanitation. With respect to access to universal primary education, all developing regions experienced improvement with the exception of East Asia and the Pacific, where access decreased by 2 percent. In terms of WDIs, all regions experienced increases in GDP, gross savings, merchandise imports, and merchandise exports. Gross capital formation also increased in all developing regions with the exception of East Asia and the Pacific.

Four developing regions—North Africa, SSA, Latin America and the Caribbean, and Southeast Asia—were used in the GCI comparison. The main findings are that SSA ranked first in business sophistication but last in health and primary education, macroeconomic environment, infrastructural development, effectiveness of institutions, higher education and training, market efficiency, technological readiness, and technological innovation.

Five developing regions—East Asia and the Pacific, the Middle East and North Africa, SSA, Latin America and the Caribbean, and South Asia—were used in the MDG comparison. The main findings are that SSA ranked first among all developing regions in contraceptive prevalence rates. On the other hand, SSA ranked last in decreasing poverty and in decreasing childhood mortality rates. In terms of access to universal primary education and improved sanitation, SSA ranked third, and the region was in fourth position in improving gender equality.

The same five developing regions were used in the WDI comparisons. In terms of the structure of production, SSA ranked first in growth in manufacturing output, third in industrial output, fourth in manufacturing output, and last in agricultural output. With respect to the structure of demand (consumption), SSA experienced the largest decrease in household consumption, the largest increase in government consumption, the second-highest growth in gross capital formation, and the slowest growth in gross savings. Finally, SSA experienced the smallest percentage increase in exports of goods and services and the third-largest percentage increase in imports.

The analyses of the best-performing SSA countries demonstrate that South Africa, which is forty-sixth in world competitiveness rankings, is the region's top-performing country. This can be attributed to its high performance in education and training, market efficiency, technological readiness, business sophistication, technological innovation, and the effectiveness of its institutions. Mauritius, which is the second-best economic performer in SSA and which ranks fifty-eighth in global competitiveness, outperformed all other countries in the region in infrastructural development and in health and primary education. Botswana, which ranks third in performance among SSA countries, had the region's best macroeconomic environment.

Notes

1. Thomas J. Bierstecker, "Globalization and the Modes of Operation of Major Institutional Actors," *Oxford Development Studies* 20 (1998): 15–31.
2. Philip G. Cerny, "The Dynamics of Financial Globalization: Technology, Market Structure, and Policy Response," *Policy Science* 27 (1994): 317–42.
3. Charles P. Klindleberger, "International Public Goods without International Government," *American Economic Review* 76 (1986): 1–13.

4. Christian M. Rogerson, "Flexible Production in the Developing World: The Case of South Africa," *Geo-Forum* 25, no. 1 (1994): 1–17.

5. John H. Dunning, "Globalization and the New Geography of Foreign Direct Investment," *Oxford Development Studies* 26 (1998): 47–69.

6. Joseph E. Stiglitz, *Public Knowledge for a Global Economy* (London: Center for Economic Policy Research, 1999).

7. D. C. Korten, "The Truth about Global Competition: The Economic Myths behind Globalization," *Development and Cooperation*, no. 3 (1996): 4–5.

8. John K. Akokpari, "Globalization and the Challenges for the African State," *Nordic Journal of African Studies* 10 (2001): 188–209.

9. Gill Hammond, Ravi Kanbur, and Eswar Prasad, *Monetary Policy Frameworks for Emerging Markets* (Edward Elgar, 2009).

10. John K. Akokpari, "Changing with the Tide: The Shifting Orientations of Foreign Policies in Sub-Saharan Africa," *Nordic Journal of African Studies* 8, no. 1 (1999): 22–39.

11. Fantu Cheru, *African Renaissance: Roadmaps to the Challenge of Globalization* (Cape Town: Zed Books, 2003).

12. Claude Ake, *Democracy and Development in Africa* (New York: Brookings Institution, 1996).

13. Yash Tandon, "Globalization and Africa's Options," in *Globalization and the Post-Colonial African State*, ed. Dani W. Nabudere (Harare, Zimbabwe: AAPS Books, 2000).

14. L. Banjo, "IMF, World Bank, WTO: The Wicked Machines of the Imperialist," *Sunday Tribune*, April 23, 2000, 19; Yash Tandon, "Global Issues and Africa's Marginalisation," presentation at the Canberra African Studies Conference, 1997, 4–5.

15. Tandon, "Globalization and Africa's Options."

16. Samuel B. Graves and Sandra A. Waddock, "Institutional Owners and Corporate Social Performance," *Academy of Management Journal* 4, no. 37 (1994): 1034–46.

17. Jean B. McGuire, Allison Sungren, and Thomas Schneeweis, "Corporate Social Responsibility and Firm Financial Performance," *Academy of Management Journal* 31, no. 4 (1998): 854–72.

18. World Economic Forum, *Global Competitiveness Report, 2007–2008* (Geneva, 2007), http://www.allianceau.com/pics/advant/2007_WorldEconomicForum.pdf.

19. World Economic Forum, *Global Competitiveness Report, 2008–2009* (Geneva, 2008), http://www.workinfo.com/Workforce/20997_devindicators.pdf.

20. Jennifer Blanke, "Assessing Africa's Competitiveness in a Global Context," *The Africa Competitiveness Report* (Geneva: World Economic Forum, 2007), 3–28, http://www.weforum.org/pdf/gcr/africa/1.1.pdf.

21. World Bank, *World Development Indicators, 2009* (Washington, DC, 2009), http://www.workinfo.com/Workforce/20997_devindicators.pdf; http://siteresources.worldbank.org/DATASTATISTICS/Resources/WDI08supplement1216.pdf.

22. World Bank, *World Development Indicators, 2009.*

3

A Two-Track Strategy for Viable Development in Africa

BENAIAH YONGO-BURE

Introduction

Globalization is the process of achieving greater interdependence among countries and their citizens.[1] It consists of increased integration of product and resource markets across countries in trade, immigration, and foreign investment—that is, via the international flow of goods and services; of people; and of investments such as equipment, factories, stocks, and bonds. It also includes noneconomic elements such as culture and the environment. It is political, technological, and cultural, as well as economic.

Globalization is not new. It is the intensification and deepening of the process of international interactions. The first and most profound influence or driving force of globalization is technology. Since the Industrial Revolution in Europe of the mid-eighteenth century, technical innovations have led to an explosion of productivity and slashed transportation costs. The steam engine, railways, and mechanization of a growing number of activities produced these developments. Later discoveries and inventions such as electricity, the telephone, the automobile, container ships, and pipelines altered production, communication, and transportation tremendously.[2] More recently, rapid developments in computer information and communications technology have further shrunk the influence of time and geography on the capacity of individuals and enterprises to interact and make transactions around the world. For services, the rise of the Internet has been a major factor in decreased communication costs and increased trade. As technical progress has extended the scope of what can be produced and where it can be produced, and advances in transport technology have continued to bring people and enterprises closer, the boundaries of tradable goods and services have been greatly extended.

Continuing liberalization of trade and investment has resulted from multilateral trade negotiations. For example, tariffs in industrial countries have been brought down from high double digits in the 1940s to about 5 percent in the early 2000s.[3] At the same time, most quotas on trade, excepting those imposed for such reasons as health and safety, have been removed. Globalization has also been promoted through the widespread liberalization of investment transactions and the development of international financial markets. These factors have facilitated global trade through greater availability and affordability of financing.

Lower trade barriers and financial liberalization have allowed more and more companies to globalize production structures through investment abroad, which in turn has provided a further stimulus to international trade. On the technology side, increased information flows and greater tradability of goods and services have had a profound influence on decisions related to the location of production. Businesses are increasingly able to locate different components of their production processes in various countries and regions and still maintain a single corporate identity. As firms subcontract part of their production processes to their affiliates or other enterprises abroad, jobs, technologies, capital, and skills are transferred around the globe.

The high degree of interdependence among today's economies reflects the historical evolution of the world's economic and political order. The rise of capitalism, the Industrial Revolution, and European overseas expansion set the stage for the internationalization of economic activities. Thus, from the 1500s to the early 1900s, various European powers dominated international economic relations. This domination was greatly shaken by World War I and did not recover until after World War II. By the end of the latter war, the United States had become economically and politically the most powerful country in the world. However, with the postwar recoveries of Western Europe and Japan, the relative size of the US economy and its overwhelming dominance declined. The formation of the European Community (later the European Union, or EU), the rising importance of multinational corporations in the 1960s, the shift of market power in regard to world oil production to the Organization of Petroleum Exporting Countries (OPEC) in the 1970s, and the creation of the euro at the turn of the twenty-first century have together contributed to the evolution of the world community into a complicated system based on growing interdependence.

Africa's Incorporation into the International Economy

Africa's incorporation into the global economy was formalized through the Berlin Conference of 1884–85.[4] Africa has thus experienced the major waves of globalization of the years 1870–1914 and of the post–World War II period. Africa's insignificant influence on the direction of global events and its consequent position as a subservient follower can be attributed largely to its balkanization resulting from the Berlin Conference and its lack of transformation in the postcolonial period. For all the talk of globalization, the process has been primarily driven by a few powerful actors in Europe and North America. Europe's early start in global economic domination and control of colonies gave Europeans advantages over other parts of the world. But as they lost their overseas possessions, their weight in the world system has been waning, although colonial legacies still give some European countries a kind of advantage.

The vast continental expanse of the United States of America has given it significant advantages in becoming a world power, aided by its tremendous natural and human resources as well as its huge domestic market. Such advantages gave the state of Michigan the ability, for many decades, to sustain three large car manufacturing companies because it is part of a large national market with unrestricted access to supplies of capital and human resources. The economic condition of the three automakers has been problematic, however, in recent years as they have suffered relative decline. Among the advantages of Michigan's being, in effect, part of a "free trade" zone include the ability to "export" freely to the huge domestic market without any market restrictions imposed by any of the other forty-nine American states and to "import" materials without tariff from any of them. Further, it can raise capital and recruit skilled labor from a large national pool. If the American states were separate countries as the African countries are, it would not have been possible for Detroit to establish and sustain a world-leading automobile industry for so long.

Although small countries can industrialize, they cannot drive their own destiny for very long. The twenty-first century is being billed by some as the "Chinese Century," just as the twentieth century was labeled the "American Century."[5] Hong Kong, Japan, Singapore, South Korea, and Taiwan could not claim the twentieth century even though their economies underwent major transformations because none of these economies were as dominant as that of the United States. To have a say in the direction of globalization, a country must have a relatively large and diversified economy with great potential for further development. For instance, if China's resources plus its actual and potential market were not so large, it would be another Hong Kong or Taiwan. The direction of China's economic development is being determined by the Chinese themselves because of their country's standing among the countries of the world. Instead of large foreign companies telling China what to do, they do what China asks them to do. Hence, they readily make their technology available to China, overlook China's pirating of their patents, and willingly undertake research and development in China. In the face of the 2007–9 economic meltdown and shrinkage of export markets, the Chinese government passed an economic stimulus package aimed at encouraging the growth of its potentially huge domestic market; as a result, the Chinese economy has continued to grow in spite of the severe global recession.

The nineteenth-century conditions that enabled small European countries to develop do not exist today, and African countries can not hope to develop as small European countries once did. As pioneers in industrialization, the Europeans faced no established competitors in the world market. As they exercised control over much of the world, they dictated the terms of international interactions. Europe's technology was the most efficient, and non-Europeans were not allowed to copy it. Europeans imported whatever resources they wanted on their terms and exported freely to all markets under their control.[6]

If they want to change significantly the living conditions of most Africans as well as to have impact on the trend and pace of globalization, African countries cannot expect to follow the past footsteps of European countries. However, they might emulate the strategic moves of Europe, such as the evolution of the European Union and the introduction of a monetary union represented by the euro. In ways similar to those Europeans have taken to enhance their welfare and influence in global affairs, the numerous African countries must undertake to transform themselves through collective self-reliance and the encouragement of viable, self-sustaining development strategies, such as "regional development poles" (RDPs). African countries may thus become significant actors within the global system and at the same time make marked improvements in the living conditions of the majority of Africans.

The quest for collective self-reliance has been advanced by African leaders in different forms since the beginnings of the various movements toward decolonization. There have been calls for African unity, as well as regional cooperation and integration, but the results have not been great. However, the Lagos Plan of Action and the Abuja Treaty, which embodied the vision of an African Economic Community (AEC) and its component regional economic communities (RECs), must be seriously pursued.[7] But given the political difficulties of separate countries pursuing a common development agenda, successes in regional and eventual continental integration has lagged. Yet, as Africa drags its feet on these fundamental issues, the processes of globalization will surely continue to unfold, and the many tiny, separate African countries will continue to be ill-prepared for its attendant challenges. Hence, the second strategy of encouraging RDPs should be given emphasis to complement the strategy of regional and eventual continental integration.

The strategy of RDPs places emphasis on accelerating the economic transformation of the few large African countries that can industrialize on their own based on their wealth of natural and human resources and large domestic markets. The creation of "development poles" within Africa could lead to the establishment of diversified industrial economies on the continent, which may in turn lead to faster diffusion of economic development to the surrounding African countries. The building of inter-African highways, railways, long-distance power transmission lines, and direct communications links could accelerate this diffusion, making it cheaper for the rest of the smaller African countries to import development inputs from the neighboring RDPs. The need to earn foreign exchange will be less desperate than at present, as it will become relatively easier to acquire the currency of the neighboring "development pole" and import from it.

Focusing on sub-Saharan Africa (SSA), as of 2010, there were only four countries with populations of approximately or above 50 million each: Nigeria (152), Ethiopia (88), Democratic Republic of Congo (DR Congo) (71), and South Africa (49). Four other sub-Saharan African countries have populations of over 30 million each: Sudan (44), Tanzania (42), Kenya (40), and Uganda (33). The rest of SSA's countries have populations below 25 million, with those above the 20 million mark being Ghana (23), Mozambique (22), Madagascar (21), and Côte d'Ivoire (21). Cameroon (19) will soon reach the 20 million mark.[8]

African Industrialization at the National Level

The economic problems of the 1970s and 1980s led African countries to revert to the economic policies of laissez faire, free trade, and encouragement of foreign investment. But these were the fundamentals of the colonial economic policies that had left African countries dependent economically as they gained political independence. Hence, it is no wonder that since the implementation of structural adjustment programs in Africa, poverty on the continent has become more widespread. The inappropriateness of the colonial-type policies was exhaustively discussed in the 1960s, but African governments that desperately wanted foreign aid were willing to disregard the arguments against such policies so they could qualify for it. The colonial economies had been based on export of primary products to the colonial metropole, with the surplus from the export earnings being channeled to the colonial power rather than reinvested in the colonial economies. This neocolonial pattern of trade still persists in most African countries. Sustainable industrialization of tiny economies is hardly possible, particularly in a world of long-established competitors in the world market. Hence, it was inevitable that the industrialization policies of the early postindependence era were unlikely to be sustainable for most countries.[9]

Conscious industrialization policy in most underdeveloped countries began in the post–World War II period. Since the developed countries were already industrialized, while the underdeveloped countries were primary producers, economic development came to be identified with industrialization. While prices of industrial exports persistently increased relative to those of primary products, prices of exported primary products were unstable and tended to decline over time. Markets for primary products stagnated as synthetic substitutes became increasingly available. For example, synthetic substitutes for cotton, rubber, sisal, jute, hides, and skins acted both as a brake against higher commodity prices and as a direct source of competition in world markets.[10] Hence, underdeveloped countries turned to industrialization as a strategy for economic growth and development.

Having decided to industrialize, the underdeveloped countries planned to substitute locally produced goods for their industrial imports. This was the policy of import-substitution industrialization. It was thought that underdeveloped economies would progress from the simpler level of manufacturing consumer goods to intermediate goods and eventually to the manufacture of capital goods.

Import substitution was expected to improve the balance of payments as more manufactured imports would be produced domestically. Tariffs were imposed to protect the infant industries from foreign competition. But these tariffs became progressively higher with advanced stages of processing. Foreign firms were encouraged to establish "tariff factories" to circumvent the protective tariffs. Their use of capital-intensive technologies resulted in limited employment opportunities. The capital-intensive industries themselves required more imports of spare parts, raw materials, and replacement capital goods, thus requiring more foreign exchange to service them. Consequently, more resources were being devoted to these urban industries than to the agricultural sector. Rural-to-urban migration increased, but because the capital-intensive industries created few jobs, urban unemployment increased. This dire economic situation led to very serious social and political problems, particularly as the unemployed migrants increasingly came to consist of politically conscious secondary-school leavers, or dropouts. With the increase in university enrollments and output, the numbers and sophistication of the politically conscious unemployed has greatly increased. They will continue to pose a serious political problem to the ruling elites unless economic development is viewed and pursued as a matter of urgency.

Because of the limitations of import-substitution industrialization, underdeveloped countries changed their industrialization strategy to manufacturing for export. The export-of-manufactures strategy was recommended particularly for small economies with limited domestic markets.[11] At the early stages of manufacturing, most underdeveloped countries produced similar products, and could not absorb much of each other's products.

Tariffs in the more industrially developed economies progressively increased along with the higher degree of value added to manufactured imports from the underdeveloped economies. For example, tariffs on processed cocoa are twice that on raw cocoa; and while tariffs on raw sugar are below 2 percent, processed sugar typically faces tariffs of 20 percent.[12]

Given the barriers to export of manufactures, underdeveloped countries embarked on promoting regional integration so as to pool their markets. But while the cooperating and integrating countries could see the joint benefits of integration, they could not easily agree on equitable sharing of these potential benefits. The partner states were at different levels of industrialization, and each partner wanted to accelerate its own rate of industrialization and development. This outlook toward economic integration has not changed much, and hence the slow pace of such integration in Africa.

Regional and Continental Integration

African integration is a strategy for African development. It is intended not to follow development but to precede it; or both integration and development are to be pursued simultaneously. The argument that each country should solve its problems before entering into integration is spurious because lack of capacity is an integral part of the failure of development. If each country could achieve its development on its own, then why integrate?

There are various degrees of regional economic integration. A preferential trade area involves two or more countries reducing or abolishing tariffs on a limited number of products. However, this form of integration is illegal under the rules of the World Trade Organization (WTO), although exceptions can be made.[13] The most common starting form of regional integration is a *free trade area*. For a free trade area to exist, the member countries reduce or eliminate trade barriers between themselves while maintaining separate tariff schedules for trade with nonmember countries. Under a *customs union* agreement, the member countries have free trade as well as a common tariff wall for commodities from outside the union. Similar to the customs union is a *common market*. The common market is a customs union with the addition of free mobility of factors of production between the member countries. The free movement of capital and labor would allow for more efficient allocation of resources, and hence faster economic growth and development can be achieved in the member countries. Finally, the member countries may upgrade their integration into an *economic union*. Under an economic union, national, social, taxation, and fiscal policies are harmonized and administered by a supranational body. The task of creating an economic union is much more difficult than achieving the other forms of integration. This is because a free trade area, a customs union, or a common market results basically from the abolition of existing trade barriers, but an economic union requires an agreement to transfer economic sovereignty to a supranational authority. The ultimate degree of economic union would be unification of national monetary policies and the acceptance of a common currency administered by a supranational monetary authority. This means the establishment of a *monetary union.*

Robert Carbaugh gives the United States as an example of a successful monetary union.[14] The fifty states are linked together in a complete monetary union with a common currency, implying completely fixed exchange rates among them. The Federal Reserve serves as the single central bank for the country; it issues currency and conducts the country's monetary policy. Trade is free among the states, and both labor and capital move freely in pursuit of maximum returns. The federal government conducts the country's fiscal policy and deals in matters concerning national defense, international affairs, retirement and health programs, and the like. Many services such as police protection and education are provided by state and local governments, thus allowing states to keep their identity within the union.

The international economic crises of the 1970s led Africa to intensify its efforts toward regional integration; one result was the adoption of the Lagos Plan of Action by the African heads of state and government in 1980. This step culminated in the signing of the Abuja Treaty of 1991 promulgating the African Economic Community (AEC), which came into effect in 1994. The full establishment of the AEC is to be phased in, in six stages.

Stage one involved the creation of regional blocs, or Regional Economic Communities (RECs), where such did not yet exist. This process was completed by 1999. The RECs are to be the building blocks of the AEC. The second stage was the strengthening of intra-REC integration and inter-REC harmonization, which was to be completed in 2007. This stage, as of 2010, has still not yet been completed as can be seen in the continued existence of multiple and overlapping groupings in various parts of the continent, shown in table 3.1. Stage three is to consist of the establishment of a free trade area and customs union in each regional bloc by the end of 2017. The establishment of an Africa-wide customs union is the fourth stage, set for completion by the end of 2019. The fifth stage is the establishment of a continent-wide common market, the African Common Market (ACM), by 2023. Stage six is to be the establishing of a continent-wide economic and monetary union by the end of 2028; and the transitional period, during which all these structures are to be established, would end by 2034 at the latest.[15]

However, as much as continental leaders seem to appreciate the importance of collective African self-reliance, their political rhetoric on African integration has so far not been accompanied by consistent actions. The duplication and overlapping of membership in the regional integration blocs that exist have hampered the progress of regional integration instead

Table 3.1. African regional economic communities

Pillar Regional Economic Communities (RECs)		Subregional communities
Arab Maghreb Union (UMA)	84.0	
Common Market for Eastern and Southern Africa (COMESA)	533.5	Indian Ocean Commission (IOC)
Community of Sahel-Saharan States (CENSAD)	359.8	
East African Community (EAC)	127.0	
Economic Community of Central African States (ECCAS)	136.7	Economic and Monetary Community of Central Africa (CEMAC) and Economic Community of Great Lakes Countries (CEPGL)
Economic Community of West African States (ECOWAS)	282.5	West African Economic and Monetary Union (UEMOA), West African Monetary Zone (WAMZ), and Mano River Union (MRU)
Inter-Governmental Authority on Development (IGAD)	201.8	
Southern African Development Community (SADC)	258.0	Southern African Customs Union (SACU) and IOC

Notes: The figures next to the pillar RECs are populations of the groups in millions (as of 2007). The African Union recognizes the pillar RECs as the building blocks of the African Economic Community. The AU's policy is for the subgroups to merge into the pillars.

Sources: United Nations Economic Commission for Africa (UNECA), *Assessing Regional Integration in Africa*, vol. 2, *Rationalizing Regional Economic Communities* (Addis Ababa, 2006), 51; World Bank, *World Development Indicators 2009* (Washington, DC, 2009), 14–16.

of facilitating it, thereby perpetuating Africa's vulnerability to global economic forces. Many countries have joined a number of groupings for political and strategic reasons. Economic reasons rank low. Duplication of membership hinders integration programs related to trade facilitation and market integration. Lack of harmonized market integration schemes means that each regional economic community has its own rules of origin or its own certification process.[16] This limits trade between communities. The duplication and overlapping of membership contribute to the underfunding of the communities as members find it difficult to pay all their dues to multiple communities. There is also the problem of adequately staffing the many RECs with their various levels of technical needs. Declarations by the African Summit of July 2007 indicated a strong desire to rationalize the existing RECs and reflect a decision not to recognize more RECs than the eight then existing as the main pillars of the AEC.[17]

Regional Economic Communities

Free trade has been the major goal of each REC. But the results have been modest. The member countries have similar production structures. Most lack a strong industrial base to produce diversified manufactured products for trade within the groupings. Their multiple currencies are not convertible. The cost of doing business within these intra- and interregional blocs is high due to a host of nontariff barriers such as poor infrastructure, duplicative border procedures, and cumbersome paperwork requirements.[18] The free movement of people and the right of establishment have progressed in some African subregional groupings, but not in many others. Some studies suggest that nontariff barriers such as customs procedures, police roadblocks, and constant harassment by immigration officials are a growing concern in Africa as they hamper free trade. Hence, the observation that tariffs are not the main problems delaying the achievement of African unity; nontariff barriers are.[19]

Growth in trade among member countries within a given intra-REC for 2000–2005 shows that on average all the RECs registered positive growth in exports to member states. The Economic and Monetary Community of Central Africa (CEMAC), the Economic Community of Great Lakes Countries (CEPGL), the Common Market for Eastern and Southern Africa (COMESA), and the Community of Sahel-Saharan States (CENSAD) all show an average increase of 40 percent or more. The West African Economic and Monetary Union (UEMOA), the Inter-Governmental Authority on Development (IGAD), the Southern African Development Community (SADC), the Economic Community of West African States (ECOWAS), the Arab Maghreb Union (UMA), and the Indian Ocean Commission (IOC) registered growth in exports to member countries in the range of 20–40 percent. The trend in intra-REC imports shows growth in all RECs, with the largest increases registered by COMESA, CENSAD, IGAD, CEMAC, and IOC.[20]

The Customs and Economic Union of Central Africa (UDEAC) was formed in 1966. UDEAC signed a treaty for the establishment of CEMAC to promote the entire process of subregional integration through the formation of a monetary union, with the Central African CFA franc as a common currency. Thus in 1999, UDEAC was officially superseded by CEMAC.

In 1981, the leaders of UDEAC agreed in principle to form a wider Economic Community of Central African States (ECCAS). ECCAS was established in 1983 by the UDEAC members, São Tomé and Príncipe, and CEPGL. Angola became a member of the ECCAS in 1999. Because of non-payment of membership dues, the ECCAS remained inactive for several years. The conflicts in the Great Lakes region, especially the conflict in the DR Congo, in which some members of the ECCAS fought on opposing sides, greatly slowed the functioning of the community.[21]

The East African Community (EAC) of Kenya, Tanzania, and Uganda was revived in 2000. Burundi and Rwanda joined the community in 2007. The EAC became a customs union on January 1, 2005, with the introduction of the EAC Customs Union Protocol. Membership in the EAC begins at a customs union level. Under the treaty, Kenya, with the strongest economy in the region, will continue to pay duties on its goods entering the other four countries until 2010, based on a declining scale. A common system of tariffs will apply to goods imported from third-party countries.

The Southern African Development Community (SADC) started as a political and security organization in 1980, under the name Southern African Development Coordination Conference (SADCC).[22] The SADCC was transformed into SADC in August 1992. Nine years later, the SADC treaty was amended. In 2000, the SADC Free Trade Area was formed with the participation of Southern African Customs Union (SACU) countries (Botswana, Lesotho, Namibia, South Africa, and Swaziland). Next to join were Madagascar, Mauritius, and Zimbabwe. In 2008, Malawi, Mozambique, Tanzania, and Zambia joined the SADC Free Trade Area. Angola, DR Congo, and Seychelles joined in October 2008, when all three regional groupings of COMESA, EAC, and SADC formed a free trade zone. This newest free trade zone will help eliminate duplicative membership and the problem that member states have in participating in other regional cooperative schemes. It represents a step forward toward the attainment of the ultimate continent-wide African Economic Community.[23]

SADC hopes to establish a customs union by 2010, but it will have to make its customs union compatible with that of its existing SACU subgrouping. COMESA had planned to have a customs union by 2008. But as reported above, COMESA, EAC, and SADC formed their free trade zone in October of that year. ECOWAS continued working to resolve a possible conflict with the existing customs union in West Africa, the West African Economic and Monetary Union (WAEMU), by adopting WAEMU's tariff bands so that a customs union for the whole region could be put in place. Efforts are ongoing to realize this goal.

Financial integration in terms of harmonizing money or capital markets on the continent would help ease financial transactions and facilitate trade among countries in Africa. There are some monetary unions among some regional blocs that use a single currency. Examples include the CFA franc zones consisting of the Communauté Économique et Monétaire de l'Afrique Centrale (CEMAC) and l'Union Économique et Monétaire Ouest Africaine (UEMOA).[24] Having a single currency can help accelerate trade and development. A single currency reinforces a common market. According to the director general of the West African Monetary Institute (WAMI), financial integration would help the African continent to withstand globalization since no one country can do it alone. Financial crises or shocks emanating from the global economy could be minimized if Africans had a common market.[25]

Some African RECs have established institutions to support regional financial cooperation. Regional development banks operate in the CEMAC, COMESA, EAC, ECOWAS, UEMOA, and UMA.[26] In SADC, the South African Development Bank serves the interests of all member countries. Established in 1984, the COMESA Clearing House provides foreign exchange support for the facilitation of intra-COMESA trade. The PTA Reinsurance Company has been providing insurance coverage and reinsurance to investors in the region since 1991.[27] The COMESA PTA Bank provides financing for trade and projects at the national and regional levels in the form of credit, credit guarantees, and minority equity participation in joint ventures. The bank also supplements the activities of national development agencies of member states through joint financing operations and the financing of development projects. It has been extending finance to manufacturing, agribusiness, tourism, mining, infrastructure, and energy sectors in the member states.

In the ECOWAS region, the ECOWAS Fund for Cooperation, Compensation, and Development (EFCCD), formed in 1975, serves as a source of finance for compensation of revenue loss accompanying regional trade liberalization. The EFCCD is also responsible for the promotion of balanced regional economic development and providing support to less developed member states of the region. The EFCCD has been reconstituted as the ECOWAS Bank for Investment and Development (EBID) with two subsidiaries: ECOWAS Regional Development Fund (ERDF) and ECOWAS Regional Development Bank (ERDB). The ERDF finances the public sector, while ERDB extends credit to the private sector. The ECOWAS Bank Group (Ecobank) has been set up to strengthen regional financial cooperation. Ecobank has subsidiaries in twelve countries in West and Central Africa. It provides commercial banking and other financial services to individuals as well as to private- and public-sector organizations. The Ecobank Foundation is a philanthropic arm of the bank that is involved in supporting scientific, cultural, and humanitarian causes across the region. The ERDF is the major shareholder of Ecobank.

In June 2009, the West African Monetary Zone (WAMZ) postponed its December 2009 deadline for the realization of a single currency (the eco) to 2015. It is planned that the entire region of the ECOWAS will adopt a single currency by 2020 with the establishment of an ECOWAS Central Bank. The plan to launch the eco was begun in 2000.[28]

The former President of Nigeria, Umaru Yar'Adua, was reported to have expressed his disappointment because thirty years after the signing of the Protocol on Free Movement of Goods and Services, cross-border bottlenecks involving member states continue to hamper effective economic integration. Yar'Adua looked to accelerated integration as a safeguard against the global economic crisis. The heads of state and government also approved a new Customs External Tariff (CET) regime of ECOWAS to be levied on certain categories of goods imported into the region. They further endorsed efforts to harmonize a value-added tax (VAT) regime in the region.

In October 2008, the COMESA, EAC, and SADC agreed to form a free trade zone spanning 26 member countries of the three RECs. They also agreed to establish joint infrastructure and energy projects for all three regional groupings and pledged to harmonize their transport, technology, and energy plans.

In August 2009, a summit by member states of these three regional groupings set up a task force to simplify and merge the rules of origin to be applied in their free trade zone. The EAC head of Customs and Trade reported that a draft of the hybrid rules of origin was ready and would come into effect as soon as the free trade area was established. The hybrid rules will replace the three separate rules for each of the three groups. The summit also agreed on a program of trading arrangements, free movement of people engaged in business, joint implementation of interregional infrastructure programs, as well as institutional arrangements on the basis of which the three RECs would foster cooperation. The summit approved the "expeditious establishment of a Free Trade Area encompassing the partner states of the three trading blocs, with the ultimate goal of establishing a single Customs Union."[29] Of COMESA's member states, 80 percent have scrapped visa restrictions as a step toward increased trade. The remaining countries are working to address the visa requirement issue.

COMESA, EAC, ECCAS, ECOWAS, and SADC, among others, are clear manifestations of African leaders' recognition of the need for larger units in Africa to achieve viable development in the current world economic environment. However, the processes of realizing the RECs and the AEC will be gradual. In the meantime, technological changes will not wait for African integration. Such a situation will perpetuate Africa's follower status in regard to the challenges of globalization. For Africans to have an impact and influence on the direction of globalization, and thus on the continent's destiny, African countries must internalize the processes of technological progress within a shorter time frame. The greater challenge of internalizing substantial technological changes within Africa should be entrusted to the large African countries that should be able to muster the political leadership to turn their potential into "regional development poles" within the continent. Development emanating from these regional poles will diffuse faster to the rest of Africa.

Regional Development Poles

The national economies of Africa were founded when the continent was partitioned into European colonies. Unfortunately, after about fifty years of formal independence, African elites have not transformed the inherited deformities in their countries' economies. These economies have either persisted or collapsed, instead of being transformed. Most African economies can hardly be transformed within the existing domestic structures, although a few large ones can. The DR Congo, Ethiopia, Nigeria, and South Africa are among the few with the human and natural resources sufficient for becoming self-sustaining economies; but the political leadership to bring this about has so far been lacking.

In light of the slow processes of regional integration, those interested in viable and sustainable development in the continent should focus their efforts on the initiation of self-sustaining development in such countries. The African Union, the New Partnership for African Development (NEPAD), the Economic Commission for Africa, and the African Development Bank, among other organizations, together with the elites of the respective countries should lead in the establishment of viable development poles. Self-sustaining development will spread from the regional development poles (RDPs) to the rest of the countries on the continent. The establishment of diversified economies, financial systems, and convertible currencies in the RDPs will help strengthen the small neighboring economies. For example, some of the small economies of southern Africa have benefited greatly from the de facto Common Monetary Area (CMA) in the region anchored on the convertible South African rand. This is because of South Africa's strong industrial economy. Had the CFA franc zones been anchored in Central Africa and West Africa instead of in France (and now on the euro), they would have had a wider impact on African economies.

The creation of development poles in Africa is to be based on the greater resource bases and populations of the larger countries. Only four African countries have populations of about or more than 50 million: Nigeria, Ethiopia, DR Congo, and South Africa. Nigeria has all it takes in terms of resources to become a major world economy, but so far its leadership has failed to effectively develop that potential. With its abundant natural resources, domestic market of some 152 million people, thousands of highly educated people in various fields, and oil export earnings upwards of $110 million per day, Nigeria could build a strong diversified economy with a profound impact on western and equatorial Africa, and even beyond. Moreover, as the Gulf of Guinea region becomes a major oil producer and exporter, Nigeria could coordinate the development of large petroleum products manufacturing industries in the area, including the islands.[30]

Before the oil industry came to dominate the Nigerian economy, the country produced its own food supplies and exported large quantities of cocoa, cotton, cattle, hides and skins, groundnuts, palm oil, and palm kernels. Reemphasis on the agricultural sector would expand the domestic market and further enhance national efforts to build a self-sustaining economy.

The DR Congo probably has the greatest potential for building a viable economy if it can efficiently develop its extraordinary richness of natural resources for the good of its people. It could learn from Brazil, a country very similar in terms of natural resource endowment. The DR Congo has the agricultural, mineral, forestry, fisheries, and hydroelectric potential to complement its large and fast-growing population and central location in Africa. Because of its potentialities and location, it suffered greatly as a consequence of the Cold War. The recent regional wars, the debt accumulated in the 1970s and 1980s, and the apparent lack of clear development-oriented leadership have continued to hamper the DR Congo's development. However, although delayed, its development might still be realized, given an informed vision and appropriate strategies.

Even a partial tapping of the renewable energy potential of the DR Congo could initiate a process of self-sustaining development. The Congo River flows around a basin that is several hundred meters above sea level. Near the Atlantic Ocean it falls about three hundred meters over a stretch of river only tens of kilometers in length. Here the Congo River, second only to the Amazon River in volume of flow, pours downward to the ocean over the Inga Falls. This is a hydroelectric site second to none in the world. Two hydroelectric plants have been built there already, but a proposed dam is planned to generate enough electricity to meet the needs of all of southern Africa.

In 1972, the Inga Dam was built. It provided electrical power for the mining area of Katanga, or Shaba. That hydroelectric installation had a capacity of 351 megawatts (MW). Ten years later, in 1982, a much larger hydroelectric installation was built with a capacity of 1,424 MW.[31]

The first two hydroelectric installations on the Congo are now known as Inga I and Inga II. There is a proposed Inga III, which will have a generating capacity of 3,500 MW. The construction of Inga III is set to begin in 2012. The African Development Bank, the European Investment Bank, and the World Bank will be major lenders for this installation in collaboration with Wescor, a utility consortium formed by the electric power corporations of Angola, Botswana, DR Congo, Namibia, and South Africa.[32] Inga III is expected to form the centerpiece of the regional partnership that envisions the interconnection of electricity grids in the five members of SADC. It is also expected to attract energy-intensive industries to the DR Congo.

Beyond Inga III, there are proposals for a Grand Inga project that would have a generating capacity of 39,000 MW, more than twice that of the Three Gorges Dam in China and more than one-third of the total electricity currently produced in Africa. It is billed as the world's largest hydroelectric project. It is listed as a priority project of SADC, NEPAD, and the World Energy Council.

Already with the Inga I and Inga II installations a project was conceived to build transmission lines across the Sahara to Egypt. The agreement was negotiated but the project was not implemented. The massive Grand Inga project is being touted not only as the solution to Africa's electricity deficit, but also as a viable source of energy for export to the Middle East and Europe as well as South Africa and countries in western Africa including Nigeria.[33]

The development of the Inga hydroelectric potential alone could earn the DR Congo billions of dollars from exports of electricity to others parts of Africa and beyond. This would both contribute to an enhanced power supply and bring in much needed foreign exchange for further development and economic diversification. Meanwhile, the country's mineral and other natural resources represent tremendous potential earnings. Overall, while the DR Congo's potential for becoming an economic powerhouse continues to be misused and underutilized, it has not been destroyed.

South Africa has already established a strong manufacturing sector. It has had, and continues to have, an important impact on development in Africa, especially in southern, eastern, and central Africa. South Africa needs to spread the benefits of its economy widely through mass education and training and land reform. Although much has been done since the end of apartheid in 1994, much more effort needs to be exerted to eradicate poverty and greatly reduce inequality so as to establish a broad-based self-sustaining economy. For development to be viable and sustainable, the bulk of the population must benefit from it. A dynamic industrial South Africa will reduce dependence of many countries in the region on long-distance imports of development inputs and hence accelerate development in the region.

Although Ethiopia has huge areas of arid land, it also has many large rivers, such as the Blue Nile, Barro, and Wabe Shebelle. It can irrigate large areas and generate large amounts of hydroelectric power, some of which can be exported. Moreover, its mineral potential has hardly been tapped. Its recent program of greatly expanding graduate programs in its universities should soon pay dividends in terms of enhanced human resources. Because of its fast-growing population, and large arid lands, industrialization is imperative to Ethiopia, as an industrial economy has greater capacity to sustain a large population.

Conclusion

For a country to chart its path in the global economy and have an influence on the terms under which globalization proceeds, it must have substantial bargaining capacity on such issues as technology transfer, research and development, trade, and finance; otherwise, it will be ignored and forced to go along under subservient conditions. For Africa to matter, and to claim a position in influencing global events, it must overcome its heritage of colonial balkanization. The insistence of African elites on the legal, but unviable, sovereignties of their existing individual countries has so far defeated the aspirations for true liberation of the African. Yet, it seems that most African elites are unprepared to shake off their current myopic nationalisms, even though their advocacy of regional economic groupings acknowledges, in effect, that their present tiny countries can not deliver prosperity for most of their populations, even if they were to be run by the most competent leaders on earth.

If the existing regional groupings were political entities, the physical and market constraints to viable dynamic development would be largely gone. What would be required to achieve development would be the appropriate vision of political leadership. However, the present regional groupings are riddled with duplication and overlapping membership, which results in a scattering of resources and efforts. Politicians make fine speeches on the need for African collective self-reliance, but they are loath to concede any of their vaunted sovereignty to a supranational body. While African countries should continue efforts toward achieving collective action to support development, those that are large enough to go it alone should spearhead a process to speed up progress. By so doing, they will create de facto situations to which the neighboring countries will have to adjust. While such unilateral directions will likely offend some African elites, the common African stands to benefit from any increase in prosperity within Africa. And that is what matters.

Notes

1. Robert J. Carbaugh, *International Economics*, 12th ed. (Mason, OH: South-Western Cengage Learning, 2009), 2.

2. John A. Perry and Erna K. Perry, *Contemporary Society: An Introduction to Social Science* (New York: Pearson Education, 2009), 269–72.

3. Carbaugh, *International Economics*, 3.

4. The Berlin Conference led to the carving up of Africa into different European colonies, establishing borders that still define the existing countries of Africa.

5. Oded Shenkar, *The Chinese Century: The Rising Chinese Economy and Its Impact on the Global Economy, the Balance of Power, and Your Job* (Upper Saddle River, NJ: Pearson Education, 2005).

6. Michael P. Todaro and Stephen C. Smith, *Economic Development*, 10th ed. (New York: Pearson Addison-Wesley, 2009), 71–77.

7. The Abuja Treaty of June 1991 established the AEC. This was a realization of the Lagos Plan of Action of 1980 adopted by the Organization of African Unity (OAU).

8. "The World Factbook," accessed August 22, 2011, https://www.cia.gov/library/publications/the-world-factbook/index.html. Sudan's forty-four million will be divided between two countries (North and South Sudan) in July 2011 as a result of the recent overwhelming vote for secession by southern Sudanese in their self-determination referendum.

9. These policies are summarized in Benaiah Yongo-Bure, *Economic Development of Southern Sudan* (Lanham, MD: University Press of America, 2007), 186–89. They are discussed at length in Todaro and Smith, *Economic Development*, 620–65.

10. Raul Prebisch, "Commercial Policy in the Underdeveloped Countries," *American Economic Review* 49 (May 1959): 251–73; and H. W. Singer, "The Distribution of Gains between Investing and Borrowing Countries," *American Economic Review* 40 (May 1950): 473–94; Todaro and Smith, *Economic Development*, 624.

11. Todaro and Smith, *Economic Development*, 588–614; Paul R. Krugman and Maurice Obstfeld, *International Trade: Theory and Policy* (New York: Pearson Addison-Wesley, 2006), 243–58.

12. Todaro and Smith, *Economic Development*, 626.

13. W. Charles Sawyer and Richard L. Sprinkle, *International Economics* (Upper Saddle River, NJ: Pearson Prentice Hall, 2009), 223–26, and Krugman and Obstfeld, *International Trade*, 232–36.

14. Carbaugh, *International Economics*, 267–68.

15. United Nations Economic Commission for Africa (UNECA), *Assessing Regional Integration in Africa*, vol. 3: *Towards Monetary and Financial Integration in Africa* (Addis Ababa, 2008), 28.

16. Rules of origin are laws that determine what country actually produced a good so that duties on the good can be assessed appropriately: as goods of either a member or a nonmember country of the integrating group.

17. UNECA, *Assessing Regional Integration in Africa*, 3:30.

18. Ibid.

19. AU Monitor, "Biofeuls and World Hunger," http://www.pambazuka.org/aumonitor/comments/many_regional_blocs_delaying_african.

20. UNECA, *Assessing Regional Integration in Africa*, 3:33–36.

21. UNECA, *Assessing Regional Integration in Africa*, vol. 2: *Rationalizing Regional Economic Communities* (Addis Ababa, 2006), 47–50; and Martina Metzger, *Regional Cooperation and Integration in Sub-Saharan Africa*, Discussion Paper no. 189 (Geneva: United Nations Conference on Trade and Development, September 2008), 17–26.

22. UNECA, *Assessing Regional Integration in Africa*, 2:35–38; and Metzger, *Regional Cooperation and Integration*, 12–16.

23. "Africa's Regional Trade Blocs Agree to Free Trade Union," http://news. alibaba.com/articles/detail/trade/100015430-1-africa%2527s-regional-blocs-agr (accessed October 22, 2008).

24. Metzger, *Regional Cooperation and Integration*, 17–26.

25. Juliana Taiwo and Dele Ogbodo, "West Africa: ECOWAS Targets 2020 for Single Currency," http://allafrica.com/stories/200906230222.html.

26. UNECA, *Assessing Regional Integration in Africa*, 3:15–17, 278.

27. COMESA was started as a preferential trade area (PTA) in 1981, and some of these institutions were formed before the name change to COMESA in 1994.

28. Taiwo and Ogbodo, "West Africa."

29. Francis Ayieko, "Africa: Trade Blocs Agree to Simplify Rules of Origin," http://allafrica.com/ stories/200908241285.html (accessed June 4, 2009); and "Africa: Plans to Harmonize Regional Blocs Underway," http://allafrica.com/stories/200906040036.html.

30. John Ghazvinian, *Untapped: The Scramble for Africa's Oil* (New York: Harcourt, 2007).

31. Thayer Watkins, "The Inga Hydroelectric Power Complex in the Democratic Republic of the Congo," San José State University, http://applet-magic.com/inga. htm.

32. Bank Information Center, "BHP Billiton Eyes Congo's Inga Dam Complex to Power New $3 Bn Aluminum Smelter," November 14, 2007, http://www.bicusa.org/en/Article.3574.aspx.

33. Nick Mathiason, "Fury at Plan to Power EU Homes from Congo Dam," August 23, 2009, http://www.guardian.co.uk/world/2009/aug/23/power-eu-congo-dam.

4

Solutions to Africa's Development Challenges

STEPHEN D. KPINPUO

Over the past few decades, the African continent has been described as being ruled by neopatrimonial regimes, a form of governance that seems not to be working for Africa.[1] Some scholars tend to attribute the ubiquitous incidence of poor governance and underdevelopment of the continent to neocolonial activities, which they claim emanate from the intervention of such development partners as the World Bank. These activities, they argue, come in the form of foreign aid that purports to assist Africa's development efforts, but with conditionalities that are more detrimental than helpful to the African economy.[2] Yet, development partners are often criticized for not doing enough for Africa. This contradiction, which labels foreign intervention as a form of neocolonialism, while at the same time blaming international intervention for inadequate funding, has dominated Africa's development literature to the extent that the role that Africans themselves ought to be playing in the process often receives little attention.

In this chapter, I explore the place of Africans in the development of Africa by examining the relationship between common misrepresentations about the continent and the types of change that would help position Africans as global citizens, as this relationship plays out in the areas of education, good governance, and self-help. The chapter draws on existing literature on misrepresentations of the African continent, as presented in some textbooks, and development discourses of international organizations and the popular Western media to examine how, in striving to enhance inclusion in a global economy, Africans end up on the periphery of the twenty-first-century knowledge economy.

The chapter is divided into three major parts: the first sets education as a foundation for Africa's development by exploring the relationship between manpower needs and development and presents the challenge of reorienting the African mind to unlearn some traditions that do not conform to modern trends of interconnectedness. The key here is to illuminate educational contributions to the development of Africa, both locally and internationally, and to suggest areas that need radical reform. The second part establishes good governance as the engine of economic growth in Africa. It places Africans' political expectations against actual development practices and examines how their differences shape the image of Africa. The third and final section examines self-help projects, highlighting efforts by both indigenous and international agencies to help Africans cultivate self-help initiatives as a way of overcoming some of the major challenges of development. Most of these challenges point to a need for Africans to let go of the long-standing tradition of being on the receiving end of other-directed initiatives. To emphasize the need for Africans to be self-reliant, I use China and other Asian countries as successful development models with a view to arguing that with the right education and a commitment to sustainable development, Africa can overcome most of her development challenges.

Education and Development in Africa

An economy without a vibrant workforce is often considered a potential failure. This is because the majority of national economies depend on their human resources to give them use value and exchange value for available natural resources. It is important to understand that unlike in the twentieth century when industrial development relied on the knowledge and skills of an elite few, in this era of globalization and interdependence, "economies depend on the skills and knowledge of all [their] people."[3] That is, the development base for most economies is now formed by mass rather than elitist interests, and such changes in the use of human capital fundamentally inform today's knowledge economy. In this postindustrial economy, "wealth is tied to knowledge workers and ultimately to educational systems." Because education takes center stage in producing skilled labor for any economy, many Africans question the efficacy of their education systems when their economies underperform. Such questions, it must be emphasized, usually result in educational reforms designed to redirect the attention of educators toward contemporary development needs.[4]

A quick look at the history of education in Ghana, for example, reveals a plethora of reforms starting from 1960s to date, albeit none that have been truly successful. Together with the two most recent reforms in the Ghana Education Service that emphasize a focus on mathematics, science, and technology education, mainly because these subjects are believed to form the core of today's development needs, the government of Ghana usually resorts to cosmetic education reforms as a strategy for avoiding blame for poor performance.[5] Regardless of any failures in curricular reforms, as I show below, changes in school curriculum alone, if at all successful, cannot prepare Ghanaians well enough for the challenges of our time. In fact, educational reforms in Ghana have often focused on one achievement or the other. Yet, they end up disappointing Ghanaians, who hardly experience the intended socioeconomic transformation promised in such reforms. Probably, Ghana's politicians need to be reminded that education is only a recipe for change; it is not the meal in itself. It is a tool that must be utilized to realize a nation's vision of good governance, economic transformation, rule of law, and so forth. In other words, although national education programs generally aim for national development, initiated by members of communities for whom such programs were designed, the same can not be said about Africans. The African people are not particularly good at taking the initiative; they often prefer to experience economic progress merely as recipients.[6] Regrettably, formal training has not been able to bring about a change in this passive approach to development in Africa. That is, although schools do not teach deviant practices, school dropouts, much like those who endeavor to graduate from school, engage in them. By simple analogy, then, we can say that it is the larger society that makes provision for such practices; state machinery does not put checks on the conduct and responsibility of Africans.

A strong society, in my view, is one that is organized on its "we" strength. It is built on social relations and a mechanism for the protection of group rather than individual interest.[7] In the education and development of a strong (economic) community, therefore, selfish interest offers very little toward constructing a dependable African society. This is probably why, in most African economies, selfish endeavors tend to be the root of corruption, greed, and most individualistic norms or development challenges. That is, individuals engage in unproductive practices and sometimes become unnecessarily violent mainly because the laissez-faire communities in which they live continue to corrupt them to the extent that they are unable to use their school-acquired knowledge to the benefit of the larger society. With school training, we need to be more radical in the pursuit of group interests, such as pan-Africanism, patriotism, national peace and security, good governance, genuine self-reliance, and the culture of sharing. Global interdependence is about sharing, collaborating, and networking among and between members of different communities, as also occurs *within* communities. Reorienting Africans' mind-set to be "each other's keeper" is therefore a prerequisite for Africa's participation in a globalizing world. Globalization, after all, is hardly brand-new to Africans, who have a history of interdependence that could be adjusted to reflect the current needs of African societies.

The barter trade and the extended family system are classic examples of how traditional African societies have relied on each other for their needs. As a system that promoted exchange of goods and services between individuals, groups, and communities, the barter trade required one not to seek exchange with empty hands; one was expected to possess something of value in order to be part of this network. The major requirements for barter trade today can be likened to the form of globalization and interdependence, which may include good governance, peace, security, sustainable economic development, and science and technology. In the global market, a nation's good governance, peace, or security may be "exchanged" for foreign investment, sustainable development for skilled labor, and science and technology for innovations.

Africans' experience with the extended family system may be seen as a great asset in today's world of interconnectedness as most Africans understand that a family member who only receives from others and never has to share is disrespected and regarded not just as a dependent, but as a nuisance. In the Dagara community of northern Ghana, such a person is called "tuurnyuur" (literally, "one who follows others for drinks," but also, broadly, someone who is always on the receiving end). I believe that most African societies and cultures do have a tuurnyuur, known in Swahili as *maskini*. Africans can easily understand, therefore, that a tuurnyuur does not command any respect even from kids, unless he is able to prove that others too can depend on him for some needs. And the only way to do so is to use whatever skills or resources are at his disposal (e.g., farming, weaving, building) to generate some income so that when he joins family members or friends for a pot of *pito* (local beer in northern Ghana), he can pay at least part of the bill. Once the tuurnyuur is able to share with others at least twice, he begins to win the respect of others in his community.

If Africa's place in the context of globalization is viewed according to the concept of the tuurnyuur, with the continent virtually dependent on foreign aid, Africans understandably occupy a marginalized position in the international community. For just as the tuurnyuur never allows circumstances to make him a condemned object of humiliation, Africans too can reorganize themselves and win the respect of the rest of the world. In debates over such issues as education, globalization, and interdependence, then, the question should not be what are others doing to relieve Africa of marginalization and misrepresentation; but rather, what are Africans doing to free themselves from such a condition.

Concerning why sub-Saharan Africa has been misrepresented in the West and elsewhere, some Africanists have attributed the stereotypical representation of the region to a Euro-American portrayal of the continent as a place of wild natives who live in jungles, forever caught in a hunter-gatherer lifestyle. They have often lamented that most Americans still have little or no knowledge at all about Africa, since they (Americans) believe that Africa is a single country where wild animals wander everywhere and the people struggle with famine and malnutrition. Against this misinformation, critics have pointed out, for instance, that many species of wildlife, such as the tiger, are not indigenous to Africa, but to Asia, and that wildlife in Africa live mostly in game reserves and zoos, which is where Africans, as with most other people, go to see them.[8] Moreover, although diseases and hunger are commonly associated with the African continent in countries like Ethiopia, Uganda, Angola, and Somalia, these may be exceptions rather than the rule, for countries such as Ghana, Nigeria, Botswana, Lesotho, and South Africa, at one time or another, have been "self-sufficient in food production."[9]

If the uninformed and ignorant, whether in the Untied States or elsewhere, continue to conjure images of Africa as a "primitive land of hot, steamy jungles inhabited by wild animals and savages" while "in truth, only 10 percent of the African continent is jungle," it is simply because Africans have failed to disclaim such misrepresentations.[10] It should be acknowledged that efforts have been made to debunk the historical misperceptions about Africa being without civilization and lacking in potential for self-government. Arguments have been put forward that ancient Africans had contacts with the Greeks, Chinese, Romans, and early Indonesians and that Africa possessed a civilization that some historians describe as "advanced," with a record of self-government as seen in the early West African kingdoms of Ghana, Mali, and Songhai.[11] However, this ancient civilization obviously failed to develop.

Why, then, does it seem difficult for Africans to build on this ancient but advanced "capacity for social organization," self-government, and international trade, "a talent that operated at the village level and in the complex kingdoms" and through which "many Africans achieved a kind of social harmony that could exist without the power of a centralized authority"?[12] As Africans seem to lack the confidence to sustain and build on early trade and interdependent initiatives and to prove to the international community that, indeed, Africa has an advanced civilization, some ideas, myths, and stereotypes about Africa, though possibly false, have "continued to flourish in Europe," North America, and elsewhere.[13] It is therefore up to Africans to educate the international community on the realities and potentialities of the continent. Before this can be done, however, Africans need to ensure that they in fact have that which they want to showcase. Otherwise, Africans will never feel accepted in the international community, no matter how well they justify their right of inclusion.

This is probably why some critical analysts have observed that despite the strong ties of political relations between China and Africa, the Chinese have a habit of looking down on Africans, an attitude that is generally attributed to a lack of knowledge on the part of the Chinese about Africa's realities.[14] According to such observers, some Chinese openly question Africans what they (Africans) have brought to the table in exchange for what they seek from China. Africans are in essence looked down upon by the Chinese because the latter do not have any confidence in the socioeconomic background of the former. The solution does not lie in insistence on respect and recognition from the Chinese, but rather in a strategic reconstruction of Africa as a self-reliant continent. Self-reliance would ensure Africa's inclusion and acceptance in today's interdependent global community.

A passive attitude on the part of Africans toward issues affecting the development of the African continent is quite widespread and worrisome, and development activists need to devote more energy to correcting this attitudinal problem. I am not suggesting that discriminatory behavior in a globalizing society should be tolerated; rather, my point is that Africans are themselves often responsible for the very discrimination they suffer, and against which they speak. This is why I see some of the suggestions made regarding certain misconceptions about and stereotypes of Africans as insufficiently responsive to Africa's development needs, at home and in the diaspora.[15]

For instance, outlining the various ways in which the American teacher of social studies may effectively teach about Africa, some researchers have tasked American teachers to discover current information on Africa, through their own library research, to supplement what is available in textbooks. Although this is clearly untenable, they contend that teachers can obtain free materials, such as current maps, hotel and tourist brochures, pictures, videos, films, and economic, educational, and demographic information, from the embassies and consular offices of African countries in New York, Washington, DC, and San Francisco because, in the view of the researchers, such materials portray the realities of life in African nations.[16]

For the most part, encouraging teachers to avoid using outdated historical texts that portray the views of colonizing Europeans and to update classroom instruction with information from primary sources is a laudable idea. However, it is very unlikely that such suggestions will motivate American or non-Africanist teachers accordingly. Since social studies teachers are likely to be responsible for teaching about the rest of the world as well as Africa, having to go through bureaucratic procedures in order to procure a video from the embassy of an African country, if such teaching materials are unavailable online, could be so discouraging that teachers might prefer using readily available (albeit outdated) information instead. Rather than passively asking foreign teachers to search for updated information on Africa, it would be better if the researchers and other Africanists worked with the proposed African embassies in a way that would bring such available instructional materials and teaching aids on Africa directly to American teachers. This could be done through a well-organized website, with print versions of essential information made available to educational institutions that may have problems with Internet connectivity.

I believe collaborative outreach programs and teaching aids for schools would help American educators teach effectively and accurately about Africa. For, if we insist that teachers avoid using outdated historical texts, then a collaborative effort of Africans in the diaspora to replace such texts is crucial.

Africans, at home and abroad, need to work with their development partners, or rather lead in the struggle to eliminate not only misconceptions and stereotypes of Africa and Africans, but also other major development challenges. NGOs and media outlets need to be more circumspect in the way they use information about African children who need aid, in order not to create the impression that such situations of dire need abound only in Africa. Television advertising and some Internet sources often create a very humiliating impression of the African child, ostensibly because exploiting such awful situations attracts donor support.[17]

Since misinformation about Africa inevitably affects its credibility in the global market, Africans must work together to correct it. One way to do so is for diasporic Africans to take up the challenge of ensuring that discussions on educational and development issues reflect an accurate image of the continent. This would ultimately eliminate the much feared misconceptions and stereotypes and extend Africans' development opportunities to greater foreign investment, external trade, and interdependence. This will require responsible leadership, however, both political and civic. In the next section, I explore how the system of rule in Africa has shaped the continent's socioeconomic transformation.

Democratization and Good Governance

Democracy is gradually gaining ground in some parts of Africa and is perceived as a better system of governance with the potential to drive the continent toward achieving its development goals.[18] Campaigns for continent-wide democratization have therefore been a major preoccupation of both local and international activists concerned with Africa's development. While some argue that the present impetus toward democratization will go a long way toward solving Africa's myriad problems, others believe it is only a different way of having authoritarian rule of the continent. In line with this latter view, the majority of African states that have adopted democracy as a system of government have been variously described as failures. A quick look at some of these arguments might help us understand why democratization is still a problem for most African states today.

In the development discourse about Africa, it is common knowledge that soon after Africa's attainment of independence, "expectations on the continent and around the world were high."[19] Leaders hoped that, through self-governance, sub-Saharan African states would 'take off' both politically and economically to become viable, independent actors in the world community. Consequently, many Africans prayed for a transition to democratic rule. It was a general conception that rule of Africa by Africans themselves would not only be potentially democratic but would also constitute an unprecedented sign of sustainable development.

Contrary to these expectations, however, the introduction and adoption of both self-rule and democracy in Africa soon morphed into serious economic and political crisis, disappointing the hopes of the already hungry and expectant multitude of Africans. Some critics call this failure "neopatrimonialism": a system of rule by personal dictatorship, military oligarchies, or plebiscitary and competitive one-party systems. In these neopatrimonial regimes, the African leader shamefully stands out as the "strongman" of the land who rules by decree; political competition and participation are taboo. Self-generated efforts at reform within these systems are also regrettably problematic, and "real political change" seems unattainable.[20]

As a result, African politics have provided repeated opportunities for greedy leaders to exploit the masses. This remains a problem today because the majority of African leaders do not really work for the interests of their people. African countries such as Uganda, Central African Republic, Equatorial Guinea, Democratic Republic of the Congo (formerly Zaire), Togo, Gabon, Zambia, Côte d'Ivoire, Nigeria, and Ghana (my own country) are just a few countries that have, at one point or another, suffered the wrath of (neo)patrimonial rule.[21] In the twenty-first century of anticipated peace, development, and global interdependence, some African states are still mired in violent conflicts, poverty, and poor governance (Zimbabwe, Kenya, and Sudan are among the continent's recent cases of political unrest and insecurity). This political legacy not only places a red flag on Africa's already ailing credibility when it comes to participation in the global market; it also undermines our expectations of the prospects for change and development.

Perhaps, we need reminding that it is unacceptable to stretch out one hand for development, interdependence, and globalization while clenching firmly with the other hand onto deviant traditions and cultures. Hoped-for improvements in African societies and economies, it is important to note, will not come "without disturbing traditional ideas, disrupting old habits, entailing sweeping organizational changes, and without posing, in turn, new problems with which we must come to grips."[22] If African governments truly believe in good governance and the socioeconomic development of Africans, they need to let go of the tradition of sycophantic leadership and follow the example of the few democratizing African states like Botswana and Ghana that have demonstrated a commitment to these goals.

Some African countries have been lauded for embracing open elections and guaranteeing universal franchise and equality before the law, an indication that good governance and economic prosperity is possible in Africa. If bright spots do exist in once extremely poor African countries like Ghana and Botswana, and in countries with deep ethnic and racial divisions along with sharp income inequalities and rampant crime like South Africa, then it becomes easier to believe that development challenges in Africa are in fact surmountable.

The recent political maturity of Ghana, where, in very keenly contested general presidential and parliamentary elections, the country voted out the incumbent on two occasions without igniting any political unrest, is a leading success case in African politics. Along with an avowed commitment to good governance, the country seems poised to eradicate lawlessness and corruption, with stronger state institutions, and increased political competition and participation. This development is what probably attracted the forty-fourth president of the United States of America, President Barack Obama, to openly compliment Ghana's development efforts by visiting the country and pledging much support for the model African nation on behalf of both his country and the international community. By agreeing to a trade partnership with Ghana in response to the country's commitment to good governance and prosperity, Obama highlighted the demands of interdependence in the global economy. According to this view, all participating nations in an interdependent world need to achieve an acceptable level of internal peace and security (through democratic rule), good governance, and development.

Until Africans are able to meet these requirements, it will be difficult for the continent to benefit considerably from globalization. In other words, these requirements are the key to the global market, and just as one would not attempt physically to "enter a market" without first opening the gate, African nations cannot be part of a system to which they lack access. Critics often hold African leaders responsible for the continent's generally weak economies, charging them with a tendency "to preside over the development of underdevelopment," rather than champion the continent's true development.[23] While African leaders have failed to meet the expectations of their people, they demonstrate much "competence" as agents of corruption, nepotism, and underdevelopment.

As we have already seen, among Africa's leadership, "the small number of individuals with power has often eroded any semblance of accountability, legitimacy, and justice," contributing to considerable disappointment on the part of planners, economists, and policymakers who expect to see African governments "introduce a reasonable and collective attack on poverty, disease, illiteracy," and other challenges of development.[24] Although, to a very large extent, African leaders could be held responsible for the worsening state of sub-Saharan Africa, it is important to point out that the inability of governments to meet the development needs of Africa is not only a problem of irresponsible leadership; it is also the result of much ignorance on the part of the masses, literates and illiterates alike.

The activities of international organizations and NGOs in Africa, though essential in educating and providing local communities with self-help strategies toward bridging this development gap, are complicated by a persistent lack of initiative on the part of their beneficiary communities. The following paragraphs explore some NGO-led development initiatives and Africans' response to such problem-solving efforts.

Self-Help and Interdependence

With natural resources to be found all over the continent, prospects for development in Africa cannot be overemphasized. We have seen in the preceding sections how Africa's ever-weakening human capital is attributable to a lack of self-confidence, resulting from the marginalization of the continent in a world of interdependence. Most African leaders and their followers have a tradition of seeking foreign intervention for solutions to local problems. This legacy has often posed problems as foreigners appear to be limited in how much help they can offer, and as Africans have often been slow to recognize that it is up to themselves to first provide that to which others may add, the narrative has often turned negative against development partners either for not doing much in terms of development aid or for taking advantage of an already bad situation to exploit the continent. Irrespective of the validity of these claims, scholarship on development in Africa has often evaded the leading role that the African people ought to play in the process. Africa's development partners are many: they include multilateral and bilateral funding agencies, NGOs, and the private sector, as well as broad-based civic organizations.[25]

The World Bank (WB) has a record of funding development projects through loans to African nations. Some scholars believe that the WB's funding of these projects does result in many quantitative and qualitative returns. In the area of education, for example, it has been providing funds for school buildings and to support teaching and learning at the primary, secondary, vocational, and higher levels of education in various countries. In spite of these positive contributions, the WB has been widely criticized for its activities in Africa, which have been described as a failure, a form of neocolonialism, or even imperialism.

The WB's critics believe that its habit of tying loans to its own policies (i.e., ideological conditions or conditionalities) for lending to African countries is both a violation of the rights of such countries and an imposition of an approach that might not work well for all borrowing countries. In general, the WB has been seen as causing more harm than good in the region; it "connotes more failure than success in Africa."[26]

In the view of some critics, the intervention of transnational agencies like the WB is a clear illustration of continued postcolonial dominance over the African continent. They believe that although many formerly colonized African countries have gained geographic and political independence, cultural and economic independence has never really been attained.[27] In other words, they argue that through the operations of these transnational organizations, former colonizers continue to dominate economically, culturally, financially, militarily, and ideologically the so-called developing world. These arguments, however, have often "missed the target"; the WB can be viewed as a development partner and need not be considered a leader in the development of Africa.[28] Perhaps we need to be reminded that "multilateral banks are just like commercial operations." They only borrow and lend money; they do not make grants. In fact, "it is easier" for such "banks to lend US$200 million than to give US$20,000 as a grant" because banks do not have "$20,000 to give, even though they have $200 million to lend."[29]

As a commercial institution with numerous clients (countries) all over the world, it is only reasonable that the WB shows concern not just about how much money to lend but, more important, about the best way to lend this money. That is, lending institutions like the WB want to encourage borrowers to fulfill the conditions of their loans, to which borrowers must initially agree, rather than to default. It is also important to note that although "banks are not worried so much about repayment, . . . they do worry about corruption, about a bad press and about people bragging that they got a free ride with the bank's money."[30] This is why each loan spells out, "in ample detail," the way the funds should be expended.

What we hardly realize is that truly poor countries of sub-Saharan African cannot really benefit from WB loans due to their lack of good governance and the acute shortcomings of their public administration. In fact, it is difficult for development banks to help poor African countries simply because development "projects require a level of bureaucratic efficacy at the receiving end" that is hardly found in Africa.[31] The fact that loans made to poor African communities often end up in private pockets of leaders of such communities is a reality of which African governments cannot claim ignorance. Yet, they continue to contract loans for politically poignant projects. As most loans are contracted for political rather than economic reasons, what outcome can we expect in terms of economic progress? Can we hold the WB or other international institutions accountable for loans legally contracted for purposes of economic development but dispensed by local authorities based on politics?

Again, the issue of poor leadership comes up. African governments, civic coalitions, NGOs, gender and community development activists, and other groups all bear responsibility for the present state of African affairs. They all understand how funds generated either locally or internationally, for development in Africa, are often diverted to servicing external debts, or simply to oil the wheels of corruption.[32] These local bodies therefore owe the continent a duty to mobilize local resources in a way that would, at the least, reduce dependency on foreign donors. The WB is sometimes described as a "fashionable" institution that is currently interested in providing a skilled workforce for a postindustrial economy. Most African nations, as frequent recipients of WB loans, are among the bank's most valued costumers and should be more concerned with establishing local procedures that would enhance greater participation in a knowledge economy.[33]

To help promote Africans' participation in a knowledge economy, critics probably need to spend more time on the crucial issue of self-help in Africa. They need to understand that international agencies are aware of the weak administrative structures in Africa and that some of the conditionalities we find unfavorable are actually designed to help keep development projects focused. For instance, if country A contracts a loan to purchase computers for its senior high schools, it is the ethical obligation of governments to ensure that that money is used to buy the computers and not to pay off debts owed to country B, much less spent on an independence day celebration of recipient country A.[34] It is to ensure, then, that funds are used for their intended purposes that financial institutions like the WB attach conditions that would compel borrowing nations to remain faithful in the administration of loans and I contend that such interventions are corrective rather than exploitative, given existing patterns of leadership in Africa. This is probably why funding agencies may put stricter conditions for loans to African nations as opposed to more liberal loan terms for other borrowers like China. The fact that lenders sometimes send their own experts and equipment purportedly to help execute projects for which they have made loans should be seen not only as exploitation, because the high cost of foreign labor and other inputs may consume virtually all of the funds for the project, but as a response by the lenders to the poor leadership and weak human resource base of the borrowers, and perhaps even an expression of a general lack of trust in their clients. In order to benefit from better loan conditions, we need a change of image. It is our leaders who do the paperwork for loans, and only they can reject loans with unfriendly terms. But those who are led also have a crucial role to play. That is, the grassroots can help or even compel governments to reject loans that do not benefit the people of Africa. Of course, we must be cautioned that change, whether top-down or bottom-up, comes with some discomfort.[35] Having to adapt to new ways of doing things inevitably creates uncertainty, fear, and anxiety, and Africans must overcome such challenges. Appropriate loans from external sources can help, for example, to expand economic capacity. However, African nations need responsible leaders, and selfless citizens, for the realization of such progress.

Conclusion

In this chapter, I have shown that Africa has the potential for development, but the development challenges facing Africans are many: ineffective leadership, poor governance, weak workforce, poverty, conflict and insecurity, and more. These problems, which have persisted over many years, have tended to bring development in most parts of the continent to a standstill. The chapter has shown that Africa's seemingly deplorable state has resulted in a kind of addiction to external aid that helps create or reinforce misrepresentation and negative stereotypes. Such misinformation affects Africa's credibility in the global market, and the African people alone can work together to correct it by changing the underlying dynamics. We have seen that Africans, at home and in the diaspora, need to take up the challenge of ensuring that discussions on educational and development issues reflect an accurate image of the continent. African leaders, and their people, must be retrained to work for peace, development, and the good of society. Such changes would ultimately eliminate the worst misconceptions and stereotypes, extend African development opportunities to attract greater foreign investment, and increase external trade and interdependence. The chapter has emphasized that although foreign aid is crucial in sustaining economic activities in Africa, providers of such aid must be positioned and seen as partners to their African recipients, and should not be misrepresented and misunderstood as leading development in Africa. Once Africans and their leaders bear the responsibility for their own economic transformation by engaging in selfless local revenue mobilization initiatives throughout the continent, they would certainly be less dependent on foreign aid. They would then be respected and recognized as participating meaningfully in a knowledge economy, for "the West respects Japan, Hong Kong, China and Taiwan today because these countries did not wait for the advice of the white man to jump into their own style of modernity. Africans, too, must find their own way in the modern world"—the world of global business and interdependence.[36]

Notes

1. Michael Bratton and Nicolas Van de Walle, "Neopatrimonial Regimes and Political Transitions in Africa," *World Politics* 46 (1994): 475–76.

2. Dambisa Moyo, *Dead Aid: Why Aid Is Not Working and How There Is Another Way for Africa* (London: Allen Lane, 2009), 7.

3. Joel Spring, "Research on Globalization and Education," *Review of Educational Research* 78 (2008): 337.

4. George Sefa Dei, *Schooling and Education in Africa: The Case of Ghana* (Trenton, NJ: Africa World Press, 2004), 28.

5. George Sefa Dei, "The Challenge of Inclusive Schooling in Africa: A Ghanaian Case Study," *Comparative Education* 41 (2005): 269.

6. Ian Palmer, Richard Dunford, and Gib Akin, *Managing Organizational Change: A Multiple Perspectives Approach* (New York: McGraw-Hill, 2009), 165.

7. Emile Durkheim, *Moral Education* (Brunel House, UK: David and Charles, 2002), 65.

8. Egerton Osunde and Josiah Tlou, "Persisting and Common Stereotypes in U.S. Students' Knowledge of Africa: A Study of Preservice Social Studies Teachers," *Professional Development Collection* 87 (1996): 121–22.

9. Ibid., 120.

10. Christine Bennett, *Comprehensive Multicultural Education: Theory and Practice* (Boston: Pearson Allyn & Bacon, 2007), 71.

11. Ibid., 72.

12. Ibid., 73.

13. Ibid.

14. Sandra Gillespie, "African Students in China—Present and Past," In *South-South Cooperation in Education and Development,* ed. Linda Chisholm and Gita Steiner-Khamsi (New York: Teachers College Press, 2009), 214.

15. Osunde and Tlou, "Persisting and Common Stereotypes," 123.

16. Ibid., 124.

17. Moyo, *Dead Aid*, 37.

18. Edmond John Keller, "Africa in Transition—Facing the Challenges of Globalization," *Harvard International Review* 29 (2007): 2, http://www.entrepreneur.com/tradejournals/article/167969659.html.

19. Ibid.

20. Bratton and Van de Walle, "Neopatrimonial Regimes and Political Transitions," 476.

21. Ibid., 457.

22. Durkheim, *Moral Education*, 3.

23. Keller, "Africa in Transition."

24. Sahr John Kpundeh, *Democratization in Africa: African Views, African Voices* (Washington DC: National Academy Press, 1992), 33.

25. David Archer, "The Impact of the World Bank and IMF on Education Rights," *Convergence* 39 (2006): 7–18.

26. Manthia Diawara, "Toward a Regional Imaginary in Africa," in *World Bank Literature,* ed. Amitava Kumar (Minneapolis: University of Minnesota Press, 2003), 66.

27. Corrine Wickens and Jennifer April Sandlin, "Literacy for What? Literacy for Whom? The Politics of Literacy Education and Neocolonialism in UNESCO- and World Bank–Sponsored Literacy Programs," *Adult Education Quarterly* 57 (2007): 276–77.

28. Claudio de Moura Castro, "The World Bank Policies: Damned if You Do, Damned if You Don't," *Comparative Education* 38 (2002): 396.

29. Ibid., 389.

30. Ibid.

31. Ibid., 390.

32. Sefa Dei, *Schooling and Education in Africa*, 6.

33. Raymond Morrow and Carlos Alberto Torres, "The State, Globalization, and Educational Policy," in *Globalization and Education: Critical Perspectives,* ed. Nicholas C. Burbules and Carlos Alberto Torres (New York: Routledge, 2000), 29.

34. John Evans Atta Mills, "White Paper on the Report of the Commission of Inquiry on the Ghana@50 Celebrations," http://www.ghanaweb.com/Ghana-HomePage/NewsArchive/artikel.php?ID=180538.

35. William Bridges, *Managing Transitions: Making the Most of Change* (Philadelphia: William Bridges and Associates, 2003), 76.

36. Diawara, "Regional Imaginary in Africa," 67.

5

Renewable Energy, Migration-Development Model, and Sustainability Entrepreneurship

RUBIN PATTERSON

Introduction

In this chapter, I attempt to illustrate and examine a plausible development strategy for Africa with the novel integration of discrete literatures that have not received much scholarly articulation. These literatures focus on renewable energy, the migration-development model, and sustainability entreprencurship. There are multiple reasons why the global economy needs to move from use of fossil fuels to embrace renewable energy sources, but the importance of this move is even greater for Africans. This chapter focuses on the innovation and commercialization of renewable energy sources in Africa as a strategic means of protecting the environment and transforming the economy. Since innovating and commercializing renewable energy is far easier said than done, a concrete strategy is needed to help pioneer a new paradigm of energizing economies, particularly for nations as poor as those on the African continent. The strategy formulated below, which is intended to help Africa lead the way with targeted renewable energy innovation, involves the migration-development model (MDM). This model was utilized by European nations early in the twentieth century and by Asian nations in the later 1900s around different industrial endeavors. I argue that Africans can begin to apply this model around renewable energy and other green or eco-industries. Finally, I contend that sustainability entrepreneurship should be the thrust behind the migration-development model in the African context today. Sustainability entrepreneurship is a concept whereby Africans in the diaspora who have amassed human, economic, and social capital can invest some of it back into the continent in support of green economic activities. Such a strategy allows diasporic Africans to "do well by doing good."

All nations place stress on environmental protection just as all nations are affected by climate change. However, the people who have contributed the least to climate change suffer more from its ill effects, while those who have had the most anthropogenic impact on the climate suffer the least due to their higher level of infrastructural development.[1] For this reason alone, Africans have an incentive to support a global shift toward renewable energy sources in order to lessen the droughts, floods, reduced agricultural yields and seasonal declines, and increased diseases that all are intensified on the continent in large part by fossil-fuel-induced changes to the environment. In addition to this, major economic gains will accrue to those nations that pioneer the new renewable energy technologies. At present, no nation has a lock on these technologies, or a substantial depth of experience vis-à-vis other nations with regard to their development. While doing so will be challenging, Africans can possibly seek and hold a pioneering position in the utilization of green technologies, and thus gain economically, rather than pursue direct competition with more advanced nations in basic industries such as steel or in digital industries such as semiconductors and computers. The idea of Africa being a leader in renewable energy industry sectors in the next decade or two is about as believable today as was the idea in the mid-1960s of South Koreans being leaders in consumer electronics by the 1980s.[2] It is possible for African nations to contribute to the development of renewable energy technologies and be among the early adopters, which would help to transform African economies and the quality of life of Africans.[3]

It is no secret that Africans lack the higher education infrastructure to produce the highly qualified, technically oriented individuals to drive green innovation. However, many Africans in the diaspora not only possess the requisite human capital to engage in the research, development, and commercialization of twenty-first-century eco-industrial technologies, but some of them have also accumulated significant economic and social capital from their years of working in high-tech institutions, universities, and R&D labs. A stratum of the next generation of African technologists on the continent can migrate to countries that are at the forefront of eco-industrial innovation in order to learn while helping to pioneer these technologies. Such an exercise of using migration as a tool of development was undertaken by several Asian nations in the late 1900s, a strategy that was itself modeled by several European nations earlier that century.

Nationalistic appeals for Africans to pursue such an agenda primarily if not exclusively for the development of the homeland are unlikely to succeed. Nevertheless, African governments can work to provide enabling environments and welcoming incentives for future sustainability entrepreneurs. Sustainability entrepreneurs are compensated for devising new means of providing services and meeting human and societal needs in an ecologically friendly manner. Several technologies that sustainability entrepreneurs are developing and deploying on the continent, which benefit both society and themselves economically, are discussed below.

Fundamentally, sustainability entrepreneurship involves identifying new opportunities to remediate environmental degradation or launch eco-friendly productive enterprises through innovative strategies. The driving impetus can be for either profit or social impact—or both. Sustainability entrepreneurship can be a vehicle for mobilizing diasporic African talent and capital for the advancement of the renewable energy industry in Africa. The integration of all three factors—innovation in developing renewable energy sources, application of MDM, and involvement in sustainable entrepreneurship—will help prepare African nations more successfully to engage the quickly transforming, complex global economy.

Industrialized Western economies have long relied for their prosperity on the unsustainable use of raw materials and energy resources from lesser developed countries. Relevant also are the huge "investments in power plants, pipelines, factories, dams, and highways to more efficiently serve the burgeoning consumption needs of those at the top of the [global] economic pyramid."[4] Multinational corporations are giving new attention to the more than three billion people in the world—nearly one-half of humanity—who survive on no more than $2.50 per day.[5] To put a finer point on this statistic, the world is growing by approximately one hundred million people a year and nearly 90 percent of that growth is occurring in the global South.[6] Without strategic plans to convert those largely third world sequestered poor people into customers in a global market, corporations are likely to miss growth opportunities in the coming decades. Without incubating and commercializing "the disruptive technologies of tomorrow that leapfrog us toward a more sustainable world," humanity is unlikely to succeed in the coming decades.[7] C. K. Prahalad makes a persuasive case:

> If we take nine countries—China, India, Brazil, Mexico . . . [Nigeria], Indonesia, Turkey, South Africa, and Thailand—collectively they are home to about 3 billion people, representing 70 percent of the developing world population. In PPP [purchasing power parity] terms, this group's GDP is $12.5 trillion, which represents 90 percent of the developing world. It is larger than the GDP of Japan, Germany, France, the United Kingdom, and Italy combined.[8]

The only way to satisfy the needs and aspirations of one-half of humanity—people who have received few benefits from the industrialization we have known to date—with affordable goods and services without accelerating environmental destruction is to progress into clean technologies that mimic rather than dominate nature.[9] Additionally, "if an industry or a firm finds the 'sweet spot'—meaning the right business model and the right combination of products and services—these markets could have explosive growth."[10] The diasporic Africans living in advanced countries who work in green technology fields have a crucial role to play. Not only can they help advance tomorrow's disruptive technologies, but they may also possess an empathetic understanding of the context of the African market (or at least this sentiment could be cultivated) that could shape how they design, manufacture, or deliver goods and services.

Over the past few years, I have researched and published ideas related to those in this chapter—namely, the migration-development model and eco-industrial advancement in Africa.[11] In building on that previous research, I traveled to India to interview and interact with government officials in the Ministry of Overseas Indian Affairs (MOIA) in February 2009. While Indians form one of the world's largest diasporas, the government of India has only recently attempted to leverage that community to benefit the homeland in direct ways. The MOIA was created to execute that leveraging of diasporic Indians for homeland development. India has learned from other Asian nations—for example, Taiwan and South Korea—that have applied MDM over a longer period of time and to great success. Insight gleaned from those interviews in India informed my subsequent fieldwork regarding the African diaspora and renewable energy in South Africa in July 2009 and then a few months later, in October 2009. During the October fieldtrip, I attended a major renewable energy conference in Johannesburg coorganized by the International Solar Energy Society and the Solar Energy Society of Southern Africa in which renewable-energy technologists, government officials with energy portfolios, sustainability entrepreneurs, and others from more than eighty countries participated. My findings from interviews with many conference participants on best practices, including methods of engaging diasporas living and working in countries at the forefront of renewable-energy R&D, are reflected in this chapter.

Renewable Energy in Africa

Renewable energy currently powers only 14 percent of the world's economy. Fears of Peak Oil (i.e., oil exhaustion) and of fossil-fuel-induced climate change, conjoined with perhaps overexuberant anticipation of an abundance of jobs in renewable energy and other parts of the burgeoning green sector, suggest that renewable energy as a percentage of global energy usage will continue surging at the expense of fossil fuels. On the whole, this could be hugely beneficial for Africans. Despite the fact that Africans contribute less than 2 percent of global carbon emissions, they suffer disproportionately from the ill effects of fossil-fuel-induced climate change. Such ill effects are manifested in more frequent, more intense, and longer duration droughts and floods, which in turn undermine agricultural out-put and increase waterborne diseases and malaria.[12] Many people in African oil-exporting states such as Nigeria, Angola, and Equatorial Guinea will be disappointed about such energy-source shifts, but on the whole, the changes will likely be to the continent's advantage, not only ecologically and biolog-ically but also economically. As the world transitions to renewable energy platforms, the question is whether Africans will have the imagination, the will, and concrete strategies to lead in some specific areas.

Renewable energy sources/technologies include solar thermal, solar pho-tovoltaics (PV), biofuels, windpower, geothermal, and wave power. These can be divided into old and new. Old renewable energy sources—namely, biomass and hydropower—are those that have been around for quite some time and do not depend on advanced science and technology (S&T). In terms of old renewables as a percentage of total energy sources, most devel-oping countries have a much higher ratio of renewables to fossil fuels than do the industrialized nations. As one study points out, "About 90 percent of worldwide biomass consumption for energy purposes takes place in non-OECD countries. In some African countries, (traditional) biomass accounts for over 90 percent of total energy consumption. Thus, the share of renew-able energy in non-OECD countries is almost four times higher than in OECD countries."[13] Unfortunately, the way that biomass is currently used in the global South is neither "renewable" nor sustainable.

As can be seen in table 5.1, with the exception of the countries of North Africa, Gabon, Mauritius, and South Africa, Africa is largely unelectrified. And to the extent that the continent is electrified, electrification is concen-trated in the principal cities. For just one example, only about 5 percent of Malians had access to electricity in 2006. In Mali's capital, Bamako, 25 per-cent of the population had access, whereas in rural areas the rate of access was less than 1 percent.[14]

Overall, only about a quarter of sub-Saharan Africans and one-half of South Asians have access to electric grids. A lack of electricity translates into, among other things, an inability to store vaccines, run computers, or study at night, all of which cripple a population's efforts to become a major partic-ipant in the global economy. Another downside of marginal electrification, particularly in rural areas, is poor health resulting from reliance on biomass and charcoal cooking. Table 5.1 shows the high percentage of energy sup-plied by biomass burning in African nations. Every year, over five million children die from respiratory ailments from accumulated smoke inhala-tion associated with such cooking. Cooking accounts for the largest use of fuel wood in Nigeria. Parents desire to have more children, in part to assist with collecting wood and other chores, but larger families require increased cooking and thus more fuel wood. New technologies are required that give people more choices and free up their time from collecting wood so that

Table 5.1. African electrification rates (selected countries), renewable energy use, and telephone access

Country	Electrification rates (2000–2005)[a] (%)	Hydro, solar, wind, geothermal (2005)[a] (%)	Biomass and waste (2005)[a] (%)	Fixed telephone lines per 100 inhabitants (2008)[b]	Mobile telephone subscriptions per 100 inhabitants (2008)[b]
Algeria	98	0.1	0.2	9.6	92.7
Angola	15	1.5	63.8	0.6	37.6
Benin	22	N/A	64.7	1.8	39.7
Botswana	39	N/A	24.1	7.4	77.3
Burkina Faso	7	N/A	N/A	1.0	16.8
Cameroon	47	4.8	78.6	1.0	32.3
Congo	20	2.5	58.3	0.6	50.0
Congo (DRC)	6	3.7	92.5	0.1	14.4
Côte d'Ivoire	50	1.6	58.3	1.7	50.7
Egypt	98	1.9	2.3	14.6	50.6
Eritrea	20	N/A	64.8	0.8	2.2
Ethiopia	15	1.1	90.6	1.1	2.4
Gabon	98	4.1	58.8	1.8	89.8
Ghana	49	5.1	66.0	0.6	49.6
Kenya	14	5.9	74.6	0.6	42.1
Lesotho	11	N/A	N/A	3.2	28.4
Madagascar	15	N/A	N/A	0.9	25.3
Malawi	7	N/A	N/A	1.2	12.0
Mauritius	94	N/A	N/A	28.5	80.7

Morocco	85	1.0	3.3	9.5	72.2
Mozambique	6	11.2	85.4	0.4	19.7
Namibia	34	10.3	13.5	6.6	49.4
Nigeria	46	0.7	78.0	0.9	41.7
Senegal	33	2.0	39.2	2.0	44.1
South Africa	70	0.2	10.5	8.9	90.6
Sudan	30	0.6	79.5	0.9	29.0
Tanzania	11	0.7	92.1	0.3	30.6
Uganda	9	N/A	N/A	0.5	27.0
Zambia	19	10.7	78.7	0.7	28.0
Zimbabwe	34	5.2	61.9	2.8	13.3

[a] UNDP
[b] ITU
N/A = not available

Sources: UNDP, *Human Development Report, 2007/2008: Fighting Climate Change*, http://hdr.undp.org/en/media/HDR_20072008_EN_Complete.pdf (2008); ITU, *Measuring the Information Society: The ICT Development Index*, http://www.itu.int/ITU-D/ict/publications/idi/2009/material/IDI2009_w5.pdf (2009).

more time and attention can be dedicated to education and other activities that enhance quality of life.

The electrification rates resemble Africa's fixed telephone lines connectivity (also in table 5.1) in the sense that the rates are minuscule in comparison to those in more developed nations. Just as the cost of massive landline infrastructure rollout proved prohibitively expensive in most African countries, so too would the expense of building massive electrification infrastructure. Additionally, similar to the way Africans are gaining telecom access through bypassing landlines and progressing directly into mobile telephony, vast numbers of Africans will only gain electrification through bypassing centralized fossil-fuel-based grids and going directly to use of renewable energy sources. The only question is whether Africans will be among the pioneers of such technologies, very early adopters, or late adopters.

Some renewable energy technologies, such as solar cookers and biogas, are operational today that bring power to rural Africans for the carrying out of the aforementioned simple, yet crucial tasks without harming their lungs. Solar cookers are often essentially parabolic mirrors that concentrate solar thermal energy at a focal point where pots are located. With these cookers, water can be boiled in a few minutes, rice can be cooked in twenty minutes, and chicken can be fried in about the same amount of time as with natural gas and electric stoves.[15] Solar cookers are an improvement in that since they are not based on fossil fuels, they neither result in carbon emissions nor harm the health of cooks and other household residents because they create no smoke.

Although prices of solar cookers vary considerably, such appliances can be obtained for around $300 and have a lifespan of about ten years. Solar cookers are an "appropriate technology" product that are somewhat simple to build and that require minimal training for potential users to operate. Solar cookers also contribute to employment through production, distribution, training, and repair. Bangladesh expects to create 100,000 new jobs from training local youth and women as certified solar technicians and repair specialists. India plans to create 150,000 jobs as a result of replacing inefficient biomass cooking stoves in nine million households.[16] If India were to scale up this operation to meet the vast energy needs of its population, millions of new jobs could be created. For only about thirty dollars a year, it is possible to improve the environment, the health of citizens, the local economy, and jobs prospects through solar cookers.

Biogas is another decentralized energy source that is ideal for rural Africa. The technology converts cattle dung, chicken droppings, and human body waste into energy to power electric devices. An important study done in Uganda determined that the following factors cause "the probability of a household adopting biogas technology" to increase: "decreasing age of head of household, increasing household income, increasing number of cattle owned, increasing household size, male head of household and increasing cost of traditional fuels."[17] A biogas digester system may cost approximately $700. Biogas digester technologies are still evolving, and Africans' contributions to the development of this technology have been somewhat minimal to date.

Although solar cookers and biogas technologies are more affordable, solar photovoltaic technology is also a major potential supplier of energy for rural Africa. Many African nations have entertained the notion of promoting the distribution and deployment of solar PV, particularly for rural, off-grid applications, but few have had much success. Cost has partially been a factor, but so too has the lack of sufficiently trained specialists for maintenance and repair. A kilowatt system installed might cost several times the household income in rural areas. Ironically, unless proper attention is given to the matter, plummeting PV prices could potentially pose a problem for Africans. The problem would be that, as prices drop to thresholds of affordability and a cost rivaling heavily subsidized fossil fuels in core and semiperipheral countries, those countries could commence to incorporate more PV supply in their energy portfolio while many African countries might not since their affordability level is significantly below that of core and semiperipheral nations. During that period when other nations would begin to rely more on PV energy, both on-grid and off-grid, African nations would still be waiting on PV prices to decrease to their level of affordability. We witnessed this phenomenon with the emergence of mobile telephones for the third world, but fortunately, once prices began tumbling, they fell somewhat quickly to levels affordable in developing countries, including Africa. Those nations of the global South that had the leadership, imagination, and concrete strategies for migrating from a sparse landline network to a national mobile platform were among the early adopters and greatest beneficiaries. This potential problem underscores the necessity for Africans to position themselves through the migration-development model and sustainability entrepreneurship to help drive renewable energy innovation.

Renewable energy is presently a minor factor in the total global energy picture, but it is likely to become the principal source of energy to power the global economy. Table 5.2 shows the low contribution of renewable energy relative to fossil fuels in the United States. Only 6 percent of total energy supplied in 2007 was from renewable sources.[18] Among the renewable sources, 47 percent was from biomass and 45 percent was hydroelectric. At some point in the future, the ratio will qualitatively change in that renewable energy will be the dominant energy source and fossil fuels will be a minor bit player. Governments in the global North as well as in China and Brazil are ramping up their R&D funding in renewable energy. Additionally, renewable energy is the fastest-growing area for global venture capitalist commercialization.[19] If Africans hope to become pioneers in some aspects of renewable energy and be among the early adopters, they would have to insert themselves with urgency into the middle of this ferment of research, development, and commercialization.

Table 5.2. Contributions of fossil fuel and renewable energy supplies (2007) in the United States

Energy supply	Percent
Fossil fuels	
Petroleum	40
Natural gas	23
Coal	23
Nuclear energy	8
Renewable energy	
Biomass	2.82
Hydroelectric	2.70
Geothermal	0.30
Wind	0.12
Solar	0.06

Source: Roger Bezdek, *Renewable Energy and Energy Efficiency: Economic Drivers for the 21st Century* (2007), http://www.greenforall.org/resources/renewable-energy-and-energy-efficiency-economic.

Table 5.3. World consumption of primary energy

1973		2004	
Fossil fuels	Percent	Fossil fuels	Percent
Oil	45	Oil	34.3
Coal	24.8	Coal	25.1
Natural gas	16.2	Natural gas	20.9
Nuclear	0.9	Nuclear	6.5
Renewable energy	13.1	Renewable energy	13.2
Biomass	11.2	Biomass	10.6
Hydroelectric	1.8	Hydroelectric	2.2
Geothermal, wind, solar, and other	0.1	Geothermal, wind, solar, and other	0.4

Source: Roland Wengenmayr and Thomas Buhrke, *Renewable Energy: Sustainable Energy Concepts for the Future* (Weinheim, Ger.: Wiley-VCH, 2008).

What is perhaps the most striking revelation from table 5.3 is how little change is evident between 1973 and 2004 in terms of movement away from fossil fuels to renewable energy. The Obama administration is calling for an energy portfolio that includes a 25 percent share from renewable energy sources.[20] Among renewable sources, the vast majority was from biomass in both 1973 and in 2004. China's allocated "stimulus spending" for renewable energy in 2009 was $221 billion, twice that of comparable US spending. Governments, venture capitalists, and global corporations are now rushing to gain leadership footing in renewable energy. None of the advanced economies, including that of the United States, can afford not to be energetically seeking to be a pioneer in this sector. Those countries with a lower renewable energy supply face prohibitive costs as great as those of companies that produce substantially more pollution than their counterparts. Pollution represents wasted materials and energy that companies spent money to purchase but that did not go directly into the production and distribution of goods and services. A competitor that cuts out pollution at various stages in the production and distribution cycle gains a cost advantage over those paying for wasted resources. Considering that some form of global cap-and-trade regime could come into existence in the future, many advanced economies and global corporations have added incentives to advance with renewable energies to be in a position to avoid extra financial penalties for CO_2 emissions.

The Role of the African Diaspora: Applying the Migration-Development Model

Presently, Africans contribute marginally to renewable-energy research, development, and commercialization. This comes as no surprise, on the one hand, in light of the low rates of general college graduation and even lower graduation rates in fields of science and technology in Africa. On the other hand, new African immigrants into the United States have higher college graduation rates than other US immigrants and Americans in general.[21] Although African immigrant concentration in S&T fields is nowhere close to the levels of Asian immigrants, it is clear that African scientists and engineers are primarily trained at advanced levels in the United States and other developed nations. Furthermore, the overwhelming majority of African universities lack the capacity to provide state-of-the-art graduate training in science and engineering, which means Africans would have to study such curriculums in core nations.

This process is not unlike situations in some western European nations— such as Italy, Switzerland, and Ireland—very early in the twentieth century and in some Asian nations—such as India, South Korea, and China—much later in the century. They too, decades earlier, lacked the academic infrastructure as well as the cutting-edge industrial capability to provide state-of-the-art graduate education and training in science and engineering. After such diasporans developed the requisite human, economic, and social capital, some of them invested a portion of this capital back into their homeland. Some countries were more skilled at and committed to courting diasporans in core nations who possessed this type of advanced capital that was in short supply and for which there was a tremendous need in the homeland.

Nations such as those cited above recognized the need fairly early on and stuck with the pursuit of those diasporans so that their accumulated capital in the core could be leveraged on behalf of homeland development. In the case of most African countries, there was a recognition in the early stages of independence that intellectually talented fellow citizens would have to be sent to the erstwhile colonizing nations for advanced study since the colonial powers judiciously avoided building universities that could immediately assist with economic development of a postindependent nation. However, after learning that the stay-rate among African nationals in the advanced countries would be too high to contribute significantly to homeland development, governments began to sour on this migration-development model. Governments turned against MDM further when a high percentage of those who returned were predisposed to try to effect fundamental political changes at home.

Many African governments have now gone full circle in that they are back to seeking implementation of some form of the migration-development model.[22] Now that African governments are poised to move in this direction, numerous critical scholars around the world and institutions such as the World Bank and International Organization for Migration (IOM) have weighed in. They have not only attached their imprimaturs to the migration-development strategy, but have also contributed to a burgeoning literature. With more policy-informing research in this area as well as more sophisticated macrolevel data and finer microlevel data available, researchers are more likely to construct accurate profiles of "typical" migrants as well as policies to elicit their homeland contributions.

As I stated in an earlier publication, "Sub-Saharan Africans cannot begin to help pioneer the future ecological economy today without first studying and working in Western universities, research institutes, and corporations any more than Asians could have helped in pioneering the information economy three decades ago without first studying and working in such Western institutions."[23] There is much to do in terms of research and development in the renewable energy industry, and Africans can position themselves to be pioneers through a sort of "green migration-development model," similar to the "digital migration-development model" that worked so well for some Asian nations, and the "basic industry migration-development model" that worked so well for some European nations. Existing hurdles to the further development of renewable energy technology include better storage capabilities, such as achieving lower cost and higher efficiency fuel cells and PV panels. Since the wind blows only intermittently and the sun does not shine all of the time, substantially better storage and recall technology of such energy sources are needed.

These renewable energy technology hurdles bring to mind those that Gordon Moore had to overcome, which became known as Moore's law. Forty-five years ago Moore, cofounder of Intel, proclaimed that the power of computer chips would double every eighteen months. Sustained R&D efforts have validated the continual accuracy of Moore's law; in turn computer advances have been the genesis of the entire information and communications technology (ICT) revolution of the past generation. Silicon Valley is where most of these innovations occurred, and the advancements were something of a global effort in that immigrants, particularly from Asia, contributed. Immigrants both helped to develop the technology and, by so doing, acquired the human, social, and economic capital to advance the ICT industry in their homelands. Renewable energy and other clean technologies represent "enabling technologies" similar to integrated circuits in that other advanced technologies depend on them. Clean technologies may encounter the level of exponential growth experienced by integrated circuits over the past few decades. The proposition advanced in this chapter is that Africans could conceivably parallel Asians with regard to clean technologies.

Sustainability Entrepreneurship Can Reinvigorate the New MDM

"Sustainability entrepreneurship" is a recent technological offshoot from the concept of "social entrepreneurship." Although social entrepreneurship was coined thirty years ago, it is just starting to be sufficiently conceptualized and it remains woefully under-theorized. As for sustainability entrepreneurship, although it is only now being fleshed out conceptually, I will demonstrate its potential utility in increasing S&T contributions from Africans of the diaspora in the renewable energy sector. But first, I will briefly discuss social entrepreneurship.

Generic "entrepreneurship" is traceable to Jean-Baptiste Say at the beginning of the nineteenth century; the French economist discussed a person or an organized group of persons who undertakes an innovative strategy to create new value for customers and profit for the entrepreneurs.[24] For another economist a century later, Joseph Schumpeter, true entrepreneurship was not about improving the status quo with slight improvements here and there; rather, it was about disrupting if not totally demolishing the status quo and the institutions that support it with the unending "gales of creative destruction."[25] As capitalist economists of capitalism, Say, Schumpeter, and their successors have designated entrepreneurship as a universal activity connoting market-oriented business practices for private gain. Consequently, the term "business" was not even needed when entrepreneurship was used in conversation: in fact, "business entrepreneurship" would be considered redundant. Since Bill Drayton, founder of Ashoka: Innovators for the Public, first used "social" as the adjective to denote a type of entrepreneurship in 1980, thereby introducing the term "social entrepreneurship," the idea has basically been to think in terms of applying the same skills, drive and determination, creativity, and innovation that entrepreneurs have historically taken to maximize profits to high-risk activities for large-scale systemic social change.

According to Roger Martin and Sally Osberg, "The critical distinction between entrepreneurship and social entrepreneurship lies in the value proposition itself."[26] That is, the distinction is between the value of engaging market forces to maximize private profit versus the value of addressing social needs by maximizing social benefit. With business entrepreneurship, where profit is sacrosanct, the goal is to innovate products for populations who can afford them or who at least have access to credit to purchase products and services now and pay for them over time. Social entrepreneurship, on the other hand, seeks to innovate products to satisfy underserved populations. Paul Light sees social entrepreneurs as having the alertness, cleverness, and determination to strategize and implement a business plan or social agenda in the following step-by-step progression.[27] These qualities have historically been seen as attributes of business entrepreneurship:

- Imagine a new equilibrium
- Discover an opportunity
- Invent the idea for change
- Scale up for high impact
- Diffuse the idea
- Sustain momentum
- Navigate the changing social ecosystem

In a sense, the business entrepreneurship versus social entrepreneurship distinction is not unrelated to Karl Marx's distinction between exchange value and use value.[28] Exchange value generates profits for the entrepreneur, as a result of innovating products that can be exchanged in the marketplace with consumers who possess sufficient money or credit. The social utility of the product exchanged is irrelevant; for example, (1) "pet rocks" or (2) drugs for erectile dysfunction—so long as they yield greater profit—can be regarded as generators of greater value than (3) malaria vaccines or

(4) off-grid renewable energy sources for the rural populations in the global South. Conversely, use value is measured more in terms of social utility for the general public, particularly those in underserved locations, rather than profits for the entrepreneurs. To date, products such as malaria vaccines or off-grid nonrenewable energy sources have been viewed as territory for social entrepreneurs as they "only" generate use value, while "pet rocks" and drugs for erectile dysfunction are potentially target-rich opportunities for business entrepreneurs since they have exchange value. If Prahalad's analysis is correct, corporations are beginning to convert what formerly would have been regarded as mere use value into exchange-value-laden products. That is, product categories such as (3) and (4) may gain exchange value based on an entirely new paradigm of production. All commodities are social products of labor; the principal distinction is whether the labor is organized and mobilized around production for profit or around satisfying social needs.

Conceptualizers and analysts of social entrepreneurship err in their conception of social entrepreneurship and business entrepreneurship as polar opposites. For instance, Eleanor Shaw and Sarah Carter define business entrepreneurship as the process of engaging market forces to maximize private profit whereas social entrepreneurship scales up and leverages community support to generate public goods to address unmet social needs.[29] Rather than thinking of business entrepreneurship and social entrepreneurship as forming a binary opposition, it is more useful to think of them as spanning a full spectrum of graduated differentiation. On the business entrepreneurship end of the spectrum, the principal imperative is profit maximization, while at the other end, social entrepreneurship, the chief impetus is the fulfillment of social needs. In between these poles are myriad points, differing ratios of profit-seeking to social-needs-addressing enterprises.

It is possible to devise different classification schemes of social entrepreneurship. Stanford University's Social Entrepreneurship Institute has a typological scheme that involves three categories. One category is social entrepreneurial activities as discussed above but executed in a manner to generate a profit for the entrepreneurial enterprise. Unlike the traditional business enterprise, the profit-seeking social enterprise may actually be stimulated by the opportunity and driven to satisfy the needs of underserved populations. A second category of social entrepreneurship involves social enterprises that are not profit-seeking yet generate sufficient income to consistently make social impacts in underserved communities. The third category of social entrepreneurship, according to the Stanford Institute, is philanthropic social action to produce profit-seeking entrepreneurs. This third approach stems from the fact that some communities simply do not produce a sufficient number of individuals with the attributes as detailed by Paul Light above. Consequently, their economies stagnate on a plateau with a huge stratum of the population underserved due at least in part to a shortage of individuals with entrepreneurial drive, skill, and seed capital, even when structural blocks are not to blame.

Sustainability entrepreneurship is a specific area of social entrepreneurship where all of the above discussion applies. That is, for instance, the orientation, skill, and ability to create novel value out of scarce resources; the willingness to take risks; and the determination to innovate and see projects through to completion, which are all attributes traditionally ascribed to business entrepreneurs, tend also to be attributes possessed by sustainability entrepreneurs. Different categories or types of sustainability entrepreneurship exist, such as those identified by the Stanford Institute. Both social entrepreneurship and sustainability entrepreneurship are concerned with addressing needs of underserved populations. Sustainability entrepreneurship has another dimension in that it sees the entire world as an underserved community with regard to renewable energy.

Populations in some impoverished countries are in more urgent need of renewable energy, such as rural populations of the global South. Actually, humanity as a whole is in dire need of renewable energy to prevent environmental collapse. There are different ways for sustainability entrepreneurs to participate, including in those ways outlined by the Stanford Institute. Some sustainability entrepreneurs are doing excellent work around the world with solar cookers and biogas. This chapter has concerned itself with the possibilities and benefits of identifying imaginative Africans among the pioneering contributors of renewable energy as well as devising a strategy for targeted innovation in this vital economic sector.

When the migration-development model was implemented on behalf of western Europeans and later of Asians, nationalism—though it has ebbed and flowed over the decades—was a much more powerful force than it is today. As Seoul, Beijing, Taipei, and other Asian capitals that benefited from MDM put this strategy into operation, they could appeal more reliably and directly to nationalist sentiment to move their diasporans on behalf of their ancestral homeland than African capitals would be able to do today. This is not to suggest that nationalism does not figure into today's migration-development strategy. Instead, since nationalist appeals to diasporans will likely be far less effective at stimulating them to make substantial and systematic contributions to their homeland's development, other inducements would likely be necessary to augment nationalist appeals. Opportunities of sustainability entrepreneurship represent such an augmentation.

Conclusion

On the whole, individuals want to see their homeland succeed. A homeland that is held in high esteem globally or that is clearly ascending in the world's economic order has a range of benefits, extending from ephemeral pride to material gain. Rightly or wrongly, individuals are judged based not only on their individual merit and character, but also on their ethnic and national heritage, and on the status of their homeland in the global hierarchy.[30]

In many respects, this is what the migration-development model is all about. That is, MDM is based on the assumption that individuals will largely be inclined to contribute to the development of their respective homelands when it is possible to do so without being too costly. In the twentieth century, certain European and Asian nations alike progressed through the application of this migration-development strategy. I have posited that an African transnational community—that is, those on the continent and in the diaspora—can similarly work together strategically so that they, too, can experience transformative development.

Africans may be centuries behind established economic powers such as the United States in basic industrial sectors and even decades behind newly industrialized powers such as South Korea in the ICT sector, but Africans are only a few years behind "leaders" in the nascent green or eco-industrial sector. Although green technologies generally subsume and embody previous technologies, they represent a paradigm shift; therefore, becoming a leader in this sector does not require leadership experience in previously reigning technologies. The Asian experience is particularly instructive in this respect since although nations such as Taiwan and South Korea missed out on the first wave of the Industrial Revolution, because the Information Revolution represented a marked paradigm shift, they were nonetheless able to gain leadership positions in key information communications technologies.

Applying this model to Africa in the present involves focusing on the next paradigm shift, namely, the ecological revolution. Diasporic Africans who already work for institutions in countries where research, development, and commercialization of green technologies are presently occurring have an indispensable role to play—according to the migration-development model. Additionally, the role of the next generation of technically oriented African intellectuals is also vitally important. African states and technology firms as well as diasporic community leaders would have to perform roles similar to their Asian counterparts a half century ago and similar to their European counterparts a century ago.

As a reflection of the key technological revolution, venture capital, and economic focus at the time, many Asian technology entrepreneurs a few decades ago concentrated on information technology with regard to circulating capital from their diasporic location to their homeland. Over time, the information technology gap was diminished. For Africans, the technology entrepreneurs may likely concentrate today on green technologies, especially those involving renewable energy sources. As a result, African governments and diasporic leaders could help produce legions of sustainability entrepreneurs. In this chapter, I noted that sustainability entrepreneurs are compensated for devising new means of providing services and meeting human and societal needs in an ecologically friendly manner. I discussed several technologies that sustainability entrepreneurs are developing and are deploying on the continent, which benefit both society and themselves economically. Finally, I have postulated a novel and plausible twenty-first-century African development strategy for examination. The postulated strategy models related strategies of twentieth-century Europeans and Asians under comparable circumstances. Adjustments in the analysis are made for differences in historical circumstances, hierarchies of power, and emerging technologies.

Notes

1. United Nations Development Programme, *Human Development Report, 2007/ 2008: Fighting Climate Change: Human Solidarity in a Divided World* (2008), http://hdr. undp.org/en/media/HDR_20072008_EN_Complete.pdf.

2. Ha-Joon Chang, *Bad Samaritans: The Myth of Free Trade and the Secret History of Capitalism* (New York: Bloomsbury, 2008).

3. Some Africanists recoil viscerally whenever the experiences of Asians are noted for comparative analysis. In response, I would point out that, first, Asians' application of the migration-development model came later in the twentieth century, decades after the Europeans utilized it. Also, Asians may have been unwilling to examine how European diasporans invested some of their human, social, and economic capital into their respective homelands. After all, they could have argued that the world was a very different place in the first half of the twentieth century when the Italians, Swiss, Irish, and others practiced this strategy than during later decades when Asians began utilizing it. Moreover, they might have argued that Europeans are the kith and kin of the US establishment, thereby making the migration-development model peculiar to peoples of European stock. Had that sentiment prevailed, Asian national economies that have been transformed may still be mired in deep-seated poverty and toiling in primary production.

Second, Africanists who reject any sort of comparative analysis with Asian nations also contend that Americans wanted specific Asian nations to succeed for Cold War reasons and that alone accounts for their economic success. Such a position imputes false, outsized power to Americans. This line of reasoning essentially posits that Americans were omnisciently powerful in that they could absolutely determine who would or would not undergo transformative development. It is one thing to concede that the United States will deploy its manifold assets globally to project power in accordance "with its interests," but it is something else entirely to contend that the United States determines which nations transform their economy and improve the quality of life of their citizens. In the end it is not about Africans attempting to emulate Asians' experiences any more than Asians previously having set out to emulate the experience of Europeans. Instead, it is about learning and applying a strategy—in this case the migration-development model—that is applicable across time and space.

4. Stuart Hart, *Capitalism at the Crossroads: Aligning Business, Earth, and Humanity* (Upper Saddle River, NJ: Wharton School Publishing, 2007), 107.

5. Anup Shah, "Poverty Facts and Stats," *Global Issues: Social, Political, Economic and Environmental Issues That Affect Us All* (1998), http://www.globalissues.org/article/26/poverty-facts-and-stats.

6. United Nations Development Programme (UNDP), *Human Development Report, 2005* (New York, 2005), 235.

7. Hart, *Capitalism at the Crossroads*, 194.

8. C. K. Prahalad, *The Fortune at the Bottom of the Pyramid: Eradicating Poverty Through Profits, Enabling Dignity and Choice Through Markets* (Upper Saddle River, NJ: Wharton School Publishing, Pearson Education, 2006), 10.

9. Janine Benyus, *Biomimicry: Innovation Inspired by Nature* (New York: Morrow, 1997).

10. Prahalad, *Fortune at the Bottom*, 50.

11. See Rubin Patterson, "Transnationalism: Diaspora-Homeland Development," *Social Forces* 84 (2006): 1891–1907; Rubin Patterson, ed., *African Brain Circulation: Beyond the Drain-Gain Debate* (Boston: Brill, 2007); and Rubin Patterson, "Historic Changes Underway in African Migration Policies from Muddling Through to Organized Brain Circulation" (paper presented at the University of Florida, Gainesville, February 2008).

12. UNDP, *Human Development Report, 2007/2008*.

13. Ulrich Laumanns, Danyel Reiche, and Mischa Bechberger, "Renewable Energy Markets in Developing Countries: Providing Green Power for Sustainable Development," in *Green Power Markets: Support Schemes, Case Studies, and Perspectives*, ed. Lutz Mez (Essex, UK: Multi-Science, 2007), 404.

14. I. M. Bugaje, "Renewable Energy for Sustainable Development in Africa: A Review," *Renewable and Sustainable Energy Reviews* 10 (2006): 603–12.

15. Information provided by Crosby Menzies, director of Sunfire Solutions, at the International Solar Energy Society conference in Johannesburg, October 13, 2009.

16. United Nations Environment Programme et al., *Green Jobs: Towards Decent Work in a Sustainable, Low-Carbon World* (2009), http://www.ilo.org/wcmsp5/groups/public/—dgreports/—dcomm/documents/publication/wcms_098503.pdf.

17. Peter Walekhwa, Johnny Mugisha, and Lars Drake. "Biogas Energy from Family-Sized Digesters in Uganda: Critical Factors and Policy Implications." *Energy Policy* 37, no. 7 (2009): 2754–62.

18. Roger Bezdek, *Renewable Energy and Energy Efficiency: Economic Drivers for the 21st Century* (2007), http://www.greenforall.org/resources/renewable-energy-and-energy-efficiency-economic. See also International Energy Agency, *World Energy Outlook* (Paris, 2008).

19. National Venture Capital Association, *Venture Capitalists are Optimistic for 2010 Despite Predictions for Industry Contraction* (2009), http://www.nvca.org/index.php?option=com_content&view=article&id=78&Itemid=102.

20. Change.gov: The Office of the President Elect, Energy & Environment: The Obama-Biden Plan (2009), http://change.gov/agenda/energy_and_environment_agenda/.

21. "African Immigrants in the United States Are the Nation's Most Highly Educated Group," *Journal of Blacks in Higher Education*, no. 26 (Winter 1999–2000): 60–61.

22. Patterson, "Historic Changes in African Migration Policies."

23. Rubin Patterson, "Preparing Sub-Saharan Africa for a Pioneering Role in Eco-Industrial Development," *Journal of Industrial Ecology* 12 (2008): 501–4.

24. Jean-Baptiste Say, *Treatise on Political Economy* (New Brunswick, NJ: Transaction Publishers, 2001).

25. Joseph Schumpeter, *Capitalism, Socialism, and Democracy* (New York: Harper and Brothers, 1947).

26. Roger Martin and Sally Osberg, "Social Entrepreneurship: The Case for Definition," *Stanford Social Innovation Review* (2007): 34, http://www.skollfoundation.org/media/skoll_docs/2007SP_feature_martinosberg.pdf.

27. Paul Light, *The Search for Social Entrepreneurship* (Washington, DC: Brookings Institution Press, 2008), 3.

28. Karl Marx, *Capital: A Critique of Political Economy*, vol. 1, trans. E. Mandel (New York: Random House, 1977).

29. Eleanor Shaw and Sara Carter, "Social Entrepreneurship: Theoretical Antecedents and Empirical Analysis of Entrepreneurial Processes and Outcomes," *Journal of Small Business and Enterprise Development* 14 (2007): 418–34.

30. Patterson, "Transnationalism," 1891–1907.

Part Two

Localities, Nations, and Globalization

6

Transborder Labor
Liberalization and Social Contracts

KAREN E. BRAVO

Introduction

The transnational labor market is characterized by the illegality and temporariness that is assigned by states to mobile and would-be mobile human providers of labor. The globalized transnational economy demands and stimulates the movement of labor from one domestic economy to another. However, individual nation-states' immigration laws that seek to barricade domestic markets from the entry of transborder labor suppliers and the near silence of multilateral trade law create obstacles to such movement.[1] The disjuncture and disequilibrium between international trade law and domestic immigration law foster illegal movement across borders and result in the vulnerability of human would-be mobile labor providers to trafficking and other forms of exploitation.[2]

The failure of states to liberalize labor as part of the multilateral trade liberalization project stands in stark contradiction to the liberalization of other fundamental economic inputs, thus undermining the vision for a globalized world. The contemporary model of globalization is facilitated and, in large part, stimulated by multilateral trade liberalization.[3] The trade liberalization begun at Bretton Woods—enhanced by successive rounds of negotiations, and to which much of the world is now committed—is focused on lowering barriers to the movement of goods, capital, services, and ideas.[4] That liberalization of the movement of inputs and products, according to trade theorists and supporters of free trade, stimulates efficient, competitive, and productive economic activity that will, ultimately, accrue to the benefit of all participants. However, the liberalization of labor (and the consequent movement of human beings) is a neglected and often feared aspect of multilateral and regional trade liberalization policies and agreements.[5] Individual human labor providers seeking to exchange their labor for value confront state barriers to their movement.

Domestic social contracts, to the extent that they exist, are subject to the pressures of transnational economic forces that have altered, fundamentally, the existing contracts between, for example, labor and capital.[6] Concepts of distributive justice require democratization of access to the benefits of trade liberalization. To the extent that individual nation-states' domestic laws demand that labor be rendered immobile or that mobile human labor providers be punished for transgressing the laws created to ensure their immobility, labor is denied full access to the benefits of trade liberalization. I propose that the path to the framing, implementation, and enforcement of a global social contract that protects labor is to liberalize labor from some of the nation-state constraints to which the transborder labor market is subject. Labor is hampered in its ability to operate in the global sphere, with a consequent negative impact on its ability to transpose domestic social contracts to the global sphere or enforce them there, or to enforce those global standards, such as International Labor Organization (ILO) conventions, that already exist.

The conflicts between the international human rights conception of humans as rights bearers and the multilateral trade regime's imposition of legal immobility, together with the immigration law and protectionist view of the migrant as a threatening profit- or benefit-devouring Pac Man–like unit creates a societal context that fosters the individual labor provider's vulnerability and exploitability. The solution proposed in this chapter addresses the following systemic tensions: (1) the gap between the rhetoric and the *reality* of trade liberalization undertaken thus far through multilateral and regional international instruments; and (2) the gap in conceptualization between humans as rights-bearing persons and as economic actors—as consumers and as labor (an economic input or commodity). The liberalization of labor will allow human labor providers to compete and collaborate with capital on the global stage. Global competition and collaboration between labor and capital are more probable sources of the formation of a global social contract than is the current framework of international labor standards.

To create a rights-protective equilibrium in the transnational labor market, I contend that the economic nature of humans—our economic roles in the global economic system—must be more fully recognized. That recognition will require that human labor providers must have the right to easily enter and exit individual domestic labor markets in response to economic stimuli.

The Contemporary Transnational Labor Market

In response to national security threats and economic development challenges, the immigration laws of many individual nation-states have become increasingly draconian. Migration scholar Douglas Massey described some of the anti-immigration measures: "patrolling the border, castigating employers who hire unauthorized workers, barring immigrants from social programs, and limiting the rights of the foreign born to housing, health care, schooling, and employment."[7] In his 2007 publication *Opening the Floodgates,* Professor Kevin R. Johnson characterized US immigration laws as both ineffectual and immoral, and called for a fundamental transformation in perspective and approach.[8] In a review of *Opening the Floodgates,* my coauthor and I contrasted the effects of domestic immigration laws with the liberalization of other factors of production, describing the plight of migrants and would-be migrants as follows:

> In *The World Is Flat...* Thomas Friedman celebrates the flattening of the world—that is, the diminution in the importance of borders, geographic boundaries, time zones, and other barriers to economic activity. The earth is *not* flat for would-be migrants, particularly migrants coming from economically vulnerable countries. In the search for economic opportunities in countries other than their own, migrants face not only physical challenges of distance and arduous land or seascapes; they face the barriers of state borders and restrictive border enforcement.[9]

Yet, restrictive immigration policies do not successfully constrain the flow of labor.[10] Instead, such policies serve to facilitate the exploitation of the migrant and would-be migrant, such that entire industries, both legal and illegal, grow from the lucrative and fruitless border enforcement.[11] Informal African migration to Europe provides a stark example of the labor flows that exist worldwide in defiance of legal and logistical barriers erected and maintained by states.[12]

Another key feature of the contemporary transnational labor market is a two-tier system that privileges skilled labor.[13] Nation-states and the owners of capital support and implement national and corporate policies that facilitate the access of skilled labor, while ignoring the needs that would be met by the liberalization of *all* labor.

Despite the imposition of barriers to movement, states, juridical persons, and humans work within the interstices and gaps of the legal framework to supply the transnational labor market through formal and informal programs, illegal transborder movement, and bilateral agreements and arrangements.[14] However, these means of access are too often narrow and exploitative exceptions to the rule. Opportunities for exploitation and conditions of inequality are increased in both the formal and informal transnational labor markets as less powerful states transmit their unequal bargaining status to their nationals.

Both Western and less developed nations participate in an extensive transborder trade in labor through, among other mechanisms, bilateral and multilateral agreements and understandings, some of which are of long standing. Those trading arrangements, formal and informal, between labor-rich sending countries and labor-poor host countries, rest upon a central premise: the human transborder labor provider will *always* be a creature (national) of his or her home country. Toward that end, a basic tenet of these arrangements is that the human transborder labor provider should never achieve the status nor enjoy the rights of a national of the host country, and may not demand from the host country the rights and privileges that come with citizenship.

Outsider status is maintained permanently through the imposition of temporal restraints and barriers to transformation into, or assimilation as part of, the host nation's privileged citizenry. The human labor provider is intentionally cabined and constrained by dependence on his or her employer for the continued legality of the former's presence, retention of the sending state's unequal bargaining power and status, and limited access to the domestic civil rights regime of the host state.[15]

Incomplete Trade Liberalization

Through the mechanism of trade liberalization, economic forces and actors are unleashed, with transnational and global effects. At the same time, through their refusal to fully implement multilateral trade liberalization and active construction of barriers, states and some vested interests oppose and encumber the transnational movement of labor. Throughout the process of continual trade liberalization, the fundamental and mostly unspoken underlying concept of labor as an immobile factor of production (truly analogous to immobile land) has not been institutionally challenged.[16] The multilateral trade liberalization undertaken through the WTO and most examples of regional trade liberalization (with the marked exception of the European Union) have neglected to liberalize labor. That neglect constrains the ability of labor—that is, individual labor providers and labor acting collectively—to respond fully to transnational economic stimuli or to participate actively in globalization as autonomous economic actors.

The failure to liberalize labor is a betrayal of fundamental trade liberalization theory as well as of classical and neoclassical economic theory. Pursuant to classical and neoclassical theory, labor is one of the principal factors of production.[17] Trade liberalization theory touts the welfare-enhancing benefits that are to be gained through removal of barriers to the movement of both factor inputs (such as capital) and finished and unfinished products or goods. However, the movement of labor, a fundamental production input, is ignored. Instead, dominant trade liberalization policy efforts assume, with little challenge, the immobility of labor as a factor of production. At the same time, mass migratory movements by labor providers representing all levels of skill reveal a deep disjuncture between the rhetoric and the reality of trade liberalization.[18]

The inability of the contemporary trade liberalization project to recognize and implement labor's status as an equal factor of production and to deploy a holistic economic conceptualization of labor undermines the entire project. As labor providers may not easily undertake transnational movement to either exit or enter particular domestic markets, this blind spot in trade liberalization also hinders the ability of individual states to flexibly adjust the factor inputs into their domestic economic production in response to changes in their economies' demand for labor. Labor liberalization would allow the unemployed in a labor-rich economy to find employment in labor-poor economies where employment openings might otherwise go unfilled. At the same time, a labor-poor economy engaged in labor-intensive production would be able to increase the supply of labor through labor liberalization polices that welcome the influx of new labor.[19]

Further, the failure to challenge the assumed immobility of labor flies in the face of evidence of the adjustability and mutability of *factor inputs* and of *comparative advantage*. For example, state intervention to adjust the quality, nature, or characteristics of factor endowments may fundamentally alter an economy's comparative advantage. Or, economies may adjust their factor inputs such that, for example, an economy that is rich in labor but poor in capital may, through the import of capital, shift its position of comparative advantage toward capital-intensive production. The liberalization of labor would enhance the flexibility and ease of adoption of different policies by individual economies, thereby also promoting economic development. A further result would be more open acknowledgment of the increasing interdependence of economies in political and economic discourse and policymaking.

The General Agreement on Trade in Services (GATS), a multilateral agreement annex to the Agreement Establishing the World Trade Organization (WTO), does provide, rather indirectly, for some liberalization of labor. Under Mode 4 of the GATS, a service supplier from state A may supply services in state B through the presence of natural persons—that is, the presence of the human labor provider necessary for the delivery of that service.[20] However, the GATS Annex on Movement of Natural Persons, although it refers to temporary admission of foreign nationals into the territory of another WTO member as part of the business of supplying services abroad, expressly excludes and disclaims an intent to affect individual member states' domestic immigration laws and any implications of the creation of rights to access the labor market of individual member states.[21] Further, to the extent that WTO member states have made commitments under the GATS, and those limited commitments have been fulfilled, liberalization of labor is restricted to highly skilled human labor providers who serve the service delivery interests of juridical (i.e., corporate) entities.[22] Finally, Mode 4 addresses only the *temporary* movement of natural persons, leaving the liberalization of human labor providers an even more neglected aspect of contemporary multilateral trade liberalization.

Regional Integration and Labor Mobility

Regional trading arrangements, which create trade groupings of small numbers of neighboring member states with greater homogeneity of cultures, economies, and interests, would appear to provide opportunities for experimentation in this neglected area of the contemporary multilateral trade liberalization and globalization project. However, with the remarkable exception of the European Union (EU), states have failed to experiment with labor liberalization even within the more controlled context of regional trading arrangements. Instead, state participants in regional trading arrangements appear to be prepared to contemplate the liberalization of labor only within the context of a drive toward deeper integration of member state economies. And, even within the context of planned enhanced integration of economies and proposed labor liberalization initiatives, the implementation of labor liberalization is stillborn—part of a rhetoric that has not yet become reality.

For example, through the African Union (AU) and subregional integration units such as the Economic Community of West African States (ECOWAS), African countries are attempting to emulate the regional integration success of the EU.[23] To that end, the AU aspires to implement the four freedoms undertaken by the EU and deemed central to economic integration—the freedom of movement of goods, persons, services, and capital.[24] However, despite the rhetoric, little has been achieved toward labor mobility on the institutional level.[25]

Some Consequences of the Omission of Labor Liberalization

The failure to liberalize labor distorts the transnational labor market.[26] While domestic capital, producers, and consumers are allowed to respond to increased competition originating from outside domestic state borders, labor is prevented from freely and fully responding to the economic stimuli in a productive manner.[27] That is, labor providers may lose their utility in the production framework of the domestic economy (i.e., become unemployed or underemployed) because of exposure of domestic producers to transborder competition in goods, services, capital, or ideas. However, labor itself is prevented from competing transnationally—that is, labor providers have limited ability to seek transborder employment opportunities. In addition, and more importantly, the dislocation of labor from overwhelmed domestic producers who decrease their production levels in response to increased external competition leads to an oversupply of labor in the domestic economy. Yet, state-constructed and state-defended borders and other barriers to entry prevent labor providers from responding productively to increased transborder economic opportunities.[28]

However, labor continues to respond to the economic stimuli posed by the contrast between the economic incentives available in domestic and transborder markets.[29] Massey and his coauthors assert that

> in the context of a globalizing economy, the entry of markets and capital-intensive production technologies into peripheral regions disrupts existing social and economic arrangements and brings about a widespread displacement of people from customary livelihoods, creating a mobile population of workers who actively search for new ways of achieving economic sustenance. Studies consistently show that international migrants [come] from regions and nations that are undergoing rapid change and development as a result of their incorporation into global trade, information, and production networks.[30]

Moreover, the legally enforced immobility of labor and its legally prohibited movement lead to exploitation of labor in both origin and destination economies. The oversupply of labor (manifested in increased unemployment or underemployment) in state A drives down or freezes the wages offered to state A's labor providers. The undocumented and quasi-personhood status of illegally mobile labor in state B, and not merely the presence of that labor, facilitates the exploitation of labor in state B and may drive down the wages of domestic labor there.[31]

In addition, the continued and contradictory assumptions about, and attempted enforcement of, labor immobility allow employers and owners of capital to interchange (and substitute) capital and labor transnationally and to "price discriminate" in their payments of compensation to labor providers trapped in individual domestic labor markets. Manufacturers and some service providers are able to outsource production to pools of cheap labor held immobile by the national borders of host states.[32] Service providers whose services must be provided in situ—for example, landscaping, roofing, and house-cleaning companies—are able to access the cheap labor of the *undocumented* worker who, due in part to the legal quasi-personhood imposed by the state, accepts lower wages than does the domestic labor force.[33] Such acceptance of lower wages by the worker who is illegally present exerts a downward pressure on the wages of some other labor providers in the host economy.[34]

Some Proposed Solutions and Critiques

The disequilibrium in transnational labor markets has not gone unnoticed. Confronted with the disjuncture in legal regimes and the disequilibrium in the labor market, together with the consequent exploitation of human labor providers, particularly migrant laborers, scholars have offered several suggestions for change. Those suggestions challenge the disequilibrium and propose reforms to address both the economic and the human (and civil) rights aspects. The proposals for reform include expansion and enhancement of existing domestic guest worker programs, liberalization of labor within the context of regional trading arrangements, and expansion of GATS Mode 4. None of the suggested reforms proffered thus far would address both the disjuncture and the contradiction between the overarching legal systems—trade liberalization and domestic immigration laws—nor do they adequately attack the economic foundations for the exploitation of individual human labor providers.

Labor must be brought front and center instead of being subsumed into other inputs into production. None of the proposals for addressing the transnational labor market disequilibrium attempt to reconceptualize and implement the role of labor in economic activity. Each of the proposed solutions offers the prospect of increased legal transborder movement of human labor providers in response to transborder economic incentives, but does not fundamentally challenge the status quo.

Ultimately, the proposed reforms fall short of addressing the economic disequilibrium that characterizes the contemporary transnational labor market; in fact, they offer the prospect of a continuation of the failed conceptualizations of the past. For example, despite calls for enhancement and expansion of the GATS Mode 4, the GATS is fundamentally ill-equipped to fulfill the role of liberalizing labor that would be required by the General Agreement on Trade in Labor proposed later in this chapter. Human labor must be truly liberalized as are the other factors of production, and that liberalization must include more than the *temporary* movement of labor. Due to its internal temporal constraints, GATS Mode 4 is inadequate to the task of liberalizing labor. As stated by one commentator, the GATS Mode 4 covers only "a subset of a subset of a subset" of the transnational labor market.[35]

The proposed reforms rely on the continued interposition of the non-omniscient state between the human labor provider and the economic stimuli to which that provider attempts to respond. For example, if an expanded guest worker program were adopted, unilaterally, by each WTO member state, the effect on labor might be similar to the effects anticipated from the coordinated multilateral labor liberalization proposed in this chapter. However, programs devised by individual nation-states would lack harmony: the scope of each program would differ, as would the terms and protections affecting individual transborder labor providers under the varied domestic legal frameworks. Furthermore, the proposed expansions of guest worker programs maintain the structures and mechanisms of exploitation, and provide inadequate recognition and facilitation of the agency of individual labor providers. As a result, the existing preconditions for exploitation would remain.

From the human rights perspective, the constraint of temporariness counters the autonomy and agency of human labor providers, and is fundamentally contradictory to the liberalization advocated here. From a political perspective, the prospect of renegotiating the GATS and of broadening the inclusiveness of its provisions is so difficult that it is preferable to aim for the most effective strategy, even if that strategy may be equally difficult to achieve.[36] Rather than amending the GATS, which addresses only a small proportion of the transnational labor market, I advocate the difficult path of enacting multilateral labor liberalization that removes temporal limitations on the mobility of human labor providers.

Regional labor liberalization solutions will exhibit the trade diversion flaws of which regional trade arrangements have been accused.[37] To the extent that labor is liberalized within a region subject to a regional trade arrangement, labor providers who, under a multilateral labor liberalization framework, might have been better compensated outside that region may instead be limited in their ability to seek "legal" economic opportunities. Further, capital may be attracted to the larger pool of liberalized labor within the regional trade arrangement to the detriment of equally qualified and otherwise competitive labor located outside the bounds of that arrangement. Nevertheless, as a second-best alternative in a nonideal world, and to overcome social and political barriers through the lens of experience, member states in regional trade arrangements should be encouraged to experiment with the liberalization of labor.

Why Liberalize Transnational Labor?

Principles of distributive justice should determine the distribution of a society's assets. Ideally, both the powerful and less powerful should derive benefits, and the less powerful should not be made less well-off. The social contract refers to the terms pursuant to which a society will operate in exchange for the relinquishment of autonomy by individual participants. The eminent philosopher John Rawls posited an ideal society in which the social contract was drawn up by participants under a "veil of ignorance." According to Rawls, such a precondition would ensure the framing of rules of interaction and governance that would be most just for both the powerful and the less powerful in a particular society.

It appears to me that the existing domestic social contracts constructed with the intent of protecting human labor providers have run out of steam—in their current form, these individual domestic contracts are unable to withstand the transnational economic forces that assail them. After industrialization took off in the nineteenth century, and the "working man" emerged from the peasantry, collective action movements, social activism, and political processes created various mechanisms aimed at protecting labor. In essence, through pensions and other contractual benefits, labor established some ownership rights in the fruits of its economic activity. Workplace safety laws and other labor protection standards (including antidiscrimination and other doctrines) operated to adjust the power differential between labor and capital. Within the individual national domestic labor markets, labor providers and the owners of capital carved out their own social contracts based on the balance of power existing between cultural and historical forces, such that rigid or flexible social divisions and the acceptance or rejection of authoritarianism, among others, all played a role in the equilibrium attained between these competing and cooperating production inputs.

Although it has achieved such benefits as cheaper consumer goods and wider consumer choice, multilateral trade liberalization has, by exposing labor and capital to transborder competition, altered, perhaps irrevocably, the social contracts wrought within individual nation-states. In the capitalist quest for a greater competitive edge, labor has been forced to surrender many of the contractual rights it had won in the past. The legal protections that were also essential to the bargain struck between labor and capital are often inadequately enforced by state authorities, which also have an interest in bolstering economic competitiveness.

Some critics have characterized this voluntary and involuntary relinquishment of protective mechanisms as a "race to the bottom." That is, in order to be competitive within a globalizing world, labor protection standards are abandoned in order to attract globally mobile *capital* and all-important *jobs.* Pursuant to this view, the glorification of cheapness and competition above quality and living wages and the failure of the multilateral trading system to impose global labor, environmental, and other linkage standards undermine the social contract created within individual states to the disadvantage of, among others, labor and the environment.

This horse—mandatory global labor standards—has already left the barn. The resistance from defenders of individual state sovereignty and autonomy and the diverse social, cultural, and historical experiences of nation-states make agreement about and adherence to global standards a long-drawn-out and nearly impossible endeavor. If a global social contract that includes prolabor protection mechanisms is to be created, the nature of labor's economic role must no longer be ignored. Like capital, labor must be liberalized to act transnationally.

Rawls appears to have disavowed a transnational social contract. According to Rawls, as summarized by Samuel Freeman:

> Each society has the duty to set up its economic and legal institutions in such a way that they make the least advantaged among its own members better off than the least advantaged would be if that society were structured according to any other distribution principle. But each society *does not have a duty to structure its system so as to maximize the position of the least advantaged in the world at large.* Though it is a universal principle that is to apply severally, or within each society, the difference principle is not global in reach, applying jointly to all societies simultaneously. To critics of many political persuasions, this seems a peculiar position. Why should principles of justice be domestically rather than globally applied?[38]

Further, Freeman notes that "for Rawls, it is simply not the role of peoples, individually or collectively, to enforce distributive justice anywhere except among their own peoples."[39] That is, those outside the territorial boundaries of a particular society are not beneficiaries of the contract forged by its members, neither as recipients of rights nor as the bearers of obligations created pursuant to the terms of that contract.

However, this principle of the nonexistence of transborder obligations toward the furtherance of a just society is inadequate to the contemporary globalized reality. Reality supersedes Rawls's ideal world;[40] the forces of globalization now are more evident, and the impact of the actions of society A on societies W, X, Y, and Z cannot be ignored. If the activities within one society's economy may negatively affect individuals and groups as well as the terms of the social contract within the sphere of another country, surely transborder obligations toward a just society must be recognized. Local and domestic factors cannot adequately explain the conditions confronting labor in either developed or less developed economies. The forces of globalization—transborder economic and other trends—are such that domestic governments, standing alone, cannot control the domestic effects on the existing social contracts. Domestic societies and economies cannot provide adequate protection for their nationals, including their labor providers. If duties do not extend beyond state boundaries, there is no obligation to intervene for the benefit of those outside the borders of a particular society. However, the reality is that activities within one country's domestic sphere *do* affect individuals in other countries. States often act as if they do have obligations—toward the individuals or groups within a state, if not toward those states themselves. Principles of global distributive justice demand that labor be liberalized to act transnationally.

The Promise of Labor Liberalization

The labor liberalization that I advocate would not commoditize labor in order to facilitate its increased *exploitation* in economic activity by other actors, such as states or multinational corporations. Instead, I propose that the liberalization of labor within the broader trade liberalization project would free labor on three levels: First, labor would be liberalized from its current conceptualization as a mere immobile input into the production of goods and services. Second, labor would be liberalized from the state border constraints that have sought to limit its transborder movement and rendered it more easily exploited.[41] Third, labor liberalization would democratize access to the benefits of trade liberalization by increasing the opportunities of individual labor providers to seek out the newly created economic benefits. Freed of the constructed state barriers, individual labor providers would be liberalized to engage in their own decision making and thereby conduct their own cost-benefit analysis and choice between the utility of movement or nonmovement to a new employment market.

The conceptual framework underpinning the exploitation of labor rests on the boundary of the conceptualization of labor and its providers as purely a commodity (evidenced by, for example, references to "human capital"), and the accepted wisdom that capital owes very little to labor (evidenced in developed countries by, for example, movement away from pension plans, toward mass layoffs, and away from health care plans for retirees). The emphases on cheapness and efficiency as well as on increasing returns and on cheaper inputs lead, at the extremes, to the conception of *people* (not just labor) as trade object.[42]

At the same time, and in contradiction, the absence of a general agreement on trade in labor or the absence of the recognition of such a role for labor in existing WTO obligations conveys the message that the international trade system rejects recognizing and conferring on labor the status of a factor of production. That message contradicts the existing economic reality. The current system allows and facilitates labor's exploitation as a factor of production while denying human providers of labor full autonomy to *explore* economic opportunity. Labor is conceptualized as subordinate to or subsumed within the production of goods and services. In order for human labor to claim its proper place (equal to the other mobile factors of production) in the world trading system, and to enjoy the human rights promised by the international human rights regime (and by some domestic civil rights regimes), labor must be recognized as a mobile and autonomous factor of production and liberalized to perform as such.

I recognize the fundamental moral, philosophical, and ethical issue that labor is not merely a commodity. However, I seek to point out and to provide a solution based on the reality that while *more* than a unit of production or economic input, human labor providers are *also* just that—economic units and production inputs. A holistic reconceptualization and implementation of that human role is absolutely necessary to the formulation of a global social contract that is protective of the interests of labor providers.

Some critics have asked whether the trade law regime is inconsistent with human rights.[43] A thorough response to this question is outside the scope of this chapter, but I identify the gap in conceptualization of humans under human rights law (as rights-bearing persons) and under international trade law (as immobile units subsumed in the production process) as a potential path toward an answer. Neither of these two legal regimes recognizes or implements the full array of human attributes. Under human rights law the individual is more than an economic unit, but it is as an economic unit that human labor providers are conceptualized under domestic immigration law (often in contravention of human rights law) and, implicitly, under international trade law.[44] Moreover, the international trade system in fact *treats* and relies upon humans as functioning economic units—producers and consumers—without explicitly recognizing and implementing the necessary steps for the economic liberalization of human labor providers.[45]

The proposed liberalization of labor would make both the international human rights and multilateral trade regimes more consistent with human rights ideals. Labor liberalization will foster the enforcement of human rights law. Liberalization of the movement of labor will give labor more economic power—the ability to respond freely and autonomously to economic conditions. Further, the right to enter and exit competing domestic labor markets will give labor the economic power of mobility, creating competitive conditions and market discipline that will increase the recognition and enforcement of labor and other human rights standards. The power of labor providers to exit individual markets will add substantive content to human rights in a manner that a static pool of labor currently is unable to do.[46]

In addition, transnational labor mobility will fundamentally transform the relationship between labor and capital. If nation-states are faced with the necessity to compete openly for labor, that competition will affect the economic policies of labor-rich states. Faced with the prospect of losing population, such labor-rich states may choose reform, and thus more equitably distribute national resources to the entrenched have-nots and not solely to the owners of capital.[47] Moreover, the declining information asymmetries will allow labor providers to both learn of and respond to economic conditions, and to avoid domestic labor markets where exploitative conditions, sexism, racism, and other discriminatory factors are not curtailed.

There is some ironic justice in the proposed labor liberalization solution. It may produce a flow of labor the reverse of that which occurred during the colonial era, which was characterized by the outward movement of Europeans to facilitate the development and industrialization of Western economies.[48] The economic growth of the formerly colonized territories and of the world economy as a whole demands the liberalization of labor.

Further, movement of labor providers from today's labor-rich countries would be less likely to exhibit the exploitative features of the mass labor movements of the colonial era (e.g., the migration of indentured servants from India to the West Indies, Fiji, and Africa within the British colonial empire). Contemporary international human rights and domestic civil rights law delineate minimum standards of treatment that did not exist in the colonial era. The liberalization of labor will enhance the legal system's capacity to implement and enforce those minimum standards within competing domestic markets. The relationship is symbiotic—liberalization would not enhance prolabor developments in the absence of the minimum standards; without liberalization those minimum standards would not be enforced.

In order for labor liberalization to be *most* effective, it should take place within a context where human rights standards are recognized and enforced. The mobile individual provider of labor would enjoy the human rights protections of the applicable domestic and international legal regimes on the same basis as the domestic labor provider.[49]

How to Implement Labor Liberalization

The beneficial participation of labor in the process of globalization would be enhanced by a reconceptualization of labor's role in the international economic system. That reconceptualization would include acknowledgment that, within the world trading system, labor should be given status analogous to that enjoyed by other production inputs, such as capital and intellectual property. Individual labor providers should be able to freely trade their labor internationally within the institutional framework of the GATT/WTO system.[50] The negotiation and implementation of a multilateral agreement on trade in labor offers the prospect of achieving the goals of both human rights protection (combating labor exploitation) and trade liberalization (more efficient use of economic resources together with welfare-enhancing effects).

This proposal demands no less than a holistic reconceptualization of labor as having the freedom to pursue economic goals while being protected by legally effective recognition of fundamental human rights. Negotiation, execution, and entry into force of a "General Agreement on Trade in Labor" would also demand reform of individual nation-states' domestic immigration laws to better reflect economic needs and realities.

Therefore, reform of the institutional framework of the WTO in further-ance of goals of global distributive justice would not conflict with Rawls's ideas about global justice.[51] Freeman notes that

> though Rawls doubted the feasibility of a world state, he did not deny that global cooperation could evolve gradually its own institutions, and that these might eventually multiply into an intricate and complex network of indepen-dent institutions with widespread effects upon peoples' future prospects. *I do not think that anything Rawls says rules out the appropriateness of standards of justice applying to those cooperative institutions, constraining economic relations in various ways to the benefit of less advantaged peoples,* or perhaps even imposing a principle of distributive justice were these institutions extensive and pervasive enough.[52]

A *"General Agreement on Trade in Labor"*

The GATT/WTO framework is the most appropriate venue for effectuat-ing the liberalization of labor. The principle of labor liberalization or labor mobility might appear to be better addressed under the auspices of some alternative international regime, such as the human rights regime (e.g., in view of the recognition of the individual right to freedom of movement) or the labor rights regime (e.g., through the ILO). However, both have proved and would continue to prove inadequate to the task of the implementa-tion of the principle of the liberalization of labor as an autonomous factor of production in the world trading system. A new "General Agreement on Trade in Labor" (or GATL) would create a framework for recognizing and increasing liberalization of labor under the auspices of the WTO. As envis-aged here, the GATL would be negotiated and adopted as a new Annex to the WTO Agreement—a multilateral agreement creating obligations for all WTO members.[53]

By advocating a new GATL, analogous to and having equal force with the Agreement on Trade-Related Aspects of Intellectual Property Rights (TRIPS) and the GATS Agreement, I reject the dominant conceptualiza-tion of the role of human labor in the international trading system. I also reject the piecemeal approach of gradual expansion of Mode 4 of the GATS, an approach that is inadequate to my goal of unleashing labor to act trans-nationally and to formulate a new accommodation with capital. The pro-posal also brings to the fore and gives substance to an attribute of labor—its transnational mobility—that is key to the formulation and enforcement of a global social contract that would benefit labor.

The GATL would untether the transnational trade in labor from the con-straints of Mode 4, including the mandated temporariness of such limited transborder labor movement as the GATS contemplates.[54] It would also untether human movement from the constraints of domestic immigration law that too often lays the foundation for the exploitation of transborder labor providers. Labor liberalization would provide legal avenues of movement for labor providers who are responding to economic stimuli.

However, there are conceptual, economic, social, psychological, and political arguments and barriers to the multilateral liberalization of labor. These arguments are based on fears of the transformative changes, including economic, social, and cultural inundation by "others"; downward wage equalization across domestic markets; and the upheaval of the existing political balance of power that would result from such a fundamental undertaking.[55]

Harnessing the WTO

Labor liberalization sits squarely within the trade liberalization raison d'être of the WTO. The equity rationale of the GATT/WTO system also speaks in favor of utilizing the WTO's institutional framework to further the liberalization of labor.[56] Features of the WTO institutional and treaty obligation framework such as "special and differential treatment" indicate the existence of such a rationale.[57] As such, the WTO provides an appropriate framework for the mechanism of labor liberalization—a mechanism aimed at widely disseminating the benefits of trade liberalization by removing the mobility constraints on labor's autonomous activity.

The GATL, as part of the GATT/WTO system, would have the advantage of the flexibility incorporated within the multilateral trade regime. Within the overarching obligations and principles negotiated by the member states, the commitments made by individual members may be tailored to the circumstances of individual nation-states so as to slow or speed up the transition challenges anticipated from the fundamental reconceptualization and liberalization of the role of labor. For example, similarly to the Agreement on TRIPS and the GATS, a transitional period would be applied to accession by the WTO's developing and least developed member states. In addition, the GATL and its interpretation would be subject to existing GATT/WTO jurisprudence and to nondiscriminatory criminal and other public order legal regimes of individual countries.

Furthermore, the GATT/WTO system possesses the power to enforce through sanctions that is missing from both the international human rights and labor rights regimes. The WTO Understanding on Rules and Procedures Governing the Settlement of Disputes (Annex 2 to the WTO Agreement) offers an avenue for effective mutual enforcement by member states of GATT/WTO obligations.

The GATL would include language expressing the commitments of member states to the tenet that labor is liberalized to respond to transborder economic forces and to the obligation to open their domestic labor market. The GATL's recognition of the application of the established nondiscrimination doctrines that are fundamental to international trade law would expressly invoke both the national treatment and most-favored-nation obligations.[58] To the extent that the national treatment and most favored nation doctrines offer insufficient protection to labor, the minimum standards of existing international human rights and labor law offer minimum standards of treatment that will strengthen such protection.

Member states would not be obligated to allow the entry of individual labor providers whom state officials reasonably determine, either as a result of inspection of their documents or evaluation of other factual circumstances, intend to participate in illegal or illegitimate enterprises. For example, the GATL would not require the entry of individual labor providers destined for industries that are illegal under the laws of the host member state. Finally, the recognition and implementation of labor's role in the global trading system must be incorporated in the treaty architecture of the existing multilateral trading regime.

Conclusion

As is clear from the foregoing discussion, the liberalization of labor may have transformative effects on the current political and economic structure of participating and nonparticipating states. Equally clearly, however, political resistance to such changes is to be expected from national governments and entrenched interests that fear competition, or loss of power and influence; some categories of capital that might lose the ability to price discriminate in compensation rates to labor; and the populations of both origin and destination-states who fear such changes to their way of life.

Nor would resistance to the GATL be limited to the domestic politics of individual states. The continuing failure of the Doha Development Round of negotiations strongly suggests that the WTO, as presently constituted, may have reached an impasse in the multilateral trade liberalization project.[59] However, it is possible that the member states whose interests have prevented resolution regarding the agricultural subsidies at the heart of the Doha negotiation difficulties would adopt different and more welcoming positions toward the prospect of liberalizing labor, which is projected to benefit both developed and developing countries. Adopting a long-term view concerning the expected benefits may help overcome this reluctance, as would a transnational perspective that transcends local and domestic interests and encompasses global concerns.

Notes

1. The GATT/WTO multilateral trading system, for example, has failed to address the liberalization of labor. See discussion below under the heading "Incomplete Trade Liberalization."

2. See US State Department, *Trafficking in Persons Report* (2009), especially its discussion of this practice in Nigeria. Nigerians are trafficked within Nigeria's borders, to other West African states, and to other regions of the world (ibid.). The individual country narratives that form the bulk of the annual reports issued by the US State Department describe the forms of human trafficking exploitation in countries throughout the world. For descriptions of human trafficking in various African countries, see 62–63, 84–85, 90–91, 93–95, 97–98, 100–103, and 109–12.

3. As used in this chapter, globalization means the increasing interdependence, interconnection, and intertwining of the economies of individual countries. Globalization is not new (throughout the centuries of human history successive waves of globalization have brought different regions of the world into greater contact), however, the technological advances of the twentieth and twenty-first centuries have quickened and deepened the relationships among states that are widely dispersed geographically.

4. The structured multilateral negotiations conducted by signatories to the General Agreement on Tariffs and Trade (GATT) addressed and attempted to remove or minimize innumerable barriers to trade liberalization. The first eight rounds of negotiations culminated in the formation of the World Trade Organization, among other trade liberalization achievements. See Raj Bhala and Kevin Kennedy, *World Trade Law: The GATT-WTO System, Regional Arrangements, and U.S. Law* (Charlottesville, VA: Lexis Law Publishing, 1998), 5–7. The member states have missed the targeted completion dates of the current round of negotiations, the Doha Development Round, but negotiations continue. See World Trade Organization (WTO), "Understanding the WTO: The Doha Agenda," http://www.wto.org/english/thewto_e/whatis_e/tif_e/doha1_e.htm. The Uruguay Round of negotiations that resulted in the creation of the WTO added the liberalization of trade in services and the recognition and enforcement of a US-dominated conception of intellectual property rights. As of July 23, 2008, 153 of the world's 192 states have joined the WTO. See WTO, "Cape Verde Becomes the WTO's 153rd Member," WTO News Items, July 23, 2008, http://www.wto.org/english/news_e/news08_e/acc_capverde_july08_e.htm.

5. For example, despite the stated regional integration purposes of the African Union (AU) and the Economic Community of West African States (ECOWAS), neither regional body has taken concrete steps to implement the mobility of labor among member states. See Rene Robert, *The Social Dimension of Regional Integration in ECOWAS*, Working Paper no. 49, Policy Integration Department, International Labor Organization, at the Social Science Research Network, http: ssrn.com/abstract=908485, 4–6, 9–10, and 19–20.

6. In the United States, these changes include labor's loss of job security and diminishment or withdrawal of pension and other contractual benefits that used to enable labor to share with capital the benefits of their joint economic production activities.

7. Douglas Massey et al., *Worlds in Motion: Understanding International Migration at the End of the Millennium* (Oxford: Oxford University Press, 1998), 288.

8. Kevin R. Johnson, *Opening the Floodgates: Why America Needs to Rethink Its Borders and Immigration Laws* (New York: New York University Press, 2007). Claiming that US immigration laws and rhetoric run counter to economic reality, Johnson points out that immigrants play a crucial role in the US economy, providing low-cost labor and supporting labor intensive industries such as construction.

9. Karen E. Bravo and Maria Pabon Lopez, "Crisis Meets Reality: A Bold Proposal for Immigration Reform," *Southern Methodist University Law Review* 61 (2008): 198.

10. See, e.g., Bridget Anderson, *Doing the Dirty Work? The Global Politics of Domestic Labor* (London: Zed Books, 2000), 138, 178. According to Anderson, "*Immigration restrictions do not stop movement,* and once migrants have entered a country only a minority are deported. The difficulty with stringent and restrictive immigration laws is that since they cannot stop migration, *they mean that migration is forced to come through irregular channels and that state control over patterns and directions of migrant labor is relinquished rather than increased.* This is clearly apparent when one contrasts Spain, where it is possible for domestic workers to enter legally, with Greece and France, where this is not so" (emphasis added).

11. On the exploitation of migrant labor, see, e.g., Theresa Hayter, *Open Borders: The Case against Immigration Controls*, 2nd ed. (London: Pluto Press, 2004), xxv ("Suffering is an inevitable consequence of immigration control"). Ginette Verstraete describes the industries that spring up and thrive around border enforcement. See "Technological Frontiers and the Politics of Mobility in the European Union," in *Uprootings/Regroundings*, ed. Sara Ahmed et al. (Oxford, UK: Berg Publishers, 2003), 235. According to Verstraete,

Not only is border control a burden for private enterprises, it can also be a gain. Lots of money is to be made in the implementation of strict borders, ranging from high-tech surveillance systems to the deployment of security guards to the deportation of illegal "aliens" by commercial airlines. Furthermore, the harder the external border, the more attractive the unofficial routes circumventing it. Smuggling people in has become a lucrative business, and not only in the countries of departure. Since the possibility of people migrating legally has become minimal, several European truckers are getting rich through organized trafficking networks.

12. For a sense of the routes taken and prices paid by Africans attempting to access the European labor market, see, BBC News, "Key Facts: Africa to Europe Migration," http://news.bbc.co.uk/2/hi/europe/6228236.stm.

13. This privileging of skilled labor occurs despite the comparatively greater demand for unskilled labor in the domestic economies of high-skilled postindustrial states. See, e.g., Joy Kategekwa, "Extension of Mode 4 Commitments to Include Unskilled Workers in the WTO: A Win-Win Situation, Especially for LDCs," OECD Development Centre Panel on Migration and Development, September 25–26, 2006, 6–8, http://www.wto.org/english/forums_e/public_forum_e/potentials_for_unskilled_worker_liberalisation_in_gats.doc.

14. Examples of such agreements include the H-2B temporary labor system in the United States and Canada's Seasonal Agricultural Workers Program, which are facilitated by intergovernmental arrangements. For a discussion of the British West Indies Temporary Labor Program, see David Griffith, *American Guest Workers: Jamaicans and Mexicans in the U.S. Labor Market* (University Park: Penn State University Press, 2006), 32; for a description of the Memoranda of Understanding between Canada and Mexico, and between Canada and individual Caribbean states, which set the legal framework for the transborder supply of temporary workers, see Veena Verma, "The Mexican and Caribbean Seasonal Agricultural Workers Program: Regulatory and Policy Framework, Farm Industry Level Employment Practices, and the Future of the Program under Unionization," *North South Institute* (December 2003): 13–16, http://www.nsi-ins.ca/english/pdf/csawp_verma_final_report.pdf.

15. For a description of the reluctance of government representatives from small Caribbean states to pursue redress for workers' grievances, see Griffith, *American Guest Workers*, 40. Griffith reports that one of the representatives explained his quandary as follows: "If I advocate too hard for that worker, I'm liable to lose that placement to Mexico or Jamaica" (ibid.).

16. Some developing countries have attempted to raise this issue in the context of the General Agreement on Trade in Services (GATS), a multilateral annex to the WTO Agreement to which all WTO members must adhere, but with limited success. For a discussion of less developed countries' attempts within the WTO negotiation frameworks to broaden the scope of GATS Mode 4 provisions in line with those countries' comparative advantage, see, generally, Kategekwa, "Extension of Mode 4 Commitments."

17. The other classical factors of production are capital and land. Labor, of course, differs from the other classical factors of production by virtue of its humanity and is more than a mere input into production. Additional inputs into production include entrepreneurship and technology. Although entrepreneurship also is human, it is most closely aligned with capital. The liberalization of capital has been a part of the multilateral trade liberalization and of the current era of globalization.

18. For discussion and charting of the education levels of immigrants to OECD countries for the years 2003–4, see, OECD, *International Migration Outlook 2007* (Paris: OECD Publishing, 2007), 132–34.

19. An obvious example of a labor-poor economy is the United States throughout most of its history: African slaves, European immigrants (including indentured servants), Asian and Latino laborers have provided a much needed, often involuntary labor supply during various eras.

20. Pursuant to Article I.2(d), trade in services is defined so as to include the supply of a service "by a service supplier of one Member, through commercial presence of natural persons of a Member in the territory of any other Member." The definitions of "person" and "natural person" included in Article XXVIII(j) and (k) of the GATS makes clear that a "natural person" is a human being. The covered natural persons are humans who are nationals of a member state or who hold reasonably analogous status (such as lawful permanent residence) pursuant to the domestic laws of another member. The other three modes of the GATS provide for the cross-border supply of a service from one member to another; the transborder consumption of a service; and the transborder supply of a service through establishment of a commercial presence.

21. The GATS Annex on Movement of Natural Persons Supplying Services under the Agreement provides that the GATS does not apply "to measures affecting natural persons seeking access to the employment market of a Member, nor shall it apply to measures regarding citizenship, residence or employment on a permanent basis." See para. 2. Pursuant to GATS Article XXIX; the annexes are "an integral part" of the GATS.

22. See Michele Klein Solomon, "GATS Mode 4 and the Mobility of Labor," in Ryszard Cholewinski, Richard Perruchoud, and Euan MacDonald, eds., *International Migration Law: Developing Paradigms and Key Challenges* (The Hague: T.M.C. Asser Press, 2007), 112. According to Solomon, "To date the commitments of nearly all WTO Members under [Mode 4] are limited to the highly skilled, and within that group most often to intra-corporate transferees, managers and executives." See also Steve Charnovitz, "Trade Law Norms on International Migration," in T. Alexander Aleinikoff and Alexander Chetail, eds., *Migration and International Legal Norms* (The Hague: T.M.C. Asser Press, 2003), 248.

23. See Craig Jackson, "Constitutional Structure and Governance Strategies for Economic Integration in Africa and Europe," *Transnational Law and Contemporary Problems* 13 (2003): 139–43.

24. Ibid. 171–72.

25. Ibid. 172.

26. See, e.g., Thomas Pogge, *World Poverty and Human Rights*, 2nd ed. (Cambridge: Polity Press, 2008), 18. Pogge states: "I do not complain that the WTO regime opens markets too much, but that it has opened our markets *too little* and has thereby gained for us the benefits of free trade while withholding these benefits from the global poor. Poor populations continue to face great barriers to exporting their products, and even greater barriers to offering their services where these would fetch a decent income."

27. See, e.g., Massey et al., *Worlds in Motion*, 14. The authors note that "border controls reduce the applicability of standard economic models by impeding the free circulation of labor as a factor of production, and, consequently preventing the development of international migration at its fullest."

28. For a discussion of the passage of a European Commission Directive mandating stricter standards and requiring the return (deportation) of migrants to their countries of origin, see Caroline Brothers, "EU Passes Tough Migrant Measure," *New York Times*, June 19, 2008.

29. However, Massey and his coauthors point to additional factors, other than those identified by classical or neoclassical economic theories, to explain the increasing flows of transborder migration. See *Worlds in Motion*, 9.

30. See, ibid., 277.

31. For a discussion of the effects of Mexican immigration on the wage levels of US domestic unskilled labor, see George J. Borjas and Lawrence F. Katz, "The Evolution of the Mexican-Born Workforce in the United States," National Bureau of Economic Research (April 2005).

32. Examples of the outsourcing of manufacturing and services include reading X-rays or executing paralegal services, such as are being performed in India. Nor is the mobility of capital limited to transnational movement. Production processes and plants may move from one region to another within a domestic market in order

to increase transnational and domestic competitiveness. See Louis Uchitelle, "The Wage That Meant Middle Class," *New York Times*, April 4, 2008, WK3. See also "Working Borders: Linking Debates about Insourcing and Outsourcing of Capital and Labor," *Texas International Law Journal* 40 (2005): 691.

33. For a discussion of the relationship among "illegality" of status, ease of exploitation, and "the extraction of cheap labor," see Hayter, *Open Borders*, 157.

34. In the United States, for example, the increase in illegal immigration stems from the increased dislocation and economic incentives created by incomplete labor liberalization and globalization in foreign (Mexican and other) labor markets coupled with the increased US border security and enforcement. That is, increased border security, coupled with limited economic activity in Mexico and economic opportunity in the United States, creates incentives for undocumented immigrants to lengthen or make permanent their stay in the United States, so that they may avoid the new border crossing difficulties. Further, once they have decided to remain, they arrange for border crossing by family members who might otherwise have remained in Mexico.

35. See Solomon, "GATS Mode 4."

36. See, e.g., L. Alan Winters et al., "Liberalising Temporary Movement of Natural Persons: An Agenda for the Development Round," *World Economy* 26, no. 8 (2003): 1137, 1149; Pradip Bhatnagar, "Liberalising the Movement of Natural Persons: A Lost Decade?" *World Economy* 27, no. 3 (2004): 459.

37. See, e.g., Helena Marques, *Migration Creation and Diversion in the EU: Are CEECs Immigrants Crowding Out the Rest?*, Loughborough University Discussion Paper No. 2005-01 (2005). Marques poses this question with respect to the European Union and analyzes empirical data. The debate regarding the trade diversion or trade promotion effects of regional trade agreements has generated a great deal of scholarly thought. See, e.g., Jagdish Bhagwati, "Preferential Trade Arrangements: The Wrong Road," *Law and Policy of International Business* 27 (1995): 865, 869.

38. Samuel Freeman, *Justice and the Social Contract: Essays on Rawlsian Political Philosophy* (London: Oxford University Press, 2007), 259 (emphasis added).

39. Ibid., 260.

40. Rawls's ideas depend on the well-ordered society that is capable of reasonable agreement. Freeman describes that society as follows:

> The way in which Rawls's justice as fairness is a social contract position has far more to do with his idea of a well-ordered society than does the original position. Rawls describes a well-ordered society as one in which all reasonable persons accept the same public principles of justice, their agreement on these principles is public knowledge, and these principles are realized in society's laws and basic social institutions. . . . A well-ordered society is then one in which everyone can justify their social, political, and economic institutions to one another on reasonable terms that all accept in their capacity as free and equal, reasonable and rational citizens. Its is . . . this "contractualist" idea of *reasonable agreement* among free and equal persons that is predominant in Rawls's social contract view, not the Hobbesian idea of rational agreement among persons motivated by their own interests that takes place in the original position. (Ibid., 4)

Left unexamined here is the question of the "justice" of the contract forged among individual nation-states and enshrined in international law principles and doctrines. Would the current formulation have been wrought had the nation-state participants agreed to the terms under Rawls's "veil of ignorance"?

41. As an autonomous economic unit, labor could seek out the markets where demand is highest and labor is most highly valued and compensated.

42. For an articulation of the view that guest worker programs lead to the commodification of the worker, see, Ruben Garcia, "Labor as Property: Guest Workers, International Trade, and the Democracy Deficit," *Journal of Gender, Race, and Justice* 10 (2006): 27–28.

43. For a discussion of the apparent and seemingly inherent conflict between market globalization and human rights, see, Frank J. Garcia, "The Global Market and Human Rights: Trading Away the Human Rights Principle," *Brooklyn Journal of International Law* 25 (1999): 51, 64–76. Garcia rejects the conflict, however, noting that "the linkage debates currently underway in trade law and policy reveal to us that international economic law is fundamentally about justice, as are human rights law and other linkage issues" (ibid., 95–96).

44. Of this conceptualization, Bridget Anderson observed:

The migrant worker is framed by immigration legislation as a unit of labor, without connection to family or friends, a unit whose production costs (food, education, shelter) were met elsewhere, and whose reproduction costs are of no concern to employer or state. In this respect, the worker who moves across continents may seem the logical result of capitalism's individual subject, the juridical person, torn from all social contexts, selling her labour power in the global market place. But while states and capitalists want workers, what they get is people. This tension between "labour power" and "personhood" is particularly striking with reference to migrant domestic workers, and I believe it has broader repercussion for migrants and for women. (*Doing the Dirty Work?*, 108)

45. Demonstrating the multilateral trading regime's treatment of and reliance on humans as functioning economic units, a central tenet of the GATT/WTO jurisprudence is founded on the notion of consumer choice—that is, humans as the creators of economic trends and competitive realities in their role as *consumers.*

46. The power of labor to exit will impose market discipline on would-be autocrats seeking to oppress the populations of their nation-states. Labor liberalization will cause nation-states to compete for labor providers, thus encouraging improvements in living conditions, including economic conditions, and in the recognition and enforcement of civil and human rights.

47. For a discussion of the market discipline that would be introduced and maintained by the ability of skilled workers to respond freely to transnational market stimuli, see Joseph E. Stiglitz, "Globalism's Discontents," *American Prospect,* January 1, 2002.

48. See Douglas S. Massey and J. Edward Taylor, *International Migration: Prospects and Policies in a Global Market* (Oxford: Oxford University Press, 2004), 95–96.

49. Here, Jennifer Gordon's concept of transnational labor citizenship would play a crucial role in maintaining transborder legal standards. See her "Transnational Labor Citizenship," *Southern California Law Review* 80 (2007): 503, 361–78. Gordon advocates the protection of migrant workers in return for the migrant workers' obligation not to undermine the minimum standards achieved by domestic labor.

50. The term "GATT/WTO" captures the continued vitality of the compromises and jurisprudence developed under the original General Agreement on Tariffs and Trade (GATT 1947). GATT 1947 is amended by and incorporated into GATT 1994, Annex 1 A to the WTO Agreement.

51. Rawls had recognized the empirical limitations of his work. According to Freeman, "Rawls did not envision the Law of Peoples as the sole element of the terms of cooperation that apply among peoples 'in our world as it is with its extreme injustices, crippling poverty, and inequalities.' Under current conditions we are in the realm of nonideal theory and partial compliance." Freeman, *Justice and the Social Contract*, 262 (quoting Rawls, *The Law of Peoples*).

52. Ibid., 321 (emphasis added).

53. Status as a plurilateral agreement, participation in which would be optional for WTO member states, would not achieve the purposes sought through this agreement.

54. The constraint of temporariness is a key source of exploitability and vulnerability of transborder labor providers.

55. Discussion and analysis of these and other arguments against the liberalization of labor can be found in Karen E. Bravo, "Regional Trade Arrangements and Labor Liberalization: (Lost) Opportunities for Experimentation?" *St. Louis Public Law Review* 28 (2008): 96–105.

56. See Charnovitz, "Trade Law Norms," 242. Charnovitz claims that "the equity rationale for the WTO is further justification for reducing barriers to the movement of people."

57. GATT Part IV and a number of the annexes to the WTO Agreement (e.g., TRIPS and the Agreement on Trade-Related Investment Measures (the TRIMs Agreement) provide for a distinction between the legal obligations of WTO member states—special and differential treatment. The distinction, which is based on the development status of member states, provides certain legal advantages to developing and less developed countries, without triggering the nondiscrimination provisions of the GATT/WTO system.

58. Article I of the GATT spells out the Most Favored Nation obligation of member states, which requires that all trade preferences extended by a member state to a trading partner be extended to all member states of the WTO. Article III lays out the National Treatment obligation. With respect to access to domestic markets, Article III:1–2, 4, creates for each WTO member state the obligation not to discriminate against other member states in favor of its own domestic industries and interests. These provisions are echoed in the GATS and the TRIPS. See Articles II (Most Favored Nation) and XVII (National Treatment) of the GATS and Articles III (National Treatment) and IV (Most Favored Nation) of the TRIPS.

59. See, e.g., Stephen Castle and Mark Landler, "After 7 Years, Talks Collapse on World Trade," *New York Times*, July 30, 2005.

7

Asante Society and the Global Market

GRACIA CLARK

Among the many pleasures associated with working with the Asante, a West African ethnic group in the nation of Ghana, as I have since 1978, is the way they offer a contrary example to so many common assumptions about how human societies work. Their matrilineal kinship system still provides a strong contrast to models assuming paternal power, since the Asante nuclear family unit features brothers and sisters with their common mother. Duolocal marriage traditions keep many husbands and wives living separately today, and thus problematize abstract models of household income pooling in several ways. Asante exceptionalism, however, cannot resolve all the challenges posed by these contradictions. While their cultural patterns made it impossible to ignore these unexpected forms, the Asante example draws attention to parallel dynamics that had often been glossed over in researching more "normal" cultures.

In a similar way, the experience of Asante society with international trade destabilizes a commonsense model of stable traditional African cultures confronting commercialization and globalization as external shocks bringing rapid changes foreign to their indigenous values and institutions. The larger Akan ethnic group in what is now Ghana can claim to be present on the world system stage before the birth of capitalism. Regular voyages by Portuguese traders to the fort they had built on the Ghana coast at Elmina provided Christopher Columbus with an opportunity for training in long-distance navigation before he set out for the New World in 1492. The gold that gave Elmina its name, and later the slaves from its famous Door of No Return, played a key part in accumulating the financial resources that eventually fueled capitalist engines and colonial empires. Asante was founded around 1700 as a political unit precisely to control trade routes running from the European coastal forts to the even older caravan trading system that stretched across and along the Sahara. These caravans had carried gold, ivory, weapons, and slaves between West Africa and the Mediterranean since the days of Carthage. Perhaps because of this history, Asante people today enter enthusiastically into global networks with no signs of disappearing, while remaining fiercely attached to a cultural identity that their neighbors emulate.

Over the decades, mature traders located at central nodes of the marketplace system, like Kumasi Central Market, accumulate significant expertise in the assessment and prediction of trends in globalization. In order to continue making a living for their families, traders like these must constantly monitor supply and demand conditions in locations ranging from remote rural villages and urban neighborhoods to shopping centers around the world. Their career experience has shown them how producers and consumers respond to a wide range of conditions, including external and internal shocks, dramatic shifts in the policy environment, and interludes of stability and expansion. The roller coaster of global economic and political change, complicated by unpredictable volatility in national commercial policies, has forced traders to confront and analyze these historical dynamics with the attention born of desperation.

While the previous chapter by Karen Bravo focused primary attention on the complexities of the transnational labor market within the context of nation-state behavior in the era of globalization, this chapter and the subsequent one written by Mary Johnson Osirim shift the focus of analysis to examine the role of female entrepreneurs in sub-Saharan Africa at the grassroots or local level of society. The African women traders featured in this chapter count as ordinary women within their local community, but their vantage point on postcolonial transformations in their society and economy is quite extraordinary. As elderly to middle-aged citizens of Kumasi, they have been living and trading in the second-largest city in Ghana, which is also the historic capital of the Asante nation. The oldest were already working there before 1957, when Ghana became the first African nation to gain independence from British colonial rule. While Ghana's national economy expanded and contracted, these women struggled continuously to keep their trading enterprises afloat and to raise their children to be healthy and prosperous. Some succeeded better than others, but each has gained a unique perspective on the processes of economic and cultural globalization.

A Global Tradition

The attention paid to globalization in social analysis during the last few decades has added an important new dimension to scholarly understanding of the transnational linkages that are so significant to local communities in every corner of the world. It has allowed social scientists to begin mapping the increasing proportion of social connections and power relations that are multilocal or global in their operation, whose absence from the map of research categories had seriously compromised the accuracy of models of social and cultural processes. Although this in itself justified the turn toward globalization, scholars newly aware of global processes also soon realized how thoroughly they penetrated the most local of contexts. Local communities also could not be accurately portrayed without sketching in those relations and institutions with roots or tentacles at the global level. The local and the global, far from having distinct populations and networks, are so intimately intertwined that the concept of mutual construction seems more appropriate than intersection.

While celebrating these highly fertile theoretical innovations, social scientists must keep in mind that it is our awareness of these factors that is new, not the global connections themselves. Global dynamics of social action and transformation appear in history long before they appeared on theoretical radar screens, although the new configurations of such influence are undeniable. What is new about these relations is not *that* they are global but *how* they are global. Likewise, the *way* gender is integrated into global and local connections takes fascinating new turns, even though gender has always played an integral part in each status quo and its transformations.

An analogous mutual construction process links the power relations of gender to those based on class, ethnicity, nation, kinship, and other principles of inequality. An individual can only be a member of a nation, an occupation, class, an ethnic or kin group as a man or a woman (or occasionally as a third gender). Conceptual understanding of this intersectionality has progressed from metaphors of a layer cake (with one aspect fundamental) or a marble cake (with mutual penetration of distinct aspects) to something more like the protons and electrons of an atom, or mass and charge as attributes of each particle. This mutual constitution means the intimate participation of gender in relations along the global/local dimension remains constant, while it also consistently changes in resonance with other aspects of the total context.

Jane Guyer proposes an alternative analytical model for West Africa in her book *Marginal Gains* that takes this insight seriously.[1] She argues that the continual unpredictability stemming from pervasive intercontinental connections shaped a distinctive fluidity and versatility in West African cultural patterns. The constant exposure to economic and political fluctuations created values and institutions capable of constant adaptation and innovation. They take change for granted and even seem addicted to it as a condition for flourishing. The Asante and their broader Akan ethnic grouping certainly confirm Guyer's interpretation, although it is by no means the only West African traditional society with commercialization woven into its cultural and social fabric.

The longstanding dominance of marketplace systems in the West African regional economy challenges the assumption that today's global informalization is a unique and recent process. For centuries, these systems managed international trade across the Sahara and via the Atlantic coast, a trade that shaped the economic and cultural institutions of West Africa in so many ways. Governing leaders were expected to promote the prosperity of their constituencies by fostering trade, yet successive governments were often suspicious of traders' wealth and influence. Besides gathering people and products destined for export, markets redistributed crops and other key resources across the ecological boundary between forest and grassland. Substantial continuities can be traced through today's markets with the locations, connections, identities, and trading practices of years past.

Yet, these markets do not simply perpetuate a timeless tradition because it is all the region's people know or can imagine. Aspects of Ghana's markets that are now firmly entrenched as traditional, such as the "market queens," evolved into their present forms at specific historical moments, in response to concrete economic pressures. The gender and ethnic demography of trade, the credit and transport patterns in specific commodities, and markets can all be shown to have changed dramatically, even within living memory. In fact, the strong networks of traders, organized around shared commodity and local interests, enable them to adapt more quickly and smoothly to abrupt shifts in commercial policy, food supply, consumer demand, or the labor market.

In Kumasi, consumers in the 1970s and 1980s were not loyal customers of open markets because of cultural conservatism or because they were unfamiliar with more "modern" grocery and department stores. The more rigid relationships and procedures of the formal sector, inspired and to some degree enforced by Western businesses, proved less capable of dealing with the challenges of contemporary political and economic turbulence. Goods kept flowing through marketplace channels even when store shelves were bare. The informal economy maintained its organizational integrity and continuity while formal institutions were falling apart. Market and street traders provided lifesaving supplements to the employment, income, food, and consumer goods that more official or formal sectors of the economy supplied, but at the same time they constituted highly visible evidence of the inadequate performance of these "modern" sectors. These paradoxes kept traders and successive governments at each other's throat, because neither could do without the other entirely.

Research Methodology

My study of the international linkages of Ghanaian market traders formed part of a larger enquiry into economic and other aspects of market life that began with my dissertation research in 1978 and continues to the present. I documented details of leadership practices such as dispute settlement most fully from 1978 to 1980, during a fieldwork period as a full-time participant observer and interviewer in Kumasi Central Market. I spent most days with traders in the market or accompanying them on buying trips to other rural supply areas or other regional markets. During this time, Ghana was led by three different heads of state: General Akuffo in 1978, followed by the brief first term in office of Flight Lt. Jerry Rawlings from June to December 1979, and ending with elected President Hillal Limann, who took office in 1980. These regime changes made possible close observation of interactions between market leaders and both military and civilian officials. The effect of price controls and other commercial policy changes on ordinary traders was also evident in their personal accounts and a sample survey of the central portion of the market, conducted in 1979.[2]

Information on historical trends presented below comes from combining ethnographic and archival sources. Dramatic price control enforcement by soldiers and police during my fieldwork in 1979 and 1983 (including confiscation of traders' goods, beatings, and market demolitions) in some ways forced traders to more openly discuss current and past market conditions. Older and more experienced traders commented on how these episodes represented an intensification of police practices they had witnessed intermittently over the past several decades, since they had started trading. Likewise, my further fieldwork with Kumasi traders on other subjects up to the present indicates that the general outlines of group activity remain recognizable, although adapting to the changing political and economic environment. My search of archival collections at the Asantehene's Record Office in Kumasi and the National Archives branches in Accra and Kumasi turned up petitions from traders to colonial officers and the Asantehene over Kumasi market disputes, wartime price controls, and market construction and taxation policies during the colonial period.[3]

Additional periods of fieldwork in Ghana enabled me to monitor changing economic and political conditions and their effects on market trade. Subsequent projects that were related to rural crop processing and women traders brought me back to Kumasi during 1982–84, 1990–91, 1994–95, 1999, and 2006. An International Labor Organization (ILO) consultancy kept me in Ghana during 1983, when the second government of Flight Lieutenant Rawlings brought the most intense attacks on traders and their national marketplace system. Life histories of older Asante women traders, recorded in 1994–95, revealed especially rich information from market leaders concerning the first half of the twentieth century. Some elderly women were able to recall stories from their mothers about times before the British came. Reorganization of several Ghanaian archives after 1984 made these collections more accessible and brought to light additional documents related to trade. The already rich historical scholarship on the

Asante during the precolonial and colonial periods continued to multiply, while over the years my ethnographic record itself became a kind of historical document. These opportunities for long-term research and the relatively deep historical record allow the identification of trends in market organization and leadership throughout the twentieth century.

The Market Queen

The market woman has been an icon of West African trading traditions in ethnographers' and travelers' accounts since Europeans first began to visit the Guinea coast.[4] The self-confidence and group solidarity of women traders was impressive to visitors partly because it contradicted European gender stereotypes, although comparable enclaves were not unknown in the European informal sector. The resilience and persistence of traders in the face of intermittently hostile colonial and national policy initiatives and other difficult conditions testified to their vital economic role. The same difficulties generated powerful loyalties among traders to their organizations based on local markets and long-distance networks.

Markets throughout Ghana were organized along consistent lines when I began this research in 1978. Leaders and elders provided valuable services on a daily basis that their members could not easily do without, and orchestrated responses to serious crises to preserve critical resources. Each basic group was identified with a single local market, and in any larger market (and certainly Kumasi Central Market, the largest single market in the country) the basic units are further specialized by the commodity or range of goods that its members sold.

The Kumasi Central Market commodity groups generally included the retailers who had stalls or tables in the market itself, the travelers who brought goods in from various supply areas, and the wholesalers who received shipments from travelers for resale to retailers. Instead of undermining group solidarity, the linking of these three categories of traders within one group reinforced that umbrella group's loyalty by strengthening its dispute settlement services. This structured internal heterogeneity meant that most buying and selling transactions took place between traders answerable to the same leader. Primary competitors also would normally be members of the same commodity group. Thus, the interactions most likely to motivate bad behavior or give rise to disputes would take place between two group members. Traders needed to remain in good standing with the group so that they could bring their own disputes to its elders in the future. Refusal to abide by a leader's decision was taken more seriously than the original offense, and punished by ostracism or fines paid to the market queen herself.

Market leadership institutions incorporate organizational features from a variety of models active within the local community, most notably ethnic traditions. Market commodity group leaders, who were elected by each group's council of elders from within their ranks, could be removed by the same council if necessary. Qualities considered positive in a potential candidate include her long experience in the market, her good reputation among her colleagues for reliability and honesty, and her demonstrated skill in settling minor disputes among her immediate neighbors as an elder. Any influential connections to the palace, the government, or a political party are legitimate assets because she may tap them later for the group's advantage.

Commodity groups also selectively incorporate elements of terminology and procedure from Christian church women's fellowships, the cooperative movement, and trade unions. The council of elders is also referred to as the "committee," with the market queen as president and other members appearing as vice president, secretary, treasurer, and sergeant-at-arms, or "police." Several of the larger groups had hired a male "secretary" who kept tactful minutes of meetings, issued membership cards, recorded dues payments in "passbooks," and sometimes recorded credit transactions. With the increase in education levels among younger women, these men are now frequently replaced by one of the women traders when they retire. Drivers and butchers (virtually all of whom are male) registered as trade unions, although most of them were also self-employed. When government policies favored cooperatives for loans and other assistance, several commodity groups registered as cooperatives. By 2006, the neoliberal policy emphasis on entrepreneurship led a few of the more up-to-date traders to call themselves microenterprises.

Several of the market leaders interviewed during my initial fieldwork (1978–80) had lived through the period of political party rivalry in the 1950s, just before and after independence, and most of them did not remember it as a particularly empowering experience. Each party tried to get its candidates elected as commodity group leaders when these offices came open, counting on them to deliver votes from their group members for the elections that began in 1951. Each party maintained gangs of young men, who roamed through Kumasi intimidating supporters of the other parties by assaulting them, blowing up their houses, and the like.[5] These rival gangs rioted in Kumasi Central Market in January 1955, and market leaders made highly visible targets. Several of the older leaders mentioned they had had to leave town for their home villages and hide there for several years, until the violence died down. These memories discouraged several market leaders from declaring any party affiliation when elections were held again in 1979, and even as late as 1994. Conversely, one elderly Convention People's Party (CPP) loyalist cheerfully resumed her place as a commodity group leader when the 1979 election of President Limann returned the CPP network to power in October, under its new name, the People's National Party (PNP).

Under military rule, published rhetoric denouncing market women became more and more extreme. In newspaper articles and letters, the image of the poor, hardworking mother trader dropped out of usage entirely, displaced by the evil "market queen."[6] She could be a group leader or simply a wealthy wholesaler, but the government-controlled newspapers and radio demonized her for her relative success in preserving a reliable income, compared to people who deserved it more: salaried, better-educated (predominantly male) formal-sector employees. As the Ghanaian economy continued to deteriorate, real incomes plummeted with no credible policy response. Official diatribes against traders constructed even ordinary ones as grasping viragoes responsible for every kind of economic hardship. A letter to the editor of the *Daily Graphic* on March 22, 1979, called them "big cheats and nation wreckers." Such discourse created an atmosphere that permitted physical repression of traders to intensify rapidly after Rawlings resumed power with the People's National Defense Council (PNDC) in 1982.

Deep Roots for Trade and Intervention

The long history of political manipulation of trade in West Africa lends legitimacy to contemporary government interventions and recent aggressive commercial policies. A ruler's responsibility for promoting the prosperity of loyal countrymen finds familiar or expected expression in protecting their commercial interests. Although the Asante were under British colonial rule for only about sixty years (1898–1957), they drew upon a very deep Akan heritage of intercontinental trade. Caravans had linked Akans to North Africa across the Sahara since before Roman times, and these carried Arab merchants and chroniclers throughout the open grasslands at least from the tenth century AD.[7] Portuguese ships first reached the West African coast in the fifteenth century, making regular trading voyages to Elmina, in present-day Ghana, and other port towns.

Early Portuguese chroniclers noted that Akans supplied a large part of the gold, kola, and slaves available, using trading skills and capital developed in the caravan trade.[8] Prominent African traders in what is now Ghana included the Akanny, who organized a tight network of diasporic communities in towns throughout the area, with parallels to the Hanseatic League, still powerful then in northern Europe, or the Aro-Chukwu financial network in eastern Nigeria, organized around shrines.[9] At least until 1700, African local authorities tightly regulated and taxed trade, protecting the trading position of their citizens and playing different European nationalities off against each other as these jostled for exclusive access.[10] Long after coastal chiefs lost the power to forbid direct trade between European and inland traders, wealthy local intermediaries still provided essential services as credit references, landlords, brokers, and negotiators. Periodic foodstuffs markets fed the growing nonfarming population and reprovisioned departing ships (even with "ship's bread" baked from local grain). DeMarees's description of reserved spaces and commodity specialization in these markets suggests their organization along the lines of contemporary market groups.

As Akans moved deeper into the forest, they founded Kumasi to control existing trade routes leading to important market towns on the northern edge of the forest, such as Salaga and Bonduku. By the eighteenth century, the Asante Confederacy had coalesced around Kumasi, becoming the dominant imperial power in the region.[11] Its chiefs actively manipulated markets by closing their borders to hostile neighbors, expelling competitive foreigners, and invading uncooperative rivals to force market access. The male *Asantehene* and female *Asantehemma*, along with their major subordinate chiefs, participated in trade directly, through designated royal treasury officials who assembled trading caravans, and indirectly, by loaning money from their official treasuries to prominent private citizens for trade.

The British colonial government promoted the commercial interests of its own citizens and officials just as openly as the Asante had. They established the Gold Coast Colony over the first half of the nineteenth century in response to the petitions and manipulations of British traders reluctant to operate within a nascent Fanti Confederacy. The reorganization of import trading along lines more favorable to Europeans began on the coast, where the larger European firms pushed aside the wealthy Africans and independent European traders during the early nineteenth century.[12] The passbook system replaced them with more reliably subordinate customers who deposited security with the firms and took that amount in goods for resale. Passbook holders were often illiterate women, while ambitious African men preferred the autonomy of the learned professions as lawyers, ministers, doctors, and bankers.[13]

Once they defeated the Asante in 1896, British colonial authorities dismantled the royal border controls and promised safe access for non-Asante traders and employees. The administration of trade through court officials and state loans collapsed, and British import-export firms now enjoyed privileged access to services and assets such as military protection, subsidized rail transport, credit, and prime downtown locations. "Northerners" moved into Kumasi from Salaga and other caravan towns, extending their connections to trading networks for "Northern" commodities such as kola, livestock, and grain. Asante men moved in large numbers into the lucrative and rapidly expanding cocoa industry, as farmers and brokers outside the marketplace system. This left market trading within the British colonial boundaries of Ashanti Region increasingly to women and to immigrant men from the Northern Territories and farther afield.[14]

Once the British established colonial institutions like barracks, prisons, and schools, they had a vested interest in keeping food prices low, so as to save money directly when buying food for these facilities and indirectly by keeping wages low. During the First and Second World Wars, military recruitment and training raised market demand for food after first siphoning off young men from the active farm labor force. The rising cost of living brought demands for wage increases in the military, civil service, and mines. British colonial authorities tried to enforce price controls in regional capitals and mining towns (including Kumasi and nearby Obuasi).[15] They also intervened openly in the 1940s to protect the market share of the leading British firms, when wartime conditions had made shipping risky and costly. Import quotas for individual firms were based on their percentage of trade before the war. Lebanese, Indian, and US firms had no success arguing for higher quotas to compensate for British wartime shortages of goods and transport or postwar rationing. British firms successfully sought higher official prices to cover their rising costs.[16] In Kumasi, population growth brought a rapid expansion in the volume of foodstuffs traded, leading traders to found more commodity groups and organize new wholesale yards.

Nationalist Alliances

The struggle for independence brought a solid and visible alliance between Gold Coast nationalists and market traders. One of the first collective actions in the Gold Coast that attracted wide international attention was the cocoa boycott of 1936–37, launched after world cocoa prices fell sharply during the Great Depression. The few international firms buying cocoa for export agreed to divide up the cocoa-producing areas to avoid direct competition between their agents, so nationalists convinced farmers and brokers to refuse to sell their cocoa.[17] The cocoa holdup was so complete partly because its organizers also boycotted consumer goods imported by the same large firms who bought cocoa. Market traders who sold these goods publicized and enforced that side of the boycott among the cocoa farmers' wives and mothers, whose demands for new lengths of cloth might have undermined their resolve. Just such family pressures eventually led laborers and caretakers to sell their shares of the cocoa harvest, and not return empty-handed to their villages far to the north.[18]

Nationalist politicians defended market traders against British charges of causing price inflation and directed African economic resentment toward British authorities and firms. J. B. Danquah, the leading nationalist figure throughout the 1940s, praised market women as heroically devoted mothers, hardworking and underpaid.[19] Market women returned this support by collecting and contributing money for the nationalist parties, making speeches at their rallies, and mobilizing their market colleagues and commercial contacts to support them.[20] Kwame Nkrumah's CPP continued to draw on market women among others for financial and political support.

Within a few years of independence in 1957, however, President Nkrumah had adopted not only colonial price controls but the colonial rhetoric that blamed selfish, parasitic traders for the high prices of food and consumer goods, with special condemnation of Lebanese and women traders. Under Nkrumah's one-party banner of African Socialism in the 1960s, commercial policies turned increasingly hostile to independent traders. He nationalized an existing chain of department stores (a Lebanese-owned, not British, chain) to found the Ghana National Trading Corporation, which also had a food section. The most direct confrontation came from the Ghana Food Distribution Corporation, which sold locally grown foodstuffs at its kiosks outside markets. The problems its male employees had securing supplies and avoiding spoilage of fresh produce still drew derisive comments from women traders in the 1980s. "They handled tomatoes like they were plantains. They had to ask their sisters how to trade." While Nkrumah's socialist initiatives never seriously challenged the commercial primacy of the marketplace organizations, they did monopolize public capital and policy support. Groups considered progressive or modern, including the state enterprises, trade unions, and business and professional associations, participated much more than market trade groups in what little political or economic consultation remained under the one-party state.

Politicians meanwhile retained important patronage connections to the marketplace system. The sheer numbers of traders and their group cohesion made their backing valuable for collecting money and turning out crowds for rallies. Officials enjoying preferential access to imports or manufactures sold them for cash to the experienced traders willing to retail them openly. Market stalls, passbooks, and "chits" or notes for allocations of factory goods and imports made well-appreciated rewards for loyal political supporters, and also good severance gifts for ex-wives and girlfriends. Traders with long market careers complained about these inexperienced upstarts who made windfall profits, but they also cultivated their own relationships with store managers and police officers through kinship links or regular gifts.

Dr. Kofi Busia and his Progress Party (PP) won the election held after Nkrumah's overthrow by a military coup in 1967, and remained in power from 1969 to 1972. President Busia was a champion of free-market policies, yet he still felt obligated to prove his good intentions immediately by enforcing price controls and arresting traders. His most famous initiative, the 1969 Aliens Compliance Order, could be interpreted as either attacking or supporting market traders. Although it sparked an exodus of foreign cocoa laborers, Busia explained that the law was aimed at traders from Nigeria or Lebanon who had market stalls, or who operated well below the level where foreign expertise or capital was arguably necessary. In Kumasi Central Market, a number of 1979 stallholders had acquired their stalls and other assets such as sewing machines very cheaply from foreigners leaving in a hurry in 1969. Although the expulsion made space for Ghanaian entrepreneurs in the short run, the Nigerians took their turn at expelling Ghanaians in 1983.

Military Regimes (1972–94)

Despite the contradictions inherent in their situation, or perhaps because of them, government policy toward market traders stabilized into a cyclical pattern during a series of military regime changes through the 1970s. After overthrowing President Busia in 1972, General Ignatius Kutu (I. K.) Acheampong led the National Redemption Council (1972–75) and the Supreme Military Council (1975–78). Raiding episodes followed each reorganization of the governing coalition, a pattern hard to predict. Attacks on the usual targets would be followed by a period of recovery, when little attention was paid to the prices and sources of goods. Traders with sufficient capital could ride out such oscillations by charging a high enough markup during quiet times to compensate for their losses from missed workdays and confiscation of their goods. Close family or business ties to well-placed soldiers also brought timely warnings to stay at home when a raid was planned.

Kumasi residents and traders reported a more predictable annual cycle of price control enforcement by 1978. In the fall, after the cocoa harvest put money in people's pockets and cocoa exports renewed the supply of foreign exchange in the Bank of Ghana, city market stalls filled with new stocks ready for Christmas shoppers. Around November, there was usually a price crackdown that lasted long enough for the soldiers to collect some money and make their own Christmas purchases at the lower official prices. Once they had finished shopping, the police and soldiers left the markets alone for the most part, so that others could buy or sell without fear.

The governing elite remained dependent on the continuing viability of the marketplace system for many unacknowledged services. Without smugglers and hoarders, this elite might run short of high-status foods, drinks, and other luxury goods. The poor might be willing to rebel if they lacked the minimum level of subsistence goods still available through these markets, as well as from overseas and local illegal sources. The market also offered the poorest citizens a means of self-employment that, although underpaid, defused or at least dampened the time bomb of rising unemployment. Meanwhile, national leaders continued to deflect blame for the country's increasingly desperate economic situation from themselves onto the convenient stereotype of the wealthy woman trader. Price controls on imports and manufactures remained on the books, always available for enforcement whenever a display of political bravado seemed called for.

These episodic raids respected another consistent limit: they always focused on the sections selling cloth and other imports or manufactured goods. Basic local foodstuffs were not standard enough in quality and quantity to permit the easy setting of official price levels, and perhaps the nationalist focus on international terms of trade had some lingering effect. Those goods listed as "essential commodities," which were subject to price controls, were a category of imports dating from World War II. Traders selling these products had adapted to the high risk with unusual selling practices that restricted the display of goods and kept most of the stock at a safe distance. A handful of empty cans on a table indicated what canned food was available, once the buyer passed inspection. Another strategy, popular for rice and sugar, was for a wholesaler to hire or sponsor a retailer with no stall to sell from a metal basin on the ground. These were always young, strong men and women, who could run away fast when inspectors arrived. Cloth sellers with stalls in prime locations learned to open their doors only a few inches, sitting inside in the dark with only a half dozen pieces. The owner was always away when known or suspected spies tried to buy something. Several traders said that their nerves could not stand the constant fear, so they decided to switch to selling local foodstuffs, which after all took up the majority of the market. Traders who flourished despite the pressure were reputed to have special protection, whether from family connections, magical paraphernalia, or sexual relationships (the so-called bottom power).

During Acheampong's rule, corruption reached levels that even other military officers suspected was unsustainable. In July 1978, the general was himself overthrown by Lieutenant Colonel Akuffo, who also arrested other notorious public figures but did not impose dramatic punishments or fines commensurate with their gains from corruption. He ordered strict enforcement of existing price controls in July and again in November 1978, maintaining the episodic rhythm of market raids. His most innovative tactic, a total currency exchange in March 1979, did target cash-hoarding corrupt ex-officials and wealthy traders, although arguably sparing those whose bank connections had stayed current.[21] The pattern of episodic price control raids on imports and manufactures traders persisted as Acheampong was succeeded by Akuffo in 1978, then Akuffo by Rawlings under the brief 1979 Armed Forces Revolutionary Council (AFRC) regime, and then Rawlings by President Limann after the 1979 election.

Markets under Attack

The AFRC "housecleaning exercise" invoked the corrupt or wealthy trader as its targeted "hoarder," but reached far beyond the familiar list of "essential commodities" with published official prices. Soldiers in Kumasi now also took over formal-sector stores and market locations devoted to local foodstuffs, not just cloth and imports. They sold off all sorts of goods at prices they set on the spot, often by figuring one-half or one-tenth the previous price. The ideological shift that turned any market traders' organization into a sinister conspiracy made any gesture toward consultation or even negotiation with market women more and more unthinkable. Market leaders scrambled to find a strategy that moderated the increasingly arbitrary price controls and unpredictable violence facing their desperate constituents.

Confiscations and forced sales destroyed many Kumasi traders' capital, and a handful endured public flogging. Those traders with any capital left tried to keep it safe by suspending trade; as long as they had savings to live on, they could stay home. The poorest traders, who lived hand-to-mouth and took goods on supplier credit, were disproportionately exposed to these dangers. They had to keep coming to the market and trying to earn something, even under the least promising and riskiest conditions, or go hungry with their families. By contrast, male occupational groups in and around Kumasi received very different treatment from the AFRC during price control enforcement. Truck drivers, spare parts dealers, butchers. and *adinkra* cloth printers, among others, negotiated their official price levels in relation to prices for their inputs. The military authorities had approached them to start talks before their control prices were announced, and the prices agreed upon were then respected.

The senior market leader (head of the yam traders' group) and her colleagues (the heads of other commodity groups) tried to negotiate official prices for local foodstuffs, since none had existed before, so traders who abided by them could then avoid harassment. They sought out meetings with the market manager, appointed by the Kumasi Metropolitan Authority, and even with the Ashanti Regional Commissioner, appointed by the head of state, as relatively neutral senior authorities who could set price levels in public that enforcers would have to accept. Unfortunately for the traders, these lawful authorities had only partial control over military personnel. After market leaders had invested considerable time in listing quality grades and agreeing on prices for sample specimens, they discovered that soldiers in the market ignored these price lists. If traders had reduced their prices in advance, the soldiers would still cut the sales price to one-half or one-quarter of their new price.

Military authorities also summoned the market queens to ad hoc meetings with delegations of farmers or soldiers, but these were quite different from military meetings called with male groups. Elderly market queens in particular complained of the time and energy consumed by such frequent meetings, but all the market elders complained bitterly of the disrespect they faced in the meetings called by soldiers.

Despite the attendance of some civilian government officials, such as the market manager, traders found that the promised negotiations were a sham. The most basic conventions of negotiation and dispute settlement were violated. The time and place were set unilaterally; the soldiers in fact commandeered the commodity group meeting room in the middle of a peak trading day. Most outrageously, the policy decisions had already been taken, and were simply being announced to them, with no opportunity to state their case in a meaningful way or propose alternatives. Traders were subjected to humiliating harangues: "They speak to us like we are children, when we are old enough to be their mothers!" Their carefully honed negotiating skills were tacitly dismissed and rendered useless; besides, they lamented, "How can you talk to a gun?" The chances of positive participation in any kind of political process seemed very remote.

As the handover to civilian rule approached, Rawlings made one last effort to leave a lasting mark on the national marketplace system. On September 5, 1979, Makola No. 1, the most famous market in Accra, was blown up with dynamite, and markets in each regional capital faced demolition over the next several days. Members of the Kumasi City Council reportedly argued successfully with the soldiers there to demolish only the outlying sections and spare the oldest section, within the original walls.

Flight Lt. J. J. Rawlings had significantly intensified the pattern of episodic price control raids from June to October 1979, but the pattern quickly reasserted itself after his handover of power to civilian rule. Incoming President Limann found it necessary to validate his political credentials with a new round of strict enforcement of price control regulations soon after taking office. When the December 31 Revolution in 1981 returned Flight Lieutenant Rawlings to power as head of state with his People's National Defense Council (PNDC) regime, he immediately reinstated the extralegal confiscations and violent harassment of the AFRC period. Since I was living in Accra (the coastal capital) from 1982 to 1984 and traveling to aid project villages in different regions, I could observe events in various parts of the country and monitor their impact on villagers as well as passing through Kumasi repeatedly. Interactions between commodity group leaders and the regime reached a new low point in 1982–83, during this early PNDC period. This time, Rawlings seemed determined to destroy or at least dethrone the marketplace system permanently.[22]

The PNDC made strenuous efforts to set up parallel distribution channels that would bypass market traders altogether. Possessing commercial quantities of food was grounds for arrest, and considered prima facie evidence of hoarding. Each farm village was exhorted to organize a Committee for the Defense of the Revolution (CDR), which would sell its produce directly to institutions and consumer cooperatives from urban neighborhoods. At first, soldiers brought trucks out with cloth, soap, and cutlasses to sell to CDRs at controlled prices, providing free transport both ways. These benefits generated some enthusiasm among farmers, but once the goods ran out and CDRs started charging for transport, farmers stopped cooperating. Newspaper reports began denouncing traders for appearing in villages with trucks loaded with consumer goods for sale and offering farmers high prices—all very unpatriotic.

It was the dry season of a second drought year by 1983, not a good time to remove price incentives.[23] The repatriation of a million Ghanaian immigrants expelled from Nigeria in February 1983 further stressed the food system. One mother described to me coming in to Kumasi Central Market with money and bursting into tears, because there was nothing to buy to make dinner for her family. Urban food supplies dried up almost completely for several months, and widespread hunger caused the prominent collarbones that were covertly referred to as "Rawlings' necklace." Soldiers were as hungry as anyone, and they began to hijack food trucks from the highways that passed by their barracks, making farmers and traders fearful of traveling at all. Without announcing any policy reversal, the PNDC quietly began to allow traders to bring and sell foodstuffs in the cities again by late 1983. This unspoken tolerance replicated the episodic enforcement pattern familiar from previous regimes, and it tacitly acknowledged that the alternative distribution channels could not do the job of feeding the nation.

Market Deregulation

The neoliberal polices next instituted under International Monetary Fund (IMF)/World Bank tutelage as the 1984 structural adjustment program (SAP) ended controls on prices and imports but still excluded traders from public policy support and investment. Such policies, which remain firmly in place after repeated and peaceful multiparty elections, continue to treat informal traders with hostility or neglect. Roadside and itinerant traders still periodically face arrest and confiscation of their goods, as part of street clearances or civic beautification campaigns in Kumasi. Yet the marketplace system remains the dominant distribution channel within Ghana's national economy, as in many developing nations.

By 1984 Rawlings capitulated to international financial and diplomatic pressures and accepted the neoliberal austerity measures recommended by the IMF. Price controls and foreign exchange controls were dismantled, with currency devaluation and price inflation rapidly surpassing previous black market levels. Austerity measures required to balance the budget brought massive layoffs of government employees and drastic cuts in health and education services, as they did for many other "adjusting" countries.[24] The buying power of the typical middle- or lower-class market patron was sharply limited by policies aimed at "demand constraint" and "cost recovery." While perhaps motivated more by the threat of bankruptcy than by a change of heart, the PNDC was thorough in its implementation of the already familiar list of IMF loan conditionalities. Ghana was soon featured prominently in World Bank publications as a structural adjustment success story, offering a good example to the rest of sub-Saharan Africa.

On the positive side, traders saw a welcome end to the physical violence of police raids and fear of confiscations. Renewed access to credit and aid funded long-needed infrastructure projects that resurfaced major highways and city streets. Rebuilding the drains that ran through the Central Market took years, but eventually the market no longer experienced regular floods that spoiled traders' stock. Gasoline rationing ended, so transport was readily available to whoever could afford it, greatly reducing the need for special transport arrangements but raising the capital requirements for efficient trading.

The promised surges in foreign direct investment and in innovative local entrepreneurship unfortunately failed to materialize. Despite Ghana's GDP growth, the living standards of ordinary people hardly budged due to the increasing polarization of income distribution. The same export sectors that colonial policy had favored (gold, cocoa, and timber) received the lion's share of World Bank investment capital under their new designation of "comparative advantage." These are also the very production sectors whose income is most concentrated in the hands of a small proportion of producers. None of their products are sold through the marketplace system, and their owners and employees are predominantly men.[25] In the case of the gold mines, new technology raised output but reduced manpower requirements, sending out laid-off workers to survive in the informal economy.

As private formal-sector employment shrank, partly under pressure from newly plentiful imports, unemployed or never-employed workers flooded into the marketplace and the streets. The influx of young men into occupations like vegetable trading, previously the domain of females, was highly visible at the market's edges. The dividing up of the restricted pool of consumer demand among more businesses meant even lower incomes for existing traders. Market traders found the new "open" economy did not open up much viable space for them, and resulted in increasing income polarization and capital dependency among their own ranks.

A Morally Challenged Economy

The availability of viable jobs that enabled people with little capital to support a family and hope to build a house appeared widely in traders' life stories as a key indicator of a good local economy. The theme of local opportunity structures emerged as a unifying framework for traders to compare different time periods or different towns they had lived in, and to debate whether one strategy or another was good or bad. Those periods when a hardworking citizen with reasonable luck and foresight could build a house were described as boom times. The economy was considered sound if people were able to earn enough to buy food for their families and lead a dignified life, at least in multiple-earner households.

These traders emphasized a wide variety of specific social and economic changes in their narratives, tacitly nominating them as significant causal factors in national decline or revival. Despite this variation, their positive or negative influence was almost always argued primarily by their impact on the range of viable work options. The Kumasi city government drew criticism from Auntie Boronya that it did not provide "real jobs," because its pay scales were too low to live on. Amma Pokuaa and Madame Ataa discussed fluctuating earnings in the cocoa industry, and in civil service and education occupations, and they worried about the higher capital now required in every type of business, due to higher prices and shrinking credit. Other careers associated with women, such as nursing or teaching, were becoming as unreliable as marriage had become.

Traders closely monitored the entry requirements for various market positions as well as other factors that might facilitate or obstruct entry for themselves or their children. They assessed these entry points to inform their immediate career decisions, not to evaluate the success of development policies. Their family accounts demonstrate that women did not follow automatically into their mothers' occupations for lack of imagination or experience. Even Pokuaa and Abenaa Ediyaa, who worked closely with their mothers for many years, had sisters in other occupations and did not expect or want their children to follow them into the market. Maame Kesiwaa, Maame Nkrumah, and Auntie Afriyε had tried several different lines of work in their youth, before settling into one that suited them. Despite their age, these women were open to changing their commodity or their position in the supply chain when this seemed to promise improvement, although the effort was not always successful. Boronya had changed her line of work quite recently, and would have liked to change again.

These Asante elders use a considerable Twi vocabulary to invoke and critique different concepts about social change processes. The word *anibue* (literally, "eye-opening") is one of the most positive terms for social change, and yet it easily reflects social prejudice and lends itself to sarcasm. Not all who use it do so naively; the irony from some would do any postmodernist proud. It has very deep roots in Asante ideas of social process and individual growth, and it is used to refer to personal qualities more often than to community growth. Children acquire *anibue* at a certain age, some more and earlier than others, as Afriyε notes. As a stage of maturation, it represents something like good judgment or common sense, but it can also mean awareness and intelligence more generally. When Pokuaa or Kesiwaa speak of a village, ethnic group, or history period as having more or less *anibue*, they mean more experience of the outside world and wider aspirations. For those without it, they literally say that "their eyes have not opened" (*n'animmue*).

Each of these women had experienced the dramatic boom-and-bust cycles of the later twentieth century in particular ways linked to her social position, as a market trader with her own level of capital and connections. Traders debate the merits of urban life and modernization in moral terms, but their moral judgments dwell in large part on economic impacts. In the more favorable assessments by Pokuaa or Nkrumah, these social changes expand opportunities for employment and material comfort. Skeptics like Ataa question their value because they seem to undermine economic stability and community autonomy.

Economic considerations cannot be separated cleanly from moral and emotional considerations, whether at the community, family, or individual level. Material wealth and progress toward modernity are viewed as positive for their own sake, but not when they undermine the commitment to mutual survival. Individual ambition is seen as consistent with group affiliation, and not normally in direct contradiction to it. Competition is expected and rewarded, but within a framework of mutual benefit that gives each person a responsibility to contribute to the common good. Traders' commitment to mutual survival and dignity has had a strong moral aspect for them, as the definitive expression of mutual respect and loyalty. Their primary financial commitment is to the survival of fellow lineage members, especially their own children but also sisters and their children. This core relationship then provides a model for the metaphorical commodity group "family" that fosters individual commercial viability within the competitive marketplace. Respect and honesty figured as moral values first for Maame Nkrumah, one of the market queens, but when she elaborated on their community benefit she shifted to their economic outcomes, in creating a social context where the ordinary citizen could make a decent living.

Inequality did not outrage these women, who were relatively poor with a few exceptions. Ediyaa and Nkrumah called it unfair that educated people were forced to come and compete for market share with "professional" career traders. The educationally advantaged, they believed, should have so many other upward paths open to them that they should be able to leave the market for illiterates, who had only this one. Traders clearly recognized the dearth of other employment options even for educated youth from the experiences of their own siblings and children. This sympathy kept most traders from organizing to exclude them. Amma Pokuaa and Abenaa

Ediyaa expressed grave concern about the lack of work options available to their maturing children. Traders often had hoped to set their children on an upward path into professional jobs, and a few had succeeded. But for many who had sacrificed to educate their children and grandchildren, the expected rewards were now monopolized by more privileged graduates, whose parents had networks of elite connections and additional money for business capital.

Even more chilling for traders was the realization that they could no longer assume that their daughters or granddaughters could at least become traders like themselves. Limited credit and consumer demand made it harder to establish an independent trading business now than when Pokuaa and Ataa had started. Supplier credit had eased the entry for these earlier cohorts, but credit was drying up for many commodities. Squeezed between higher capital demands and the capital losses they had suffered during price raids and other political upheavals, many older women like Pokuaa had been forced to reduce the scope of their own businesses. They could not afford to employ younger relatives or even extend them credit, and there might be few assets left to inherit when they died. Ediyaa was not sure that trading was even a viable option now for supporting a young family. Without capital, even the market stall itself could not be put to very profitable use by a successor. Although well aware of the risks of emigration, these mothers suspected that the accessible occupations within the local economy were a sure dead end.

All but the most successful traders experienced this as a crisis of reproduction: biological reproduction had little meaning without social reproduction. They felt impotent, because they could not finish raising their children into properly functioning adults. Their frustration underlines the fact that creating this basic level of independence is seen as a primary obligation of parents and elders to the next generation. Pokuaa remarked poignantly that her younger daughters did not even know what the satisfaction of feeding a family was like, and so they didn't miss it. As things stood, literate and illiterate children alike could not count on appropriate jobs to care for their own needs, indicating the truly deplorable state of the national economy.

Although traders could accept a lack of success in addressing underemployment, they could not accept the neoliberal politicians' disavowal of any binding obligation to address it. The World Bank no longer recognized the low incomes and inadequate diet of traders and their urban neighbors as a major problem to be solved. In fact, Ghana's situation in 1989 was celebrated as a success story and promoted as a global model by the UN and other multilateral agencies. To many Ghanaians, the priorities of neoliberal technocrats seemed immoral and corrupt, not just unfortunate, because they denied any responsibility for community welfare outcomes.[26]

Political Inclusion Begins

Although suspension of price controls has made trading legal, traders' moral values and economic concerns still found little influence on national development planning or international assistance. While they bore no political responsibility, their political isolation continued. The much replicated Program of Action to Mitigate the Social Costs of Adjustment (PAMSCAD), which began in Ghana in 1987, specifically disqualified traders from its 1988 small loan program aimed to encourage entrepreneurship and risk taking. Market repairs moved as slowly and corruptly as ever, and traders' material interests seemed to be ignored as completely as ever. Those trading in the outer precincts of the marketplace, who operated from flimsy stalls or who stopped for a few hours in a regular spot, remained subject to repeated clearances, with little warning, despite the rent they paid to the city.

Some incidents suggest that market traders may have begun making progress toward more political integration as the country settled into a stable electoral democracy. In 1989, women traders from Accra were appointed to a few government advisory and planning commissions. A few traders won seats on rural district assemblies through local government elections also held in 1989. Under decentralization measures district assemblies began operating in local languages and gained control of some funds.[27] Traders' organizational representatives also joined those appointed in 1991 to the constituent assembly that convened to draft a new constitution before the return to national elections.

In Kumasi, the yam queen was also appointed for one term to a city council seat not filled by election, and still enjoyed her air-conditioned office in 1994. Debates were always held in English, which she did not understand, so she sat near a family friend who could interpret for her. She was satisfied to make occasional remarks, which she considered analogous to the final summing up by the senior chief presiding over a traditional council. Her impromptu interpreter, conversely, reported that the English-speaking members ignored her comments, so they had little impact on council decisions.

A local nongovernmental organization registered in Kumasi, the Center for the Development of People (CEDEP), made several interventions intended to raise awareness and respect for market women. Its Women's Forum collected life stories of successful local women as inspiring examples in 1995, deliberately including the yam queen in the forum launch celebration and in an eventual publication. A subsequent CEDEP initiative organized participatory workshops for market leaders at which they prioritized their problems and identified potential solutions and partners. A corresponding workshop for city officials at the Kumasi Metropolitan Authority aimed to raise their awareness of traders' contributions to local development, stressing that approximately half the total city budget came from market revenues.[28]

Increased official awareness did not negate the underlying political inequalities and tensions. City officials reacted in 1999 by trying to squeeze even more money out of traders with a dubious security guard scheme. Market leaders had already stated flatly that real progress was unlikely under the longtime city council chairman. Regardless of that (unrecorded) consensus, the assessment exercise may have stiffened their resolve to reject the security guard proposal. In June 2006, a new city leader had not been in office long enough to make long-term policy changes evident.

Without the burden of overt government hostility, however, the long history of local rulers promoting local prosperity through trade seemed to slowly reassert itself during the 1990s. Some chiefs of farming districts that grew local food crops for sale tried to protect the commercial territory of their hometown traders against urban-based buyers. Techiman and Gonja chiefs, at different times, forbade Kumasi yam traders from buying directly from farmers in villages or town markets, insisting they buy through local traders. In these instances, urban/rural and north/south rivalries overshadowed the occupational divide between traders and farmers. Traders based in small towns and villages also often farm themselves.

A violent confrontation took place in early March 2006 between tomato buyers from the southern cities, like Auntie Boronya, and tomato farmers from the distant Upper East Region. The negotiations to end it indicate that women traders may now be regaining some access to government officials. These traders (from the national capital, Accra, and nearby southern cities) successfully asked high-ranking public officials to intervene on short notice. The leader of one of the traders' associations advised me that she took a cell phone call reporting the attack from one of the traders from her town who was there. She immediately headed for Accra to alert her superior, head of the National Tomato Traders' Association, who had already been informed by her Accra colleagues who were in a group ambushed near Paga.[29] Within hours, they were able to contact national and regional officials to ensure police protection and mediate the dispute.

These farmers grew dry season tomatoes on the irrigation projects fed by the Volta River. Promises that a long-defunct tomato cannery nearby would be rehabilitated had induced them to plant large quantities that year. Some had sold or mortgaged assets like land to finance larger farms, expecting higher prices promised by the cannery manager. Meanwhile, women traders from the southern cities had organized to buy tomatoes in bulk across the nearby border in Burkina Faso, as customs agreements allowed. When the harvest started but the cannery was not ready to buy, farmers became desperate. The member of Parliament for that area spoke on the house floor of riots and suicides.[30]

These remote farmers had little leverage to hasten the construction of power lines to connect to their local cannery, but the roads from Burkina Faso brought the more vulnerable traders right through their villages. On March 1, a group of male farmers blockaded the Paga border post, trapping traders with at least forty-one of their tomato trucks. After local police escorted these trucks through the nearest large town, Navrongo, farmers ambushed them again farther south, stealing the traders' money and cell phones and sending several traders to the hospital.[31]

The attack brought an immediate response from regional and national officials, starting with the Upper East Regional Security Council, the Regional Director of Agriculture, the Deputy Regional Minister, and the Regional Minister. Before a week had passed, the president of the National Tomato Traders and Transporters Association had extended a compromise offer to farmers and concluded impressive negotiations in Bolgatanga and Accra that involved the Minister of Trade, the minister of Food and Agriculture, and the president of the National Farmers and Fishermen Award Winners Association. The agreement announced March 7 set up procedures for local purchases and imports that accommodated traders and farmers but paid little heed to international treaties or free-market principles.[32] It was hard to imagine in 1990 or 1999 that only a few years later public figures of this stature would be openly sitting down with traders' leaders, and expressing a willingness to respect their perspectives.

Conclusion

The complex historical dynamics of market organizations in Ghana show a continuing ambivalence in the relations between individual traders, their local commodity groups, and the various governments that have sought to control them. Notorious episodes of price control and market demolitions from 1979 to 1984 were only the most dramatic moments in a long series of interventions in trade that public opinion often legitimated. Meanwhile, market rents and daily fees supplied a steady source of public revenue that funded local government institutions. Traders' tenacious resistance to regulation and the resilience of their autonomous organizations advertised the limits of government control of the economy. The shifting contours of this contestation shaped traders' organizational and ideological strategies throughout the twentieth century and into the twenty-first.

In Ghana, open marketplaces remain the primary economic institution delivering the basic foods and consumer goods without which urban residents (and most rural communities) cannot survive. Marketplaces revive so rapidly after periods of violent crisis not just because traders can deploy a priceless cultural repertoire of transactional and organizational praxis, but because market systems can and do change swiftly.[33] The historical record suggests that public policy toward markets needs to accommodate this flexibility and continuity in supporting traders' access to public space, customers, transport, storage facilities, credit, sanitation, and other social infrastructure.

The complicated historical dynamics that constructed this mutual distrust also support a more encouraging prognosis. Market commodity groups represent neither an eternal tradition nor an imitation of modernity, but rather an indigenous innovation and a reservoir of considerable economic expertise. If their recent configuration responds to specific late-twentieth-century conditions, this suggests that traders can and will continue to generate creative shifts in their organizational practices in response to twenty-first-century changes in their political, economic, and cultural environment. Just such a complex interaction of many factors brought the situation to this pass, making a precedent for future change that promises to be equally complex. Such future innovation by traders will be needed to preserve the resilience that has been so conspicuous and valuable a feature of market trade in the past.

Overcoming such deep-rooted antagonism is a complicated process that will probably take a long time and comprise many different strategies and cultural changes. Traders contribute best to sustainable economies as active participants creatively meeting contemporary global challenges, not as folkloric anachronisms in out-of-the-way preserves. Traders' leaders and organizations should be recognized as legitimate stakeholders in urban and regional planning, and as central participants in all relevant consultation processes. Such inclusion needs to take culturally and historically appropriate forms, but these particular inflections do not negate its global character.[34] As a general principle, full inclusion would mean a substantial step forward in the often volatile and destructive relations between traders and their governments.

Notes

1. Jane Guyer, *Marginal Gains* (Chicago: University of Chicago Press, 2004).

2. More details on these research methods are included in my doctoral thesis and a subsequent book: Gracia Clark, "The Position of Asante Women Traders in Kumasi Central Market, Ghana" (PhD diss., University of Cambridge, 1984); and Gracia Clark, ed., *Onions Are My Husband: Survival and Accumulation by West African Market Women* (Chicago: University of Chicago Press, 1994). I would like to thank the ESRC (UK), the ILO, the SSRC, the Fulbright Commission, and the US Department of Education for funding various of my fieldwork opportunities.

3. I am especially grateful to historians Gareth Austin, Larry Yarak, and Thomas McCaskie for directing my attention to valuable files.

4. Pieter DeMarees, *Chronicle of the Gold Coast of Guinea*, trans. A. Van Dantzig and Adam Smith (1602, repr., Oxford: Oxford University Press, 1985); and Kenneth Little, *African Women in Towns* (Cambridge: Cambridge University Press, 1973).

5. Jean Allman, *The Quills of the Porcupine* (Madison: University of Wisconsin Press, 1993).

6. Jennifer Hart, "Hoarding Mothers? Shifting Images and Public Discourses of Ghanaian Market Women, 1952–1979" (unpublished class paper, Indiana University–Bloomington, 2006).

7. Anthony Hopkins, *An Economic History of West Africa* (New York: Columbia University Press, 1973), 79–87.

8. DeMarees, *Chronicle of the Gold Coast.*

9. K. Onwuka Dike and Felicia Ekejiuba, *The Aro of South-eastern Nigeria, 1650–1980* (Ibadan: Ibadan University Press, 1990).

10. Sylvia Harrop, "The Economy of the West African Coast in the 16th Century," *Economic Bulletin of Ghana* 8 (1964): 15–29.

11. Ivor Wilks, *Asante in the Nineteenth Century* (Cambridge: Cambridge University Press, 1975).

12. Rhoda Howard, *Colonialism and Underdevelopment in Ghana* (London: Croom Helm, 1978).

13. Margaret Priestley, *West African Trade and Coast Society* (London: Oxford University Press, 1969).

14. Gwendolyn Mikell, *Cocoa and Chaos in Ghana* (New York: Paragon, 1989).

15. District Commissioner, Obuasi, to Chief Commissioner, Ashanti, November 13 and 25, 1939, "Foodstuffs and Meat Regulation," item 33, NAK12: No. 1136, Ghana National Archives, Kumasi.

16. "Irregularities in Import Control," Motion by Hon. Dr. J. B. Danquah, March 26, 1947, NAA6: No. 0028 SF8, Ghana National Archives, Accra.

17. Anthony Hopkins, "Economic Aspects of Political Movements in the Gold Coast and Nigeria, 1918–39," *Journal of African History* 7 (1965): 133–52.

18. Howard, *Colonialism and Underdevelopment in Ghana.*

19. See "Irregularities in Import Control," Motion by Danquah, March 26, 1947.

20. St. Clair Drake and Leslie Lacy, "Government vs. the Unions: The Sekondi-Takoradi Strike, 1961," in *Politics in Africa: 7 Cases*, ed. Gwendolyn Carter (New York: Harcourt, Brace, 1966).

21. For observations of the November 1978 and March 1979 events, and more traders' narratives of earlier episodes, see Clark, *Onions Are My Husband*; and Gracia Clark, "Price Control of Local Foodstuffs in Kumasi, Ghana, 1979," in *Traders versus the State* (Boulder, CO: Westview, 1988), 57–80.

22. For more detailed analysis of the AFRC and PNDC periods, see Claire Robertson, "The Death of Makola and Other Tragedies: Male Strategies against a Female-Dominated System," *Canadian Journal of African Studies* 17 (1983): 469–95; and Clark, "Price Control of Local Foodstuffs," 57–80.

23. Gracia Clark, "Food Traders and Food Security in Ghana," in *The Political Economy of African Famine*, ed. R. E. Downs, D. O. Kerner, and S. P. Reyna (London: Gordon and Breach, 1991), 227–56. Clark compares food shortages in 1979 and 1983 to regular dry seasons.

24. Gracia Clark and Takyiwaa Manuh, "Women Traders in Ghana and the Structural Adjustment Programme," in *Structural Adjustment and African Women Farmers*, ed. Christina Gladwin (Gainesville: University Press of Florida, 1991), 217–36.

25. Ibid.

26. Gracia Clark, "Gender and Profiteering: Ghana's Market Women as Devoted Mothers and 'Human Vampire Bats,'" in *"Wicked" Women and the Reconfiguration of Gender in Africa*, ed. Dorothy L. Hodgson and Sheryl A. McCurdy (Portsmouth, NH: Heinemann, 2001), 293–311.

27. Maxwell Owusu, "Democracy and Africa: A View from the Village," *Journal of Modern African Studies* 30, no. 3 (1992): 369–96.

28. Rudith King, "The Role of Urban Market Women in Local Development Processes and Its Implications for Policy: A Case Study of Kumasi Central Market, Ghana" (PhD diss., University of Sussex, 1999).

29. Confidential interview with anonymous tomato trader, 2007. The association sometimes included its contracted drivers, as the National Tomato Traders and Transporters Association.

30. Ghana News Agency, news item, March 3, 2006.

31. Ghana News Agency reports from March 1–7, 2006, were compared with oral reports from a participating traders' organization leader to prepare this summary account of events.

32. Ghana News Agency, news item, March 7, 200.

33. Clark, "Food Traders and Food Security."

34. Examples of confrontations in many parts of the world can be found in Clark, "Price Control of Local Foodstuffs."

8

Enterprising Women in Zimbabwe

Confronting Crisis in a Globalizing Era

Mary J. Osirim

Although not a new phenomenon on the world stage, globalization and its effects have become an increasingly important focus of study for social scientists over the past twenty-five years.[1] While initially thought of in primarily economic terms as referring to the emergence of a worldwide capitalist economic system that integrated markets and encouraged the free movement of goods, services, and corporations around the globe, in recent years it has taken on broader meaning in studies of politics, culture, and gender.[2] In its current iteration, globalization also refers to the movement of populations, organizations, and ideas across national boundaries, regions, and cultures.

Given the importance of globalization in overall processes of economic, political, and social transformation, social scientists have been particularly eager to chart the impact of such changes on national and transnational populations. In this regard, feminist scholars have sought to document the effects of globalization on women around the world, especially those whose lives are plagued by the intersection of race, class, and gender—women thus positioned at the bottom of the socioeconomic hierarchies in their nations. On the one hand, while feminist researchers such as Valentine Moghadam have demonstrated that globalization has increased women's labor force participation rates in many nations, her work also indicates that most of this employment has been created in low-status, low-wage occupations, which in the global North has meant more jobs at the bottom of the tertiary sector of the economy.[3] Other gender studies theorists have examined the impact of globalization on women's work in such fields as child and elder care, factory assembly, and sex work. Most of this research has focused on these activities in the global North and such global South regions as Latin America, the Caribbean, and Asia.[4] While the microenterprise sector constitutes the second major area of income earning for sub-Saharan African women, most of the attention in this sector has focused on women's work as market traders.[5] Outside of the microenterprise sector, beyond market and long-distance trade, less attention has been given to the impact of globalization on women's work in sub-Saharan Africa.[6]

Based on intensive fieldwork conducted in Harare and Bulawayo, Zimbabwe, in the 1990s, this chapter intends to move beyond the field of trade in assessing the impact of globalization on women's work in Africa. As Gracia Clark has demonstrated in chapter 7, African women have made significant contributions to the enhancement of economic growth and development in their communities. Over the past nearly two decades, women entrepreneurs in such fields as hairdressing, sewing, and crocheting have borne a disproportionate share of the impact of globalization, in the form of the imposition of the economic structural adjustment program implemented in Zimbabwe in late 1990/early 1991 and the enhanced structural adjustment facility in 1995. Businesswomen in these fields have suffered under neoliberalism, as mandated by the International Monetary Fund (IMF) and the World Bank, which has had a negative impact on their enterprises and their personal lives. They have faced increased costs and competition, higher user fees for social services, and increased un/underemployment, all of which affected the operation of their firms. Despite these problems, however, the entrepreneurs in this study demonstrated exceptional resilience, creativity, and business acumen in maintaining their firms in the midst of economic crisis. At the same time, they made many important contributions to the development of human and social capital as well as to material culture. In the sections that follow, this chapter will examine the theoretical and historical background that informs this work, as well as the profile of these entrepreneurs in the microenterprise sector. The chapter will further explicate their contributions to their businesses and communities, as well as the impact of globalization on their enterprises.

Feminist Political Economy: How Theory and History Shed Light on Zimbabwean Women's Status

Within the sociology of development and stemming from the earlier paradigms of world systems theory and comparative political economy (what the American Sociological Association today calls the political economy of the world system), feminist political economy provides a new, critical lens through which to understand the historical and contemporary experiences of women and men in societies of the global North and South.[7] In my work, I have defined three major aspects of this theory: (1) how feminist political economy expands the parameters of the political economy of the world system perspective; (2) the role of intersectionality within feminist political economy; and (3) the role of women's agency in activities and social movements in which they resist the power of the state, particularly in the global South.[8]

First, feminist political economy builds on the political economy of the world system perspective in maintaining that both external factors—such as relations among states in the global South, the Northern hegemonic powers, and the international financial system—and internal ones—that is, such problems as class, race, and gender inequality within states—must be considered in assessing a nation's prospects for development. Feminist political economy takes this idea a step further in noting the gendered international division of labor that exists between global North and global South nations that has differential impacts on women and men depending on where they are situated, globally speaking. Thus, feminist theorists increasingly draw our attention to the fact that young women, particularly those in East Asia, South Asia, and Latin America, have increasingly become important as global assembly-line producers in the mass production of textiles, electronics, and footwear sold in global markets. These women occupy low-status positions in the labor hierarchies in their countries and, as such, earn low wages. Unlike their male counterparts, they seldom hold positions as managers in such plants.

Second, feminist political economy considers how gender, race, and class (among other factors) intersect in the lives of women especially in global South nations, often trapping poor women of color on the lowest rungs of the socioeconomic hierarchy. Black African women in such former settler-colonies as Zimbabwe and South Africa were often the most marginalized populations in these areas, receiving little to no formal education and being relegated to the least desirable, lowest-paid positions in their societies. Feminist political economy draws our attention to the fact that the disadvantages these populations experienced owed not to the mere addition of these factors, one to another, but rather to the interaction that exists among these variables in women's lives. While this intersectionality is a dominant theme in the research of many feminist scholars in the United States, it has also been a critical focus of the works of African feminist scholars.[9] In fact, such works from the African continent predated many of the studies by feminists in the United States. African gender studies scholars have paid particular attention to how colonialism, capitalism, and patriarchy combined to limit the life chances of black women on the continent.

Third, those working within the feminist political economy perspective also pay particular attention to women's acts of resistance against oppressive states, state policies, and global capitalism in sub-Saharan Africa as well as other areas.[10] Gender studies scholars within this tradition have examined such actions as coalitions formed among market traders, students, and other workers to protest structural adjustment policies in African and Latin American nations in the 1980s and 1990s. More recently, researchers in this tradition have also studied the resistance of women in the Niger Delta to the activities of the Nigerian state and multinational oil corporations.[11]

Feminist political economy is particularly useful in analyzing the historical development of Zimbabwe from its British colonial status as Rhodesia to its postindependence position in the broader world economy. Rhodesia (Zimbabwe) entered the capitalist world economy on the periphery as a colony of Britain, largely restricted to the production of primary products. Feminist political economy is especially beneficial in charting the experiences of black Zimbabwean women (and men) over time.

Under British settler colonialism in the late nineteenth century and first half of the twentieth century, Rhodesia established a race- and gender-based system of stratification, which positioned black women at the bottom of the socioeconomic hierarchy. A system of internal colonialism prevailed in the colony, which not only established a class-color system whereby blacks were relegated to the most marginalized positions, with black men being recruited to the cities and rural areas to serve as cheap labor for white-owned mines and cash crop farms.[12] Black male labor migration was strictly controlled by the state. Such laws as the Land Apportionment Act of 1930 reserved the vast majority of the most arable land (over twenty million hectares) to the minority white population while blacks were left with the smaller portion (about nine hectares) of the least arable land.[13] Most black women were forced to remain in the black areas, the "Tribal Trust Lands," to eke out a living in small-scale farming to the best of their ability, while black men had to sell their labor to meet the taxation demands of the colonial state.[14]

The class-color-gender system of stratification also disadvantaged black Zimbabwean women in education. Under this system, black men were likely to receive more formal education compared to their female counterparts since the former had to serve the needs of the colonial state.[15] Even when black women were able to obtain a few years of primary education, it was highly gendered, with most of their instruction being in basic reading, writing, computation, and domestic skills.[16]

By the 1940s, as black women and men began to lose farmlands to larger cultivators, some black women joined men in migrating to the cities.[17] The women who migrated began to establish makeshift markets to sell locally produced foodstuffs, particularly those grown indigenously, to the male laborers. Thus, Zimbabwean market traders, as well as beer brewers or "shebeen queens," became some of the earliest women entrepreneurs in the urban areas, indeed in the nation. Over time, the white authorities began to ignore the black women migrants who were satisfying the needs of the black male workforce for "home" foods—those that were unique to the Shona or Ndebele diet.[18] Although women began to establish themselves as traders in markets in the high-density suburbs (black areas) of Harare and Bulawayo, they typically remained the nation's poorest residents.

Poor and low-income women, however, held out much hope for a change in their status with the coming of independence in 1980. After all, women fought alongside men in the Liberation War and were promised that if the Zimbabwe African National Union (ZANU) was victorious, women would achieve equality and an overall improvement in their standard of living.

In many ways, the early postindependence Zimbabwean state delivered on these promises. In 1981 the government established the Ministry of Community and Cooperative Development and Women's Affairs to end all forms of state-sanctioned discrimination against women and to ensure women's meaningful participation in all realms of the state and the society. This agency was particularly concerned with enhancing the prospects for women's employment and entrepreneurship, as well as their access to social services.[19] In this regard, the Women's Affairs Ministry was especially committed to expanding the number of poor and low-income women who had access to child care and community centers for their children as well as to primary health care. They were major proponents of the state's efforts to expand educational opportunities to young Zimbabweans, especially female children. This ministry also served as a "broker" to other ministries, such as the Ministry of Trade and Commerce, in promoting women's income-generating activities and providing vital supports for business development. All in all, it fostered women's empowerment.

The Zimbabwean state further attempted to promote entrepreneurship through the provision of business loans to women under the auspices of ZIMBANK, in which the government was the major shareholder. Such small-scale lending, or microloans, did not require women to put up collateral. The Small Enterprises Development Corporation also provided training for women in business. Again, the Women's Affairs Ministry was very involved in encouraging other ministries and local governments to support women's small businesses and microenterprises.[20]

Zimbabwean women experienced a monumental change in their status with the passage of the Legal Age of Majority Act in 1982. This act removed black Zimbabwean women from their previous status as minors and thereby enabled them to engage in contracts and own property in their own names. It also recognized women's contributions to family wealth and thus provided them with a share of the family property in the case of divorce.[21]

Although Zimbabwe did undergo some economic downturns in its first postindependence decade, due to droughts and other problems, for the most part the nation enjoyed a boom period. Thus, it could afford the massive expansion of the state in the 1980s—the major increases in public employment and spending on health care, education, and housing. The economic boom, however, was short-lived, and by 1989 the nation found itself on the brink of economic crisis with approximately 50 percent of the potential labor force unemployed.[22] Declining prices for Zimbabwe's primary exports, continued violent incursions into the nation by the apartheid regime in South Africa, and frequent droughts seriously hindered the nation's Growth with Equity Agenda. Therefore, at the behest of the IMF and the World Bank, Zimbabwe established an economic structural adjustment program (ESAP) in late 1990/early 1991 in an attempt to get the economy back on track. As had been the case for many other global South nations previously, Zimbabwe found itself having to enact the same conditions that had plagued other countries including major reductions in the size of the state, massive devaluations of the currency, trade liberalization, and restrictions on trade unions.[23]

Feminist political economy provides us with the tools to explore ESAP as part of the larger worldwide process of globalization and its particular impact on the lives of poor and low-income women in Zimbabwe. First, under this program, more than forty thousand individuals lost their jobs in the public sector. Men constituted the majority of those retrenched from the state, and they were strongly encouraged to begin micro- or small-scale enterprises as a means of sustaining themselves and their families. Second, women, especially mothers who believed they had a responsibility to assist in the support of the family, also sought to sustain or begin microbusinesses as a way of keeping their families afloat. As men began increasingly to enter this sector and, in fact, started businesses in areas traditionally controlled by women such as market trade in foodstuffs, they posed increased competition for women. Finally, because of the dominance of patriarchy in the precolonial, colonial, and postindependence periods, despite the nation's attempts to promote equality in the latter, women remained in a disadvantaged position relative to men. Because men had greater access to capital, whether material, human, or social, they were more likely to succeed in business.

In addition to the difficulties that poor and low-income women experienced with respect to the operation of their businesses during the economic crisis and adjustment, they were further disadvantaged in their roles as mothers and caregivers. With the growing unemployment of husbands and fathers, women increasingly shouldered the costs of food, household expenses, and school fees, even though such responsibilities were clearly the purview of men in Shona and Ndebele culture. Severe cuts in the state's support for social services meant the imposition of, and in some cases increases in, user fees for education and health care. Some social services that families had been able to obtain for free during the 1980s now had high fees attached to them. As a result, under adjustment and persistent patriarchy, many young women in Zimbabwe, as in other nations, were disproportionately removed from schools in favor of educating boys.[24] Under such severely constrained economic conditions, families preferred to educate sons rather than their female siblings since males were expected to care for aging parents and families.

The economic crisis and adjustment also took their toll on the health care of poor women and children. In the first three years after ESAP was implemented, the share of the national budgets devoted to health, housing, and transportation decreased by 20, 25, and 40 percent, respectively. As a result, Zimbabwe's status in health care declined precipitously with fewer and fewer children receiving basic immunizations against diseases, such as measles.[25] The prohibitive cost of pharmaceuticals and the significant migration of health professionals left the nation in even direr straits under adjustment. These negative costs of globalization were very disproportionately borne by women and children at the bottom.

These experiences with the impact of the economic crisis and ESAP were quite common for businesswomen in the microenterprise sector in Zimbabwe in the 1990s and beyond. Despite these dilemmas in their personal lives and with respect to their enterprises, the entrepreneurs in this study exhibited the resilience to maintain their enterprises and their families and to contribute to community and national development. The following sections of this chapter will explore how they succeeded in these tasks.

Discovering the Zimbabwean Women Entrepreneurs: Who Are They? Where Do They Work?

During three fieldwork visits in 1991, 1994, and 1997, my research assistants and I conducted intensive interviews with 157 entrepreneurs who worked in market trade, hairdressing, sewing, and crocheting about their family, educational, and occupational histories; the establishment and operation of their firms; their relationship to nongovernmental organizations (NGOs); and the impact of the state and globalization on their businesses.[26] We conducted in-depth interviews and participant observation of their sites in Harare and Bulawayo, the two largest cities in Zimbabwe. In this analysis, only the hairdressers, seamstresses, and crocheters will be considered.

In this study, hairdressers and seamstresses are grouped together and distinguished from crocheters, since the former owned businesses located in buildings in which they either shared space as seamstresses or generally had freestanding shops as hairdressers. Crocheters and knitters (who will generally be referred to as crocheters in this study since this is the major activity in which they were engaged) generally operated their businesses within a market. These crochet markets differed from outdoor food markets, however, in that the former did not contain stalls. Rather, crocheters worked, displayed, and sold their goods from locations on the bare ground. The only item that designated their space as a market was a large erected signboard stating that the space they occupied was provided by the city council of either Harare or Bulawayo. Crocheters worked outdoors at the mercy of the elements—they had no stalls, sheds, or protective covering to shield themselves or their goods.

The crochet markets were usually located adjacent to shopping centers or, in some cases, near a major government building or tourist area, such as in front of the Bulawayo City Hall. Thus, crochet markets were mainly found in the downtown areas of these major cities or in the low-density suburbs, formerly known as "white areas." Such locations were logical choices since the majority of the crocheters' customers were white residents, tourists, or South African merchants. South African traders or wholesalers frequented such markets, where they purchased such highly treasured items as handmade sweaters from the Zimbabwean businesswomen to be resold in South Africa.

Although many black Zimbabweans were hairdressers, few at the time of my study actually owned shops located in the central business district of the city. One was more likely to find them in the outer rim of the downtown commercial establishments, closer to the "black areas" of the metropolis. On occasion, though, one would find many black-owned beauty parlors occupying several flats within a large downtown building, such as Broadwell Lodge in Harare. In the downtown areas, one was more likely to find one or two buildings in which black seamstresses were clustered, such as Robin House in Harare. Sometimes these entrepreneurs would be concentrated in a few rooms within a large building, with each sewing machine in some cases demarcating a separate business.

In this chapter, the business activities of thirty-nine hairdressers and seamstresses will be considered alongside the activities of fifty-seven crocheters. The vast majority of businesswomen in this study were Shona, the largest ethnic group in the country, constituting 72 percent (twenty-eight) of the hairdressers and seamstresses and 70 percent (forty) of the crocheters. Of the hairdressers and seamstresses, 15 percent (six) were Ndebele, the second-largest ethnic group in the nation, compared to 18 percent (ten) of the crocheters. Other participants in this study were mainly from ethnic groups based in other southern African nations, such as Zambia. The median ages of entrepreneurs in these sectors ranged from thirty-seven to forty, with hairdressers as the oldest of these populations with a median age of forty. For crocheters, the median age of their enterprises was eight years, compared to seven years for sewing and hairdressing establishments.

About 70 percent (forty) of the crocheters had completed at least primary school; nearly half of them (nineteen) had also received some secondary education. Four crocheters actually completed their Ordinary Level (O-level) certificates, a prerequisite for higher education and to enter formal-sector occupations. One crocheter had not received any formal education. For their part, all of the hairdressers and seamstresses had received formal education. Two-thirds of the hairdressers had received some secondary education, while three of them had completed their O-level) certificates. Half of the beauty salon owners in this study had received specialized training in their field. Among the seamstresses, 78 percent (nineteen) had received some secondary education, while two seamstresses had earned their O-levels. In this study, a few seamstresses and hairdressers appeared to constitute a more "middle-class" segment of the population given their higher levels of educational attainment, their generally higher earnings, and the location and size of their businesses.

Although the entrepreneurs had been engaged in these businesses for some time, these positions were generally not aspirations that they had held in their youth. Most women in this sample wanted to enter largely gendered occupations, aspiring to become nurses, teachers, or flight attendants. Such occupations were unattainable for the vast majority of these participants, because they had not successfully completed the first level of high school and received their O-level certificates. The feminist political economy perspective draws our attention to the blocked opportunity structure that precluded high levels of educational attainment for black Zimbabwean women coming from poor and low-income families. First, education was not free at the time these women were in primary or secondary school. Parents would have to pay to send them to school, and if they came from large families, this was far more difficult. Patriarchal beliefs and practices meant that boys were given preference to attend school over their sisters. Sons remain a part of the father's family until death and have an obligation to support them, while daughters, once they marry, become part of their husband's family. This situation was even more problematic for young women in secondary schools, which were more expensive and, for some, would overlap the period during which they would be considered marriageable.

The second limit on educational attainment for poor and low-income black Zimbabwean women involved the requirements to receive the O-level certificate. Young students would have to pass five academic subjects, with English being one of them. Patriarchal practices made this a very difficult feat for young women from economically disadvantaged backgrounds, because they were generally saddled with many daily domestic and child care responsibilities that left little time for their studies. While their male counterparts also had some domestic chores, these young men were more likely to have assignments such as car washing and home repairs that were less time-consuming.[27] Even if a young woman was able to take her O-level examinations, if she failed any one of the required five, she would have to reenroll in school and pay the fees for tuition and testing before taking the test(s) again. This was out of reach for most low-income parents. The third factor blocking educational achievement was early pregnancy, which many young women experienced in secondary school. For the women in this study, such an occurrence meant that they had to leave school. A young woman could eventually return to attain her secondary school certificate, but again because of the costs involved, this remained prohibitive for young women from poor families.

The entrepreneurs in this study had a strong commitment to education over their lives. Although the majority of them were unable to complete the first level of secondary school, these women attained additional training at various points in their lives. While some attended schools or training programs and developed their skills in typing, bookkeeping, and sometimes shorthand, others learned how to crochet, knit, sew, and embroider from churches, community centers, or local clubs or from members of their extended families. Most of these women used these skills to pursue occupations in the microenterprise sector or to establish their businesses; a very few sought work in the formal sector.

Before starting their enterprises, most of the crocheters worked either in other sales positions, often involving some form of trade; in domestic work; or as teachers, laundresses, or farmers. Seamstresses and hairdressers had prior experience either in teaching or nursing, or as typists, sales workers, cashiers, or apprentices. Again, the somewhat higher educational attainment of the hairdressers and seamstresses meant that they had greater access to formal-sector positions.

All in all, although these entrepreneurs did encounter structural blockage due to their gender, class, and race in the educational and occupational systems in their youth and early adulthood, they manifested a very strong commitment to education and hard work over their life course, which would later enable them to achieve some success in their enterprises. Feminist political economy, though, enables us to see how Zimbabwe's historical and contemporary position in the global economy coupled with the realities of intersectionality limited the social mobility of these women. At the same time, they managed to build and sustain microenterprises and contribute to the development of the larger society. How did they operate their firms during a period of economic crisis and adjustment?

Entrepreneurship in the Microenterprise Sector under Globalization: Coping with Crisis

The 1990s to the present have posed some major challenges to the development and maintenance of enterprises in Zimbabwe's microenterprise sector. What began as an economic crisis in the early 1990s was soon compounded by a devastating political upheaval at the end of the decade that persisted into the new millennium. Many women who owned enterprises in sewing, hairdressing, and crocheting during this period, however, managed to keep their businesses afloat throughout the 1990s and survive the crisis. How did they succeed in this task? Although there are several responsibilities involved in the operation of a microenterprise, this paper will consider only a few in which these businesswomen were involved: employment generation, innovation, and the (re)investment of profits in their firms and in other activities. The detailed financial indicators of the firms' performance will not be examined here.

These enterprises were very much the invention of the women studied here. The majority of these businesswomen started their activities with capital from their own savings. As stated earlier, these entrepreneurs held previous positions in which they worked in sales, trading, teaching, nursing, or domestic work, among other duties, and their commitment to having something of their own led them to save as much as possible. Some of these enterprises, such as crocheting, did not require much start-up capital, since the business could essentially be run with the purchase of wool, cotton, and knitting and crochet needles. Some forms of hairdressing—for example, full-scale beauty salons—did involve a substantial initial capital investment to purchase sinks, dryers, furniture, and hair products to operate the business. For the most part, these women provided most of this capital themselves. Husbands and other relatives were of secondary importance in paying start-up costs, while banks played an extremely minor role.

One of the major contributions of micro- and small-scale enterprises around the world is employment creation. Collectively, such businesses provide the majority of jobs in nations, even in such economic powers as the United States. During the period of this study, microenterprises were the second major area of income earning for Zimbabwean women, and approximately two-thirds of microbusinesses were owned by women. While the firms in this study provided only a few jobs on average, they did generate some employment and contributed to the development of human capital. How did they accomplish this?

Unlike the other segments of the microenterprise sector examined here, crocheters made a rather unique contribution in this area through the provision of subcontracting. Historically, subcontracting arrangements were not common in sub-Saharan Africa but were more commonplace in East Asia.[28] Thirty of the crocheting firms in this study provided an average of two subcontracting positions per business. These crocheters hired subcontractors particularly when they had to make very large garments, such as tablecloths and bedspreads, and during the peak holiday periods, when demand for these and other goods was especially high. Under subcontracting arrangements, the task of making a large tablecloth might be given to two or three women. Each woman would crochet dozens of squares—possibly of three inches by three inches—which were later stitched together by the entrepreneur to make the tablecloth. Women who crocheted the individual squares were paid on a piecework basis averaging a few cents per square. Crocheters also subcontracted the knitting of sweaters, particularly during the Christmas season, paying each woman the equivalent of about two dollars per sweater. These subcontracting arrangements increased efficiency in the firms, added to the entrepreneur's profits, and increased her social capital. The latter was expanded since businesswomen often subcontracted some or part of their work to other female relatives, neighbors, and friends, women who could be relied on to accept and complete such assignments on relatively short notice. Although these subcontracting positions were temporary and generally low-paying, they did contribute to employment generation, poverty alleviation, and human and social capital formation in these low-income communities.

All of the hairdressers in this study provided paid employment with an average number of four workers per enterprise. Another hairdresser also provided apprenticeship training in her salon. One example of the business acumen of these women is illustrated in the division of labor in their firms. Beauty salons employed women in a number of different specialized positions—as shampooers, braiders, cleaners, receptionists, and bookkeepers. In fact, a number of the employees in these salons were also trained hairdressers with certificates from cosmetology programs.

Seamstresses were less likely than hairdressers to provide employment in their enterprises; 46 percent (eleven) of seamstresses employed workers in their firms, with a median of two employees per enterprise. There is some division of labor in these sewing establishments, although less than one would find in the beauty salons in this study. A few seamstresses did hire tailors, embroiderers, knitters, and sales clerks.

One of the more fascinating aspects of the businesses in this chapter was the extent to which entrepreneurs engaged in innovation in their enterprises. This was perhaps most evident among crocheters, who demonstrated their business acumen, their knowledge of the market, and their creativity through their innovative products and practices, such as adding batiks to the roster of goods for sale. In the mid-1990s, crocheters witnessed an increase in tourist clientele, made up mostly of Europeans, as well as more frequent visitors and merchants coming from South Africa. With the coming of majority rule to South Africa in 1994, overall tourism to the southern African region increased, and these crocheters believed this was just the beginning of a large wave to follow. To attract tourists and others, they made large, brightly colored batiks with designs that appeared uniquely African and in many cases southern African. For example, it was not unusual to see batiks featuring the Zimbabwe bird. These batiks could be used as wall hangings, bedspreads, or tablecloths and to appeal to the tourists, the entrepreneurs hung these on their long clotheslines in their crochet market spaces immediately adjacent to the handmade sweaters, which continued to be in great demand among South Africans.[29] In making and selling these batiks, which contributed to local material culture, the crocheters exhibited not only their understanding of the market, but their creativity and business acumen as well. Knowledge of the market and of the range of handmade goods sold is demonstrated by a crocheter from Harare: "In 1983, making crochet dresses only. Added batiks in 1995; five years ago with money, I added carvings. Sell batiks, jerseys, tops, sets, dresses, carvings, necklaces, woodcarvings. Yes, I also change the patterns and colors."[30]

During this same period, from the mid-1990s, crocheters also began to sell Shona carvings, a unique art form from the region. Although these goods had been sold at crochet markets in the past, they were sold mostly by the male artists. These soapstone carvings became a major attraction for tourists, who admired the carved figures of individuals and families as well as animals from the region. Not only were women increasing their profits by selling these goods, but they also were crossing gender boundaries in engaging in such sales, since this had been the purview of men. Again, their knowledge of the market is revealed in the following: "[I] started with crocheting only, but realized white foreigners wanted more items and so started selling jerseys and other carving items. Now, I sell woodcarving, stone carvings, jerseys, all crochet work, bedspreads, tops, tablecloths."[31]

With respect to hairdressers and seamstresses, the former were more innovative than their counterparts in sewing. About 70 percent of the beauty salon owners had engaged in innovation compared to only 30 percent of the seamstresses. For the vast majority of hairdressers, innovation meant the introduction of new styles and products and an increased variety of goods sold in their salons. Some that began by mainly providing permanent relaxers for their clients then expanded to include various styles of braiding. Braiding became increasingly popular in the country in the 1990s. For those beauty salon owners who had achieved more "middle-class" status in their businesses, their foreign travels also facilitated innovation. Some examples of innovation can be noted in their statements:

> When I went to the UK, I came back with ideas and different chemicals. I concocted some hair treatments, scalp treatments, and braiding styles. When I went to the U.S., I learned more braiding styles and treatments.
>
> I do braiding, perms, relaxers and weaving. Now, I do weaving, tints, and highlights. I introduced new products. Use Revlon Dark and Lovely products now. Used to use only local products.[32]

Although seamstresses' rate of innovation was lower than that of their counterparts in hairdressing, some of them also added new lines of clothing to the repertoire of goods that they made or added new designs, such as embroidery, to their garments: "I have improved with time because I can sew jackets and trousers. When I began, I just used to sew skirts and other small things, but now, I have diversified in line with my experience and growing demand."[33] Seamstresses were apt to discuss the difficulties they experienced due to the nation's austerity and adjustment programs, which restricted the importation of some raw materials, including certain fabrics. They also relied on other imported goods that, though not banned, had greatly increased in cost due to the devaluation of the Zimbabwe dollar.

Another example of the strong dedication that these businesswomen brought to their enterprises is revealed in their use of profits from their firms. The majority of crocheters, hairdressers, and seamstresses reinvested profits in their businesses, with crocheters reporting the smallest percentage that did so—51 percent (compared to over 75 percent for each of the other categories of entrepreneurs). Reinvested profits were used to expand stocks of hair products, fabrics, threads, wool, or cotton as well as to add machines to their enterprises, such as sewing, knitting, and embroidery machines and hair dryers. Crocheters reported that reinvested profits were also used to hire subcontractors, especially during the peak Christmas holiday season.

Since most of these businesswomen, especially those in crocheting, did not draw a set salary from their firm's receipts, they also used profits to meet family obligations. At the top of this list was providing education for their children, particularly during this period of economic crisis and adjustment when many husbands and fathers who faced unemployment (or underemployment) were unable to meet their responsibilities. While entrepreneurs in this study were devoted to all of their children, they especially expressed the need to pay school fees for their daughters, who were more likely during this period of economic crisis to be pulled out of school in favor of their male siblings' education. The participants in this study also indicated their belief in the value of education over the course of their lives; they therefore frequently invested in further schooling and training programs for themselves and their extended family members. As stated by a Bulawayo hairdresser: "I have tried to educate myself in an effort to supplement the O-levels. I am educating myself to improve this business."[34] Their dedication to relatives exceeds their spending on education for themselves since the vast majority of entrepreneurs also give their parents and in-laws regular gifts of money, as well as bring them food and clothing when they visit.

Given their efforts in employment generation, innovation, and the use of profits, these Zimbabwean women entrepreneurs not only maintained their firms during difficult financial times but also contributed to the development of human and social capital, material culture, and local and national development. For many, they have provided a haven in the midst of the economic crisis.

Globalization Zimbabwe Style: Taking a Toll on Business Development and Personal Lives

As stated above, in response to the economic crisis at the end of the postindependence decade, the Zimbabwe state established an economic structural adjustment program (ESAP) in late 1990 and early 1991 at the behest of the International Monetary Fund and the World Bank. This program, which included such conditions as massive devaluation of the currency, reductions in government spending, and trade liberalization, wrought many negative effects that were disproportionately borne by poor and low-income women and children in the nation. ESAP is one facet of globalization in the 1990s, when the international financial institutions (IFIs) and the Northern hegemonic powers attempted to more fully integrate nations such as Zimbabwe into a global capitalist system.

Businesswomen in this study also experienced the impact of ESAP in many ways that substantially affected their enterprises and their personal lives: their customer base declined and their sales shrank, leading to lower or no profits; the devaluation of the currency caused rampant inflation in the cost of raw materials; bans on certain imported raw materials and other goods disrupted supplies; costs of import and business licenses went up; competition increased; and the unemployment rate rose. These factors are clearly related to each other and in broad terms affected all segments of the microenterprise sector investigated here.

While participants indicated above that they earned profits in the operation of their firms, profits did not increase unabated throughout the period of this research. In fact, the unemployment and currency devaluation resulting from ESAP led to smaller numbers of customers in all of these areas, especially since their products and services were not viewed as essential for survival. Many entrepreneurs expressed such concerns:

ESAP is here to make people suffer. Profits in 1992 were Z$600; in 1993, they were Z$200, in 1994, I estimate that they are Z$100.

ESAP affects business—we lose customers because they have no money to come in, because ESAP closes factories. These other people are possibly stranded; this affects business here. If you have a job in the formal sector, you have to look nice—have your hair done. If people are out of work in Bulawayo, they can't afford to do their hair. A person who does their hair is a person who is working.[35]

The devaluation of the currency made the costs of renting space in which to work as well as the cost of raw materials for production significantly higher. Furthermore, given the number of banned goods due to the austerity program, both the process and the cost of obtaining import licenses for such inputs was beyond the reach of many women in this study. These issues caused by globalization had a major negative impact on the financial health of these firms:

> Because of all the bans on imports, then what is happening is that there are magazines available for new products, which you want to introduce and become the most popular. It is a problem because you can't get these products and it is very frustrating. I have considered going into manufacturing of hair products, but premises would be a problem and I would have to be a hairdresser full-time.[36]

With the imposition of ESAP and the retrenchment of tens of thousands of workers from the national government, the Zimbabwean state encouraged the establishment of small businesses and microenterprises as a means of stemming the tide of poverty. In this regard, more women and men started enterprises—in markets and along the downtown streets. Crocheters, hairdressers, and seamstresses experienced significant increases in competition as more and more women began these types of businesses in Harare and Bulawayo:

> Things are too expensive, so too many people are crocheting to sell the same goods, like doilies. There is something wrong. Everything is going up. My husband earns little money, people don't have much money.
>   There is a lot of competition, especially from establishments that can afford to charge lower prices for garments. This means that those who place orders for resale from the Republic of South Africa will flock there to buy at lower prices. I have no embroidery machine and therefore must go and get this done at an extra charge. This machine is about Z$25,000.[37]

Not only did ESAP lead to major increases in unemployment throughout the nation as the state retrenched forty-thousand-plus workers, its other conditions caused ripple effects of unemployment. Unemployment in these businesswomen's families created its own share of problems. As previously stated, participants in this study had to substantially increase their contributions to maintaining their households and families, particularly in the areas of providing food, clothing, and the payment of school fees. Entrepreneurs in this study, though, were adamant that state officials bore responsibility for ESAP. The words of a combined seamstress and hairdresser sum up the feelings expressed by many in this research:

> Under ESAP, retrenchment resulted in loss of customers. With hairdressing as a luxury business, no one can make themselves attractive while the stomach growls with hunger. ESAP has destroyed so many families; some of my

relatives are out of work, and people have lost property due to inability to pay the increase in rates. They tell us that it will end next year, but who knows. I see the government as being responsible for ESAP. They have cheated us. Ministers live rent-free with healthy allowances and they backdated a 54 percent pay hike by seven months. They live well, and the rest of us suffer.[38]

The Economic and Political Crisis and the Microenterprise Sector since 1999: The Role of Cross-Border Trade

My larger project on the impact of globalization on women entrepreneurs in the Zimbabwean microenterprise sector ended in 1999, a year that witnessed the beginning of the political crisis in that nation. Over the next few years, the Mugabe administration experienced the greatest challenges of its political life—a constitutional crisis, significant global criticism over the seizure of white-owned farms, "corrupt elections" at every level, as well as the growing HIV/AIDS pandemic. Hyperinflation became the buzzword to describe the Zimbabwean economy, which had an inflation rate of over 100 million percent in late 2008.[39] Massive food shortages accompanied Zimbabwe's ever-increasing unemployment situation in the new millennium, and in the past two years cholera reared its ugly head.

Despite these devastating social, political, and economic conditions, the microenterprise sector actually grew during this period. More and more traders sold a variety of goods along the city streets with men increasingly joining the ranks of women who were previously dominant in this sector.

One of the major coping strategies of businesswomen in this sector, which enabled them to keep their families and enterprises afloat, at least to some extent, was cross-border trade. Cross-border trade between Zimbabwe and South Africa was already prominent during the period of my research.[40] Over the past decade, however, cross-border trade with South Africa and Zambia as well as other southern African countries has multiplied many times over. What used to be primarily an activity engaged in by crocheters transporting their doilies, tablecloths, sweaters, and other items to Johannesburg for sale and buying such goods as computer software to sell back home in Harare has now become an activity that supplies supermarkets, hotels, and even boarding schools.

Moreover, these cross-border traders have recently formed an organization called the Zimbabwe Cross-Border Traders Association (ZCBTA), which boasts over fifteen thousand members.[41] The ZCBTA is linked to the Southern African People's Solidarity Network (SAPSN), which promotes grassroots participation in development. As feminist political economy indicates, Zimbabwean women in this organization are again demonstrating their agency both in their country and transnationally. They are currently lobbying sub-Saharan African governments and the Southern African Development Community (SADC) to ease border restrictions and create a regional passport that will facilitate their activities as cross-border traders. In turn, such action would recognize Zimbabwean women's efforts as entrepreneurs in the microenterprise sector and strengthen meaningful southern African economic cooperation.

Conclusion

Using a feminist political economy perspective, this chapter illustrates that despite the harsh toll that globalization, especially in the form of the economic structural adjustment program, enacted on businesswomen in urban Zimbabwe in the 1990s, they were able to maintain their firms and make vital contributions to employment generation, the creation of material culture, and local and national development. They made these contributions in the midst of a severe economic crisis (later accompanied by a political crisis) that led to declining sales, increased competition, shortages of raw materials for production, and personal sacrifice. Their strong business acumen, creativity, and determination to improve their lives and those of their families enabled (and continues to enable) them to move beyond simple survival in maintaining their enterprises and to engage in cross-border trade. These female entrepreneurs are the true, unsung heroines of Zimbabwe!

Notes

1. Although the current phase of globalization contains many aspects, in this chapter the use of the term "globalization" mainly refers to its economic aspect—the creation of a world system that strives for the integration of national economies under the auspices of the free market into one unified system. The integration of nations into this system occurs through production, trade, and financial channels. See Mary J. Osirim, *Enterprising Women in Urban Zimbabwe: Gender, Microbusiness, and Globalization* (Washington, DC, and Bloomington: Woodrow Wilson Center Press and Indiana University Press, 2009).

2. Esther Ngan-ling Chow, "Gender Matters: Studying Globalization and Social Change in the 21st Century," *International Sociology* 18, no. 3 (2003): 443–60; Valentine Moghadam, "Gender and Globalization: Female Labor and Women's Mobilization," *Occasional Papers No. 11* (Normal: Illinois State University, Women's Studies Program, 2000); Christopher Chase-Dunn, *Global Formation: Structures of the World Economy* (Lanham, MD: Rowman & Littlefield, 1998); Saskia Sassen, *Globalization and Its Discontents* (London: New Press, 1998).

3. Moghadam, "Gender and Globalization."

4. Evelyn Hu-Dehart, "Surviving Globalization: Immigrant Women Workers in Late Capitalist America," in *Women's Labor in the Global Economy: Speaking in Multiple*

Voices, ed. Sharon Harley (New Brunswick, NJ: Rutgers University Press, 2007); Mary Zimmerman, Jacquelyn Litt, and Christine Bose, eds., *Global Dimensions of Gender and Care Work* (Stanford: Stanford University Press, 2006); Rhacel Parrenas, *Servants of Globalization: Women, Migration, and Domestic Work* (Stanford: Stanford University Press, 2001).

5. Gracia Clark, ed., *Onions Are My Husband: Survival and Accumulation by West African Market Women* (Chicago: University of Chicago Press, 1994); Nancy Horn, *Cultivating Customers: Market Women in Harare, Zimbabwe* (Boulder, CO: Lynne Rienner, 1994); Bessie House-Midamba and Felix Ekechi, eds., *African Market Women and Economic Power: The Role of Women in African Economic Development* (Westport, CT: Greenwood Press, 1995); Claire Robertson, *Trouble Showed the Way: Women, Men, and Trade in the Nairobi Area, 1890–1990* (Bloomington: Indiana University Press, 1997).

6. Microenterprises in this chapter are defined as businesses that employ no more than five workers; some of the activities in this study contain only one person as owner-operator. Akosua Darkwah, "Trading Goes Global: Ghanaian Market Women in an Era of Globalization," in *Global Gender Research: Transnational Perspectives*, ed. Christine Bose and Minjeong Kim (New York: Routledge, 2009); Kaendi Munguti, Edith Kabui, and Mabel Isoilo, "The Implications of Economic Reform on Gender Relations: The Case of Poor Households in Kisumu Slums," in *Gender, Economic Integration, Governance, and Methods of Contraceptives*, ed. Aicha Tamboura Diawara (Dakar: AAWORD Book Series, 2002); Zine Magubane, "Globalization and the South African Women: A Historical Overview," in *Visions of Gender Theories and Social Development in Africa: Harnessing Knowledge for Social Justice and Equality* (Dakar: AAWORD Book Series, 2001); Mohau Pheko, "Privatization, Trade Liberalization and Women's Socio-Economic Rights: Exploring Policy Alternatives," in *Africa: Gender, Globalization, and Resistance*, ed. Yassine Fall (Dakar: AAWORD Book Series, 1999).

7. Valentine Moghadam, *Globalizing Women: Transnational Feminist Networks* (Baltimore: Johns Hopkins University Press, 2005); Esther Chow, ed., *Transforming Gender and Development in East Asia* (New York: Routledge, 2002).

8. Osirim, *Enterprising Women in Urban Zimbabwe*, 22–25.

9. For feminist scholarship in the United States, see Margaret Andersen and Patricia Hill Collins, eds., *Race, Class, and Gender: An Anthology* (Belmont, CA: Wadsworth Publishing, 1992); and Elizabeth Higginbotham and Lynn Cannon, *Rethinking Mobility: Towards a Race and Gender Inclusive Theory* (Memphis, TN: Center for Research on Women, 1988). For African scholarship, see Desiree Lewis, "Review Essay: African Feminist Studies, 1980–2002," *Gender and Women's Studies Africa* (2002), http://www.gwsafrica.org/knowledge/africa%20review/history.html.

10. Amina Mama, *Women's Studies and Studies of Women in Africa during the 1990s*, Working Paper Series (Dakar: CODESRIA, 1996); Patricia McFadden, *Patriarchy: Political Power, Sexuality, and Globalization* (Port Louis, Mauritius: Ledikasyon Pu Travayer, 2001); Charmaine Pereira, "Configuring 'Global,' 'National,' and 'Local,' in Governance Agendas in Nigeria," *Social Research* 69, no. 3 (2003): 781–804.

11. Terisa E. Turner, "The Land is Dead: Women's Rights and Human Rights: The Case of the Ogbodo Shell Petroleum Spill in Rivers State, Nigeria, June–July 2001," July 2001, http://www.uoguelph.ca/~terisatu/ogbodospill.pdf.

12. Robert Blauner, *Racial Oppression in America* (New York: Harper and Row, 1972); Edna Bonacich, "Class Approaches to Ethnicity and Race," in *Majority and*

Minority: The Dynamics of Race and Ethnicity in American Life, ed. Norman Yetman (Boston: Allyn and Bacon, 1991); Ian Phimister, *An Economic and Social History of Zimbabwe, 1890–1948* (London: Longman, 1988).

13. Christine Sylvester, *Zimbabwe: The Terrain of Contradictory Development* (Boulder, CO: Westview, 1991), 35; Osirim, *Enterprising Women in Urban Zimbabwe*, 33.

14. Horn, *Cultivating Customers*; Mary J. Osirim, "Carrying the Burdens of Adjustment and Globalization: Women and Microenterprise Development in Urban Zimbabwe," *International Sociology* 18, no. 3 (2003): 535–58; Osirim, *Enterprising Women in Urban Zimbabwe*, 33–34 .

15. Elizabeth Schmidt, *Peasants, Traders, and Wives: Shona Women in the History of Zimbabwe, 1870–1939* (Portsmouth, NH: Heinemann, 1992).

16. Carol Summers, "Native Policy, Education, and Development: Social Ideologies and Social Control in Southern Rhodesia, 1890–1934" (PhD diss., Johns Hopkins University, 1991); Schmidt, *Peasants, Traders, and Wives*, 122–54.

17. Ian Phimister and Charles van Onselen, "The Labour Movement in Zimbabwe: 1900–1945," in *Keep on Knocking: A History of the Labour Movement in Zimbabwe, 1900–1997*, ed. Brian Raftopoulos and Ian Phimister (Harare: Baobab Books, 1997), 45–48.

18. The Shona and Ndebele populations are the largest black ethnic populations in the nation, comprising about 80 percent and 18 percent of the population, respectively.

19. Zimbabwe Ministry of Community and Cooperative Development and Women's Affairs (MCCDWA), *Policy Statement* (Harare, 1981); Mary J. Osirim, "Women, Work, and Public Policy: Structural Adjustment and the Informal Sector in Zimbabwe," in *Population Growth and Environmental Degradation in Southern Africa*, ed. Ezekiel Kalipeni (Boulder, CO: Lynne Rienner, 1994), 61–84; Osirim, *Enterprising Women in Urban Zimbabwe*, 43–44.

20. MCCDWA, *Policy Statement*.

21. Patricia Made and Myorovai Whande, "Women in Southern Africa: A Note on the Zimbabwe Success Story," *Issues: A Journal of Opinion* 17, no. 2 (1989): 26–28.

22. Andrew Meldrum, "Mugabe's Maneuvers," *Africa Report* (May–June 1989): 38–41.

23. Godfrey Kanyenze, "The Performance of the Zimbabwean Economy, 1980–2000," in *Twenty Years of Independence in Zimbabwe*, ed. Staffan Darnolf and Liisa Laakso (New York: Palgrave Macmillan, 2003), 34–77; Osirim, *Enterprising Women in Urban Zimbabwe*.

24. Rudo Gaidzanwa, "Gender Analysis in the Field of Education," in *Engendering African Social Sciences*, ed. Ayesha Imam, Amina Mama, and Fatou Sow (Dakar: CODESRIA Book Series, 1997); N'dri Assie-Lumumba, "Educating Africa's Girls and Women: A Conceptual and Historical Analysis of Gender Inequality," in *Engendering African Social Sciences*, ed. Imam, Mama, and Sow; Marjorie Mbilinyi, "Searching for Utopia: The Politics of Gender and Education in Tanzania," in *Women and Education in Sub-Saharan Africa: Power, Opportunities, and Constraints*, ed. Marianne Bloch, Josephine Beoku-Betts, and B. Robert Tabachnick (Boulder, CO: Lynne Rienner, 1998); Joy Kwesiga, *Women's Access to Higher Education in Africa: Uganda's Experience* (Kampala: Fountain, 2002).

25. UNICEF, *The Progress of Nations* (New York, 1993); Richard Kamidza, "Structural Adjustment without a Human Face," *Southern Africa: Political and Economic Monthly* 7, no. 6 (1994): 11–12.

26. Advanced undergraduate students in the social sciences from Bryn Mawr College and graduate students from the University of Zimbabwe worked with me as research assistants on this project.

27. In her study on the division of labor among women and men in US families, *The Second Shift: Working Parents and the Revolution at Home* (New York: Viking Penguin, 1989), Arlie Hochschild discussed how women most often bear the major responsibilities for chores that have to be done on a daily basis compared to men, who have greater flexibility in completing their household tasks that do not require daily attention.

28. Alejandro Portes, Manuel Castells, and Lauren Benton, eds., *The Informal Economy: Studies in Advanced and Less Developed Societies* (Baltimore: Johns Hopkins University Press, 1989).

29. Handmade sweaters and other goods were a much rarer find in South Africa. Most of the sweaters were machine-made, especially those found in the department stores, and were far more expensive than those made in Zimbabwe.

30. Interview with Kisyedza, a crocheter, Harare, 1997.

31. Interview with Maud, a crocheter, Harare, 1997.

32. Interview with Deena, a hairdresser, Harare, 1991; interview with Rite, a hairdresser, Bulawayo, 1991

33. Interview with Tsitsi, a seamstress, Harare, 1997.

34. Interview with Irish Best, a hairdresser, Bulawayo, 1997.

35. Interview with Sibusiso, a crocheter, Bulawayo, 1994; interview with Susan, a hairdresser, Bulawayo, 1997.

36. Interview with Deena, a hairdresser, Harare, 1991.

37. Interview with Priscilla, a crocheter, Bulawayo, 1994; interview with Tenda, a seamstress, Harare, 1994.

38. Interview with Miriam, a seamstress and hairdresser, Bulawayo, 1994.

39. The more recent economic crisis is discussed in my book, *Enterprising Women in Urban Zimbabwe: Gender, Microbusiness, and Globalization*, xiii–xv, 221–28.

40. This cross-border trade is well documented in my book *Enterprising Women in Urban Zimbabwe*, 195–98.

41. Tonderai Kwidini, "Zimbabwe's Women Traders Keep Economy Afloat," April 14, 2009, http://www.huffingtonpost.com/2009/03/05/zimbabwes-women-traders-k_n_172169.html.

9

Sustainable Strategies in a Postconflict Environment

Fostering Local Entrepreneurship in Côte d'Ivoire

Ulf Richter

Introduction

Private-sector logic and dynamics could become the single largest contribution to the accomplishment of the Millennium Development Goals in Africa by 2015. Market-based solutions for poverty alleviation have attracted much positive attention and have been received both among academics and practitioners, paralleling the success of the systematic adoption of microfinance around the world.[1] Moreover, a favorable business climate can be considered both a comparative advantage and a key public good in emerging markets.[2] Following these arguments, development and human rights organizations have become increasingly receptive to the concept of private-sector strategies to improve the lives of the poor. However, it is of crucial importance that the creation, implementation, and functioning of private-sector strategies are pro-poor, and do not resemble a new form of colonialism—a common critique—that only advantageously serves foreign multinational companies (or large foreign multinationals). Often, doing business at the "bottom of the pyramid" may threaten local culture and independence while providing nowhere near the economic or societal advantages that some suggest.[3]

In this chapter, I argue that a much more powerful angle to alleviate poverty might be, instead of concentrating on large foreign multinational corporations, to foster local entrepreneurial activity to allow for the emergence of inclusive, pro-poor markets, and indeed promote local cultures and local autonomy for sustained change. The importance of locally based entrepreneurial activities and initiatives is highlighted by Gracia Clark in chapter 7 of this volume and by Mary J. Osirim in chapter 8. While expanding the discussion on this major theme, I examine the general potential and impact of triggering entrepreneurial activity, as well as financial, operational, and management constraints on entrepreneurship in Côte d'Ivoire. This chapter concentrates on the following major research questions: what is the potential of professional, interactive e-commerce for local artisanal products from West Africa to create economic opportunities, foster entrepreneurship, and help alleviate poverty? and what are the major constraints that must be overcome? For this chapter, it is assumed that social transformation can be achieved through various axes: empowering the local population by creating economic opportunities, promoting local artisanal work and African culture in general, knowledge transfer, improving business and technological skills, and integrating African entrepreneurs into the global economy. Tools for social impact assessment are presented and analyzed. I conclude that if such challenges to conducting business in Côte d'Ivoire as political instability and ubiquitous corruption can be overcome, an inclusive e-commerce may have high potential for creating substantial economic opportunities and initiating social transformation by connecting African artists to the global economy.

I identify common impediments to establishing business in the Ivorian environment, integrating insights from active research on ICT dissemination for creating economic opportunities and fostering entrepreneurship at the International University of Grand Bassam (IUGB) in Côte d'Ivoire. Thereby, I aim to synthesize the frameworks of corporate social responsibility (CSR) and social entrepreneurship in a developing country context. Data were collected through a one-year action research project at IUGB. I, along with other researchers, was highly involved in interacting with artisans and meeting with representatives of local cooperatives, community officials, and vendors of artisanal products. Besides participating in more than a hundred meetings, we also promoted artisanal products around the world, in particular in western Europe, to assess their market potential and possible ways to improve their quality. In order to maintain a certain degree of researcher neutrality, we regularly sat down and discussed our experiences, observations, and concerns. I also continuously wrote down summaries of our research activities and cross-checked the results with external experts. Finally, I collected secondary data from local archives, community officials, local nongovernmental organizations, and corporate and governmental websites.

The Research Setting

Côte d'Ivoire

Today, Côte d'Ivoire is a postconflict environment (while technically still in civil war) with substantial unemployment (often reaching 40–50 percent), widespread poverty, a large informal sector, an alarming HIV/AIDS rate, high malaria risk, substantial pollution, high corruption, low trust in governmental institutions, large immigration and strong social tensions.[4] Negative reporting on the impediments of African corruption and incompetence are commonplace. Côte d'Ivoire ranks 151st out of 193 countries in the 2008 corruption index of Transparency International. Daily small-scale corruption is being accompanied by accusations of large-scale corruption in the public as well as private sectors.[5] Recently, chief executives in the Ivorian cocoa industry were detained on corruption charges for the defalcation of over $224 million that had been allocated for the purchase of a chocolate factory in the United States. A particularly problematic form of corruption is racketeering, which according to a World Bank study cost Côte d'Ivoire between $230 million and $363.3 million in 2008.[6] Further serious impediments include environmental and conflict-related issues, poverty, labor conditions, and the state of public health.[7]

Grand Bassam

Grand Bassam is a small city with about seventy thousand inhabitants, covering about 11,300 hectares and located about thirty kilometers east of Abidjan, Côte d'Ivoire's main city with four million people and West Africa's major port. Grand Bassam was the first French colonial capital from 1893 to 1900 and remained a key seaport until the growth of Abidjan beginning in the 1930s. With its beautiful setting, fifteen kilometers of fine (but polluted) sand beach and surrounding Ébrié lagoon, it remains a key destination for local tourism and an active artisanal center. Grand Bassam's facilities include a number of two- to four-star hotels (local standard) with more than nine hundred rooms, swimming pools, and conference rooms; a number of restaurants for European and local cuisine; four local and international banks and money transfer agencies; a hospital; primary and high schools; an outdated electricity grid; and a broken wastewater network; a limited number of telecommunication companies and cyber cafés; and a police station. Grand Bassam is also known for its artisanal village that is located two kilometers from the entrance to the town on the main road to Abidjan. There are about two hundred stands that display artisanal products made of wood, bronze, ivory, silver, or gold, including masks, statues, furniture, batik cloth, paintings and jewelry, that represent the diversity and richness of West African tribal culture. Local cultural highlights include the "Fokwe," a warrior dance in the Abouré village, and "Abissa," a one-week street carnival of the N'zima people, including a royal ceremony by the local king and a street art and international cartoon festival.[8]

Current Problems

Despite its rich heritage and culture, Grand Bassam is in decline. This historical gem of the "Quartier France," which contains many historical buildings from colonial times, is in severe decay. Almost all the colonial buildings are in ruins and will soon rot away. The reasons for this deterioration include low budgets for regional development, little expertise on how to access programs sponsored by multilateral institutions, and an absence of synergy between initiatives of the government, cities, and the private sector.[9] To reverse the decay, on November 26, 2006, Grand Bassam submitted its application for classification as a UNESCO World Heritage Site. Even though the history of the site, as Côte d'Ivoire's first capital, certainly helps its candidacy, the decision is still pending since many historic buildings have been changed by their inhabitants and would need a major investment to return them to their original state.

Local culture is weakening and gradually vanishing. The quality of artisanal products has worsened substantially. Wealthy foreign tourists have virtually disappeared while local customers are few and pay less. Moreover, young artisans are not educated anymore in the cultural significance and the specificities of the products that they produce. In addition, the local celebrations such as Abissa are gradually losing their traditional historical and spiritual context. The general problem encountered is often described as "a psychology of poverty," a lack of understanding of the importance of preserving local, national, and regional (West African) heritage, or the complete disregard of it.[10] This is worsened by the lack of engagement by government institutions with the local (ethnic) people to understand their specific needs and wants. A number of recent initiatives and projects, however, provide hope that the situation might improve in the near future.

Signs of Hope

The International University of Grand Bassam

IUGB strives to be a regional center of excellence that will help educate and train the human capital required for sustained growth and development in West Africa. IUGB prepares its graduates to participate and to assume leadership roles both nationally and globally. Its mission is "to provide internationally recognized higher education through technology-enhanced English medium instruction in fields critical to regional development, international success and life-long learning."[11] IUGB follows a pragmatic approach and aims to serve the needs of the local labor market. IUGB opened in January

2005 and was formally established as an accredited institution of higher education by Presidential Decree 2007-477 of May 16, 2007. In the fall semester of 2009, IUGB had 136 students, up from about 120 students in the previous year. A partnership for technical assistance with Georgia State University was signed in early 2009 and the first IUGB student graduated from GSU in June 2009.[12]

The School of Business, International Relations, and Economic Policy (BIREP) at IUGB, aims to establish a comprehensive entrepreneurship center to trigger entrepreneurial activity in West Africa by offering pertinent know-how, tools, and networking activities for active and nascent entrepreneurs. The goals of the entrepreneurship center are to establish a comprehensive entrepreneurship program, a regular regional business plan competition, and an incubator for small and medium-sized enterprises as well as to offer advice and consulting services. The entrepreneurship program will consist of a major in entrepreneurship at the undergraduate level, certificate programs in entrepreneurship, executive and professional training programs, and a graduate program in entrepreneurship. Special attention will be paid to the potential of the following sectors: information and communications technologies, biotechnology, agribusiness, and renewable energy. A key concern will be to support female entrepreneurship. In addition, the relevance of corporate entrepreneurship and entrepreneurial activity within organizations will be explored. Aiming for regional excellence, the IUGB entrepreneurship program will be specifically tailored to the West African business environment, taking into account local needs and challenges such as the importance of small and medium-sized enterprises (SMEs) and the informal sector. The strategic plan for the BIREP entrepreneurship center at IUGB is currently being developed. Implementation is envisioned to start by the end of 2011 due to the ongoing postelectoral crisis.[13]

Free Trade Zone and VITIB

A free trade zone, the Mahatma Gandhi VITIB (Village des Technologies de l'Information et de la Communication et des Biotechnologies) was created as a public company on November 30, 2006, with a number of national and international partners. The Ivorian government holds a minority interest in VITIB. Other partners include eighteen companies from Côte d'Ivoire, four from India, three from China, and one each from the United Arab Emirates and South Africa. The mission of VITIB is to construct the technological infrastructure necessary for the commercial exploitation of the ZBTIC (Zone franche des Biotechnologies et des Technologies de l'Information et Communication)—a free trade zone created by the Ivorian government within the territory of Grand Bassam. VITIB aims to turn the free trade zone into a center for information and communications technology for both local and multinational companies. It is searching for companies that want to use its facilities for production and other industrial activities, R&D, "offshore" financial services, and training and capacity development at the VITIB Academy. While hailed in the beginning, VITIB has not been able to take off as envisioned at its founding due to the general political and internal struggles that hampered decision-making. However, as of 2010 there are a number of companies operating in the VITIB. For instance, the South African telecommunications company MTN is currently setting up a new data center to be operated from VITIB.

Kachile

Kachile is a social venture dedicated to alleviating poverty and raising environmental consciousness in West Africa. It aims to create opportunities in the digital economy through the targeted application of information and communication technology (ICT). Kachile regards itself as a hub for entrepreneurs and change agents who drive social innovation and transformation in fields such as education, health, ecology, and enterprise development. A focal element of Kachile is its multistage approach to building lasting and sustainable business solutions through knowledge transfer and empowerment in ICT and entrepreneurial learning centers. This will be achieved through three major axes: (1) setting up of IT infrastructure, technological support, and necessary ICT instruction; (2) business coaching and incubation for local SMEs, focusing on female entrepreneurs; and (3) introduction and application of advanced mobile phone technologies. The name *Kachile* stems from the local language, Baoulé, and means "change." Gradual and lasting social transformation is expected to come through a number of projects. Current projects include: kachile.com, an e-commerce website for local artists in postconflict Côte d'Ivoire; ICT learning courses to serve as educational hubs for local entrepreneurs; research on mobile technology for microfinance to provide access to capital; and the analysis of "green" ICT business solutions for foreign direct investment (FDI) that will help to redress West Africa's environmental problems. Typically, in a developing country context, the ratio of problem-focused information to solution-focused information is strongly imbalanced.[14] Kachile aims to move beyond these common identifiable struggles in order to substantially help the poor. Thereby, Kachile will direct ICT dissemination toward development goals by fostering entrepreneurship, spurring endogenous growth, reversing a psychology of poverty, and ensuring that these changes last. Moreover, Kachile strives to address the imbalance between problem-focused versus solution-focused information by providing the insights and knowledge required to properly assess risks and recognize opportunities in francophone West Africa.

Kachile was founded in January 2009 and is mainly operating in Côte d'Ivoire. Since its inception a number of milestones have been achieved. First, an initial placeholder website has been programmed. The site is estimated to be operational for beta testing e-commerce by the end of July 2011. Kachile has assembled an international and local team of students, academics, international IT and development experts, and business professionals. Local stakeholders such as the International University of Grand Bassam, the mayor of Grand Bassam, and the president's office have been engaged to provide support. Kachile has also initiated negotiations with distinguished international and local potential partners such as the World Bank and VITIB. A first partnership with the Fondation TAPA (which represents a large number of Ivorian artists) on joint projects to promote Ivorian artists was struck in June 2009. Both a local company to operate the e-commerce site and a foundation in Switzerland have been established to provide the legal frameworks for its operations.

Kachile.com: E-Commerce for Artisanal Products

Kachile.com is envisioned as an e-commerce site for traditional ethnic and contemporary art and artisanal products from West Africa. The central problem that kachile.com addresses is the current lack of direct access for local African artists to global markets and the lack of promotion of African culture to mainstream consumers in Europe or the United States. High-quality artisanal products from West Africa are being sold at enormous price differentials between what the local artist is paid and what the consumer in Europe or the United States pays; a product may sell for up to ten times its original value. Products are mostly brought to the European and American markets either by individuals, chiefly diasporic Africans, or by merchants who fill whole containers with products and ship them to Europe or North America to retail in smaller shops. The solution: Kachile will provide a data-rich, transparent online platform providing access to potential customers around the world, using the latest Web 2.0 technologies. An Internet-based business allows direct connections between consumers, small shops, art galleries, and other potential customers such as banks or corporations to the supplier operating on the ground. This will allow for higher profit margins for local artists and lower prices for European and US customers. Income generated will partially be repatriated to support local artists. The site will operate as a social enterprise. Consumers will be able to access biographies, stories, and videos of the artists. The artists will be able to access global markets through the e-commerce platform. Kachile.com will generate income through online sales of artisanal products.

Initially, kachile.com will sell artisanal products from West Africa. It will start sourcing its products from the artisanal village of Grand Bassam, one of the major centers for Ivorian artisanal products. Côte d'Ivoire, despite its current temporary social tensions, remains the economic engine of West Africa, accounting for about 40 percent of its GDP. Products include objects of African art such as masks, ceramics, local clothing fashions, fabric, musical instruments, figurines and statues, furniture, and jewelry. The target markets consist of West African corporations and philanthropists that are interested in promoting local African culture and, in Europe and the United States, middle-class consumers, wholesalers, and art galleries that are interested in African or, more generally, ethnic products. Kachile aims to organize (a) fashion shows with models wearing African-style fashion and jewelry; (b) African product-distribution parties where African culture is presented in a private setting hosted by individuals, ideally with African roots, and with an ambiance set through African music, movies, and presentations; (c) expositions of African paintings in art galleries as well as in restaurants, banks, schools and universities, and retail shops, ideally on a no-fee basis; and (d) product fairs for Kachile products located in city markets, administrative buildings, banks, corporate headquarters, and shopping centers. Finally, Kachile aims to use Web 2.0 tools for online marketing such as through Facebook, Google AdSense, Twitter, or social bookmarking.

Kachile.com aims to create a substantial social impact through its operations, beginning first in Grand Bassam. In the city alone there are about one thousand artists working to support their families and relatives, equating to a total potential impact of five to ten thousand people. Lifting their living standards is a major immediate goal. At a later stage, Kachile aims to replicate its model across West Africa.

The Kachile Foundation

The Kachile Foundation plans to initially set up well-equipped ICT learning centers that will provide instruction and serve as cyber cafés in major cities in West Africa. They will be operated as for-profit businesses half of the time and used as classrooms for teaching computer and business skills the other half. The courses to be taught are envisioned to offer varied levels of difficulty in adapting both to different age groups and education levels and to business training requirements and individual needs. A pilot is planned in local schools, some of which have up to six thousand students. The foundation will then expand its activities to the rest of Côte d'Ivoire, in particular to the areas that have been affected by conflict. Kachile plans to serve as an incubator for the small businesses that it hopes will be one outcome of its entrepreneurship courses and venture plan competitions, with seed funding provided to help nascent entrepreneurs to succeed. Kachile will take an equity position in those businesses generated out of its activities, and the sales of Kachile's stakes in those ventures could become a main source of income in the mid term. Alternatively, cooperation with established partners such as VITIB might help to overcome the initial operational obstacles and infrastructural challenges.

The Kachile Foundation will mainly target the young adult population, ages eighteen to thirty, with attention to the requirements of the politically unstable environment in Côte d'Ivoire. The country, which underwent a violent internal conflict from 2002 to 2004, was effectively cut into a northern and a southern half. The dire situation continues despite a peace treaty signed by the opposing parties and the promise of elections. Not only is unemployment higher than average in this age group, but also the adoption of and adaptability to new information and communications technologies is assumed to be higher than in the older population. The foundation also aims to be able to provide new skills to ex-combatants who are looking to reintegrate into Ivorian society. Special courses will be provided to female entrepreneurs to create an enabling learning environment. Ultimately, Kachile aims to empower the local (in particular female) population by creating economic opportunities, improving knowledge transfer and business and technological skills, and integrating African entrepreneurs into the global economy.

The Kachile Foundation will generate income through four means: (1) revenues generated by tuition for entrepreneurship courses and fees for Internet usage in ICT learning centers, (2) microfinance and successful investment in SMEs, (3) repatriation of funds from kachile.com, and (4) donations, grants, sponsorships, and partnerships. To be successful in the long run Kachile aims to partner with a number of different entities, among them local cooperatives, universities, development organizations and UN agencies, and corporations active in West Africa. Through teaching computer and basic business skills, Kachile hopes to direct microenterprise creation toward social and environmental goals, including but not limited to creating jobs for young adults, in particular women; improving access to essential medicines; and fostering entrepreneurial ventures that focus on waste management and renewable energy.

Preliminary Results and Observations

Our preliminary analysis demonstrates that the greatest hurdles faced in Côte d'Ivoire are political instability, ubiquitous corruption, lack of a trained workforce and access to capital—not necessarily in that order. Entrepreneurial thinking and activity is, by nature and definition, risky and involves strategic thinking. Nevertheless, given persistent high levels of unemployment and little foreign direct investment, entrepreneurship is an essential force for job creation and economic development in Africa.

Financial Constraints

Access to capital for ordinary citizens is difficult since large parts of the population do not qualify for a regular bank account because they either do not have the minimum amount required for an initial deposit or receive a regular income too low according to local bank standards. Even small investments are very often delayed or made impossible since most microfinance institutions operating in Côte d'Ivoire broke down with the start of the hostilities in 2002. On the other hand, Western Union (WU) is expanding rapidly due to the transfers from the rapidly increasing Ivorian diaspora, in particular from France. Also WU's competitor MoneyGram is entering the market on a big scale.

Management and Operational Constraints

The first lessons from the Kachile project indicate that when attempting to strengthen capabilities at the grassroots level, it is easy to initially overestimate local skills. When seeking local stakeholders a high degree of supervision and mentoring is required. In order to preserve the sense of ownership and pride, and in light of our pilot research, we recommend locating the strongest, most capable person in the social group to act as mentor to his or her peers, rather than advocate structures based on authority. Only by initially adapting to, and gradually changing, local conditions will it be possible to implement long-lasting entrepreneurial programs that are viable in the nation's postconflict climate. Moreover, a number of operational problems relating to the operation of e-commerce in Côte d'Ivoire have arisen that are specific to this environment: For instance, PayPal does not operate in Côte d'Ivoire; any attempt to access a PayPal account from Côte d'Ivoire is blocked, because the user is detected as a potential criminal (fraud). Also certain software companies do not allow the activation of their software in Côte d'Ivoire due to the fear of copyright infringement. Also, logistics remains a challenge, since Côte d'Ivoire is considered a remote country with low shipping volumes (notwithstanding its important harbor at Port Bouet), leading to high transportation costs when working with established international shippers such as DHL or UPS.

Cultural Constraints

The pace of business in West Africa is slowed by kinship ties and the tendency of employers to hire within circles of family and friends. Rather than prescribe an overhaul of these culturally deep-seated business traits, incremental reforms such as on-site evaluation and assessment of employees and colleagues could be implemented to overcome stagnation and raise productivity.

Tools for Social Impact Assessment

Kachile is experimenting with the tools that might help in assessing the impact of the above-described initiatives. These tools focus on social return on investment and make use of analytical tools developed by the nongovernmental organizations and UN agencies.

Social Return on Investment

STV Consulting is a firm offering services in the area of project and strategic management, policy formulation, training and mentoring, and general management. The company proposes to go through a four-step methodology to calculate the social return on investment (SROI) that will allow Ivorians to improve the ratio between money invested and the creation of social impacts.[15] The first step is to quantify the nonfinancial impact per unit. Second, proxy data or actual evidence is used to calculate what is the real, unique outcome. The third step that STV Consulting proposes is to translate social impact into dollars per unit to achieve "social cash flows." Finally, for SROI, the different "social cash flows" are totaled, then discounted to provide value, and divided by investment to date. For these calculations, four levels of value creation must be distinguished in relation to quantifiability: (1) easy—for example, cost savings, capital assets, profit-sharing, emission reductions, investment returns, or goodwill; (2) relatively easy—for example, insurance, liability costs, investment projections, landfill use, healthcare costs, addiction treatment costs, potential earnings, employment rates, or welfare expenditures; (3) relatively hard—for example, health, physical safety, biodiversity, clean air, safe water, green space, mobility, availability of electricity, or political stability; and (4) hard—for example, self-sufficiency, quality of life, dignity, life, or privacy.

Variety of Assessment Tools

UNEP analyzes a number of social impact assessment tools and methods based on World Bank materials.[16] It distinguishes between analytical tools (e.g., stakeholder analysis, gender analysis, secondary data review), community-based tools (e.g., participatory rural appraisal), consultation methods (e.g., beneficiary assessment), observation and interview tools (e.g., participant observation, focus groups, semistructured interviews, village meetings), participatory methods (e.g., role playing, wealth ranking, access to resources, analysis of tasks, mapping, needs assessments, pocket charts, tree diagrams), and workshop-based methods (e.g., objectives-oriented project planning).

Challenges and Recommendations

The Rockefeller Foundation and the Goldman Sachs Foundation discuss sixteen social impact assessment methods currently used in the nonprofit and for-profit sectors based on findings from the Double Bottom Line Project.[17] They argue that the existing methods can be measured regarding three variables: the type of venture, the investment stage, and functional content (e.g., outcome-oriented vs. process-oriented, level of social responsibility). Regarding the conceptual, operational, structural, and practical challenges of the field of social impact assessment, they offer six main recommendations: (1) align goals, assessment tools, and best practices; (2) acknowledge evaluation expenses as part of the cost of doing business where appropriate; (3) invest in measurement systems and tools; (4) develop examples of proven impact; (5) balance breadth with consistency; and (6) commit to outcomes assessment. Due to its early stage, Kachile has not yet embarked on one particular method for measuring its own social impact but is committed to applying the highest level of scrutiny to guarantee a maximum impact in the communities and provide a solid method for continuous learning and improvement.

Discussion and Strategies for Success

Private-sector development strategies, focusing on triggering entrepreneurial activities, first must concentrate on training the local workforce and access to capital, taking into consideration low literacy and the current lack of entrepreneurial endeavor. To both cultivate inclusive markets and nurture more sustainable long-term value for producers, private-sector development strategies should be tailored to build up human capital by fusing modern management methods to realities on the ground. While improving human capacity is important, competition and regulatory factors also need to be addressed to usher in a culture of entrepreneurship. In the case of Côte d'Ivoire, only building an environment that is conducive to promoting entrepreneurship in a postconflict situation will allow sustainable free markets to emerge. Ultimately, efforts to attain human development goals must take into account current capabilities and skills as well as sensitivities to the Ivorian civil war.

Partnership Strategy

Kachile is negotiating partnerships with the local investment and donor community, including the World Bank and the International Finance Corporation, to ensure its financial viability. Other potential partners include the Ministère de la Culture et de la Francophonie, the Direction du Patrimoine Culturel, the Archives Nationale de Côte d'Ivoire, the Association Quartier France, the Fondation Borremans, the Université de Cocody, the Préfecture de Grand Bassam, the Cour Royale de Moossou, the Archevêché de Grand Bassam, the Ministère de l'Urbanisme et de l'Habitat, and the mayor of Grand Bassam.

Local Embeddedness and State-of-the-Art Technology

Kachile will provide extensive background information including videos on artists and local African culture, available for public perusal on kachile. com. Currently, Kachile is building up a database that is researched and completed by local team members and by partner institutions. Kachile.com works with local artists and with a local team who help with finding sources of quality products. Kachile has signed a partnership agreement with the local stakeholders of the artisanal sector. Kachile is well positioned to access local resources and gain credibility for kachile.com locally. Kachile also uses state-of-the-art software solutions for e-commerce, e-mail marketing, small business administration, database management, and graphics and design.

Conclusion

Based on the preliminary research, I conclude that if the above-mentioned challenges to entrepreneurial activity in Côte d'Ivoire can be overcome, the potential for the successful creation of new businesses to serve the poor could be tremendous as shown by the success of the telecommunications sector in the whole of Africa. The experience of the (ongoing) research project of Kachile shows that a holistic and yet focused concept is needed to tackle development challenges in a postconflict environment. Fostering entrepreneurship becomes a highly complex task with regard to the interplay of financial, managerial, operational, and cultural constraints. While it is hoped that Kachile's e-commerce solution will have an immediate impact, and could be considered as a rather minor innovation, the ICT learning centers fill a much broader need of the West African region for connections to the global knowledge-based economy. Understanding the need for digitizing, structuring, and storing information in more efficient ways for administrative, commercial, and educational purposes is one thing; implementing it will be a massive task that represents tremendous opportunities for capable and courageous entrepreneurs. Given Kachile's limited resources, strategic local partnerships will most likely play a crucial role in guaranteeing local embeddedness and real social impacts. A successful collaboration with IUGB as well as with the local operator of the free trade zone VITIB might prove to be crucial to ensure lasting success.

Notes

1. Allan Gerson, "Peace Building: The Private Sector's Role," *American Journal of International Law* 95 (2001): 102–19; Juliette Bennett, "Public Private Partnerships: The Role of the Private Sector in Preventing Funding Conflict," *Vanderbilt Journal of Transnational Law* 35 (2002): 711–17; Aneel Karnani, "The Mirage of Marketing to the Bottom of the Pyramid: How the Private Sector Can Help Alleviate Poverty," *California Management Review* 49, no. 4 (2007): 90–111; and CSR Initiative, *The Role of the Private Sector in Expanding Economic Opportunity through Collaborative Action: A Leadership Dialogue* (Cambridge: John F. Kennedy School of Government, Harvard University, 2007). See also C. K. Prahalad and Stuart L. Hart, *Strategies for the Bottom of the Pyramid: Creating Sustainable Development* (1999), http://pdf.wri.org/2001summit_hartarticle.pdf.

2. Benn Eifert, Alan Gelb, and Vijaya Ramachandran, "Business Environment and Comparative Advantage in Africa: Evidence from the Investment Climate Data," Working Paper No. 56. Washington, DC: World Bank, Center for Global Development, 2005.

3. Prahalad and Hart, "Strategies for the Bottom"; Michael D. Gordon, "Management Education and the Base of the Pyramid," *Journal of Management Education* 32, no. 6 (2008): 767–81.

4. International Monetary Fund, "IMF Executive Board Approves US$565.7 Million PRGF Arrangement for Côte d'Ivoire," Press Release No. 09/96, March 27, 2009, Washington, DC; UNOCI, "Côte d'Ivoire—UNOCI Facts and Figures," http://www.un.org/en/peacekeeping/missions/unoci/facts.shtml; UNICEF, "Côte d'Ivoire," http://www.unicef.org/infobycountry/cotedivoire.html (accessed April 18, 2009); World Bank, "The World Bank and Côte d/Ivoire Wage War on Racketeering,"

July 25, 2008, http://web.worldbank.org/WBSITE/EXTERNAL/COUNTRIES/
AFRICAEXT/CDIVOIREEXTN/0,,print:Y~isCURL:Y~contentmDK:21852817~page
PK:1497618~piPK:217854~thesitePK:382607,00.html.

5. Lancine Bakayoko, "Côte d'Ivoire: Affaire 1 milliard detourne au Crou-A
La Direction generale du Budget mise en cause, http://fr.allafrica.com/stories/
200901220745.html.

6. World Bank, "War on Racketeering."

7. Amnesty International, *Côte d'Ivoire: Les femmes, victimes oubliées du conflit* (London, 2007); Déclaration de Berne, *Chocolat suisse: Le scandale du travail des enfants* (2009), http://www.evb.ch/fr/p25015371.html; Global Witness, *Hot Chocolate: How Cocoa Fueled the Conflict in Côte d'Ivoire* (Washington, DC, 2007); Jean-Pierre Stroobants, "Affaire du 'Probo-Koala': L'affréteur mis en examen pour corruption," *Le Monde*, April 10, 2009; UNICEF, "Côte d'Ivoire," http://www.unicef.org/infoby-country/cotedivoire.html; UNOCI, "UNOCI Facts and Figures"; "World Bank, "War on Racketeering."

8. Kouadio N'Da N'Guessan, *Grand Bassam: Ville culturelle, Ville de patrimoine* (City of Grand Bassam, 2003); Jean-Michel Moulod, Joselyn Kongo, and Sylvain N'Guessan, *Akwaba à Grand Bassam* (City of Grand Bassam, 2007).

9. N'Guessan, *Grand Bassam.*

10. Ali Banuazizi, "Psychology, the Distant Other, and the Dialectic of Change in Non-Western Societies," in *Myths about the Powerless: Contesting Social Inequalities*, ed. M. B. Lykes et al. (Philadelphia: Temple University Press, 1996).

11. International University of Grand Bassam, *Mission Statement* (Grand Bassam, 2010), http://iugb.org/iugb-missi.php.

12. International University of Grand Bassam, *International University of Grand Bassam: School of Business, International Relations, and Economic Policy: Strategic Plan FY 2010–2014* (2009).

13. Ulf Richter, *Entrepreneurship Program at the International University of Grand Bassam* (Grand Bassam: International University of Grand Bassam, 2009).

14. David Bornstein, *How to Change the World: Social Entrepreneurs and the Power of New Ideas* (London: Penguin Books, 2004).

15. Sara Olson, *Social Return on Investment: Partnership on Nonprofit Ventures* (Athlone, Ireland: STV Consulting, 2004).

16. United Nations Environment Program, *Environmental Impact Assessment Training Resource Manual*, ed. Barry Sadler and Mary McCabe, 2nd ed. (Geneva, 2002).

17. The Rockefeller Foundation and The Goldman Sachs Foundation, *Social Impact Assessment: A Discussion among Grantmakers* (New York: The Rockefeller Foundation, 2003).

Part Three

Industrial and Financial Networking

10

Globalization and Monetary Convergence

Independent Currency Union or Dollarization?

CHRISTOPHER E. S. WARBURTON

Introduction

This chapter investigates the prospects of setting up an independent currency union for West Africa. The prospects of such a union in Africa and Europe have been found to be contingent on internal reforms and convergence criteria. Using time series data from the World Bank for the period 2000–2006, this chapter shows that the much more globalized French-speaking countries have comparatively low rates of inflation, though some West African states collectively continue to have higher rates of inflation. The empirical evidence shows lack of beta and sigma convergence of inflation rates in states that are aspiring to form a monetary union when intra- and extragroup comparisons are made. The chapter concludes that some West African countries are already *dollarized* (using convertible foreign currency rather than local currency) and that *dollarization* provides greater potential for global economic integration than an independent currency union. As such, globalization is consistent with monetary convergence—that is, the elimination of inconvertible or less competitive currencies in favor of highly competitive and convertible ones. Here, globalization is precisely defined as economic integration of national economies into the international economy through trade, foreign direct investment, capital flows, and mobility of factors of production. This definition is consistent with what is loosely characterized as economic integration.

Although currency selection is normally overshadowed by technological innovation and outsourcing in the explanation of the scope of globalization, the type of currency being used for international transactions is integral to the pace at which nations on the periphery of international economic activity can be integrated into the global economy.

This chapter maintains that de jure (official) dollarization, more than an optimum currency area (OCA) or de facto (unofficial, but expedient) dollarization, enhances the prospects of globalization for the nations of West Africa that aspire to form a monetary union. This argument is premised on the fact that inconvertible currencies or the semblance of them can no longer compete in the changing global economy and that efforts to postpone the embracing of convertible currencies can only prolong the economic decline of states that are having great difficulties with inflation, lack of credibility, capital outflows, and lack of access to international capital markets. Of course, the currency impediment subjects these nations to the so-called original sin, which makes it impossible for them to borrow in their inconvertible currencies from global capital markets.

To raise capital and become competitive, countries must now be integrated into the global economy, but the failed attempts to establish a currency union prolongs the adverse consequences of monetary nationalism and inconvertible currencies. The effects of inconvertible currencies and the inability to raise capital evidently lead to seigniorage and currency substitution (de facto dollarization)—a situation in which foreign convertible currencies are extensively used in place of local ones—although sovereign governments have not officially renounced the use of local currencies.

The members of the West African Monetary Zone (WAMZ)—Nigeria, Sierra Leone, Guinea, and Ghana (Gambia being an exception)—continue to have higher rates of inflation relative to the de facto dollarized optimum currency area of the former French colonies and the de jure dollarized Latin American countries. As a result, the inability to attain convergence criteria consistently endangers timely investments or capital inflows. This problem, which is also symptomatic of the lack of a credible exchange rate regime, greatly reduces the capacity for nations to be integrated into global markets in order to earn the much coveted reserves that are crucial for stabilizing their economies—that is, maintaining stable prices (and therefore credibility) while increasing output or reducing the level of unemployment.

A closer look at convergence criteria for the WAMZ currency area shows that inflation is a much more refractory problem for WAMZ's membership. As such, the empirical focus of this chapter analyzes the prospects of convergence based on inflation disparities while evaluating de jure dollarization and the sustainability of an optimum currency area.

The rest of the chapter is structured to account for the following: (a) relevant aspects of the prevailing literature on globalization—early forms of integration, OCA, and dollarization; (b) the quest of convertible currency for globalization; (c) empirical evaluation of the criteria for monetary union in West Africa; (d) implications of the failure of monetary convergence for globalization; and (e) evaluation of competing arrangements for price stability and globalization. Concluding remarks are provided at the end of the chapter.

The Globalization and Currency Literature

Although the modern content of globalization has been given considerable attention, globalization has undergone important phases of development. When these phases are put in perspective, they tend to show how some nations have benefited from innovation more than others because of a rapid reaction to technological innovation and economic transformation.

Robert Carbaugh identifies three significant phases: 1870–1914, 1945–80, and the post-1980 period.[1] All of these periods are characterized by innovation and reduction in the cost of production and exchange. In the first period, steam replaced wind as a means of transportation and led to reduced tariffs and transportation costs. The second phase witnessed considerable specialization in trade, as rich countries specialized in manufacturing and industrial agglomeration. Most developing countries did not participate significantly in global trade in manufacturing and services.

During the third phase, some developing countries, such as China, India, and Brazil, have been able to utilize labor to create comparative advantage in labor-intensive industries. Some countries benefited from outsourcing and capital flows and minimized the effects of constrained labor mobility. The WAMZ countries have not been significant beneficiaries of this phase of globalization.

In the 1940s the WAMZ countries were still colonized, and after independence, they have struggled with civil wars or structural problems to compete with industrialized countries. Yet, the most recent phase of globalization has provided tremendous opportunities to transform human capital and tap into the technologically advanced service sector to reduce unemployment and increase national welfare.

However, the literature on globalization has not been monolithic. It presents discontents and optimism, which makes it imperative for nations to decide how they want to weigh the marginal costs and benefits of embracing economic integration. Jagdish Bhagwati extols the virtues of international trade and global integration within reasonable limits. He notes that many poor countries that turned away from international trade and investment flows made the wrong choice, unlike countries of East Asia that used international opportunities to great advantage.[2]

Trade is not inherently harmful, but undesirable policies and terms of trade may further *immiserize* (decrease the welfare of) a country and its poor.[3] Nevertheless, the capitalist structure of globalization and the expansion of multinational corporations into more and more countries have created apprehension. Multilateral institutions have not always been very careful or sensitive to the needs of poor countries that seek ways to be integrated into the global economy.

Joseph Stiglitz recounts some of the many downsides of globalization, which include the financial architecture for global trade finance and liberalization as well as structural adjustments to maintain long-term growth. Much more pointed is Stiglitz's analysis of how the International Monetary Fund (IMF) and the World Bank (WB), through their policies of imposing conditionalities and structural adjustments, have made some of the developing nations worse off in the process of promoting global trade and stabilization of national economies—policies that are noticeably conceived of as contractionary and inflationary.[4]

Since inflation is triggered by excess money relative to output, it is logical to analyze the role of monetary policy, exchange rate regime, or currency selection in the quest of price stability and globalization. Central to an understanding of inflation in West Africa is the nexus of fiscal and monetary policies—a connection that shows how expansionary monetary policy is induced by deficit spending in order to compensate for shortfalls in tax revenue or government income—a situation in which governments spend more than they collect in taxes or revenues and then use seigniorage to finance deficits through nonautonomous central banks.

Inflation has always been a nuisance to economic integration. It is a symptom of financial trouble, and once it mutates into hyperinflation countries must then find ways to arrest its rapid growth or ascertain a reasonable measure of credibility in exchange rates. The ocular signs of trouble are de facto dollarization or a movement to a monetary union, both of which are choices to arrest uncontrollable price increases and loss of credibility in the efficacy of a currency.

The theory of OCA was first comprehensively outlined by Joseph Mundell long after the *colonies françaises d'Afrique* (French Colonies of Africa, or CFA) had a union of their own. He put it forward at a time when the Europeans were nursing their union.[5] His theory presents an optimum currency area as one within which currencies of a group of nations are permanently fixed to an international currency or currencies under conditions that will make the exchange rate of the monetary union an optimum arrangement against nonmember currencies.

The OCA theory has been used by many economists to evaluate the costs and benefits that may be derived from forming monetary unions in Africa. David Fielding and Kalvinder Shields applied the theory to the two francophone monetary unions in Africa in order to identify and compare the impact of macroeconomic shocks on different members of the CFA zone and on Kenya.[6] They focused on shocks to aggregate output growth and to aggregate price inflation by constructing a structural vector autoregression (VAR) representation of the macroeconomy of each member of the CFA and Kenya.[7] They concluded that the cost of lost monetary autonomy can be larger in comparison to monetary response to an immediate shock.

John Anyanwu extends the monetary union literature by estimating the beneficial macroeconomic effects of monetary unions with respect to trade and output and suggests that a monetary union (the use of a single currency within a region) is good for bilateral trade and economic growth. In his study, panel economic indicators are used for individual members of the West African Economic and Monetary Union (WAEMU), otherwise known as Union Économique et Monétaire Ouest Africaine (UEMOA), as well as non-UEMOA ECOWAS counterparts to determine whether the monetary union brought about stabilization between 1990 and 2001.[8] His findings indicate that stable economic growth was greater in the WAEMU countries than in non-WAEMU countries during the period of the analysis, but the same result was not observed in terms of inflation.

Other authors have developed extensive modeling efforts to focus on price stability, cost-benefit (CB) analysis, and the desirability and prospects of monetary unions. A significant example for the CB assessment can be found in the work of Paul Masson and Catherine Pattillo.[9] In their influential work, they examine the CB analysis of monetary union in West Africa in terms of trade patterns, asymmetric shocks, labor mobility, fiscal transfers, and exchange rate stability. They express doubts about the sustainability of the union given macroeconomic fluctuations and institutional arrangements prior to 2004.

Absent the prospects of price stability, some nations of the world have traditionally turned to official dollarization so that they can rapidly restore price stability and be integrated into the global economy. The literature on dollarization is diverse, but it demonstrates widespread agreement on price stability and enhanced prospects of integration.

Robert Rennhack and Masahiro Nozaki tested several explanations for financial dollarization and found it to be a rational response to inflation uncertainty.[10] Yet, the restoration of confidence in a domestic currency may take many years and consistently sound policies. Confidence is normally shaped by the ability or inability of social planners or governments to freely print money to finance deficits. However, lacking the strong will to resist the temptation of seigniorage, nations can quickly experience "original sin." Dollarization insulates against that temptation.

The value of dollarization for globalization rests on the ability of nations to tap into money and capital markets and attract investment. Barry Eichengreen and Ricardo Hausmann highlight the credibility gap in terms of currency mismatches and "original sin."[11] The ultimate question confronting nations in the belated quest for economic integration is how their currencies of choice can best restore financial credibility and influence investments. OCA does not quite explain the answer convincingly, even though it may well lead to comparative price stability. The next section discusses the problems with convergence criteria and choice of currency for globalization.

Money and the Quest for Globalization

The fundamental challenge of creating an OCA like that of the eurozone or the CFA area for the WAMZ members is attaining convergence criteria—the criteria that will put the members on a sound enough footing to give up their local currencies in favor of the eco. But in the globalized world of formidable convertible currencies, the new currency will have to compete with the US dollar, the euro, the British pound, and the Japanese yen.

The ECOWAS treaty of 1975, like the Treaty of Rome in 1957, was designed to achieve an economic union (monetary integration).[12] Although the West African and Central African colonies of France (CFA) had an OCA in the 1940s, the bases for an economic union or OCA were not given considerable scrutiny until the 1960s. The preconditions for the use of a single currency or exchange rate regime in both regions can however be attributed to different conditions after the Second World War.[13]

The surrender of monetary policy to a regional central bank is a much welcomed idea to ensure the credibility of monetary authorities in attaining some measure of price stability. Of course, the leaders must first genuinely come to terms with the idea of relinquishing monetary sovereignty, after which they must deal with the political and cultural problems that lurk beneath a sustainable monetary union in a culturally diverse region of the world.

Convergence criteria are preconditions for the alignment of monetary and economic policies prior to the circulation of a common currency for the members of a monetary union. These criteria are broadly intended to limit money growth to check inflation and to put a lid on deficit financing by the monetary authorities of prospective members to ensure credibility and healthy economic prospects.

The objective is to obtain a high degree of symmetry against a pegged currency that is not expected to move or adjust adversely to idiosyncratic shocks. It is therefore necessary, as Mundell points out, for shocks to be symmetric rather than asymmetric. Otherwise, wages and labor movement must be flexible enough to compensate for divergent idiosyncratic shocks. In 1969, Peter Kenen added within-country diversification of export capacity as a mitigating factor for lack of flexibility.[14]

The convergence criteria of the European Union (EU) are currently used as a modified template for the WAMZ. The Accra summit of 2000 established the criteria that were supposed to have been achieved by the members in 2003, but the criteria were subsequently extended to December 2005, December 2009, and (at the time of this writing) January 2015. The criteria include: (a) the accumulation of gross official reserves to cover at least six months of imports of goods and services after 2003; (b) a maximum budget deficit that is no more than 4 percent of GDP; (c) a rate of inflation not exceeding 5 percent; and (d) central bank financing of a budget deficit not exceeding 10 percent of a previous year's tax revenues.[15]

The long-run inflation situation is significant because fiscal policy (taxing and spending) will remain in the hands of individual national governments—as do policies about labor, pensions, and capital markets—though they are stripped of the ability to make monetary policy. Fiscal policy, like monetary policy, is capable of destabilizing prices in the long run. As such, it is vital for governments to commit to commonly agreed-upon rules about public finances that are intended to obtain price stability, growth, and external balance.[16]

The yardsticks of measurement for convergence indicate that the WAMZ countries are precariously poised for a monetary union. Labor mobility may not be as flexible as it is presently conceived in the face of wage rigidity.[17] History teaches that immigration and instability in one country can quickly degenerate into xenophobic hostility and expulsion of foreigners in another in times of grave political and economic peril.

Language and cultural barriers impose additional restrictions—just as persistent inflation, compromising monetary policies, and untrammeled fiscal policy can create significant disturbances within a monetary union. These precautions are noteworthy and indicate that although monetary unions like that of the CFA zone have a better record on inflation, they also tend to be less than optimal in the race to achieve global economic integration. The following section evaluates the prospects of monetary union in West Africa, given the preconditions.

Empirical Analysis: Are Convergence Criteria Attainable?

The empirical analyses in this section report data on convergence criteria and then evaluate the prospects of convergence by using World Bank data on inflation for the WAMZ countries from 2000 to 2006. To assess the desirability of OCA or dollarization the rates of inflation in three regions—WAEMU, WAMZ, and Latin America—are considered for analysis. The preferred measure of inflation is the average annual percentage change of the gross domestic product deflator (the ratio of nominal GDP to real GDP), which is a broader measure of inflation than the consumer price index (CPI) or the producer price index (PPI).

Convergence is measured by two approaches both within and outside the WAMZ and WAEMU regions: (1) the rate at which inflation changes (beta, β, convergence) over time; and (2) the deviation of inflation over time from an average value (sigma, σ, convergence). In mathematical notation these measures can be denoted as follows:

$$\beta = \frac{\Delta\mu_{ijt}}{\mu_{ijt}} \text{ (beta convergence),} \tag{1}$$

$$\text{and } s = \sqrt{\frac{\sum(x-\mu)^2}{(n-1)_{ijt}}} \text{ (sigma convergence);} \tag{2}$$

where Δ is for change, μ is the mean of a variable for a category of countries, x is for a raw score, n is for the number of countries or categories considered, ijt indexes two groups of countries (i and j) for comparison over time (t), and sigma $(\sum)$ is the usual summation operator.[18]

These measures indicate whether initially high inflation rates in some countries tend to fall over time to converge with relatively low inflation rates in other countries and whether the disparities in rates of inflation are getting smaller over time when they are evaluated against an average rate of inflation.

Although convergence is desirable for global economic integration, the 2008 convergence report indicates that the WAMZ members have collectively performed poorly on the inflation target (table 10.1). Only Gambia was able to meet the target for two out of three years. Gambia and Nigeria did well on deficit financing and the accumulation of gross reserves. Without external or asymmetric shocks, fiscal restraint is a good complement of independent monetary policy, but evidently inadequate for long-term stability. Guinea and Sierra Leone are evidently facing steep challenges to meeting convergence targets.

Empirical analysis shows beta convergence of inflation rates for Nigeria and Gambia over the six-year period (table 10.2). Nigeria started with a higher rate of inflation in 2000 but reduced the rate substantially by 2006, while the growth of inflation in Gambia was virtually stagnant. This is not the case for the other members, particularly Guinea and Sierra Leone, which registered a positive growth rate of inflation.

The results of beta convergence mirror those of sigma convergence. Table 10.3 shows that there is also no sigma convergence for the period of analysis. The spread or dispersion of inflation rates for Nigeria and Gambia decreased by a standard deviation (SD) of approximately 21.66, from 24.40 SD in 2000 to 2.74 SD in 2006, but this was not the case for the remaining members of the WAMZ, for which dispersion in average annual inflation rates actually increased from 11.03 SD in 2000 to 13.84 in 2006, a net increase of 2.81 SD.

Table 10.1. Convergence report, 2006–8

	Inflation (≤ 5%)			Fiscal deficit/GDP (≤ 4%)		
	2006	2007	2008	2006	2007	2008
Gambia	Y	N	Y	Y	Y	Y
Nigeria	N	N	N	Y	Y	Y
Ghana	N	N	N	N	N	N
Sierra Leone	N	N	N	N	N	N
Guinea	N	N	N	Y	Y	Y

	Central bank financing (≤ 10%)			Gross reserves (≥ 6 months)[*]		
	2006	2007	2008	2006	2007	2008
Gambia	Y	Y	Y	Y	Y	Y
Nigeria	Y	Y	Y	Y	Y	Y
Ghana	Y	N	Y	N	N	N
Sierra Leone	N	N	Y	N	N	N
Guinea	N	N	Y	N	N	N

Y = yes; N = no

Note: Three months required by 2000 and six months as of 2003.

[*] *Source:* West African Monetary Agency, http://www.amao-wama.org (accessed August 15, 2009).

Table 10.2. Beta convergence and divergence in WAMZ

Country	2000	2006	β	Country	2000	2006	β
Nigeria	38.17	7.94	−0.79	Sierra Leone	6.11	14.13	1.31
Gambia	3.66	4.07	0.11	Ghana	27.23	14.63	−0.46
Cumulative Average	20.91	6.00	−0.71	Guinea	11.13	38.36	2.45
				Cumulative Average	14.82	22.37	0.51

Table 10.3. Sigma convergence and divergence in WAMZ

	Nigeria	Gambia	σ	Sierra Leone	Ghana	Guinea	σ
2000	38.17	3.66	24.40	6.11	27.23	11.13	11.03
2006	7.94	4.07	2.74	14.13	14.63	38.36	13.84

Table 10.4. Beta and sigma convergence and divergence in WAMZ and WAEMU

Beta (inflation, average annual percentage)			
	2000	2006	β
WAEMU	1.85	2.23	0.21
WAMZ	17.26	15.82	–0.08
WAMZ (2)[a]	14.82	22.37	0.51

Sigma (inflation, average annual percentage)					
	2000	σ1		2000	σ2
WAEMU	1.85		WAEMU	1.85	
WAMZ	17.26	10.90	WAMZ(2)[a]	14.82	9.17
	2006			2006	
WAEMU	2.23		WAEMU	2.23	
WAMZ	15.82	9.61	WAMZ(2)[a]	22.37	14.24

[a] Without Nigeria and Gambia (converging WAMZ countries)

A broader analysis of convergence in the West African region (table 10.4) shows that although the inflation rates are significantly different, there is a tendency for the inflation rates in the WAMZ and WAEMU regions to converge as a group when the performance of Nigeria and Gambia are taken into consideration, but not when the other WAMZ states are collectively factored into consideration.

The WAMZ countries started with a very high average inflation rate relative to their CFA counterpart, but they actually experienced an increase in the growth rate of inflation when Nigeria and Gambia, the two converging countries, are not taken into consideration. The result changes when these two are included, suggesting a negative growth rate of inflation (–0.08).

The finding of divergence is replicated for sigma convergence when Nigeria and Gambia are not taken into consideration. When the two countries are included, variance in the rate of inflation over the two periods contracts by about 1.29 SD (10.9 SD in 2000 to 9.61 SD in 2006). By excluding the two countries, the dispersion in inflation rates increases by 5.07 SD (9.17 SD in 2000 to 14.24 SD in 2006).

These findings are not very optimistic and they are generally indicative of lack of beta or sigma convergence in the short run within the WAMZ or outside the WAMZ for the ECOWAS region. The numbers indicate that Nigeria and Gambia currently hold the key to regional convergence with the WAEMU. But the lack of convergence portends problems for regional economic integration and increased volume of global trade. The implications of failure are discussed in the next section.

Implications of the Failure of Monetary Convergence for Globalization

The immediate consequences of persistent failure can ultimately be found in the levels of inflation, de facto dollarization, and foreign direct investment (FDI), as economic agents try to hedge against inflation, secure convertible currencies, or find ways to reduce transaction costs or maximize profits. In actual fact, these indicators are already evident in the region. The CFA optimum area and dollarized Latin American states maintain much more stable prices though they tend to struggle with fiscal policy and asymmetric shocks. Table 10.5 gives a comparative result of the average levels of inflation for the period under review.

It can be seen that the WAEMU countries and the officially dollarized Latin American countries have inflation in the single digits while the WAMZ countries have inflation in double digits, for the most part. The broader

Table 10.5. Inflation, GDP deflator, 2000–2006 (average annual percentage)

WAEMU	Inflation	WAMZ	Inflation	Latin America (dollarized)	Inflation
Benin	3.56	Gambia	12.12	Panama (1904)	1.26
Burkina Faso	2.51	Ghana	22.50	Ecuador (2000)	9.03
Côte d'Ivoire	2.94	Nigeria	18.22	El Salvador (2001)	3.34
Guinea-Bissau	0.63	Sierra Leone	7.92	Guatemala (2001)	7.12
Mali	4.08	Guinea	17.33		
Niger	2.88				
Senegal	1.95				
Togo	0.50				

[a] Without Nigeria and Gambia (converging WAMZ countries)

Source: World Bank, *World Development Indicators CD-ROM* (2008).

Table 10.6. De Facto dollarization in West Africa

Country	Foreign currency deposit (broad money [M2] in millions US$)
Gambia (2008)	15,017/9,287 = 1.62
Ghana (2007)	993/4,774 = 0.21
Sierra Leone (2008)	307,444/1,013,797 = 0.30

Source: Annual Reports of Central Banks (local currency units).

measure of inflation shows a significant variation for Gambia, but this is due also to the extended period of analysis. Not surprisingly, some of the West African states are already dollarized as a result of inflation and currency inconvertibility.

To assess the level of de facto dollarization, the ratio of foreign currency deposit to broad money measure (M2) is computed. The broad money measure is used because it captures the definition of money as a medium of exchange and store of value. This algorithm of de facto dollarization is consistent with that of Andrew Berg and Eduardo Borensztein's estimate of dollarization for Argentina, Bolivia, Costa Rica, Nicaragua, Peru, and Uruguay.[19] Table 10.6 shows that at least three countries in the region are already dollarized substantially: Gambia (2008), Sierra Leone (2008), and Ghana (2007).

The ratio for Gambia is 1.62; Sierra Leone, 0.3; and Ghana, 0.21—the higher the ratio, the greater the degree of dollarization. The ratio in Gambia is noticeably high because of its degree of financial market liberalization and the ability of residents and nonresidents to freely open accounts in local and foreign currencies. The former CFA franc also had a substantial presence in the country before the implementation of the euro.

Generally, the magnitude of unofficial dollarization in West Africa is unknown and more likely to be greater than official estimates because of the surreptitious circulation of foreign currencies outside the banking system in the underground economy. Substantial de facto dollarization has destabilizing consequences for any macroeconomy.

On the fiscal side, unofficial dollarization increases participation in the underground economy and reduces the cost of tax evasion. On the monetary side, when de facto dollarization is widespread, the effective money supply is difficult to measure and expansionary policy can create procyclical destabilizing effects rather than countercyclical stabilizing effects. That is, expansionary monetary policy can actually cause inflation instead of increasing output, thereby reinforcing a trend of low output and inflation in the business cycle rather than preventing it. These consequences have effects on transaction costs and capital flows.

Inflation and exchange rate instability affect the transaction costs of international exchange and long-term capital flows. Nervous governments may impose capital controls to regulate the flow of capital, and in so doing increase the incidence of corruption. Desai and colleagues estimate that transnational affiliates that are located in countries with capital controls face 5.25 percent higher interest rates on local borrowing than do affiliates of the same parent borrowing locally in countries without capital controls.[20] Higher interest rates discourage investment in countries with capital controls on trade in financial assets in forward and exchange rate markets, and corruption in turn affects the flow of foreign direct investment, such that the combination of inflation, capital controls, and corruption impinges on FDI, though the saving-augmenting effect of FDI for poorer countries is well known. This means that because poorer countries have low levels of aggregate saving for capital formation, relatively long-term inflows from abroad (FDI) can actually help to augment national saving.

Property, plant, and equipment tend to grow faster at an annual rate following liberalization or globalization. Liberalization of controls or globalization checks investment outflows and reduces transaction costs. Reduced transaction costs facilitates increased international trade and investments in countries with common convertible currencies.

Table 10.7. Average FDI stock, 2000–2007 (in millions US$)

Latin America	Average	WAMZ	Average	WAEMU	Average
El Salvador	3,593.98	Sierra Leone	359.65	Benin	270.62
Guatemala	4,751.57	Nigeria	35,767.63	Burkina Faso	147.78
Panama	9,569.94	Gambia	328.82	Côte d'Ivoire	3,685.98
Ecuador	8,918.80	Guinea	468.20	Mali	683.60
Cumulative Average	6,708.57	Ghana	2,183.17	Guinea-Bissau	52.94
		Cumulative Average	7,821.49	Niger	102.50
				Senegal	363.58
				Togo	630.04
				Cumulative Average	742.13

Source: United Nations Conference on Trade and Development (www.unctad.org).

Descriptive statistics in table 10.7 (without the outlier effect of Nigeria) show that the value of the average stock of FDI is higher in the dollarized states of Latin America relative to the other categories of states for the period 2000–2007. The average stock of FDI in the WAMZ region is comparatively higher than that of the WAEMU countries because of FDI in oil-rich Nigeria. Nigeria's FDI asset aside, the value of FDI stock in the WAMZ region drops precipitously to approximately $667.97 million (a value to be demonstrated, *quod erat demonstrandum*), which is significantly less than that of all the regions.[21]

The European story of monetary harmonization lends support to the empirical report of table 10.7. Hisham Foad observes that since 1999, the UK's share of FDI heading into Europe has declined dramatically, while the eurozone's share has increased, essentially because the formation of the eurozone eliminated nominal exchange rate volatility between member states and increased export market access within the monetary union.[22]

For source countries outside of Europe, eurozone countries are more attractive destinations for export-oriented FDI, as operations within the union are insulated from destabilizing currency fluctuations. Foad estimates that as exchange rate volatility between a non-euro country and local export markets increases, or as the market size of the eurozone increases, more and more investment will be diverted toward eurozone countries.[23]

There are specific ways through which monetary convergence can enhance globalization. With monetary convergence households and businesses reduce the transaction costs that are associated with the exchange of currencies, including the need to hedge against foreign exchange risk; capital controls are minimized; the destabilizing effect of de facto dollarization is eliminated; and resource mobility is significantly enhanced. The next section takes a look at a menu of currency arrangements to ascertain the net benefit of dollarization for globalization.

Globalization by OCA, Currency Board, or Dollarization?

The controversy over the currency arrangement that best fosters globalization is persistent, but a comparison of three major competing options— OCA, currency boards, and dollarization—is revealing of the prospects for macroeconomic stability, pace of globalization or economic integration, and sustainability.[24] Table 10.8 summarizes the main arguments. Under any of the arrangements a government can make fiscal policy, but not monetary policy *and* fiscal policy. Dollarization is largely irreversible, but not the other arrangements.

Examples of failed OCA and currency boards can be found in East Africa in the 1960s, and, more recently, in Argentina; the South American

Table 10.8. Currency arrangements for stability and globalization

	OCA	Currency board	Dollarization
Stability indicators reversible	Yes	Yes	Unlikely*
External shock	Yes	Yes	Yes
Need for reserves	Substantial	Substantial	Less substantial*
Risk premium	Higher	Higher	Lower*
Monetary and fiscal policies	No	No	No
Transaction costs	Higher	Higher	Lower*
Balance of payments difficulties	Severe	Severe	Less severe*
Concessional financing	Yes	No	No*
Devaluation	Yes	After dissolution	No*

* Important for credibility and macroeconomic stability

country's currency board lasted from 1991 until 2001. In the 1980s and 1990s some larger economies of the West African CFA zone enjoyed concessional financing of their fiscal deficits that are reminiscent of questionable monetary expansion in East Africa of the 1960s—a system whereby central governments borrow from commercial banks that then obtain refinancing from the regional central banks.

Table 10.8 shows that at some point in time, all countries experience the effects of external shocks or cycles. This may be as a result of currency devaluation, collapse of financial markets, adverse prices for primary products and fuel, or weak foreign absorption (demand), but dollarized countries with a good measure of fiscal responsibility tend to be well situated for the acquisition of foreign reserves. Even when risk of external shocks cannot be eliminated, full dollarization absorbs the impact of shocks more favorably and lowers the risk of contagion by eliminating exchange rate risk.

The acquisition of reserves is crucial to resolving current and capital account imbalances because nations must pay for their imports or outflows of capital in foreign currencies. Dollarized economies can afford to hold relatively fewer reserves. Panama enjoyed stability for about sixty years after it dollarized, and Juan Luis Moreno-Villalaz notes that Panamanian banks hold 5 percent lower reserves than they would have without dollarization.[25]

The inability to acquire reserves imposes severe challenges for the settlement of payments imbalances. Sovereign debt and financial instability compromise the ability of poorer West African governments to provide urgently needed social and infrastructural services—health, education, roads, bridges, and high-speed rail. These drawbacks contribute to political instability. The potential for acquiring reserves under OCA or a currency board arrangement is less robust relative to a dollarized system (see table 10.8).

Shortfalls in reserve earnings have forced governments to resort to trade and capital controls in the form of tariffs and nontariff barriers and restrictions on capital outflows via rationing of currencies and multiple exchange rate regimes to minimize the importation of less-essential goods and to defend the local currency in forward markets. This is not an entirely peculiar phenomenon to any West African state. For example, in February 2009, the Nigerian Central Bank restricted the sale of foreign currency as the naira depreciated in value because of falling oil prices.[26] It is uncertain whether the country will see the repatriation of emigrating or flight capital.

As a result of the problems of the black market in the foreign exchange market, the Sierra Leonean government introduced the two-tier exchange rate system—an official rate and a commercial rate—in December 1982. The government merged the two exchange rates at a rate of Le 2.50 = US$1 in 1983 and required residents to obtain central bank permits to buy foreign exchange in order to import essential goods into the country. A thriving black market still exists for foreign exchange, though a policy of financial liberalization including open market operations is pursued by the central bank.

In Ghana, foreign exchange transactions are regulated under the Exchange Control Act of 1961 (Act 71). The Bank of Ghana is the main regulatory authority, though certain regulatory approvals under this law, such as equity investment by nonresidents, require the approval of the bank and the ministry of finance.

An important advantage of dollarization is that interest rates and risk premiums are relatively lower in dollarized countries. The dollarized country accepts inflation and interest rates that are synchronized or similar to those of the United States or the global economy because of arbitrage opportunities. Price disparities are more often than not indicative of transaction costs.

Though the effects of an exchange rate regime or currency arrangement are not generally identical, nations must carefully evaluate the costs imposed by the adoption of a currency or exchange rate mechanism. The cost of setting up an OCA depends on convergence criteria and the probability of sustainability. The cost of establishing a currency board is closely contingent on the balance of payments situation of a country, capital inflows, external shocks, and the extent to which spending obligations can be sustained. Small economies with uncontrollable money supply, loss of credibility, inconvertible currencies, and weak investments that seek global integration are well suited for dollarization.

Dollarization costs involve the redemption of local currency in circulation, the degree of de facto dollarization, access to foreign credit markets, wage rigidity, and the sequencing of the process of dollarization. Dominick Salvatore reports the (immediate) cost of dollarization to be about 4 to 5 percent of GDP for Latin American countries.[27] The tabular representation of stability indicators in table 10.8 shows that dollarization has the greatest net benefit for the maintenance of price stability, capital inflows, economic growth, and globalization.

Conclusion

The contemporary global economy is rapidly being shaped by enduring or irreversible globalization as businesses try to harness technological innovation to reduce the cost of production and gain competitive advantage. Nations that prefer to be integrated into the circuits of innovation and development must now find ways to speedily foster economic transactions, maintain price stability, increase employment (internal balance), and increase foreign reserves for bringing capital and current accounts into equilibrium. As such, a nation's selection of a currency arrangement is integral to the process of growth and globalization.

The West African OCA that is sought for globalization is largely suboptimal because of preexisting economic and social conditions, but also because of the transaction costs and the low probability of a new currency successfully competing against the major convertible currencies that already play dominant roles in the global economy. Empirical evidence shows that inflation is a much more refractory problem for the WAMZ countries and that convergence by beta and sigma measures is not very promising. Currency harmonization like that of the CFA zone guarantees a greater degree of price stability, but is inadequate to arouse confidence in the viability of a monetary arrangement. Nations that provide assurances of fiscal responsibility and require price stability and globalization must now seriously consider the use of convertible currencies if they desire to maintain internal and external balance in order to expeditiously attain global economic integration.

Notes

1. Robert J. Carbaugh, *International Economics*, 12th ed. (Mason, OH: South-Western Cengage Learning, 2009), 1–8.
2. Jagdish Bhagwati, *In Defense of Globalization* (New York: Oxford University Press, 2004), 9.
3. Ibid., 55.
4. Joseph E. Stiglitz, *Globalization and Its Discontents* (New York: W. W. Norton & Company, 2003), 3–22.

5. Robert A. Mundell, "A Theory of Optimum Currency Areas," *American Economic Review* 51, no. 4 (1961): 509–17.

6. David Fielding and Kalvinder Shields, "Modelling Macroeconomic Shocks in the CFA Franc Zone," *Journal of Development Economics* 66, no. 1 (2001): 199–223.

7. The VAR specification is presented as an atheoretic representation of macroeconomic relationships with multiple dependent variables—real interest rate, nominal money stock, income, and inflation in domestic consumer prices.

8. John Anyanwu, "Estimating the Macroeconomic Effects of Monetary Unions: The Case of Trade and Output," *African Development Review* 15, nos. 2–3 (2004): 126–45. The WAEMU members are Benin, Burkina Faso, Côte d'Ivoire, Guinea-Bissau, Mali, Niger, Senegal, and Togo. The non-WAEMU members of ECOWAS are Cape Verde, Gambia, Ghana, Guinea, Liberia, Nigeria, and Sierra Leone.

9. Paul Masson and Catherine Pattillo, *Monetary Union in West Africa: Is It Desirable and How Could It Be Achieved?* (Washington, DC: IMF, 2001), 4–25.

10. Robert Rennhack and Masahiro Nozaki, "Financial Dollarization in Latin America," *International Monetary Fund Working Paper 06/7* (January 2006), http://imf.org/external/pubs/ft/wp/2006/wp0607.pdf.

11. Barry Eichengreen and Ricardo Hausmann, "Exchange Rate and Financial Fragility," *Proceedings* (Federal Reserve Bank of Kansas City, 1999), 329–68.

12. Economic integration is a gradual process that may go through several stages: free trade area (removal of tariff /taxes on goods among members); customs union (harmonization of trade policy toward the rest of the world); common market (free mobility of economic resources among members); and economic union (the use of a common currency and harmonization of monetary policy); see Dominick Salvatore's *Introduction to International Economics* (Hoboken, NJ: John Wiley and Sons, 2010), 179–80. The goal of using a single currency for the region was proposed by the ECOWAS Monetary Cooperation Program (EMCP) and duly adopted in 1978.

13. The CFA franc was created for the French colonies on December 26, 1945, to spare them the costly devaluation of the French franc associated with the setting up a fixed exchange rate with the US dollar after World War II. Europe was emerging from an era of competitive devaluation and assorted forms of trade restrictions. Economic integration became an attractive alternative to trade restrictions for economic prosperity. The ECOWAS countries of Ghana (then Gold Coast), Nigeria, Sierra Leone, and Gambia were party to a 1913 West African currency board, which was responsible for the money supply in the British colonies until the institutionalization of their respective central banks.

14. Mundell, "Theory of Optimum Currency Areas," 509–17; see also Peter B. Kenen, "The Theory of Optimum Currency Areas: An Eclectic View," in *Monetary Problems of the International Economy*, ed. Robert A. Mundell and Alexander K. Swoboda (Chicago: University of Chicago Press, 1969).

15. Similar convergence criteria for price stability and long-term interest rates before the issue of the euro were based on the performance of three prospective member countries with the best records. For example, the rate of inflation and long-term interest rates must be no more than 1.5 percent and 2 percent, respectively, above the average of those countries. Stable exchange rates and government finances have different standards. Exchange rates must be within target bands with no devaluation for two years prior to becoming a member. On the fiscal side, budget

deficits should be no more than 3 percent of GDP and outstanding government debt should be no more than 60 percent of a year's GDP.

16. External stability is a balance of payments position that is not likely to cause disruptive adjustments in exchange rates. A balance of payments position is externally stable when the underlying current account is in equilibrium and the capital and financial or reserve account do not create risks for precipitous capital reversals and speculative attack.

17. Aderanti Adepoju notes that in many cases national political exigencies supersede community interests; for example, Nigeria expelled nationals of the ECOWAS community in 1983 and 1985 as its economic conditions worsened. In 1999 Ghana requested all aliens in the country to be registered in order to obtain identity cards. This was done after foreigners were expelled under its 1969 Alien Compliance Order. In border disputes between Senegal and Mauritania and Ghana and Togo, foreign nationals had to be dislodged despite the free-movement-of-persons provisions of the ECOWAS protocol. Sierra Leoneans faced hostility in Guinea as a result of the decade-long civil war in their country. Moreover, colonial experiences and language barriers limit poverty-induced migration to Francophone and Anglophone countries in the region or advanced economies abroad; see Adepoju, "Migration in West Africa," *Global Commission on International Migration* (Lagos: Human Resources Development Centre, 2005).

18. In situations where only two countries are analyzed, the raw scores from the base year (2000) are computed relative to 2006.

19. Andrew Berg and Eduardo Borensztein, "The Pros and Cons of Full Dollarization," in *The Dollarization Debate*, ed. Dominick Salvatore, James Dean, and Thomas Willet (New York: Oxford University Press, 2003), 72–97.

20. Mihir Desai, Fritz Foley, and James Hines Jr., "Capital Controls, Liberalization, and Foreign Direct Investment," NBER Working Paper No. 10337, Washington, DC (2004).

21. Actual increases in FDI flow as a result of integration are also evident in Southeast Asia. The Chinese did not pursue monetary convergence/union, but as an alternative, they sought global integration by increasing regional cooperation and global economic relations simultaneously after the 1990s. China proposed the free trade area of the Association of Southeast Asian Nations (ASEAN) in November 2000 and shortly thereafter China became a destination of FDI inflows that became a hallmark of its low production costs. By the end of 2006, Japan became the largest source country of FDI for China and China accounted for 40 percent of FDI from the South Korea (the fourth largest); see UNCTAD's *Trade and Development Report* (2007), 91.

22. Hisham S. Foad, "Export-Oriented FDI, the Euro, and EU Enlargement," Working Paper 0022 (San Diego State University, Department of Economics, 2007), 1–31.

23. Foad uses detailed data on the operations of foreign affiliates of US transnationals across seventeen European countries from 1983 to 2004 to test his theory. See ibid.

24. Apart from dollarization, a currency board arrangement is an extreme form of fixed exchange rate system in which a nation pegs its exchange rate to a convertible currency or basket of currencies and turns over the functions of an independent central bank to a currency board (usually by statute). The money supply is

then made to be contingent on balance of payments surpluses or deficits and reserve inflows or outflows. For further discussion, see Salvatore, *Introduction to International Economics*, 412; and Carbaugh, *International Economics*, 490–91.

25. Juan Luis Morreno-Villalaz, "Lessons from the Monetary Experience of Panama: A Dollar Economy with Financial Integration," *Cato Journal* 18 (1999): 421–39.

26. It is worth noting that the restriction occurred about fourteen years after the movement to financial market liberalization or the repeal of the Exchange Control Act, which regulated foreign currency transaction in Nigeria long after ECOWAS was formed in 1975.

27. See Dominick Salvatore, "Which Countries in the Americas Should Dollarize?" in *The Dollarization Debate*, ed. Salvatore, Dean, and Willet, 198. This percentage of GDP is considered to be the stock cost. The low-end flow cost can be obtained by multiplying national currency in circulation by interest rate on foreign assets, which is estimated to be about 0.2 percent annually for the average Latin American country. The high-end flow cost is a product of the monetary base (e.g., M2, money as a medium of exchange and store of value) and the domestic inflation rate or domestic interest rate that is presumed to be higher than the interest rate on foreign assets. For Argentina this was estimated to be about 0.5 percent of GDP per year; and for Ecuador, 7.4 percent of annual GDP.

11

The Impact of Globalization on Emerging Markets

The Case of Côte d'Ivoire

ULF RICHTER

Introduction

Globalization is changing the African political and economic landscape. The global resource and energy challenge for emerging economic powers has turned many African countries into desirable partners for investment in exchange for development cooperation and political partnerships.[1] Not only governments but also private equity funds explore new opportunities in Africa.[2] As former colonial powers gradually leave the field, space is opening up for new players in the global arena. New global rivalries, in particular between China and the United States, have not left Africans untouched.[3] Conferences such as the China-Africa Business Summit in 2009 underscore the new importance that is given to the African countries and their resource riches.[4] Specifically, India and China have strongly increased their efforts to develop ties with Côte d'Ivoire, and such emerging relationships are the focus of this chapter.[5]

These recent developments have raised substantial concerns over which model for development and industrialization policies will determine the future of Africa.[6] The academic business literature, beyond the development field, that accounts for changes in Africa is limited, and relevant literature on Côte d'Ivoire is virtually nonexistent.[7] Since the outbreak of the country's political crisis in 2002, few researchers have found their way into Côte d'Ivoire. The country went through a time of civil conflict from 2002 to 2004 and since then has been split in two. The first postconflict democratic elections in November 2010 did not solve the conflict but created a political stalemate between the major opponents, Alassane Ouattara and Laurent Gbagbo.

In this chapter, I provide a detailed outlook at the investment patterns in Côte d'Ivoire in order to contribute to the wider analysis of changes in emerging countries in Africa. I collected data for this chapter during my work at the International University of Grand Bassam in Côte d'Ivoire in 2009. I concentrated on archival data and interviewed crucial people from government, academia, and the private sector. Herein, I focus primarily on the status quo in Côte d'Ivoire, outlining the shifts that have occurred with regard to investment and business in general. I place particular emphasis on the arrival of Indian and Chinese companies. I first discuss the current setting, explaining some of the predominant social and environmental challenges, then turn to recent developments and the evidence of investment patterns and business practices. Finally, I account for some of the expected impacts of globalization.

Côte d'Ivoire: A Country Profile

Côte d'Ivoire is a coastal country situated in West Africa, bordering the countries of Liberia, Ghana, Guinea, Burkina Faso, and Mali. The official administrative capital is Yamoussoukro, while its largest city and economic engine is Abidjan, with about four million inhabitants. Côte d'Ivoire is an ethnically diverse country with more than seventy native languages spoken. According to CountryWatch, its major ethnicities include the Akan, Voltaiques or Gur, Krou, Northern Mandes, and Southern Mandes.[8] The major religions practiced are Christianity (34 percent), Islam (27 percent), and local religions (39 percent). Its climate is tropical, and its surface area roughly equals that of Germany.[9] Estimates of Côte d'Ivoire's population vary from 18.7 million to about 20 million as of 2007; it is projected to surpass 21 million by 2011.[10] The population growth has been estimated at an average of 2.7 percent from 2005 to 2009.[11]

Traditional export goods of Côte d'Ivoire include agricultural commodities such as cocoa, coffee, cotton, palm oil, pineapples, bananas, tuna, raw rubber, and tropical woods.[12] Côte d'Ivoire is the largest cocoa producer in the world. For many years, cocoa was the main source of national income (up to 40 percent). The sector employs about six hundred thousand people and directly affects an estimated six million people.[13] In recent years, newly discovered oil reserves have created a new source of national income. Côte d'Ivoire also has substantial refinery capacity and produces a significant amount of natural gas, extracted mainly by American and French companies. Further export products include diamonds, iron ore, manganese, cobalt, copper, and bauxite.[14]

Côte d'Ivoire had long been a symbol of political stability, ethnic peace, and an open economy in West Africa since its independence from France in 1960. A military coup in 1999, however, ended this period of relative prosperity and led to political instability and civil conflict. Following a failed coup in 2002, the country lapsed into civil war and basically split in two. During the hostilities an estimated three thousand persons were killed and up to seven hundred thousand persons were displaced.[15] In the years 2003–6, the different parties competed to take control of the struggling country.[16]

In order to stabilize the war-torn country, the international community established a United Nations mission in Côte d'Ivoire. The first mission, MINUCI, was based on UN resolution 1479 and lasted from May 2003 to April 2004. It included 184 international and local staff with a budget of $29.9 million. The current mission, UNOCI, succeeded MINUCI in April 2004, authorized by UN resolution 1865 until July 31, 2009; UNOCI has since been extended. The strength of the UNOCI mission as of February 28, 2010, was 8,544 total uniformed personnel with a budget of $497.46 million. In addition, there are about 1,000 French troops, out of an original 3,500 that were stationed in Côte d'Ivoire as a stabilization force. According to local observers, the French troops will leave the country once the elections turn out to be peaceful.[17]

In 2005 the World Bank, African Development Bank (ADB), the Agence Française de Développement (AFD), and other bilateral partners suspended dealings with Côte d'Ivoire because it had defaulted on its debt obligations to ADB.[18] In March 2007 Ivorian president Laurent Gbagbo and the country's rebel leader, Guillaume Soro, signed the Ouagadougou Accord to establish peace between the government and the rebel forces.[19]

Economic activity had slowed down tremendously with the outbreak of the crisis due to increased political and security risks.[20] Foreign direct investment (FDI), mainly from France, accounted for 40–45 percent of total capital of Ivorian firms before the crisis. On November 6–8, 2004, anti-French demonstrations erupted, and subsequent plundering caused several deaths and the departure of eight thousand Europeans, most of them French nationals. According to the Ivorian Chamber of Commerce (CCI-CI), the immediate employment loss amounted to ten thousand jobs and the disappearance of about a hundred companies.[21] This economic blow was aggravated by the fact that in Côte d'Ivoire one employed person usually supports at least ten people. Out of 147 subsidiaries of French companies in the country at the time, 135 massively cut back their activities; as a result, 95 percent of the 350 expatriates employed by these companies left.

The true victims of the French-Ivorian conflict in Côte d'Ivoire were the small and medium-sized French enterprises (SMEs) that employed about thirty-six thousand people. The consequences were severe. The already struggling economy slowed down even more. Cocoa exporters experienced difficulties in bringing their goods to the port of Abidjan. The fiscal authorities experienced a substantial decline in tax revenues, to which French companies had contributed up to 50 percent before the crisis.[22] Many local companies that were serving the French market had to decrease production.

Côte d'Ivoire used to be known for its outstanding infrastructure, but today that infrastructure is deeply insufficient. There are 50,400 kilometers of highways (but only 4,889 km paved), 660 kilometers of railways, and two active ports (Abidjan and San Pedro).[23] The port of Abidjan, Africa's largest between Cape Town and Casablanca, is the key entry point to West Africa. However, the crisis delayed necessary investments, particularly in roads. General infrastructure challenges include inadequate supplies of electric power and water. Energy costs are high, especially in areas that are not yet fully electrified. Traditionally an electricity exporter, Côte d'Ivoire had to cut electricity exports to neighboring countries, such as Ghana, Burkina Faso, Togo, and Benin, due to the increasing difficulties in satisfying its own needs. Waste management in the city of Abidjan broke down. Moreover, inland transport continues to be hindered through barricades and ubiquitous corruption. Tourism, in particular from France, has almost completely ceased.[24]

Massive Social and Environmental Problems

Environmental Degradation

Côte d'Ivoire is facing massive environmental problems. The timber industry has largely destroyed the nation's rain forests, once among the largest in West Africa.[25] In addition, the setting up of plantations for cash crops to be exported to Europe and the United States has accelerated deforestation. Combined with the conflict-induced breakdown of institutional control, these conditions have had disastrous consequences for biodiversity. For instance, chimpanzees that once numbered in the tens of thousands in the rain forest were decimated to an estimated population of two hundred to three hundred, and local observers fear they will be extinct within the next five years. More recently, industrial pollution has become a major problem. Water pollution from industrial and agricultural effluents combined with poor waste management, contamination of water supplies, and deteriorating urban conditions have turned parts of Abidjan, once the "Paris of West Africa," into cesspools. In addition, natural hazards such as heavy surf along the coast and torrential flooding during the rainy season are aggravated by the overexploitation of coastal resources and the lack of natural harbors.[26]

Corruption: The Trafigura Case

In August 2006 the cargo vessel *Probo Koala*, owned and operated by the Dutch commodities trading company Trafigura (headquartered in London), unloaded an estimated five hundred tons of highly toxic liquid waste in the port of Abidjan.[27] Its Ivorian subsidiary, Puma Energy, contracted the disposal of the waste to a local company, Tommy (which had been set up for this task through the help of the Waibs company). The toxic waste was loaded onto trucks and dumped at twelve sites around Abidjan.

According to Greenpeace, at least fifteen people died and thousands of victims suffered from contamination due to the toxic waste.[28] Even after two years, only the families of the recognized victims had received compensation, and much of the waste still had not been removed.[29] The government of Côte d'Ivoire received 152 million euros in return for dropping all charges against Trafigura and the executives of its Ivorian subsidiary.[30] The executive of Tommy and an employee of Waibs were sentenced to twenty years and five years in prison, respectively.[31] Moreover, Trafigura was accused of corruption, for having offered luxury vacations in Morocco and weekly salaries of 750 euros to witnesses for falsified testimonies, as well as ignoring a hearing at the jury court.[32]

Subsequently, the government of Côte d'Ivoire decided to revoke the original decision and demand the compensation sum of 564 million euros from Trafigura and its partners in the affair.[33] Moreover, the law firm Leigh, Day filed a class-action suit against Trafigura in London's High Court on a no-win, no-fee basis on behalf of thirty-one thousand residents; this lawsuit was eventually settled for $48.7 million in compensation.[34] However, Trafigura never did accept any liability or responsibility for the dumping.[35] The company officially states: "It has always been, and remains, Trafigura's position that it is not liable to the claimants."[36] The final settlement states that "independent experts are unable to identify a link between exposure to the chemicals released from the slops and deaths, miscarriages, birth defects, loss of visual acuity or other serious and chronic injuries."[37] Trafigura pointed to counterevidence;[38] however, this engendered new criticisms of Trafigura for denial of responsibility, and of the Leigh, Day firm for profiteering.[39]

Conflict-Related Issues

The unresolved political conflict between the opposition and the government that practically split the nation in two and the outstanding elections continue to affect business activity in Côte d'Ivoire. For instance, in 2007 the Washington-based NGO Global Witness published a report on the contribution of the cocoa sector to the armed conflict in Côte d'Ivoire since 2002.[40] Global Witness emphasized that the lack of transparency about the flow of funds and the institutions involved had facilitated the purchase of arms to prolong the conflict. The Ivorian government reacted by publishing its revenues from the cocoa sector and their utilization.[41] Moreover, conflict diamonds continue to be traded even today in Côte d'Ivoire according to my own research and former studies such as that by the NGO Partenariat Afrique Canada.[42] Diamonds from the north of Côte d'Ivoire, which are banned by the Kimberly Processes, continued to appear on the world market, notably in the United Arab Emirates, the NGO reported. The smuggled diamonds represent an estimated value of $9–23 million that are believed to have sustained the armed conflict. Furthermore, about three thousand children are estimated to have been abused as child soldiers.[43] Violence against children and women (in particular sexual abuse) not only by the local population but also by UN peacekeepers and Ivorian government forces has been reported frequently.[44]

Poverty and Labor Conditions

The political instability and civil strife have caused an economic decline that has reduced living standards and increased levels of poverty. According to the International Monetary Fund (IMF) and World Bank (WB), poverty increased from 38.2 percent in 2002 to 48.9 percent of the whole population in 2008.[45] (The poor are defined as those earning less than $480 per year.) Due to fallouts from the crisis, the country dropped from its 154th rank in 1999 to 166th in 2007 (out of 177 countries) in the UN Development Index. The extent of the decline is indicated by the following World Bank statistics: the unemployment rate is estimated at 40 percent (60 percent among young adults); 32 percent of Ivorians do not have access to primary school education; and 26 percent do not have access to a hospital.[46] The degree of adult literacy is estimated to be only about 48.7 percent.[47] A particularly alarming aspect of poverty is the continued existence of child labor in many areas of the economy, in particular in the cocoa sector.[48]

Public Health

Côte d'Ivoire is facing tremendous challenges with regard to public health, as is borne out in the following statistics: life expectancy in 2007 is reported at 47.4 years; child mortality for those under age five is estimated at about 18 percent, among the highest in the world, and rising; and only 50 percent of children are fully immunized.[49] At the end of 2005, an estimated 750,000 Ivorians carried the HIV/AIDS virus, and 7.1 percent of the population aged fifteen to forty-nine were HIV positive.[50] Some local observers state that the official figures are much too low, and that local hospitals in Abidjan report HIV/AIDS infection rates up to 25–30 percent in the poorer districts. Overall, deaths in Côte d'Ivoire caused by HIV/AIDS are estimated at 38,000, resulting in about 420,000 orphaned children below the age of seventeen.[51] Moreover, malaria is a common disease that is often fatal, disproportionately afflicting the poor.[52]

Corruption

Côte d'Ivoire ranks 151st out of 193 countries in the 2008 corruption index published by Transparency International.[53] Routine small-scale corruption is now being accompanied by alleged large-scale corruption in the public as well as private sectors.[54] The case of Trafigura is a tragic example of how corruption can lead to severe, long-lasting damages to the local population. Recently, company executives in the cocoa sector were detained on corruption charges for the defalcation of more than $224 million that was allocated for the purchase of a chocolate factory in the United States.[55] A particularly problematic form of corruption is racketeering, which according to a WB study costs between $230 and $363.3 million annually.[56]

Recent Economic Development

New Optimism

The Treaty of Ouagadougou signed in March 2007 fostered a new optimism that has significantly revived the Ivorian economy.[57] To support the efforts of the Ivorian government, the WB approved a grant of $120 million for a crisis recovery program.[58] According to the IMF, real GDP in 2008 amounted to $23.5 billion, or $1,132 per capita.[59] Real per capita GDP had fallen by 15 percent in 2000–2006 but started growing again by 1.6 percent in 2007, increasing to 2.3 percent the following year.[60] For the first time since 1999, private investments grew substantially. In particular, Côte d'Ivoire's telecommunications and construction sectors grew considerably. The telecommunications industry has been growing rapidly due to the existence of a public data communications network, cellular phones, and ADSL broadband services with speeds of up to 8 Mb/s. Cellular phone use in Côte d'Ivoire is above the African average with currently five operators doing business in the country. The arrival of two new international fiber-optic submarine cables, together with the likely auction of the WIMAX spectrum in the near future, should further boost the telecommunications sector.[61] Côte d'Ivoire also has a regional stock exchange, which, as of May 2010, was composed of thirty-eight companies with 12,683 shares being traded. Its market capitalization was at about $3.2 billion.[62] However, the economic takeoff has been accompanied by increasing inflation, which topped 9 percent at the end of 2008 due to the food crisis and high prices for crude oil.[63]

Debt Relief

On March 27, 2009, the IMF approved a three-year arrangement worth SDR 373.98 million (about $565.7 million) under the Poverty Reduction and Growth Facility (PRGF) for Côte d'Ivoire.[64] The country would be allowed to immediately draw the equivalent of SDR 159.348 million (about $241.1 million) from the IMF. Four days later, the IMF announced that Côte d'Ivoire reached the decision point under the enhanced HIPC Debt Relief Initiative.[65] This meant the country could begin to access relief under the Multilateral Debt Relief Initiative (MDRI) in order to improve security, regain political stability, and reunite the country through economic recovery. Debt relief under the MDRI was estimated at $3.0 billion, equivalent to a 23.6 percent reduction. However, half of the debt relief for Côte d'Ivoire has already been received through past debt rescheduling and concessional arrears and clearance operations.[66] Côte d'Ivoire's external debt was estimated at $14.3 billion as of the end of December 2007.[67] Despite the relief through HIPC, reintegrating the north of the country will remain a major challenge for economic recovery.

Who Invests? The Evidence

Many potential investors are still hesitant to undertake large investments in Côte d'Ivoire because the first postconflict elections that occurred in October and November 2010 could not solve the political crisis. The elections had earlier been scheduled for November 29, 2009.

Increasing levels of violence, political instability, and mass unrest ensued as Laurent Gbagbo refused to gracefully exit the Office of the Presidency after the 2010 elections took place, even though the Independent Electoral Commission in the country indicated that opposition candidate, Alassane Outtara, was the legitimate winner of the elections. The United States, France, as well as a number of international organizations have shown support for Alassane Outtara.[68]

French Influence

French companies continue to be the leading investors in Côte d'Ivoire, holding about 28 percent of shares in Ivorian companies.[69] In 2008 France lost its position as Côte d'Ivoire's primary trading partner to Nigeria, due to the increase in Nigerian oil exports to Côte d'Ivoire.[70] However, Côte d'Ivoire continues to be France's leading trading partner in Africa with a market share of 18 percent. According to Maison des Français de l'Étranger, on December 31, 2008, there were 11,248 French residents registered in Côte d'Ivoire.[71] There are more than five hundred businesses and 143 subsidiaries of French companies that account for 68 percent of foreign capital. They are most active in agriculture, construction, energy, oil, transport, telecommunications, banking, insurance, and the hotel industry. Important companies that have remained despite the conflict include banking institutions such as SGBCI (a subsidiary of Société General), Total (as major shareholder of the Ivorian refinery company Société Ivoirienne de Raffinage), EDF, SOMDIAA, Compagnie Fruitière, COLAS, VINCI, SATOM, Thales, Rougier Bouygues, France Télécom, the liquor company Castel, and the investment and industrial holding company Bolloré.[72] Many of these firms entered into joint ventures with the government or Ivorian entrepreneurs to set up local companies. For instance, Côte d'Ivoire Telecom is a joint venture between France Télécom and the Ivorian government, and is the number one mobile phone operator in the country with a national presence in all major cities and more than five hundred villages.[73]

Lebanese Takeover

Much of the void left by the departure of the French has been filled by Lebanese businesspeople who took over former French operations. The Lebanese immigrated to Côte d'Ivoire in two waves. The first occurred in colonial times, and most who came were relatively well off Christians. The second wave occurred after 1975 when Côte d'Ivoire opened its doors to refugees from the Lebanese civil war.[74] Their population was estimated to be between sixty thousand and one hundred thousand by the end of the 1980s and has remained stable. The Lebanese are well integrated into Ivorian society and often act behind the scenes on behalf of projects that are attributed to local (Ivorian) businessmen. One reason for this arrangement is that Ivorian entrepreneurs frequently do not have the means to start their own businesses and thus involve Lebanese in financing their activities. Alternatively, the Ivorians rent out their licenses against a commission.[75]

Indian "Charm Offensive"

India established diplomatic relations with Côte d'Ivoire on November 30, 1962, and opened its first embassy there in 1987.[76] Côte d'Ivoire is the major supplier of raw cashew nuts for the Indian market, with exports of 295,791 tons to India in 2002. It also exports cotton, wood (in particular teak wood), and cocoa. From India, Côte d'Ivoire mainly imports "semi-blanchi" rice, pharmaceutical products, chemicals, metallic products, ceramic, glass, stone, and vehicles.

On March 19–21, 2008, the largest-ever India-Africa conclave took place in New Delhi to discuss the India-Africa Project Partnership 2008. Over nine hundred delegates, among them the vice presidents of Tanzania and Ghana and thirty-seven African ministers, came together to discuss more than 130 investment projects in Africa worth $10 billion.[77] Already in 2002, the Indian government was offering assistance to Côte d'Ivoire in the small-scale industrial and engineering sectors.[78]

In 2004 the Indian government initiated a $500 million development initiative with eight African countries—Burkina Faso, Côte d'Ivoire, Ghana, Guinea-Bissau, Equatorial Guinea, Mali, Senegal, and Chad—under the name TEAM 9 (Techno-Economic Approach for Africa-India Movement).[79] In Côte d'Ivoire, TEAM 9 financed the following projects: (a) provision of 400 buses to SOTRA, the Abidjan Transport Company, by TATA Motors; (b) transformation of cashew nuts into finished products, with National Federation of the Producers of Cashews (FENOPACI); (c) oil extraction from seeds of palm trees, with the National Federation of the Producers of Palm Oil (FENACOPAH-CI); (d) transformation of cassava (manioc) plants into various semifinished and finished products (e.g., starch and glucose); (e) production of chips from local fruit and vegetables; and (f) establishment of a center to demonstrate Indian machinery, with Société Ivoirienne de Technologie Tropicale (I2T) of Côte d'Ivoire and the National Research Development Corporation (NRDC) of India.

The TEAM 9 initiative also provided $20 million in financing for the free trade zone and technology park Mahatma Gandhi VITIB (Village des Technologies de l'Information et de la Communication et des Biotechnologies) in Grand Bassam. The park was created as a public company on November 30, 2006, with a number of national and international partners. The Indian companies involved include Shapoorj Pallonji & CL, United Telecoms Limited, and Software Technology Parks of India. Other partners include the Ivorian government, eighteen companies from Côte d'Ivoire, three from China, one from the United Arab Emirates, and one from South Africa.[80]

Finally, the TEAM 9 initiative is providing a credit line of $200 million for infrastructure and rural development to assist the New Partnership for Africa's Development (NEPAD).[81] According to the *Financial Express*, the TEAM 9 initiative is driven by India's energy and resource needs.[82] In the future, India is planning to invest $1 billion in Côte d'Ivoire to develop oil operations.[83] The oil of the Gulf of Guinea is of high quality and is mostly located offshore, far away from conflict regions. Moreover, Côte d'Ivoire is not a member of OPEC, which makes it more open to bilateral negotiations.

Currently, the largest Indian company active in Côte d'Ivoire is Olam International. Olam, headquartered in Singapore, is a leading global supply chain manager of agricultural products with extensive operations across Africa.[84] Olam dominates the cocoa trade, buying directly from local farmers and selling to larger companies such as Nestlé or Cargill. In order to increase the output of local farmers, the company follows a very pragmatic approach. For instance, it provides low-technology solutions such as cocoa-drying facilities powered by solar energy free of charge to local farmers. It also helps by financing warehouses and providing interest-free loans to farmers to help them buy farm inputs.

China's First Steps

The Chinese presence in Côte d'Ivoire is rather modest. According to Bénédicte Châtel, there are about six hundred to one thousand Chinese who work mainly for about fifteen Chinese companies officially operating in Côte d'Ivoire.[85] Côte d'Ivoire and China established diplomatic relations on March 2, 1983. In 1984 and 1996, bilateral trade agreements were signed. In December 1997, the China Investment and Development Center for Trade Promotion was inaugurated. Since then, a number of important Chinese statesmen, including Hu Jintao, then vice president of the PRC (January 1999), have visited Côte d'Ivoire. Also, Ivorian leaders made official visits to China, including former president Henri Konan Bedie in May 1997 and president, Laurent Gbagbo, in April 2002.

During the China-Africa summit in 2006 in Beijing, China announced a general offer of bilateral cooperation for its African partners, including Côte d'Ivoire. The participating governments announced a plan on how to sustain and develop their relationships for the coming three years. The second China-Africa summit took place at the Cape Town International Convention Center in South Africa, October 22–23, 2009. This event focused on how Chinese activities in Africa could be intensified. Recently, the legal consulting firm PKD Conseil organized its second forum on primary resources in Côte d'Ivoire, held in Shanghai.[86]

Currently, joint ventures between Chinese and Ivorian companies in Côte d'Ivoire include the Hua-Ke Vehicles Co. Ltd and the Agro-machinery Assembling Co. Ltd. Moreover, the China Road and Bridge Construction Corporation and China Overseas Engineering Corporation are operating in Côte d'Ivoire. As mentioned above, Chinese companies are also strongly interested in Côte d'Ivoire's newly discovered oil resources and recently completed a project for petroleum prospecting there. Chinese construction companies have also been involved in building the new presidential palace and the parliament building in Yamoussoukro. However, construction has been temporarily suspended since the Ivorian government did not pay its part of the construction costs due to a shortage of finances.

Recently, the Chinese government offered to ship materials ranging from mobile phones to lamps in support of the elections that took place in November 2010.[87] Despite this fact, China has offered aid of $65,000 to every developing country interested in participating in the World's Fair in Shanghai taking place from May 1 to October 30 in 2010. Côte d'Ivoire will be among the countries attending and thus benefiting from the Chinese benefaction, exhibiting mainly artisanal products. China is welcoming Ivorian students, offering about twenty scholarships a year to attend Chinese universities, at the same time that France is closing more of its universities to applicants from West Africans.[88] Moreover, China is providing about three thousand scholarships to African government officials every year, among them about thirty Ivorians. The main goal is to teach the Chinese language so that these individuals will be better able to establish relationships with Chinese businesses.

Both Indian and Chinese mobile phone companies are looking to Africa for investment opportunities.[89] However, African operators have to bear high infrastructure costs, particularly since existing infrastructure such as base stations, various exchanges, or other kinds of networks are not shared among companies.

Russian and Venezuelan Attempts

The Russian-Ivorian relationship, traditionally rather distant, has intensified in recent years.[90] Russian oil companies are becoming increasingly interested in Côte d'Ivoire since the discovery of oil in the Gulf of Guinea. In 2006 LUKOIL Overseas signed an agreement for the acquisition of a significant stake (63 percent) in the exploration, development, and production of the Baobab field of Côte d'Ivoire.[91] However, there has been no follow-up to this agreement. In addition, Venezuela's Arevenco is considering the possibility of investing $7 billion into a San Pedro refinery over the next five years.[92] Ivorian PETROCI Energy, the American company Energy Allied International, and WCW International announced their intention to invest $1.3 billion into an oil refinery in Abidjan from 2008 to 2011. Due to the political crisis the investment has been postponed.

Swiss and American Agricultural Dominance

Swiss-based Nestlé, the largest food company in the world, is among the largest companies operating in Côte d'Ivoire. The company announced that it will invest $26.3 million in cocoa and coffee processing factories through the end of 2010.[93] However, currently all investments are on hold.

Cargill and ADM (Archer, Daniels, Midland) have a strong presence in Côte d'Ivoire. Cargill is an agro-industrial giant that sources and processes cocoa and produces cocoa products including cocoa liquor, butter, cake, and powder in Côte d'Ivoire. Cargill started operating in Côte d'Ivoire in 1998 and today has about 450 employees.[94] It acknowledges the challenging political and economic circumstances in Côte d'Ivoire that have led to a deterioration of the health and education systems. ADM, one of the world's leading agricultural processors, has substantial operations in Côte d'Ivoire, mainly crushing and exporting cocoa and shea nuts.[95] In 2001 ADM bought the cocoa operations of SIFCA, which at the time was the primary cocoa producer in Côte d'Ivoire. Today, ADM operates a cocoa-processing facility in Abidjan and three conditioning and storage plants in Abidjan and San Pedro.[96]

ADM, Cargill, and Nestlé are members of the World Cocoa Foundation, which was established in 2000 to facilitate the development of public-private partnerships to benefit cocoa-farming communities through training programs and research.[97] Presently, Nestlé and Cargill also work with the Ivorian government through the International Cocoa Initiative (ICI)—a partnership between industry, NGOs, and trade unions established in 2002—to prevent the worst forms of child labor.[98]

ADM emphasizes its efforts to improve the lives of cocoa farmers in Côte d'Ivoire on its website, highlighting the Sustainable Tree Crop Program and Socially and Environmentally Responsible Agriculture Practices (SERAP) Program, which has grown to more than twelve thousand participants. Suppliers are asked to commit to the elimination of the worst forms of child labor, and noncompliant contracts are terminated. Cargill provides free training seminars for local farmers on how to improve the quality of the cocoa beans and transparent information on international cocoa market prices. Cargill also partners with local truck companies, the German firm GTZ, and the national rural development agency, ANADER.[99] In 2007 Cargill joined a new certification program for supply chain transparency to the farm level with nearly fifty multinational companies and organizations. It is designed to ensure that prices paid to Ivorian farmers are fair and that Côte d'Ivoire cacao is grown in a sustainable manner.[100]

Following its "creating shared value" directive, Nestlé is committed to sustainable cocoa growing through its partnership programs in order to benefit local cocoa and coffee farmers and increase production. Currently, the company is funding a three-year project with three cooperatives of about three thousand farmers in Côte d'Ivoire together with the International Cocoa Organization (ICCO), the ICI, and cocoa exporter ECOM.[101] Nestlé wants to distribute ten million cocoa plants to Ivorian farmers to replace aging trees over the next decade since trees are getting older and have been harmed by diseases including black pod and swollen shoot and by poor weather, which have led to lower harvests.[102]

Dutch Presence

Unilever, another large multinational with considerable operations in Côte d'Ivoire, announced in 2008 that it had sold its palm oil business to PALMCI and plantation interests and had acquired a regional soap business in exchange.[103] The palm oil operations were sold to SIFCA and to a fifty-fifty joint venture of Singapore's Wilmar International and Olam International. In addition, SIFCA announced that it will invest $85.28 million with financing from Wilmar into a palm oil processing factory until 2012 in order to double palm oil output to five hundred thousand tons over the next three years.[104] The SIFCA Group operates in major sectors of agribusiness in Ghana, Benin, Liberia, and Nigeria. In 2008, it employed approximately seventeen thousand people with revenues of more than $500 million in 2007.[105] Unilever remained a minority stakeholder of PALMCI. At the same time, Unilever announced that it is working toward the sustainable cultivation of palm oil to fight deforestation.[106] The company stated that it had been promoting sustainability in palm oil cultivation through such initiatives as the Roundtable on Sustainable Palm Oil. However, PALMCI, Unilever's new supplier, was strongly accused by environmentalists of planning to set up a palm oil plantation in the Tanoé forest wetlands of southern Côte d'Ivoire.[107] The company responded that it would use its influence to "ensure adherence to best practices in terms of sustainability and Environmental Impact Assessment," which would also be "stipulated in the sale of our plantations."[108]

Canadian Oil Operations

According to PETROCI, the national oil company, there are four major active oil fields that are currently being exploited: the fields of Lion and Panthère, Foxtrot, Espoir, and Baobab.[109] The major operator is Canadian Natural Resources Limited Côte d'Ivoire (CNR), which started working in Côte d'Ivoire in 2002;[110] currently CNR operates the blocks CI-26 and CI-40.[111] The Lion and Panthère field is managed by a consortium of DEVON, IFC, SK Corp, and PETROCI. The Espoir field is operated by CNR, Tullow Oil, and PETROCI. And a consortium of CNR, Svenska, and PETROCI operates the Baobab field. Phase II of the Baobab field development is on track, according to CNR.[112] The Ivorian government is officially committed to sustainable development and announced that it would dedicate the majority of the income from its oil operations to the fight against poverty.

Future and Present Government Projects

According to Business Monitor International (BMI), the government of Côte d'Ivoire announced important infrastructure investments. It aims to boost the electricity generating capacity from 1,200 megawatts today to 2,415 megawatts by 2016; it charged Electricité de France to improve drinking water supply systems in Daloa, San Pedro, and Tabou; and it intends to improve five thousand kilometers of roads. In addition, a transmission line is planned from Boba Dialasso to Ouagadougou worth $100 million; although it was supposed to be constructed from 2007 to 2009, it has yet to be started. CIPREL (Compagnie Ivoirienne de Production d'Electricite), a gas turbine power station, announced it would build a thermal plant in Abidjan worth $96 million. Finally, the Ivorian port-management firm SETV will make a $62.3 million investment in the port of Abidjan to be realized by 2012.[113]

Additional New Players

The Swiss-based Aga Khan Development Network (AKDN) has recently increased its activities in Côte d'Ivoire, aggressively providing loans of CFA 150,000 (US$300) to a $225 million dollar investment in the country's infrastructure.[114] AKDN directed the financing to Azito Energie, a joint venture between Swiss ABB, French Electricité de France, British CDC group, AKDN, and Ivorian IPS SA. The joint venture set up the largest gas-fired power station in West Africa, the Azito power plant, which is part of Côte d'Ivoire's long-term development program. It currently produces a power output of 300 megawatts, representing 39 percent of the nation's energy production. Azito Energie aims to mobilize stakeholders' support through dialogue in order to contribute to development and become better rooted in local communities.[115] AKDN also recently launched a microfinance operation in the region of Boundiali and Dianra in northern Côte d'Ivoire, providing loans of 150,000–250,000 CFA francs ($300–500) for six months to two years.[116] Finally, in the telecommunications sector, Côte d'Ivoire saw the entrance of the South African mobile phone operator MTN as well as Moov, operated by Atlantique Telecom, in which Etisalat holds a 50 percent share. Both operators have been extremely successful, cutting substantial market share from former monopolist Côte d'Ivoire Telecom.[117]

Discussion

The new market entrants from developing countries are bringing about changes in the economic, social, environmental, and political realm that are difficult to assess. The entrance of China and India already has caused new competition on the political level with regard to which economic lead the government of Côte d'Ivoire will follow. International conferences and business summits exclusively organized by the Chinese and Indian governments for African leaders show that emerging countries are not only trying to create new political ties but also purposively excluding the established powers in Europe and North America. The logic is simple and plausible—in the global competition for oil, food, and other primary resources, these emerging powers can negotiate without the burden of a colonial (Europe) or imperialistic (United States) heritage. According to former Ugandan ambassador to China Phillip Idro, the warnings of China's hunger for Africa's resources were "borne of fear, based on ignorance and are an old hangover."[118] Moreover, China's and India's rise to power represents a role model that many African leaders look up to. The new relationships being forged have substantially contributed to Africa's growth in the recent past.[119] A number of further observations can be made.

Employment

The new entrants are likely to create new job opportunities and contribute to social stabilization in a country where youth unemployment is estimated at 60 percent. For instance, growth in telecommunications has created an enormous amount of new jobs for low-skilled labor. However, Chinese companies in particular have a very bad track record in Africa when it comes to labor rights, worker safety, and wage levels.[120] While these countries are welcome for their pragmatism and "just do it" mentality, in the long run it will be of crucial importance to create and enforce existing policies and sanction mechanisms to avoid the continuous disregard of internationally recognized labor standards.[121]

Consumer Prices and Availability of Goods and Services

In the telecommunications sector, new entrants like Etisalat and MTN are driving prices down and bringing new product and service innovations to the market. New cost-saving offers are constantly being announced. Ivorian consumers benefit not only from lower prices but also from the greater selection of services offered. Today many Lebanese import-export businesses concentrate on importing cheap goods from China, simultaneously broadening the array of available products to choose from and making accessible products that were formerly inaccessible (because too expensive). Even artificial hair for African women is largely imported from Asia. But dependence on cheaper imports has its negative effects as well. For example, Chinese textiles are much cheaper than those produced locally due to economies of scale and better production technology, but their success has put many local companies out of business. Many industry sectors in manufacturing and services cannot compete with the imports from China or India on a price level.

Competition

In the cocoa sector, new entrants such as Olam International have increased competition for established players like ADM and Cargill. But Olam is very new to the field of corporate social responsibility and thus is much less involved in institutional processes that have been set up to redress the lack of good governance in many developed countries. Moreover, companies from emerging economic powers are well prepared for such obstacles as infrastructure deficiency that they encounter in Africa. They understand the specific challenges and have proved highly flexible in reacting to them.

Technology and Skill Transfer

Little technology or skill transfer to the African continent has occurred in recent decades, and Côte d'Ivoire is no exception. The level of professional training is low despite the activities of many multinational companies, international agencies like the IMF and World Bank, and nongovernmental organizations. Field research shows that many Ivorian companies have a human resources problem; the task of finding qualified employees is consistently difficult. What, then, is the promise of companies from emerging economic powers? The potential advantage is that, based on their home market experience, they have developed techniques to operate in difficult environments. This may allow local companies to imitate successful strategies for increasing efficiency, identifying market opportunities, and achieving growth. For instance, at VITIB, Indian entrepreneurs plan to offer training courses for information and communication technologies for local entrepreneurs.

Environment

The environmental track record of companies from emerging countries is rather questionable.[122] There are several reasons for this fact. First, Indian and Chinese companies are not under the same pressure by the general public or civil society organizations such as Greenpeace to establish policies to account for the social and environmental impact of their operations that many Western companies face. Second, their governments for a long time relied on a development model that put environmental concerns at a very low priority. Third, investor capital is not necessarily tied to social or environmental concerns. It will be a major challenge for Côte d'Ivoire to assure that companies from emerging countries that are not subject to close public scrutiny and vigilance of nongovernmental organizations comply with internationally recognized environmental standards.

Conclusion

Once called the African miracle, Côte d'Ivoire has descended into stagnation at a low level of development. The country has been economically ruined by the combination of a violent internal conflict, mismanagement by the political elites, and neocolonial policies forced upon the Ivorian government by the WB and the IMF.[123] As part of the "bottom billion," the people of Côte d'Ivoire are desperately looking for ways out of the economic and political crisis.[124] On the one hand, the new economic powers of China and India are seen as both threat and opportunity; their involvement in the Ivorian economy may allow Côte d'Ivoire to regain its former pride. On the other hand, many Western institutions, including multinational companies, are deeply mistrusted. Although the "charm offensives" launched by the Chinese and Indian governments are clearly of a strategic nature, and admittedly so, Ivorians appreciate the offer of aid for development and technology transfer. The impacts are yet unknown. The Western-style development model that has failed has not yet been replaced by a true alternative. The rise of India and China provides hope to many Africans: African countries may finally be able to fulfill the promise of peace and prosperity the people of the continent have held since the times of decolonization. However, African leaders should be wary. Experience from around Africa shows that Chinese investors in particular have followed aggressive agendas and have not hesitated to collaborate with corrupt and illegitimate regimes.

Notes

1. Walden Bello, "China Eyes Africa," *Multinational Monitor*, 28, no. 1 (2007): 23, 26; Harry G. Broadman, "China and India Go to Africa," *Foreign Affairs* 87, no. 2: (2008): 95–109; Lucy Corkin and Sanusha Naidu, "China and India in Africa: An Introduction," *Review of African Political Economy* 35, no. 115 (2008): 115–16; Martyn

Davies, "China's Developmental Model Comes to Africa," *Review of African Political Economy* 35, no. 115 (2008): 134–37; Clifton W. Pannell, "China's Economic and Political Penetration in Africa," *Eurasian Geography and Economics* 49, no. 6 (2008): 706–30; Ian Taylor, "China's Oil Diplomacy in Africa," *International Affairs* 82, no. 5 (2006): 937–59; Harry G. Broadman, "Africa's Silk Road: China and India's New Economic Frontier," *Foreign Affairs* 87, no. 1 (2008): 196–97.

2. J. Marshall, "Private Equity Pushes into India, Africa," *Financial Executive* 24, no. 1 (2008).

3. Horace Campbell, "China in Africa: Challenging U.S. Global Hegemony," *Third World Quarterly* 29, no. 1 (2008): 89–105.

4. Corporate Africa, "China-Africa Business Summit 2009" (2009; accessed May 20, 2010).

5. Mohit Joshi, "India-Africa Conclave to Discuss Projects Worth over 10 Billion Dollars," TopNews.in, March 14, 2008, http://www.topnews.in/india-africa-conclave-discuss-projects-worth-over-10-billion-dollars-225681; Kamini Krishna, *India-Africa Partnership in the Twenty-First Century: Expanding Horizon* (Lusaka: University of Zambia, 2009); Sushant K. Singh, *India and West Africa: A Burgeoning Relationship* (London: Chatham House, 2007); "Team 9 Opens a New Innings [*sic*] in India-West Africa Relations," *Financial Express*, March 4, 2004; Bénédicte Châtel, "Chine/Afrique: L'ouverture," *African Business* 5 (2009): 32–36; C. Lapeye, "La Côte d'Ivoire demeure: La plus grande économie," *Marchés Africains* 12 (2009): 6–7.

6. Alemayehu Geda and Atnafu G. Meskel, "China and India's Growth Surge: Is It a Curse or Blessing for Africa? The Case of Manufactured Exports," *African Development Review* 20, no. 2 (2008): 247–72.

7. For exceptions see Cristian Chelariu, Abodulaye Ouattarra, and Kofi Q. Dadzie, "Market Orientation in Ivory Coast: Measurement Validity and Organizational Antecedents in a Sub-Saharan African Economy," *Journal of Business and Industrial Marketing* 17, no. 6 (2002): 456–70; Urbain Kiswend-Sida Yameogo, *Report of the African Case Study: Company and Stakeholder Involvement in Territory Social Development* (Paris: University of Paris XII, Val De Marne, 2008).

8. Country Watch, "Country Overview," chap. 1 in *Côte d'Ivoire Review 2007* (2007).

9. Auswaertiges Amt, "Côte d'Ivoire" (2009), http://www.auswaertiges-amt.de/diplo/de/Laenderinformationen/01-Laender/CoteDIvoire.html.

10. Ibid.; Country Watch, "Country Overview"; International Monetary Fund (IMF), "IMF and World Bank Consider Côte d'Ivoire Eligible for Assistance under the Enhanced Heavily Indebted Poor Countries (HIPC) Initiative" (Washington, DC, 2008); "IMF Executive Board Approves US$565.7 Million PRGF Arrangement for Côte d'Ivoire," Press Release No. 09/96, March 27, 2009, Washington, DC.

11. IMF, "IMF Executive Board Approves Arrangement."

12. Business Monitor International (BMI), "Soft Commodities Likely to Perk Up," No. 13, 13590006, 2007.

13. World Bank, "World Bank Vice-President for Africa Calls for Far-Reaching Reforms in Côte d'Ivoire's Cocoa-Coffee Sector" (September 25, 2008); http://web.worldbank.org/WBSITE/EXTERNAL/COUNTRIES/AFRICAEXT/CDIV OIREEXTN/0,,contentMDK:21916156~pagePK:1497618~piPK:217854~theSit ePK:382607,00.html.

14. Country Watch, "Country Overview"; Country Watch, "Environmental Overview," chap. 6 in *Côte d'Ivoire Review 2007*.

15. BMI, "Soft Commodities Perk Up."

16. Ibid.; PRS Group, *Côte d'Ivoire: Country Forecast Scenarios* (2003).

17. MINUCI, "Côte d'Ivoire—MINUCI—Facts and Figures" (2004).

18. Africa Research Bulletin, "Africa-China: 'Win-Win' Strategy," *Economic, Financial, and Technical Series* 43, no. 6 (2006): 16999–17001.

19. Ibid.; International Crisis Group, *Côte d'Ivoire: Can the Ouagadougou Agreement Bring Peace?* (Brussels: International Crisis Group, 2007).

20. BMI, "Soft Commodities Perk Up"; Chambre de Commerce et Industrie Français en Côte d'Ivoire, "Economie" (2009), http://www.ccifci.org/index.php?var=EconomieCI (accessed October 25, 2009).

21. Ibid.; Marc Balzer, "Les conséquences des pillages du 6 au 8 novembre 2004 en Côte d'Ivoire" (2004), http://www.izf.net/pages/criseivoirienne/5876/.

22. French Embassy, "France and Côte d'Ivoire" (2009), http://www.ambafrance-uk.org/France-and-Cote-d-Ivoire.html#outil_sommaire_1.

23. BMI, "Soft Commodities Perk Up."

24. Ibid.; World Bank, "President Gbagbo Praises World Bank for Support in Tackling Solid Waste Management" (2009); Auswaertiges Amt, "Côte d'Ivoire."

25. Country Watch, "Environmental Overview."

26. World Bank, "President Gbadebo Praises World Bank"; Country Watch, "Environmental Overview."

27. Jean-Pierre Stroobants, "Affaire du 'Probo-Koala': L'affréteur mis en examen pour corruption," *Le Monde*, April 10, 2009.

28. Greenpeace, "Greenpeace Vows to Pursue Trafigura" (2009), http://www.rnw.nl/int-justice/article/greenpeace-vows-pursue-trafigura.

29. Norbert Navarro, "Procès du Probo Koala: Douze accusés mais Trafigura absent" (2008), http://www.rfi.fr/actufr/articles/105/article_72891.asp.

30. Thijs Bouwknegt, "Côte d'Ivoire Pollution Trial Suspended" (2008), http://static.rnw.nl/migratie/www.rnw.nl/internationaljustice/081008-probokoala-redirected.

31. FIDH, Sherpa, Greenpeace, Mouvement ivoirien des droits Humains, and Ligue ivoirienne des droits de l'Homme, *Communiqué: Côte d'Ivoire / Affaire des déchets toxiques*, press release, October 28, 2008 (Paris, Abidjan, Amsterdam).

32. Ibid.

33. Marc Yevou, "Déchets toxiques: Les avocats de l'état réclament 370 milliards aux accusés" (2008); http://actu.atoo.ci/larticle.php?id_ar=4202.

34. Guy Chazan, "Firm to Pay $48.7 Million in Ivory Coast Pollution Case," *Wall Street Journal*, September 21, 2009, Eastern ed., 254, 13; Leigh, Day & Co. and Trafigura, *Agreed Final Joint Statement* (London, 2009); "Trafigura Close to Settling Lawsuit over Waste Dumping," *Wall Street Journal–Eastern Edition*, September 17, 2009, 254, 17.

35. Abidjan.net, "Déchets toxiques: Trafigura peut encore être poursuivie (avocat de l'Etat)" (2008), http://news.abidjan.net/article/?n=305740; abidjan.net, "Séance de cotation du vendredi 3 Avril 2009" (2009), http://business.abidjan.net/ (accessed May 21, 2010); Stroobants, "Affaire du 'Probo-Koala.'"

36. Trafigura, "Probo Koala Updates: Statement—UK Legal Update" (November 2008), http://www.trafigura.com/our_news/probo_koala_updates.aspx (accessed April 18, 2009).

37. Leigh, Day & Co. and Trafigura, *Agreed Final Joint Statement.*

38. See Karel Knip, "Trafigura's Ivory Coast Disaster—Not So Toxic after All," *NRC Handelsblad,* October 19, 2009 (also cited on Trafigura's website).

39. Greenpeace, "Greenpeace Vows to Pursue Trafigura"; Greenpeace, "Trafigura Director Knew about Toxic Waste" (2009), http://www.rnw.nl/africa/article/greenpeace-trafigura-director-knew-about-toxic-waste; "Litigation: Trafigura Settlement: A Drop in the Ocean?," *Lawyer* (2009): 6.

40. Global Witness, *Hot Chocolate: How Cocoa Fueled the Conflict in Côte d'Ivoire* (Washington, DC, 2007).

41. Global Witness, "Côte d'Ivoire: La réforme de la filière cacao insuffisante tant que les exportateurs évitent la transparence" (2008), http://www.globalwitness.org/media_library_detail.php/666/fr/cote_divoire_la_reforme_de_la_filiere_cacao_insuff.

42. Partenariat Afrique Canada, *Les diamants et la sécurité humaine: Revue Annuelle 2008* (2008), http://www.pacweb.org/.

43. UNICEF, "Côte d'Ivoire" (2009), http://www.unicef.org/infobycountry/cotedivoire.html.

44. Amnesty International, *Côte d'Ivoire: Les femmes, victimes oubliées du conflit* (London, 2007); Amnesty International, *Amnesty International Report 2008* (London, 2008); UNICEF, "Côte d'Ivoire."

45. IMF, "IMF Executive Board Approves Arrangement"; World Bank, "Ivoirian Government Commits to Reducing Poverty Rate to 16 Percent in 2015" (January 28, 2009), http://web.worldbank.org/WBSITE/EXTERNAL/COUNTRIES/AFRICAEXT/CDIVOIREEXTN/0,,contentMDK:22047895~pagePK:1497618~piPK:217854~theSitePK:382607,00.html.

46. World Bank, "Ivoirian Government Commits to Reducing Poverty Rate."

47. Amnesty International, *Amnesty International Report 2008.*

48. Déclaration de Berne, *Chocolat suisse.*

49. UNICEF, "Côte d'Ivoire."

50. UNAIDS, "Drive for AIDS Funding in Côte d'Ivoire" (2007), http://www.unaids.org/en/KnowledgeCentre/Resources/FeatureStories/archive/2007/20070509_cote_dIvoire_funding_NSP.asp.

51. UNAIDS, *Ivory Coast* (Geneva, 2009), http://www.unaids.org/en/CountryResponses/Countries/ivory_coast.asp.

52. World Health Organization (WHO)/AFRO, *Malaria Country Profiles: Côte d'Ivoire* (Geneva, 2004).

53. Transparency International, *Corruption Perceptions Index 2008* (Berlin, 2009).

54. See, e.g., Lanciné Bakayoko, "Côte d'Ivoire: 'Affaire 1 milliard détourné au Crou-A'—La Direction générale du Budget mise en cause" (2009).

55. World Bank, "Reforms in Côte d'Ivoire's Cocoa-Coffee Sector."

56. World Bank, "The World Bank and Côte d'Ivoire Wage War on Racketeering" (July 25, 2008), http://web.worldbank.org/WBSITE/EXTERNAL/COUNTRIES/AFRICAEXT/CDIVOIREEXTN/0,,contentMDK:21852817~pagePK:1497618~piPK:217854~theSitePK:382607,00.html.

57. "L'économie ivoirienne a étonnamment résisté à la crise," *Le Monde*, April 25, 2007, 19.

58. Africa Research Bulletin, "Africa-China."

59. IMF, "IMF Executive Board Approves Arrangement."

60. IMF, "Côte d'Ivoire Reaches Decision Point under the Enhanced HIPC Debt Relief Initiative" (2009); IMF, "IMF Executive Board Approves Arrangement."

61. Totel, "Cote d'Ivoire (Ivory Coast)—Telecoms Market Overview and Statistics" (2008), http://www.totel.com.au/cote-divoire-telecommunications-research.asp?cid=CI&toc=1086.

62. abidjan.net, "Séance de cotation du vendredi 3 Avril 2009" (2009), http://business.abidjan.net/.

63. IMF, "IMF Executive Board Approves Arrangement."

64. Ibid.

65. IMF, "Côte d'Ivoire Reaches Decision Point."

66. Ibid.

67. Ibid.

68. BMI, "Soft Commodities Perk Up"; Brian Klaas, "From Miracle to Nightmare: An Institutional Analysis of Development Failures in Côte d'Ivoire," *Africa Today* 55, no. 1 (2008): 109–26; see also, Adam Nossiter, "Standoff Set Up with 2 Ivory Coast Presidents," published December 3, 2010. Accessed at http://www.nytimes.com/2010/12/04/world/africa/04ivory.html.

69. Chambre de Commerce et Industrie Français en Côte d'Ivoire, "Economie"; French Embassy, "France and Côte d'Ivoire"; Maison des Français à l'Etranger, "Côte d'Ivoire" (2009).

70. Chambre de Commerce et Industrie Français en Côte d'Ivoire, "Economie."

71. Maison des Français de l'Etranger, "Côte d'Ivoire."

72. BMI, "Soft Commodities Perk Up"; IZF.net, "Investissement Directs Étrangers Et Présence Française" (2002).

73. Côte d'Ivoire Telecom, "Côte d'Ivoire Telecom" (2009).

74. Marie Miran, *Islam, histoire et modernité en Côte d'Ivoire* (Paris: Karthala, 2006).

75. abidjan.net, "Déchets toxiques."

76. Ambassade de Côte d'Ivoire New Delhi, "Ivoiro-Indian Cooperation" (2007), http://www.amb2ci-inde.org/en/ambcicooperation.php.

77. Joshi, "India-Africa Conclave."

78. Government of India, Ministry of Commerce and Industry, Department of Commerce, "India to Offer Assistance to Côte d'Ivoire in Drugs and Pharmaceuticals" (2002), http://commerce.nic.in/PressRelease/pressrelease_detail.asp?id=806.

79. Krishna, *India-Africa Partnership*.

80. VITIB SA, "Nos Partenaires" (2009), http://www.vitibsa.com/nos-partenaires/nos-partenaires-56.html (accessed May 20, 2010).

81. Krishna, *India-Africa Partnership*; NEPAD, "NEPAD Programs and Projects" (2009), http://www.nepad.org/Nepad+Projects/sector_id/3/lang/en (accessed May 20, 2010).

82. "Team 9 Opens New Innings."

83. BBC, "Country Profile: Ivory Coast" (2009), http://news.bbc.co.uk/2/hi/africa/country_profiles/1043014.stm.

84. David E. Bell and Mary Shelman, *Olam International* (Cambridge: Harvard Business School, 2008).

85. Châtel, "Chine/Afrique."

86. Ibid.

87. "China Offers Aid to Côte d'Ivoire's Nov. 29 Election," *People's Daily*, September 28, 2009, http://english.people.com.cn/90001/90776/90883/6771883.html.

88. Châtel, "Chine/Afrique."

89. Ekow Spio-Gabrah, "Connecting Rural Africa," *NEPAD Business and Investment Guide 2009* 4 (2009): 92–93.

90. Ambassade de Côte d'Ivoire en Russie, "L'Ambassadeur Fagnidi rend hommage à Madame Korzun: Intensification de la coopération ivoiro-russe" (2009), http://www.ambaci-russie.org/fr/?p=27#more-27.

91. LUKOIL, "LUKOIL Overseas Signs Agreement to Acquire Exploration Project in West Africa" (2006), http://www.lukoil-overseas.com/press.asp?div_id=3&id=371&year=2006 (accessed April 17, 2009).

92. BMI, "Soft Commfodities Perk Up."

93. Ibid.

94. Cargill, "Côte d'Ivoire" (2009), http://www.cargill.com/worldwide/cote-divoire/index.jsp.

95. ADM, "Africa" (2010), http://www.admworld.com/en-US/worldwide/africa/Pages/default.aspx.

96. ADM, "Côte d'Ivoire" (2010), http://www.adm.com/en-US/worldwide/cote_divoire/Pages/default.aspx.

97. World Cocoa Foundation, "World Cocoa Foundation Member Companies" (2009), http://www.worldcocoafoundation.org/who-we-are/members.html.

98. Cargill, "Responsible Cocoa Sourcing and Production" (2009), http://www.cargill.com/commitments/pov/cocoa-sourcing/cote-divoire-wafrica/labor-practices/index.jsp; International Cocoa Initiative, "Structure, Membership, and Financing" (2009).

99. Cargill, "Sustainable and Responsible Cocoa Sourcing" (2009), http://www.cargill.com/commitments/pov/cocoa-sourcing/cote-divoire-wafrica/sustainable-farming/index.jsp.

100. Cargill, "Responsible Cocoa Sourcing and Production."

101. Nestlé, "Nescafé Factory in Côte d'Ivoire" (2009), http://www.nestle.com/SharedValueCSR/FarmersAndAgriculture/Coffee/Nescaf%C3%A9+factory+in+C%C3%B4te+d%E2%80%99Ivoire.htm; Nestlé, "Sustainable Cocoa: Côte d'Ivoire" (2009), http://www.nestle.com/SharedValueCSR/CSVatNestle/InAction/AllCaseStudies/SustainableCocoaCotedIvoire.htm (accessed April 17, 2009).

102. BMI, "Soft Commodities Perk Up."

103. Unilever, "Unilever Disposes of Oils Business and Plantation Interests and Acquires Regional Soap Business" (2008), http://www.unilever.com/mediacentre/pressreleases/2008/UnileverinCoteDIoire.aspx.

104. Reuters Africa, "Ivory Coast's SIFCA Seeks to Double Palm Oil Output" (2009), http://af.reuters.com/article/nigeriaNews/idAFL6276778200907o6?pageNumber=2&virtualBrandChannel=0.

105. SIFCA, "A Regional Agribusiness Stakeholder in West Africa" (2009), http://www.groupesifca.com/ (accessed May 20, 2010).

106. Unilever, *Unilever Buys First Batch of Certified Sustainable Palm Oil* (Rotterdam, 2008); Unilever, "Sustainable Palm Oil: Unilever Shares the Widespread Concerns about the Destruction of the World's Rainforests from Expanding Palm Oil Production" (2009), http://www.unilever.com/sustainability/environment/agriculture/sustainablepalmoil/.

107. mongabay.com, "Environmental Campaign Blocks Palm Oil Project in Côte d'Ivoire Wetland" (2009), http://news.mongabay.com/2009/0425-cote_d_ivoire_palm_oil.html.

108. Unilever, *Unilever Statement on Concerns about the Protection of the Tanoé Forest in the Ivory Coast* (Rotterdam, 2008).

109. PETROCI, "Champs in Exploitation" (2009), http://www.petroci.ci/index.php?numlien=43 (accessed May 20, 2010).

110. Canadian Natural Resources Limited, *Canadian Natural Resources Limited Commences Oil Production in Côte d'Ivoire* (Calgary, 2002).

111. Bamba Mafoumgbé, "Exploitation pétrolière en Côte d`Ivoire: Une compagnie remet un chèque de un milliard de Fcfa à l`Etat" (January 29, 2009), http://news.abidjan.net/article/imprimer.asp?n=317966.

112. Offshore, "Re-drills Lift Baobab Output" (2009), http://www.offshore-mag.com/index/article-display/361314/articles/offshore/drilling-completion/africa/re-drills-lift-baobab-output.html.

113. BMI, "Soft Commodities Perk Up."

114. Aga Khan Development Network (AKDN), "AKDN in Côte d'Ivoire" (2009), http://www.akdn.org/cote_d'ivoire.asp.

115. Yameogo, *African Case Study.*

116. AKDN, "Economic Development" (2009), http://www.akdn.org/cote_d'ivoire_economic.asp; AKDN, "Lancement d'une Agence de Microfinance en Côte d'Ivoire par le Président Gbagbo et l'Aga Khan" (2009), http://www.akdn.org/Content/451.

117. Etisalat (Atlantique Telecom), "'MOOV' in Cote d'Ivoire Sees Half a Million Subscribers" (October 10, 2006), http://www.ameinfo.com/98659.html.

118. Idro, quoted in Wanetsha Mosinyi, "Continent Must Engage China with Win-Win Strategies" (2009), http://allafrica.com/stories/200910210934.html.

119. Peter Bosshard, "China's Environmental Footprint in Africa," *Pamabzuka News*, no. 376 (2008).

120. Ibid.; Kelvin Kachingwe, "Controversial Chinese Firm Given Another Copper Mine" (2009), http://allafrica.com/stories/200906020324.html.

121. Mosinyi, "Continent Must Engage China." See, e.g., International Labor Organization, *International Labor Standards* (2009).

122. Bosshard, "China's Environmental Footprint in Africa."

123. Klaas, "From Miracle to Nightmare."

124. Paul Collier, *The Bottom Billion: Why the Poorest Countries Are Failing and What Can Be Done about It* (Oxford: Oxford University Press, 2007).

12

Globalization and Industrial Development in Nigeria

KOLA SUBAIR

We've seen the result [of globalization]. The spread of sweat-shops. The resurgence of child labor, prison, and forced labor. Three hundred million more in extreme poverty than 10 years ago. Countries that have lost ground. A boom in busts in which a generation of progress is erased in a month of speculation. Workers everywhere trapped in a competitive race to the bottom.
—John Sweeney, speech to International Confederation of Free Trade Unions Convention, April 4, 2000

Introduction

Globalization has been viewed as an instrument that accelerates economic growth, most especially among those countries that are technologically advanced. It can also aid a country as it makes the transition from a primarily extractive economy to one that has a significant manufacturing sector. This has not been the case with sub-Saharan African countries, including Nigeria. They have been relegated to the background in the international arena. They could not even determine the prices of their primary commodities that earn them the largest percentage of their foreign exchange. These countries have also weakened their economies as they are constantly faced with problems of policy inconsistency and political instability. Hence, their primary commodities are sold at very cheap and unsustainable prices. This disadvantage has led to a series of interrelated negative impacts on their economic growth, which include, among others, very low industrial development. Just as it succeeded in increasing the tempo of low-scale manufacturing activities in Nigeria, as existing evidence has shown, so globalization has equally put several large-scale industries out of operation.

Though in theory globalization is expected to integrate all economies of the world into a self-sustainable equilibrium market and promote growth through reduction in barriers to trade, in reality it has led to the deindustrialization of Nigeria by emphasizing liberalization, privatization, and deregulation (three factors that are together referred to as LPD). It is against this backdrop that I seek to examine in this chapter the interconnections between globalization and industrialization by testing for their extent of correlation. I will conclude by offering recommendations about what steps should be taken in the Nigerian manufacturing sector in order for Nigeria to compete more effectively in the global economy.

Concept and Processes of Globalization

The concept of interdependence of nations due to differences in resource endowment is a fundamental principle upon which globalization has been conceived. Globalization has accelerated and sustained growth especially in the European, North American, and Japanese economies. Evidence has, however, shown that the continuous economic hardship experienced by developing countries as a result of globalization is also having its effect on the Asian, European, and North American economies. Hence, globalization promotes the interests of a few powerful countries while at the same time jeopardizing the interests of weaker nations. Globalization forces all of the countries of the world into a common economic "order" with little governmental participation and few border restrictions. Consequently, high rates of inflation, especially of prices for basic necessities, and increasing inequalities in income distribution have ensued. Globalization is believed by its advocates to be an avenue for generating increased specialization with efficiency, better quality products, competitiveness, technological improvement, and economies of scale. All these benefits are attainable, it is claimed, only by increasing economic integration through reduction of barriers to trade, migration, capital flows, technological transfer, and direct investment.

According to the United Nations Development Programme (UNDP), globalization is defined as a multidimensional process involving intensive and extensive interactions, interconnections, and integration of countries on a global scale through democracy, ideological shifts, technological revolutions, cultural adaptations, and above all, economic interdependence.[1] Economic globalization is by all accounts the increasing international integration of markets for goods, services, and capital propelled by trade, financial flows, technology and information, and the movement of people.[2] The extent of globalization can ably be measured by the levels of foreign direct investment, foreign trade, and private capital flows.[3] Peter Lindert describes globalization as a simple process whereby economic decision making regarding such issues as consumption, investment, and savings is integrated all across the world, thus forcing all states to participate.

In the interest of achieving a global economic system, and based on broad governmental consensus, the United States promoted a policy of liberalization, privatization, and deregulation (LPD). This subsequently exposed any nation to two forms of globalization—the shallowest and the deepest.[4] The shallowest form is where "an economic entity in one country engages in arm's-length trade in a single product with another economic entity in one other country."[5] The deepest form of globalization, as distinguished from other forms of "internationalization," is "where an economic entity transacts with a large number of other economic entities throughout the world; where it does so across a network of value-added chains; where these exchanges are highly coordinated to save the worldwide interests of [the] globalizing entity; and they consist of a myriad of different kinds or forms of transactions."[6] This is a clear indication that globalization is an advanced stage of capitalism that influences national sovereignty and reduces the democratic participation of citizens in national economic and political affairs through the substitution of "the market" for the people.[7]

Since the integration of world economies began, globalization has promoted competition and cooperation among nations, as earlier mentioned, through LPD. These three self-contained and mutually interdependent policy tools have been the core foundation for structural adjustment programs (SAPs) in the third world. But based on comparisons across countries, the utilization of SAPs has rather impoverished and cut off these countries from global competition. Liberalization as a follow-up is meant to eliminate trade restrictions whether they are unilateral, bilateral, regional, or multilateral. According to Stephen Thomsen, the less inimical an agreement is to the pattern of trade and investment, the more beneficial it is to globalization.[8] Economic liberalization later enhanced the proliferation of multinational corporations (MNCs) that engaged in a systematic attempt to control third world economies through their huge investments in extractive ventures rather than in manufacturing activities. While the economies of Japan, Europe, and North America were sustainably developed, the countries of Africa, Nigeria included, were retrogressing without any hope of witnessing development. Deregulation, for its part, emphasizes the reduction of administrative controls and greater reliance on market forces. By implication, this will reduce government intervention in economic activities that tend to encourage market inefficiencies, corruption, and waste. And with the promotion of privatization, greater economic efficiency could be attained through private-sector participation.

Interconnections between Globalization and Industrialization

Globalization is further characterized by an emphasis on financial benefits arising from the liberalization of capital movement from the Japanese, European, and North American axes. Companies from these countries are more interested in the repatriation of their profits and dividends while simultaneously encouraging capital flight through their activities, to further sustain the economies of their respective countries. Proactively, this promotes growth and enhanced manufacturing activities in these countries while the poor countries see their natural resources depleted. These poor countries cannot simply transform their resources into manufactured products due to a lack of specified skills and required technology. Since industrialization expands manufacturing activities that are not easily attainable by these poor countries, the need arises for mobilization of foreign capital. As posited here, industrialization as a corollary of growth requires adequate funding to enable the move from extractive industry to secondary and tertiary industries. But since most developing countries are faced with capital constraints, it is imperative that they attract additional funds from outside their economies. According to this scenario, it follows that the problem of capital constraints on industrialization can be resolved through mobilization of private capital inflows. This is further emphasized in the Harrod-Domar growth model.[9] This model is based on the premise that a nation's economic growth rate will be warranted by incremental savings-capital-output ratios. But where savings are inadequate, the economy could seek to fill the gap in savings through either foreign aid or private foreign investment. Michael Todaro and Stephen Smith have also upheld this argument that the "capital constraint stages approach to growth and development became a rationale and an opportunistic tool for justifying massive transfers of capital and technical assistance from the developed to the less developed nations."[10]

The Harrod-Domar growth model has been further reinforced by the balanced growth model, which basically emphasizes the removal of limitations to aggregate demand caused by the small size of markets in the developing countries.[11] In view of these limitations, the balanced growth model recommends sufficient large-scale investments in various complementary and competitive industries in order to overcome inadequate demand and to create external economies. This investment must, however, "be able to achieve balances between the agricultural sector and industrial sector, between capital goods and consumer goods, and between social overhead capital and directly productive activities."[12]

Considering the massive investment required by developing countries to overcome their inadequacies in order to industrialize, they have no choice but to borrow from external sources. This is often facilitated by financial globalization that positively influences the development of the real sector, consequently causing economic development and growth. Financial globalization augments domestic savings, reduces the cost of capital, transfers technology from advanced to developing countries, and develops domestic financial sectors. It has equally undermined the initial gains expected by the developing countries.[13] It has created wide inequality within and between nations, exacerbated unemployment, thwarted social progress, increased financial markets' volatility and capital flows while also furthering the pauperization of these already poor nations.

For John Naisbitt, however, all these deficiencies are "a global paradox" that is being experienced by all the countries of the world. He retorts that "across the globe, for developed and developing countries alike, change is bringing economic hardship."[14] But it is evident that the pressure is greater on the poor and developing countries as their industries are faced with low capacity utilization with no end in sight. Given the trend toward the realization of a single world economic system, it would be fair to say the developing countries have been recolonized.

Methodology

Data Collection Procedure

The arguments against effects of globalization on developing countries are far-reaching considering the extent of its negative impacts on third world economies. In this chapter I have thus used time series data to determine whether globalization has any significant effect on the manufacturing sector in Nigeria. Since annual time series data are static in nature, I decided to incorporate a nonstatic condition of the data on industrial output, capacity utilization rate, interest rate, consumer price index, foreign-direct-investment/gross-domestic-product ratio, private-capital-inflows/gross-domestic-product ratio, and gross-degree-of-openness-measured-by-total-trade/ gross-domestic-product ratio so as to determine if there are any potential integrating links among the variables.

The data on these variables were extracted and computed from the National Bureau of Statistics' *Annual Abstract of Statistics*, and the Central Bank of Nigeria *Statistical Bulletin*.[15] All these data are from the period 1981–2006, which coincides with the era of trade liberalization and the time when most African countries were undergoing various structural adjustment measures.

Model Specification

This study required, first, that the extent to which Nigeria is integrated with the rest of the world be determined before the impact of globalization on its manufacturing sector could be considered. To this end, I adopted Ismihan, Olgun, and Utku-Ismihan's model to derive a single economic globalization index (EGI) for Nigeria for selected periods.[16] Based on these authors' submission, the core elements of economic globalization—trade, investment (production), and finance—have been used to measure the dimensions of globalization in the following order:

$$FTR_{it} = \frac{FTR_{it} - Min_{FTR}}{Max_{FTR} - Min_{FTR}} \text{ X } 1000 \quad\quad (1)$$

$$FDIR_{it} = \frac{FDIR_{it} - Min_{FDIR}}{Max_{FDIR} - Min_{FDIR}} \text{ X } 1000 \quad\quad (2)$$

$$PCFI_{it} = \frac{PCFI_{it} - Min_{PCFI}}{Max_{PCFI} - Min_{PCFI}} \text{ X } 1000 \quad\quad (3)$$

Where:

FTR_{it} = foreign trade index for country i at time t
$FDIR_{it}$ = foreign direct investment index for country i at time t
$PCFI_{it}$ = private capital inflows index for country i at time t

Based on equations (1)–(3), EGI is derived by finding the average of the three subindexes (FTR_{it}, $FDIR_{it}$, $PCFI_{it}$). Hence, economic globalization index (EGI_{it}) for country i at time t is:

$$EGI_{it} = \frac{FTR_{it} + FDIR_{it} + PCFI_{it}}{3} \quad (4)$$

The maximum value of EGI is 1,000 and the minimum is 0. So whenever its value is close to 0, the level of global integration is low, but if close to 1,000, the level of integration is high. EGI is further used to measure a country's performance such that if for two years $EGI_2 - EGI_1 > 0$, then country i has improved its integration. It can also be used to rank the level of countries' global integration.[17]

Two models were also constructed to give a clearer picture of the issues at stake. The first model presents the situation of Nigerian industry prior to globalization by simply tracing the impact of the capacity utilization rate, interest rate, and consumer price index on the performance of Nigeria's manufacturing sector. By contrast, the second model presents the industrial situation during globalization by examining the impact of the foreign-direct-investment/gross-domestic-product ratio, private-capital-inflows/gross-domestic-product ratio, and total-trade/gross-domestic-product ratio on the performance of the manufacturing sector in Nigeria. These models are therefore presented in the following structural equations:

$$INDQ_t = f(CUR_t, INT_t, CPI_t) \qquad (5)$$

But technically, equation (5) can otherwise be stated as:

$$INDQ_t = \alpha_0 + \alpha_1 CUR_t + \alpha_2 INT_t + \alpha_3 CPI_t + \mu_t \qquad (6)$$

$$INDQ_t = f(GFDI_t, GPCI_t, GDPN_t) \qquad (7)$$

Equation (7) can also be technically specified as:

$$INDQ_t = \beta_0 + \beta_1 GFDI_t + \beta_2 GPCI_t + \beta_3 GDPN_t + v_t \qquad (8)$$

Where:

$INDQ_t$ = industrial output index at time t
CUR_t = capacity utilization rate at time t
INT_t = interest rate at time t
CPI_t = consumer price index at time t
$GFDI_t$ = foreign-direct-investment/gross-domestic-product ratio at time t
$GPCI_t$ = private-capital-inflows/gross-domestic-product ratio at time t
$GDPN_t$ = total-trade/gross-domestic-product ratio at time t
$\alpha_0, \alpha_1, \alpha_2, \alpha_3; \beta_0, \beta_1, \beta_2, \beta_3$ = technical coefficients
$\mu_t; v_t$ = error specifications

Analytical Techniques and Theoretical Expectations

Going by the specified models above, the estimation techniques adopted were ordinary least square technique and cointegration analysis. The cointegration analysis was based on the Augmented Dickey-Fuller (ADF) test to determine the degree of integration among the aforementioned variables.[18]

The theoretical expectations about the technical coefficients of all the equations are stated inter alia: for equation (5), $\alpha_1 \geq 0$; α_2, $\alpha_3 \leq 0$. It was expected that capacity utilization rate and industrial output index would be positively related to each other. This is because CUR_t measured the (weighted) average of the ratio between actual output of industries to the maximum that could be produced per unit of time with existing plant and equipment. All other coefficients, such as INT_t and CPI_t, were expected to have negative signs implying that the higher the values of these indexes, the lower the level of industrial output.

For equation (7): β_1, β_2, $\beta_3 \geq 0$. This implied that the industrial output index should be positively related to every change in $GFDI_t$, $GPCI_t$, and $GDPN_t$ as indicated by the technical coefficients.

Empirical Results and Issues

A review of Nigeria's industrial policy reveals that the sector was characterized by high geographical concentration of industries, high production costs, low value added, low capacity utilization, high import content of industrial output, and low level of foreign investment in the manufacturing sector.[19] Most of these problems could be traced to the various self-contradictions inherent in Nigerian industrial policy. In other words, the policy had contributed to weakening the base for a solid development in the manufacturing sector even before the adoption of trade liberalization in 1981. The haphazard nature of these various policies that had failed to conform to basic economic principles, optimization rules, veritable objectives of development, and nonrecognition of peculiar environmental constraints led to deindustrialization of the country.[20] For instance, the policy of indigenization emphasized the buying up of many businesses rather than encouraging self-reliance. Without considering the prospects of these businesses in the future, Nigeria invested in many, varied industries: Iwopin paper mills, Aladja and Ajaokuta steel companies, Volkswagen and Peugeot automobile companies, Osogbo Steel Rolling Mills, textile companies, and more. Many of these companies vanished into thin air with time while those that survived could neither produce at the minimum capacity level nor export their goods to other countries, not to mention compete with imported goods.

It was against this background that the structural adjustment program was introduced with the aim of restructuring and diversifying "the productive base of the economy in order to reduce dependence on the oil sector and on imports."[21] But the almost immediate effect of this policy was

Table 12.1. Growth and share of manufacturing sector output: selected years, 1981–2006

Indicator	1981	1986	1991	1996	2001	2006
Index of manufacturing output (1990 = 100)	117.4	96.1	178.1	138.7	142.2	145.7
Output share of manufacturing sector in GDP (%)	5.31	4.22	4.69	3.62	3.32	3.71
Annual growth rate of manufacturing sector[a]	N/A	1981–86 −22.3%	1986–91 46.04%	1991–96 −28.41%	1996–2001 2.5%	2001–6 2.40%

[a] Author's computation

N/A = not available

Sources: National Bureau of Statistics, *Annual Abstract of Statistics* (Abuja, 2006); Central Bank of Nigeria, *Statistical Bulletin* (Abuja, 2006).

to impact the country's economy in a negative way. As a matter of fact, the output share of the manufacturing sector in GDP declined all through the selected years of analysis. This performance could not even be halted during the trade liberalization period. In 1981 the output share of the manufacturing sector in GDP was 5.3 percent, but this share declined to 4.2 percent by 1986. This change implied that prior to the liberalization period, the sector was to some extent better off, as is shown in table 12.1. The sector's contribution declined further from 4.2 percent in 1986 to 3.3 percent by 2001. The growth rate of the manufacturing sector for the years also buttressed the decline in its contribution. In fact, the years 1986 and 1996 witnessed negative growth rates of 22.3 percent and 28.4 percent, respectively. Except for 1991, which witnessed a 46 percent growth rate, 2001 and 2002 experienced negligible growth rates of 2.5 percent and 2.4 percent, respectively.

The decline had been traced to the problem of imported inputs, in which costs were forced to increase with very low manufacturing value added. Nigerian industries such as these could not earn foreign exchange. Out of all the manufacturing subsectors, only soap and detergent, beer and stout, as well as soft drinks performed very well. Based on table 12.2, none of the other subsectors' performance was anything to write home about. But considering the comparative growth rates of manufacturing subsectors, virtually

Table 12.2. Comparative performance of manufacturing subsectors based on index of manufacturing products (1985): selected years, 1981–2006

Manufacturing subsector	1981	1986	1991	1996	2001	2006
Sugar/confectionary	219.2	71.8	129.1	57.5	47.5	47.5
Soft drinks	104.2	71.2	243.5	160.9	194.0	193.8
Beer/stout	101.6	128.1	100.7	107.5	125.7	134.5
Cotton/textiles	193.5	31.9	147.5	102.1	93.5	94.7
Synthetic fabrics	303.1	196.1	1921.1	815.6	665.6	670
Footwear	377.5	75.4	85.9	52.0	44.9	45.4
Paints	266.3	79.1	98.0	122.2	114.4	115.8
Cement	76.6	108.1	98.7	88.8	93.5	106.6
Vehicle assembly	128.5	46.8	17.1	14.2	15.1	15.5
Soap and detergent	263.9	49.3	153.9	183.3	210.1	214.4
Refined petroleum	93.6	50.3	116.0	131.4	133.0	144.7
All manufacturing	117.3	78.2	178.1	138.7	137.7	145.9

Sources: National Bureau of Statistics, *Annual Abstract of Statistics* (Abuja, Nigeria, 2006); Central Bank of Nigeria, *Statistical Bulletin* (Abuja, Nigeria, 2006).

all the industries' growth rates were unimpressive. Sugar and confectionary declined all through the years.

For instance, it declined further from −7.5 percent in 1986 to −125 percent in 1996 and later bounced back somewhat to −75 percent. While a majority of the various manufacturing subsectors witnessed negative growth rates, beer and stout, refined petroleum, and cement managed to witness positive growth but at a reducing rate. From table 12.3, the growth rate for beer and stout increased from 6.3 percent to 14.5 percent between 1996 and 2001 but decreased to 6.5 percent by 2006. Refined petroleum increased from 1.2 percent in 2001 to 8.1 percent in 2006, while the cement subsector also increased from 5 percent to 12 percent between those years. This situation has remained so because of inadequate foreign exchange to procure their inputs. In fact, the capacity utilization rate of the few existing manufacturing industries has remained very low to date.

Another interesting issue is the protracted problems generated by trade liberalization, such as rampant dumping and smuggling of fake and sub-standard products in the Nigerian markets. Used products, popularly called "Tokunboh," including electrical and electronics appliances, matches, cars,

Table 12.3. Comparative growth rates of manufacturing subsectors (percent)

Manufacturing subsector	1981–86	1986–91	1991–96	1996–2001	2001–6
Sugar/confectionary	−205	44.3	−125	−74.0	0.0
Soft drinks	−46.0	70.8	−51.3	17.1	−0.10
Beer/stout	18.8	−24.2	6.3	14.5	6.5
Cotton/textiles	−410	74.3	−44.5	−9.2	1.3
Synthetic fabrics	−55.0	90.0	−136.0	−23.0	0.66
Footwear	−400.7	13.22	−66.1	−15.8	1.10
Paints	−237	19.3	19.8	−6.8	1.2
Refined petroleum	−86.1	56.6	−12.5	1.20	8.1
Cement	29.1	−9.5	−0.15	5.03	12.4
Vehicle assembly	−175.0	−174.0	−20.4	5.96	2.58
Soap and detergent	−435.0	9.8	16.0	12.8	2.0
All manufacturing	−50.0	56.0	−284.0	−0.73	5.62

R20 batteries, and drinks, flooded the markets. The local manufacturers were thus exposed to unfair competition from these imports since they were cheaper than locally produced ones. This was further complicated by the import-substitution strategy. Its adoption failed to compel manufacturing firms to vigorously develop local substitutes for imported inputs. This also contributed to the persistent capacity underutilization of the sector (see table 12.4). As at the peak period of trade liberalization, capacity utilization for the entire manufacturing sector declined from 78.2 percent in 1986 to 42 percent in 1991. It declined further to 32.5 percent in 1996.

FDI had been concentrated more in mining and oil than in other sectors. John Cantwell held that most investments from the United States focused on oil, accounting for more than two-thirds of the total stock of US FDI in Africa in 1993.[22] In particular, Nigeria received about 31 percent of its FDI stock in oil and 16 percent in other mining industries in the early 1980s. Where the FDI stock diversified from the primary sector to the manufacturing sector, the share of the selected subsectors in total FDI declined all through the period of liberalization. (Evidence for these developments abounds in table 12.5.)

The share of these subsectors markedly reduced from 27.9 percent to 15.4 percent between 1986 and 1996, but slightly increased to 16.9 percent in 2001.

Table 12.4. Capacity utilization rates of manufacturing subsectors: selected years, 1981–2006 (percent)

Manufacturing subsector	1981	1986	1991	1996	2001	2006
Sugar/confectionary	84.2	32.9	47.5	27.8	35.6	45.0
Soft drinks	N/A	26.7	38.6	50.4	40.2	35.0
Beer/stout	100	49.8	62.4	30.5	54.6	57.5
Cotton/textiles	76.9	41.3	54.9	46.5	31.8	56.6
Synthetic fabrics	N/A	N/A	N/A	N/A	N/A	N/A
Footwear	84.4	73.0	38.2	N/A	22.9	76.17
Paints	71.1	79.1	20.1	38.5	49.2	51.88
Refined petroleum	65.4	47.1	41.5	32.9	47.6	90.5
Cement	70.3	66.9	33.2	33.5	48.8	53.13
Vehicle assembly	79.1	24.9	19.6	51	41.4	16.0
Soap and detergent	N/A	30.6	32.6	38.2	48.2	53.8
All manufacturing	73.3	78.2	42.0	32.46	42.7	53.3

N/A = not available

Source: Central Bank of Nigeria, *Statistical Bulletin* (Abuja, Nigeria, 2006).

All these scenarios in the Nigerian manufacturing sector had drastically limited the country's participation and competition in the world economy. Through modification of the EGI by multiples of 10, instead of 1,000, the extent of the country's participation in the world economy is presented in table 12.6. The closer the value is, this time, to around 0, the lower the level of integration. But if closer to 100, the level of integration attained is higher.

Between 1981 and 1989, the EGI_t was 25.2 percent at the early stage of trade liberalization and the early part of the SAP period based on the mean value of indicators in table 12.6.

Considering that the value of EGI_t for this period was closer to 0 percent than 100 percent, the level of integration was low compared to the period 1998–2006 when it was 38.5 percent.

The outstanding performance of the FTR_t index of 55.6 percent could be attributed to the high growth rate of imports at the expense of exports. At the peak of liberalization, imported goods from Asia, especially fake and substandard ones, flooded the Nigerian markets. Nigeria's exports at this time increased at a very slow pace, only in primary commodities and with the manufacturing sector gradually fading.

Table 12.5. Foreign direct investment (FDI) in selected manufacturing and processing sectors: selected years, 1986–2001 (in millions ₦)

Activity sector	1981	1986	1991	1996	2001	2006
Nonmetal mineral products	119,949.0	221,631.0	345,111.0	1,577,160.0	1,680,489.3	5,676,463.8
Cotton/textiles	356,637.0	470,515.0	2,032,001.0	3,306,677.0	5,151,187.1	16,751,754.2
Footwear	N/A	7,700.0	18,737.0	44,066.0	45,997.3	2,667,862.5
Petroleum products	3,946.0	2,433.0	8,071.3	683,034.0	70,660.3	2,344,688.3
Total FDI	1,725,033.0 (27.9%)	2,513,088.0 (27.9%)	9,121,579 (26.4%)	36,346,604.0 (15.4%)	44,576,484.4 (16.9%)	125,508,669.6 (21.9%)

N/A = not available

Table 12.6. Economic globalization index: selected years, 1981–2006 (percent)

Indicator	1981–89	1990–97	1998–2006
FTR[a]	38.4	36.1	55.6
PCFI[b]	8.4	11.2	20.2
FDIR[c]	28.9	34.8	39.5
Total	75.7	82.1	115.3
$\sum X / N^d$ = EGI	25.2	27.4	38.5

[a] Foreign trade index
[b] Private capital inflow index
[c] Foreign direct investment index
[d] Mean of value of indicators (EGI)

Extension and Robustness

I carried out stationarity tests to corroborate facts using ADF test procedures. For the first model, application of the ADF test to the variables $INDQ_t$, CPI_t, CUR_t, and INT_t found them to be stationary at first difference [I(1)]. This was due to the greater values recorded for the test statistics as against the critical values at 1 percent, 5 percent, and 10 percent. However, these variables with the exception of CUR_t attained stationarity at all percentage levels of critical values, as indicated in table 12.7. Therefore, regression could be carried out without any spurious results. The ADF test was also applied to the second model with the variables $GFDI_t$, $GPCI_t$, $GDPN_t$, and $INDQ_t$. They were also found to be stationary at all percentage levels of critical values, as shown in table 12.7.

Table 12.7. ADF unit root test results

Variable	ADF test statistics	Critical value @ 1%	Critical value @ 5%	Critical value @ 10%	Level
$INDQ_t$	–5.592298	–3.7343	–2.9907	–2.6348	I(1)
CUR_t	–3.353836	–3.7497	–2.9969	–2.6381	I(1)
INT_t	–5.283418	–3.7497	–2.9969	–2.6381	I(1)
CPI_t	–4.666671	–3.7343	–2.9907	–2.6348	I(1)
$GFDI_t$	–8.798458	–3.7343	–2.9907	–2.6348	I(1)
$GPCI_t$	–8.445470	–3.7343	–2.9907	–2.6348	I(1)
$GDPN_t$	–7.852990	–3.7343	–2.9907	–2.6348	I(1)

Correlation and Regression Results

The results further examined the performance of the manufacturing sector and extent of its contribution to the integration of Nigeria with the rest of the world. In this way, the study establishes the relationship between industrial output (dependent variable) and its various determinants (independent variables) before and after trade liberalization.

Based on tables 12.8 and 12.9, models 1 and 2 explained about 49 percent and 57 percent of all variations in the industrial performance, respectively. This implied that, to a greater extent, the low level of Nigeria's integration globally through its manufacturing sector was largely influenced negatively by globalization; hence, its inability to compete in the world market. In model 1, the CPI_t remained unstable and negatively correlated with $INDQ_t$ as shown in table 12.8. This was reinforced by its ordinary least square estimated value of −30 percent and correlation value of −14.7 percent, thus indicating its negligible impact. All other variables were positive and significantly influenced the level of performance of the manufacturing sector, especially interest rate (INT_t) with its 210 percent value.

For model 2, by contrast, all the independent variables with the exception of $GPCI_t$ were positive and significantly influenced the performance of the manufacturing sector more than did model 1. While $GFDI_t$ was 32,360 percent, $GPCI_t$ was −17,129 percent while $GDPN_t$ was 5,790 percent. By these extreme values, model 2 showed that the manufacturing sector faced the danger of exposure to proliferation of cheap products while its exports could hardly penetrate the world market. This is a confirmation to the claim that for every seven hundred containers that came into Nigeria from Europe, almost five hundred were returned empty. This showed that the manufacturing sector would need to be given serious attention for Nigeria to reap the benefits of globalization (see tables 12.9 and 12.10). This situation was worsened by the negative value of $GPCI_t$, which by implication means that the repatriation of profits and dividends were greater than injected funds into the economy. This was also reinforced by its negative correlation (−7.8 percent) with $INDQ_t$ as shown in table 12.8. This situation had been responsible for the persistent capital flight from the country and thus increased the exposure of the manufacturing sector to global shocks.

Conclusion and Recommendations

The importance of industrialization in any economy is enormous and as such should be given appropriate support. In particular, the manufacturing sector had contributed significantly to Nigeria's economic development through employment generation, increased income, and diversification of the economy. But for reasons ranging from poor financing, policy inconsistency,

Table 12.8. Correlation matrix among variables

Variable	CUR_t	INT_t	CPI_t	$GPCI_t$	$GFDI_t$	$GDPN_t$
$INDQ_t$	0.051066	0.557135	–0.146576	–0.077993	0.585244	0.724722

Table 12.9. Multiple regressions for model 1

Variable	Coefficient	Std. error	t-Statistic	Probability	$R^2 = 0.488510$
α_0	74.29630	17.83548	4.165646	0.0004	Adjusted $R^2 = 0.418761$
CUR_t	0.455383	0.271338	1.678288	0.1074	S. E. = 13.76960
INT_t	2.102951	0.469304	4.481001	0.0002	F- Statistic = 7.003862
CPI_t	–0.298114	0.155204	–1.920794	0.0678	Durbin-Watson = 1.054590

Table 12.10. Multiple regressions for model 2

Variable	Coefficient	Std. error	t-Statistic	Probability	$R^2 = 0.566651$
β_0	90.17598	8.190623	11.00966	0.0000	Adjusted $R^2 = 0.507558$
$GFDI_t$	323.5950	223.1774	1.449945	0.1612	S.E. = 12.67423
$GPCI_t$	–171.2859	344.1448	–0.497715	0.6236	F- Statistic = 9.589123
$GDPN_t$	57.89711	18.88899	3.065125	0.0057	Durbin-Watson = 1.011289

technological backwardness, lack of interfirm linkages, infrastructural decay, high level of corruption and inflation, limited markets, debt problems, political instability, and harsh operating environment, the manufacturing sector could no longer fulfill these roles adequately.

All these factors have been responsible for Nigeria's very low participation in the world economy, outside its oil sector. The inability of the country's industries to compete and integrate well into the global economy stemmed from the country's overreliance on exporting oil while neglecting its nonoil sectors. The situation worsened by the time SAP, an element of LPD, was adopted. However, prior to the liberalization era, the performance of the country's industrial sector had not been encouraging, as shown by the estimated result of model 1 above. In fact, the sector's performance has worsened during the globalization era due to inequitable trade relations based on those factors mentioned above.

If Nigeria is to be integrated more effectively with the rest of the world in order to benefit from globalization, solutions must be proffered to counter the specific problems faced by the manufacturing sector. The present state of infrastructure must be overhauled for any meaningful industrialization and development to take place. Electricity generation and distribution must first be vigorously pursued as it is the basis for the functionality of all other strategic infrastructures like transport and communication. The decrepit power supply has remained a source of such increased overhead costs to many industries that at one point or another most of them were forced to operate below their minimum capacity level. In pursuance of an adequate power supply, private-sector participation with government must be encouraged while also sourcing for alternative electricity supply through solar energy.

The disjointed nature of industrial and corporate linkage must be eliminated for any meaningful industrialization in Nigeria. Because the Nigerian economy is dominated by the informal sector, there is need to encourage SMEs to establish connections with various government agencies in charge of empowerment programs within their immediate communities. These agencies must become aware of those enterprises' needs in order to "diffuse and process" their products. The agencies should further be encouraged to develop indigenous technology adaptable to the local environment.

The import-substitution strategy must be refocused to concentrate on strategic sectors of the economy. For instance, Nigeria's government must be able to support various automobile plants like Anambra Automobile Corporation (ANAMCO) and Peugeot Automobile Nigeria (PAN). Funds should be injected into this sector in order to enhance its capacity to generate higher output and employment. Furthermore, protectionist policies like the imposition of higher tariffs on the importation of fully assembled vehicles should be implemented, encouraged by the formulation of policies to set up factories in Nigeria to manufacture other automotive products.

For industrialization to succeed in Nigeria, the spate of corruption must be eradicated. Various studies have shown that this destructive social vice distorts economic growth and development. Therefore, fiscal discipline and rationalization are called for, along with improved provisions for social and economic welfare. The punishment of corrupt officials will further serve as deterrent to others.[23]

One condition paramount to others for the development of the manufacturing sector is maintenance of a strong and stable macroeconomic framework. This will pave the way for accelerated development and use of local raw materials and intermediate inputs rather than continuing dependence on imports. Other necessary requirements for global integration are strong institutional and social reforms that encourage political stability, good governance, transparency, and accountability; sound banking practices; and industrial capacity building and technological development. The fulfillment of these specific recommendations would improve the country's manufacturing sector and bring about the necessary conditions for Nigeria to reap the benefits of globalization.

Notes

1. United Nations Development Programme, *Nigerian Human Development Report, 2000/2001* (Lagos, 2001), 2.

2. Mike I. Obadan and E. Chuks Obioma, "Contemporary Issues in Global Trade and Finance and Their Implications," *Journal of Economic Management* 6, no. 1 (1999): 6–8.

3. Several works have used these elements to explain globalization; for example: Mustafa Ismihan, Hassan Olgun, and M. Fatma Utku-Ismihan, "Globalization of National Economies, 1975–2005," paper presented at the international conference for the State University of New York, Cortland, June 18–20, 2007, 64–82; Peter Dicken, *Global Shift: Transforming the World Economy* (New York: Guildford Press, 2003), 16; and International Monetary Fund, "Globalization," *IMF Survey* 29, no. 19 (2000): 304.

4. John H. Dunning, "The Advent of Alliance Capitalism," in *The New Globalism and Developing Countries*, ed. John Dunning and Khalil Hamdani (Tokyo: United Nations University Press, 1997), 13.

5. Ibid.

6. Ibid., 14.

7. Sam Aluko, "Background to Globalization and Africa's Economic Development," paper presented at the annual conference for the Nigerian Economic Society, Abuja, Nigeria, August 18–20, 2003, 36–37.

8. Stephen Thomsen, "Attracting Investment in an Integrating World Economy," in *New Globalism and Developing Countries*, ed. Dunning and Hamdani, 219–23.

9. For further details, see Evsey Domar, *Essays in the Theory of Economic Growth* (New York: Oxford University Press, Inc., 1957), 29–57.

10. Michael P. Todaro and Stephen C. Smith, *Economic Development* (New York: Pearson-Addison-Wesley, 2009), 112–15.

11. See K. Gerald Helleiner, *Peasant Agriculture, Government, and Economic Growth in Nigeria* (Homewood, IL: Richard Irwin, 1966), 52–53.

12. Further details are found in M. Adebayo Adejugbe, "Industrialization, Distortions, and Economic Development," in *Industrialization, Urbanization, and Development in Nigeria: 1950–1999*, ed. M. Adebayo Adejugbe (Lagos: Concept Publications Limited, 2004), 330; and Ragner Nurkse, *Problems of Capital Formation in Under-developed Countries* (New York: Oxford University Press, 1953), 39.

13. This is against the backdrop that financial integration, despite its necessity, may not after all guarantee fast economic growth, according to K. Edward Prasad et al., "Effects of Financial Globalization on Developing Countries: Some Empirical Evidence," *Finance and Development* 27 (2003): 17–21.

14. John Naisbitt, *Global Paradox: The Bigger the World Economy, the More Political Its Smallest Players* (New York: William Morrow, 1994), 97.

15. National Bureau of Statistics, *Annual Abstract of Statistics* (Abuja, Nigeria, 2006), 19–23; Central Bank of Nigeria, *Statistical Bulletin* (Abuja, Nigeria, 2006), 10–23; 132–36; 162–66; 179–80; 211–38.

16. Ismihan, Olgun, and Utku-Ismihan, "Globalization of National Economies," 68–76.

17. Ibid.

18. David Dickey and Wayne Fuller, "Likelihood Ratio Statistics for Autoregressive Process," *Econometrica* 49 (1981): 1052–72.

19. See Federal Republic of Nigeria, *Industrial Policy of Nigeria* (Abuja: Federal Ministry of Industries, 1988), 1.

20. A. Mashood Fashola, "A Schema for Nigeria's Optimal Industrial Development," in *Industrialization, Urbanization, and Development*, ed. M. Adebayo Adejugbe (Lagos: Concept Publications Limited, 2004), 293–320.

21. Details on the instruments and implementation of structural adjustment program in Nigeria are elaborated in Federal Republic of Nigeria, *Structural Adjustment Program for Nigeria, July 1986–June 1988* (Lagos: Federal Press, 1986), 13.

22. See John Cantwell, "Globalization and Development in Africa," in *New Globalism and Developing Countries*, ed. Dunning and Hamdani, 159.

23. See Kola Subair, "Economic Revival and Management in Nigeria: An Islamic (I-E) Model," *Hamdard Islamicus, Quarterly Journal of Studies and Research in Islam* 24 (2001): 80–83.

13

Interest Rates, Fiscal Policy, and Foreign Private Investment in Nigeria

IYIOLA ALADE AJAYI AND ADEYEMI BABALOLA

Introduction

A fundamental requirement for economic development in any economy is an adequate rate of capital formation relative to that of population growth. Adequate capital formation is essential because it helps accomplish the following economic goals, among others: to build up capital equipment needed for purposes of development; to enhance capital progress, which in turn helps to ensure sustained production on a large scale; to ensure expansion of the market; to remove market imperfections by creating economic and social overhead capital; and to break the vicious circle of poverty from both the demand and the supply side.

The process of capital formation involves three distinct phases: first, the volume of savings increases; next, savings are mobilized by financial and credit institutions; and lastly, those savings are invested. Savings can be mobilized in an economy from two distinct sources, domestic and foreign. Domestic sources include but are not limited to an increase in national income, a reduction in consumption, and fiscal and monetary measures to encourage savings. However, foreign sources involve attracting capital from abroad, which may take the form of private investment, official loans, or grants. Private capital may be direct or indirect investment. Direct investment means that foreign investors exercise de facto or de jure control over the assets created in the capital-importing country by means of their investments; this typically involves setting up a company or subsidiary of a company hitherto operating in the capital-importing country in which the foreign investor maintains majority control. It may also involve acquiring fixed assets in the target countries by nationals from the investing country. Such companies are called multinational corporations (MNCs) or transnational corporations (TNCs).

Nigeria's economy is a monocultural oil-rich economy that, in spite of the massive revenues realized from crude oil export over the last three and a half decades, still lags in terms of poor development in all ramifications of development. The oil boom of the 1970s brought with it fundamental changes in the Nigerian economy such that, prior to July 1986, the country witnessed a traumatic economic crisis. Nigeria suffered a dip in foreign exchange earnings and government revenues due to the global economic recession of the early 1980s that resulted in the collapse of the world oil market, erosion of competitiveness of its agricultural sector and that sector's ultimate neglect, as well as from the effects of inappropriate policies of the past such as economic stabilization and economic emergency measures in 1982 and 1985, respectively, and the structural adjustment program in 1986.[1]

Consequently, revenues of the government, the prime mover of Nigeria's economy, dipped significantly, external reserves fell, and efforts to contain these adverse developments impacted the macroeconomy in negative ways. These impacts were further compounded by the autocratic and undemocratic military leadership that ruled the country for about two-thirds of the years since independence was achieved in 1960. Hence, with its revenues in decline and facing consequent low domestic capital formation and mounting challenges to economic development, the government resorted to external sources of funding to bridge the savings-investment gap and put the economy on the desired trajectory.[2]

Issues at Stake

Foreign direct investment (FDI) has, over the years, proved to be a major stimulus of economic growth in developing countries through its contribution to technology transfer, enhanced balance of payment position, employment generation, and diversification of the industrial base, among other factors. The emphasis on these resources for economic growth has made FDI the focus of policymakers in many low-income countries. One of the recent questions confronting economic researchers is how do African countries increase their share of global foreign direct investment.[3] By and large, Nigeria has the potential to attract FDI but has not been successful in doing so despite efforts toward liberalizing its FDI regime and intensifying the enabling environment. Even though Nigeria had embarked on policies and structural reforms favoring increased openness and lower barriers to trade, and had liberalized its domestic financial markets and removed restrictions on the movement of capital, FDI flows have occurred mainly in the oil sector of the economy, from which the country derives over 90 percent of its export earnings. In terms of diversification of FDI to other sectors of the economy, Nigeria has not benefited commensurately to its potential. Factors such as overdependence on the oil sector, inadequate and dilapidated infrastructure, government corruption, unstable regulatory and institutional environment, and other security concerns including civil unrest and crime have been responsible in part for the lackluster flow of FDI into the economy.[4]

The first response of the Nigerian government to these deteriorating economic conditions was to introduce stabilization, austerity, and protectionist measures between 1982 and 1984. The Economic Stabilization Act (1982) imposed more stringent exchange controls and import restrictions supported by appropriate monetary and fiscal policies. A rejection of IMF loans and their draconian conditionalities resulted in the introduction in 1986 of a structural adjustment program (SAP) with its major policy thrust of liberalization, deregulation, privatization, commercialization, and exchange rate flexibility. However, the economy appears not to have fared better in the post-SAP period in comparison to the pre-SAP period because the structural adjustments negatively affected real investment. Gross domestic investment (GDI) fell from 48.5 percent during the period 1981–85 to 13 percent by 1988 and increased only slightly to 16.2 percent in 1990. The major underlying factor was the rapidly declining level of foreign investment that had been projected to complement domestic savings.[5]

Foreign capital could usefully help less developed countries (LDCs) bridge simultaneously their gaps in domestic savings and foreign exchange. However, in spite of decades of foreign capital inflows, LDCs as a group are no nearer to overcoming their savings or foreign exchange need. The gap in resources is still wide, and, in some cases, it is also widening in comparison with savings and foreign exchange resource availability. This explains the rise in the rate of unemployment, near collapse of infrastructure, closures of factories, low capacity utilization in the manufacturing sector, and inadequate funding for education, all of which have resulted in gloomy overall macroeconomic indexes.[6]

The question then should be: Has the nation not attracted sufficient capital to take it to the desired level of development or has the capital that flows into the country been misapplied? To answer this question, this study examines the global trends in foreign direct investment; identifies specific policies adopted over the years by successive governments in Nigeria regarding the enhancement of FDI; and traces the magnitude of FDI, its application, and impact on the economy with a view to ensuring steady development and macroeconomic stability.

Conceptual Framework, Theoretical Framework, and the Literature on Globalization and FDI

It is a commonplace to say that globalization has turned the world into a global village; countries and peoples are integrated such that barriers of all kinds are downplayed. Foreign direct investment, or the flow of capital and labor from abroad to another country, is the engine of globalization. Ownership of such capital can be by an individual or a corporate body or a government.[7] Basically, what defines FDI is that a foreign firm or individual must control a majority shares in the firm receiving the investment funds.

There are three traditional schools of thought on FDI—namely, dependency, modernization, and integrative. Generally, the theories argue that the flow of FDI requires profitable opportunities and a regulatory framework that facilitates investment transactions. It further requires policies that ensure general macroeconomic stability, integrate markets, and open sectors to private investment that can help expand the range of profitable enterprises.

The Dependency School

The dependency school, which comprises *dependencia* (neo-Marxist) and structuralist theories that flourished from the 1960s into the 1980s, seeks to achieve more equitable wealth, income, and power distributions through the self-reliant and collective actions of developing nations. Dependency theory sees the cause of underdevelopment primarily as exploitation by the industrialized nations. Its major contribution to the study of FDI is its focus on the consequences of FDI in developing countries and its critical analysis of Western development paradigms that regard FDI as explicitly positive. The dependencia or neo-Marxist subschool states that developing countries are exploited either through international trade, which leads to deteriorating terms of trade, or through multinational corporations transferring profits out of developing economies. This subschool posits that industrialized countries extract resources from the periphery (the poor countries). The theory does not criticize capitalism outright but rather points out that the periphery does not gain from capitalism as much as the center does. According to this view, modernization, capitalization, and industrialization are limited to the export-driven economy and other sectors according to the export needs of the core.[8]

The Modernization School

The modernization school is reflected in the "perfect market" approach as represented by neoclassical theories, and it remains widely influential to the present day. It holds that there is a natural order through which countries ascend to what is seen as higher developmental stages. The theorists recommend the way to exogenously motivated development is through industrialization, liberalization, and the opening up of these countries' economies.

A country's ability to overcome these barriers will depend on how well endowed it is in terms of production factors—that is, labor, capital, and natural resources. The modernization school views FDI as a prerequisite and catalyst for sustainable growth and development. For FDI to fulfill its crucial role, economies have to be freed from distorting state interventions and opened to foreign investment and trade. The approach of the modernization school rests on both neoclassical and perfect market theories.[9]

The Integrative School

The integrative school, which is represented by the diverse FDI and negotiation paradigm, attempts to transform thinking on foreign direct investment by analyzing it from the perspectives of host countries as well as investors. It integrates those dependency and modernization concepts that are applicable to current FDI analysis. Accordingly, integrative theory accounts for the multiplicity of heterogeneous variables involved in the FDI process. An integrative FDI theory considers microeconomic and macroeconomic variables that determine FDI. The macrolevel envelops the entire economy, while the microlevel denotes firms and institutions that link the two variables. However, what distinguishes integrative FDI theory from the other schools is that it accords more importance to the microlevel, the sphere where macrovariables and microvariables meet and the public and private sectors interact. It is in this arena that public policies are established and implemented. Thus, the microlevel is pivotal to the successful implementation of public policies. Integrative theories shed more light on the perspective of the institutional arrangement in the host nation and view FDI at the microlevel, which is where the day-to-day challenges in FDI policy implementation occur and where structural rigidities often are expressed such as corruption, nepotism, and ignorance. According to this school, despite its importance, the microlevel has not received the attention it deserves because theorists are not always aware of the daily challenges that developing countries encounter in implementing economic and investment reforms.[10] This chapter intends to explain FDI in Nigeria based on integrative theory.

Literature Review

Economic growth can be attributed to the level of acceptance of globalization within a country. Globalization has been described as one of the good developments that have happened in recent world history.[11] However, others see development as nothing more than a modern version of the slave trade practiced for centuries by many developed countries. They see nothing good in globalization and even accuse the developed countries of using the expansion of global trade to destroy barriers to enlarging their spheres of control. Globalization entails these five major areas:

- Growth in trade
- Capital flows and increased financial capacity
- Easy migration
- Information technology and the Internet
- Diffusion of technology

Thus understood, according to Shahid Yusuf, globalization has the potential to influence all parts of the world, though its impacts are felt by only a relatively small proportion of the world's population due to countries' varying levels of integration. Of particular importance is the effect of globalization in promoting economic growth in developing countries.[12]

The flow of FDI to a country depends largely on the presence in that country of certain critical minimum requirements. Among the requirements are the presence of economic, political, and social stability as well as rules regulating the entry and operation of business enterprises. Other factors that help create an attractive environment for FDI are fair treatment of foreign affiliates; facilitation of business activity; investment incentives; sufficient market size, growth, structure, and accessibility; a supply of raw materials; a low-cost but efficient labor force; and adequate physical infrastructure in the form of ports, roads, utilities, and telecommunications.[13] The incentives that are available to foreign investors include tax relief and repatriation of earnings on appreciation of capital investment. In some cases, import or export licenses are waived, and up to 100 percent foreign ownership of enterprises is allowed. Furthermore, concessions are also available on the development of local raw materials, and on local value-added, labor-intensive, or export-oriented activities that involve significant training.[14]

Foreign private investment has had mixed results for LDCs. On the positive side, it has been seen as filling the gap between the domestically available supplies of savings and the planned level of these resources necessary to achieve developmental strategies.[15] A counterargument is the "suction pump" thesis that asserts that the capital created in LDCs is transferred or pumped out from the host economy via dividends and profits relative to capital inflows into these countries.

The bulk of private foreign direct investment in many LDCs is now increasingly identified with MNCs, especially those with strong historical connections to the period of colonial economic administration.[16] The following were identified as the major determinants of foreign private investment (FPI): size of the domestic market, inflation, exchange rate volatility, interest rate, and macroeconomic policies.[17] Pfeffermann and Madarassy indicate that size of domestic market is positively related to FPI, while inflation and volatile exchange rates have negative effects. High and rising inflation rates heighten fears of cost increases for imported capital goods and other inputs, while unstable exchange rates create foreign exchange risks and an uncertain investment climate.

John Dunning, F. Root, and A. Ahmed demonstrated that FPI exercises a dominant influence over the host country's market.[18] Furthermore, they stressed that high inflation rates reduce international competitiveness in terms of export earnings and foreign earnings. This also puts pressure on current account and exchange rates. Michael Obadan also confirmed the importance of market size and trade policies on raw materials as a determinant of foreign private investment in Nigeria.[19] Harold G. Osuagwu traced the determinant of investment demand in Nigeria to expected rate of return, supply of funds, absorptive capacity, and government policies.[20] Rising bank lending rates were noticed to have discouraged productive investment because a lower lending rate in the host economy is expected to have an overall effect on higher internal rate of return on investment and thus boost investment flows.[21]

Adeoye Akinsanya argued that large external debt plays a vital role in reducing investment activities. This is because higher debt service payments associated with large external debt reduces funds available for investment. He also produced evidence to show that from 1965 to 1970, yearly inflows of investment into oil-producing countries were negative. The growth of foreign private investment in the developing world has been rapid in recent decades. It rose from $2.4 billion in 1962 to $35 billion in 1990 before surging to over $147 billion in 2002 and reaching $334 billion in 2005.[22] Accompanying this enormous advance of FPI over time to various regions of the world is the great volatility of investment flows. A majority of FPI flows from one developed country to another and of flows to developing countries are heavily concentrated in just a few destinations. For example, in 2005 well over a third ($118 billion) of the record amount of FPI that flowed to developing countries was invested in Hong Kong and mainland China alone. Africa, as usual, received only a small fraction of inflows. In 2005, although FPI in Africa reached a record $31 billion, Africa's share of global FPI was little more than 3 percent; and most of the thirty-four African LDCs received very little foreign investment. This is not surprising given the fact that private capital gravitates toward countries and regions that offer the highest financial returns and greatest perceived safety. Where debt problems are severe, governments are unstable, and economic reforms are only beginning, the risk of capital loss can be high.

The global trend in foreign direct investment flows is presented in table 13.1. FDI flows represent new additions to the existing stock of FDI. As the table shows, during the five-year period 1997–2001, total annual worldwide FDI flows amounted to about $830 billion on average. As can be expected, several developed countries are the dominant sources of FDI *outflows*. The United States, on average, invested $139.2 billion per year, with the UK following close behind at $134.5 billion. France, Germany, and the Netherlands also invested heavily overseas, at about $91.0 billion, $65.8 billion, and $46.6 billion per year, respectively. Spain invested $31.1 billion; Canada, $29.4 billion; Japan, $28.5 billion; Switzerland, $25.3 billion; Sweden, $21.0 billion; and Italy, $12.6 billion. The developed countries mentioned above account for about 90 percent of the total worldwide FDI outflows during the period. This implies that MNCs domiciled in these countries should have certain comparative advantages in undertaking overseas investment projects. It is interesting to note that China, itself considered a developing country, had begun to undertake FDI during this period, albeit on a modest scale.

Table 13.1 also shows FDI *inflows* by country. The United States received the largest amount of FDI inflows, $202.3 billion per year on average, among all countries. The next most popular destinations of FDI flows were the United Kingdom ($71.7 billion), Germany ($62.2 billion), China ($43.5 billion), France ($38.8 billion), the Netherlands ($37.1 billion), Canada ($29.3 billion), Sweden ($25.5 billion), and Spain ($18.6 billion). These nine countries account for about 60 percent of total worldwide FDI inflows, suggesting that they must have location advantages for FDI over other countries. In contrast to its substantial role as an originating country of FDI, Japan plays a relatively minor role as a recipient of FDI: Japan received annually only $6.7 billion worth of FDI, on average, reflecting a variety of Japanese legal, economic, and cultural barriers to foreign investment. It is noted that FDI flows declined in 2001, reflecting a slowdown of the world economy.

Eun Cheol and Resnick Bruce affirmed that FDI flows into China have dramatically been on the increase over time. The amount of FDI increased from $3.5 billion in 1990 to $46.8 billion in 2001. By 1993 China had emerged as the third most important recipient country for FDI, trailing only the United States and the United Kingdom. MNCs might have been lured to invest in China not only by lower labor and material costs but also by the desire to preempt the entry of rivals into China's potentially huge market.[23]

Among developing countries, Mexico is another country that experienced substantial FDI inflows, $15 billion on average per year for 1997–2001. It is well known that MNCs are investing in Mexico, a low-cost country, to serve the US as well as Mexican markets. It is also noteworthy that MNCs invested heavily, $18.6 billion per year for the period, in Spain, where the costs of production are relatively low compared to other European countries such as France and Germany. Most likely, MNCs invested in Spain in part to

Table 13.1. Foreign direct investment: outflows (inflows), 1997–2001 (in billions US$)

Country	1997	1998	1999	2000	2001	Annual Average
Australia	5.9	2.5	3.0	5.1	11.2	5.5
	(8.6)	(6.6)	(5.7)	(12.0)	(4.1)	(7.4)
Canada	22.1	26.6	15.6	47.5	35.5	29.4
	(11.5)	(16.5)	(24.4)	(66.6)	(27.5)	(29.3)
China	2.6	1.6	1.8	0.9	1.8	1.7
	(44.2)	(45.5)	(40.3)	(40.8)	(46.8)	(43.5)
France	35.6	40.6	120.6	175.5	82.8	91.0
	(23.2)	(28.0)	(47.1)	(42.9)	(52.6)	(38.8)
Germany	40.3	86.6	109.5	49.3	43.3	65.8
	(9.6)	(19.9)	(54.8)	(195.1)	(31.8)	(62.2)
Italy	10.2	12.1	6.7	12.3	21.5	12.6
	(3.7)	(2.6)	(6.9)	(13.4)	(14.9)	(8.3)
Japan	26.0	24.2	22.7	31.6	38.1	28.5
	(3.2)	(3.2)	(12.7)	(8.3)	(6.2)	(6.7)
Mexico	1.1	1.4	1.5	1.0	3.7	1.7
	(12.8)	(10.2)	(12.5)	(14.7)	(24.7)	(15.0)
Netherlands	21.5	38.3	57.7	71.3	44.0	46.6
	(9.4)	(31.9)	(41.3)	(52.5)	(50.5)	(37.1)
Spain	12.5	18.4	42.1	54.7	27.8	31.1
	(6.4)	(11.3)	(15.8)	(37.5)	(21.8)	(18.6)
Sweden	12.6	22.5	21.9	40.6	7.2	21.0
	(10.9)	(19.4)	(60.9)	(23.4)	(12.7)	(25.5)
Switzerland	16.7	17.4	33.3	42.7	16.3	25.3
	(4.9)	(3.7)	(11.7)	(16.3)	(10.0)	(9.3)
United Kingdom	63.6	114.2	201.4	253.9	39.5	134.5
	(37.0)	(63.1)	(87.9)	(116.6)	(53.8)	(71.7)
United States	110.0	132.8	174.6	164.9	113.9	139.2
	(109.3)	(193.4)	(283.4)	(300.9)	(124.4)	(202.3)
World	475.1	648.9	1,042.1	1,379.5	620.7	833.3
	(464.3)	(643.9)	(1,088.3)	(1,491.9)	(735.1)	(884.1)

Source: Adapted from UNCTAD, *World Investment Report 1999: Foreign Direct Investment and the Challenge of Development,* www.unctad.org/en/docs/wir1999_en.pdf.

gain a foothold in the huge single market created by the European Union, of which Spain is a member country.[24]

As shown in the IMF's "Foreign Direct Investment Trends and Statistics" published in 2003, the flow of foreign direct investment has grown faster over the recent past.[25] Higher global flows of FDI always reflect a better economic environment in the presence of economic reforms and investment-oriented policies. Such flows reached an appreciable level of about $1.3 trillion in the year 2006.[26] The trend has slowed down as a result of the global recession experienced in the last several years. The increase in FDI was largely fueled by cross-border mergers and acquisitions. FDI in 2006 increased by 38 percent more than the previous year. Most of the developing and least developed countries worldwide participated equally in the process of direct investment activities.

- FDI inflows to the Latin American and Caribbean region increased by 11 percent on average in comparison to the previous year.
- In Africa, FDI inflows set a record in the year 2006.
- Flows of FDI to South, East, and Southeast Asia and Oceania maintained an upward trend.
- Both Turkey and oil-rich states of the Persian Gulf continued to attract high FDI inflows.
- The United States, the world's largest economy, also attracted larger FDI inflows from the eurozone and Japan.[27]

Higher inflows of FDI to a country typically generate employment in the nation. FDI in the manufacturing sector creates more employment opportunities relative to other sectors. For the year 2006, countries such as Luxembourg, Hong Kong, China, Suriname, Iceland, and Singapore ranked toward the top of the Inward FDI Performance Index of the United Nations Conference on Trade and Development (UNCTAD). In recent years, most countries have made their business environment investment friendly for absorbing global opportunities.

The recently released *World Investment Report 2010* estimates that FDI inflows worldwide plummeted by 37 percent to $1.1 trillion in 2009—following a 16 percent decline in 2008.[28] During recession-plagued 2009, global FDI outflows fell some 43 percent to $1.1 trillion, outpacing even the 37 percent drop in inflows. Global FDI declined across the primary, secondary, and services sectors, and most FDI components—equity investment, intra-company loans, or reinvested earnings—contracted. FDI by private equity funds decreased by 65 percent, although flows from sovereign wealth funds rose by 15 percent. These funds together accounted for one-tenth of global FDI flows, compared to less than 7 percent in 2000, but were down from 22 percent in the peak year of 2007.

FDI Flows and Multinational Corporations

Two central characteristics of MNCs are their large size and the fact that their global operations and activities tend to be centrally controlled by parent companies. They are the major force in the rapid globalization of world trade. They are not in the development business per se; rather, their objectives are to maximize their returns on capital and to seek out the most profitable opportunities. Generally speaking, they are not necessarily concerned with issues such as poverty, inequality, employment conditions, and environmental problems, except as these affect their bottom line.

Foreign direct investment flows to developing countries have remained a small fraction of these countries' total investment, most of which is accounted for by domestic sources. Through the years, FDI has become by far the largest source of foreign funds flowing to developing countries. The role of MNCs in filling in the so-called foreign exchange gap between targeted foreign exchange requirements and those derived from net export earnings plus net public foreign aid is also important. The inflow of foreign direct investment is capable of not only alleviating the deficit on the balance of payments current account, either in part or in full, but also of functioning to relieve debts over time if the foreign-owned enterprise can generate net positive export earnings.[29]

Unfortunately, as noted in the case of import substitution, the overall effect of permitting MNCs to establish subsidiaries behind protective tariff and quota walls producing goods for domestic consumption is often a net worsening of both the current and capital account balances. Such deficits generally result from the importation of capital equipment and intermediate products (normally from an overseas affiliate and often at inflated prices) and the outflow of foreign exchange in the form of repatriated profits, management fees, royalty payments, and interest on private loans.

Over the years, foreign capital investment has helped tremendously the fiscal condition of LDC governments. It has helped fill the gap between targeted government tax revenue and locally raised taxes. By taxing MNCs' profits, for instance, and participating in their local operations, LDC governments are thought to be better able to mobilize public financial resources needed for development projects. Terisa Turner has noted that the activities of MNCs also disrupt or impede governance in many LDCs. The instability of the Nigerian state is due primarily and principally to the alliance between MNCs, government bureaucrats, and local elites, a trend that is prevalent in many LDCs.[30] This argument was further buttressed in the work of John Ohiorhenuan and Hugh Stephenson.[31] Also worthy of mention is the utter disregard and abuse of environmental quality by a great number of multinational corporations in their production activities. A specific case in point here has occurred in the Niger Delta region of Nigeria. MNCs involved in oil exploration activities have left massive oil spillages, uncontrolled gas flaring, destruction of the region's biodiversity, and worsening unemployment, all of which contribute to poverty. This issue was also passionately discussed in the work of Akin Oshuntokun.[32] These impacts have snowballed into a crisis of very serious social dimensions that threatens the very fabric of the Nigerian state. The deterioration of security promotes restiveness among youth in the oil-producing communities and has spawned armed militancy, kidnappings, and hired killings, pushing Nigeria to the verge of becoming a failed state.

Private Portfolio Investment

Private portfolio investment (PPI) consists of foreign purchases of stocks (equity), bonds, certificates of deposit, and commercial paper of LDCs. PPI as a type of investment has favored middle-income countries while neglecting sub-Saharan Africa, the poorest region of the world.[33] Just as in the case of FDI flows through MNCs, the benefits and costs of PPI flows to both investors (primarily from developed countries) and LDC recipients have been a subject of rigorous debate.[34] From the point of view of investors, investing in the stock market of emerging countries (another term for LDCs) gives investors an opportunity to increase their returns while diversifying their risks.

However, from the recipients' point of view, private portfolio flows in local stock and bond markets are welcome as a means for raising capital for domestic firms. Their desirability depends on the level of development and depth of the local stock and bond markets; their vitality also facilitates local domestic investors to diversify their assets and can help to improve the efficiency of the whole financial sector by serving as a screening and monitoring device for allocating funds to industries and firms with the highest potential returns.

Foreign private financial flows have been fluctuating in recent decades. Similar to multinational corporations, foreign portfolio investors are not in the development business. Their decisions are guided by variations in rates of return and profit projections across the global economy. For example, if the interest rate in a developed country rises or the perceived potential profit in an LDC declines, foreign portfolio speculators can withdraw their investment as quickly as they bought in. Private portfolio financial flows are very volatile and respond to global interest rate differentials as well as to investors' perception of political and economic stability, variables that provide a tenuous foundation on which to base medium- or long-term development strategies.[35] Asia's financial collapse in 1997, Russia's in 1998, Brazil's currency turmoil of 1999, and Argentina's crisis of 2001–2 underlined the fragility of global financial markets.

Foreign Remittances

A World Bank report in 2006 pointed out that wage levels in high-income economies are approximately five times those of similar occupations in the developing nations, after adjusting for purchasing power parity. This differential in wage levels between high-income countries and developing countries has provided an incentive for migration from low-income developing countries to high-income developed countries. It is estimated that there were more than 250 million migrants at the end of 2006. This migration of (mostly) skilled workers could accentuate brain drain and manpower development problems as highly skilled workers who might have driven the development process in their home countries are often lost to out-migration due to the attraction of higher wages elsewhere. This further complicates and skews the development pivot in favor of the developed and rich nations of the world, thus perpetuating underdevelopment and trapping poor countries in a vicious circle.

On the positive side, especially when migrants are low-skilled workers, there are clear advantages for potential development and poverty reduction. When such migrants make remittances to relatives in the migrants' countries of origin to build houses, pay for education, and ensure their families are well fed, these remittances are helping to provide a significant pathway out of poverty. The World Bank reports that, based on household surveys, remittances substantially reduced poverty in such countries as Guatemala, Uganda, Ghana, and Bangladesh.

Empirical Analysis

The distribution of various activities into which foreign private investment flowed in the Nigerian economy during 1998–2006 is shown in table 13.2. Mining and quarrying was the largest recipient of inflows throughout the period covered. However, the importance of this sector has been declining over time; as a percentage of total FPI flow (in monetary terms), it dipped from 39.3 percent in 1998 to 22 percent in 2006. This drop-off may be connected to the spate of violence and upheaval in the Niger Delta, where most economic activity is oil production, the dominant subsector in the mining and quarrying sector of the economy. The uncertainty and insecurity in the area have caused the loss of quite a number of investments. Transportation and communications has the least importance, though this sector was stable for the first three years from 1998, only to pick up slightly from 2001 (0.6 percent) to 1.7 percent in 2006. This could be attributed to the liberalization of the telephone industry and impact of the global system for mobile communications (GSM) in the economy.

Table 13.2. Nigeria's cumulative foreign private investment by type of activity, 1998–2006 (in millions ₦)

Activity\year	1998	1999	2000	2001	2002	2003	2004	2005	2006
Mining & quarrying	59,970.5	58,855.4	60,710.9	61,611.9	61,611.9	61,809.1	62,145.7	80,789.4	105,668.4
Manufacturing & processing	34,503.9	36,282.1	37,333.6	37,779.6	39,953.6	45,719.4	102,995.8	133,894.5	212,729.4
Agriculture, forestry, and fisheries	1,209.0	1,209.0	1,209.0	1,209.0	1,209.0	1,209.0	1,209.0	1,209.0	12,090.0
Transportation & communications	689.2	820.3	820.3	955.3	1,736.3	2,890.5	4,281.1	3,565.4	8,291.0
Building & construction	3,888.3	3,995.9	3,995.9	4,211.9	4,293.9	4,545.8	5,194.1	6,713.3	1,0461.1
Trading & business services	10,460.5	10,927.3	11,201.3	12,016.3	12,317.3	14,457.3	20,242.4	26,315.1	41,309.3
Miscellaneous services	41,689.5	42,100	42,237.6	43,657.6	45,509.6	49,056.5	53,571.2	69,642.6	102,780.0
Total	152,410.9	154,190	157,508.6	161,441.6	166,631.6	166,631.6	249,220.6	324,656.7	481,239.1

Source: Central Bank of Nigeria, *Statistical Bulletin 2009*, http://www.cenbank.org/OUT/2010/PUBLICATIONS/STATISTICALBULLETINS/2009/PartD/PartD.html.

Manufacturing and processing also witnessed continuous growth, rising from 22.6 percent in 1998 to 44.2 percent by 2006, a near doubling. The overwhelming importance of trading and business services to the economy cannot be overemphasized. This sector's share of the total FPI is next to that of manufacturing and processing during the early years (34.3 percent in 1998).

The volume of investment inflows increased from ₦152,410.90 in 2004 to ₦249,220.60 the next year and peaked at ₦481,239.10 in 2006, a leap of 93 percent from 1998. This is reflective of a growing confidence in the economy and could be attributed to the burgeoning of democracy, especially with successive transfers of power (though not without hitches) from one civilian regime to another. The inflation rate declined at the turn of the transition from a military to a civilian regime, from 1998 to 1999 as indicated in table 13.3. Inflation began to climb thereafter, however, peaking at 18.9 percent in 2001. This development may be connected to expenditure most especially by politicians' preparing for reelection and campaigning for office in 2003. Domestic savings witnessed strong growth, as shown in table 13.4, throughout the entire period. This growth is nominal and may have been exaggerated by the rising inflation being experienced at the same time.

The summary of the correlation coefficient for this study is shown in table 13.9 (based on data included in tables 13.3, 13.5–13.8). The correlation coefficient of the relationship between foreign private investment (net foreign inflows used as proxy) and the minimum rediscount rate (MRR, as a proxy for interest rate) shows a negative relationship of 60 percent. This implies that foreign private investment declines as MRR goes up and vice versa. This result is corroborated by Iyoha and by Ajakaye.[36]

Table 13.3. Inflation rate in Nigeria, 1998–2006 (percent)

Year	1998	1999	2000	2001	2002	2003	2004	2005	2006
Rate (%)	10.0	6.6	6.9	18.9	12.9	14.0	15.0	17.9	8.2

Source: Central Bank of Nigeria, *Statistical Bulletin 2009* (see table 13.2).

Table 13.4. National savings statistics for Nigeria, 1998–2006 (in millions ₦)

Year	1998	1999	2000	2001	2002	2003	2004	2005	2006
Total savings	200,065.1	277,667.5	385,190.9	488,045.4	592,094.0	655,739.7	797,517.2	1,078,330.1	1,604,174.5

Source: Central Bank of Nigeria, *Statistical Bulletin 2009* (see table 13.2).

Table 13.5. Nigeria's minimum rediscount rate (MRR), 1998–2006 (percent)

Year	1998	1999	2000	2001	2002	2003	2004	2005	2006
MRR (%)	14.3	18.0	13.5	14.3	19.0	15.8	15.0	13.0	12.2

Source: Central Bank of Nigeria, *Statistical Bulletin 2009* (see table 13.2).

Table 13.6. Debt profile of the Federal Government of Nigeria, 1998–2006 (in millions ₦)

Year	Domestic	External	Total
1998	537,490.9	633,017.0	1,170,507.9
1999	794,806.6	2,577,374.4	3,372,181.0
2000	898,253.9	3,097,383.9	3,995,637.8
2001	1,016,974.0	3,176,291.0	4,193,265.0
2002	1,166,000.7	3,932,884.8	5,098,885.5
2003	1,329,680.0	4,478,329.3	5,808,009.3
2004	1,370,325.2	4,890,269.6	6,260,594.8
2005	1,525,906.6	2,695,072.2	4,220,978.8
2006	1,753,259.0	451,461.7	2,204,720.7

Source: Central Bank of Nigeria, *Statistical Bulletin 2009* (see table 13.2).

Table 13.7. Electricity generation, 1998–2005 (megawatts per hour)

Year	1998	1999	2000	2001	2002	2003	2004	2005
Rate	1,724.9	1,859.8	1,738.3	1,689.9	2,237.3	6,180.0	2,763.6	2,779.3

Source: Central Bank of Nigeria, *Statistical Bulletin 2009* (see table 13.2).

The correlation coefficient for foreign private investment and gross domestic product showed a strong positive relationship of 84 percent. Growth in foreign private investment had a very strong and positive influence on GDP growth in the Nigerian economy during the period covered.[37] Also, weak relationships of 21 percent and 32 percent, respectively, exist between FPI, on the hand, and electricity generation and debt profile, on the other. The weak relationship of FPI and electricity generation may be a result of the Nigerian government's inability or lack of commitment to

Table 13.8. Nigeria's gross domestic product (GDP), 1998–2006 (at 1990 basic prices, in billions ₦)

Year	GDP
1998	388,468.1
1999	393,107.2
2000	412,332.0
2001	431,783.1
2002	451,785.6
2003	495,007.1
2004	527,576.0
2005	561,931.4
2006	595,821.6

Source: Central Bank of Nigeria, *Statistical Bulletin 2009* (see table 13.2).

Table 13.9. Correlation results: correlation coefficient $(r_{xy}) = \Sigma xy / \sqrt{\Sigma x^2} * \sqrt{\Sigma y^2}$

Correlate	r Coefficient
FDI net inflow vs. MRR	– 0.60
FDI net inflow vs. GDP	0.84
FDI net inflow vs. Inflation	0.00
FDI net inflow vs. Electricity production	0.21
FDI net inflow vs. Debt profile	0.32

Note: Data for computations extracted from tables 13.3, 13.5, 13.6, 13.7, and 13.8.

Source: Central Bank of Nigeria, *Statistical Bulletin 2009* (see table 13.2).

liberalize the power industry. In the final analysis, the correlation coefficient showed zero or no relationship between FPI and the rate of inflation in the Nigerian economy.[38]

Lessons from Other Countries

Generally, there has been unprecedented growth in global flows of foreign private investment in the last two decades, and these flows have become more widely dispersed among host countries in recent years. Asia has received the lion's share of FPI flows to developing countries. The overall flow of FDI to developing countries has declined by 26 percent since 1999, while China's share has increased from 21 percent to 39 percent. FPI to China amounted to $55 billion, while FPI to sub-Saharan Africa was only $11 billion, and for Economic Community of West African States it was only $3 billion—of which Nigeria's amount, $1.88 billion, was the highest.[39] This is against the backdrop of the uneven distribution of world FPI among developing countries that is skewed negatively when it comes to recipients in Africa.[40]

There is a consensus of opinion among analysts and researchers that East Asian countries have attracted massive and growing flows of FPI because they were (already) growing rapidly, have sound economic fundamentals, and macroeconomic environments conducive to investment, as well as high per capita incomes, among other factors.[41] China is one leading example of a country that has benefited immensely from increasing FPI flows. The erstwhile sleeping giant of Asia reported a spectacular 10.5 percent average growth rate of real per capita income between 1997 and 2001.

Foreign capital and technology have been playing a useful role in India's economic development. The policy of the government of India regarding foreign capital was first enunciated in the industrial policy statement of 1948. A restatement of this industrial policy in 1973 defined the country's clear-cut stance toward its foreign concerns and subsidiaries for the first time. Foreign capital has also been instrumental in facilitating India's drive toward self-reliance and import substitution as well as filling the gap between domestic savings and the capital needed for development. For example, during the second, third, and fourth plans, its contributions have been very substantial: 28 percent, 27 percent, and 34 percent, respectively.[42]

Conclusion

The nonattraction or inadequate attraction of available and scarce foreign capital investment not only to the Nigerian economy but to the economies of many other developing countries that lack domestic surplus and savings has been the bane of development efforts.[43] Given this situation, we offer the following recommendations that may help ensure that Nigeria is able to attract sufficient foreign capital investment and optimize its economic potential.

Ensure a Stable, Responsible, and Transparent Polity

The hallmark of stability, responsibility, and transparency for Nigeria is situated in democratic governance built on the tenets of the rule of law, democratic participation, confidence in leadership, and public accountability that is amenable to constructive criticism. Strengthening these factors would go a long way toward building trust in the Nigerian government and the state by its citizens. This emerging society may also be tapped into by foreign companies by investing in the economy.

Adequate Security and Social Framework

A stable economy where strife, war, violence, and civil and military brigandage is not the order of the day is imperative to any country hoping to receive inflows of foreign capital. Investors, whether local or foreign, can only do business in a peaceful and crime-free environment. Therefore, fostering a security framework comprised of a well-trained and well-equipped force that protects life and property, removes impediments to free enterprise, and also guarantees and defines property rights, should be a priority for Nigeria. The crisis of confidence in the Niger Delta has disrupted the activities of multinational corporations in the area through kidnappings, armed militancy, rent-seeking behavior, and other unwholesome acts with the end result that some MNCs have pulled out of the country, while foreign embassies publish on a daily basis the security risks that Nigeria as a whole poses to business interests.

Elimination of Bureaucratic Costs

The bureaucracy in Nigeria, like that in a host of other developing countries, is structured in a manner that is often incompatible with the needs of the modern day or that frustrates legitimate economic activities and creates room for graft and rent-seeking. These activities increase the cost of doing business in the country. Therefore, a properly oriented and well-trained civil service that is responsive and useful to the economy should be put in place to complement a highly liberalized and deregulated economy that in turn will attract much-needed foreign capital for development.

A Sound Macroeconomic Policy Climate Conducive to Development

Nigeria's macroeconomic environment should be such that it promotes, both in the short and long term, rapid growth and sustainable development through low inflation, sound and prudent monetary and fiscal policies, and a sustainable current account/balance of payments position. Furthermore, it should be transparent and capable of reducing the instability engendered by externally generated shocks. Monetary policy should be designed so that the attainment of a low rate of inflation, as well as low but positive interest rates in a liberalized and deregulated framework, is promoted. Unsustainable fiscal deficits, usually a by-product of reckless and wasteful government spending, should be discouraged because ultimately such spending only leads to higher interest rates and reduces credit to the private sector, thereby crowding out private investment.

Expenditure on enduring infrastructural development should be encouraged as this will enhance the attractiveness of the investment climate for both local and foreign capital. Also, policies of guided deregulation, liberalization, commercialization, and transparent privatization of mismanaged public enterprises should be encouraged. Collectively, these steps would, as the experience of some countries that have benefited extensively from foreign capital flows has shown, attract foreign capital flows, particularly portfolio flows.

Investment promotion in the economy should be intensified; India's development path provides a worthy example to follow. The attention of foreign investors should be drawn to investment opportunities in Nigeria, even as limits in the Nigerian economy are acknowledged. Information on factors affecting the investment climate should be readily available and easily accessible to any willing investor. The government should support and encourage the strengthening of institutions to facilitate this transparency through policies that are timely, proactive, and sincere.

Cultural Rebirth

Nigerian society, like that of many developing countries, possesses certain values, attitudes, and traits that have proved counterproductive to modern development, while tarnishing the image of the average Nigerian citizen, and putting off willing investors. To cite just one well-known example, Internet scams, and the get-rich-at-any-cost attitude behind these fraudulent practices, many of which go unpunished, have a tendency to make the typical foreign investor wary and skeptical about the intentions of Nigerian businesspeople. What is needed from the Nigerian government is excellent leadership, as exemplified in transparent dealings and concerted efforts to create a corruption-free society.

Notes

1. I. F. Olaniyan, "Beyond SAP: A Policy Framework," *Nigerian Economic Society* (1996): 143–58.

2. John C. Anyanwu et al., *The Structure of the Nigerian Economy, 1960–1997* (Onitsha, Nigeria: Joanee Educational Publishers Limited, 1997), 453–54.

3. O. Iyoha, "Policy Environment, Direct Foreign Investment, and Economic Growth in Sub-Saharan Africa," *Finance and Banking Review* 1, no. 1 (July 2007): 1–19; O. Ajakaiye, *Structural Adjustment Programme and Changes in the Structure of Production in Nigeria, 1986–1994*, NCEMA Monograph Series No. 9 (Ibadan: National Center for Economic Management and Administration, 1997).

4. Anyanwu et al., *Structure of the Nigerian Economy*, 3–6.

5. Ibid., 468–70.

6. Ojetunji Aboyade, *Integrated Economics* (London: Addison-Wesley, 1986).

7. M. U. Yakub, "Foreign Direct Investment Flows to Nigeria: Issues, Challenges, and Prospects," *Bullion: A Publication of the Central Bank of Nigeria* 29, no. 4 (2005): 54–64.

8. G. Pfeffermann and A. Madarassy, "Trends in Private Investment in Developing Countries," *IFC Discussion Paper No. 19* (World Bank, November 30, 1992), 1–55.

9. I. A. Moosa, *Foreign Direct Investment: Theory, Evidence, and Practice* (New York: Palgrave, 2002); E. Borensztein, J. De Gregorio, and J. W. Lee, "How Does FDI Affect Economic Growth?" *Journal of International Economics* 45 (1998): 115–35.

10. Yakub, "Foreign Direct Investment Flows"; Saskia K. S. Wilhelms, "Foreign Direct investment and Its Determinants in Emerging Economies," African Economic Policy Discussion Paper no. 9 (Washington, DC: United States Agency for International Development, 1998).

11. Oluitan, "Globalisation and Human Capital Development," *Nigerian Banker: Journal of The Chartered Institute of Bankers of Nigeria* (January–March 2007): 21–27.

12. Shahid Yusuf, "Globalisation and the Challenge for Developing Countries," Policy Research Working Paper Series No. 2618 (Washington, DC: World Bank Development Economics Research Group, 2001).

13. Yakub, "Foreign Direct Investment Flows."

14. United Nations Conference on Trade and Development, *World Investment Report* (1999).

15. Michael Todaro, *Economies of a Developing World* (London: Longman, 1977).

16. Aboyade, *Integrated Economics*, 189.

17. Pfeffermann and Madarassy, "Trends in Private Investment," 265–68.

18. John H. Dunning, *Multilateral Enterprises in the Global Economy* (London: Addison-Wesley, 1993); F. Root and A. Ahmed, "The Influence of Policy Investment on manufacturing: Direct Foreign Investment in Developing Countries," *Journal of International Business Studies* (Winter 1988): 91–93.

19. Micheal Obadan, "Direct Investment in Nigeria: An Empirical Analysis," *African Studies Review* 25, no. 1 (1994): 167–81.

20. Harold G. Osuagwu, "Determinants of Investment Demand in Nigeria, 1960–1975," *Quarterly Journal of Administration* (October–January 1983).

21. Ajakaiye, *Structural Adjustment Programme*.

22. Adeoye A. Akinsanya, *Multinationals in a Changing Environment: A Study of Business-Government Relations in the Third World* (New York: Praeger, 1984).

23. S. C. Eun and B. J. Resnick, *International Financial Management* (New York: McGraw-Hill, 2004), 352–61.

24. Ibid.

25. IMF, *Foreign Direct Investment Trends and Statistics*, October 28, 2003, 6–9.

26. UNCTAD, *World Investment Report 2007: Transition, Corporations, Extractive Industries.*

27. IMF, *Foreign Direct Investment Trends and Statistics*, October 28, 2003.

28. http://www.unctad.org/en/docs/w.r.2010_en.pdf.

29. S. Fajana, *Industrial Relations* (Lagos: Labofin and Company, 2005).

30. Terisa Turner, "Multinational Corporations and the Instability of Nigerian State," *Review of African Political Economy* 5 (January–April 1976): 63.

31. John Ohiorhenuan, "The Political Economy of Military Rule in Nigeria," *Review of Radical Political Economics* 16, nos. 2–3 (1984): 1–28; Hugh Stephenson, *The Coming Clash: The Impact of the International Corporation on the Nation State* (London: Weidenfeld & Nicolson, 1972), 120–25.

32. A. Oshuntokun, *Environmental Problems of the Niger-Delta* (Lagos: Friedrich Ebert Foundation, 1999).

33. S. Claessens, "The Emergence of Equity Investment in Developing Countries: An Overview," *World Bank Economic Review* 9 (1995): 1–17.

34. Ibid.

35. Paul Krugman, "Dutch Tulips and Emerging Markets," *Foreign Affairs* 74, no. 4 (1995): 74.

36. Iyoha, "Policy Environment, Direct Foreign Investment"; Ajakaiye, *Structural Adjustment Programme.*

37. M. Fry, "Foreign Direct Investment, Financing, and Growth," in *Investment and Financing in Developing Countries*, ed. Bernhard Fischer (Baden-Baden, Germany: Nomos Verlagsgesellschaft, 1994).

38. Iyoha, "Policy Environment, Direct Foreign Investment."

39. World Bank, *FDI Trends: Looking beyond the Current Gloom in Developing Public Policy for the Private Sector* (Washington, DC, 2004), 24–25.

40. Padma Mallampally and Karl P. Sauvant, "Foreign Direct Investment in Developing Countries: Policy Perspectives," *Finance and Development* 36, no. 1 (March 1999).

41. Iyoha, "Policy Environment, Direct Foreign Investment."

42. M. L. Jhingan, *The Economics of Development and Planning* (Delhi: Vrinda Publications, 2005), 827–37.

43. Anyanwu et al., *Structure of the Nigerian Economy*, 468–70.

14

Why Nigeria Does Not Work

Obstacles and the Alternative
Path to Development

CHARLES J. MAMBULA

Introduction

To its advocates, globalization is a "positive-sum game," whereby every country is expected to benefit equally on a comparative basis, while pessimists see it as a "zero-sum game" that only exploits poorer countries for the benefit of the richer ones.[1] Both arguments seem to hold true with practical examples for each. African economies seem only to qualify as cheap sources of low-value-added raw materials for processing products in industrialized countries and end up becoming markets for finished products.[2] Due to the lack of a solid entrepreneurial and technological base to foster innovative and creative abilities, most African countries continue to remain backward, dependent, and at a competitive disadvantage in this age of globalization. In Nigeria, entrepreneurial development has not advanced much beyond the basic craft or artisan levels. Nor has foreign direct investment (FDI) grown appreciably, due to a dearth of both facilities and the factors that support them. This apparent disadvantage, according to Walter Rodney, has its origins partially in the legacy of slavery and colonialism in Africa, as those institutions and individuals responsible for economic activity basically exploited Africa's natural resources and deliberately refused to encourage the practice of industrial manufacturing and technical development in Africa.[3]

Entrepreneurs as development agents and globalization as an interdependent network of people, institutions, and markets are concomitant.[4] Entrepreneurs in countries that have been able to discover beyond their borders what consumers in other countries need and are able to trade such goods through appropriate channels are economically the most prosperous, because they generate wealth, create employment opportunities, and improve the standard of living of their country's citizens.[5] In a similar way, those countries with a supportive enabling environment tend to attract FDI. However, the attention of foreign investors in large numbers has not been attracted or drawn to most of Africa like it has been to China and India. This chapter seeks to identify the factors that are constraining the development process in sub-Saharan Africa (SSA), particularly in Nigeria, and to suggest ways that an entrepreneurial society and foreign-investment-based economy can be developed in the twenty-first century.

Methodology of Study

To conduct this study, I have used an environmental-scanning approach to survey the global, regional, national, and local levels. I have researched the relevant literature in international business, entrepreneurship, economics, and related areas in order to discover the contributions of other scholars, practitioners, and professionals in terms of theories and explanations as to why certain outcomes have been achieved in African development, with particular focus on SSA. I also utilized the participant observation approach through visits to Nigeria, during the ending years of the twentieth century (1990–99) and early years of the twenty-first century (2000–2010). Practical applications and results derived from studies of entrepreneurship and FDI in various countries that serve as examples and lessons are also noted from the literature. Having observed ongoing trends and events in relevant key environments, I present and discuss the effects and influences of these observed variables and factors on countries under different specific situations and circumstances and compare them to the Nigerian context. Comments and opinions from a variety of stakeholders on the particular effects of entrepreneurship and FDI in the globalization era on general development are also discussed. Finally, I make recommendations based on these findings concerning what needs to be done to achieve progressive and sustainable development in Nigeria/SSA in view of the roles of entrepreneurship and FDI.

Review of Related Literature

Companies of all sizes go global for different reasons, some which are reactive (or defensive) like responses to the globalizing actions of competitors, the imposition of trade barriers, enactment of difficult regulations and restrictions, and increasing customer demand. Other companies go international for proactive (or aggressive) reasons, such as to achieve economies of scale; reduce costs; increase profits; and take advantage of growth opportunities, resources, and cost savings as well as incentives provided by host countries. In addition to other factors that influence entry into global markets, multinational corporations (MNCs) are attracted to host countries that offer the most stable and supportive environment with attractive, lucrative opportunities for investment. Most of the literature looks at factors that influence entrepreneurship and FDI as options for development, to examine whether Nigeria will be able to meet its seven-point Millennium Development Goals agenda and thus reach "developed country" status by the year 2020.

Tables 14.1 and 14.2 highlight some of the commonly observed factors that are known to affect entrepreneurship, FDI, and general development. Table 14.3 provides recommended actions that can ameliorate the condition of underdevelopment. These influencing factors gathered from the literature and listed in the tables will be discussed and supported with factual evidence of their roles in the development of sub-Saharan Africa in general and Nigeria in particular.

A Question of Image

What perception does the outside world have of Nigeria? Where does the country rank on the scorecard of nations? Nigeria was shunned from attending both the G-8 in July 2009 and the G-20 meetings of industrialized nations that took place in L'Aquila, Italy, also in the summer of 2009, thus tarnishing its image. Another setback occurred when US president Barack Obama decided to visit Ghana instead of Nigeria on his first official visit to the continent. Nigeria's poor status was recently underscored when it was rated as the world's fifteenth "most failed nation" out of a total of 177 countries surveyed. The index's rankings are based on twelve indicators of state vulnerability—four of which are social; two, economic; and six, political. The indicators are not designed to forecast when states may experience violence or collapse. Rather, they are meant to measure a state's vulnerability to collapse or conflict. Out of the fifteen most failed nations surveyed, ten were in Africa. The Crisis States Research Center defines a "failed state" as a condition of "state collapse"—that is, a state that can no longer perform its basic security and development functions and that has no effective control over its territory. The index's twelve indicators of state cohesion and performance were compiled through a close examination of more than thirty thousand publicly available sources.

The Fund for Peace, a US-based think tank and independent research organization, and the magazine *Foreign Policy* have published the Failed State Index since 2005; the 2009 ed. is the fifth.[6] The index does not

Table 14.1. Environmental factors and variables affecting entrepreneurial and foreign direct investment

S/N	FACTOR	DESCRIPTION
		National variable
1.	Political factor	Form of government/governance, Rentier/Political stability/Foreign policy/State companies/ Role of military/Level of terrorism/Restrictions on imports and exports/Management/Risk
2.	Economic factor	Economic system/State of development/Economic stability/International financial standing/ Monetary and fiscal policies/Foreign investment/Volatility/Risk
3.	Physical situation	Climate/Infrastructure/Markets
4.	Technology	Know-how/Status/Level of technology/Availability of local technical skills/Technical requirements of country/Appropriability/Transfer of technology/Infrastructure/ Development level
5.	Legal/Regulatory	Legal system/Prevailing international laws/Protectionist laws/Tax laws/Role of contracts/ Protection for proprietary property/Law and order/Degree of enforcement/Environmental protection
		Sociocultural variable
6.	Religion	Conflicts/Discrimination
7.	Education	Level of development, e.g., Entrepreneurial/ Technological/R&D
8.	Health	Availability of facilities locally/Quality of health standards
9.	Language	Multilingual, heterogeneous, diversity

	Cultural variable
10. Values	Ideas of what is good or bad, acceptable, taboos
11. Norms	Economy of affection
12. Beliefs	Traditional/Natural/Superstitious
Attitudes	Treatment of foreigners, hospitality, humane, friendliness
13 Work	Ethic/Performance standards/Quality consciousness
14. Time	Speed/Bureaucracy/Red tape
15. Materialism	Demonstration effect ("me too" or "wannabe" effect) encourages corruption and crime to satisfy needs.
16. Individualism/Collectivism	Freedom, nepotism, group or independent approach
17. Change	Slow/Resistant
Individual and employee job behavior	Sense of responsibility, initiative, independence (e.g., South Koreans)
18. Motivation	Personal interest/Greed/Money
19. Commitment	Patriotism/Sacrifice/Level of involvement
20. Productivity	GDP/Value-added/Level
21. Ethics	Work/Relational

Table 14.2. Examples of some mitigating factors currently affecting Nigeria's entrepreneurial and FDI development

S/N	Factor	Effect
1.	Economic factors	Inconsistent fiscal and monetary policies; exchange rate volatility; cumbersome banking procedures; repatriation restrictions
2.	Weak enforcement of laws	Laws not strictly enforced, e.g., for intellectual property and standards
3.	Inappropriate decision making	Sale of strategic establishments, e.g., Ajaokuta Steel & NNPC complexes
4.	Security issues	Niger Delta conflicts, kidnapping; robbery; regional, ethnic, and religious conflicts
5.	Political conflicts	Assassinations of people like Abiola, Yar'Adua, Bola Ige
6.	Corruption	Impunity breeding widespread corruption
7.	Performance standards	High versus low standards. e.g., in production and manufacturing
8.	Future orientation	Myopic vision affecting the fulfillment of 7-point agenda of the Millennium Development Goals
9.	Infrastructure	Basic infrastructure inadequate: water; electricity; roads
10.	Rentier	Government interference disruptive to business and development
11.	Patriotism	Lack of sacrifices; capital flight; brain drain; lack of patronage of made-in-Nigeria products
14.	Smuggling/Scams	Of imported products against domestic products and exporting of crucial products like petroleum and other natural resources for domestic production, oil bunkering, money laundering, fraud, code "419"
15.	Neglect of diaspora input	Hijacking projects from diasporic Nigerians who cannot participate or vote in Nigerian elections

16.	Education	Inconsistent school periods due to strikes; inadequate educational equipment; paucity of resources for research; lack of global or entrepreneurial curriculum in schools
17.	Entrepreneurial opportunities are not maximized	Waste of entrepreneurial opportunities: e.g., agricultural produce through lack of preservation; other natural resources or exporting
18.	Foreign MNCs	Shell involvement in MOSSOP and fine; Halliburton and Siemens bribery scandal; dumping of waste deposits at Koko
19.	Health	Poor facilities and medical system
20.	Neglect of inventions	Helicopter invention in Kano, car invention in the southeast, etc., ignored
21.	Corruption	Corrupt customs practices at ports and corruption by other government functionaries
22.	Image concern	Obama shuns Nigeria during Africa visit; G–8 shuns invitation of Nigeria; G–20 shuns Nigeria
23.	FDI equity participation	51/49 sharing formula in favor of Nigeria is against interests of MNCs with wholly owned subsidiaries
24.	Dutch disease	Nigerian dependence upon its own natural resources (notably oil) coupled with an inflow of foreign aid has given rise to a less competitive manufacturing sector

Table 14.3. Recommended actions for correcting obstacles to entrepreneurship and FDI in Nigeria

Factor
1. Harness local resources for domestic production.
2. Produce for export markets.
3. Involve diasporic Nigerians in elections and planning, and curb brain drain.
4. Develop an entrepreneurial society as development agents (cf. Schumpeter) through education, research, training, and awareness.
5. Tackle corruption, mismanagement, misappropriation, and embezzlement.
6. Improve image of the country through proper governance, legal enforcement of rules and regulations against anarchy.
7. Import appropriate technology and training.
8. Support and encourage inventions with rewards.
9. Provide adequate infrastructure: roads, electricity, water, and ports.
10. International networks involving diasporic Nigerians—like the Chinese and Indians.
11. Provide incentives, taxes, security, protection, repatriation, and copyrights.
12. Avoid loans, debt by being independent.
13. Avoid dependency on aid by being innovative and by creating new wealth, not by redistributing existing wealth (cf. A. Sen); innovation is key to recovery (cf. Obama); Africa has to find its own road to prosperity.
14. Standardization of quality, e.g., ISO, Six Sigma.
15. Improve key sectors of health, education, agriculture, and industry for development.
16. Curb brain drain and discourage capital flight.
17. Recognize talents and reward achievements.
18. Equity sharing should be open and up to 100% for FDI.
19. Step up with internal security measures and protection.
20. Encourage patronage of homemade goods.

provide all the answers, nor does it claim to; but it is a starting point for a discussion about why states fail and what should be done to keep them from doing so.[7]

Political risk for global business is described as any governmental action or politically motivated event that affects the profitability of companies doing business in a particular country.[8] When the World Bank published its compilation of Worldwide Governance Indicators (WGI) for 1996–2008, collectively entitled "Governance Matters," it reported that the future development of Nigeria would be directly linked to good governance. According to the statistics released by the World Bank, about 97 percent of 212 countries that were surveyed performed better than Nigeria on "political stability and absence of violence" in 2008. The report ranked Nigeria in the third percentile on political stability—in other words, it was better off than only 3 percent (or worse off than 97 percent) of the countries surveyed on the issue.

Many questions have arisen concerning the transparency of political elections and the succession of power in Nigeria. Ethnic and religious instability together with controversial and questionable handling of political matters have been the main issues that have tarnished Nigeria's image internationally. Political instability and risk events, which include terrorism, are often fueled by two factors, ethnicity and religion. For business, however, it is usually the actions of government toward businesses that are of more concern. William Shreeve noted seven typical events involving political risk that are common today, and likely will be in the future, that companies must consider before doing business in host environments.[9] Each of these is discussed in turn.

Expropriation of Corporate Assets without Prompt and Adequate Compensation

In the oil-producing Niger Delta areas of Nigeria, there have been reports of confiscation and threats of destruction of property owned by foreign companies for ransom money.

Forced Sale of Equity to Host-Country Nationals, Usually at or below Depreciated Market Value

The Nigerian Indigenization Decree (1971) promotes indigenous property ownership by Nigerians. This measure is meant to discourage foreign partners from gaining more control in their attempts to avoid imperfections and maintain high-quality standards in production.

Discriminatory Treatment against Foreign Firms in the Application of Regulations or Laws

At times, indigenous or home-based companies are not required to observe certain regulations or rules while foreigners are made to do so—that is, informal organizations operate in Nigeria without formal registration, while foreign firms are penalized.

Barriers to Repatriation of Funds (Profits or Equity)

Nigerian banking standards until recently have been very ineffective and cumbersome. Transferring money in or out of the country is not easy. Only a certain amount can be remitted at a time. Companies who borrowed money in their home countries to do business in another country will find this arrangement very difficult to comply with as they may not be able to transfer enough money to cover their loan payments.

Loss of Technology or Other Intellectual Property

Most MNCs invest heavily in R&D, especially in high technology and pharmaceuticals. Countries with lax laws do not penalize intellectual property infringement. Countries can be members of the International Convention for the Protection of Intellectual Property (ICPIP), or the Paris Union. Under this organization, the legitimacy of appropriability of technology is maintained, which states that the inventing company has the right to profit from its own inventions and thus should be protected. Although Nigeria is a member of this union, it does not enforce the standard seriously. Some Nigerian producers still fabricate and improvise products under the unsanctioned name of "Taiwan" typically used for imitation products. Countries that are not members of this organization or that pay only lip-service to its rules pose a risk for MNCs that own costly patents through their investment in R&D; such firms are unlikely to invest in such countries.

Interference in Managerial Decision Making

Through the practice of nepotism certain countries mandate or decide who should be hired even if the employee lacks qualifications, which can negatively affect performance levels in the workplace. Nigeria operates in a "rentier"-based type of economy, where the government controls practically everything.

Casmir Igbokwe, who studied the obstacles being confronted in running a profitable business in Nigeria, observed, "Ask any Nigerian entrepreneur what their major headache is, and the answer will be government."[10]

Collectively, public officials, according to Igbokwe, by omission or commission, have made the Nigerian environment a difficult place in which to do business. He quotes the executive chairman of Fenguru Nigeria Ltd, Alhaji Mohammed Koiranga Jada: "The problem we have is that government owns these parastatals that are so useful to Nigerians and yet it cannot manage them."[11] Alhaji Jada adds that Mobile Telecommunications Ltd (M-TEL) is not doing as well as the other mobile telecom companies because the government has a hand in it. "The fact is that government business is seen as no man's business."[12] Yet the public sector is the main driver of wealth creation in Nigeria. According to the minister of solid minerals development, Mrs. Oby Ezekwesili, "Despite the existence of a private sector, what we actually have is a pseudo-private sector. This is because those who claim to be private sector players only survive by their linkage to the resource provided to them by the public sector."[13] This kind of situation hardly fosters economic growth. Every year, hundreds of thousands of graduates come out of the universities to search for nonexistent jobs. The Fenguru CEO puts it this way: "The industries are not working. The government cannot and will never accommodate the graduates. It's all about government interference in business. There were about 140 companies in Kano. Today, there are about 22 or so. We are not talking of other cities. These companies are a source of employment." But Igbokwe continues to say that "for any chalk to write well on this board, government must first provide the enabling environment for businesses to thrive."[14] Any firm that is paying 10 percent in value-added tax, sales tax, and corporate income tax, plus the environmental sanitation fee, refuse disposal levy, local government development levy, area boys empowerment levy, generator fee, and other sundry taxes may not survive. If it does, the cost of its products and services will be so high that demand for them will be low.

Dishonesty by Government Officials, Including Canceling or Altering Contractual Agreements, and Extortion Demands

The global corruption barometer in 2005 showed the position of Nigeria as among the most corrupt countries in the world. On a scale of 1 (not corrupt at all) to 5 (extremely corrupt), Nigeria was rated 4.5.[15] Given the very strict laws like the Foreign Corrupt Practices Act (FCPA) in the United States and injunctions of the Serious Fraud Office (SFO) in the United Kingdom, companies from these countries are understandably wary of doing business in Nigeria, with its lax laws and resultant high level of corruption, because American or British citizens could be arrested and punished with fines and jail terms whenever they return home.

Whether or not a country is viewed as an economic risk depends, among other things, on its creditworthiness or its ability to pay its foreign debt. Since Nigeria adopted a World Bank/IMF structural adjustment program (SAP) in 1986, the national currency has been unstable. Exchange rate volatility and currency translation exposure occur when the value of a country's currency depreciates against another currency. The more frequently a country's exchange rate fluctuates, the less confident and willing investors will be to invest in that country. In the early 1980s, the value of the Nigerian naira was under one naira to the US dollar. By September 2009 the naira had depreciated to ₦155 to one US dollar.

Many of the modern financial instruments that one finds in the Western world that facilitate doing business and transferring money are simply not available in Nigeria. The Governor of the Central Bank of Nigeria dismissed several CEOs of the country's largest banks in August 2009 within weeks of his appointment when he discovered gross mismanagement and incompetence in the overall handling of the banking system. People are at risk of losing their money to dishonest banking personnel who are operating in a weak system that seems to lack professional transparency, accountability, and controls. Fiscal and monetary policies change frequently in Nigeria, and this volatility would also affect FDI because of the uncertainty of the effect of new policies that are inconsistent or unsustainable in the long run. An even more serious problem faced by foreign investors is that the currencies of most SSA nations are not recognized in the international monetary system for conducting business.

I have noted that the Nigerian banking system was partly responsible for the underdevelopment of the country's entrepreneurial sector, due to the underfunding of prospective entrepreneurs.[16] Because there is no law to protect bankers against defaults by small businesses, banks are reluctant and selective in their loan disbursements, according to bank officials. Igbokwe recounts the claim of Jada, who is also a director of Guaranty Trust Bank, that when he started business in 1980, there were fewer scam cases.[17] "For this reason, whatever idea you had," he says, "banks would support you. You could walk into a bank in those days and get bank credit facility without collateral if a reputable company gave the contract to you. All you needed then was for such companies to sign that the payment must pass through the bank. Today, it is easier for a camel to pass through the eye of a needle than for a budding entrepreneur to get loans from banks."[18]

The Legal Environment

In 1999 the World Bank reported that Nigeria could not grow without the rule of law.[19] The World Bank's report shows that Nigeria ranks in the lower percentiles for perceptions of voice and accountability (31 percent), political stability (3.3 percent), government effectiveness (13.3 percent), regulatory quality (29.5 percent), rule of law (11.5 percent), and control of corruption (17.9 percent).[20] These World Bank indicators reveal problems for the future growth of Nigeria's economy unless it can achieve improvements in the rule of law, accountability, and political stability.

The country also needs to improve on governance effectiveness, regulatory quality, and the control of corruption with a special focus on improving the public service. The compilation of Worldwide Governance Indicators (WGI) for 1996–2008 entitled "Governance Matters" rated Nigeria as "still low" on the rule of law.[21] If the rule of law is weak in a country, it is an indication that true justice will not be upheld at most times. The justice system in Nigeria has been brought into question on many occasions. For example, many corrupt government officials have escaped retribution for their misdeeds. A justice minister's assassination in 2007 has not been resolved to this day, as no culprits have been arrested or convicted for the crime. The impression that most people get about Nigeria's justice system is that freedom can be bought with money. In the Siemens and Halliburton scandal, people involved in the case paid fines and even went to jail in the UK and the United States, but no one among those involved was apprehended for any crimes in Nigeria. This scandal involved top-level government personnel, who allegedly accepted bribes to allow foreign MNCs to get government contracts in Nigeria. Former US vice president Dick Cheney was implicated as then CEO of Halliburton, and was to be extradited to Nigeria for questioning. The case was later dropped altogether. Examples like these forewarn foreign investors to beware of countries where law and order are not highly esteemed. "No person wants to live in a society where the rule of law gives way to the rule of brutality and bribery. That is not democracy, that is tyranny, and now is the time for it to end," President Obama said to Ghanaians (and to a wider audience of Africans) on July 11, 2009, during his visit to Ghana.

Societal Culture

Philip Harris and Robert Moran identified eight subsystems that influence societal culture that are also crucial for the successful implementation and management of global businesses.[22] These factors include kinship, education, economy, politics, religion, health, associations, and recreation. Some of these are examined and discussed briefly below as they apply to the Nigerian context and environment for promoting entrepreneurship and FDI.

Infrastructure

While expressing regrets over a torrent of relocation of companies from Nigeria to Ghana, Alhaji Bashir Borodo, president of the Manufacturers Association of Nigeria (MAN), said that the development is the outcome of the breakdown of infrastructure in Nigeria.[23] This should serve as a wakeup call for Nigeria to remove the infrastructure roadblocks and provide incentives. An adequate and steady supply of infrastructural amenities and facilities will serve as incentives to lower overhead costs for investors. Such facilities as (a) good roads, (b) constant electricity, (c) regular water supply, (d) suitable ports, and (e) steady communications are in acutely short supply in Nigeria.

Roads

Simply put, the state of most roads in Nigeria is bad. Dipo Kolawole reported that the World Health Organization (WHO) claimed that traffic accidents kill thirty-two thousand people yearly.[24] However, it seems as if the high casualty figures as given by the WHO are for deaths and injuries combined, as explained by the president of the Nigerian Union of Road Transport Workers Alhaji Gidado Hamman. Speaking at the official launch of the Road Accident Health Insurance Scheme in Abuja, Hamman said, "Despite the fact that not all deaths and accidents on our roads are officially reported, 8,672 people were said to have lost their lives to road accidents in Nigeria in 2003, while another 28,215 people sustained different degrees of injuries within the period."[25]

Statistics from the Federal Road Safety Commission reveal that in 2006 alone, a total of 4,955 people lost their lives in road accidents in the country, while 17,390 were injured during the same year.[26] Transportation for the timely distribution and delivery of goods and supplies is only possible with good roads; otherwise, their absence literally slows down progress and business development.

Electricity

"Never Expect Power Always" is the name that frustrated Nigerians have given to the country's National Electric Power Authority (NEPA) due to the erratic nature of the utility when it comes to power supply. NEPA supplies less than about three thousand megawatts of electricity generating on average just one thousand megawatts to the entire country of nearly 150 million people, which comes to about three hours of electricity a day per person. Most houses and businesses have no choice but to operate gasoline-powered generators, which leads not only to pollution but also to health hazards caused by inhalation of fumes from generators. The shortage of electricity continues to persist because the utility officials enjoy the lucrative benefits of marketing power generators. Foreign investors, especially manufacturers that heavily depend on electrical power, clearly are frustrated. One reason manufacturing industries are attracted to a country like Trinidad and Tobago, although it is not heavily populated or as developed as the G-8 countries, is its steady, low-cost energy supply. Lack of electricity has undermined Nigeria's domestic economy, forcing local businesses to resort to costly diesel generators, while rural people use candlelight and kerosene lamps for light and firewood or charcoal for cooking.

Paradoxically, the oil sector continues to flare between 40 and 60 percent of gas associated with oil production: an economic loss of $2.5 billion per annum. Gas flaring causes acid rain, which acidifies lakes and streams and damages crops and vegetation. It reduces farm yields and seriously harms human health. The shortage of power-generating facilities should have provided ample opportunities for Nigerian entrepreneurs to develop alternative sources, but it has not. Most generators, however, even simple ones, that are used in Nigeria are imported, and effective technologies to control gas flaring have yet to be invented or installed. In all these cases, the creative and innovative capabilities of Nigerian entrepreneurs could be tapped and utilized.

Water

Good water for human consumption as well as industrial use is another important resource that both indigenous and foreign investors look for before making investments. In Nigeria, the water supply situation is like that of inadequate electricity. For those who can afford it, digging a water borehole or well powered by a machine that stores water in overhead tanks is the only way to ensure a regular supply. All these inadequacies, however, only increase overhead costs, which discourages companies from investing.

Education Sector

To attract investment, countries need to ensure a stable education system that offers good quality education and training; this saves companies money and time in training and retraining their employees. In addition, foreign investors and company personnel who travel with their families on overseas assignments hope to find good educational institutions for their children as well. A key reason that many American information technology jobs are outsourced to India is that India has an ample supply of highly trained IT professionals who are available to work at lower costs than their counterparts in the United States. In Nigeria, by contrast, the educational system is flawed with many problems and inadequacies that make the country unattractive for foreign investors. For instance, it would take almost twice as long for the average Nigerian student to graduate from a university compared to a student in a country with a stable system. The educational environment is marred by demonstrations, strikes, financial difficulties, and other problems. In September 2009, for example, the Academic Staff Union of Universities (ASUU) was on strike. Lack of facilities and other amenities have also contributed to the low quality of Nigerian graduates. Most students lack access to computer hardware because it is unaffordable or is unavailable for general use in universities. Books are outdated and scientific equipment and even standard classroom furniture are either unavailable, very substandard, or in bad condition. Perhaps worse than the inadequacy of facilities is the growing corruption: in certain cases, students pay fixed amounts to obtain degree certificates, and brilliant but unfortunate students who cannot afford to pay lose out. Recently, the comptroller of the Nigerian customs service, like many other government officials, was suspected of having forged his certificates. A ranking list of the top 500 universities in the world published by the Center for World Class Universities at Shanghai Jiao Tong University in China had only three African universities listed on it, and all three were from southern Africa; none were from Nigeria.[27] Nigeria has therefore not earned a passing mark in the management of this important sector because its educational system is in a state of constant deterioration.

Health Sector

A country's health care system needs to put all its focus on ensuring the well-being of its citizens. A key area is the threat of communicable diseases, like the Asian flu, that in an era of globalization can be exported from one country to another, thereby stalling international travel, especially to countries with poor health facilities.[28]

The health sector in Nigeria has serious problems, which translate into obstacles for FDI. The functioning hospitals in Nigeria are mostly controlled by private clinics and are very expensive. The malfunctioning of Nigeria's hospitals can be blamed directly on the federal ministry of health, which is in charge of coordinating the health care system. Most government officials and other Nigerian elites travel outside of the country to get proper treatment, even for simple medical checkups. The late president Umaru Musa Yar'Adua had himself gone abroad for treatment. Nigeria's Ministry of Health has been described as the most corrupt ministry in the government. At one time, the health minister and other senior ministry officials had to resign because of their involvement in the embezzlement of state funds. The Health Ministry is also notorious for hijacking project master plans that are the original innovative ideas of other people, especially of Nigerians in the diaspora. Examples of such plans include establishing health research centers for the control and prevention of tropical infectious diseases in addition to specialist hospitals for the treatment of different types of illnesses. The Health Ministry invites proposals that have the potential to attract foreign grants and government allocations, but once the funds are collected, the projects are abandoned and never implemented. For instance, the ministry obtained a $1 billion World Bank loan to fight malaria in 2009 but no significant achievement has been reported as of yet. Life expectancy in Nigeria is low compared even to many other developing countries. The *CIA World Factbook* (https://www.cia.gov) reports life expectancy at birth in Nigeria as 46.94; Nigeria is 216th out of 224 countries in the world by this source's rankings. Foreign-based MNCs worry about the economic disadvantages of having to provide health care benefits to potential employees in Nigeria if they make investments there. The high cost of medical care has an indirect negative effect on entrepreneurs, who cannot afford both to cover health care expenses for themselves and their families and to reinvest in their businesses for further growth and expansion.

Industrial Sector

In the Nigerian economy, most manufacturing equipment and materials need to be imported, and the process of doing so requires navigating cumbersome banking formalities. Small firms find it very difficult to survive due to various constraints. One of the main problems for Nigerian businesses is that they import and consume but do not export manufactured goods, except for a few within Africa. Most exports and FDI are by MNCs in the oil industry. There are very few MNCs in other business sectors. It has been observed that after ships offload at Nigerian ports from overseas, they return virtually empty. There are no goods to take back from Nigeria. This situation causes a huge unfavorable hit to Nigeria's balance of payments position. The formation of strategic alliances between small and large companies in Nigeria, such as for subcontracting, is not a common practice. Finally, the government, which should be a chief customer of Nigerian producers (to encourage domestic production), is not.

The Manufacturers Association of Nigeria is the body that represents indigenous manufacturers in the country, but it does not carry much influence to change any negative effects on its membership. MAN has no major role in policymaking. The *Daily Trust* reported that about 820 manufacturing companies in Nigeria either closed down or temporarily suspended production between 2000 and 2008, according to MAN's figures.[29] The president of the association, Alhaji Bashir Borodo, while commenting on the disruptions in the supply of petroleum products to his members, said the problem has shattered the prospects of some of MAN's members to stay in business. According to him, from the period of deregulation to date, industrial consumers have witnessed three price hikes, especially for gasoline and fuel oil.

Internal Security

Internal security in Nigeria has been overwhelmed in recent years especially by concerns of political, ethnic, and religious clashes; kidnappings and armed robberies; as well as militant uprisings in certain areas. Although most of the kidnappings have occurred in the southern part of the country, especially in the Niger Delta's rich oil-producing areas, the religious clashes have happened primarily in the northern part of Nigeria, like the recent "Boko Haram" crisis, which spread across several states in the North. Radical Islamists in Nigeria like those of Boko Haram (literally, "Western education is sinful") could pose a strong threat to the federal government, in turn weakening the government's role as regional economic engine.

The aims of this Islamist sect, which is at the heart of the disturbances, are to wage holy war against the Nigerian state, impose a strict form of sharia law, and extirpate all Western cultural influences.[30] Nigeria is notorious for interreligious and ethnic crises. Such eruptions are by nature unpredictable, due to inadequate surveillance and proactive security measures to at least help to stop any such threats. Among the important, obvious needs of both domestic and foreign businesses is the assurance of security for their properties and assets.

Foreign Partnership Formula

Except for the petroleum industry, which has a formula for revenue sharing that favors the majority of Nigerians, implementation of revenue sharing in other sectors, where currently foreign investors can hold up to 100 percent ownership, would only discourage the growth of Nigerian entrepreneurship. Most foreign companies that strive to stay competitive in global markets prefer majority ownership in the joint ventures of which they are a part, but these arrangements prevent indigenes from developing in key areas like operations and research.

Most host countries require that a 51 percent stake in joint ventures with foreign companies be owned by nationals, but some countries, such as Abu Dhabi and other UAE sheikdoms, which are attracting both tourists and investors today, allow 100 percent foreign ownership.[31] In Japan, foreign companies can repatriate up to 100 percent of their profits without going through a cumbersome process like Nigeria's, but foreign entry to compete in Japan is very restricted.

Project Globe Study

The Project Globe Study was performed by a team of 170 researchers who collected data over seven years on cultural values, practices, and leadership attributes from eighteen thousand managers in sixty-two countries from every corner of the globe.[32] The team identified nine areas that categorize countries in terms of cultural value dimensions. These dimensions could further explain some of the factors that serve as instruments for attracting or discouraging FDI or entrepreneurship development. Three of these dimensions are future orientation, performance orientation, and gender differentiation.

Countries that plan for the future should be visionary and calculating. Singapore and Switzerland are examples of forward-thinking countries. Among the qualities of a future-oriented country is its efficiency in use of its resources. A future-oriented society invests in its citizens and resources to provide continuous improvement for sustainable development such as entrepreneurship. Nigeria, by contrast, does not manifest the qualities of such a society. The country displays a marked tendency to waste and mismanage resources. Donald Payne, a US congressman (D-NJ), reported that 20 percent of Nigeria's oil production in the Niger Delta is lost daily from bunkering, or the illegal siphoning of oil by tampering with and vandalizing oil distribution pipelines. He added that this illicit trade has the tacit backing of the Nigerian government, which is aware of such dealings but does not seem to be very concerned about it.[33]

Entrepreneurial opportunities that might have provided employment for citizens in downstream and upstream sectors of the oil industry are not being utilized effectively to the benefit of the Nigerian people, even on a small-scale basis. In addition to the waste of oil resources (e.g., through excessive flaring), agricultural resources such as meat and dairy products also are being wasted. With supportive government action—such as provision of start-up funds, job training, and technical facilities—these problems could have been turned into entrepreneurial opportunities.

Performance-oriented countries like the United States, Singapore, Hong Kong, and Germany strive for perfection, excellence, and quality in economic production. The International Organization for Standardization (ISO) and Six Sigma provide measures of world-class quality standards. With the exception of National Agency for Food and Drug Administration and Control (NAFDAC), which closely monitors the quality of pharmaceuticals, Nigeria's standards organization has not been as active in emphasizing quality as it should. To be competitive at the global level, MNCs must get quality inputs from suppliers and vendors; if Nigerians cannot offer them, companies will look elsewhere.[34] And for Nigerian products to be accepted in global markets, they must measure up to world quality standards.

Societies that emphasize gender inequality raise red flags for MNCs that value social freedoms when considering where to invest. Many Muslim-majority countries deny women equality as part of religious practice or custom, especially where sharia law is imposed. Given that about half of the Nigerian population is Muslim, living predominantly in the northern part of the country, visitors from non-Muslim countries such as in the Western world may find it an uncomfortable environment in which to do business.

Foreign Multinational Corporations

Citizens of host countries have observed that the majority of foreign companies that establish business activities in West Africa do not seem to have the region's best interests at heart when it comes to development. By their practices, they appear only to be interested in immediate economic gain at the expense of underdeveloped African countries. The following list presents the most common criticisms of such MNC subsidiary activities, whether in lesser developed or more developed countries:

1. MNCs raise their needed capital locally, causing interest rates to rise in host countries.
2. The majority (sometimes even 100 percent) of the stock in most subsidiaries is owned by the parent company. Consequently, host-country populations have little or no control over the operations of corporations within their borders.
3. MNCs usually reserve the key managerial and technical positions for expatriates; as a result, they do not contribute to the development of host-country personnel.
4. MNCs do not adapt their technology to the conditions that exist in host countries.
5. MNCs concentrate their research and development activities at home, restricting the transfer of modern technology and technical know-how to host countries.

6. The actions of MNCs give rise to demand for luxury goods in the host countries at the expense of essential consumer goods, thus encouraging materialism among host-country citizens.

7. MNCs start their foreign operations by purchasing existing firms rather than by developing new productive facilities in host countries.

8. MNCs dominate new industrial sectors, and earn excessively high profits and fees, thus contributing to inflation by stimulating demand for scarce resources.

9. MNCs are not accountable to their host countries but only respond to home-country governments and thus are unconcerned with host-country plans for development.[35]

In addition, some multinational companies, together with corrupt government officials, have contributed to the damaging of Nigeria's reputation and image. For example, Royal Dutch Shell was ordered by a US court to pay millions of dollars in compensation and fines to the Ogoni people for environmental destruction and for bearing partial responsibility for the unlawful execution of eight environmental activists, including Ken Saro-Wiwa.[36] An MNC (name withheld) was ordered to remove hazardous polychlorinated biphenyl (PCB) wastes it had deposited in the Koko area of Nigeria; the toxins had claimed many lives before the cause was discovered.[37] Monsanto Chemical, a American-based corporation, has exported DDT to many foreign destinations, even though its use in the United States has been essentially banned. Apart from the brazen absence of social responsibility toward the people and the environment in the countries that import DDT, this action is also irresponsible toward US citizens because many of their fruits and meat products are in turn imported from those countries.[38] Halliburton and Siemens were also involved in bribery scandals in collaboration with some corrupt Nigerian government officials. More recently, the Sony Corporation referred to Nigeria in its advertisements as a scamming nation, adding to the country's bad publicity. Pfizer Inc. was ordered to pay fines for selling medicine that was linked to more than fifty deaths of children in Nigeria.[39] All these types of negative actions of MNCs in Nigeria and Africa are made possible by taking advantage of the lax laws and standards. These incidents demonstrate the controversial nature of FDI, as to whether it promotes development or not. They also serve to underscore why developing countries should avoid becoming overly dependent and instead find their own prosperity through entrepreneurship and resourcefulness.[40]

Responsible policymakers should regularly update and make available to prospective investors information that will encourage their participation. At the same time, the government should embark on productive entrepreneurial activities and internal economic development leading to higher GDP and national income aimed at maintaining sustainable growth and development especially for exports by utilizing local resources. These programs should be designed to involve a network of educational institutions, research centers, financial institutions, entrepreneurs, foreign affiliations, and the government. These institutions together should ensure that the country meets international standards in all areas of production as measured by the recognized institutions like the ISO and immediately address any anomalies that need corrective action. If Nigeria wants to take FDI as a serious route toward its development goals, it needs to embark on an aggressive marketing mission to convince and attract investors and take strict measures to eliminate practices like corruption and insecurity to improve the investment climate in Nigeria. Question-and-answer sessions should be held for potential investors during trade missions. Government officials from relevant ministries like commerce and industry, foreign and internal affairs, should be ready to answer those who want to know about Nigeria's present conditions. Where things have improved, along the lines of the recommendations herein as well as others, supporting evidence and documentation should be provided to prospective investors.

For entrepreneurship to flourish in Nigeria, the country needs a strong currency to facilitate acquisition of the technologies available in other economies. Nigeria's lack of exports other than oil and its present exchange-rate woes make goods and raw materials too expensive, and raise prices of Nigerian goods.

National and international observers have identified the most serious obstacle hampering Nigeria and Africa's development: lack of good governance. President Obama and Secretary of State Hillary Clinton in their respective speeches to Africans repeatedly emphasized this issue.[41] A first step, which would also be very helpful for business, would be to establish a practice of auditing all public resources, backed by efforts to reward competent and honest officials while removing corrupt, unscrupulous ones. This has already been attempted in the Nigerian banking industry. The central bank governor, Lamido Sanusi, while endeavoring to sanitize dubious financial dealings, dismissed corrupt CEOs of some of the nation's leading banks. The move has begun to pay dividends through the recovery of billions of dollars' worth of shareholders' and depositors' money. Within the short period of this exercise, investors' confidence was boosted and the Nigerian banking sector suddenly earned international credit for its commitment to achieving progressive change. Needless to say, all other sectors should follow this approach.

Common Nigerians perceive that the reason for their country's low-quality educational standards is that public officers in charge care less about improving the system than about lining their own pockets. Not only have they embezzled funds meant for that purpose, but they can afford to send students in their own families to foreign countries to study. As an exemplary action, Nigerian public officials should instead, out of a show of loyalty to their country, refrain from sending their family members to study abroad. If public officials were stakeholders in this way, they would be more inclined to emphasize improvements to the educational system, thus enabling more people to get a good education at home. In the meantime, Nigeria's failed education system has led to the emigration of most practicing professionals (so-called brain drain); many of these individuals have become permanently ensconced in foreign countries, particularly in North America and western Europe. Nigerians should take a lesson from Barack Obama, the US president, who said, "The countries that out-teach us today will out-compete us tomorrow."[42] Education as an essential investment for any country's human capital cannot be overemphasized. However, the educational curriculum in the Nigerian school system does not emphasize global business or entrepreneurship as a nationwide program for training. By comparison, the entrepreneurial economies of Europe and North America were founded on deliberate and concerted efforts to develop entrepreneurship, supported broadly through state-provided education.[43]

African leaders should learn to develop their economies with minimal reliance on foreign aid and model after a fellow developing country like Cuba. Notwithstanding the Western economic blockages against Cuba, very few lesser-developed countries in SSA have approached or even come close to Cuba's achievements in health and education. At one point, there were more than twenty thousand Cuban medical doctors working in over twenty-five countries of the third world.[44]

Odidison Omankhanlen reported that Nigerian citizens living abroad sent home ₦1.5 trillion, or the equivalent of US$10 billion, as remittances in 2008, but they are not even allowed to vote in their home country's elections.[45] Diasporic Nigerians should be taken seriously and allowed to be included in policymaking decisions. Overseas citizens have been known to play a crucial role in the development of many countries, especially in terms of remittances. According to Dilip Ratha, coauthor of a World Bank report on the subject, "Remittances provide a lifeline to many poor countries." Many Nigerians in the diaspora are doing well in the countries where they live. Some such Nigerians, however, have been frustrated because of attempts by government officials to hijack the projects and ideas they have brought back to Nigeria, in which they have invested time and money developing blueprints and master plans. In some cases, funds earmarked for these programs have been embezzled or misappropriated by the public officials or ministries in charge of their implementation. The Nigerian Ministry of Health, especially from the 1990s up to the year 2009, has been rife with this type of fraudulent practice.

Entrepreneurial talents and ideas of Nigerians both abroad and at home should be recognized and rewarded. In the United Kingdom, the Prince of

Wales provides official recognition to those with especially innovative ideas on an annual basis, and in the United States, the Malcolm Baldridge National Quality Award recognizes the same. There are no such awards in Nigeria to recognize and encourage promising talents to surface. Some notice was given to the student in Kano who invented a model helicopter using scrap metal, and the Nigerian from the southeast who produced a car using local resources. However, the celebration of these successes was short-lived. Israel Agwamba, a Nigerian in the diaspora based in the US state of Maryland, created AfroTrading.net for entrepreneurs all around the world to do business, exchange ideas, or form alliances online. That achievement was never announced or celebrated by Nigeria's Ministry of Commerce and Industry, Ministry of Foreign Affairs, or the Economic and Research Institutes. Diasporic Indians and Chinese (the so-called bamboo network) are credited for their immense contributions to the development of their home economies.[46]

Nobel Prize laureate Muhammad Yunus, in his book *Banker to the Poor*, elaborated on how he started the Grameen Bank in Bangladesh as a microfinancing institution to combat world poverty.[47] Both rich and poor countries alike met with resounding successes when they adopted the Grameen model. Malaysia, for example, reduced the number of its citizens who live below the poverty line by more than half as a result of using this method for alleviating poverty. Nigerians could learn from these successes as they work to develop an entrepreneurial base and alleviate poverty by starting on a small scale.

Conclusion

Entrepreneurship and foreign direct investment are among the essential tools to achieve sustainable development in countries, especially in the era of globalization. Countries should not continue to depend on loans, grants, and aid to sustain general economic growth and development. Nor should they depend on foreign investors alone to supply the investment funds that shape the economic development landscape. FDI and entrepreneurship could be cultivated and practiced either as separate phases or simultaneously. However, in order for either approach to be successful, it requires the existence of an environment that is supportive and enabling. An investment-friendly climate represents the credentials, or calling card, of a country that can attract and persuade investors from other countries to want to invest outside their own country. Nations like Nigeria that are serious about achieving developed country status by 2020 must rebuild their foundation by eliminating obstacles that discourage foreign investors or that frustrate entrepreneurs. Some of these mitigating factors, or barriers to FDI and entrepreneurship, have been identified in this chapter. Additional in-depth, country-by-country comparisons need to be done to arrive at the best examples to emulate and the worst examples to avoid. Nigeria in particular needs to be more proactive in its development planning by looking ahead into the future with a more articulate vision. Above all, Nigeria needs to invest significantly in its entrepreneurial talent by training its people to learn how to harness and mobilize the country's ample resources for development.

Notes

1. Charles Hill, *International Business: Competing in the Global Marketplace*, 7th ed. (Boston: McGraw-Hill Irwin, 2009).

2. Walter Rodney, *How Europe Underdeveloped Africa* (Washington, DC: Howard University Press, 1981).

3. Ibid.

4. Joseph Schumpeter, *Theory of Economic Development* (Cambridge: Cambridge University Press, 1934).

5. Tony Sagami, "A New Fundamental Change in China That Could Make You Rich," http://www.uncommonwisdomdaily.com/a-new-fundamental-change-in-china-that-could-make-you-rich-3-6342 (2009).

6. 2009 Failed States Index, *Foreign Policy* (Washington, DC: Slate Publishing Group, 2009). The Fund for Peace, a US-based think-tank and independent research organization, and the magazine *Foreign Policy* began publishing the Failed States Index in 2005.

7. Abimbola Akosile, "Nigeria Sinks Deeper, Ghana Rated Best in Africa," *Osun Defender Newspapers*, July 16, 2009, http://www.osundefender.org.

8. Helen Deresky, *International Management: Managing across Borders* (Upper Saddle River, NJ: Prentice Hall, 2008).

9. William Shreeve, "Be Prepared for Political Changes Abroad," *Harvard Business Review* (July–August 1984): 111–18.

10. Casmir Igbokwe, "Nigeria Must Not Go," *Nigerian Punch*, December 23, 2005.

11. Ibid.

12. Ibid.

13. Ibid.

14. Ibid.

15. Transparency International, *Corruption Perceptions Index 2005*, http://www.transparency.org (accessed August 6, 2006).

16. Charles J. Mambula, "Perceptions of SME Growth Constraints in Nigeria," *Journal of Small Business Management* 40 (2002): 58–65.

17. Igbokwe, "Nigeria Must Not Go."

18. Ibid.

19. World Bank, Annual Reports (2008–9).

20. World Bank, *Worldwide Governance Indicators* (Washington, DC, 1996–2008).

21. Ibid.

22. Phillip Harris and Robert Moran, *Managing Cultural Differences* (Houston: Gulf Publishing, 1987).

23. Editorial, *Daily Trust Newspapers*, July 24, 2009.

24. Kolawale Dipo, *Nigerian Tribune*, August 7, 2009.

25. Ibid.

26. Ibid.

27. "Academic Ranking of World Universities—2008," http://www.arwu.org/ARWU2008.jsp.

28. Phillip Cateora, Mary Gilly, and John Graham, *International Marketing*, 14th ed. (Boston: Richard D. Irwin, 2009).

29. Editorial, *Daily Trust Newspapers*, July 24, 2009.

30. David Smith, "Nigerian 'Taliban' Offensive Leaves 150 Dead," http://www.guardian.co.uk/world/2009/jul/27/boko-haram-nigeria-attacks, July 27, 2009.

31. "UAE Approves Final Draft of Foreign Ownership Bill," http://www.arabianbusiness.com (Dubai: ITP Publishing Group).

32. Mansour Javidan and Robert J. House, "Cultural Acumen for the Global Manager: Lessons from Project Globe," *Organizational Dynamics* (Spring 2001): 289–305.

33. Rafiu Ajakaye and Adela Yusuf, "20% of Nigeria's Oil Lost Daily," News Agency Reports (associated with Nigerian Punch Publishing), 2009.

34. Bennet Lientz and Kathryn Rea, *International Project Management* (Singapore: Academic Press, an Imprint of Elsevier Science, 2003).

35. Editorial, *Wall Street Journal*, December 29, 2000, 3, cited in Deresky, *International Management*.

36. "Shell Reports Record Oil Spillages in Nigeria," http://www.guardian.co.uk/environment/2010/may/05/shell-oil-spill-niger-delta, May 5, 2010 (Associated Press).

37. S. Tifft, "Who Gets the Garbage?" *Time*, July 4, 1988, 42–43.

38. Reza Vaghefi, S. K. Paulson, and W. H. Tomlinson, *International Business Theory and Practice* (New York: Taylor and Francis, 1991), 249–50.

39. BBC News, "Pfizer in Nigeria Case," August 30, 2001, http://www.bbc.co.uk/news/world-africa-11971805.

40. Theodore Moran, Edward Graham, and Magnus Blomstrom, eds., *Does Foreign Direct Investment Promote Development?* (Washington, DC: Institute for International Economics, Center for Global Development, 2005).

41. Sandra Waddock, *Leading Corporate Citizens: Vision, Values, Value Added*, 3rd ed. (Singapore: McGraw-Hill Irwin, 2009).

42. President Barack Obama, Address to Joint Session of Congress, February 24, 2009, http://www.whitehouse.gov/the_press_office/Remarks-of-President-Barack-Obama-Address-to-Joint-Session-of-Congress/.

43. David Audretsch et al., *Entrepreneurship: Determinants and Policy in a European–U.S. Comparison* (Dordrecht: Kluwer Academic Publishers, 2002).

44. Sara Carrillo de Albornoz, "On a Mission: How Cuba Uses Its Doctors Abroad," *British Medical Journal* 333 (2006): 464.

45. Odidison Omankhalen, "Nigerians Abroad Remit 10 Billion US Dollars Home in 2009," *Nigerian Tribune*, July 17, 2009.

46. Tarun Khanna, *Billions of Entrepreneurs: How China and India Are Reshaping Their Future and Yours* (Boston: Harvard Business School Press, 2007); Deresky, *International Management*.

47. Mohammed Yunus, *Banker to the Poor: Micro-Lending and the Battle against World Poverty* (New York: Public Affairs, 1999).

Part Four

Insecurity and Conflicts

15

The Impact of Globalization on International Security

JOHN BABATUNDE BAMIDELE OJO

"The fracturing of the Western alliance over Iraq and the huge
anti-war demonstrations around the world . . . are remind-
ers that there may still be two superpowers on the planet: the
United States and world public opinion." Apparently factual, this
statement should be seen rather as interpretive reconstruction.
It framed these empirical events in a globally civil way. They are
presented as transpiring on the public stage of the world, America is portrayed, not as an elect but as a particularistic nation,
confronting not the evil of an Iraqi dictator but the world as a
civil, rationally-organized society: "President Bush appears to
be eyeball to eyeball with a tenacious new adversary: millions of
people who flooded the streets of New York and dozens of world
cities to say they are against war based on the evidence at hand."

—Jeffrey C. Alexander

There's a certain pride you take in the wealth of experience.
That's kind of nice. That you belong all over the world rather
than a little part. You're proud of the world, not just proud of
your neighborhood. Proud to be part of it. It's not like you're
saying, "Go Bronx." It's "Go World."

—Esther Dyson

Introduction

Globalization involves a myriad of transnational processes which although
are global in their scope but are distinct from one another. Through these
processes, globalization generates systemic forces that affect all states. While

it is beyond the scope of this study to address each process and issue in detail, we shall delve into some of those that are most pertinent to the complexity of international security in the contemporary world. This chapter examines military, economic, health, information technology, and cultural components of human security, as they interact with terrorism, all through the prism of globalization. While many students of international security consider globalization itself as one of the elements of security, it occupies a unique position among these other security components not only because of its ability to overshadow them but because of its impact on their dynamics and its capacity even to enslave (each one of) them as mere expressions of its own processes.

In today's world, making a distinction between national and international security is like drawing a line in the water. Both conflict and peace have become borderless just as stability and instability have. By the hour, globalization is weakening the hegemonic order of the Westphalian state system. This is an indication of a robust and unprecedented civilization. We are moving away from an international into a global era. The word *international* recognizes only the nation-state as the basic building block of world affairs. The word *cooperation* usually means international cooperation among governments. This framework has become inadequate. The connotations and parameters of the term *cooperative* have to become *global* for it to carry meaningful weight. Global security entails a common and comprehensive security worldwide. In the new global equation, there are significant players other than nation-states that are involved in contemporary world affairs.

Today, we can move literally across borders in minutes or hours, and can connect to each other through cyberspace instantaneously. Interconnectedness has profound benefits and costs. Innovative and constructive ideas can be transmitted quickly through our social networks, but such connections can also rapidly spread disease and the seeds of conflict and devastation. Globalization is not only ubiquitous in our daily lives but is germane in confronting security-related global problems that cannot be overcome by traditional methods or in isolation. For example, in the first epigraph above, Jeffrey C. Alexander captures the reaction of those around the world who opposed the 2003 invasion of Iraq as a rogue American action against a sovereign state that they believed posed no regional or global threat. Globalization also is a cooperative challenge directly facing humanity in the sense of a global village, as imagined by Esther Dyson in the second epigraph. I share the vision of Dyson regarding our current world. This work holds that the interactive and cumulative effects of globalization not only affect the security of individual nation-sates but have created a relatively novel global security environment in which, to a certain extent, such states are defenseless (e.g., to environmental insecurity, negative effects of the illicit economy, threats of terrorism and irregular military forces, and so on).

The goal of this chapter is to examine the impact of globalization on international security. I first present a workable definition of globalization that transcends disciplinary divides and examine the competing theoretical postulations. I then discuss the impact of globalization on international security by examining the elements that constitute security in the contemporary period. To understand globalization's impact, it is imperative to grasp fully the comprehensive connotation of the term *security* in its current usage. The components of security manifest the characteristics of globalization in their different forms. This examination is aimed toward illuminating both negative and positive effects of globalization on international security and their implications for Africa. Finally, I provide empirical analysis of tangible regional effects of globalization on Africa.

Our point of departure is the contention that globalization has ushered us into a post-Westphalian order. The emerging global configuration is diminishing the power and influence of the conventional sovereign state. Annie-Marie Slaughter argues that while the state is not necessarily disappearing, it is disintegrating into its "separate, functionally, distinct parts. These parts—courts, regulatory agencies, executives, and even legislatures—are networking with their counterparts abroad, creating a dense web of relations that constitutes a new, trans-governmental order."[1] In this emerging order, the process of globalization has reshaped the costs, benefits, and consequences of pursuing various policy choices.

States can limit their exposure to globalization to a certain extent. "Globalization does not impose openness; rather it raises the opportunity costs of closure."[2] If the forces of globalization produce more opportunities and benefits than limitations and risks, as I will argue, then the advantages of cooperation are immense vis-à-vis a state's assumption of autarky (e.g., North Korea). Essentially, the core value of globalization should be cooperation at the global level.

The German-American political theorist Hannah Arendt delineates that, symbolically, three events can be identified as the main indicators of the emergence of the globalization phenomenon: the death of Ayatollah Ruhollah Khomeini, the collapse of the former Soviet Union, and the emergence of the Internet. The death of Khomeini marked the end of exclusive religiosity and theocracy. The fall of the former Soviet Union marked the failure and rejection of extreme secularism and the materialist world perspective. Arendt argues that the creation of the Internet fulfilled the promise of a new way of thinking "and a new sphere for both the *vita activa* and the *vita contemplativa* [the active life and the contemplative one]."[3]

The concept of globalization has attracted remarkable attention and has been popularized in part because of the ambiguity surrounding it and its ability to assume different connotation depending on the contextual usage. Generally, it serves as shared vocabulary to express the increasing sense of connectedness among the world's human inhabitants.[4] There is no single driver of globalization, but rather a combination of factors are working together to produce the new sense of global interconnectedness. Globalization impacts every aspect of human life: culture, religion, the economy, the environment, communications, health, immigration, and ultimately, security in all its ramifications.[5] Different schools of thought have offered different definitions of globalization.

Definition

George Ritzer of the University of Maryland offers a (postcapitalist) definition of globalization as "the worldwide diffusion of practices, expansion of relations across continents, organization of social life on a global scale, and growth of a shared global consciousness."[6] From an international political economic perspective, Henry Veltmeyer defines globalization as "the process of integrating societies in the world, and their economies and cultures, into one system."[7] For our purposes, Richard Tiplady's definition will suffice: globalization refers to the increased interconnectedness whereby developments and events that take place in one part of the world affect and influence other parts of the world and to "an increasing sense of a single global whole."[8] By focusing on the essence of globalization at large, Tiplady's definition accommodates different perspectives and the field of international security.

The mission of understanding globalization is not a simple one. Tony McGrew attests to this when he states that globalization "is in many respects an idea in search of a theory." He observes that "despite the fact that, in a little over a decade, it has colonized the intellectual imagination of the social sciences, it remains for the most part largely under- [if not un-] theorized."[9] To this, Veltmeyer suggests that it is probably "un-theorized" rather than "under-theorized." J. Hobson and M. Ramesh argue that much, though not all, of the "literature on globalization is cast in terms of two main theoretical propositions: either (i) a strong globalization/decline of the state or (ii) weak globalization/strong state thesis."[10] Theorizations of globalization are as variegated as its definitions.

Theory

The realist theoretical framework woefully failed to predict globalization because its hypotheses center on "power"; that is, power in the context of empire and imperialism (or neoimperialism), relative gains, self-help, anarchy, and so on. Realist tradition conceives the world as riddled with conflicts; nothing can be in everyone's interest. If one group does well, it must be at another's expense. In the realist world, political decision makers see a zero-sum game rather than the opportunities of collaboration, collectiveness, or integration. The fundamentals of realism as theorized by staunch advocates like Kenneth N. Waltz, John Mearsheimer, and Joseph Grieco are insufficient and too narrow to explain either the contemporary character of the international system or states' behavior as rational actors.[11] Citing Grieco's work, Lee Ryan Miller delineates and criticizes the realist-neorealist fundamental assumptions as follows:

1. In anarchy, states are preoccupied with power and security and are inclined toward conflict and competition, often failing to cooperate even when faced with common interests.
2. States are the major actors in international arena.
3. The international system is characterized by anarchy, and anarchy is the principal force that shapes states' actions.
4. International institutions have marginal effect on cooperation.
5. As "unitary rational agents" states act to protect their individual "vital interest."[12]

Confessing to being a recovering realist himself, Miller rejects the above tenets and argues that realist assumptions are at best misleading. In fact, the realists' doctrine was fatally wounded by the end of the Cold War, an event that they "neither predicted nor expected." In his book *Confessions of a Recovering Realist: Toward a Neo-Liberal Theory of International Relations*, he offers mounting evidence to prove that each of these assumptions lacks universal validity and therefore must be discarded.[13]

Elsewhere, I have similarly argued that realism, whether classical, motivational, neorealist (i.e., structural realism), is too narrow a concept to explain the affairs of international security. The precept of neorealism, an environment-based theory, that "whatever the state behavior that cannot be explained by anarchical structure of the system, is trivial" is anachronistic to the contemporary world and therefore misleading. Neorealist structural constraints are at best static and monolithic. The theoretical preeminence on security that realism enjoyed prior to the end of the Cold War, I contend, was a periodic coincidence without lasting value or utility.[14] Although neoliberalism subscribes to the neorealist view that anarchy is the cause of insecurity and of states' self-help behavior, it goes beyond this causational view. Neoliberals rightly argue that states are inclined to cooperate especially through the aid of international institutions.[15] Michael Doyle asserts that unlike nondemocracies, democracies do not go to war against one another.[16] The emergence of the constructivist epistemology strengthens the realist opposition camp although it slightly differs from that of the neoliberals' arguments.

The constructivist school of thought, a critical theory, postulates that social practices will dictate material outcomes and not the other way around as realism would have us believe.[17] Norms, as either outcome or inducer of social interactions, are collective understandings that shape actors' behavior and define their identity and interest. Seen this way, there are good and bad norms.[18] Constructivist globalization is in line with the constructivist theoretical postulation of the possibility that norms are generated or at least reinforced by sustained and repeated social interactions. In contrast, the theoretical tradition of natural law (which supports globalization) sees human communities as bound together by common values that might coincide with a divine plan. Remarkably, globalization is standing on and flourishing within the integrative liberal tradition.[19] The neoliberal hypothesis on states' ability to cooperate becomes the launching pad of liberal institutionalism and economic liberalism. This cooperation is reaching a global level of maturation.

The most accommodating and germane theories regarding globalization are neoliberal institutionalism, economic liberalism, and constructivism, all of which pose challenges to traditional international relations theory. As articulated by Edward Koloziej, there is no particular theoretical framework that can solely explain the globalization phenomenon. However, he advocates that no security theories should be rejected. Globalization theory should be multidisciplinary in perspective and as such derivable from multiple academic fields.[20] Globalization covers a range of phenomena that epitomize a paradigm shift. Proglobalization theoretical perspectives generally shift away from the traditional divides of North-South, East-West, and so on. A theoretical framework capable of conceptualizing globalization would have to account for its many processes that have greatly reduced time and distance thus rendering the world increasingly "smaller." The ideal framework cannot confine the world to the territorial spaces of traditional realist boundaries. Layers of theoretical postulations and hypotheses are needed that are capable of exploring the technological aspects of global dynamics, such as information flow and mobility, among others, that contribute to the collapsing of time and space.[21]

James N. Rosenau's group of self-described (globalization) Cutting-Edgers anticipates an encompassing cosmopolitan framework. They argue that not all nongovernmental organizations (NGOs) have the necessary cosmopolitan attributes, especially those whose leaders advocate for globalization but whose orientations are not necessarily cosmopolitan. Rosenau and his colleagues have adopted a framework that hardly distinguishes between the local-global divide because they see such distinctions as no longer useful.[22] These Cutting-Edgers are more sensitive to globalization than others who attend more to what falls within the scope of localization.[23]

According to Farhang Rajaee, utilizing a comprehensive approach avoids the reductionist tendency to rely on a single cause to explain social phenomena while equally avoiding the one-dimensional purpose of theorizing that endeavors for socialization and conformity. A framework that identifies opportunities for bridging and interacting rather than for separating and distinguishing would be sublime for globalization. It is easy to create an exclusive framework for the future, but quite challenging to create a participatory context in which everyone will feel welcome and accepted. Rajaee asserts "that globalization has given us such an opportunity, provided we make proper use of it."[24] The opportunity presented by such a framework would bring together perspectives that complement rather than contradict each other as seen in parochial theories. Let us examine some of these other parochial theoreticians, some of whom hypothesize that the end of the Cold War ended an era. Francis Fukuyama in "The End of History" argues that capitalism and liberal-pluralist politics triumphed over the dialectic of history thereby putting an end to history itself. The universalization of Western civilization as encapsulated by Western liberal democracy, he contends, would become the final form of human government.[25] In *The End of History and the Last Man*, Fukuyama points to Western liberal democracy as "the ultimate faith of humanity as a whole."[26]

Rajaee rebuts this optimistic model as short-lived, claiming it has been replaced by a pessimistic paradigm, as evidenced by the phrase "the end of civility," a paradigm developed by Robert D. Kaplan, Samuel Huntington, and Farid Zakaria. On the surface, globalization appears to have enveloped everybody and enfranchised those who were formerly voiceless. According to Zakaria in his essay "The Rise of Illiberal Democracy," this occurrence has given rise to democratic polities that do not necessarily guarantee democratic values such as human rights and individual freedom.[27] Nonetheless, they are democratic insofar as a democratic process was employed in bringing them about. Rajaee expresses that globalization brought about mob politics, and thus populist democracies that do not necessarily guarantee the rule of law have replaced pluralistic ones.[28]

Kaplan's article "The Coming of Anarchy" claims that the existing order has collapsed and been replaced by environmental crises and huge population movements. In short, globalization has divided the humanity into two classes, the privileged and the downtrodden. The breakdown of the Westphalian state system loosed the possibilities of warfare in which warmaking is not restricted to a specific territory or nation. Today, nonstate entities are capable of conducting formidable battles because both the technologies and weaponry that enable such are more available than in the past. Parochial nonstate entities can freely engage in warfare, and technological advances are "used toward primitive ends."[29]

Another pessimistic view is that articulated by Samuel Huntington. Like Kaplan, he contends that the state system has lost most of its authority. Culture and civilization have become the attractive foci for loyalty. The world has divided in two, pitting the West as the hitherto dominant civilization against all others. The post–Cold War globalization signifies the clash of civilizations.[30]

Rajaee makes crucial observations about all these approaches. First, these paradigms tend to be one dimensional and exclusionary. Rajaee argues that "one should take multiplicity as integral to the human condition, using a sophisticated, integrative, and interactive approach." His second criticism of these approaches relates to their "internal logic." Despite their differences, they claim in common that globalization has eroded politics, thereby insinuating what may be called "the end-of-politics." Such a view is both extreme and dangerous. The end of-politics paradigm presumptuously aggrandizes one aspect of human essence, whether it is the political, cultural, or religious dimension, thus "considering one of these dimensions, predominant." Each approach overemphasizes "the will to power" aspect that displays a Hobbesian pessimism toward human nature—that is, man's perennial desire to compete and to hate.[31] Although it may be human to hate, it is also human to love and to care. To overemphasize the aggression aspect and neglect the caring and loving part twists the true picture of humanity as portrayed by contemporary globalization. The Cutting-Edgers see themselves as being above this type of theoretical parochialism with its constraints.

Globalizing Security: The Dynamics

Until recent decades, security has been defined mainly in terms of military security. However, security today covers a gamut of nontraditional issues ranging from military, political, social, technological, environmental, biological, and economic aspects, among others. Despite their diverse nature, these issues share some things in common; that is, they are global concerns that cannot be unilaterally or even regionally addressed. Dealing with these challenges sometimes elicits discord but ultimately requires extensive global cooperation. Managing these security issues has being facilitated by the globalization phenomenon that P. J. Simmons and Chantal Oudraat call "a magnified version of interdependence." While the interdependence of peoples and nations is not new, globalization is marked by unprecedented political, economic, and technological integration, which enables nation-states, corporations, and individuals to reach around the world, farther and faster, deeper and cheaper than at any time in the past.[32] While the phrase might provoke semantic arguments, many authors on the subject of globalization concur that management of global issues is inevitably a product of "many hands trying to move levers—not always in sync and not always with the desired results." Given the turmoil of the arenas in which various issues surface, their complexity and overlapping nature defy tidy theorizing.[33]

Individuals at the cutting edge of globalization do not conceive it narrowly in economics terms alone. Typically, a Cutting-Edger has undergone a transformation in his or her orientation toward the larger world that involves a broader conception of how to address human concerns beyond national boundaries. This is done by using a broad and global as opposed to a narrow and national perspective as the yardstick of analysis. The numerous processes that constitute this expansive view include cultural conflicts, communications, economics, and scientific, political, and social activities that result in flows of people, ideas, norms, goods, money, and so on across the borders.[34] Leaders who focus on systematic inquiries and operate at the cutting edge of globalization by giving directions, structure, and meaning to theoretical dynamics and framework's boundary-setting differ from the other scholars and antiglobalization network, that is, the "other leaders."[35] Unlike the Cutting-Edgers, the other scholars and antiglobalization theorists promote frameworks that are less than global. According to Rosenau and colleagues, scholars who focus on global systemic inquiries like themselves are phenomenally the Cutting-Edgers of this subfield of globalization.[36] They are the seers that look beyond the boundaries of their countries in putting the contemporary world into perspective.

The precision of the individuals constituting the cutting edge cannot be estimated. Rosenau and associates argue:

> This understanding rests on the basic premise that globalization's powerful boundary-spanning processes are sustained by concrete and identifiable people—by public officials who frame issues, make choices, negotiate outcomes, and implement policies; by corporate executives who generate resources, sell products, and focus on market shares; by technological specialists who facilitate communications and analysis of policy alternatives; by pundits who speak out on public issues; by entertainers, artists, and academics whose works are disseminated abroad and may express political support or dissent; by consumers who purchase goods and by workers who produce them; by tourists and immigrants who travel extensively; by citizens who join protest marches; and by a host of other individuals who contribute to a vast diversity of transnational and international processes.[37]

Taken together, the insights, attitudes, and activities of these myriad individuals generate the orientation of processes that constitute globalization. These individuals give direction to and sustain the dynamics of globalization. Their preoccupation with globalizing dynamics appears to have lessened states' authority and increased globalizing activities.

The acceleration of globalization was brought about by the collapse of communism in Eastern Europe and the Soviet Union beginning in the late 1980s that ended the Cold War. Moreover, the new opportunities facilitated by technological developments, especially in communications, enhance the process.[38] To examine the impact of globalization on international security, one must examine its impacts on the variegated subsets that constitute security in the contemporary world. In this way, we can thoroughly dissect and discern how globalization influences global security and how security itself has become globalized. We shall first consider the impact of globalization on the military sphere of security, followed by the other aspects.

Military

Globalization has marked a decline in the popularity of military adventurism. It is refocusing states' attention to redirecting national treasure into investment in needed domestic infrastructure. This shift may open a wider path to nations' cooperation in the area of curtailing military weapons, particularly nuclear weapons.[39] The mere fact that globalization has created a context viable to constructive dialogue among states and peoples that face common threats and have common interests is confounding the readily accepted Western and realist conflict model of operation. The cooperative model of conflict resolution that people of vision have hoped for, whereby the peoples of a global village interact, borrow, and profit from one another as they have done throughout history, is now challenging the realist suggestion that they must clash in a zero-sum game of unending war.[40]

In the past, issues of security and political instability enjoyed higher priority, while economic and social issues took a back seat. In the contemporary world, these priorities have been reversed. There are those (nation-states and students of international security) who endorse the use of a multidisciplinary approach that is more inclusive of what the priorities should be. Nonetheless, with the advent of globalization, no one appears to be buying the idea of the zero-sum approach of the past any longer. A case in point, the abysmal theory of the "clash of civilizations" conceived by Samuel Huntington is fading out of today's reality.[41] The lack of uniformity in civilization has not resulted in any significant clash capable of slowing down globalization. In a globalized world, a "battle of ideas" is more conducive to stability than the "battle of worldviews" as pessimistically postulated by Huntington. The former leads to flourishing and the latter leads to Huntington's conventional zero-sum concept wherein only one civilization can prevail.[42]

In terms of global institutions, the United Nations still reflects the weakening Westphalia state system. The UN Security Council is often handicapped by the veto power of its permanent members as well as weak enforcement of its resolutions on its member and nonmember states alike. Similarly, the International Court of Justice (ICJ), which is the world's sole legal body designed specifically to discourage war and use international law to resolve disputes, lacks enforcement power. Thus states, including the United States, exercise their sovereign right to refuse, and have refused, to accept the jurisdiction of the ICJ.[43]

The European Union typifies how intergovernmental organizations are eroding the Westphalian system. The level of international security and stability obtainable among its members is more predictable than that obtainable among the UN's membership.[44] In other words, the EU's security arrangements are cohesive and guarantee stability among the EU's members, unlike the UN's. The reason is that globalization works in favor of all the EU membership, leaving no room for dangerous Hobbesian competition and warfare, whereas such competition and warfare are still common features among UN member states. Louis P. Pojman contends that despite all its accompanying promises and problems, globalism is moving the world toward a cosmopolitanism that demands greater international cooperation "based on enforceable international law."[45] Such cooperation can diminish if not eradicate threat perception and the urge to prepare for war.

Intrastate conflicts became dominant in the immediate post–Cold War era. At the dawn of the twenty-first century, there were twenty-seven major armed conflicts around the globe. With the exceptions of two international wars, the remaining twenty five were intrastate conflicts; all were in Asia or Africa (with five being in the Middle East). Contemporary civil wars pose serious global consequences including refugee migrations, regional instability, and trade impediments. Based on the decisions and choices of powerful countries, intervention was strong in some instances (e.g., Bosnia in 1991–95; Kosovo in 1999), while in other cases, there was reluctance to intervene (e.g., the 1994 Rwanda genocide; the ongoing Darfur genocide). The scale of global consequences of civil wars is such that no single state can possibly muster the "external legitimacy, resources, and staying power to intervene for peace. Single-state intervention has not been very successful."[46] For example, India's peacekeeping forces became embroiled in the Sri Lanka conflict during India's unilateral intervention (1987–90). The mainly US invasion of Iraq has been nothing but more trouble, such that both the Iraqi and the US image are worse for it. Only multilateral intervention through institutions such as a functional and effective UN can provide the required external legitimacy or legal authority and spread the risk and costs of intervention. Globalization provides the atmosphere to establish international norms, institutions, and capacities required for effective management of internal conflicts in the long term. By attempting to foster liberal democratic values, globalization could create the conditions that undermine the emergence of intrastate conflicts.[47]

From the perspective of conventional weapons, globalization is assistive in the formation of a more positive international security environment. It is more conducive to transparency in interstate arrangements, which mitigates both interstate and intrastate conflicts and promotes confidence- and security-building measures. For example, organizations like the Conference on Security and Cooperation in Europe and Conventional Armed Forces in Europe specialize in such endeavors. This new cooperative global security environment is more helpful for managing weapons proliferation as well as for preventing or terminating conflict.

The Cold War era's perceptions and misperceptions of relative gains and inequality were used to justify cheating on agreements, which also exacerbated issues of trust. In a nutshell, globalization is conducive to disarmament, which helps in preventing wars and in mitigating the use of weapons that cause "unacceptable human suffering."[48] Where disarmament is currently impossible, globalization enables a better performance in arms control vis-à-vis the unsuccessful endeavors of the twentieth century that were for the most part marked by failure and distrust. Where and when disarmament is not feasible, arms control is critical because of its benefits: reducing the risk of war; limiting the destructiveness of war when it does occur; and helping to channel resources away from destructive weapons to productive and peaceful ends.[49]

Considering the intensity of the Cold war rivalry that polarized the major powers over the issues of weapons of mass destruction (WMD) until the late 1980s, globalization has tempered the global security concerns that surrounded this specific security threat to humanity. Great effort was made over decades to control or eliminate the risks posed by nuclear, biological, and chemical (NBC) weapons. In the process, three regimes were established to manage such risks: the 1968 Nuclear Nonproliferation Treaty (NPT); the 1972 Biological Weapons Convention (BWC); and the 1992 Chemical Weapons Convention (CWC). Combining the benefits of open markets with safeguards against the abuse of technologies, globalization can influence international collaboration of both governmental and nongovernmental organizations in addressing the variety of risks—humanitarian, security, and environmental—posed by NBC weapons.[50] Some of the emerging effects of globalization have drawn worldwide attention to the danger of NBC materials falling into the hands of terrorists and making the issue more critical. Thus the context of globalization can help resolve the challenges of confronting WMD in the policy area by first attracting the holdout nation-states of NPT, BWC, and CWC to participate in these nonproliferation regimes. Second, through its collaborative attribute, a globalized world order can enhance policy implementation and compliance. Third, it can help ensure that the private actors that have increasingly become part of the problem of proliferation become instead part of the solution. Finally, by its networking characteristic, it can help prevent WMD or related materials from falling into terrorists' hands.[51] The impact of globalization on international actors has the potential to help resolve the inherent weaknesses of the international measures associated with the three global WMD regimes.[52] However, the major factors influencing countries like Iran and North Korea in their pursuit of nuclear weapons capability arguably are the United States' reluctance to reduce its own arsenal and its pursuit of a selective policy on nonproliferation. The United States ignores its friends with nuclear weapons but punishes its "enemies" that are attempting to acquire them. This double standard is a barrier to NPT compliance in some quarters.[53] On the whole, globalization has doused states' appetite for military adventurism and territorial aggrandizement.

Economics

The crux of globalization rests on its ability to produce a peaceful environment in which the world's countries can trade and the interchange of ideas can flourish. Simultaneously, trade and investment interdependence increase mutual confidence, the sense of common interests and partnership, and shared risks, opportunities, vulnerabilities, and consequently, security. This interdependency mitigates the chances of conflict and war and feeds into sustainable peace and stability. Although the risks for a global war may exist as the critics would argue, the nature of economic interdependence and integration puts constraints on such manifestations for the most part. International actors gravitate toward the positive gains to be had from globalization far more than to its conflictual tendencies. While the increased flow of people, goods, and capital that is part of economic globalization may harbor obvious threats to security (e.g., sleeper-cell terrorists, contagious diseases, global organized crime networks), the existence of these threats is not a sufficient reason to roll back globalization. (No one can seriously propose rolling back globalization anyway; the genie is out of the bottle.)

The institutional rules of the World Trade Organization (WTO) guide the operation of economic globalization. The WTO is dominated by wealthy countries like the United States, Japan, Canada, and the nations of the EU. Because the WTO's headquarters are in Switzerland, which has one of the highest costs of living in the world, many poor countries cannot afford to have permanent representatives there as the wealthy countries do. According to Ruth Valerio, on any issue of trade negotiation, the poor countries are consequently outweighed from the start and are hemmed in by perpetual discrimination.[54] The poor countries that have no resources to participate are pushed to the edge of poverty.[55] Valerio contends that economic globalization is sustained by the policies of trade liberalization, privatization, and financial market deregulation, meaning free trade between nations without protective barriers is most conducive to the profit-driven globalization. The growth of the global economy has led to, and in part resulted from, the emergence of powerful multinational corporations (MNCs). Whereas the home bases of these MNCs are located in the advanced and industrialized countries, as a consequence, the developing countries and particularly African states are at an economic disadvantage from the perspective of either governmental organizations or nongovernmental organizations. This puts the poor countries in double jeopardy, economically speaking.

Economists see globalization as increased economic interdependence and the integration of national economies into one gigantic framework of the global capitalist market. Sovereign territorial spheres are gradually losing their relevance, although individual nation-states continue to pursue their national interests, including through trade partnerships. Globalization is restraining unhealthy competition and harmonizing the global market arena. Market rules no longer apply to nation-states only but to all participating institutions as well.[56] For example, the era of "buy American" or "buy British" is over. Few global middle-class consumers are influenced by such patriotic campaigns. Instead, families want the best goods at the cheapest price. In the present global market, it can be difficult to identify a product's "nationality." One typical example is a Reebok sneaker bearing an African name and exhibiting a Union Jack on its label that was made by an American company whose operations are located in South Korea.[57]

Remarkably, the ongoing globalization of finance has put a leash on the likelihood of armed conflict by creating a strong disincentive for states to risk either militarized crises or war. On the one hand, as Jonathan Kirshner elucidates, "states are more beholden to the preferences of the international financial community" and thus are very sensitive to preserving those international economic policies that preserve the value of their assets. On the other hand, war threatens the very macroeconomic environment in which finance is able to profit and thrive. The risk of war is most likely to result in the restriction of capital flow and a downgrading of combatants' creditworthiness by international agencies like the IMF or World Bank. While there is no certainty that any of these factors might prevent a state from initiating a conflict with another nation, nonetheless, financial globalization raises the "costs and opportunity costs of choosing such a path." A state (rational actor) that is very sensitive to its financial interests at home and abroad will be more hampered by these constraints than would a state (irrational actor) that is not. This represents another, albeit limited, mechanism by which globalization can influence the pattern of an armed conflict.[58]

The globalized environment is generally conducive to the expansion of market sphere and diminishes the possibility of military conflict. Ordinarily, increased cultural contact contributes more to harmony than to disharmony.

For example, as of 2008, "Hollywood studios . . . earn half of their income from foreign markets"; consequently, cultural sensitivity plays a vital role in how the products are made and marketed.[59] The greater penetration of societies by foreign cultural products enhances and is itself a remarkable consequence of globalization. Globalization of finance has tremendously increased the opportunity costs of going to war. As a result, globalization has recalibrated the costs and benefits of interstate warfare. It has reduced the expected gains from interstate war and territorial conquest, rendering such adventurism unprofitable.

The Environment

The global and transboundary nature of contemporary climate change underscores the need for international coordination and cooperation to reverse or cope with it, especially involving the world's most industrialized nations. Some states, such as the EU member states, are proactive while others, like the United States and China, have been hesitant. There is no clear picture of how the current diffusion of policies and approaches can converge to attain a policy framework that is universal and uniform.[60] In recent decades, climate change has been identified as an environmental cause of human conflict and insecurity. The scientific research that pointed to troubling evidence of global warming in the 1970s and 1980s was initially ignored by policymakers as a peripheral issue. Today, however, climate change has being recast as a serious threat to global security. Some scientists and security analysts have claimed that the region most likely to suffer from its worst effects is Africa. Globally, climate change is contributing to conditions including "drought, desertification, land degradation, failing water supplies, deforestation, fisheries depletion, and even ozone depletion" that can be causally related to conflict. Climate change is thus threatening "water and food security, the allocation of resources, and coastal populations. These threats can amplify forced migration, raise tension, and trigger conflict."[61] African states that produce the least greenhouse gas emissions have been identified as the most likely victims of the negative effects attributable to the excessive consumption and carefree attitudes of the rich countries. "On the average, each resident of sub-Saharan Africa produces less than a ton of CO_2 per year, as compared with an average European's output 8.2 tonnes of CO_2 and the average North American's of 19.9 tonnes."[62] The effects of these outputs will impact the stability of African states by producing or protracting conflicts.

Officials of the United Nations Environment Program (UNEP) have suggested that the Darfur genocide was driven, in part, by climatic change and environmental degradation.[63] In about the last forty years, rainfall has been reduced by 30 percent in the region while the Sahara Desert has advanced by more than a mile every year. The eruption of violence that pitched farmers and herders against each other over the disappearing pasture and declining water holes underscored the genesis of Darfur conflict. It threatens to reignite Sudan's century-old war between the North (home to Arab nomads) and the South (where the Nuba tribe lives) that had been quieted by the fragile peace accord of 2005.[64] And with respect to Rwanda, several analysts have argued that resource scarcity caused by human impacts on the environment in addition to increasing population pressures contributed to the 1994 genocide.[65] Similarly, water scarcity has for decades been identified as a potential trigger for conflicts in the Middle East. Without equivocation, when a condition of scarcity arises, whether as a result of increased consumption or environmental change, competition for scarce resources between rival groups of users ensues, provoking potentially deadly outcomes. To some, environmental wars are likely to result because "climate change requires military solutions, to secure by force one's own resources or erect solid barriers to large-scale distress migration." Such conflict further depletes human resources, damages infrastructure, slows economic development and innovation, and thereby exacerbates insecurity.[66]

The rapid globalization of human civilization by means of industrialization and other activities with human environmental impacts is causing unintended negative consequences. Rapid economic development accompanied by lax environmental laws or lax enforcement of such laws as exist is a recipe for environmental disaster. Climate change, like many other global problems, requires global solution. Addressing the effects of climate change on international security in June 2007, the UN secretary-general, Ban Ki-Moon, observed that we must see the Darfur conflict beyond the convenience of "military and political short-hand—an ethnic conflict pitting Arab militias against black rebels and farmers. Look to its roots, though, and you discover a more complex dynamic. Amid the diverse social and political causes, the Darfur conflict began as an ecological crisis, arising in part from climate change."[67] In 2007 the UN Security Council authorized a large armed force to maintain and enforce peace in the region.

The prospect of stabilizing and eventually reducing global emissions lies in a global approach. Specifically, the advanced industrialized countries such as the United States, Japan, Russia, and major European nations and the large developing countries like Brazil, China, India, and Mexico must meet their fair quotas in reducing global emissions. Global measures to reduce greenhouse gas include the Kyoto Protocol, which requires the developed countries to embark on the emission-reduction strategy. The first period of caps on emissions started in 2008 and expires in 2012.[68] Such global cooperation is important to continue in the approaching post-Kyoto period. Katharina Holzinger and colleagues rightly observe that while increasing international linkage has driven environmental policies toward greater similarity, only international harmonization and communication through international institutions can provide the needed convergence of environmental policies rather than states' competing regulatory regimes.[69]

Terrorism

The manifestations of so-called Terror-Culture that include militancy and terrorism are increasingly ubiquitous. Gun culture, media violence, school shootings, gangster and rebellious groups, organized crime networks, and so forth also share in this ethos of violence. Sam George elucidates that "both globalization and religion have a reciprocal relationship with Terror-Culture, shaping it and being shaped by it."[70] Globalization has spread terrorism around the planet, and religious fundamentalism, as Anthony Giddens claims, is a child of globalization.[71] Notwithstanding, most religious fundamentalist movements (e.g., Wahhabism) have their origins before this present era of globalization, though within the modern era. Although globalization provides some incentive opportunities for terrorism, it is not the causative factor. The hopelessness and other conditions that underpin terrorism—ignorance, poverty, injustice, oppression—must be addressed at the national and regional levels, as well as globally.

Pojman argues that "our deepest reflections do permit certain types of violent responses to evil under certain situations. We are permitted (and even enjoined) to defend ourselves against harm by resorting to measured violence."[72] This is only applicable to cases of just war theory (*jus in bello*). Horrific violence like the 9/11 attacks against targets in the United States is beyond the scope of this morality. Pertinent international institutions must endorse the most widely accepted principles of morality. Primarily, we are all human beings, and secondarily, accidental citizens of different countries. Building on this sentiment, Pojman argues for the creation of institutional cosmopolitanism (world government) in order to bring about lasting global peace and justice.[73]

Terrorism as a tactic is associated with asymmetric conflict.[74] It has been in existence for many centuries prior to the emergence of globalization. Old-style terrorism goes after specific targets. The new genre, suicide bombing, obliterates the distinction between combatants and civilians. One particular school of thought considers terrorism a social problem. From the constructivist perspective, terrorists are concerned less with causing material damage than with causing fear (terror) among their targets. Therefore, instead of focusing on the terrorist, research should focus on terrorism discourse as a social construction, a social fact rather than a material fact. In the light of the constructivist epistemology, focusing on terrorist actors instead of the discourse by which the terrorist actor and his actions are constituted is misleading. Most of what has been written on al-Qaeda by experts on terrorism has been based "neither on interviews nor on field research conducted inside the organization." Rather, it was based on less-direct information: "veranda terrorism research." Also, this school of thought criticizes the (contestable) metaphorical shift of terrorism from war to crime in 2004 that it only normalizes terrorist groups like al-Qaeda.[75] Terrorism from the constructivist framework is an act of war and should be seen and treated as one.

The present challenge posed by terrorism is for the community of nations to recognize it for what it is, a global problem and an act of war. Responsibility for criminal prosecution of terrorists should be delegated to international institutions such as the International Criminal Court (ICC). There are thirteen international conventions that prohibit terrorism, each of which demands all states to either prosecute or extradite any individual or organization that contravenes such convention to the right authority. However, the lack of coherent and effective judicial institutions to enforce prosecution of alleged terrorists has weakened the efforts at the national and international levels.

The failure of the cooperation demanded by the UN resolutions to condemn and deal with act of terrorism as a threat to international peace and security is directly related to this vacuum. Over the years, the UN deliberations on the subject have resulted in comprehensive prohibitions condemning terrorism as a means of effecting political change regardless of how laudatory the purpose or sought-for change might be. Nonetheless, post-9/11, the realization has set in that UN antiterrorist declarations alone without adequate action are insufficient. However, the failure to create an adequate legal regime or grant the ICC the necessary jurisdiction to try terrorist criminals is due not to incapacity to do so but to a lack of political will. In the spirit of cooperative globalization, the international community should move to address terrorism by creating a central judicial authority capable of bringing terrorists to account. The legal activity of such a body will produce a deterrent effect that goes beyond the historic ad hoc antiterrorist measures that have in the past failed to prevent terrorists from indiscriminately killing civilians with impunity.[76] Although terrorists take advantage of globalization, it is only through global cooperation, cross-cultural exposure, and broad economic prosperity (i.e., positive effects of globalization) that terrorism can be eradicated.

Health

A downside of global dynamics is that disease is no longer a local phenomenon. The faster movement of more and more people across borders serves, unfortunately, as a perfect conduit for the spread of communicable diseases. Migrant workers may carry contagious diseases common in their locale to neighboring states (e.g., Egyptians brought the Hepatitis C virus to the Gulf States). People in nation-states far and near contract contagious and fatal diseases whether from humans, animals, products, or imported foodstuffs (e.g., the bovine spongiform encephalopathy—mad-cow disease—first found in 1986 in beef from the UK). Health interdependence has become one of the features of globalization that is most feared, since the spread of certain diseases may threaten international peace and security. At the same time, the successful spread of knowledge and technical information about the prevention and cure of communicable diseases (e.g., HIV, Ebola virus, TB, or swine flu), itself made possible by globalization, highlights strategic approaches to combating health threats to international security especially in the developing world.[77]

HIV/AIDS is a global epidemic and the first disease of the modern era of globalization. Its securitization was inaugurated by the United Nations Security Council on January 10, 2000 (although it began to be a global crisis before 2000). The rationale for treating it as a political problem is that it can cause huge social welfare costs and further attenuate already weakened states, undermine economic growth, amplify social tensions, and diminish military preparedness. It is estimated that between 40 and 60 percent of some African armed forces are infected with the virus, raising concerns about their combat readiness and the implications for peacekeeping mission capabilities.[78] To make matter worse, these soldiers can serve as vectors of the illness wherever they are deployed. Considering the astronomical number of cases in third world countries, certain degree of correlation exists between poverty and poor health as typified by the cases of some African states. The disease, comments Steven Fouch, is inextricably linked to poverty. Quoting an African woman about her experience with HIV/AIDS, Fouch recounts: "People do not have more sex in Africa than in Europe, we are not less moral, yet we have a worse AIDs problem. The difference between AIDS/HIV in the West and the developing world is one of poverty. Why do Christians always emphasize sex as the primary prevention issue and not poverty?" The majority of victims of this disease are in the developing and poor countries of the world.[79] The faster movement of travelers, including sex tourists, has enabled infectious diseases to be imported from one corner of the globe to another. For example, sex tourists from the Western world introduced AIDs to Haiti and Thailand.[80] The increasing impact of health crises by means of the complex dynamics of global human relationships has elevated health issues to the level of international security concerns.

Second to the problem of the spread of disease is the cost of advanced modern health care and medicines. Most medications are not available to many people who need them because they cannot afford them. To make matters worse, in such countries as Angola, the Democratic Republic of the Congo, Somalia, and Sudan, a good number of hospitals and clinics have been bombed or destroyed as a result of conflicts. To further compound the problems faced by conflict-torn areas, protracted civil wars also cause the destruction or loss of transportation infrastructure and clean water supplies and curtail access to food. The massive migration of populations to urban areas also exacerbates the spread of HIV, the current pandemic of swine flu virus (H1N1), and the spread of such diseases as anthrax, hepatitis, tropical malaria/dengue/yellow fevers, SARS (severe acute respiratory syndrome) as well as a myriad of sexually transmitted diseases.[81] Without any doubt, the modern sex industry, contemporary travel and tourism practices, and the international market in blood products (partially supplied by China) are fueling the HIV/AIDS pandemic.

Ironically, despite its "evils," it is modernization that holds the promise of overcoming these pandemics, in particular, in developing countries. During my research for this study, it was announced by the British Broadcasting Corporation World Service that a new vaccine that holds the promise of preventing HIV has been developed in Thailand. On September 24, 2009, researchers announced that the vaccine can reduce by about one-third the chances of contracting HIV. The joint United Nations Program on AIDS (UNAIDS) is particularly keen in promoting awareness through its "HIV/AIDS Awareness Cards" to address the contribution of peacekeeping missions to the spread of HIV. These cards' risk-prevention messages are written in English, Swahili, and other languages.[82] UNAIDS is the leading advocate for global action against HIV/AIDS. The hope of preventing and curing these epidemics lies largely in the global spread of advanced technology.

Empirical Analyses

In this segment, we shall examine some particular security-related activities to make concrete sense of how globalization is unfolding in Africa. Harold James observes that "the big ideological debate about globalization is largely over. . . . The authentic voice of anti-globalization is now that of a very different global vision, that of Islamic fundamentalism. Many former critics now see at least some advantages in globalization." The more intelligent critics are now focusing on the need for a "better globalization" rather than turning their back on globalization entirely.[83]

With regard to Africa, third world advocates generally want more and not less globalization. The remarkable economic growth of China and India has demonstrated that opening one's economy to the world market produces benefits and alleviates poverty. African countries in particular desire the dismantling of the industrialized countries' trade barriers. Africa can benefit tremendously from the opportunities of Western economies' outsourcing as did China and India. However, in the near term, the prospects for globalization for sub-Saharan Africa are much less sunny compared to those for the advanced industrialized democracies. Free market and media pressure on authoritarian and weak states in this region will tend to create an environment that is unfortunately more conducive to civil war, insurgency, and violent crises associated with atrophy of national governments than to development. According to Kirshner: "The inescapable disruptions of globalization, felt most acutely by small economies and vulnerable elements of society, will threaten national cohesion and identity, and exacerbate existing regional, distributive, and ethnic conflicts."[84] Potential refugee flows will result from failed state systems faced with challenges to their functionality, ranging from transnational forces to atomizing internal loyalties. Thus the deterioration of the classic asylum-centered refugee regime signals troubling future unless both the governments and refugee advocates from NGOs, humanitarian organizations, and transnational networks converge around new rules and practices so as to create the effective capacity to meet the needs of future refugees. The office of the United Nations High Commissioner for Refugees still relies for refugees' protection on the ineffective 1951 Convention Relating to the Status of Refugees. With a history of noncompliance by states, these weak principles are insufficient to confront the potential series of potential megacrises on the African horizon.

Also, by addressing the issue of chronic poverty, the world's elite states can help douse the continued perception of marginalization of Africa from the globalization process. However, globalization cannot be blamed for the inefficient, undemocratic, and corrupt governments in Africa that have afflicted its peoples with perpetual poverty, political instability, and armed conflict. The so-called marginalization of African states is, for the most part, a consequence of their own weaknesses and vulnerabilities to security threats that were incubated internally. The numerous irregular military forces operating on the continent, including insurgent groups, ethnic militias, and separatist movements, have emerged in reaction to years of authoritarian rule, tyranny, oppression and repression, corrupt leadership, embezzlement, and mismanagement of national resources. Until the lingering mistakes of the past and anomalies of the present are corrected, any tangible development will be unattainable. Only Africans can help Africans through the process of regional integration, if they aspire to become a regional economic bloc similar to the EU model. Even so, the African Union cannot expect to be a significant force if it is a conglomeration of failed states. National economies must become integrated into the global system as opposed to being defined by geographic locality. Overtime, if necessary measures are taken at the local, national, and regional levels, and if it is cushioned by external supports, there is no reason why Africa cannot rise from the status quo. We must be cognizant, however, of the destructive pandemic of HIV/AIDS that threatens some African states with collapse if appropriate and timely action is not taken. For many African states on the verge of failure, globalization has not improved the regional security environment, and many observers think it has even made it worse. Internal remedies must come before external remedies.

Conclusion

This study acknowledges that, whether we like it or not, globalization is an inescapable constituent of the contemporary world order. The challenges of national and international security cannot be overcome by unilateral or bilateral endeavor but only by concerted and collective global cooperation. We should embrace globalization because it is good for international security; it is good for humanity. It marks not an abrupt change but a historical shift from traditional to modern society in the quest to fulfill a vision of universalism. In realistic terms, globalization is providing humanity a way out of the Westphalian territorial cul-de-sac and warfare into an integrated world civil society. The neorealist zero-sum theory postulates that for a state to do well, it must do so at other states' expense; this negative assumption does not jibe with the reality of the contemporary world with players that are increasingly bound together by common values. The evolving global world order ascertained above is supported by the neoliberal positive analysis of collective cooperation and the constructivist normative approach.

In the final analysis, globalization is a multidimensionally contested subject. This discussion has examined how globalization affects international security through the multifaceted dynamics covering the military, economics, ecological concerns, terrorism, and health, among others. According to its critics, globalization perpetuates and intensifies armed conflict, epidemics, unemployment, environmental degradation, cultural annihilation, poverty, financial crises, crime, and social disintegration. Intensified globalization, they say, has afforded terrorists new tools and an elevated profile. While these claims might be true in some respects, globalization is not the only source of human insecurity but just one among many interrelated factors. Through its extensive connections, however, globalization has enhanced international security by providing: disincentives to war, improving economic efficiency, assisting humanitarian relief, and helping create new employment opportunities, spread democratic values, advance technology, heighten ecological sensitivities, encourage greater cultural pluralism, and so on. Globalization is ushering the world into a postterritorial conception of social geography. Consequently, the dynamics of globalization is globalizing security and thus enhancing stability and peace.

The context of globalization has enhanced the possibilities of arms control and disarmament. Globalization brings clarity to global security problems by enabling the costs and benefits to be properly distributed. It promotes the formation of regional and continental alliances (collective defense) and thereby helps states avoid military competition and wars. Regional organizations like the African Union and the Organization for Security and Cooperation in Europe (OSCE) have undertaken conflict management initiatives in their respective regions. The fact that the states that comprise the Organization for Economic Cooperation and Development (OECD) have not gone to war against each other since 1945 and that military conflicts between "states of East Asia, Europe, and North America" are unlikely, empirically attests to the potential positive impact of large-scale globalization on international security. In agreement with Jan Aart Scholte, the empirical analyses in this study demonstrate that there is a correlation between globalization and "greater peace."[85] Despite the ability of globalization to promote security, absolute security is not attainable. Nonetheless, globalization will continue to have important repercussions for various aspects of international security in the future.

Notes

Epigraphs: Jeffrey C. Alexander, "Globalization as Collective Representation: The New Dream of a Cosmopolitan Civil Sphere," *International Journal of Political Culture* 19 (2005): 81–89. Esther Dyson quoted in James N. Rosenau et al., *On the Cutting Edge of Globalization: An Inquiry into American Elites* (New York: Rowman & Littlefield, 2006). Dyson was originally quoted in Joel Garreau, "Home Is Where the Phone Is: Roaming Legion of High-Tech Nomads Takes Happily to Ancient Path," *Washington Post*, October 17, 2000, A1; she is an entrepreneur and a former chairwoman of the Internet Corporation for Assigned Names and Numbers.

1. Anne-Marie Slaughter, "The Real New World Order," *Foreign Affairs* (September–October 1997): 194–95.

2. Jonathan Kirshner, "Globalization, American Power, and International Security," *Political Science Quarterly* 123, no. 3 (2008): 363–89.

3. Farhang Rajaee, *Globalization on Trial: The Human Condition and the Information Civilization* (Ottawa, ON: Kumarian Press, 2000), 6. Farhang extracted the concept of *vita activa* and *vita contemplativa* from the work of Hannah Arendt, *The Origins of Totalitarianism* (New York, NY: Harcourt, Brace and World, 1951). Other works cited include Hannah Arendt, *The Human Condition* (Chicago: The University of Chicago Press, 1958).

4. Mathias Koenig-Archibugi, "Introduction: Globalization and the Challenge to Governance," In *Taming Globalization: Frontiers of Governance*, ed. David Held and Mathias Koenig-Archibugi (Cambridge, UK: TJ International, Padstow, Cornwall, 2003), 1.

5. Richard Tiplady, ed., *One World or Many: The Impact of Globalization on Mission* (Pasadena, California: William Carey Library, 2003), 2.

6. F. Lechner, "Globalization," in *Encyclopedia of Social Theory*, ed. George Ritzer (Thousand Oaks, CA: Sage, 2005), 330–33, in George Ritzer, *The Globalization of Nothing 2* (Thousand Oaks, CA: Pine Forge Press, 2007), 4.

7. Henry Veltmeyer, introduction to *New Perspectives on Globalization and Antiglobalization: Prospects for a New World Order?*, ed. Henry Veltmeyer (Burlington, VT: Ashgate, 2008), 1.

8. Tiplady, *One World or Many*, 2.

9. T. McGew, "Review of *Globalization: A Critical Introduction* by Jan Aart Scholte," *New Political Economy* 6 (2001): 293–301, in Veltmeyer, introduction to *New Perspectives*, 14.

10. J. Hobson and M. Ramesh, "Globalization Makes of States What States Make of It: Between Agency and Structure in the State/Globalization Debate," *New Political Economy* 7, no. 1 (2002): 5–22.

11. Kenneth Waltz, John Mearsheimer, and Joseph Grieco are realists and leading scholars of the neorealist school of thought. Waltz is credited as the leading prophet of structural realism. See Kenneth Waltz, *Theory of International Politics* (New York: McGraw-Hill Publishing, 1979).

12. Lee Ryan Miller, *Confessions of a Recovering Realist: Toward a Neo-Liberal Theory of International Relations* (Bloomington, IN, Author House, 2004), 1–38; Joseph M. Grieco, "Anarchy and the Limits of Cooperation: A Realist Critique of the Newest Liberal Institutionalism," *International Organization* 42, no. 3 (1988): 458–508.

13. Ibid.

14. John Babatunde Bamidele Ojo, "The Correlation between the Strategic Security Environment and Extent of Weapons Acquisition: A Theoretical Reformulation of Competing Theories in International Security" (PhD diss., Howard University, 2000), 11–30.

15. Robert Axelrod and Robert O. Keohane, "Achieving Cooperation under Anarchy: Strategies and Institution," in *Neorealism and Neoliberalism: The Contemporary Debate*, ed. David A. Baldwin (New York: Columbia University Press, 1993), 85–115.

16. Michael Doyle, "Liberalism and World Politics," *America Political Science Review* 80 (December 1986): 1151–69.

17. Ronald L. Jepperson, Alexander Wendt, and Peter Katzenstein, "Norms, Identity, and Culture in National Security," in *The Culture of National Security: Norms and Identity in World Politics*, ed. Peter Katzenstein (New York: Columbia University Press, 1996), 33–75.

18. Jeffrey T. Checkel, "The Constructivist Turn in International Relations Theory," *World Politics* 50, no. 2 (January 1998): 325–26.

19. Harold James, "Globalization, Empire, and Natural Law," *International Affairs* 84, no. 3 (2008): 421–26.

20. Robert Daniel Wallace, review of *Security and International Relations*, by Edward Kolodziej, Themes in International Relations series, *Intelligence and National Security Book Reviews* 23, no. 2 (April 2008).

21. Rosenau et al., *On the Cutting Edge of Globalization*, 16–17.

22. Ibid., 19.

23. Ibid., 20.

24. Rajaee, *Globalization on Trial*, 16–17.

25. Francis Fukuyama, "The End of History," *National Interest* 16 (Summer 1989): 3–35 (in ibid., 21–22).

26. Francis Fukuyama, *The End of History and the Last Man* (New York: Free Press, 1992), 48.

27. Farid Zakaria, "The Rise of Illiberal Democracy," *Foreign Affairs* 76, no. 6 (1997): 22.

28. Rajaee, *Globalization on Trial*, 22.

29. Robert D. Kaplan, "The Coming of Anarchy," *Atlantic Monthly* 273, no. 2 (1994): 73.

30. Samuel Huntington, "The Clash of Civilizations," *Foreign Affairs* 73, no. 3 (1993); and Samuel Huntington, *The Clash of Civilizations and the Remaking of World Order* (New York: Simon and Schuster, 1996).

31. Rajaee, *Globalization on Trial*, 34–36.

32. P. J. Simmons and Chantal de Jonge Oudraat, "Managing Global Issues: An Introduction," in *Managing Global Issues: Lessons Learned*, ed. P. J. Simmons and Chantal de Jonge Oudraat (Washington, DC: Carnegie Endowment for International Peace, 2001), 3–22.

33. Ibid., 14.

34. Rosenau et al., *Cutting Edge of Globalization*, 2.

35. Ibid., 18.

36. Ibid., 2.

37. Ibid., 3.

38. Tiplady, *One World or Many*, 5.

39. James W. Skillen, "To Look at the World Entirely Afresh," in *Prospects and Ambiguities of Globalization: A Critical Assessment at a Time of Growing Turmoil*, ed. James W. Skillen (New York: Lexington Books, 2009), 1–8.

40. Rajaee, *Globalization on Trial*, 10.

41. Huntington, "Clash of Civilizations."

42. Farhang Rajaee, *Ma'rekeye Janhanbiniha: dar Kheradvarziye Siyassi va Hoviyate Ma Iranian* (Battle of World Views: On Political Rationalism and Our Iranian Identity), 2nd ed. (Tehran: Ehya Ketab, 1997), 3–4, in Rajaee, *Globalization on Trial*, 14. Zero-sum means that one group benefits at the other's expense.

43. Keith Suter, *In Defence of Globalization* (Sydney: UNSW Press, 2000), 27–28.

44. Ibid., 33.

45. Louis P. Pojman, *Terrorism, Human Rights, and the Case for World Government* (Boulder, CO: Rowman & Littlefield, 2006).

46. Timothy D. Sisk, "Violence: Intrastate Conflict," in Simmons and Oudraat, *Managing Global Issues*, 534–38.

47. Ibid., 538–55.

48. Joanna Spear, "Warfare: Conventional Weapons," in Simmons and Oudraat, *Managing Global Issues*, 564–68.

49. Ibid.

50. Thomas Bernauer, "Warfare: Nuclear, Biological, and Chemical Weapons," in Simmons and Oudraat, *Managing Global Issues*, 610–59.

51. Ibid., 628–29.

52. Ibid., 654.

53. Richard J. Payne, *Global Issues: Politics, Economics, and Culture*, 2nd ed. (New York: Pearson Longman, 2009), 159.

54. Ruth Valerio, "Globalization and Economics: A World Gone Bananas," in Tiplady, *One World or Many*, 17.

55. Ibid., 21.

56. Rajaee, *Ma'rekeye Janhanbiniha*, 25.

57. Suter, *In Defence of Globalization*, 21.

58. Kirshner, "Globalization, American Power," 377.

59. Ibid., 384.

60. Katharina Holzinger, Christoph Knill, and Thomas Sommerer, "Environmental Policy Convergence: The Impact of International Harmonization, Transnational Communication, and Regulatory Competition," *International Organization* 62, no. 4 (2008): 553–54.

61. Oli Brown, Anne Hammill, and Robert McLeman, "Climate Change as the 'New' Security Threat: Implication for Africa," *International Affairs* 83, no. 6 (2007): 1141–54. See also Homer Dixon, "On the Threshold: Environmental Changes of Acute Conflict," *International Security* 16, no. 2 (1991): 76–116.

62. World Bank, *The Little Green Data Book 2007* (Washington, DC, June 2007), in Brown, Hammill, and McLeman, "Climate Change," 1145.

63. United Nations Environment Programme, *Sudan: Post-Conflict Environmental Assessment* (Nairobi, 2007), in Brown, Hammill, and McLeman, "Climate Change," 1143.

64. Ibid.

65. P. Uvin, "Tragedy in Rwanda: The Political Ecology of Conflict," *Environment* 38 (1996): 6–15, in Brown, Hammill, and McLeman, "Climate Change," 1147.

66. Brown, Hammill, and McLeman, "Climate Change," 1147–54.

67. Ban Ki Moon, op-ed, "A Climate Culprit in Darfur," *Washington Post*, June 16, 2007, http://www.washingtonpost.com/wp-dyn/content/article/2007/06/15/AR2007061501857.html.

68. Brown, Hammill, and McLeman, "Climate Change," 1144.

69. Holzinger, Knill, and Sommerer, "Environmental Policy Convergence," 584.

70. Sam George, "TerrorCulture: Worth Living or Worth Dying For," in Tiplady, *One World or Many*, 55.

71. Anthony Giddens, *Runaway World: How Globalisation Is Shaping Our Lives*, Reith Lectures (London: Profile Books, 1999), http://www.bbc.co.uk/radio4/reith1999/.

72. Pojman, *Terrorism*, 12.

73. Ibid., 28.

74. Kirshner, "Globalization, American Power," 389.

75. Rainer Hulsse and Alexander Spencer, "The Metaphor of Terror: Terrorism Studies and the Constructivist Turn," *Security Dialogue* 39, no. 6 (2008): 571–92.

76. Michael Lawless, "Terrorism: An International Crime," *International Journal* 63, no. 1 (Winter 2007–8): 139–59.

77. Octavio Gomez-Dantes, "Health," in Simmons and Oudraat, *Managing Global Issues*, 392–94.

78. Stephan Elbe, "Risking Lives: AIDS, Security, and Three Concepts of Risk," *Security Dialogue* 39, no. 2–3 (2008): 177–79.

79. Steven Fouch, "Globalization and Healthcare Mission," in Tiplady, *One World or Many*, 134.

80. Ibid., 123–29.

81. Ibid., 132.

82. Elbe, "Risking Lives," 182–95.

83. James, "Globalization, Empire, and Natural Law," 424.

84. Kirshner, "Globalization, American Power," 386.

85. Jan Aart Scholte, *Globalization: A Critical Introduction*, 2nd ed. (New York: Palgrave Macmillan, 2005), 282–85.

16

Resource Curse, Globalization, and Conflicts

Ricardo Real Pedrosa de Sousa

Conflict is a malady that afflicts societies and individuals with incommensurable pain and stress. Over the last few decades, there has been an increased interest in understanding the mechanisms of conflict as a way to engage in preventive policy initiatives. Within this context, this chapter seeks to uncover the mechanisms associated with the initiation of conflict as identified in the literature. Contemporary academic writing associated with the term "resource curse" (which has been used to describe the failure of resource-rich countries to benefit from their natural wealth) and the "greed and grievance" model of conflict, significantly developed by the economist Paul Collier, are reviewed. The chapter concludes by evaluating the mechanisms identified, illustrating their possible effects on the dynamics of the initiation of intrastate conflict, normally referred to as civil war.

The chapter is divided into six parts, each corresponding to a category that groups related and relevant factors: the external environment, governance, economic factors, social factors, geography, and history. Based on this assessment, I conclude with a summary of factors that have been identified as the key contributors to conflict.[1]

External Environment

Accepting the conceptualization of the nation-state for this analysis, the external environment encompasses all the factors and mechanisms that fall outside of a state's control (especially in the case of poorer countries) and that directly conditions the domestic policy options of the actors in the country. Specifically, it includes the international markets, agreements, and behavior of key industries in the context of regional and global economic conditions and international relations.

Since the 1950s, the theory of the declining terms of trade has argued that resource-based growth is inefficient because world prices of primary exports relative to manufactures show a profound tendency toward decline, while rich countries are more protectionist against primary imports than manufacturing imports.[2] Recent studies now agree that the aggregate terms of trade for primary commodities have been declining since at least the beginning of the 1900s (measured at an estimated 0.1 percent to 1.3 percent per annum), and although the impact of this phenomenon on economic growth needs further examination at the case study level, it is "statistically robust at the global level."[3]

Furthermore, since the mid-1960s, some studies have argued that the instability of commodity markets in poor countries, which rely significantly on their commodity export earnings, creates unstable revenues for the government and makes private investment too risky, therefore harming economic growth. Contesting this perspective, other studies have shown that export instability paradoxically produces economic growth. More recent research has shown that export instability either harms economic growth or has no impact at all.[4] Furthermore a model developed by Enrique Mendoza predicts that terms-of-trade instability will reduce social welfare, regardless of its effects on growth.[5]

This commodity price cycle may even directly promote civil conflict because the boom-and-bust effect of revenue destabilizes the political center and presents motives and opportunities for opponents to seize power. In this way, conflict could be said to be more closely associated with more volatile commodities, with commodities that are more easily taxed, with higher levels of commodity dependence, and with lower levels of macroeconomic discipline.[6] Furthermore, imperfect market operations, such as the specific concentrations of buyers or sellers, unbalanced powers of negotiation, the uneven distribution of value throughout the value chain, and trade barriers and subsidies have produced mixed results, but it seems that the benefits (if any) resulting from such imperfection have only trickled down to the poorest developing countries.

Moreover, the financial markets have proved to be a mixed blessing. Although they create opportunities for developing countries to access finance and investment, the benefits have not materialized in some regions. For instance, sub-Saharan Africa suffers from low domestic and foreign investment, high capital flight, and low remittance flows.[7] At the same time, their operations have been prone to misuse and mismanagement, where some of the consequences have been "odious" debt or financial crisis.[8] Furthermore, the volatility in the flows of foreign direct investment has been identified as harmful to economic growth, even though most of the investment in developing countries is of a domestic nature.[9]

International agreements or initiatives have also been subject to different responses. While some are considered to enable peaceful development, others such as the TRIMs, GATS, and TRIPs have been scrutinized since their objectives seem "aimed at limiting the development policy options of developing country governments" and "are likely to lock in the position of Western countries at the top of the world hierarchy of wealth" by "kicking away the ladder" of development.[10] Combined with this analysis is the evidence that peace initiatives may need to be coordinated with international trade agreements. Otherwise, the trade policies chosen by industrial countries may undermine peace efforts abroad.[11]

The development paradigm and practices of the international aid industry have changed steadily over the last few decades. Academically at least, one can state that up to the 1970s, the focus was on a country's physical capital, or "hardware" whereas during the 1980s and early 1990s, the paradigm shifted to center more on the "Washington Consensus" on structural adjustment programs that focused on pursuing economic liberalism. In the late 1990s, the predominant note was the New Institutionalism, which sought to tackle poverty directly through social investment and a renewed state role. Finally, the current emphasis is now on the "software" of an economy: the institutions, customs, laws, and social cohesion needed to create and sustain markets.[12] However, there is sometimes a lag between the academic, political, and institutional formulation of development thinking and the actual development practices themselves and vice versa.

Also of relevance here is the scope of today's prescribed interventions in the "development process" which grow by agglomeration and together amount to "what may be considered the constant preoccupations of development theory—for example, in international economics (trade, investment, and today—above all?—capital markets), macroeconomics (exchange, interest, inflation and savings rates, employment, productivity), and social policy (health, education)."[13] In addition to these factors, "state reform, the (re) design and management of public institutions, clear and properly enforced property rights, democratization, civil society and the sources of social capital, small-scale credit, nongovernmental organization (NGO) management, (environmentally) sustainable development, women/gender and development, children and development, refugees and development, humanitarian emergencies and interventions, and post-conflict resolution" may be added, among others.[14]

It is within this particular environment that the Millennium Development Goals (MDGs) have, to some extent, set the development agenda for the foreseeable future, and therefore the discussion is dominated less by notions of "what to do" and more by notions of "how to do it."[15] As far as implementation mechanisms are concerned, the Commission for Africa report recommends that support should be given directly to open and transparent budgets with a clear strategy in place instead of sector wide approaches, and only as a last resort to projects.[16] These recommendations do not exclude the complementary roles that the private sector, third sector (the sphere of social and economic activity undertaken by organizations that are non-profit), and donors can play in meeting the MDGs.[17]

In the case of the arms industry, Paul Collier, Anke Hoeffler, and Mans Soderbom conclude that the viability of the conflict enterprise, which is based on its financial and military circumstances, will determine the duration of conflict.[18] Therefore, the emergence of a global and unpoliced market in armaments after 1980 may have given rebels advantages while at the same time contributing to the viability of the conflict enterprise.[19] Both the Commission for Africa report and the *Human Development Report*, both of 2005, consider control of the trade of small arms to be a priority.[20] The efficiency and effectiveness of peace efforts will likely improve substantially if both demand and supply factors are controlled.

There is increasing evidence that extractive natural resource industries, particularly in the form of multinational corporations operating in the oil and gemstones industries, are contributing either directly or indirectly to conflict. There is broad agreement in the literature on gemstones about the role of these industries in financing conflict, especially if they are lootable (e.g., alluvial diamonds). Nancy Birdsall and Arvind Subramanian draw attention to the need for the international community to put greater pressure on oil companies, which too often abet local corruption, and, one could add, disrupt local communities' livelihoods during resource extraction.[21] In the SIDA Report, emphasis is placed on the need for developing countries to have "institutional frameworks for factor and product markets that provide stable and secure conditions for exchange that prevent narrow self-interest from damaging public interest."[22]

The configuration of political relations can foster and maintain many of the peace and development efforts and will determine the extent of a country's influence. Membership in regional organizations can also provide a decisive push in this direction. In 1995, William Easterly and Ross Levine noted that the improvement of policies by one country alone can substantially boost growth, but that if neighboring countries act together, the effects on growth are much greater.[23] Other nonregional groupings, anchored in legacies of the past (like colonialism) or other factors (like language), seem to work ambiguously. On the one hand, these groupings can benefit a country's security and influence, while also allowing greater access to labor, product, and service markets. On the other hand, they implicitly perpetuate associations that may prove complex to manage in the long run. The length of such relations and the manner in which they are cultivated need to be judged carefully on a case-by-case basis so as not to deconstruct balances of power without first identifying a country's sustained, substantive and locally accepted and developed alternatives. Optimal or improved proposals are only better if they work effectively.

All the factors addressed throughout this chapter are linked to the question of globalization. This is frequently associated with modernization, but the concept is too broad and ill-defined in many aspects (see the above mentioned scope of intervention of the international aid industry). One important consideration is the degree of change that this dynamic requires of people. To cope with change is a human attribute, but one's degree of tolerance to change and associated tensions varies depending on many factors. Among these is an individual's or group's awareness of their capacities for dealing with such changes. Another factor is how groups or individuals perceive themselves during the course of change and in the envisaged future. Although positive changes in individual well-being are normally readily accepted, this may not always be the case. Examples are to be found among those actors who attach more value to relative rather than absolute changes in their conditions. For these people, either the pace of change or some particular aspect of it may be unacceptable, being perceived as something that cannot be disentangled from the overall process.

Finally, as far as regional and global politics are concerned, the literature finds evidence that wars in neighboring countries can have a distinct influence on a country's peace and security, both politically and through rebel incursions.[24] Also the existing configuration of world powers directly affects the nature of conflict. While on the one hand there were fewer onsets of war during the 1990s (only eleven from a data set of seventy-nine large-scale conflicts occurring between 1960 and 1999), on the other hand the average duration of civil wars increased after 1980.[25] In addition, funding mechanisms have changed, as alluvial diamonds seem to have played an increasingly major role in the onset of civil wars since the end of the Cold War.[26] James Fearon asserts that

> it remains reasonable, on both theoretical and anecdotal grounds, to think that the availability of finance for would-be rebels affects a country's prospects of civil war. We still do not know, however, if rebel finance is a "critical constraint" that varies a great deal from place to place, or if it is easily satisfied provided other conditions are satisfied (e.g., weak central government with little rural presence, a sudden increase in grievances due to changed government policy, or a prevalence of unemployed young males). Indeed, we still know little about the sources of rebel groups' incomes. How much comes from local donations and "revolutionary taxes," how much from foreign governments or companies, how much from diasporas?[27]

Governance

Resource-rich countries develop specific processes in terms of democracy, institutions, quality of policies, and rule of law and human rights, which interact not only with socioeconomic planning but also with conflict. Most of the literature identifies that the type of regime to be found in countries rich in oil (but not necessarily other commodities) is more likely to be less democratic, because such countries: (a) tend to be less accountable to the people; (b) use rents to buy political support;[28] (c) spend more money on the military;[29] (d) develop an elite that delays the transition to democracy;[30] (e) are prone to more corruption;[31] and (f) use executive discretion in the distribution of rents.[32] Nevertheless, Alan Gelb and colleagues conclude that it is difficult to infer the relationship between the political system and political efficiency from the use that is made of rents.[33] Silje Aslaksen and Ragnar Torvik recently added that a key factor could be the comparative payoffs accrued from conflict versus from democracy, whereas "countries will not pass this test [of self-sustaining democracy] if their resource wealth is sufficiently high, labor productivity sufficiently low, political competition sufficiently strong or politicians sufficiently short-sighted."[34] This could mean, for instance, that rational decision makers would most likely opt for conflict if there is significant oil or gemstone wealth in the country, in the cases where (a) low costs of labor (normally found in poor countries) facilitate the recruitment of would-be rebels; (b) a very competitive political culture exists that leads to violent forms of contestation; and (c) politicians opt for short-term political gains instead of agreements on long-term benefits.

Additionally, institutions such as those composing the three branches of the state, legislative, executive, and judicial, have been identified as playing a major role at the heart of the resource curse. Resource-rich countries are under less pressure (from below and above) to develop sound institutions. This fact limits their capacity to formulate good policies and further increases rent-seeking and parasitic activities.[35] At the same time, low national income results in weaker military resources and technological infrastructure for repressing rebellions.[36] These circumstances can lead to a downfall or breakdown of the system of law and wealth creation.[37] The challenge thus lies in reverting to the equilibrium point; however, "only countries with grabber-friendly institutions [i.e., bad institutions that divert scarce entrepreneurial resources out of production into unproductive activities] are captured by the resource curse, while countries with producer-friendly institutions escape the resource curse."[38]

The quality of policies in developing countries has been poor in many cases, which observers have found puzzling.[39] Given that most problems of resource-rich countries have "remedies" that have been studied in some depth, one can conclude that more should have been done about solving their problems. Together with the dynamics affecting regime type and institutions, possible explanations for the failure to improve the quality of policies are to be found in the fact that the "easy rich" tend to become short-sighted and exuberant, as well as averse to risk taking; engage in lax economic planning; and prefer "egalitarian current consumption policies" over "development policies." In other words, resource-rich countries will focus less on long-term accumulation and growth due to the availability of resources. This availability removes pressure to have proper economic management and allows opting for current consumption over long-term policies. Another possible explanation is that the investment needed to offset the problems is intuitively large for politicians. Appropriate policies might not be in compliance with the aid industry development paradigm of the time (and therefore might become more difficult to finance), or else the government agency responsible for instituting the change process is apparently too dependent on factors out of its control (for instance, changing international terms of trade might render an otherwise good investment option in the country a less promising economic venture). The "big push" needed to move equilibrium from a negative to a positive trend (a change in the economic structure of the country wherein synergies can be generated and more than proportional growth can be aimed at) is dependent on many other actors besides the government (from national private actors to international multilateral and private actors). If these several elements are not aligned, the "rational" choice of a politician might just be to engage in business or politics "as usual" (for instance, managing the short-term political processes of executive office contestation) if the "break-even" point does not seem reachable.

In analyzing what might be considered the requirements of this initial "big push," James Robinson highlights the economics of the new institutionalism, what the governments and international institutions are expected to deliver and why.[40] In particular, it is widely recognized that governments (with the encouragement and support of the World Bank) need to invest in services to the poor. But furthermore, incorporating a social constraint into their economic analysis, Ernesto Dal Bó and Pedro Dal Bó explain why these and other policies, which would seem to be counter-optimal in a frictionless society, might be appropriate options in societies faced with social conflict.[41] Finally, conflict, of whatever type, needs to be viewed along a continuum of the nonobservance of the rule of law and human rights. Through this lens crime or civil war are, above all, symptomatic of a social conflict over the direct or indirect appropriation of resources.

Economic Factors

Resource-rich countries face the challenges not only of integration into the world economy and modernization but also of the careful management of newfound wealth and the volatility of revenues. Compounding these management challenges is the constant political rivalry over the appropriation of resources and rents.

All of the factors presented so far are necessarily linked to the question of economic modernization. There are different paths, identified elsewhere, for a country's development. Of particular relevance here are those developmental choices that lead to growth that favors the poor, generally characterized as a form of economic development where the private business sector enjoys broad-based growth, resulting in wealth creation for all sections of society, which is then dispersed geographically and reaches poor parts of the country in particular.[42]

Also salient in the literature are the rentier states or petro states (which could be considered a particular form of rentier state), which do not necessarily embark on a process of industrialization. Different definitions have been offered for this concept: "a rentier state is characterized by a high dependence on external rents produced by a few economic actors. Rents are typically generated from the exploitation of natural resources, not from production (labor), investment (interest), or the management of risk (profit). Rentier states tend to be autonomous, more detached and less accountable; because they do not need to levy taxes";[43] and "in a rentier economy [i.e., where the territory is for sale or rent], income accrues through the provision of services and/or by withholding these from undesirable third parties."[44]

Increasing internal revenue is generally not achieved through production but through various nonproductive activities. The latter include foreign aid, remittances from abroad, dividends on foreign securities, licenses, stamp duties, customs receipts, land and fishing tax, leases, loans, and payments. Income is also derived from the provision of services, licenses, or specific activities that generate fees known as "invisible receipts," including tourism, banking, tax havens, military bases, casinos, yacht berths, space tracking facilities, transshipment, flags of convenience, bunkering, waste dumping sites, and various collectors' items.[45] Rather than focusing on exports of highly competitive commodities such as coffee and sugar, exports may be extraordinary commodities such as postage stamps, exotic shells, handicrafts, and even migrant workers. This approach, however, may make some small states vulnerable to being taken advantage of by money launderers and drug traffickers.[46]

Of particular concern in a resource-rich country is the impact of what has become known as the Dutch disease. In the standard model, when an economy experiences a resource boom (either in terms-of-trade improvement or as a result of a resource discovery), both the manufacturing and agricultural sectors tends to shrink (depending on the level of industrialization) and the nontraded-goods sector tends to expand.[47] Additionally, backward and forward linkages seem difficult to achieve in countries where highly capital-intensive extractive industries result in little additional growth in the nontradable sector.[48]

Furthermore, significant relationships have been identified between a dependence on different types of natural resource exports and conflict (although such relationships may be explained differently and may not be found in other studies). Examples of these relationships include:

1. Oil increases the risk of the onset of conflict;[49] the risk of conflict increases with oil dependence;[50] the risk of conflict increases in lower-income countries,[51] particularly in the case of separatist conflict.[52] The chief examples in Africa include conflicts for control of the government in Angola and the secessionist conflicts in Cabinda in Angola, Biafra in Nigeria, and the South of Sudan.[53]
2. Lootable gemstones increase the risk of the onset of ethnic conflict and its duration, chief examples in Africa being Sierra Leone and Democratic Republic of the Congo.[54]
3. Case studies suggest that drugs (cocaine, opium, and cannabis) and timber can be associated with the duration of conflict, the latter in the cases of Liberia and Democratic Republic of the Congo.[55]
4. Both the onset and the duration of conflict are very strongly linked to increases in the quantity of some agricultural goods, especially coffee, cotton, and (in low-income countries) cocoa, while other agricultural goods seem to be unrelated to conflict in Latin America and Africa.[56]

Export dependence exacerbates the problem of managing revenue shocks. In the case of oil windfalls, the most important recommendation drawn from the past is that spending levels should have been adjusted to fast rises in oil income much more carefully than they actually were.[57] Furthermore, decisions about subsidies or levels of expenditure should take into account other factors, such as the composition of consumption (traded versus nontraded) and its potential growth through learning by doing, the absorptive capacity of governments, or the volatility of revenues.[58] The mechanisms for the management of such funds seem to be essentially reliant on good governance, consensual support, and the stability of government policies. Finally, the use of part of the revenues for direct distribution to the populations seems to have both positive and negative economic effects in the short term;[59] however, this application of funds also has the potential to trigger a generalized societal phenomenon of sloth, whereby "men of a fat and fertile soil are most commonly effeminate and cowards; whereas contrariwise a barren country makes men temperate by necessity, and by consequence careful, vigilant, and industrious."[60]

This context is not the same as managing sizable, but temporary, windfall gains in agricultural products. If properly managed, institutional arrangements such as stabilization funds, marketing boards, or private producers' organizations can make it possible to engage in counter-cyclical policies and, in particular, to secure producer prices during negative shocks and to channel, through producers, temporarily high revenues to the capital markets.[61]

Furthermore, rent-seeking activities and parasitic rent appropriations can induce slow economic growth, reduce net returns on capital, and produce a "voracity effect," whereas under a windfall gain there is more than a proportional increase in fiscal redistribution and illegal appropriations. The level of income, the distribution of power and interest groups, and the continuity of government all interact with the institutional capacity to manage this "voracity effect."[62]

Additionally, James Robinson and Ragnar Torvik developed a model where resource rents may make it politically efficient to build "white elephants" (investment projects with negative social surplus) as a way for a politician to secure power through credible redistribution, rather than by building efficient investment projects that would then be followed by all politicians.[63] Gelb and associates identified three important roles for nonresident equity participation in resource-based, export-oriented projects, which could be more broadly applied (a) to check on the realism of feasibility studies by scrutinizing the assessment of the rate of return risk, (b) to facilitate construction, startup, and operation, and (c) to reduce risk by securing markets and reducing the government's stake.[64] Foreign equity should be considerable, at least 30 percent.

The economic conditions in the country—measured in terms of GDP per capita, rate of growth, and income shocks—are found to have a statistically significant correlation with conflict in most studies, especially in low-income countries.[65] Edward Miguel, Shanker Satyanath, and Ernest Sergenti discovered that the link between GDP growth and the incidence of civil war is extremely strong: a 5 percent drop in annual economic growth increases the likelihood of a civil war (more than twenty-five deaths per year) breaking out in the following year by one-half.[66] Other variables, such as GDP per capita, democracy, ethnic diversity, and oil exporter status do not display a similarly robust relationship in sub-Saharan Africa. Christopher Blattman also concludes that (a) rising primary commodity prices are associated with less violence, while falling prices are associated with more violence; (b) the inverse relationship between prices and violence is decreasing with the level of income; and (c) oil exports are associated with lower levels of conflict in middle-income countries, and higher average conflict in low-income countries, among other findings.[67] Additionally, Dal Bó and Dal Bó found that "both theoretical models and empirical evidence suggest that, all else equal, a lower opportunity cost in terms of wages in the labor market should increase the chance that an individual engages in activities such as rebellion or crime."[68]

Complementing the opportunity cost perspective, rather than competing with it, is the argument of the state's weak capacity for repression in its management of conflict. In this sense, it has been argued that the "weak repressive capabilities of African states constitute the background conditions under which poor young men choose between fighting and conventional economic activities. Negative growth shocks make it easier for armed militia groups—which are often major combatants in Africa's civil wars—to recruit fighters from an expanding pool of underemployed youth."[69] Data on regional levels of poverty, hunger and inequality, formal and informal sector structures, composition of income, and household or regional unemployment will certainly provide more insight into these processes.

A related dimension, but inconsistently found to be significant in the statistics of conflict, is inequality. This lack of statistical proof means that Amartya Sen's assertion that "the relation between inequality and rebellion is indeed a close one" remains unproven.[70] Explanations for such disparities have been presented by, among others, Gudrun Ostby, who has concluded that instead of the commonly used indicator for inequality—economic inequality measured by the GINI coefficient—horizontal social inequality is positively related to conflict outbreak.[71] This finding supports Sen's suggestion that the coupling of cultural identities and poverty increases the significance of inequality and may contribute to violence.[72]

Social Factors

Several studies have identified different social characteristics to be significant in the analysis of conflict: these characteristics are either associated with it directly (like ethnic dominance), indirectly (working through the economic, governance, or educational factors), or compounded with other factors (like economic inequality with social fractionalization). For instance, rebel groups in countries without an economic base on which to organize themselves, like in Ethiopia, Eritrea, Uganda, or Rwanda, had to rely on noneconomic means to mobilize and meet the needs of the insurgency.

One interesting conclusion is that societies that are characterized by ethnic and religious diversity are safer than homogeneous societies, so long as they avoid dominance.[73] Ethnic dominance, together with social fractionalization, is found to be associated with conflict onset.[74] Social fractionalization and horizontal social inequality are positively related to conflict outbreak, and variables for ethnic polarization, inter-individual inequalities, and combined ethnic/socioeconomic polarization are not significant.[75] Other studies restrict ethnicity relevance mainly to increase in risk of (ethnic) wars in countries with alluvial diamonds, especially poor countries.[76]

A recent survey done in Africa by Edward Miguel and Daniel N. Prosner reinforces the need for a multivariable approach regarding the analysis of the ethnic factor in conflict studies; it shows that (1) only 41 percent of twenty-four thousand respondents rank their ethnic group as their most important associational membership, and (2) the source of this ethnic identification lies both in exposure to competition for jobs in the nontraditional sectors and in disputing political power such as by participating in a competitive national election.[77] Furthermore, over this same issue of ethnicity Alberto Alesina et al. identifies that

> in general it does not matter . . . whether ethnic differences reflect physical attributes of groups (skin color, facial features) or long-lasting social conventions (language, marriage within the group, cultural norms) or simple social definition (self-identification, identification by outsiders). When people persistently identify with a particular group, they form potential interest groups that can be manipulated by political leaders, who often choose to mobilize some coalition of ethnic groups ("us") to the exclusion of others ("them").

And that

> politicians can also mobilize support by singling out some groups for persecution, where hatred of the minority group is complementary to some policy the politician wishes to pursue.[78]

Finally, two other relations have been identified: population size is positively associated with conflict onset, as it is easier to reach the threshold of conflict deaths;[79] and higher concentration of population corresponds to a lower risk of conflict, as it is easier for the state to provide security.[80]

On the economic and governance side, GDP per capita growth has been found to be inversely related to ethnolinguistic fractionalization, and ethnic and linguistic fractionalization has been associated with negative outcomes in terms of quality of government whereas religious fractionalization has not.[81] William Easterly and Ross Levine have identified that Africa's ethnic diversity tends to slow growth and reduce the likelihood that good policies will be adopted.[82] Of the education indicators, secondary school enrollment has been found to be significantly associated with reducing the onset and duration of conflict.[83] Other social variables, such as health or housing, do not produce significant results in some of the tests, with the exception of the infant mortality rate, which is frequently referred as a good indicator of a country's level of health or development.

Surprisingly, diasporas have been found to be statistically significant in relation to conflict renewal, and it should be stressed that such a result is not related to the intensity of the conflict.[84] One hypothesis put forward to explain this relationship is that diasporas are a source of funding for rebel movements; however, it is not clear how and why diasporas, namely refugees from civil wars living in industrialized nations, have the capacity or interest to finance rebel movements in their home countries. For their part, gender issues are rarely mentioned in relation to conflict. Data unavailability is certainly a major limitation here, but such information could be useful for understanding the broader patterns of violence. For instance, data on domestic violence might denote male and female tensions over their social positioning and circumstances, and could provide information about the degree and trends of violence in a country.

Furthermore, patterns of migration, whether as refugee movements or not, seem to correlate with conflict only when there are neighboring countries at war. However, in this case, the explanations found are either political ones or else relate to rebels operating in more than one country. Also, reintegration policies for ex-combatants can help to reduce the availability of individuals with particular knowledge accumulated throughout the conflict.

More broadly, social capital, defined as the intangible assets available to individuals as a result of their membership in groups, has been identified as a primary factor in determining social processes.[85] A report by the World Bank in 2000 distinguishes between three different types of social capital, all deriving from the concept that membership in groups is important for development: (1) bonding social capital—that is, strong horizontal ties between members, which is important for resource sharing and security; (2) bridging social capital—those horizontal ties that connect individuals more weakly, which is still positive for sharing of information and resources not available from within a country; and (3) linking social capital—the vertical ties between groups for access to markets and resources not otherwise available.[86]

Finally, other less quantifiable processes or characteristics, such as a country's traditional rules and norms, reliance on and characteristics of leadership, levels of trust, rules regarding marriage and its significance, linguistics, networks of formal and informal influence, social support networks (and how, for example, HIV/AIDS is destroying them), behavior and attitude toward animals, as well as many others, have all the potential of being informative about the dynamics of conflict.

Geography

There are specific geographic conditions that favor the activity of rebels and determine their strategies for gaining control over resources. The climate and in particular the resulting environmental conditions affecting livelihoods, have been found to be of particular relevance in determining the likelihood of conflict. Among these geographic factors, the one that has been found by some studies to have an influence on the duration of conflict is forest cover.[87] Another notable variable is proximity to key urban areas; in fact, the further a conflict is from the capital, the longer it lasts.[88] Although, intuitively, mountainous terrain would seem to provide a useful hiding place for rebels, it does not appear to be statistically significant. Nor is the existence of communication channels highlighted in the literature, apart from the possible effect that roads may have on the military's capacity to suppress a rebellion. The level of communication of information—namely, the extent of its penetration into remote regions—could also be of interest, as some studies highlight the finding that a concentration of population decreases conflict. One possible explanation of this finding might be that since poor people are normally less well informed, if rebels are organizing a violent action, the overall quality of information and perceptions about grievances and opportunities will be vital for the success of the techniques of the recruitment process employed by the insurgents. Techniques of manipulation of perceptions through the use of information and propaganda, both by rebels and government, will impact the decisions that people will make whether to adhere to or support a side in the conflict.

Other geographic features, such as adverse weather conditions, seasonal flooding, droughts, arid land, lack of water, low quality agricultural land (with low productivity), and deforestation, are rarely referenced in the literature. This may be due to the fact that they are associated only with minor violence or, more likely, that the effect of these conditions is proxy for the use of the standard economic variables of income. For instance, with drought or flooding the economic activity of the country will decline and such will be captured in the GDP. This is the case with rainfall, which has been found to be statistically related to conflict in sub-Saharan African societies, measured by the resulting economic conditions.[89]

Also relevant to the generation of conflict is the type and distribution of natural resources and the possible strategies for gaining control of them (through conflict) in comparison with their value. Strategies for control will depend on the extent of the state's presence in the region, the concentration of the target resources, whether they are lootable or not, if they are obstructable, and the payoff from control of the resources. The latter will be greatly determined by (a) the value-to-weight ratio, meaning that, for instance, a gemstone may have a high value but little weight, making it easily transportable to market; and (b) the technology cost of the extraction process, which is related to the amount of investment and the complexity of operations necessary to acquire the resources. For instance, the complexities associated with operating deepwater oil wells makes it impossible for non-professional operators to access the oil, in contrast with alluvial diamonds.[90]

History

Time elapsed since last conflict is the most relevant variable in predicting the reemergence of conflict. In addition, insofar as the dynamics of conflict are concerned, directly after a civil war there is a higher probability for a conflict to resume, which likelihood then declines over time.[91] This can be explained by the gradual depreciation of "war capital" as time passes, both physical capital (e.g., weapons) and human capital (e.g., an established rebel group). Also to be taken into account is the progressive fading away of conflict hatreds and the inevitable changes from a wartime to a peacetime economy.

Nevertheless, frequently it is the long narrative of a society that tends to determine current processes. One historical factor studied in the literature is whether and how the colonial legacy has affected the varied institutional settings (the formal and informal mechanisms a society deploys to manage its tensions) of different countries. For instance, James Robinson highlights how, historically, land was not scarce in Africa, and therefore there was no pressure for the development of property rights.[92] Also, during the colonial era, boundaries were determined top down by the colonial powers over the negotiation table, reinforcing the lack of pressure for the development of state administration to secure territory. After independence, the United Nations, the Cold War, or the concern for territorial integrity would stop any issues from arising over borders in Africa. This perspective on history contributes to an explanation of the reduced pressure for the development of institutional settings and instead of the reinforcement of the "personal rule paradigm."[93]

Less quantifiable factors affecting the incidence of conflict are the country's more remote history. For example, past incursions into territories or invasions by others, national or ethnic heroes, traditional strategic alliances, symbolic historical moments, and so on can provide a more "in-depth" body of "subjective" information that can shape the underlying attitudes and behaviors in the present.[94] The same consideration applies to the broader understanding of how regional or world history can shape decisions in the present. As George Orwell asserts in his book *Nineteen Eighty-four*, whoever controls the present controls the past, and whoever controls the past controls the future; Orwell goes on to describe some dynamics of becoming "more equal than others" in his book *Animal Farm*.[95]

In summarizing the critical dynamics of the process of conflict, the main motive for violent conflict seems to be the need to exercise control in a context of poverty. In such cases, we have two extreme kinds of people who are more prone to violent conflict: first, those who have almost no control over the circumstances of their lives, who are living in extreme poverty, who might take part in rebellious activities; and second, people who are in positions to exercise almost absolute control over their own and others' lives, such as an elite in an authoritarian regime, who might take part in rebellions or become involved in coups. This relationship is symbiotic.

The assessments made by either group in taking action are: (a) time and trend dependent—that is: (1) dependent on the instability of control or the volatility of the revenue from resources, such as negative shocks to

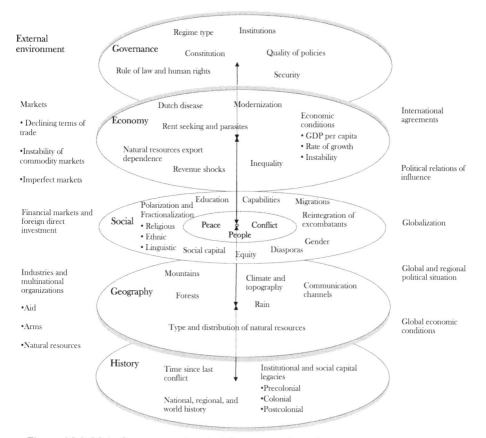

Figure 16.1. Main factors associated with peace and conflict in countries rich in mineral resources or dependent on commodity exports.

agricultural commodity prices, which can result in both increased poverty and the instability of the political center, and (2) dependent on expectations for the future, such as for continued positive or negative economic growth; and (b) based on the viability of conflict—namely, how much can be gained in return from a rebellion or coup, as determined by (3) ongoing domestic and foreign finance during the conflict, (4) the capacity to maintain a conflict group, (5) the likelihood of failure (effective state resistance or the probability of death), and (6) the prize of victory.

Within this assessment, a possible dynamic process focused on the opportunity costs of absolute and relative grievances involving the two groups identified above, wherein the opportunity cost to fight is low if there is too little or too much to lose. Normally, with too little to lose (having virtually no control over one's livelihood), violence is channeled through rebellions, and with too much to lose (having virtually complete control over one's livelihood) violence is channeled through the state or paramilitary forces. There is an "equilibrium" point at which a form of "soft warfare" takes place. In such a case, both absolute and relative grievances are kept in check with some level of violence, crime, or repression (perhaps classified as a "peace episode"), corresponding to a country's specific combination of social grievances and institutional arrangements.

The onset of more violent conflict (i.e., when the "equilibrium" is broken, and the situation moves into a "conflict episode")—hard warfare—is triggered by an unfortunate combination of such diverse factors as poverty, income shocks, the financial viability of fighting, the potential of group cohesion, the instability of the political center, and a weak state apparatus, or by an individual or group capacity to formalize, speculate, or capitalize on these factors.[96] In this case, the situation can move to a higher level of violence (e.g., coups, civil wars, or separatist movements) until either victory or a settlement is achieved (indicating a return to "soft warfare equilibrium"); or it could even move to a state of "hard warfare equilibrium," which can only be broken by a change in the military and financial viability of fighting. Collier, Hoeffler, and Soderbom found that "both peace and civil war are highly persistent states."[97]

There is, however, another type of "equilibrium," or what has been called "soft peacefare," a condition of less inequality, where the likelihood of rebellion is virtually nil and the extent of state violence (human and civil rights violations, for example) and incidence of nonstate violence (crime) decrease significantly (as can be seen in some industrialized nations).[98] The alleviation of the tensions of "soft warfare" in developing countries could mean increasing the opportunity cost of fighting, necessarily through a decrease in relative grievances (e.g., decreasing corruption or rent seeking) and absolute grievances (e.g., improvements in the Human Development Index or a decrease in the percentage of the population living below the poverty line).

Notes

1. I would like to thank the promoters of the PhD course on the "Resource Curse" held June 20–24, 2005, at the Norwegian University of Science and Technology (NUST) and organized jointly by the NUST Department of Economics; the Center for the Study of Civil War at the International Peace Research Institute, Oslo (PRIO); and the Nordic network on the Political Economy of Governance and Conflict (PEGC). Also I would like to thank fellow participants at conferences and one anonymous reviewer for their valuable comments on an earlier version of this text, previously entitled "Managing Conditional Trust: The Resource Curse and the Factors Affecting Conflict." Any remaining errors are my own.

This review does not look into the series of limitations affecting the collection and analysis of data that have been identified elsewhere. See, for example, James Fearon, "Primary Commodities Exports and Civil War," *Journal of Conflict Resolution* 49, no. 4 (2005): 483–507; Edward Miguel, Shanker Satyanath, and Ernest Sergenti, "Economic Shocks and Civil Conflict: An Instrumental Variables Approach," *Journal of Political Economy* 112 (2004): 725–53; Christopher Blattman, "Commodities and Conflict: A Re-examination of the Facts," unpublished working paper, March 2005 (preliminary results), accessed at the PhD course on the "Resource Curse"; Halvard Buhaug and Paivi Lujala, "Accounting for Scale: Measuring Geography in Quantitative Studies of Civil War," *Political Geography* 24, no. 4 (2005): 399–418; Paul Collier and Anke Hoeffler, "Greed and Grievance in Civil War," Oxford Economic Papers, Oxford University Press, vol. 56, no. 4 (October 2004), 563–95; Paivi Lujala, Nils Petter Gleditsch, and Elisabeth Gilmore, "A Diamond Curse? Civil War and a Lootable Resource," *Journal of Conflict Resolution* 49, no. 4 (2005): 538–62; Michael Ross, "Does Oil Hinder Democracy?" *World Politics* 53 (2001): 325–61; and Paul Collier, Anke Hoeffler, and Mans Soderbom, "On the Duration of Civil War," paper prepared for the World Bank, Development Research Group, University of California, Irvine, Center for Global Peace and Conflict Studies, Workshop on "Civil Wars and Post-Conflict Transitions," May 18–20, 2001: 1–31. One should also add to these the limitations of both a time bias (the analyses cover a period of a few decades) and a space bias, since most of the writers reviewed are from developed countries and devote their time to analyzing the dynamics of developing countries.

2. Jeffrey D. Sachs and Andrew M. Warner, "Natural Resource Abundance and Economic Growth," NBER Working Paper No. 5398 (1995), 4. This is often referred to as the Prebish-Singer thesis.

3. Michael Ross, *The Political Economy of the Resource Curse* (Baltimore: Johns Hopkins University Press, 1999), 304.

4. Ibid.

5. Enrique Mendoza, "Terms-of-Trade Uncertainty and Economic Growth," *Journal of Development Economics* 54, no. 2 (December 1997): 323–56.

6. Blattman, "Commodities and Conflict."

7. Commission for Africa, *Our Common Interest*, March 11, 2005, 229.

8. The term *odious* is commonly used to refer to the debts of illegitimate governments that have illegitimately borrowed money in the country's name.

9. Robert Lensink and Oliver Morrissey, "The Volatility of FDI, Not the Level, Affects Growth in Developing Countries," *CDS Research Report Series no. 13* (2002), http://www.rug.nl/cds/_shared/pdf/Respap13.pdf. In developing countries, investment is about 80 percent domestic and 20 percent foreign.

10. TRIMs: Trade-Related Investment Measures; GATS: General Agreement on Trade in Services; TRIPs: Trade-Related Aspects of Intellectual Property Rights. Robert Hunter Wade, "What Strategies Are Viable for Developing Countries Today? The World Trade Organization and the Shrinking of 'Development Space,'" *Crisis States Programme*, Working Paper No. 31 (London: London School of Economics, 2003), 1. This is not to say that development and industrialization are unattainable, as is shown by the number of newly industrialized countries.

11. Ernesto Dal Bó and Pedro Dal Bó, "Workers, Warriors, and Criminals: Social Conflict in General Equilibrium,," paper presented at Sixth Jacques Polak Annual

Research Conference, International Monetary Fund, Washington, DC, November 3–4, 2005, 5.

12. Nancy Birdsall and Arvind Subramanian, "Saving Iraq from Its Oil," *Foreign Affairs* 83, no. 4 (July–August 2004): 77–89.

13. Henry Bernstein, "Studying Development/Development Studies," *African Studies* 65, no. 1 (July 2006): 55.

14. Ibid.

15. Nevertheless, attention must be paid to the concerns about "palliative economics" that the MDG agenda can induce, as illustrated by Erik S. Reinert in "Development and Social Goals: Balancing Aid and Development to Prevent 'Welfare Colonialism,'" paper prepared for the High-level UN Development Conference on MDGs, New York, March 14–15, 2005.

16. Commission for Africa, *Our Common Interest*, 361.

17. Further analysis needs to be made, however, of the different aid mechanisms and the negative effects that these can induce in developing countries.

18. Collier, Hoeffler, and Soderbom, "On the Duration of Civil War."

19. Ibid., 19.

20. Commission for Africa, *Our Common Interest*, 12; United Nations Development Programme, *Human Development Report, 2005* (New York, 2005), 13.

21. Birdsall and Subramanian, "Saving Iraq from Its Oil," 77–89.

22. Swedish International Development Cooperation Agency (SIDA), *Approach and Organisation of SIDA Support to Private Sector Development: Emerging Market Economics in Co-operation with AF-Swedish Management Group*, SIDA Evaluation Report, January 14, 2001, 33.

23. William Easterly and Ross Levine, "Africa's Growth Tragedy: A Retrospective, 1960–89," *Policy Research Working Paper 1503* (Washington, DC: World Bank, 1995), 4.

24. Collier, Hoeffler, and Soderbom, "Duration of Civil War," 11.

25. Paul Collier and Anke Hoeffler, "Greed and Grievance in Civil War," *World Bank Policy Research Working Paper 2355* (May 2004): pp. 563–95, esp. 569; Collier, Hoeffler, and Soderbom, "Duration of Civil War," 12.

26. Lujala, Gleditsch, and Gilmore, "A Diamond Curse?" 538–62, esp. 559.

27. Fearon, "Commodities Exports and Civil War," 483–507, esp. 505.

28. For both (a) and (b), see Richard Damania and Erwin Bulte, "Resources for Sale: Corruption, Democracy, and the Natural Resource Curse" mimeo, University of Adelaide, 2003, 1–28, esp. 7.

29. Ross, "Does Oil Hinder Democracy?" 325–61, esp. 335.

30. Leonard Wantchekon, "Why Do Resource-Abundant Countries Have Authoritarian Governments?" *Yale University Leitner Center Working Paper No. 99-12* (New Haven: Yale University, 1999); in Nathan Jensen and Leonard Wantchekon, "Resource Wealth and Political Regimes in Africa," *Comparative Political Studies* 37, no. 7 (September 2004): 817.

31. Daniel Treisman, "The Causes of Corruption: A Cross-National Study," *Journal of Public Economics* 76, no. 3 (2000): 399–457, in James A. Robinson, "Politician-Proof Policy?" background paper to *World Development Report 2004* (2003), 22.

32. Jensen and Wantchekon, "Resource Wealth and Political Regimes," 821.

33. Alan Gelb et al., "Summary of Findings," chap. 9 of *Oil Windfalls: Blessing or Curse?*, World Bank Research Publication (New York: Oxford University Press, 1988), 134–43, esp. 139.

34. Silje Aslaksen and Ragnar Torvik, "A Theory of Civil Conflict and Democracy in Rentier States," *Scandinavian Journal of Economics* 108, no. 4 (2006): 571–85, esp. 584.

35. Ross, *Political Economy of the Resource Curse*, 321.

36. James Fearon and David Latin, "Ethnicity, Insurgency, and Civil War," *American Political Science Review* 97 (March 2003): 75–90, esp. 75; Herschel I. Grossman, "A General Equilibrium Model of Insurrections," *American Economic Review* 81 (1991): 912–21, esp. 915.

37. Such a downfall is referred to as a negative equilibrium in Halvor Mehlum, Karl Moene, and Ragnar Torvik, "Cursed by Resources or Institutions," *Working Paper Series No. 5705* (Norwegian University of Science and Technology, Department of Economics, 2005).

38. Ibid., 16.

39. Another direction of possible research is into the types of electoral systems, political competition, and the identity or "citizen candidate" pattern, as well as into how these affect the quality of policies and institutions. See John M. Carey and Matthew Soberg Shugart, "Incentives to Cultivate a Personal Vote: A Rank-Ordering of Electoral Formulas," *Electoral Studies* 14 (2006): 417–39. Edwin S. Mills also points out that we can "make much of history intelligible" by assuming "that governments extract from economies under their jurisdiction as much surplus or output as possible and use this surplus to benefit the smallest group possible." Mills, *The Burden of Government* (Stanford: Hoover Institution, 1986), 138.

40. Robinson, "Politician-Proof Policy?"

41. Dal Bó and Dal Bó, "Workers, Warriors, and Criminals," 23.

42. SIDA, *Support to Private Sector Development*, 16.

43. Jensen and Wantchekon, "Resource Wealth and Political Regimes," 817.

44. Robert Hunter Ward, "Earth's Empty Quarter? The Pacific Islands in a Pacific Century," *Geographical Journal* 155, no. 2 (1989): 235–46, esp. 242.

45. Godfrey Baldacchino, "Bursting the Bubble: The Pseudo-Development Strategies of Microstates," *Development and Change* 24, no. 1 (1993): 29–51, esp. 40.

46. Stephanie Fahey, "The Future of East Timor: Threats and Opportunities for Economic Development of a Small Island State," *RIAP Briefing Paper 3*, no. 2 (July 2000): 1–28, esp. 26.

47. Macartan Humphreys, Jeffrey Sachs, and Joseph Stiglitz, eds., introduction to *Escaping the Resource Curse* (New York: Columbia University Press, 2007): 1–21, esp. 5.

48. Ross, *Political Economy of the Resource Curse*, 302; Sachs and Warner, "Natural Resource Abundance," 5.

49. Fearon, "Primary Commodities Exports and Civil War," 18; Michael Ross, "What Do We Know about Natural Resources and Civil War?" *Journal of Peace Research* 41 (2004): 337–56.

50. Collier and Hoeffler, "Greed and Grievance in Civil War," 580.

51. Blattman, "Commodities and Conflict."

52. Ross, "What Do We Know about Natural Resources and Civil War?" 352.

53. Africa's main oil exporters are Angola, Chad, Equatorial Guinea, Gabon, Nigeria, Republic of the Congo, and Sudan.

54. Furthermore, African countries with secondary diamond production where internal conflicts started between 1946 and 2002 are Angola, Central African Republic, Côte d'Ivoire, Democratic Republic of the Congo, Gabon, Ghana, Guinea, Republic of the Congo, Lesotho, Liberia, Mali, Namibia, Sierra Leone, and South Africa, with Tanzania as the only country where conflict was not initiated in the period. For primary diamonds those African countries that initiated conflict in the period were Côte d'Ivoire, Congo, Lesotho, Namibia, Sierra Leone, and South Africa, while Botswana, Tanzania, and Zimbabwe managed to avoid the initiation of conflict. Lujala, Gleditsch, and Gilmore, "Diamond Curse?" 549.

55. Ross, "What Do We Know about Natural Resources and Civil War?" 345–46.

56. Blattman, "Commodities and Conflict"; the following specific resources have been linked to civil war between 1990 and 2000 in Africa: Angola—oil and diamonds; Republic of the Congo—oil; Democratic Republic of the Congo—copper, coltan, diamonds, gold, cobalt and timber; Liberia—timber, diamonds, iron, palm oil, cocoa, coffee, cannabis, rubber, and gold; Sierra Leone—diamonds; and Sudan—oil. Michael Ross, "How Do Natural Resources Influence Civil War? Evidence from Thirteen Cases," *International Organization* 58 (Winter 2004): 35–67, esp. 48.

Additionally, in some situations, such as has been identified for Angola, Liberia, Sierra Leone, Republic of the Congo, and Democratic Republic of the Congo, the use of booty futures—exploitation rights to natural resources that the combatants expect to capture in battle—contributed to both the onset and duration of civil wars. Michael Ross, "Booty Futures," *Working Paper*, May 6, 2005, 4, http://www.sscnet.ucla.edu/polisci/faculty/ross/bootyfutures.pdf.

57. Gelb et al., "Summary of Findings," 139. It has also been suggested that "the optimal share of national wealth consumed each period needs to be adjusted down" and that "the optimal spending path may be increasing or decreasing over time." Egil Matsen and Ragnar Torvik, "Optimal Dutch Disease," *Journal of Development Economics* 78 (2005): 494–515, esp. 494.

58. Matsen and Torvik, "Optimal Dutch Disease," 18. Learning by doing is an economic concept that refers to the capability of workers to improve productivity by regularly repeating the same action. It has been applied to growth theory to explain effects of innovation and technical change. S. van Wijnbergen, "The 'Dutch Disease': A Disease after All?" *Economic Journal* 94 (March 1984): 41–55, esp. 53.

59. For macroeconomic considerations see Gelb et al., "Summary of Findings"; and on the difficulties of managing such systems, see Ross, "What Do We Know about Natural Resources and Civil War?"

60. Jean Bodin, *Six Books of a Commonwealth*, ed. and trans. M. J. Tooley (1576, repr.; New York: Barnes and Noble, 1967), in Sachs and Warner, "Natural Resource Abundance," 4.

61. Jeffrey Davis analyzes the effects of increases in beverages prices (1975–78) in a sample of countries highly dependent on these commodities. See Davis, "The Economic Effect of Windfall Gains in Export Earnings, 1975–1978," *World Development* 11, no. 2 (1983): 119–39.

62. Aaron Tornell and Philip R. Lane, "The Voracity Effect," *American Economic Review* 89, no. 1 (1999): 22–46.

63. James A. Robinson and Ragnar Torvik, "White Elephants," *Journal of Public Economics* 89 (2004): 197–210.

64. Gelb et al., "Summary of Findings," 140–41.

65. Collier and Hoeffler, "Greed and Grievance in Civil War," 588; Collier, Hoeffler, and Soderbom, "Duration of Civil War," 253.

66. Miguel, Satyanath, and Sergenti, "Economic Shocks and Civil Conflict," 725–53, esp. 725.

67. Blattman, "Commodities and Conflict."

68. Dal Bó and Dal Bó, "Workers, Warriors, and Criminals," 2.

69. Miguel, Satyanath, and Sergenti, "Economic Shocks and Civil Conflict," 728.

70. Amartya Sen, "Violence, Identity, and Poverty," *Journal of Peace Research* 45, no. 1 (2008): 5–15, opening page in Collier and Hoeffler, "Greed and Grievance in Civil War," 572.

71. Gudrun Ostby, "Polarization, Horizontal Inequalities, and Violent Civil Conflict," *Journal of Peace Research* 45, no. 2 (2008): 143–62; horizontal inequality occurs when power and resources are unequally distributed between groups that are also differentiated in other ways—for instance, by race, religion, or language.

72. Other theoretical models also analyze this relationship. For instance, Dal Bó and Dal Bó, "Workers, Warriors, and Criminals," 23, developed a model compatible with the positive correlation between crime and inequality, although the theory also predicts that reducing inequality without affecting the incentives to undertake productive activities may not diminish conflict (as with social programs that provide lump-sum redistributions).

73. Collier, Hoeffler, and Soderbom, "Duration of Civil War," 4.

74. Ethnic fractionalization increases when the number of ethnic groups in a society increases, and it can be interpreted as the probability that two randomly selected individuals belongs to different ethnic groups. Ethnic polarization increases when there are few (equally) large groups with homogeneous characteristics within each group, and differences in a cluster of characteristics among groups. Indexes of polarization are highest when there are two relatively large groups of exactly the same size. Ibid., 14.

75. Ostby, "Polarization, Horizontal Inequalities, and Conflict," 143.

76. Lujala, Gleditsch, and Gilmore, "Diamond Curse?" 559.

77. Edward Miguel and Daniel N. Prosner, "Sources of Ethnic Identification in Africa" (unpublished), accessed at the PhD course on the "Resource Curse" (see note 1).

78. Edward Glaeser, "The Political Economy of Hatred," *Quarterly Journal of Economics* 120, no. 1 (January 2005): 45–86.

79. Fearon and Latin, "Ethnicity, Insurgency, and Civil War," 75.

80. Collier and Hoeffler, "Greed and Grievance in Civil War," 588.

81. Alberto Alesina et al., "Fractionalization," *Journal of Economic Growth* 8 (2003): 155–94, esp. 183.

82. Easterly and Levine, "Africa's Growth Tragedy," 4.

83. Collier, Hoeffler, and Soderbom, "Duration of Civil War," 266.

84. Collier and Hoeffler, "Greed and Grievance in Civil War," 588.

85. SIDA, *Support to Private Sector Development*, 40. There are diverse definitions of social capital, but most are associated with some sort of benefit or resources (effective or potential) that an individual or group can access by sharing or have relationships within a certain group or network.

86. World Bank, *World Development Report 2000/1: Attacking Poverty* (New York: Oxford University Press, 2000), 128.

87. Collier, Hoeffler, and Soderbom, "Duration of Civil War," 11.

88. Buhaug and Lujala, "Accounting for Scale," 399–418, esp. 412.

89. See Miguel, Satyanath, and Sergenti, "Economic Shocks and Civil Conflict," 728.

90. For an analysis of these factors, see Philippe Le Billon, "The Political Ecology of War: Natural Resources and Armed Conflicts," *Political Geography* 20, no. 5 (2001): 561–84.

91. Collier and Hoeffler, "Greed and Grievance in Civil War," 589.

92. Robinson, "Politician-Proof Policy?" 24.

93. The "personal rule paradigm" concept emerged in the 1980s to denote what scholars had previously labeled "patrimonialism" or "neopatrimonialism." In the African context it is a short description to describe patronage politics where the distribution of public goods is made based on loyalty.

94. "Objective" information refers to the hard currency of information-processing devices of all kinds, is used to transmit impersonal knowledge and is readily quantifiable and ultimately reducible to binary digits; "subjective" information is inextricably bound up with issues of meaning, value, and perspective, and thus would seem to defy such universal quantification. Robert Jahn and Brenda Dunne, "Science of the Subjective," *Journal of Scientific Exploration* 11, no. 2 (1997): 201–24.

95. George Orwell, *Nineteen Eighty-four* (1949; repr., London: Penguin Books, 2000); George Orwell, *Animal Farm* (1945; repr., New York: Houghton Mifflin, 2003).

96. Political conditions, where this individual and group agency takes form, is the least studied of the three effects of the "resource curse" according to George Soros. The other two are the economic factors of the "Dutch disease" and fluctuations in commodity prices. George Soros, foreword, in Humphreys, Sachs, and Stiglitz, *Escaping the Resource Curse*, xi.

97. Collier, Hoeffler, and Soderbom, "Duration of Civil War," 5.

98. In "Greed and Grievance in Civil War," Collier and Hoeffler present a model that "predicts that a hypothetical country with all the worst characteristics found in our sample have [*sic*] a near-certain risk of war, while one with all the best characteristics would have a negligible risk" (580).

17

The Politics of Oil and Development and Visual Metaphors of the Crisis in Nigeria's Niger Delta

ADERONKE ADESOLA ADESANYA

Introduction

Nigeria's Niger Delta is an engaging phenomenon in view of its history, complexities, paradoxes, and challenges. Although much has been discussed in the existing literature about the region, it has continued to generate fresh debates and new issues over the politics of representation, the politics of oil, and the appropriation of political space and control of conflict theaters by a select few. With this contextual background, in this chapter I examine the situation of Niger Delta women, especially the rural poor, and how their art mirrors this situation and the oil conflict in the region. I will structure my arguments around five key issues: First, I provide an overview of what is known about the Niger Delta (ND), in particular its history of violence and unrest, and a characterization of the different politics that have marked the region's struggles. Second, using images that explicate and articulate my arguments, I will identify what is largely ignored in the ND crises to which some artistic representations point, and explain why. The muting of the female voice in the ND, the underdevelopment of women, and their omission or underrepresentation in policy and intervention concerning the region are tangential issues that have not been discussed in the context of resolving the ND crises. Third, I shall underscore the importance of addressing this largely ignored segment of the Niger Delta, and my argument will interface with the conflict economy that has emerged in the region, as well as the amnesty program instituted by the federal government of Nigeria in August 2009 to grant state pardon to militants in the Niger Delta. Fourth, I will attempt to outline the complications that are apparent in the ongoing amnesty project and how the current efforts by the Nigerian government may not abate the crisis in the area. Finally, I will discuss the fragility of hope in the region, the implications of compromising and undermining significant vulnerable groups, especially women, in the Niger Delta population, and the overarching importance of this phenomenon for globalization and sustainable development. The issues of peace, development, and the influence of globalization in the region cannot be comprehensively addressed without factoring women into the overall equation. Moreover, both development and globalization are ideological battlegrounds where power and resources, among other things, are contested by many actors and won by the privileged few. Power controls and shapes development as it does globalization. Those who have it dispossess, delegitimize, disenfranchise, and even demonize others in order to maintain their hegemony, as is clearly observable in the Niger Delta.

This chapter benefits from existing literature, archival records, and direct field investigation. A lot has been written on the Niger Delta, and in addition to presenting an overview, I set forth new arguments and proffer a way forward. The arguments are advanced within the context of two theoretical models: greed and grievance theory as canvassed by Paul Collier and Anke Hoeffler and patriarchy.[1]

The Niger Delta Paradox: Resource Wealth and Resource Curse

The Niger Delta is a region of geopolitical significance to Nigeria in view of the oil wealth it generates (see fig. 17.1).[2] This wealth, derived from oil exports, has made the Nigerian economy heavily dependent on the oil sector, while underscoring the country's importance to the world oil economy.[3] The oil-rich region is also a tension zone and is at the center of contemporary Nigerian politics, especially as major political upheavals emanate from this conflict hub or are indirectly connected to the confrontations experienced elsewhere within the country. Since the time when oil was discovered at Oloibiri in 1956 by Shell Petroleum Development Company, Nigeria has experienced a mixture of blessings and curses arising from its oil wealth. Confrontations between the Nigerian state and the people of the ND are commonplace, and the literature has documented the various dimensions of conflict in the region.[4]

The root cause of the unrest in the ND has been identified as the high level of environmental degradation that occurs as a result of oil exploration and exploitation and the sheer neglect of the area in spite of local outcries for the state to intervene. These issues, above all others, have led to repeated demands by the people in the ND on both the federal government and multinational oil companies operating in the region, including Royal Dutch Shell and Chevron Corporation, to ameliorate the prevalent

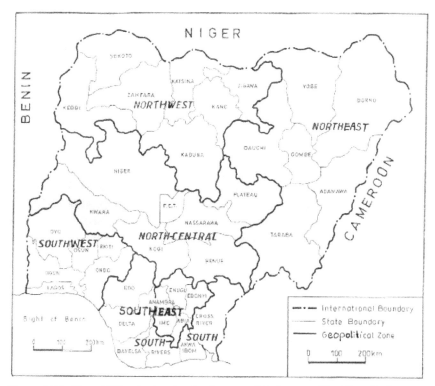

Figure 17.1. Map of Nigeria showing its six geopolitical zones. The Niger Delta states are in the South-South (Akwa Ibom, Bayelsa, Delta, Edo, Cross River, and Rivers), the Southwest (Ondo), and the Southeast (Abia and Imo). Map courtesy of Aderonke Adesanya.

dehumanizing conditions, poverty, and suffering. Critics charge the oil companies with responsibility for widespread pollution including oil spills, toxic waste dumping, and excessive gas flaring, all of which constitute great hazards to the region's people.

Indeed, one could say that greed (i.e., "profit maximization") alone goes a long way toward explaining the actions of the oil companies in the way they externalize their waste to reduce their operating costs. Max Spielbichler has argued that "the most probable reason" for companies' dumping of "their waste in the delta for the past 50 years is to reduce their cost of production. Externalizing is when a firm is pushing its costs off to a third party, so in this case, the oil companies are pushing the costs of taking care of the waste off onto society, which has disastrous effects on population and environment."[5] No serious attempt has been made either by the oil companies or by the federal government to stop the environmental degradation and clean up the oil spillage. Observers and analysts blame the oil spills on poor maintenance of pipelines (that become corroded after protracted use) and other infrastructure weaknesses. Other dangers result from deliberate vandalization of equipment. The scale of pollution and environmental harm has never been properly assessed; figures vary considerably depending on sources. However, it is widely acknowledged that the number of spills each year is in the hundreds.[6]

To cushion the effects of the loss of land and livelihood and to guard against the threat of food insecurity, the Nigerian government has been pressured at various times to ensure that adequate resource allocation, commensurate with what the region contributes to the national treasury, be given to the ND for necessary development. To date, in spite of the many entreaties and the successive agitations that have occurred, the region lays in waste, denuded of its natural resources. It is arguably now the least developed of the geopolitical regions in Nigeria.[7] Indeed, the degree of neglect confirms the reality that the people there are impoverished amidst great wealth. In addition to neglect, the massive pollution constitutes a major threat to food, health, and human security.[8]

Embattled on all fronts, the people of the ND are being pushed to the limits by the dehumanizing and hazardous conditions in their immediate environment. As a result, their anger over the high degree of corruption and looting of oil wealth (which could have been used for development and to save the inhabitants from peril) has raised the level of tension in an already tense region. It was apparent since the early 1990s that the agitation of the ND people would eventually erupt in violence. Several warnings were sounded against the apathy displayed by the Nigerian government. For instance, a year before the events of September 11, 2001, the US State Department in its annual assessment of global terrorist threats identified the Niger Delta—the geographic heart of oil production in Nigeria—as a breeding ground for militants, noting the "impoverished ethnic groups" who had already been involved in numerous terrorist acts (e.g., abductions, hostage taking, kidnapping, and extrajudicial killings).

As predicted, a spate of violent reactions from different groups and stakeholders, including restive youths in the region, has created continual unrest within the country. Young militants, obviously irked by the gross neglect and indifference shown by the federal government, have repeatedly vandalized pipelines and engaged federal troops in a series of battles in the creeks.

From the foregoing, one could deduce that grievance against the Nigerian state for its inattention to issues of the region's development is the underlying factor motivating the militants. However, later actions that involve hostage taking and oil bunkering are symptomatic of the theory of greed.[9] "Greed" here is shorthand for the argument that combatants in armed conflicts are motivated by a desire to better their own situation and thus perform an informal cost-benefit analysis in deciding whether the rewards of joining a rebellion are greater than what might be lost from not joining. This is different from grievance, which may arise from injustice or tyranny visited on a group, community, or region, and could cause militants or combatants to launch a rebellion or revolution. Grievance stands for the argument that people rebel over issues of identity—ethnicity, religion, social class, and so on—rather than over economics.

Given the scenario that oil-related crime and criminality now pervades the region, whereby politicians, soldiers, and militants alike compete for control of the oil for personal gain, the rebels have since abandoned their initial grievance motivation. Statistics that support this view are staggering: The International News Service Agency reports that in the course of their struggle, the militants have kidnapped hundreds of people and carried out attacks on numerous oil installations. The Niger Delta Technical Committee—a forty-five-person body established by the federal government to seek a solution to the Delta crisis—found that in 2008 alone, three hundred hostages were taken and about one thousand people are estimated to have been killed in violence committed by the Delta militants.[10] Hostage taking and attacks on oil pipelines continued into 2009, with victims including civilians, celebrities, and relatives of businessmen.[11]

To intensify the effect of their rebellion, the militants in June 2009 moved farther south to attack oil stations in Lagos, to the chagrin of the Lagos state government and indeed other Yoruba groups who felt that the attack was misguided. They unequivocally condemned it and warned that a repeat of such an act would generate an unprecedented strong reaction. Basically, the sympathy that the Niger Delta people received from those in other regions, particularly in the Southwest, eroded in the wake of the attacks on oil stations in Lagos. In the same month, the federal government extended an olive branch to the restive youths in the region promising them amnesty if they would surrender their guns and ammunition to assigned centers in the nine ND states. The amnesty program ended in October 2009. Although some rebels responded and surrendered various weapons, many observers question the sincerity of both parties, that is, the government and the militants.

I shall return to the issue of amnesty later in this chapter. Suffice it to say that four major political issues come to the fore in the Niger Delta crisis, apart from the aforementioned degradation of land and the indigenous communities' loss of livelihood—namely, territoriality and identity, marginalization, self-determination, and resource control. Resource control is the quest for autonomy and power by a people to administer the economic resources within their geographical, political, and cultural space. From the viewpoint of the Niger Delta people, it exemplifies their struggle to gain autonomy, to control the exploitation of oil in the region, and to have a substantial part of the income generated from oil prospecting used to develop the area.

The periods before and immediately after oil was discovered in the Niger Delta region were characterized by the politics of territoriality and identity. The politics of territoriality manifested itself in the confrontations between groups, principally the Ijaw and the Itsekiri. Prolonged internecine wars broke out between these groups over land allocation and dividends of development. The Ijaw, the most dominant group in the Niger Delta and largely domiciled in the creeks, had accused the Itsekiri, who live on the land, of being unduly favored by the government above other ethnic groups in the region. The Ijaw believed that owing to their sheer numbers, they deserved to have greater access and control over social benefits. Their struggle waned after the two groups decided that their common enemy was the government and that all groups in the region were grossly neglected; as a result, pressure groups emerged in different parts of the region to pursue a pan-Delta agenda for reclamation, restoration, resource control, and an end to official neglect. The politics of identity began in the late 1950s after the discovery of oil as different groups laid claim to the Niger Delta region in view of the prospective oil revenues that would necessarily accrue to groups that resided within the territory. Historically and cartographically, the original Niger Delta currently comprises six Nigerian states: Akwa Ibom, Bayelsa, Cross River, Delta, Edo, and Rivers. The region was expanded in the year 2000 by former President Obasanjo to include three other states, namely Abia, Imo, and Ondo. The rallying point of these states is that they are oil-producing communities and thus deserve percentages from the federal government. The Nigerian government granted the states oil revenues of 13 percent as against the 27 percent they demanded, but the clamor for greater revenue has not stopped.

The leading figure in the campaign protesting political marginalization was Ken Saro-Wiwa, the late environmental activist, who along with others (popularly known as the Ogoni Nine) became victims of judicial murder during the regime of General Sanni Abacha, Nigeria's enfant terrible, authoritarian leader, and maximum ruler. Saro-Wiwa and his compatriots, championing their people's cry of having endured many years of gross neglect and underdevelopment, formed the formidable group called Movement for the Survival of the Ogoni People (MOSOP) in 1992. Under the aegis of MOSOP, they called on the Nigerian state to end the political and economic marginalization of the Niger Delta, make good the (empty) promises of the 1970s and 1980s, and cease the escalating military repression taking place in the region. The challenge was a costly confrontation with Abacha's despotic regime. State-sponsored violence worsened in 1994 causing more than two thousand civilian deaths, the internal displacement of more than one hundred thousand residents, and the destruction of at least thirty villages. In the context of the protests, violence, counterviolence, and military repression, Ken Saro-Wiwa and his group were framed for the gruesome plot that claimed the lives of four Ogoni chiefs. They were tried without fair hearings and sentenced to death by hanging on November 10, 2005. Their executions ended their quest for the actualization of their dream of an emancipated Niger Delta and truncated the advancement of the MOSOP's ideology.[12] But the politics of marginalization did not die with the exit of those who conceived the idea within the Niger Delta theater of conflict. Rather, the movement gained momentum in later struggles by other stakeholders in the region. It is this ideology that influenced the campaign of the South-South people and their demand for equity, fairness, and justice in the administration of the Nigerian state. The politics of marginalization is underscored by the way policies inimical to the progress and development of the Niger Delta are made by Nigeria's majority ethnic groups against the interests of the region's minorities. Iyenemi Wokoma captures the situation in an essay on women's nonviolent protests in the ND:

> Nigeria is a monocultural economy that relies on oil as the main source of its revenue. Nearly all of the nation's oil reserves are found in the Niger Delta or the South-South geopolitical zone, which is primarily inhabited by ethnic minority communities of southern Nigeria, including, among others, the Ijaw, Ibibio, Efik, Bini, Urhobo, Itsekiri and Ogoni. Yet, decisions concerning ownership and/or allocation of the revenues derived from oil are made in a National Assembly where, together, the three major ethnic groups (Hausa-Fulani, Yoruba, and Igbo) amongst Nigeria's approximately 350 ethnic nationalities form a collective majority. Since independence, agitations by the indigenes of the Niger Delta region have centred on guaranteeing fairness and equity in the distribution of political power and economic resources.[13]

The politics of self-determination began in the late 1990s through the struggle of the Ijaw against the Nigerian state over unbridled exploitation of their land.[14] The Ijaw in Bayelsa State began a conscious struggle for self-determination and resource control with the formation of the Ijaw Youth Council (IYC) and the issuing of the Kaiama Declaration. They called for the suspension of operations and withdrawal of the oil companies from Ijaw territory. They commemorated the struggle with what was known as Operation Climate Change in December 1998. The government saw this as a challenge to its sovereign authority and moved its troops, numbering over ten thousand, to occupy Bayelsa and Delta states in order to contain the protesting IYC. The military occupation of these regions resulted in grave casualties.[15] Concurrent with the politics of self-determination is the politics of marginalization. Indeed, one could argue that the latter gave rise to the former in the sense that the quest for self-determination was informed by the refusal of the Nigerian state to grant the Niger Delta people any meaningful recognition within the nation's polity and to enable them to enjoy the enormous wealth that their communities contribute to the state.

The politics of resource control—that is, direct political power by the people of the area in question over resource production, management, and utilization, in order to ensure regeneration of the environment and overall sustainable human development—is an offshoot of the politics of self-determination. The latter concerns conscious efforts by Niger Delta peoples to confront the reality of inequity in the oil-revenue-sharing formula of the Nigerian state and demand change. When the revenue sharing began in 1958, the ND region received a 50 percent share. However, things took a downward turn; from 1968 to 1989 the states in the region earned as low as 10 percent. Resistance and agitation by local people had some impact on the federal government, which raised the stake from 10 percent to 13 percent (see table 17.1). However, the increased allocation still did not appear commensurate to the degree of decimation observable in the region and did not translate into any meaningful development. Thus, having realized that the Nigerian state was not ready to accede to their request, and in view of the fact that the control of all petroleum activities and revenue generation is vested in the Nigerian state by virtue of the Petroleum Act of 1969 and Section 40(3) of the 1979 Constitution of the Federal Republic of Nigeria, ND stakeholders began campaigning for greater involvement of the region in determining how national oil revenues are shared. Indeed, in tandem with the concept of resource control, the people demanded autonomy to control whatever is generated from oil prospecting within the oil-producing states. Itse Sagay sheds further light on the concept:

> While resource control should naturally result in increased revenue from the proceeds of the resource for the communities where it is located, the more important aspect of this concept is the involvement of the communities in the actual control and management of the resource. It is about the right of states and communities most directly affected to have a direct and decisive role in the exploration, exploitation and disposal, including sales, of the resource. The argument for resource control is that it is those who live with the devastating consequences of irresponsible exploitation practices who must control the method and management of commercial production to ensure an environment-friendly production process, elimination of pollution, protection of the land, forests, rivers and atmosphere.[16]

To the four major political issues discussed above, I add the politics of development, a concept that describes the activities of the federal government, leaders in the ND states, and youth militants, and through which I question the genuineness of the actions of all stakeholders on the one hand, and the appropriateness and effectiveness of various interventionist development projects on the other.[17] The argument being advanced here is that the federal government of Nigeria as well as the stakeholders and militants in the Niger Delta have, thus far, been playing varying degrees of politics when it comes to regional development.

Table 17.1. Nigeria's oil-revenue-sharing formula, selected years, 1958–2001 (percent)

Year*	Federal	State	Local	Special projects	Derivation formula**
1958	40	60	0	0	50
1968	80	20	0	0	10
1977	75	22	3	0	10
1982	55	32.5	10	2.5	10
1989	50	24	15	11	10
1995	48.5	24	20	7.5	13
2001	48.5	24	29	7.5	13

* Indicates period when oil revenue–sharing formula was implemented (1958) and reviewed (1968–2001).
** Annual percentage; for example, the oil-derivation-sharing formula was 50 percent in 1958, but was then reduced drastically (e.g., to 13 percent in 2001).

It is significant to note the change in the allocation curve. From 1968 forward, more of the revenue went to the federal government's coffers than to the states'. This is a root cause of conflict between the Niger Delta region and the Nigerian government.

Source: Federal Republic of Nigeria, *Official Gazette* 96, no. 2 (February 2, 2009).

On several fronts, the government has been criticized for being more concerned with safeguarding the interests of multinational corporations operating in the region than with securing the health and wealth of its people. While this is understandable from a business standpoint as the oil companies are in a joint venture with the Nigerian National Petroleum Corporation (NNPC), thus tying the government's fortunes to those of the companies, an attack on any of the multinational oil companies is perceived by the government as an attack on the state and its financial base. The government has therefore promptly responded to such attacks by ordering troops to contain the militants in the Niger Delta. It did so in May 1994 when it sent in troops and unleashed brutal repression on the Ogoni people. Later that year, in November, a massacre occurred at Odi in Rivers State. In order not to be seen as repressing its citizens, to douse the tension in the region, and to create an enabling atmosphere for the MNCs to work, President Olusegun Obasanjo's regime established the Niger Delta Development Corporation (NDDC) in the year 2000. The NDDC was to replace the comatose Oil Mineral Producing Areas Development Commission (OMPADEC), which was set up in 1989 to enhance development in the oil-producing communities. It was funded with

3 percent annual allocation from the federal budget but yielded little or no development. The government also set up the Petroleum Trust Fund (PTF) on March 21, 1995, to finance infrastructure projects. The PTF gets a certain percentage of the profits from the local sale of refined petroleum products. Unlike OMPADEC, the PTF was not intended to cater exclusively to the oil communities, but undertakes projects in all parts of the country. The oil communities themselves, however, clearly did not consider OMPADEC and PTF to be sufficient. OMPADEC in particular was criticized for its wastefulness, massive mismanagement, and corruption.

The failure of OMPADEC led to the formation of the NDDC. It was hoped that through this agency, most of the concerns and demands of the people from the region would be met. But very little has been achieved since its inception. The Ministry of Niger Delta Affairs (also known as Niger Delta Ministry) was also created in 2008 by former president Umaru Yar'Adua (with the NDDC becoming one of its units). This, too, has failed in terms of matching the realities and expectations of the region's embattled peoples; indeed, they see the NDDC and the ministry as "white elephant" projects. Concerning the activities of the ministry, the editorial comment of the *Vanguard* of July 31, 2009, puts it succinctly:

> Efforts at redeeming the damage done to the Niger Delta region are increasingly becoming facades, charades and circuses—government actions consistently fail to match the intent of those acclaimed efforts. The activities of the Ministry of Niger Delta Affairs, starting from the location of its headquarters in Abuja, rather than the ravaged Niger Delta, serve as premium examples of how the Federal Government develops the Niger Delta with words.[18]

The editorial notes that the ministry, under the leadership of Chief Ufot Ekaete, instead of hosting its multimillion-dollar project (which it tagged the Job Creation Fair/Training Expo 2009) somewhere in one of the nine states in the Niger Delta, held it at the International Conference Center, Abuja.[19] The choice of a venue outside the Delta seriously marred the initiative since those meant to benefit from the exercise could not even afford to travel to Abuja. Had the fair been held in state capitals of the Niger Delta states (e.g., Akure, Yenagoa, Calabar, Asaba, Benin City, Owerri, Port Harcourt, Uyo), many of the job seekers would have been able to participate. Having summarized the collective travails of the peoples of the Niger Delta, I will now turn to what has been ignored in the struggle.

Imaging and Imagining Gender and Development in the Niger Delta

In the vanguard of the movement to end exploitation of the Niger Delta and of the quest for self-determination are the leadership of communities and militant youths, predominantly men. Men, more than women, occupy a central position in the ND's struggles. Yet, it must be said that the problems at issue impact women as much as men, and that women, too, have staged protests at various times to condemn the precarious conditions in the region and to demand change.[20] The history of women's struggle and movement in Nigeria is well documented, especially in the excellent studies by Nina Mba and Bolanle Awe.[21] Taking their cue from examples in other parts of the country, ND women have adopted a nonviolent approach to bringing positive changes to their environment. Literary and artistic works have commented on the nonviolent protests these women have staged. For instance, Bruce Onabrakpeya's *Nude Protest* (fig. 17.2) is a visual commentary on a typical revolutionary protest in which women marched through the streets naked to the site of an oil company to decry the environmental pollution of the ND and the denial of jobs to ND indigenes in the oil companies operating in the region.[22] In representing the neglected communities in the context of development and interventions in the Niger Delta, they chose to act based on their solidarity with these communities; the particularities of their needs as caregivers, and their vulnerability during and in the aftermath of conflict.

In dealing with the issue of women in the Niger Delta, I will first set forth the parameters of my assessment lest this argument be categorized along with those dismissed by Olufemi Taiwo as advancing a prima facie oppression of women.[23] Women are not a homogeneous group, and their experiences at different places and times are not monolithic. Even when they live within the same areas, variations in their experiences and socialization do occur, based on such factors as class.

Guided by these considerations, I will delineate those women I view as being subjected to hardship in the Niger Delta. These are the poor rural women of the oil-bearing communities who are the focus of several existing studies that have confirmed the precarious conditions in which they live.[24] The experiences of men and women are not the same. And there is a big difference in the daily experiences of poor rural women in comparison to those of the female elites. Thus, in view of these differences, ignoring or undermining the rural women who suffer most in the Niger Delta crises invariably subjects them to the double jeopardy of denial and pain—in terms of their vulnerability and the indignities they have undergone. Indeed, it could be argued that these women suffer more than anyone else in the calamities, dislocations, exploitation, and land degradation afflicting the Niger Delta. To cite just one example, oil spillage, this recurrent problem leads to scarcity of basic amenities, which in turn creates physical and psychological trauma for women. When there is no drinking water and water for cooking, washing clothes and dishes, bathing, and doing other household chores, women are thrown into chaos. They must seek alternatives for meeting their

Figure 17.2. *Nude Protest* by Bruce Onabrakpeya (media: plastograph). © by the artist, reproduced with permission.

basic domestic needs and the requirements of those to whom they cater in their homesteads.

Even these daily discomforts are negligible compared to the deepening crisis engendered by other fallouts of oil spills and oil exploration mishaps. When these occasion grave loss of livelihood, the women and their vulnerable dependents are hardest hit. They have to seek other avenues for survival, which may mean migrating to other regions within the country or to other countries in search of menial jobs; or worse, to the commoditizing of their bodies such as when girls resort to prostitution or child labor. With such negative impacts on their health, pregnant women end up giving birth to children with congenital defects. And worse still, in the midst of the frequent confrontations between militants and federal troops over territorial space, women and girls, especially those living in villages, suffer at the hands of invading soldiers who seek out women and girls to sexually assault. The militants, whose offensives attract government reprisals, often escape to hideouts in the creeks leaving women, children, and the aged at the mercy of irate soldiers.

The question thus arises: if women suffer so much, why are they not taken into account in the efforts to bring lasting peace to the Niger Delta? A number of reasons could be adduced. One reason is their lack of voice and outright denial. Their protests are largely ignored, and this official neglect is underscored by women's lack of access to the structures of development. In view of the patriarchal society in which they live, it is difficult for women to access the opportunities that male-dominated pressure groups obtain from government or from multinational oil companies. Unless the power structures within the region are reformed, resistance approaches employed by women will continue to be less effective than those by men.

Pivotal to my discussion are two artworks (figs. 17.3, 17.4 and 17.5) that foreground the nexus between art and the politics of oil and development in the Niger Delta. During one of my visits to the Niger Delta area, I saw two sculptures of note among the garden statuary created by art students of Delta State University, at Abraka. I was struck by their visual power as carriers of meaning; their apprehension and representation of time; their articulation of the social reality of the Niger Delta region; and their codification of the notions of power, politics, and gender. Art, above everything else, has always provided a viable window for looking at various societies. As an art historian, I use artistic expressions to understand phenomenon; examine communities; contemplate their nuances and challenges, in order to tease debates on the moments and events that are played out in such localities; theorize; and arrive at logical conclusions. Images are subject to multiple interpretations, manifestations, and manipulations that can be literal or metaphorical, implicit or explicit. As regards the interpretation of art, meaning—that is, the message or idea in a work of art—can be derived in two key ways: through the expressive qualities and aesthetics employed by the artist, and its relationship to the social context in which the art piece was made.

Figure 17.3. *Resource Control/Bunkering* by Philip Nzekwe (media: metal, cement fondue). Photograph courtesy of Aderonke Adesanya, at Delta State University, Abraka, Nigeria, January 2009.

Figure 17.4. *Resource Control/Bunkering* by Philip Nzekwe. Photograph courtesy of Aderonke Adesanya, at Delta State University, Abraka, Nigeria, January 2009.

Figure 17.5. *Peasant Female* by Benedicta Okotie (media: polyester). Photograph courtesy of Aderonke Adesanya, at Delta State University, Abraka, Nigeria, January 2009.

In looking at the two sculptures, I take a cue from the synchronic tradition, a Western formal criterion for studying art forms that evolved in the mid-1900s and that advocates examination of artworks within their specific historical and geographic contexts. The meaning for these two artworks is drawn from the events that shape the socioeconomic conditions in the Niger Delta region. These images articulate well the realities, paradoxes, and complications of the Niger Delta situation. Although the images do not fully represent the cultures in the nine states that make up the Niger Delta, they explicate the nuances, differences, and similarities inherent in them. They reference the prevailing conflict economy in the region, as well as gender and class issues.

Figure 17.3, *Resource Control/Bunkering*, is a visual metaphor of dramatic personae in the politics of oil in the Niger Delta. Chieftains of the ND communities who have been identified in literature as a significant group among those largely behind oil bunkering in the region typically dress in this fashion.[25] Although generally Niger Delta adult males wear long shirts over wrappers and fedora-style hats as traditional garb for special ceremonies, the rows of beads on the neck of the sculpted figure are distinctive of leaders in the communities rather than any anonymous figure.[26] Indeed, the artist did not hint at the anonymous; his choice of visual idiom is deliberate to underscore the fact that the affluent and influential are those responsible for the chaos in the Niger Delta. The oil drums that the person drags behind him (fig. 17.4) evoke his nefarious engagements and speak to the larger issue of oil bunkering in the Nigerian state. Many oil bunkerers apprehended by law enforcement agencies have been caught with truckloads of oil drums stacked and being carted away to various destinations. Their illegal exploitation of oil is well established in the literature. For instance a report by Eghosa Osaghae et al. note that

> from the coastal states of Nigeria, specifically in the swamps of the Niger Delta in Delta, Rivers, Cross River, Akwa Ibom, Ondo, and Bayelsa States, large inventories of stolen crude oil or petroleum products are typically trans-shipped into larger ocean-faring marine vessels, waiting patiently on stand-by, either mid-stream, or offshore, for their booty. In the hinterland, particularly in Abia, Benue, Delta, Enugu, Edo, Kogi, Ondo, Lagos, and Ogun States, large inventories of refined petroleum products (petrol, kerosene and diesel oil) are loaded directly into tanker trucks from the point of deliberate rupture of petroleum products pipelines that traverse the length and breadth of Nigeria.[27]

Lastly, the oil pipes laid out behind the figure are visual codes that reference the vandalization of pipelines, a common practice in the region. There is a broad consensus that a "crimogenic" environment has been created in the Niger Delta with the sponsors being principally the political class—namely, the leadership of the Niger Delta communities (chiefs and traditional rulers), politicians, businessmen, police, and military personnel—all of whom struggle to control bunkering routes and illegally acquire oil blocs.[28] These people have been identified as powerful "shadow" parties in the orchestration of violence and unrest in the region;[29] they sponsor criminality to further their economic as well as political ambitions and sponsor crises because they profit from it. They incite militant youths to vandalize oil pipelines, in order to draw the attention of both the state and the oil companies and obtain privileges and favors. They are essentially *conflict entrepreneurs* who profit from the chaos in the Niger Delta. For them, to end the crises in the region is not an attractive option. The amnesty program introduced by the Nigerian government in June 2009 threatens their hegemony. The gender makeup of these groups is predominantly male, with negligible female participation. Hence, the artist Phillip Nzekwe has chosen the male figure dressed in chiefly robes to typify and satirize the bunkerers, the leadership, and the political class. *Resource Control/Bunkering* dramatizes the oil politics in the Niger Delta and satirizes what was initially a collective agenda and has now become a private and personal agenda of a few elites who appropriate resource wealth in order to increase their economic power and political clout. It comments on the greed of a few (elite/political class) and their access to capturable oil wealth.

The image *Peasant Female* showing a woman guiding a bicycle (fig. 17.5) is an eloquent expression on the position of women in the Niger Delta region. Before the oil boom, the region had a primarily agrarian economy, with fishing and farming being its mainstays. Ever since the dislocation of the traditional economy, more men have abandoned fishing and embraced the modalities of the conflict economy as described above, while women have continued their work in subsistence farming where it is still possible to do so. In cases where few opportunities exist for women, they have looked for other means of survival, sometimes within the communities and sometimes outside. Because of the area's patriarchal culture, women have had little or no part in decision making, and thus have not been able to benefit significantly from the interventions (palliative measures) coming through government agencies and even through the multinational oil companies. These companies also connive with community leaders to deny people their rights. Isaac Albert notes in his study on emancipatory social movements that women charged the leadership of the Niger Delta communities with being too corrupt to be trusted with any information on civil protests because they receive land royalties and bribes from oil companies.[30]

The plight of women in the region is shaped by patriarchy.[31] Taking a cue from some feminist theorists on patriarchy, I argue that women in the Niger Delta region have faced confrontations with the universe of men at different levels, spaces, and situations.[32] They experience patriarchy of culture, patriarchy of religion, and patriarchy of colonialism.

Patriarchy of culture derives from traditional institutions headed by men for the control of the society and perpetuation of male hegemony. It finds expression in all aspects of cultural life where women take second place to men, resources and spaces are controlled by men, and decisions are largely made by men. Patriarchy of colonialism began during the colonial era when the colonialists, importing their own patriarchal ideology, instituted political and other structures that excluded women. Patriarchy has always been about domination and exclusion, dynamics between the sexes that are sometimes hinged on the notion of difference—conflicting interests between men and women. Colonialism encouraged the restriction of women to the private sphere while giving prominence to men in the public arena. It also "undermined the solidarity of the women by introducing new divisions based on education, wealth, and, in some areas, religious affiliations. Educated women subscribed to different social and occupational codes than their uneducated sisters. In the political area, colonialism not only deprived women of much of their precolonial authority in their own sphere, but by its exclusion of them from the colonial order, it served to reinforce their consciousness of being separate."[33] Patriarchy of religion unites and further entrenches the nuances of cultural institutions and colonial legacies such that, on all fronts, women were grossly disadvantaged.

Within this three-dimensional patriarchal structure, and facing the region's tensions, challenges, and confrontations, how can women achieve development in the Niger Delta? What is their hope in the context of globalization? Can they remain calm or passive when violent, aggressive militant groups, by their violent actions and armed struggle with the state, threaten the security and lives of those under their care, particularly the vulnerable groups: children and the aged? Can they afford to be onlookers while men make decisions that impact significantly on and compromise their livelihood and survival? Can they afford to remain passive members of the society in the throes of violence, frequent hostage taking, terrorism, ruthless dictatorship, and exploitation of resources? In view of the fact that women are more affected where there is no peace, they are more likely to work for the attainment of peace especially as this ensures security not only for them but for those whom they traditionally take care of.

Angela King, assistant secretary-general of the Peace Research Institute, Oslo, in a foreword to the book *Gender, Peace, and Conflict*, advanced the following germane arguments:

> Most women appear to have a somewhat different understanding of peace, security and violence than most men. This has led to the assumption that if women were involved in a sufficient number in peace, security and conflict resolution, these definitions would be transformed and so would all related policies, activities and institutional arrangements. Broadening both these concepts and participation in conflict resolution would open new opportunities for dialogue. It would replace the traditional model of negotiations aimed at ceasefire or crisis management by a real conflict resolution model, where the root causes of conflict are addressed, all aspects of human security are taken into consideration, and the process of negotiation is inclusive, involving representatives of civil society, including women's organizations.[34]

Excluding the indigenous women from the conflict resolution approaches adopted in the Niger Delta impasse may not yield lasting peace or promote the desired development in the region. Their exclusion threatens or greatly compromises their survival and that of their dependents, including children and the aged. Besides, they have major stakes in the survival of the communities. As rightly argued by Errol Miller, "The low representation of women represents a deficit in representation itself because women have special qualities to contribute to political affairs; qualities that are not being tapped."[35] Women, in view of their life-giving and life-preservation attributes, tend to accommodate, cooperate, conciliate, and demonstrate all-inclusive skills that are sorely needed in today's world. Basically, what the world needs are political and not military solutions in the conduct of human affairs. The culture of peace would be better served by gender equality in the political apparatus of nations. What the Niger Delta therefore needs goes far beyond the amnesty that the federal government has offered warring militants.

From a simplistic point of view, the amnesty appears to be a positive step toward ending the long struggle between the Nigerian state and the militants. Observers have expressed reservations, however, that chances are slim that criminality and violence will not reoccur. The reasons are clear. Militants have become used to getting "free money" through their various escapades in the creeks. The guns they carry are their meal tickets, and criminality their means of livelihood. The monthly stipend of ₦60,000 per head offered to the militants is a far cry from what most of them purportedly make even from a single raid. Rita Lori Ogbebor, an Itsekiri chieftain, reasoned that asking militants to lay down their weapons is a waste of time because the militants are no fools. She argued that "if they ever drop one, they will keep five," therefore rendering the amnesty exercise a mere waste of effort, time, and resources.

However, there is more to the Niger Delta issue than the surrender of weapons by militants and the rehabilitation of those who surrender. Quite a number of people have suffered during past skirmishes and violent outbreaks, and the degree of pain and trauma endured by women and their dependents at various times can no longer be ignored by the Nigerian state. While one hopes that the amnesty will lead to a lasting peace in the region, for a full peace it is necessary that the travails of women be recognized and addressed. Unfortunately, the government has chosen to focus thus far on the militants who unleash terror on the immediate oil-bearing and oil-producing communities and the Nigerian state. A surer path to peace and development in the region would ensure that the needs and grievances of all stakeholders be met and redressed, not that the interests of the greedy few be catered to. Development can translate to freedom and choice, but as the situation now stands, who will guarantee freedom and choice for the most vulnerable?

Niger Delta Women in the Context of Globalization and Sustainable Development

Globalization is a process that theoretically enables the world to harness, harmonize, and advance economic, technological, and political concerns for the benefit of most people. It makes possible the democratization of market forces, the breaking down of trade barriers, and the opening up of territorial borders for migration. Globalization is a paradox: in practice, it negates the very ideology that it promotes. Although globalization's proponents argue that it encourages the integration of homogeneous entities in the spheres of economy, culture, technology, and governance for the common good, what is apparent is that strong nations continue to wax stronger and bond together while weak nations remain on the periphery. Besides, strong nations have greater control and ability to manipulate the processes of globalization, and benefit more from its practice and progression, than do weak nations. Globalization mocks the weak, exploits the poor and the disadvantaged, and privileges the few ultra-imperialists who are its major beneficiaries. Within this frightening and disenfranchising structure, where do indigenous women in the Niger Delta stand? While it could be argued that globalization has made inroads into the Niger Delta through oil prospecting by multinational corporations, the people of the region are still struggling to survive, their livelihood, access to education, and health security all threatened by the very forces that hold out the promise of equal participation and prosperity. Market forces under globalization are essentially capitalist, typically vicious, discriminatory, and exploitative, thereby encouraging the survival of the fittest.

How then is the Niger Delta, and by extension Nigeria, situated within the rubric of globalization? Global market forces controlled by strong nations seek from weak ones, including Nigeria, cheap labor, cheap raw materials, maximum profit, and a well-cultivated taste for Euro-American culture. These are components of the capitalist agenda that explain the gross neglect experienced by the Niger Delta region. The inability of the people to realize their human potential leads to frustration, and in the case of ND militant youths, to violence and criminality. For those who cannot wield weapons of warfare and who necessarily have to wait for assistance in order to access wealth and development, such as the women and other vulnerable groups, globalization is like a mirage. Although Nigeria has a Ministry of Women Affairs and there are several NGOs working on women's issues, there has been no appreciable transformation in the conditions of indigenous women in the region. The mission statement of the Federal Ministry of Women Affairs pledges "to serve as the national vehicle to bring about speedy and healthy development of Nigerian women, in the mainstream of national development process, ensure the survival, protection and participation of all children as preparation for meaningful adult life"; however, what happens to women in the region implicates the ministry as well as its policies for women not only in the Niger Delta but in the country as a whole. The vision of the ministry is anchored on building a Nigerian society devoid of gender discrimination, ensuring equal access to wealth-creation opportunities, developing a culture that places a premium on the protection of the child, and focusing attention of both the public and the private sector on issues that promote full participation of women and children in the national development process.[36] Nonetheless, in view of the reality on the ground and the obvious underdevelopment of women, having a ministry is just one step toward addressing the inequalities between men and women; actualizing the goal is another matter. How this broad agenda takes care of intragender differences, class issues, regional needs, and cultural specificity is not well articulated in the policy document of the Ministry of Women Affairs.

A look at the impact of globalization on women worldwide as presented by Cecilia Ng in her essay "Women: Globalization and Women" is helpful for understanding how women in the Niger Delta respond to the forces of globalization. Ng argues that though the twentieth century has brought enormous gains in the quest for empowerment for women and representation within the political arena, the globalizing process is not grafting women firmly into "homogeneous entities in the spheres of economy, culture, technology and governance."[37] Though there is increasing feminization of employment, which is thought to impact positively on women's empowerment and visibility, the literature on women and globalization presents a grim picture. Ng, citing a 1997 report of the United Nations Development Programme (UNDP), informs: "Out of the 1.3 billion poor people in the world, 70 percent are women, the majority of whom are illiterate with no access to basic amenities like safe drinking water. Two-thirds of the 130 million children worldwide who are not in school are girls. Between 75 and 80 percent of the world's 27 million refugees are women and children."[38] From the 2008 UNDP report one notes that there are still 1.2 billion people around the world who live on less than a dollar a day, while about 850,000 go hungry every night. Poverty is not just about money: lack of access to essential resources goes beyond financial hardship to affect people's health, education, security, and opportunities for political participation. The fact that the report stressed the need to address many dimensions of global poverty while remaining targeted, measurable, and sensitive to the wider impact of poverty on women shows that women still constitute a significant number of the world's poor. The feminization of poverty clearly has attendant consequences including the feminization of cheap labor and the attraction and integration of women into such negative aspects of globalization as human trafficking and prostitution. Women's entry into the sex industry is identified through established patterns: forced and voluntary.

Commoditization of women has become rampant in the era of globalization, and many of the females who enter the sex industry are drawn from ravaged economies including those in Africa. More and more females from Nigeria's Niger Delta, notably from Edo State, are being drawn into the sex trade in Europe, and Nigeria continues to develop measures and apply sanctions in order to eradicate the practice. But the battle against female prostitution is a complex one. It is very much like the illicit trade in oil and foreign currency popularly called "black market." The buyers and sellers have a common understanding of their means of exchange. In Warri and arguably Port Harcourt, the presence of foreigners working in the multinational oil corporations seems to encourage commoditization of the female body.[39] Attempting to avoid being caught up in the sex trade, women migrate to other towns and cities in the country where they take menial jobs.

Of major concern are the young girls taken abroad by "madames" to foreign countries, most especially to Italy, to join the prostitution racket. This group illustrates the paradigm of the forced sex trade. The parents or guardians of the young females are usually told that they are leaving to get respectable jobs in Europe that will earn their families good income. However, they get to their destinations only to find that they have been lured into a thriving sex racket. Most of the girls usually submit as they do not have the means to return home.

These developments essentially point to the need to rethink policies and interventions that concern the ND. A gender lens must be applied to short- and long-term strategies being developed to address the various challenges in the area. The approach of the federal government to the militants in the region—paying them immediate attention now that their violent actions pose an ongoing major threat to the fabric of the Nigerian state—is basically short-sighted. The current government policy for the ND assumes that focusing on such a group is adequate to addressing the basic needs of other groups, but this is neither forward looking nor realistic.[40] It also highlights the inequalities between the sexes in the region and the shortcomings of a government approach that fails to apply a gender lens to issues of development.

Conclusion

I have argued in this chapter that tensions in the Niger Delta region have more far-reaching implications for holistic regional development, and for all of Nigeria, than have been imagined. I also noted that a "crimogenic" environment engendered by greed and grievance of various stakeholders further complicates the crisis in the region. I argued that the creation of a conflict economy sustained by militancy poses major threats to the success of the federal government's amnesty program aimed at winning the cooperation of the ND militants. I underscored the neglect of women as an important element in the failure of interventions in the Niger Delta. Women have a vital role to play in furthering the process of the institutionalization of a peace that has the potential to ultimately bring about both freedom and development. Finally, I argued that the forces of globalization have both positive and negative impacts on women in the Niger Delta and that for women to achieve their potential within the context of globalization, development initiatives must be all-embracing.

The Nigerian state can no longer pretend that women do not matter. Neither can men continue to hold sway over all members of Nigerian society. Promoters of future peace initiatives and interventions in the Niger Delta region should factor women and their concerns into their agenda; better still, women should be among those who set agendas for such initiatives. Peace agreements will only be durable when women as well as men have key roles to play. To ensure this, there is an evident need for a coalition of women's groups from different states of the federation to draft a forward-looking development agenda for women. Although it has been suggested that the way to end the crises in the ND is to let the resources be controlled by the region's people, I aver that such an action will not resolve the problem as the sheer consideration of it will threaten the cohesion of the nation and generate further crises. In rethinking the development of the region, the state can explore a more equitable sharing of revenues generated from the its oil resources; in particular, it could increase the allocation to the region from the present paltry 27 percent to 40 percent and ensure that these revenues are invested wholly in the development of the region and do not end up lining the pockets of the political class, or in the hands of men more than women.

Notes

1. Paul Collier and Anke Hoeffler, "Greed and Grievance in Civil War," Oxford Economic Papers, Oxford University Press, vol. 56, no. 4 (October 2004): 563–95.

2. This region, formerly called the Oil Rivers as it was a major producer of palm oil, is made up of nine states: Abia, Akwa-Ibom, Bayelsa, Cross River, Delta, Edo, Imo, Ondo, and Rivers. From the figures indicated in the *Official Gazette* of the Federal Republic of Nigeria released on February 2, 2009, the total population of these states is 31,277,901.

3. Since the 1960s Nigerians have increasingly shifted from an agrarian-based to an oil economy. In contrast to the traditional agricultural practices that yielded appreciable income, the oil economy propelled Nigeria into the league of oil-rich states. In spite of the degree of oil exploration, with huge oil revenues running upwards of $1 trillion to date, and the employment of large number of skilled, well-paid Nigerians by the oil corporations drilling in Nigeria, the oil wealth has had little or no significant positive impact on majority of Nigerians, most especially the people of the Niger Delta states and of the far north, who have become poorer since the 1960s. In "The Nature of the Nigerian State and Its Economy," S. T. Akindele, C. Uwasomba, and Mete Feridun reasoned that since that era "Nigeria is supposed to have realized $300 billion from the oil sector alone" (in *Nigerian Economy: Essays in Economic Development*, ed. Mete Feridun and S. T. Akindele [Morrisville, NC: Lulu Press, Inc., 2005], 22). However, this is not the case, as they go on to point out:

Thirty per cent of this amount is unaccounted for. Nigeria is regarded as the third-largest economy in Africa. It is also the sixth-largest producer of oil in OPEC. Ninety per cent of the country's earnings come from oil, which makes the economy susceptible to the vagaries of the international oil market. But the rent-seeking mentality of the state operator will not allow them to creatively open the economy by way of diversification and prudent management of resources at their disposal. The control of the economy especially after the civil war years provided a formidable instrument for inducement for selfish, corrupt behaviour. (22–23)

4. See, e.g., the studies of D'arcy Doran, "Nigerian Women Take on Oil Corporation—and Win" (November 19, 2004), http://www.namibian.com.na/2002/july/africa/02726ACCD6.html; Eghosa E. Osaghae, "The Ogoni Uprising: Oil Politics, Minority Agitation, and the Future of the Nigerian State," *African Affairs* 94 (1995); O. Ibeanu, "Oil, Conflicts and Security in Rural Nigeria: Issues in Ogoni Crisis," *AAPS Occasional Paper Series* 1, no 2 (1997): 10; Victor Isumonah, "The Making of the Ogoni Ethnic Group," *Africa: Journal of the International African Institute* 74, no. 3 (2004): 433–53; Ben Naanen, "The Niger Delta and the National Question," in *The Management of the National Question in Nigeria*, ed. Eghosa E. Osaghae and Ebere Onwudiwe (Ibadan: PEFS, 2001); and Sola Adebayo, "$3 Billion Project: Delta Warns Oil Firm," *Punch* 17, no. 19 (May 16, 2006): 12.

5. Max Spielbichler, "Nigerians Angered over Waste Dumping," *ZIS Economists*, May 26, 2009, http:/welkerwickinomics.com/students.

6. According to UNDP, a total of 6,800 spills occurred between 1976 and 2001. See UNDP, *Niger Delta Human Development Report* (Abuja, 2006), 76; and *Nigeria Human Development Report 2000/2001* (Lagos, 2001). The National Oil Spill Detection and Response Agency, in March 2008, noted that there were at least two thousand sites in the Niger Delta that required treatment because of oil-related pollution. The true figure may be far higher than what is reported in the literature.

7. Nigeria since independence has taken in more than $1 trillion in oil revenues with little or no impact on the standard of living of most Nigerians. Minimally paid workers in the country earn a basic salary of ₦7,500 (or about $50) per month. The sharp contrast between the huge oil revenues and the degree of poverty in the country confirms Transparency International's ranking of Nigeria as the world's "most corrupt" state. Evidently the country has little to show for its resource wealth, which to many, especially people in the ND, has turned out to be a "resource curse."

8. Gas flaring releases carbon dioxide and methane into the air. The air pollution generates acid rain; the constant glow created by flaring makes it difficult for people in the area to differentiate between night and day; and exposure of pregnant women to oil pollution and gas flaring engenders congenital malformations, including neurofibromatosis, in their children.

9. Foreign employees of multinational oil companies and their relatives have been prime targets. See, for example, Shyamantha Asokan, "Nigerian Kidnapping Culture on the Rise," *Global Post*, December 19, 2009, http://www.globalpost.com/dispatch/nigeria/091217/nigerias-kidnapping-culture; and Kathleen Houreld, "Ransoms Fuel Surge in Nigerian Kidnapping," Associated Press, July 11, 2007,

http://www.washingtonpost.com/wp-dyn/content/article/2007/07/11/ AR2007071101271.html; see also accounts in UNDP, *Niger Delta Human Development Report* (2006), 2.

10. These reports have been culled from *Report of Technical Committee on the Niger Delta*, vol. 1, November 2008, 9. See also *Crisis Group Africa Briefing*, no. 60 (April 30, 2009): 2.

11. Chief Pete Edochie, a notable Nollywood actor, was abducted in Awka, Anambra state, on August 16, 2009, though he was released the next day when his family could not come up with the ₦50m (about $3.5 million) ransom demanded by the kidnappers (*Vanguard*, August 19, 2009, 12). A gang of three kidnappers on August 18, 2009, also whisked away Mrs. Grace Mamah, aged sixty-five, the wife of Igwe James Mamah, who is the ruler of Umuozzi in Igbo-Eze North Local Government Area of Enugu state and chairman of the Ifesinachi Group of Companies (ibid.).

12. Ledum Mittee, one of the founders of MOSOP who survived the General Sanni Abacha military dictatorship and went into exile, tried unsuccessfully to get MOSOP back on track when he returned in 1998. The best the group under his leadership could do was to enjoin the Ogoni to vote in the 1999 elections.

13. Iyenemi Norman Wokoma, "Assessing Accomplishments of Women's Non-violent Direct Action in the Niger Delta," in *Gender and Peace Building in Africa*, ed. Dina Rodriguez and Edith Natukunda-Togboa (San Jose, Costa Rica: University for Peace, ALPI, 2005), 168.

14. Osaghae et al. put the date at 1998. See "Youth Militias, Self-Determination, and Resource Control Struggles in the Niger Delta Region of Nigeria" (2007), http://www.ascleiden.nl/Pdf/cdpnigeriaRevisedOsaghae[1]2.pdf.

15. Villages were razed, many people were killed, and women and girls were assaulted by invading federal troops. See Wokoma, "Women's Non-violent Direct Action."

16. Itse Sagay, "The Niger Delta and the Case for Resource Control," *Vanguard*, June 13, 2005, http://www.vanguardngr.com/articles/2002/politics/june05/ 14062005/p414062005.html; see also http://www.waado.org/NigerDelta/Essays/ ResourceControl/Sagay.html.

ALE These projects include developing local industries where people living in communities devastated by oil prospecting could be gainfully employed, providing portable water since the streams in the locale were already populated, awarding scholarships to children in the communities to be able to attend school, granting financial aid to men and women to start small-scale businesses, and creating health care units in the communities; all are geared to cushion the effect of environmental degradation in the region. The so-called interventions are basic infrastructures that a community should have and that should have been taken for granted.

18. See Vanguard News Online, "Niger Delta—Unfair Fair," *Vanguard*, July 31, 2009, http://www.vanguardngr.com/2009/07/31/niger-delta-unfair-fair/.

19. The fair was aimed at equipping the youths of the region with the capacity to gain employment in the oil and gas industry and ultimately make them relevant to businesses within their locality.

20. See Doran, "Nigerian Women Take on Oil Corporation." Isaac Albert also made this observation (see "Emancipatory Social Movements in the Niger Delta:

Goals, Strategies, and Critical Lessons for Peace Practice," typescript submitted to IFRA, University of Ibadan, 2008).

21. Bolanle Awe, ed., *Nigerian Women in Historical Perspective* (Ibadan: Sankore/Bookcraft, 1992).

22. When women go naked in public, their nakedness is understood as the height of provocation and as a last resort that portends grave consequences for whoever triggered the provocation. See Wokoma, "Women's Non-violent Direct Action," 173, where she reports on the 1984 nude protest of Ogharefe women in Delta State.

23. Olufemi Taiwo, "Feminism and Africa: Reflections on the Poverty of Theory," in *African Women and Feminism: Reflecting on the Politics of Sisterhood*, ed. Oyeronke Oyewunmi (Trenton, NJ: Africa World Press, 2003), 53.

24. Albert, "Emancipatory Social Movements"; Wokoma, "Women's Non-violent Direct Action."

25. Various personalities and groups including expatriate and local business-men, high-ranking politicians and military personnel, and even employees of oil companies are implicated in oil-bunkering activities in the Niger Delta. See Human Rights Watch interviews, Port Harcourt, November 23 and 28, 2004. Also see "Peace and Security in the Niger Delta: Conflict Expert Group Baseline Report," Working Paper for SPDC (Shell Petroleum Development Company), December 2003, 46; and Report of the Special Security Committee on Oil Producing Areas, submitted to President Olusegun Obasanjo (unpublished), February 2002.

26. Materials used for the shirt range from simple cotton to expensive lace fabrics while wrappers are imported from overseas. The fedora hats are called "resource control" hats.

27. Eghosa Osaghae et al., "Youth Militias, Self-Determination," 25–26.

28. The term "crimogenic" refers to the attraction to and creating of enabling structures for criminality. It also concerns the institutionalization and unification of crime, criminality, and corruption for monetary gain. For the perpetrators of various heinous activities linked with the politics of oil in the Niger Delta, criminality is like a business from which investors must derive benefits. "Crimogenism" may or may not be violent but its outcome must essentially attract economic returns.

29. See Osaghae et al., "Youth Militias, Self-Determination," 25–26.

30. Albert, "Emancipatory Social Movements."

31. In *The Theory of Social and Economic Organization* (New York: Free Press, 1947), Max Weber defined patriarchy as women and younger men being ruled by older men who were heads of households. Deviating a little from the Weberian definition, some feminist theorists, such as Drude Dalherup and Slyvia Walby, adopt the now more common approach that discards Weber's generational difference between men and defines patriarchy as that system of social structures and practices in which men dominate, oppress, and exploit women. See Errol Miller, "Gender, Power and Politics: An Alternative Perspective," in *Gender, Peace, and Conflict*, ed. Inger Skjelsbaek and Don Smith (London: Sage Publications, 2001), 81.

32. See Drude Dahlerup, "Confusing Concepts-Confusing Reality: A Theoretical Discussion of a Patriarchal State," in *Women and the State: The Shifting Boundaries of Public and Private*, ed. Anne Showstack Sassoon (London: Hutchinson, 1987); and Sylvia Walby, *Theorizing Patriarchy* (Oxford: Basil Blackwell, 1990).

33. Nina Emma Mba, *Nigerian Women Mobilized: Women's Political Activity in Southern Nigeria, 1900–1965* (Berkeley: University of California, Institute of International Studies, 1982), 291.

34. Angela King, foreword to Skjelsbaek and Smith, *Gender, Peace, and Conflict,* viii.

35. Miller, "Gender, Power, and Politics," in Skjelsbaek and Smith, *Gender, Peace, and Conflict,* 102.

36. See the National Commission for Women Act of 1989 (later repealed, and replaced by the National Commission for Women Decree of 1992).

37. Cecilia Ng, "Women: Globalization and Women," *Human Rights Solidarity* 11, no. 2 (February 2001): 2, http://www.hrsolidarity.net/mainfile.php.2001vol11no.2/25/ (accessed November 24, 2009).

38. Ibid.

39. Observations are based on reports from the fieldwork I carried out in January and August 2009.

40. While the case of men (militants) receives immediate attention, issues concerning women, who generally are nonviolent actors in the region, are grafted into the long-term policy developed by the federal government to address the ND problem.

18

Islam and the "Global War on Terror" in West Africa

Despite over four centuries of exchange relations initially with the Middle East, Europe and Asia, including the intercontinental European slave trade and subsequent colonization, Africa was never fully integrated into the global economy—Africa was probably the most globally penetrated continent, yet on the other hand, she remains the world's least developed continent.

> —Ghelawdewos Araia, "Africa in the Global Economy"

The worst of the Muslim militants are extremists out to kill their perceived adversaries. But the most rational of the Islamists do believe that the world system has lost the restraints of checks and balances that the United States has become too powerful, and that Islam must introduce a countervailing force to the American empire.

> —Ali Mazrui, *Islam: Between Globalization and Counterterrorism*

Introduction

Both as a concept and a process, the term "globalization" is among the most hotly discussed and debated in the social sciences. It is often defined, generally, as involving an ever deepening and accelerating phenomenon in cross-border economic, political, and cultural relations that are made possible by innovations in technology. As a process, it is often perceived as the integration of all the above and characterized by intensified interactivity and interdependence. James Mittelman defines globalization as "the spatial reorganization of production, the interpenetration of industries across borders, the spread of financial markets, the diffusion of identical consumer goods to distant countries, massive transfer of populations mostly within the South—as well as from the South and the East to the West—resultant conflicts between immigrants and established communities."[1]

While many scholars contend that globalization is not entirely new, and that it began as early as the fifteenth century, what is new is the pace, depth, breadth, and generalized synergistic impact in communications, technology, culture, and commerce.[2] To many analysts, it is the best thing to have occurred in the development of human societies, as it has provided to many the opportunity for improved lives through economic and other forms of interaction.[3] Others lament its incomplete or partial character insofar as only a few countries are fully integrated and receive most of the benefits from it. Many scholars see it as "old wine in a new wineskin"—an ideology aimed at justifying American, as well as Western, hegemony in the global economy—a sanitized "imperialism" used to conceal continued exploitation of weaker states by the powerful and the rich.[4]

This chapter explores the link(s) between globalization, development, and the "War on Terror" in West Africa. It argues that Islamist movements in West Africa are in large measure the outcome or response to socioeconomic and political conditions that have been aggravated by rapid urbanization and globalization in Muslim-majority countries, both Arab and non-Arab.[5] And while many analysts argue, and rightly so, that globalization through communication and other technologies enhance terrorism, what is often lost in these debates is the contention that international asymmetries, global inequality, and underdevelopment are important contributory factors to the rise of terrorism.[6]

This chapter is divided into five subsections: the first provides a synopsis of Africa's position in the global economy and the social, political, and economic effects globalization has had on the continent as a whole and West Africa specifically. In the second, I undertake a brief survey of the terrorist presence in Africa as a backdrop to a discussion in the third subsection, which focuses on terrorism in West Africa. In the fourth subsection, I provide a dynamic analysis of the intersection between globalization, development, and the "War on Terror," and I conclude in the fifth by suggesting key ways to make globalization and a new development initiative work for Africans in order to curb oppositional political violence.

Africa in the Global Political Economy: A Synopsis

For centuries, Africa has remained on the periphery of the global system, and globalization may have only deepened African nations' dependence and marginalization, except perhaps for South Africa. Granted, globalization in communication technologies has increased interaction between Africa and the rest of the world. Yet, the fact remains that Africa's role as a producer of raw materials—from slavery, through colonialism, to the post independence era—has remained relatively the same. Paradoxically, this situation continues at a time when the continent today enjoys the fastest growth in cell phone use and is home to some of the fastest-growing economies in the world. At the same time, Chinese capital outlays have almost overtaken those of the West in Africa.[7] In spite of these factors, Africa's performance on key economic indicators remains low. Take, for instance, Africa's share of global trade: it remains low, particularly when precious metals and crude oil are not factored in; or consider the ratio of foreign direct investment. Here, too, the picture is not encouraging. And such investment has tended to create dependency of African states on Chinese capital with few positive linkage effects. One of the positive aspects of Chinese investments in Africa is the fact that it is not accompanied by austerity measures or conditionalities that are often associated with Western investment in the continent. This gives African policymakers greater flexibility in trade decisions. Consequently, China is quickly replacing the West as a more favorable source of investment. As a result, poverty rates, rather than improving, remain high and are deteriorating, leaving more than two hundred million Africans poorly nourished.

The reasons for this less than optimal outcome are multiple. Post independence development strategies rather than being internally driven have generally followed an extroverted and Western-driven model that is at variance with Africa's realities.[8] In some countries even where there are abundant resources—as in Angola, Nigeria, Sudan and the Democratic Republic of the Congo—mismanagement, corruption, and lack of accountability may eclipse, at least for the foreseeable future, what potential there is to improve people's living standards; this reality has been called the "resource curse" (as was discussed more fully in chapter 16 by Ricardo de Sousa). In other states (Gambia, Niger, Chad, Burkina Faso, to name a few), size, climate, and location have conspired to keep entire populations poor. And yet in too many countries, such as Côte d'Ivoire and Uganda, for instance, conflict and internal strife have undermined the prospects for development.[9]

Just as important, however, are the effects of decades-long military rule and intervention in many countries that has left in their wake deep-seated ethnic, class, and regional cleavages. Witness the political impasse that currently engulfs Côte d'Ivoire, once one of Africa's most prosperous countries. Some called it the "Ivorian Miracle." To this list must be added failed ideologies or "isms" (capitalism, African socialism, Afro-Marxism) and everything in between that sought to lift Africans in the years following independence. Indeed, capitalism and economic globalization have not improved the lives of poor Africans.

Today, however, there is the ideology of "developmentalism," the new fundamentalism. As William Easterly cogently argues:

Like all ideologies, development promises a comprehensive final answer to all of society's problems, from poverty and illiteracy to violence and despotic rule. It shares the common ideological characteristics of suggesting that there is only one answer, and it tolerates little dissent. It deduces this unique answer for everyone from a general theory that purports to apply to everyone, everywhere. There is no need to involve local actors who reap its costs and benefits. Development even has its own intelligentsia, made up of experts at the IMF, World Bank and UN.[10]

The emphasis on free markets; a minimalist, noninterventionist state; and structural adjustment have together exposed African states generally to further control by these transnational institutions—leaving little room for creative local and regional solutions. Thus, the admirable concerns of rich countries over the tragedy of world poverty are thus channeled into fattening the international aid bureaucracy, the self-appointed priesthood of development.[11]

Also, in the first decade of the twenty-first century, many African states and peoples find themselves beholden to ruinous policies of autocratic rulers. These combined with the aforementioned challenges of size, location, conflict, poor governance, and increased external dependence set in motion a vicious circle of underdevelopment. Add to this the relatively new player in the continent—China, which today, not unlike the Scramble for Africa by European powers in the 1800s, is gobbling Africa's precious resources and establishing settler colonies to compete with African industries. And like Western multinational corporations before them, Chinese companies are undermining the competitiveness of local industries and taking them over. China is today building infrastructure just as the West did to ease the transport and export of Africa's valuable resources.[12] Here, too, African leadership is complicit. Leaders are being wooed by the Chinese into accepting another unequal trade relationship, with its own dependency structures. And with China's growing influence and rivalry with the United States for global hegemony, Africa once more stands to be marginalized.[13]

In sum, globalization as currently constructed has deepened preexisting economic challenges more so in Africa than perhaps in Asia and Latin America. Fundamentally, the ideology that informs contemporary theories and practices of globalization and development—the "Washington consensus"—promised more than it could deliver. According to Joseph Stiglitz, many of the problems with globalization are of our own making, a result of the way in which globalization has been managed by international financial institutions, the G-7, governmental and nongovernmental aid agencies, and their underlings on the ground.[14]

This has in turn precipitated a backlash against globalization, as witnessed in numerous popular protests against the World Trade Organization (WTO) in cities like Seattle, Prague, Washington, DC, and Pittsburgh, to name a few. Political and economic leaders in industrialized countries are finally coming to grips with the not so good side of globalization that critics and laypersons alike have long identified. On April 2, 2009, then Prime Minister Gordon Brown of Britain stressed the need for deep financial reforms, and President Nicolas Sarkozy of France, in another setting, made a similar remark. Both agreed to the need for a new global economic order, and for changing the rules of the game to allow for more participation of emerging powers— China, India, and Brazil.[15] These concessions are important, as they recognize third world demands from the 1970s for a new international economic order. This global crisis should once and for all put to rest the "developmentalist" ideology that has dominated development discourse since the end of World War II.

For the most part, emphasis on free markets and Africa's place in the current wave of modernization/globalization has weakened and thrown off balance many communities. The result, as in the Middle East, is conflict, international terrorism, and violence—all by-products of globalization. This could very well be the linchpin of globalization, that is, the intersection of globalization and terrorism. The latter is in part a byproduct of globalization, and it also, like culture and ideas, is being globalized through communications technology.[16] It is sometimes aided indirectly by growing global inequality, the hegemonic unilateralism of the United States, and policies of the European Union and international financial institutions. Steven Weber and colleagues put it cogently:

> The world today is more dangerous and less orderly than it was supposed to be. Ten or fifteen years ago, the naive expectations were that the "end of history" was near. The reality has been the opposite. The world has more international terrorism and more nuclear proliferation than it did in 1990—cleavages of religious and cultural ideology are more intense and the global financial system is more unbalanced and precarious.[17]

Peril of International Terrorism in Africa: An Overview

Following the deadly terrorist attacks on New York's World Trade Center and the Pentagon near Washington, DC, on September 11, 2001, the United States under its former commander in chief, President George W. Bush, embarked upon a global strategy to combat what it viewed as the growing peril of international terrorism. Key to this strategy is the United States Africa Command (AFRICOM). Established in October 2007, and headquartered in Stuttgart, Germany, AFRICOM is the newest US regional military command with a goal of creating in Africa a stable environment in which economic and political development can take place.[18] AFRICOM, according to Department of Defense officials, seeks to strengthen the porous borders of states in West Africa in order to stem the flow of terrorists and secure core US national interests in West Africa. And unlike earlier US military programs in Africa, AFRICOM will focus on war prevention rather than war fighting and is supported by several agencies of the US government, including the Department of State.[19] Therefore, as Africa's importance has grown in recent years, so has the competition between China and the United States to access Africa's valuable resources. AFRICOM can be seen as the American antidote to increased Chinese economic engagement in Africa, and in West Africa specifically.

Yet, the peril of international terrorism is present and real in Africa. On August 7, 1998, two massive bombs exploded outside of the US embassies in Dar es Salaam, Tanzania, and Nairobi, Kenya, killing 224 people, including twelve Americans, and injuring some 5,000. Responsibility was quickly traced to al-Qaeda. Four years later, al-Qaeda operatives struck again in Africa, killing fifteen people in an Israeli-owned hotel in Mombasa, Kenya, while simultaneously firing missiles at an Israeli passenger jet taking off from Mombasa's airport.[20]

In 2003, internationally linked Moroccan terrorists conducted suicide attacks in Casablanca, killing forty-three. In South Africa, groups affiliated with al-Qaeda are said to be making inroads into Muslim communities.[21] To this litany of attacks must be added Somalia and Sudan, which for several years provided refuge for international terrorists, both foreign and home-grown. In fact, Sudan, from 1991 to 1996, allegedly provided shelter for Osama bin Laden, prompting several US missile attacks, including one in retaliation for the embassy bombings in Kenya and Tanzania. What is in doubt, however, among African leaders and many Africanist scholars, is whether "Islamic terrorism" in Africa has in fact reached the magnitude that the United States alleges.[22]

In West Africa where there are high concentrations of Muslims, the link with international terrorism is assumed by some Westerners as a matter of course. Here, the most heavily Islamized countries or Muslim-majority states include Mauritania, which is 98 percent Muslim, and landlocked Niger and Mali, which have Muslim populations around 95 percent. In Senegal and Gambia, Muslims account for 95 and 90 percent, respectively, while Nigeria is approximately 47–50 percent Muslim. Nigeria's seventy million Muslim population is larger than the total number of Muslims in Mauritania, Niger, Mali, Senegal, Gambia, and even Guinea, which is 95 percent Muslim.[23]

Partly because of this large Muslim population and the grinding poverty that pervades the lives of many West Africans, US policymakers, as well as some academics, assume a causal link between these factors and terrorism. The implication is that Muslim-majority countries, compared to predominantly Christian

states, are more prone to produce or harbor terrorist operatives. This conclusion has not been borne out by evidence. Instead, Muslims in West Africa,
though spiritually linked to the *Umma* (Muslim world)—that is, the Middle East
including Saudi Arabia, specifically—do not constitute a monolithic bloc with
them and, therefore, are less likely than their Arab and other coreligionists to
engage in anti-Western violence or rhetoric.

Even in Nigeria, where many of its states in the North have adopted sharia
law, it is *oppositional political violence* rather than terrorism that is common.
To a large extent oppositional violence in the Niger Delta is a consequence
of deep-rooted inequalities in Nigeria itself, and in northern Nigeria, specifically. Growing poverty, marginalization, and underdevelopment in the
North is expressed through religion and competition/tensions between
Muslims and Christians. Thus, it is to the political, economic, social, and
military setup in Nigeria that we must look for the underlying grievances
expressed through violence and militant Islamist rhetoric. Even though the
Islamist group Boko Haram (translated roughly as "Western education is a
sin") favors the imposition of Sharia law across the country, its activities do
not target Westerners. As Scott Johnson has argued, "The death-to-the-West-
erners mantra just has no constituency here, and West Africa has not been
fertile ground for jihadism."[24] According to Johnson:

> What Nigeria does have, and what the Boko Haram attacks actually reflect
> is the immensely complicated (and often very nasty) nature of local politics.
> Nigeria's mean poverty rate—the number of people living below $1.25 a day,
> soars above 70 percent, as a tiny minority of wealthy and often very corrupt
> officials live decadently. Nowhere is the discrepancy between the haves and
> have-nots more pronounced than in Nigeria's fertile northern regions, where
> the Boko Haram attacks are occurring. Unemployment is rife, even among
> college-educated youth. That's partly why northerners opted for alternative
> political systems and Shari'a law in particular—hoping that bypassing the exist-
> ing system would guarantee them a bigger piece of the pie.[25]

The Nigerian case clearly suggests that acts of violence by such groups
as the Boko Haram have their own underpinning in social and political
imperatives based in local experiences. Political interests were acted out
through religious mobilization, and justifications offered by referring to the
Quran.[26] In Senegal, by contrast, according to Linda Beck, marabouts (Muslim clergy) had more to gain from using their positions in society to extract
political resources from the state than from establishing a theocracy.[27]
According to Leonardo Villalon, Momar Coumba Diop and Mamadou Diouf
put it succinctly: "Contrary to Iran or Syria where the leaders of religious
orders came together to form politico-Islamic organizations and introduced
social projects, the advent of which required the overthrow of their political

systems, in Senegal the marabouts have abstained from playing any role in the destabilization of politico-administrative power."[28] Linda Beck also contends that unlike the Middle East and South Asia where Islamic reformism has resulted in political challenges by Muslim leadership, the piety associated with Islamic resurgence in Senegal has been translated into criticism of self-interested marabout-politicians corrupted by their clientelist relations with the secular state.[29]

Senegal's religious landscape, like those in the Muslim-majority states of West Africa, is constituted by several Sufi sects that include the Muridyya, Tijaniyya, and Qadiriyya. In Senegal, and Gambia, in particular, these Sufi orders have historically maintained a symbiotic relationship with secular political elites, with the religious leadership often serving as political brokers between the political class and the mass *tallibe* (student body) under their tutelage. And while these Muslim-majority states have had an Islamist strand, its influence has waned, in part because its "radical" message of an Islamist state has thus far not resonated with the larger Muslim population in these countries. This may change, however, as economic hardship becomes more pervasive, especially among the rural and urban poor.

Religious currents in Gambia follow those of Senegal closely, albeit on a smaller scale. Here, according to Momodou Darboe, religious leaders and politicians exploit the emotions of the faithful for their specific agenda of political gain or survival, reorganization of society, and sometimes conformation to religious doctrine.[30] As in Senegal, religious leaders in Gambia use politics in the interest of their religion and its followers, and politicians use Islamic symbols or rationales to gain or maintain political power.[31] But none of these Muslims in these or other Muslim-majority countries are waging war on the United States, Western Europe, or Israel. They do not demand the release of Taliban fighters captured in Pakistan's Swat Valley. Nor do they behead captured soldiers, and they do not slaughter civilians to terrify the populace—these groups "are not the latest front in the Global War on Terror."[32]

In sum, while West Africa is home to approximately 150 million Muslims, this fact has not translated into terrorist attacks against Westerners, nor has it affected relations with Washington. Also, "radical" politics in the Middle East have not, so far, impinged on politics in West Africa to the extent that relations between West African states and the Western world are adversely affected. Rather, countries like Senegal, Mali, Niger, Nigeria, and Mauritania have sought to strengthen ties with the West. In fact, Mali and Senegal are both relatively stable democracies, and Senegal has recognized Israel's right to exist. More important, al-Qaeda's activities in the region have involved, not the fomenting of terrorism, but the exploitation of conflict and political instability in such countries as Liberia and Sierra Leone to expand its finances.[33] Even in the Middle East where so-called terrorism is rife, it is oppositional political violence rather than actual terrorism that is the norm. And even here, such movements also are responses to power imbalances, US unilateral policy, the war in Iraq, and the Israeli-Palestinian conflict.

It should be noted again that Muslims, while united by the Five Pillars of Islam and the Hadith (practices and sayings of the Prophet Muhammad), are not a monolithic group, just as Christianity and Judaism are not homogeneous faiths. In West Africa specifically, Islam takes on syncretistic colorations embodying traditional religious and cultural practices and beliefs. It is the followers of this blended brand of Islam who are often the targets of Islamist reformists or "purists" who practice a strain of Wahhabism (a puritanical version of Islam).

Islam in much of West Africa does not exclude women, nor are women required to wear the *Hijab* (veil). Women, despite their second-class status, generally hold important positions of power, drive automobiles, and are an important constituency that politicians court during elections. Many educated Muslim women in West Africa are also professed feminists/womanists and openly challenge male domination and harmful traditional practices, such as female circumcision.

While Islamism is generally perceived as a movement of "fundamentalists" bent on bringing down corrupt secular governments and harming Westerners, many Muslims reject the fundamentalist label because it tends to convey the wrong impression that Islam is a violent religion.[34] What this brief survey reveals about Islam in West Africa is that uniformity is not its strong suit. Muslims are differentiated along several lines, albeit united by key central pillars and principles such as human rights and equality.[35] Wahhabism, as noted earlier, is a "radical" strain of Islam that has its roots in Saudi Arabia but is practiced also in Pakistan, Afghanistan, Indonesia, and Sudan.[36] In Gambia and Senegal, for instance, Wahhabism is predominantly an urban phenomenon, while in the rural areas Islam of a more tolerant mold is practiced amid endemic poverty, especially among the youth.[37]

While poverty pervades the lives of many West African youth, they have not succumbed to terrorist recruitment appeals to become suicide bombers lured by unbridled luxury in the afterlife. Nor have terrorist groups mushroomed in the region. Rather than joining terrorist groups en masse and training in al-Qaeda terrorist camps, Muslim youth from Gambia, Mali, Niger, and Guinea brave the open seas, often under perilous conditions, plying rickety boats to Europe in search of a better life for themselves and their families. Gregg Mills and Jeffrey Herbst argued cogently that what is most notable, given the vast number of marginalized people who suffer extraordinary deprivations south of the Sahara, is how few Africans have been associated with international terrorism.[38]

Therefore, the causal relationship often assumed between poverty and terrorism is overstated. Part of the problem in linking West Africa specifically with international terrorist networks and as a haven for terrorists has to do with what David J. Kilcullen terms the US policy of "aggregation"—that is, the amalgamation of local and regional African insurgent groups into a monolithic enemy. This approach, he argues, suffers from overly simplistic assumptions concerning Africa as the next front on the "War on Terror." Kilcullen contends, therefore, that these perspectives and an overemphasis on hard power have only heightened long-standing ethnic tensions and resulted in clientelism and unviable military interventions.[39] Such is the case in Mali, where a precarious balance or truce exists between a Berber group fighting for its share of development and rights against the central government. Recent US military aid to help Mali fight militants in its northern desert only complicates what is already a volatile situation.[40]

AFRICOM and West Africa's Strategic Importance to the United States

Since 2001 West Africa has grown steadily in strategic importance to US policymakers, as a major supplier of crude oil to the United States. Similarly, China is looking to Africa to meet its growing crude oil needs, which has in turn increased Africa's strategic importance to China's leadership.[41] Partly because of this growing recognition, China has canceled about $1.2 billion of debt held by thirty-one African states to date and has overtaken the World Bank as the lender of last resort; by 2009 China's investments in Africa totaled over $100 billion.[42] The most recent Chinese financial outlay was in Guinea, where a $7 billion investment package was undertaken to explore for oil and extract precious stones.[43]

Pointing to US interventions in Iraq and Afghanistan, many Africans worry that AFRICOM may represent the expansion of a militarized US foreign policy.[44] Clearly, current African suspicions over the goals of AFRICOM echo deep-seated antipathies over US military objectives in Africa and the earlier US Military Assistance Program (MAP) for the continent during the Cold War era. In the 1950s and up until the end of the Cold War around 1990, the United States and its allies provided military training for army officers as well as arms to back certain dictatorial regimes as part of its "containment strategy" to thwart Soviet interests and influence worldwide. One of the enduring consequences of US military relations with Africa was that African security concerns were, at best, subsumed under US interests, and, at worst, fomented regional insecurity, delaying resolution of endemic problems.

African militaries played an important role in securing US security and economic interests not only in wars of proxy against Soviet allies in the region but also in maintaining repressive regimes in apartheid South Africa and Zaire under Mobutu Sese Seko. The resulting militarization of Africa fueled interstate conflict in West Africa. And part of the justification for the support of dictatorial civilian and military regimes, in particular, lay in the presumption that armies in African societies were better positioned than their civilian counterparts to provide the leadership needed to modernize decaying political economies.[45] Could the US-led global "War on Terror" deflect attention away from the more pressing development and security needs in West Africa? Indeed it could, and to some extent it already has. Let me explain.

Thousands of miles from the battlefields of Iraq and Afghanistan another side of America's fight against terrorism is unfolding in West Africa. US Green Berets, according to Eric Schmitt, are training African armies to guard their borders and patrol vast desolate expanses against infiltration of al-Qaeda militants. In five West African countries (Mauritania, Mali, Niger, Nigeria, and Senegal) counterterrorism training and funding has intensified.[46] While US efforts at countering the specter of terrorism in West Africa are not limited to military means alone, as it includes instruction for teachers and job training for young Muslims, the military component of the policy trumps all others. The US concern over securing "ungoverned spaces" and strengthening weak states has led to the deployment of dozens of American and European trainers who conduct military exercises to curb the entry of militants who are likely to take refuge in countries along the vast Saharan north.[47] A US policy that targets Muslims and Islam could, in the end, prove counterproductive. Surely it is time to reconceptualize the term terrorism and distinguish it from legitimate political and economic grievances for self-determination in West Africa and other regions of the world, including the Middle East.

Conclusion

In place of the "Washington consensus," a new globalization ethos is needed, one centered on improving living standards and reducing rates of infant mortality.[48] These national strategies must be driven not by constructed and imposed models but by policies that are internally and democratically chosen. Each country in the continent must determine its own priorities and (learning from others and mistakes of the past) improve education, health, and nutrition in both rural and urban areas while maintaining its viable traditional values.[49]

Clearly, this alternative view emphasizes social justice, greater social equality, and careful use of resources to ensure societal and environmental balance. It is also imperative that national strategies be supported by a democratic institutional framework that empowers the poor and women in the decision-making process. Furthermore, there is nothing sacred about "markets" necessarily. What is important is how these markets are used to satisfy human needs, which, ultimately, is a political decision. As Stephen Marglin puts it so well:

> One has only to examine the assumptions that underlie contemporary economic thought. Economics is simply the formalization of the assumptions of modern Western culture—it is not surprising that a culture characterized in this way is a culture in which the market is the organizing principle of social life—the rise of the market system is bound with the loss of community.[50]

Markets in Africa were and still are an integral part of communities and are built on mutual obligation to the group and society. Social relations were traditionally based, and still are to some extent, on responsibility to the whole with strong emphasis on interpersonal relations, though people in a community are bound to one another economically, socially, and politically as well.[51]

There are three important lessons from this discussion on globalization. First, globalization needs to be reconceptualized to focus on local initiatives to emphasize core community values. Second, globalization must be redefined and remade to benefit the poor and those groups and countries that have benefited little. And third, development practitioners and theorists must recognize that current economic theory is rooted in the values and historical experiences of the West and if it is to be applied at all to other contexts, that application must be done with caution.[52]

More important, the recent US policy focus on Islam and Muslims as the targets of the US-led "War on Terror" is for all practical purposes misplaced, perhaps even dangerous. West African countries are home to moderate Sunni Muslim populations. For the most part, these populations have historically maintained good relations with the United States specifically, and the West in general. Therefore, a policy that constructs and targets West African Muslims and Islam as the enemy could backfire and undermine efforts to stem actual terrorism US policy should instead give priority to the nonmilitary component of AFRICOM. It is also likely that the "War on Terror" may very well spur a rapid flow into this region of foreign terrorists while simultaneously sparking resentment and emboldening homegrown resisters. The confluence of interest(s) between these groups could not only undermine regional and national stability, it could exacerbate military disorder and weak democratizing regimes in West Africa.

To overcome such an outcome and misgivings, AFRICOM must demonstrate a commitment to programs mutually beneficial to both African and American interests. Yet a shrewd strategic communications campaign will not be enough to convince a skeptical African public that AFRICOM's priorities mirror their own.[53] If the military strategy to win the "War on Terror" is not tempered with the use of American soft power, then the role of African militaries stands to be distorted in support of an agenda that may subvert national security goals of development, peace, and stability—and contributory directly to the increase of oppositional violence in the continent.

Conversely, it is also conceivable that more training for soldiers and senior military officers under AFRICOM could enhance professionalism, inculcate military discipline, and support and strengthen democratic institutions. Yet this is possible only if West African security priorities are at the heart of AFRICOM. Therefore, US policy must address West Africa's precarious economic challenges, which leave the bulk of its population in abject poverty. It is poverty, marginalization, and material deprivation that are at the crux of much of the conflict and violence in West Africa, which is then often expressed through religion.

Therefore, it is crucial that West Africa's peripheral and marginalized status in the global economy be alleviated over time through the reduction of US and European farm subsidies to enable African commodities to compete fairly and effectively. The United States must also support the New Partnership for Africa's Development and the UN Millennium Development Goals, as both focus on poverty reduction. What Muslim-majority states in West Africa must counter strongly is the presumption that poverty and the prevalence of "ungoverned spaces" predispose Muslims to engage in acts of terrorism or make their countries terrorist havens. These states also must dispel the widely held belief that Islam and democracy are inherently irreconcilable, in part because Islam lacks "separation of mosque and state." In all the Muslim-majority states, except Mauritania, secularism rather than theocracy is the norm. And in Mali and Senegal specifically, democracy and democratic norms are taking root. Even in Nigeria, with all its democratic deficits, religious tolerance is its defining feature. Therefore, the distinguishing element of Islam in West Africa specifically, and in Africa generally, is its predominantly tolerant outlook.

This chapter has also argued against the presumption that poverty and terrorism correlate strongly in West Africa or, more important, that Muslims and Islam are both inherently violent. We must look to the underlying historical, political, and economic imperatives and to globalization in order to get a handle on why people in acute conditions of deprivation sometimes resort to oppositional political violence to register legitimate grievances against the state when all else has failed. Therefore, US antiterrorism policy must distinguish between oppositional violence and real terrorist activity so as not to downplay legitimate grievances over self-determination and a just distribution of national wealth. By strengthening both the human capital and the democratic state institutions of West African nations, the United States stands to reap the important dividend of winning people's hearts and minds. This is already taking place, but more efforts are needed.

Finally, the United States has to tap its Africanist scholarly community and simultaneously train young Americans to speak African languages and to study and understand Islam as well as the particular cultures of West Africa—so as to tailor and influence policies that enhance mutual US and African interests. Verbal assurances will go only so far toward assuaging people's fears, so backing this kind of policy initiative with actions and support for strengthening national democratic institutions and economic development is the surest way to win the hearts of Africans and curb both terrorism and oppositional violence. Only then will globalization in West Africa in concert with the US military policy become partners in a reconceptualized AFRICOM strategy to win the "War on Terror" in the region. Finally, scholars must begin to unpack or deconstruct the assumptions and meanings that undergird the terms "terrorist" and "terrorism." Both are totalizing terms that often do not make fine distinctions between legitimate struggles for self-determination, as in Gaza or Boko Haram in Northern Nigeria, and indiscriminate and senseless use of violence, such as the attacks on the Twin Towers in New York and the Pentagon on 9/11. We must also be wary as scholars when repressive states and their agents use the terms in an effort to silence or discredit views held by their opponents or to overshadow protests over acute political and economic repression. In this regard, the term "oppositional political violence" is more appropriate.

Notes

Epigraphs: Ghelawdewos Araia, "Africa in the Global Economy: Aid," in *Globalizing Africa,* ed. Malinda Smith (Trenton, NJ: Africa World Press, 2007), 199. Ali Mazrui, *Islam: Between Globalization and Terrorism* (Trenton, NJ: Africa World Press, 2006), xix.

1. James Mittelman, *The Globalization Syndrome: Transformation and Resistance* (Princeton, NJ: Princeton University Press, 2000), 15.

2. James Petras, "Globalization: A Critical Analysis," in *The Political Economy of Imperialism: Critical Appraisals,* ed. Ronald H. Chilcote (Lanham, MD: Rowman & Littlefield, 2000), 181.

3. Thomas Freidman, *The World Is Flat: A Short History of the Twentieth Century* (New York: Farrar, Straus & Giroux, 2005), 8; Jagdish Bhagwati, *In Defense of Globalization* (New York: Oxford University Press, 2004), 28.

4. Mazrui, *Islam,* 35; Samir Amin, "Capitalism, Imperialism, Globalization," in Chilcote, *Political Economy of Imperialism,* 165.

5. Kayhan Delibas, "Conceptualizing Islamic Movements: The Case of Turkey," *International Political Science Review* 30, no. 1 (2009): 89–103; Anouar Boukhars, "Islam, Jihadism, and Depoliticization in France and Germany," *International Political Science Review* 30, no. 3 (2009): 297–317.

6. I use the term "terrorism" with much reservation. Very often, the term conflates legitimate struggles for self-determination or struggles by groups for a fair share of a country's wealth. The adage "One person's terrorist is another's freedom fighter"

calls attention to the power of naming. Abdoulaye Saine, *The Paradox of Third-Wave Democratization in Africa: The Gambia under AFPRC-APRC, 1994–*2008 (Lanham, MD: Lexington Books, 2009).

7. Ali Zafar, "The Growing Relationship between China and Sub-Saharan Africa: Macro-Economic Strategies in Africa," in *Clashing Views in African Issues*, ed. William G. Mosley (New York: McGraw-Hill, 2009), 119; Padraig Carmody and Francis Owusu, "Competing Hegemons? Chinese versus American Geo-Economic Strategies in Africa," in Mosley, *Clashing Views in African Issues*, 134.

8. Paul Nugent, *Africa since Independence: A Contemporary History* (New York: Palgrave Macmillan, 2004), 69.

9. Saine, *Paradox of Third-Wave Democratization*, 82.

10. William Easterly, "The Ideology of Development," in *Developing World 09/10*, ed. Robert J. Griffiths (New York: McGraw-Hill, 2008), 6.

11. Ibid., 6–8.

12. Carmody and Owusu, "Competing Hegemons?" 134.

13. Ibid.

14. Joseph Stiglitz, *Making Globalization Work* (New York: W. W. Norton & Company, 2006), 24.

15. CNN World, April 2, 2009.

16. Judy Duncker, "Globalization and Its Impact on the War on Terror," in *Africa and the War on Terrorism*, ed. John Davis (Burlington, VT: Ashgate, 2007), 65.

17. Steven Weber et al., "How Globalization Went Bad," in *Taking Sides: Clashing Views in Global Issues*, ed. James E. Harf and Mark Owen Lombardi (New York: McGraw-Hill, 2009), 263.

18. United States Africa Command, "Questions and Answers about AFRICOM," http://www.africom.mil/africomFAQs.asp, 1.

19. Ibid.

20. Princeton N. Lyman and J. Stephen Morrison, "The Terrorist Threat in Africa," *Foreign Affairs* 83 (2004): 75.

21. Robert G. Berschinski, "AFRICOM's Dilemma: The 'Global War on Terrorism,' 'Capacity Building,' Humanitarianism, and the Future of U.S. Security Policy in Africa" (2007), http//www.StrategicStudiesInstitute.army.mil/, 17.

22. Abdelkerim Ousman, "The Potential of Islamist Terrorism in Sub-Saharan Africa," *International Journal of Politics, Culture, and Society* 18, nos. 1–2 (2004): 70; Gregg Mills and Jeffrey Herbst, "Africa, Terrorism, and AFRICOM," *Royal United Services Institute Journal* 152, no. 2 (2007): 42.

23. William F. S. Miles, "West African Islam: Emerging Political Dynamics," in *Political Islam in West Africa: State Society Relations Transformed* (Boulder, CO: Lynne Rienner, 2007), 7.

24. Scott Johnson, "The Islamist Rebellion Isn't the Latest Front in the Global War on Terror," *Newsweek Web Exclusive*, August 3, 2009, 3.

25. Ibid., 2.

26. Alex Thomson, *An Introduction to African Politics* (New York: Routledge, 2004), 67.

27. Linda Beck, *Brokering Democracy in Africa: The Rise of Clientelism in Senegal* (New York: Palgrave, 2008), 86.

28. Leonardo Villalon, "Senegal: Shades of Islamism on a Sufi Landscape," in Miles, *Political Islam in West Africa*, 161; Beck, *Brokering Democracy in Africa*, 86.

29. Beck, *Brokering Democracy in Africa*, 86.

30. Momodou Darboe, "The Gambia: Islam and Politics," in Miles, *Political Islam in West Africa*, 129.

31. Ibid., 130.

32. Johnson, "Islamist Rebellion."

33. Lyman and Morrison, "Terrorist Threat in Africa," 83.

34. Ousman, "Potential of Islamic Terrorism," 65–105.

35. Ibid., 72–73.

36. Duncker, "Globalization and Its Impact," 66.

37. Darboe, "The Gambia," 146.

38. Mills and Herbst, "Africa, Terrorism, and AFRICOM," 44.

39. Berschinski, "AFRICOM's Dilemma," 12.

40. "World Briefing/Africa; Mali: More U.S. Military Aid," Reuters/New York Times, October 21, 2009, 1.

41. Berschinski, "AFRICOM's Dilemma," 4.

42. Zafar, "China and Sub-Saharan Africa," 127; Berschinski, "AFRICOM's Dilemma," 5.

43. US Africa Command, "Questions and Answers about AFRICOM," 3.

44. Berschinski, "AFRICOM's Dilemma," 8.

45. Saine, *Paradox of Third-Wave Democratization*; and Abdoulaye Saine, "The Gambia's 'Elected Autocrat Poverty, Peripherality, and Political Instability,' 1996–2006: A Political Economy Assessment," *Armed Forces & Society* 34, no. 3 (2008): 450–73.

46. Eric Schmitt, "U.S. Training in Africa Aims to Deter Extremists," *New York Times*, December 13, 2008, 1–3.

47. Ibid.; Eric Schmitt and Souad Mekhennet, "Al-Qaeda Branch Steps Up Raids in North Africa," *New York Times*, July 9, 2009, 1–3.

48. Stiglitz, *Making Globalization Work*, 44.

49. Ibid., 45.

50. Stephen Marglin, "Development as Poison," in *Developing World 09/10*, ed. Robert J. Griffiths (New York: McGraw-Hill, 2008), 23.

51. Ibid., 20.

52. Ibid., 22.

53. Berschinski, "AFRICOM's Dilemma," v.

Selected Bibliography

The following compilation includes some of the significant sources utilized in this book.

Adejugbe, M. Adebayo. "Industrialization, Distortions, and Economic Development." In Adejugbe, *Industrialization, Urbanization, and Development in Nigeria*, 330.

———, ed. *Industrialization, Urbanization, and Development in Nigeria, 1950–1999*. Lagos: Concept Publications Limited, 2004.

Akindele, S. T., C. Uwasomba, and Mete Feridun. "The Nature of the Nigerian State and Its Economy." In *Nigerian Economy: Essays in Economic Development*, edited by Mete Feridun and S. T. Akindele, 14–26. Morrisville, NC: Lulu Press, 2005.

Akokpari, John K. "Changing with the Tide: The Shifting Orientations of Foreign Policies in Sub-Saharan Africa." *Nordic Journal of African Studies* 8, no. 1 (1999): 22–39.

———. "Globalization and the Challenges for the African State." *Nordic Journal of African Studies* 10 (2001): 188–209.

Alesina, Alberto, Arnaud Devleeschauwer, William Easterly, Sergio Kurlat, and Romain Wacziarg. "Fractionalization." *Journal of Economic Growth* 8 (2003): 155–94.

Alexander, Jeffrey C. "Globalization as Collective Representation: The New Dream of a Cosmopolitan Civil Sphere." *International Journal of Political Culture* 19, nos. 1–2 (December 2005): 81–89.

Amsden, Alice. *Escape From Empire: The Developing World's Journey through Heaven*. Cambridge: MIT Press, 2007.

———. "The Tyranny of Empire." *Challenge* 50, no. 5 (September–October 2007): 24–25.

Anand, Sudhir, Paul Segal, and Joseph Stiglitz. *Debates on the Measurement of Global Poverty*. New York: Oxford University Press, 2010.

Anderson, Bridget. *Doing the Dirty Work? The Global Politics of Domestic Labor*. London: Zed Books, 2000.

Anyanwu, John. "Estimating the Macroeconomic Effects of Monetary Unions: The Case of Trade and Output." *African Development Review* 15, nos. 2–3 (2004): 126–45.

Araia, Ghelawdewos. "Africa in the Global Economy: Aid." In *Globalizing Africa*, edited by Malinda Smith, 199–216. Trenton, NJ: Africa World Press, 2007.

Archer, David. "The Impact of the World Bank and IMF on Education Rights." *Convergence* 39 (2006): 7–18.

Aslaksen, Silje, and Ragnar Torvik. "A Theory of Civil Conflict and Democracy in Rentier States." *Scandinavian Journal of Economics* 108, no. 4 (2006): 571–85.

Audretsch, David, Roy Thurik, Ingrid Verheul, and Sander Wennekers. *Entrepreneurship: Determinants and Policy in a European–U.S. Comparison*. Dordrecht: Kluwer Academic Publishers, 2002.

Axelrod, Robert, and Robert O Keohane. "Achieving Cooperation under Anarchy: Strategies and Institution." In *Neorealism and Neoliberalism: The Contemporary Debate*, edited by David A. Baldwin, 85–115. New York: Columbia University Press, 1993.

Baldacchino, Godfrey. "Bursting the Bubble: The Pseudo-Development Strategies of Microstates." *Development and Change* 24, no. 1 (1993): 29–51.

Beck, Linda. *Brokering Democracy in Africa: The Rise of Clientelism in Senegal.* New York: Palgrave, 2008.

Bell, David E., and Mary Shelman. *Olam International.* Cambridge: Harvard Business School, 2008.

Bennett, Christine. *Comprehensive Multicultural Education: Theory and Practice.* Boston: Pearson Allyn & Bacon, 2007.

Bennett, Juliette. "Public Private Partnerships: The Role of the Private Sector in Preventing Funding Conflict." *Vanderbilt Journal of Transnational Law* 35 (2002): 711–17.

Bernstein, Henry. "Studying Development/Development Studies." *African Studies* 65, no. 1 (July 2006): 45–62.

Bhagwati, Jagdish. *In Defense of Globalization.* New York: Oxford University Press, 2004.

———. "Preferential Trade Arrangements: The Wrong Road." *Law and Policy of International Business* 27, no. 6 (1995): 865–71.

Bhala, Raj, and Kevin Kennedy. *World Trade Law: The GATT-WTO System, Regional Arrangements, and U.S. Law.* Charlottesville, VA: Lexis Law Publishing, 1998.

Bhatnagar, Pradip. "Liberalising the Movement of Natural Persons: A Lost Decade?" *World Economy* 27, no. 3 (2004): 450–72.

Bierstecker, Thomas J. "Globalization and the Modes of Operation of Major Institutional Actors." *Oxford Development Studies* 20 (1998): 15–31.

Birdsall, Nancy, and Arvind Subramanian. "Saving Iraq from Its Oil." *Foreign Affairs* 83, no. 4 (July–August 2004): 77–89.

Blanke, Jennifer. "Assessing Africa's Competitiveness in a Global Context." In *The Africa Competitiveness Report*, 3–28. Geneva: World Economic Forum, 2007.

Bloom, John, and Jeffrey Sachs. "Geography, Demography, and Economic Growth in Africa." *Brookings Papers in Economic Activity* 2 (1998): 207–95.

Borensztein, E., J. De Gregorio, and J. W. Lee. "How Does FDI Affect Economic Growth?" *Journal of International Economics* 45 (1998): 115–35.

Bornstein, David. *How to Change the World: Social Entrepreneurs and the Power of New Ideas.* London: Penguin Books, 2004.

Bosniak, Linda, et al. "Working Borders: Linking Debates about Insourcing and Outsourcing of Capital and Labor." *Texas International Law Journal* 40, no. 4 (Summer 2005): 691–805.

Boukhars, Anouar. "Islam, Jihadism, and Depoliticization in France and Germany." *International Political Science Review* 30, no. 3 (2009): 297–317.

Bravo, Karen E. "Regional Trade Agreements and Labor Liberalization: (Lost) Opportunities for Experimentation?" *St. Louis Public Law Review* 28 (2008): 71–114.

———. "Free Labor! A Labor Liberalization Solution to Modern Trafficking in Humans." *Journal of Transnational Law and Contemporary Problems* 18 (2009): 545–616.

Bravo, Karen E., and Maria Pabon Lopez. "Crisis Meets Reality: A Bold Proposal for Immigration Reform." *Southern Methodist University Law Review* 61 (2008): 191–206.

Bridges, William. *Managing Transitions: Making the Most of Change.* New York: William Bridges and Associates, 2003.

Brown, Oli, Anne Hammill, and Robert McLeman. "Climate Change as the 'New' Security Threat: Implication for Africa." *International Affairs* 83, no. 6 (2007): 1141–54.

Brune, Nancy, and Garret Geoffrey. "The Globalization Rorschach Test: International Economic Integration, Inequality, and the Role of Government." *Annual Review of Political Science* 8 (2005): 1–5.

Bugaje, I. M. "Renewable Energy for Sustainable Development in Africa: A Review." *Renewable and Sustainable Energy Reviews* 10 (2006): 603–12.

Buhaug, Halvard, and Paivi Lujala. "Accounting for Scale: Measuring Geography in Quantitative Studies of Civil War." *Political Geography* 24, no. 4 (2005): 399–418.

Campbell, Horace. "China in Africa: Challenging U.S. Global Hegemony." *Third World Quarterly* 29, no. 1 (2008): 89–105.

Cantwell, John. "Globalization and Development in Africa." In Dunning and Hamdani, *New Globalism and Developing Countries*, 158–77.

Carbaugh, Robert J. *International Economics.* 12th ed. Mason, OH: South-Western Cengage Learning, 2009.

Carey, John M., and Matthew Soberg Shugart. "Incentives to Cultivate a Personal Vote: A Rank-Ordering of Electoral Formulas." *Electoral Studies* 14 (2006): 417–39.

Castro, Claudio de Moura. "The World Bank Policies: Damned if You Do, Damned if You Don't." *Comparative Education* 38 (2002): 387–99.

Cateora, Phillip, Mary Gilly, and John Graham. *International Marketing.* 14th ed. Boston: Richard D. Irwin, 2009.

Chang, Ha-Joon. *Bad Samaritans: The Myth of Free Trade and the Secret History of Capitalism.* New York: Bloomsbury, 2008.

Charnovitz, Steve. "Trade Law Norms on International Migration." In *Migration and International Legal Norms*, edited by T. Alexander Aleinikoff and Alexander Chetail, 241–54. The Hague: T.M.C. Asser Press, 2003.

Chase-Dunn, Christopher. *Global Formation: Structures of the World Economy.* Lanham, MD: Rowman & Littlefield, 1998.

Chelariu, Cristian, Abodulaye Ouattarra, and Kofi Q. Dadzie. "Market Orientation in Ivory Coast: Measurement Validity and Organizational Antecedents in a Sub-Saharan African Economy." *Journal of Business and Industrial Marketing* 17, no. 6 (2002): 456–70.

Cheru, Fantu. *African Renaissance: Roadmaps to the Challenge of Globalization.* Cape Town: Zed Books, 2003.

Chilcote, Ronald. *The Political Economy of Imperialism: Critical Appraisals.* Lanham, MD: Rowman & Littlefield, 2000.

Chirot, Daniel. "The Debacle in Côte d'Ivoire." *Journal of Democracy* 17 (2006): 63–77.

Chow, Esther Ngan-ling. "Gender Matters: Studying Globalization and Social Change in the 21st Century." *International Sociology* 18, no. 3 (2003): 443–60.

———, ed. *Transforming Gender and Development in East Asia.* New York: Routledge, 2002.

Clark, Gracia. "Food Traders and Food Security in Ghana." In *The Political Economy of African Famine*, edited by R. E. Downs, D. O. Kerner, and S. P. Reyna, 7–56. London: Gordon and Breach, 1991.

———. "Gender and Profiteering: Ghana's Market Women as Devoted Mothers and 'Human Vampire Bats.'" In *"Wicked" Women and the Reconfiguration of Gender in Africa*, edited by Dorothy L. Hodgson and Sheryl A. McCurdy, 293–311. Portsmouth, NH: Heinemann, 2001.

———, ed. *Onions Are My Husband: Survival and Accumulation by West African Market Women.* Chicago: University of Chicago Press, 1994.

Clement, Henry H., and Robert Springborg. *Globalization and the Politics of Development in the Middle East.* Cambridge: Cambridge University Press, 2001. In Jonathan Kirshner, "Globalization, American Power, and International Security." *Political Science Quarterly* 123, no. 3 (2008): 363–89.

Cohen, Stephen. *Multinational Corporations and Foreign Direct Investment: Avoiding Simplicity, Embracing Complexity.* New York: Oxford University Press, 2007.

Collier, Paul. *The Bottom Billion: Why the Poorest Countries Are Failing and What Can Be Done about It.* Oxford: Oxford University Press, 2007.

Collier, Paul, and Anke Hoeffler. "Greed and Grievance in Civil War." Oxford Economic Papers 56, no. 4 (October 2004): 563–95.

Corkin, Lucy, and Sanusha Naidu. "China and India in Africa: An Introduction." *Review of African Political Economy* 35, no. 115 (2008): 115–16.

Darkwah, Akosua. "Trading Goes Global: Ghanaian Market Women in an Era of Globalization." In *Global Gender Research: Transnational Perspectives*, edited by Christine Bose and Minjeong Kim, 41–48. New York: Routledge, 2009.

Davies, Martyn. "China's Developmental Model Comes to Africa." *Review of African Political Economy* 35, no. 115 (2008): 134–37.

Delibas, Kayhan. "Conceptualizing Islamic Movements: The Case of Turkey." *International Political Science Review* 30, no. 1 (2009): 89–103.

DeMarees, Pieter. *Chronicle of the Gold Coast of Guinea.* Translated by A. Van Dantzig and Adam Smith. 1602; repr., Oxford: Oxford University Press, 1985.

Deresky, Helen. *International Management: Managing across Borders.* Upper Saddle River, NJ: Prentice Hall, 2008.

Diawara, Manthia. "Toward a Regional Imaginary in Africa." In *World Bank Literature*, edited by Amitava Kumar, 64–81. Minneapolis: University of Minnesota Press, 2003.

Dicken, Peter. *Global Shift: Transforming the World Economy.* New York: Guildford Press, 2003.

Doyle, Michael. "Liberalism and World Politics." *American Political Science Review* 80 (December 1986): 1151–69.

Drake, St. Clair, and Leslie Lacy. "Government vs. the Unions: The Sekondi-Takoradi Strike, 1961." In *Politics in Africa: 7 Cases*, edited by Gwendolyn Carter, 67–82. New York: Harcourt, Brace, 1966.

Drake, William J. *Communications.* In Simmons and Oudraat, *Managing Global Issues*, 25–74.

Duncker, Judy. "Globalization and Its Impact on the War on Terror." In *Africa and the War on Terrorism*, edited by John Davis, 63–78. Burlington, VT: Ashgate, 2007.

Dunning, John H. "The Advent of Alliance Capitalism." In Dunning and Hamdani, *New Globalism and Developing Countries*, 12–43.

———. "Globalization and the New Geography of Foreign Direct Investment." *Oxford Development Studies* 26 (1998): 47–69.

———. *Multilateral Enterprises in the Global Economy.* London: Addison-Wesley, 1993.

Dunning, John H., and Khalil A. Hamdani, eds. *The New Globalism and Developing Countries.* Tokyo: United Nations University Press, 1997.

Durkheim, Emile. *Moral Education.* Newton Abbot, UK: David and Charles, 2002.

Easterly, William. "Are Aid Agencies Improving?" *Economic Policy* 52 (September 2007): 633–68.

———. "Can the West Save Africa?" *Journal of Economic Literature* 47, no. 2 (2009): 373–417.

———. *The Elusive Quest for Growth.* Cambridge: MIT Press, 2001.

Elbe, Stephan. "Rsking Lives: AIDS, Security, and Three Concepts of Risk." *Security Dialogue* 39, nos. 2–3 (2008): 177–98.

Eun, S. C., and B. J. Resnick. *International Financial Management.* New York: McGraw-Hill, 2004.

Fajana, S. *Industrial Relations.* Lagos: Labofin and Company, 2005.

Falola, Toyin, and Aribidesi Usman, eds. *Movements, Borders, and Identities in Africa.* Rochester, NY: University of Rochester Press, 2009.

Fashola, A. Mashood. "A Schema for Nigeria's Optimal Industrial Development." In Adejugbe, *Industrialization, Urbanization, and Development in Nigeria*, 293–320.

Fearon, James. "Primary Commodities Exports and Civil War." *Journal of Conflict Resolution* 49, no. 4 (2005): 483–507.

Fearon, James, and David Latin. "Ethnicity, Insurgency, and Civil War." *American Political Science Review* 97 (March 2003): 75–90.

Feige, Edgar, Michael Faulend, Velimir Šonje, and Vedran Šošić. "Unofficial Dollarization in Latin America." In *The Dollarization Debate*, edited by Dominick Salvatore, James Dean, and Thomas Willet, 72–97. New York: Oxford University Press, 2003.

Fielding, David, and Kalvinder Shields. "Modelling Macroeconomic Shocks in the CFA Franc Zone." *Journal of Development Economics* 66, no. 1 (2001): 199–223.

Freeman, Samuel. *Justice and the Social Contract: Essays on Rawlsian Political Philosophy.* London: Oxford University Press, 2007.

Freidman, Thomas. *The World Is Flat: A Short History of the Twentieth Century.* New York: Farrar, Straus & Giroux, 2005.

Ganzle, Stefan, and Steffi Retzlaff. "'So, European Union is 50 . . .': Images of the EU and the 2007 German Presidency in Canadian News." *International Journal* 62, no. 3 (Summer 2008): 627–44.

Garcia, Ruben. "Labor as Property: Guest Workers, International Trade, and the Democracy Deficit." *Journal of Gender, Race, and Justice* 10 (2006): 27–65.

Geda, Alemayehu, and Atnafu G. Meskel."China and India's Growth Surge: Is It a Curse or Blessing for Africa? The Case of Manufactured Exports." *African Development Review* 20, no. 2 (2008): 247–72.

Ghazvinian, John. *Untapped: The Scramble for Africa's Oil.* New York: Harcourt, 2007.

Giddens, Anthony. *Runaway World: How Globalisation Is Reshaping Our Lives.* Reith Lectures. London: Profile Books, 1999.

Gilbert, Erik, and Jonathan T. Reynolds. *Africa in World History: From Prehistory to the Present.* Upper Saddle River, NJ: Pearson Prentice Hall, 2004.

Glaeser, Edward. "The Political Economy of Hatred." *Quarterly Journal of Economics* 120, no. 1 (January 2005): 45–86.

Global Witness. *Hot Chocolate: How Cocoa Fueled the Conflict in Côte d'Ivoire.* Washington, DC, 2007.

Goldberg, Pinelopi K., and Nina Pavcnik. "Distributional Effects of Globalization in Developing Countries." *Journal of Economic Literature* 45, no. 1 (March 2007): 76–77.

Gomez-Dantes, Octavio. "Health." In Simmons and Oudraat, *Managing Global Issues,* 392–423.

Gordon, Jennifer. "Transnational Labor Citizenship." *Southern California Law Review* 80 (2007): 503–87.

Gordon, Michael D. "Management Education and the Base of the Pyramid." *Journal of Management Education* 32, no. 6 (2008): 767–81.

Grieco, Joseph M. "Anarchy and the Limits of Cooperation: A Realist Critique of the Newest Liberal Institutionalism." *International Organization* 42, no. 3 (Summer 1988): 458–508.

Griffith, David. *American Guest Workers: Jamaicans and Mexicans in the U.S. Labor Market.* University Park: Penn State University Press, 2006.

Griffiths, Robert J., ed. *Developing World 09/10.* New York: McGraw-Hill, 2008.

Guyer, Jane. *Marginal Gains.* Chicago: University of Chicago Press, 2004.

Hammond, Gill, Ravi Kanbur, and Eswar Prasad. *Monetary Policy Frameworks for Emerging Markets.* Edward Elgar, 2009.

Harley, Sharon, ed. *Women's Labor in the Global Economy: Speaking in Multiple Voices.* New Brunswick, NJ: Rutgers University Press, 2007.

Hart, Stuart. *Capitalism at the Crossroads: Aligning Business, Earth, and Humanity.* Upper Saddle River, NJ: Wharton School Publishing, 2007.

Hayter, Theresa. *Open Borders: The Case against Immigration Controls.* 2nd ed. London: Pluto Press, 2004.

Held, David, and Mathias Koenig-Archibugi, eds. *Taming Globalization: Frontiers of Governance.* Cambridge, UK: TJ International, Padstow, Cornwall, 2003.

Higginbotham, Elizabeth, and Lynn Cannon. *Rethinking Mobility: Towards a Race and Gender Inclusive Theory.* Memphis, TN: Center for Research on Women, 1988.

Hill, Charles. *International Business: Competing in the Global Marketplace.* 7th ed. Boston: McGraw-Hill Irwin, 2009.

Hobson, J., and M. Ramesh. "Globalization Makes of States What States Make of It: Between Agency and Structure in the State/Globalization Debate." *New Political Economy* 7, no. 1 (2002): 5–22.

Holzinger, Katharina, Christoph Knill, and Thomas Sommerer. "Environmental Policy Convergence: The Impact of International Harmonization, Transnational Communication, and Regulatory Competition." *International Organization* 62, no. 4 (2008): 553–87.

Hopkins, Anthony. "Economic Aspects of Political Movements in the Gold Coast and Nigeria, 1918–39." *Journal of African History* 7 (1965): 133–52.

———. *An Economic History of West Africa*. New York: Columbia University Press, 1973.

Horn, Nancy. *Cultivating Customers: Market Women in Harare, Zimbabwe*. Boulder, CO: Lynne Rienner, 1994.

House-Midamba, Bessie, and Felix Ekechi, eds. *African Market Women and Economic Power: The Role of Women in African Economic Development*. Westport, CT: Greenwood Press, 1995.

Houssa, Romain. "Monetary Union in West Africa and Asymmetric Shocks: A Dynamic Structural Factor Model Approach." *Journal of Development Economics* 85 (2008): 319–47.

Howard, Rhoda. *Colonialism and Underdevelopment in Ghana*. London: Croom Helm, 1978.

Hubson, Andrew. "One World? Many Worlds? The Place of Regions in the Study of International Society." *International Affairs* 83, no. 1 (2007): 127–46.

Hu-Dehart, Evelyn. "Surviving Globalization: Immigrant Women Workers in Late Capitalist America." In Harley, *Women's Labor in the Global Economy*, 85–102.

Hufbauer, Gary C. "Globalization Facts and Consequences." *Petersen Institute of International Economics* (March 13, 2001).

Hulsse, Rainer, and Alexander Spencer. "The Metaphor of Terror: Terrorism Studies and the Constructivist Turn." *Security Dialogue* 39, no. 6 (2008): 571–92.

Humphreys, Macartan, Jeffrey Sachs, and Joseph Stiglitz, eds. *Escaping the Resource Curse*. New York: Columbia University Press, 2007.

Huntington, Samuel. "The Clash of Civilizations." *Foreign Affairs* 73, no. 3 (1993).

———. *The Clash of Civilizations and the Remaking of World Order*. New York: Simon and Schuster, 1996.

Isumonah, Victor Adefemi. "The Making of the Ogoni Ethnic Group." *Africa: Journal of the International African Institute* 74, no. 3 (2004): 433–53.

Iyoha, O. "Policy Environment, Direct Foreign Investment, and Economic Growth in Sub-Saharan Africa." *Finance and Banking Review* 1, no. 1 (July 2007): 1–19.

Jackson, Craig. "Constitutional Structure and Governance Strategies for Economic Integration in Africa and Europe." *Transnational Law and Contemporary Problems* 13 (2003): 139–77.

James, Harold. "Globalization, Empire, and Natural Law." *International Affairs* 84, no. 3 (2008): 421–26.

Jensen, Nathan, and Leonard Wantchekon. "Resource Wealth and Political Regimes in Africa." *Comparative Political Studies* 37, no. 7 (September 2004): 816–41.

Jepperson, Ronald L., Alexander Wendt, and Peter Katzenstein. "Norms, Identity, and Culture in National Security." In *The Culture of National Security: Norms and Identity in World Politics*, edited by Peter Katzenstein, 33–75. New York: Columbia University Press, 1996.

Jhingan, M. L. *The Economics of Development and Planning*. Delhi: Vrinda Publications, 2005.

Johnson, Kevin R. *Opening the Floodgates: Why America Needs to Rethink Its Borders and Immigration Laws*. New York: New York University Press, 2007.

Kanyenze, Godfrey. "The Performance of the Zimbabwean Economy, 1980–2000." In *Twenty Years of Independence in Zimbabwe*, edited by Staffan Darnolf and Liisa Laakso, 34–77. New York: Palgrave Macmillan, 2003.

Keller, Edmond John. "Africa in Transition—Facing the Challenges of Globalization." *Harvard International Review* 29 (2007).

Khanna, Tarun. *Billions of Entrepreneurs: How China and India Are Reshaping Their Future and Yours*. Boston: Harvard Business School Press, 2007.

Kirshner, Jonathan. "Globalization, American Power, and International Security." *Political Science Quarterly* 123, no. 3 (2008): 363–89.

Klaas, Brian. "From Miracle to Nightmare: An Institutional Analysis of Development Failures in Côte d'Ivoire." *Africa Today* 55, no. 1 (2008): 109–26.

Krishna, Kamini. *India-Africa Partnership in the Twenty-First Century: Expanding Horizon*. Lusaka: University of Zambia, 2009.

Krugman, Paul. "Dutch Tulips and Emerging Markets: Another Bubble Bursts." *Foreign Affairs* 74, no. 4 (1995): 74.

Krugman, Paul R., and Maurice Obstfeld. *International Trade: Theory and Policy*. New York: Pearson Addison-Wesley, 2006.

Kuepie, Mathias, C. J. Nordman, and F. Roubaud. "Education and Earnings in Urban West Africa." *Journal of Comparative Economics* 37, no. 3 (2009): 491–515.

Kull, Irene. "About Grounds for Exemption from Performance under the Draft Estonian Law of Obligations Act." *Juridica International*, no. 1 (2001): 44–52.

Kurlantzick, Joshua. "The World Is Bumpy: Deglobalization and Its Dangers." *New Republic* 240, nos. 12–13 (July 15, 2009): 19–21.

Kwesiga, Joy. *Women's Access to Higher Education in Africa: Uganda's Experience*. Kampala: Fountain, 2002.

Lapeye, C. "La Côte d'Ivoire demeure: La plus grande économie." *Marchés Africains* 12 (2009): 6–7.

Laumanns, Ulrich, Danyel Reiche, and Mischa Bechberger. "Renewable Energy Markets in Developing Countries: Providing Green Power for Sustainable Development." In *Green Power Markets: Support Schemes, Case Studies, and Perspectives*, edited by Lutz Mez, 403–13. Essex, UK: Multi-Science, 2007.

Lawless, Michael. "Terrorism: An International Crime." *International Journal* 63, no. 1 (Winter 2007–8): 139–59.

Legrain, Philippe. *Immigrants: Your Country Needs Them*. London: Little, Brown, 2007.

Levy, Pierre. "Collective Intelligence, A Civilization: Towards a Method of Positive Interpretation." *International Journal of Politics* 18, nos. 3–4 (Spring–Summer 2005): 189–98.

Light, Paul. *The Search for Social Entrepreneurship*. Washington, DC: Brookings Institution Press, 2008.

Lindert, Peter H., and Jeffrey Williamson. "Does Globalization Make the World More Unequal?" In *Globalization in Historical Perspective*, 227–76. Cambridge, MA: National Bureau of Economic Research, 2001.

Lujala, Paivi, Nils Petter Gleditsch, and Elisabeth Gilmore. "A Diamond Curse? Civil War and a Lootable Resource." *Journal of Conflict Resolution* 49, no. 4 (2005): 538–62.

Lyman, Princeton N., and J. Stephen Morrison. "The Terrorist Threat in Africa." *Foreign Affairs* 83, no. 1 (2004): 75–86.

MacEwan, Arthur. *Neo-Liberalism or Democracy? Economic Strategy, Markets, and Alternatives for the 21st Century.* New York: St. Martin's Press, 2000.

Made, Patricia, and Myorovai Whande. "Women in Southern Africa: A Note on the Zimbabwe Success Story." *Issues: A Journal of Opinion* 17, no. 2 (1989): 26–28.

Magubane, Zine. "Globalization and the South African Women: A Historical Overview." In *Visions of Gender Theories and Social Development in Africa: Harnessing Knowledge for Social Justice and Equality,* 73–94. Dakar: AAWORD Book Series, 2001.

Mallampally, Padma, and Karl P. Sauvant. "Foreign Direct Investment in Developing Countries: Policy Perspectives." *Finance and Development* 36, no. 1 (March 1999).

Mambula, Charles J. "Perceptions of SME Growth Constraints in Nigeria." *Journal of Small Business Management* 40 (2002): 58–65.

Martin, Roger, and Sally Osberg. "Social Entrepreneurship: The Case for Definition." *Stanford Social Innovation Review.* April 20, 2007.

Marx, Karl. *Capital: A Critique of Political Economy.* Vol. 1. Translated by E. Mandel. New York: Random House, 1977.

Massey, Douglas, Joaquin Arango, Graeme Hugo, Ali Kouaouci, Adela Pellegrina and J. Edward Taylor. *Worlds in Motion: Understanding International Migration at the End of the Millennium.* Oxford: Oxford University Press, 1998.

Massey, Douglas S., and J. Edward Taylor. *International Migration: Prospects and Policies in a Global Market.* Oxford: Oxford University Press, 2004.

Masson, Paul, and Catherine Pattillo. *Monetary Union in West Africa: Is It Desirable and How Could It Be Achieved?* Washington, DC: International Monetary Fund, 2001.

Matsen, Egil, and Ragnar Torvik. "Optimal Dutch Disease." *Journal of Development Economics* 78 (2005): 494–515.

Mazrui, Ali. *Islam: Between Globalization and Counterterrorism.* Trenton, NJ: Africa World Press, 2006.

McFadden, Patricia. *Patriarchy: Political Power, Sexuality, and Globalization.* Port Louis, Mauritius: Ledikasyon Pu Travayer, 2001.

Melitz, Jacques. "The Theory of Optimum Currency Areas, Trade Adjustment, and Trade." *Open Economies Review* 7, no. 2 (1996): 99–116.

Mendoza, Enrique. "Terms-of-Trade Uncertainty and Economic Growth." *Journal of Development Economics* 54, no. 2 (December 1997): 323–56.

Micklelethwait, John, and Adrian Woodridge. *God Is Back: How the Global Revival of Faith Is Changing the World.* New York: Penguin Press, 2009.

Miguel, Edward, Shanker Satyanath, and Ernest Sergenti. "Economic Shocks and Civil Conflict: An Instrumental Variables Approach." *Journal of Political Economy* 112 (2004): 725–53.

Milanovic, Branko. "The Two Faces of Globalization: Against Globalization as We Know It." *World Development Journal* 31, no. 4 (2003): 667–83.

Miles, William F. S., ed. *Political Islam in West Africa: State Society Relations Transformed.* Boulder, CO: Lynne Rienner, 2007.

———. "West African Islam: Emerging Political Dynamics." In Miles, *Political Islam in West Africa,* 1–18.

Miller, Errol. "Gender, Power, and Politics: An Alternative Perspective." In *Gender, Peace, and Conflict,* edited by Inger Skjelsbaek and Don Smith, 103. London: Sage Publications, 2001.

Miller, Lee Ryan. *Confessions of a Recovering Realist: Toward a Neo-Liberal Theory of International Relations.* Bloomington, IN: Author House, 2004.

Mittelman, James. *The Globalization Syndrome: Transformation and Resistance.* Princeton, NJ: Princeton University Press, 2000.

———. *Globalizing Women: Transnational Feminist Networks.* Baltimore: Johns Hopkins University Press, 2005.

Moosa, I. A. *Foreign Direct Investment: Theory, Evidence, and Practice.* New York: Palgrave, 2002.

Moran, Theodore, Edward Graham, and Magnus Blomstrom, eds. *Does Foreign Direct Investment Promote Development?* Washington, DC: Institute for International Economics, Center for Global Development, 2005.

Morrow, Raymond, and Carlos Alberto Torres. "The State, Globalization, and Educational Policy." In *Globalization and Education: Critical Perspectives,* edited by Nicholas C. Burbules and Carlos Alberto Torres, 27–56. New York: Routledge, 2000.

Mosley, William G., ed. *Clashing Views in African Issues.* New York: McGraw-Hill, 2009.

Moyo, Dambisa. *Dead Aid: Why Aid Is Not Working and How There Is a Better Way for Africa.* London: Allen Lane, 2009.

Mundell, Robert A. "A Theory of Optimum Currency Areas." *American Economic Review* 51, no. 4 (1961): 509–17.

Naim, Moisés. "Think Again: Globalization." *Foreign Policy* 171 (February 16, 2009): 32.

Naisbitt, John. *Global Paradox: The Bigger the World Economy, the More Political Its Smallest Players.* New York: William Morrow, 1994.

———. "Women: Globalization and Women" *Human Rights Solidarity* 11, no. 2 (February 2001).

Nugent, Paul. *Africa since Independence: A Contemporary History.* New York: Palgrave Macmillan, 2004.

Nurkse, Ragner. *Problems of Capital Formation in Under-developed Countries.* New York: Oxford University Press, 1953.

Obadan, Mike I. "Direct Investment in Nigeria: An Empirical Analysis." *African Studies Review* 25, no. 1 (1994): 167–81.

Obadan, Mike I., and E. Chuks Obioma. "Contemporary Issues in Global Trade and Finance and Their Implications." *Journal of Economic Management* 6, no. 1 (1999): 6–8.

Olaniyan, I. F. "Beyond SAP: A Policy Framework." *Nigerian Economic Society* (1996): 143–58.

Orwell, George. *Animal Farm.* 1945; repr., New York: Houghton Mifflin, 2003.

———. *Nineteen Eighty-four.* 1949; repr., London: Penguin Books, 2000.

Osaghae, Eghosa E. "The Ogoni Uprising: Oil Politics, Minority Agitation, and the Future of the Nigerian State." *African Affairs* 94 (1995): 325–44.

Oshuntokun, A. *Environmental Problems of the Niger-Delta.* Lagos: Friedrich Ebert Foundation, 1999.

Osirim, Mary J. "Carrying the Burdens of Adjustment and Globalization: Women and Microenterprise Development in Urban Zimbabwe." *International Sociology* 18, no. 3 (2003): 535–58.

———. "Creatively Coping with Crisis and Globalization: Zimbabwean Businesswomen in Crocheting and Knitting." In Harley, *Women's Labor in the Global Economy*, 134–57.

———. *Enterprising Women in Urban Zimbabwe: Gender, Microbusiness, and Globalization.* Washington, DC, and Bloomington: Woodrow Wilson Center Press and Indiana University Press, 2009.

———. "Women, Work, and Public Policy: Structural Adjustment and the Informal Sector in Zimbabwe." In *Population Growth and Environmental Degradation in Southern Africa*, edited by Ezekiel Kalipeni, 61–84. Boulder, CO: Lynne Rienner, 1994.

Ostby, Gudrun. "Polarization, Horizontal Inequalities, and Violent Civil Conflict." *Journal of Peace Research* 45, no. 2 (2008): 143–62.

Osunde, Egerton, and Josiah Tlou. "Persisting and Common Stereotypes in U.S. Students' Knowledge of Africa: A Study of Preservice Social Studies Teachers." *Professional Development Collection* 87 (1996): 121–22.

Ousman, Abdelkerim. "The Potential of Islamic Terrorism in Sub-Saharan Africa." *International Journal of Politics, Culture, and Society* 18, nos. 1–2 (2004): 65–105.

Palmer, Ian, Richard Dunford, and Gib Akin. *Managing Organizational Change: A Multiple Perspectives Approach.* New York: McGraw-Hill, 2009.

Pannell, Clifton W. "China's Economic and Political Penetration in Africa." *Eurasian Geography and Economics* 49, no. 6 (2008): 706–30.

Parrenas, Rhacel. *Servants of Globalization: Women, Migration, and Domestic Work.* Stanford: Stanford University Press, 2001.

Parternariat Afrique Canada. *Les diamants et la sécurité humaine: Revue Annuelle 2008.* 2008.

Patterson, Rubin, ed. *African Brain Circulation: Beyond the Drain-Gain Debate.* Boston: Brill, 2007.

———. "The Migration-Development Model Can Serve Two Masters: The Transnational Capitalist Class and National Development." In *The Nation in the Global Era: Conflict and Transformation*, edited by Jerry Harris, 101–19. Boston: Brill, 2009.

———. "Preparing Sub-Saharan Africa for a Pioneering Role in Eco-industrial Development." *Journal of Industrial Ecology* 12 (2008): 501–4.

———. Payne, Richard J. *Global Issues: Politics, Economics, and Culture.* 2nd ed. New York: Pearson Longman, 2009.

Pereira, Charmaine. "Configuring 'Global,' 'National,' and 'Local,' in Governance Agendas in Nigeria," *Social Research* 69, no. 3 (2003): 781–804.

Perry, John A., and Erna K. Perry. *Contemporary Society: An Introduction to Social Science.* New York: Pearson Education, 2009.

Petras, James. "Globalization: A Critical Analysis." In *The Political Economy of Imperialism: Critical Appraisals*, edited by Ronald Chilcote, 181–214. Lanham, MD: Rowman & Littlefield, 2000.

Pheko, Mohau. "Privatization, Trade Liberalization, and Women's Socio-Economic Rights: Exploring Policy Alternatives." In *Africa: Gender, Globalization and Resistance*, edited by Yassine Fall, 89–99. Dakar: AAWORD Book Series, 1999.

Phimister, Ian. *An Economic and Social History of Zimbabwe, 1890–1948.* London: Longman, 1988.

Pogge, Thomas. *World Poverty and Human Rights.* 2nd ed. Cambridge, UK: Polity Press, 2008.

Pojman, Louis P. *Terrorism, Human Rights, and the Case for World Government.* Boulder, CO: Rowman & Littlefield, 2006.

Portes, Alejandro, Manuel Castells, and Lauren Benton, eds. *The Informal Economy: Studies in Advanced and Less Developed Societies.* Baltimore: Johns Hopkins University Press, 1989.

Prahalad, C. K. *The Fortune at the Bottom of the Pyramid: Eradicating Poverty through Profits, Enabling Dignity and Choice through Markets.* Upper Saddle River, NJ: Wharton School Publishing, Pearson Education, 2005.

Prasad, K. Edward Kenneth Roggof, Shang-Jin Wei, and A. Mary Kose. "Effects of Financial Globalization on Developing Countries: Some Empirical Evidence." *Finance and Development* 27 (2003): 17–21.

Przeworski, Adam, and James Raymond Vreeland. "The Effect of IMF Programs on Economic Growth." *Journal of Development Economics* 62 (2000): 385–421.

Rajaee, Farhang. *Globalization on Trial: The Human Condition and the Information Civilization.* Ottawa, ON: Kumarian Press, 2000.

Rauch, James E., and Scott Kostyshak. "The Three Arab Worlds." *Journal of Economic Perspectives* 23, no. 3 (Summer 2009): 165–88.

Ritzer, George. *The Globalization of Nothing 2.* Thousands Oaks, CA: Pine Forge Press, 2007.

Robertson, Claire. "The Death of Makola and Other Tragedies: Male Strategies against a Female-Dominated System." *Canadian Journal of African Studies* 17 (1983): 469–95.

———. *Trouble Showed the Way: Women, Men, and Trade in the Nairobi Area, 1890–1990.* Bloomington: Indiana University Press, 1997.

Rodrik, Dani. "Symposium on Globalization in Perspective: An Introduction." *Journal of Economic Perspectives* 12 (Fall 1998): 3–8.

———. "Trading in Illusions." *Foreign Policy* 123 (March–April 2001): 55–62.

Rosenau, James N., David C. Earnest, Yale H. Ferguson, and Ole R. Holsti. *On the Cutting Edge of Globalization: An Inquiry into American Elites.* New York: Rowman & Littlefield, 2006.

Ross, Michael L. "Does Oil Hinder Democracy?" *World Politics* 53 (2001): 325–61.

———. "How Do Natural Resources Influence Civil War? Evidence from Thirteen Cases." *International Organization* 58 (Winter 2004): 35–67.

———. "What Do We Know about Natural Resources and Civil War?" *Journal of Peace Research* 41 (2004): 337–56.

Sachs, Jeffrey. *The End of Poverty.* New York: Penguin, 2005.

Saine, Abdoulaye. "The Gambia's 'Elected Autocrat Poverty, Peripherality, and Political Instability,' 1996–2006: A Political Economy Assessment." *Armed Forces & Society* 34, no. 3 (2008): 450–73.

———. *The Paradox of Third-Wave Democratization in Africa: The Gambia under AFPRC-APRC Rule, 1994–2008.* Lanham, MD: Lexington Books, 2009.

Salvatore, Dominick. *Introduction to International Economics.* 10th ed. Hoboken, NJ: John Wiley and Sons, 2010.

Salvatore, Dominick, James Dean, and Thomas Willet, eds. *The Dollarization Debate.* New York: Oxford University Press, 2003.

Samli, Coskun. *Entering and Succeeding in Emerging Countries: Marketing to the Forgotten Majority.* Singapore: Thompson, Southwestern, 2004.

Sassen, Saskia. *Globalization and Its Discontents: Essays on the New Mobility of People and Money.* London: New Press, 1998.

Sawyer, W. Charles, and Richard L. Sprinkle. *International Economics.* Upper Saddle River, NJ: Pearson Prentice Hall, 2009.

Saxenian, Anna Lee. *The New Argonauts: Regional Advantage in a Global Economy.* Cambridge: Harvard University Press, 2006.

Say, Jean-Baptiste. *Treatise on Political Economy.* New Brunswick: NJ: Transaction Publishers, 2001.

Schmidt, Elizabeth. *Peasants, Traders, and Wives: Shona Women in the History of Zimbabwe, 1870–1939.* Portsmouth, NH: Heinemann, 1992.

Scholte, Jan Aart. *Globalization: A Critical Introduction.* 2nd ed. New York: Palgrave Macmillan, 2005.

Sefa Dei, George. "The Challenge of Inclusive Schooling in Africa: A Ghanaian Case Study." *Comparative Education* 41 (2005): 267–89.

———. *Schooling and Education in Africa: The Case of Ghana.* Trenton, NJ: Africa World Press, 2004.

Sen, Amartya. *Development as Freedom.* Oxford: Oxford University Press, 1999.

———. "Violence, Identity, and Poverty." *Journal of Peace Research* 45, no. 1 (2008): 5–15.

Shaw, Eleanor, and Sara Carter. "Social Entrepreneurship: Theoretical Antecedents and Empirical Analysis of Entrepreneurial Processes and Outcomes." *Journal of Small Business and Enterprise Development* 14 (2007): 418–34.

Shenkar, Oded. *The Chinese Century: The Rising Chinese Economy and Its Impact on the Global Economy, the Balance of Power, and Your Job.* Upper Saddle River, NJ: Pearson Education, 2005.

Shiva, Vandana. *Stolen Harvest: The Hijacking of the Global Food Supply.* Cambridge, MA: South End Press, 2000.

Simmons, P. J., and Chantal de Jonge Oudraat, eds. *Managing Global Issues: Lessons Learned.* Washington, DC: Carnegie Endowment for International Peace, 2001.

Singh, Sushant K. *India and West Africa: A Burgeoning Relationship.* London: Chatham House, 2007.

Skillen, James W. "To Look at the World Entirely Afresh." In *Prospects and Ambiguities of Globalization: A Critical Assessment at a Time of Growing Turmoil,* edited by James W. Skillen, 1–8. New York: Lexington Books, 2009.

Skjelsbaek, Inger, and Don Smith, eds. *Gender, Peace, and Conflict.* London: Sage Publications, 2001.

Solomon, Michele Klein. "GATS Mode 4 and the Mobility of Labor." In *International Migration Law: Developing Paradigms and Key Challenges*, edited by Ryszard Cholewinski, Richard Perruchoud, and Euan MacDonald, 107–27. The Hague: T.M.C. Asser Press, 2007.

Spio-Gabrah, Ekow. "Connecting Rural Africa." *NEPAD Business and Investment Guide 2009* 4 (2009): 92–93.

Spring, Joel. "Research on Globalization and Education." *Review of Educational Research* 78 (2008): 330–63.

Steger, Manfred B. *Globalism: The New Market Ideology.* Lanham, MD: Rowman & Littlefield, 2002.

Stiglitz, Joseph E. "Globalism's Discontents." *American Prospect* 13, no. 1 (January 1, 2002): A16–A21.

———. *Globalization and Its Discontents.* W. W. Norton & Company, 2002.

———. *Making Globalization Work.* New York: W. W. Norton & Company, 2006.

Suter, Keith. *In Defence of Globalization.* Sydney: UNSW Press, 2000.

Taiwo, Olufemi. "Feminism and Africa: Reflections on the Poverty of Theory." In *African Women and Feminism: Reflecting on the Politics of Sisterhood*, edited by Oyeronke Oyewunmi, 45–56. Trenton, NJ: Africa World Press, 2003.

Taylor, Ian. "China's Oil Diplomacy in Africa." *International Affairs* 82, no. 5 (2006): 937–59.

Thomas, Vinod, Yan Wang, Nalin Kishor, Dani Kaufmann, Ramon Lopez, and Ashok Dhareshwar. *Quality of Growth.* New York: Oxford University Press for the World Bank, 2000.

Tiplady, Richard, ed. *One World or Many: The Impact of Globalization on Mission.* Pasadena, CA: William Carey Library, 2003.

Todaro, Michael P., and Stephen C. Smith. *Economic Development.* 10th ed. New York: Pearson-Addison-Wesley, 2009.

Treisman, Daniel. "The Causes of Corruption: A Cross-National Study." *Journal of Public Economics* 76, no. 3 (2000): 399–457.

Veltmeyer, Henry. Introduction to *New Perspectives on Globalization and Antiglobalization: Prospects for a New World Order?* Edited by Henry Veltmeyer, 1–10. Burlington, VT: Ashgate, 2008.

Verstraete, Ginette. "Technological Frontiers and the Politics of Mobility in the European Union." In *Uprootings/Regroundings*, edited by Sara Ahmed, Claudia Castenada, Anne-Maria Fortier, and Mimi Sheller, 225–50. Oxford, UK: Berg Publishers, 2003.

Waddock, Sandra. *Leading Corporate Citizens: Vision, Values, Value Added.* 3rd ed. Singapore: McGraw-Hill Irwin, 2009.

Walekhwa, Peter, Johnny Mugisha, and Lars Drake. "Biogas Energy from Family-Sized Digesters in Uganda: Critical Factors and Policy Implications." *Energy Policy* 37, no. 7 (2009): 2754–62.

Wallensteen, Peter. *Understanding Conflict Resolution: War, Peace, and the Global System.* London: Sage Publications, 2002.

Wallerstein, Immanuel. "Culture as the Ideological Battleground of the Modern World-System." In *Global Culture: Nationalism, Globalization and Modernity*, edited by Mike Featherstone, 31–55. London: Sage Publications, 1990.

Waltz, Kenneth. *Theory of International Politics.* New York: McGraw-Hill, 1979.

Ward, Kerry. *Networks of Empire: Forced Migration in the Dutch East India Company.* Cambridge: Cambridge University Press, 2009.

Weber, Steven, Naazneen Barma, Matthew Kroenig, and Ely Ratner. "How Globalization Went Bad." In *Taking Sides: Clashing Views in Global Issues,* edited by James E. Harf and Mark Owen Lombardi, 263–69. New York: McGraw-Hill, 2009.

Wengenmayr, Roland, and Thomas Buhrke. *Renewable Energy: Sustainable Energy Concepts for the Future.* Weinheim, Germany: Wiley-VCH, 2008.

Winters, L. Alan, Terrie Louise Walmsley, Zhen Kung Wang, and Roman Grynberg. "Liberalising Temporary Movement of Natural Persons: An Agenda for the Development Round." *World Economy* 26, no. 8 (2003): 1137–61.

Yongo-Bure, Benaiah. *Economic Development of Southern Sudan.* Lanham, MD: University Press of America, 2007.

Zalik, Anna, "The Niger Delta: 'Petro-Violence' and Partnership Development." *Review of African Political Economy* 31, no. 101 (2004): 401–24.

Zhao, Hong. "China-U.S. Oil Rivalry in Africa." *Copenhagen Journal of Asian Studies* 26, no. 2 (2008): 97–119.

Zimmerman, Mary, Jacquelyn Litt, and Christine Bose, eds. *Global Dimensions of Gender and Care Work.* Stanford: Stanford University Press, 2006.

Contributors

ADERONKE ADESOLA ADESANYA is assistant professor of art and art history in the College of Visual and Performing Arts at the James Madison University. Her areas of specialization include African art history, peace and conflict studies, folklore, and gender and cultural studies. She has published several essays in her areas of specialization and contributed to international scholarly journals and book projects including *Yoruba Religious Textiles*, edited by Elisha P. Renne and Bahatunde Agbaje Williams; *Perspectives on Peace Conflict Studies*, edited by Isaac Olawale Albert; and *African Civilization*, edited by Ademola Ajayi. She is the coauthor of *Migrations and Creative Expressions in Africa and the African Diaspora* with Toyin Falola and Niyi Afolabi, and the coauthor of a collection of poems titled *Etches of Fresh Waters* with Toyin Falola.

BAIYEE-MBI AGBOR-BAIYEE is the president and chief executive officer of the African University Foundation in Indianapolis, Indiana. He is responsible for setting the strategic vision of the foundation including planning, organizing, implementing, and monitoring the fund-raising operations to mobilize resources to launch an African university in Cameroon. He holds a PhD in agricultural economics from the University of Illinois, Urbana-Champaign, an MS in agribusiness management, and a BS in agricultural economics from Alabama A&M University, Normal. He is an associate faculty member in the Department of Economics at Indiana University–Purdue University Indianapolis (IUPUI). He teaches applied business statistics, principles of economics, and international economics courses. He is also a consultant to business ventures in Cameroon.

IYIOLA ALADE AJAYI received his BS and MS from the University of Ibadan, Nigeria. He also studied industrial relations and personnel management at the University of Lagos, Nigeria. He is an associate of The Chartered Institute of Personnel Management of Nigeria. Currently he teaches economics in the College of Business and Social Sciences, Crawford University, in Ogun State, Nigeria. His research areas of interest are the public sector, development, health, labor, and environmental economics. He has attended and presented scholarly papers at conferences both in and outside of Nigeria.

ADEYEMI BABALOLA is a graduate of both the University of Lagos and Obafemi Awolowo University, Ile-Ife Nigeria. He is currently pursuing his MPhil/PhD degree at Obafemi Awolowo University and his area of specialization is financial management. He has attended several conferences and has a reasonable number of publications (local and international) to his credit. He is a Lecturer 1 in the Department of Accounting and Finance at Crawford University in Ogun State, Nigeria, where he teaches business finance, financial management, capital market, and portfolio theory among other subjects.

KAREN E. BRAVO is a professor of law and John S. Grimes Fellow and Dean's Fellow at the Indiana University School of Law–Indianapolis, where she teaches business organizations and public and private international law courses, including illicit international markets (concerning the transborder traffic in people, money, and drugs). Professor Bravo practiced corporate law with international law firms in New York and Massachusetts before joining the American Bar Association Central European and Eurasian Law Initiative (ABA/CEELI) in the Republic of Armenia, where she worked with domestic judiciary and advocates, and local and international NGOs on legal reform and education programs and strategies. Following her return from Armenia, Professor Bravo received her LLM in international trade regulation from New York University School of Law in 2004. Her research interests include human trafficking, labor liberalization, and regional integration. Her publications include *Exploring the Analogy between Modern Trafficking in Humans and the Trans-Atlantic Slave Trade; Free Labor! A Labor Liberalization Solution to Modern Trafficking in Persons; Regional Trade Arrangements and Labor Liberalization: (Lost) Opportunities for Experimentation?*; and *International Economic Law in U.S. Law Schools: Evaluating Its Pedagogy and Identifying Future Challenges.* Professor Bravo is a graduate of the University of the West Indies, Columbia University School of Law, and New York University School of Law.

GRACIA CLARK is an associate professor of anthropology at Indiana University in Bloomington. She has studied the Kumasi Central Market in Ghana, West Africa, since 1978. Her thesis research in social anthropology at the University of Cambridge highlighted the regional dominance of this daily market and the relations of credit, leadership, and domestic work that kept its twenty thousand traders in their stalls. She consulted for the ILO and UNIFEM for several years before teaching at University of Wisconsin, Parkside and the University of Michigan, Ann Arbor. Subsequent fieldwork addressed development issues of food security and trade liberalization and lastly recorded life stories from older traders. A 2010 volume of life stories titled *Asante Market Women* (IUP) complements her 1994 book, *Onions Are My Husband*.

TOYIN FALOLA is the Frances Higginbotham Nalle Centennial Professor of History and Distinguished Teaching Professor at the University of Texas at Austin. He is the Nelson Mandela Professor of African Studies at Large, the Julius Nyerere Chair in Modern African Studies at Benue State University in Nigeria, and the Ibn Khaldun Distinguished Research Professor. He is the author/editor of more than 114 books, numerous journal articles, and book chapters. He has received numerous teaching awards, including the 2000 Jean Holloway Award for Teaching Excellence, the 2001 Texas Excellence Teaching Award, the 2003 Chancellor's Council Outstanding Teaching Award, and the 2004 Academy of Distinguished Teachers Award. He is the recipient of numerous awards through the years including the 2008 Quintessence Award, the 2007 Distinguished Africana Award, the 2007 Amistad Award for Academic Excellence in Historical Scholarship on Africa and the African Diaspora, the 2007 SIRAS Award for Outstanding Contribution to African Studies, and the Africana Studies Distinguished Global Scholar Lifetime Achievement Award from Indiana University–Purdue University Indianapolis.

BESSIE HOUSE-SOREMEKUN is the director of Africana Studies, the Public Scholar in African American Studies, Civic Engagement, and Entrepreneurship, professor of political science, and professor of Africana studies at Indiana University–Purdue University Indianapolis. She is also the founding executive director of the Center for Global Entrepreneurship and Sustainable Development at IUPUI. She has published six books, numerous journal articles, and book chapters. Over the past fifteen years, she also created four other entrepreneurial centers, including the National Center for Entrepreneurship, Inc., the Center for the Study and Development of Minority Business at Kent State University, the Entrepreneurial Academy of the Cleveland Empowerment Zone, and the Youngstown Entrepreneurial Academy, in collaboration with a host of community partners. These centers have helped to create many new businesses and contributed to economic development processes in the United States. She has written and received twenty-one grant awards and other funding support totaling more than $1.2 million from federal, state, and local agencies/foundations, as well as several universities to conduct research on globalization and entrepreneurship and to develop business training programs to create jobs, enhance economic development, and promote economic self-sufficiency.

STEPHEN D. KPINPUO is a doctoral student at the Department of Organizational Leadership and Supervision, Purdue University, Indiana. His research interests lie in the use of technology transfer, organizational effectiveness, and workforce development in promoting sustainable development in sub-Saharan Africa and beyond. He attained an interdisciplinary background in linguistics, educational studies, and organizational leadership through international education and research in sub-Saharan Africa, Europe, and the United States.

CHARLES J. MAMBULA currently serves as associate professor and chair of the Department of Management at Langston University's School of Business in Langston, Oklahoma. Before he came to Langston, he taught at various educational institutions in Massachusetts, including Suffolk University, Merrimack College, Fisher College, and Salem State College. He briefly worked with the Small Business Development Institute at Morgan State University in Baltimore, Maryland, before coming to Massachusetts. Mambula has worked with the Nigerian National Petroleum Corporation (NNPC) at the Eleme Petro-Chemicals Company Limited (EPCL) in Port Harcourt as the chief marketing officer. Before this, he worked as a civil servant with the Borno State Government Civil Service as registrar for cooperatives, commercial officer, and senior planning officer in charge of research. His work has been published in a number of journals and other publications, which include *International Journal of Entrepreneurship, Journal of Small Business Economics, Journal of African Business, Journal of Social Economics* (Special Issue), and *the International Journal of Nigerian Studies and Development.*

JOHN BABATUNDE BAMIDELE OJO received his PhD at Howard University in Washington, DC. He is the author of "Confronting the Future: An Advocacy Agenda and Program" in *The Yoruba Transition: History, Values, and Modernity,* edited by Toyin Falola and Ann Genova. His research interests include international security, arms control and disarmament, global politics, and international relations. Currently, he works for the government of the District of Columbia in Washington.

MARY J. OSIRIM is professor of sociology, codirector of the Center for International Studies, and faculty diversity liaison at Bryn Mawr College. Her teaching and research interests have focused on gender and development, race and ethnic relations, immigration, the family, and economic sociology in sub-Saharan Africa, the English-speaking Caribbean, and the United States. During the past twenty years, she has conducted fieldwork on women, entrepreneurship, and the roles of the state and nongovernmental organizations in the microenterprise sectors of Nigeria and Zimbabwe in which Bryn Mawr students participated as research assistants. She has many publications in these areas in such journals as *International Sociology, Gender and Society,* and *Women's Studies International Forum* and in a coedited special edition of *African and Asian Studies.* Her book in this field, *Enterprising Women: Gender, Microbusiness, and Globalization in Urban Zimbabwe,* was published by the Woodrow Wilson Center Press and Indiana University Press in 2009. Currently her research focuses on transnationalism and community development among African immigrants in the northeastern United States. Her research was included in her recently published book *Global Philadelphia: Immigrant Communities, Old and New,* coedited with Ayumi Takenaka. She has received several awards and fellowships, including grants from the National Science Foundation, a Pew Faculty Fellowship in International Affairs, a Carter G. Woodson Fellowship at the University of Virginia, and a fellowship at the Woodrow Wilson International Center for Scholars.

RUBIN PATTERSON is professor of sociology, director of Africana studies, and chair of the Department of Sociology and Anthropology at the University of Toledo. He was associate editor of the *Journal of Developing Societies* for several years, and he is currently chief editor of *Perspectives on Global Development and Technology*. His areas of research are sustainability entrepreneurship, eco-industrial development, migration and African development, environmental justice and sustainable development, and comparative diaspora studies.

ULF RICHTER is visiting assistant professor of management at Portland State University. He previously taught at CENTRUM Catolica, Pontifica Universidad Catolica del Peru, and at Centre de Recherche et d'Action pour la Paix and the International University of Grand Bassam in Côte d'Ivoire. He received his doctorate in economic sciences from the University of Lausanne. His research interests include corporate social responsibility, corporate strategy, global supply chains, and sustainable entrepreneurship in emerging markets. He recently founded Kachile, a social enterprise dedicated to alleviating poverty through creating digital opportunities in West Africa, and NunaLab, which focuses on sustainable product development in Peru.

ABDOULAYE SAINE is professor of African studies and international political economy in the Department of Political Science at Miami University of Ohio. He received BA (honors), MA, and PhD degrees from the University of Denver. He is the author of numerous journal articles and several books, including *The Paradox of Third-Wave Democratization in Africa: The Gambia under AFPRC-APRC Rule, 1994–2008*, which was nominated for two book awards. He is completing a book for Greenwood Press on the Gambia. His coedited book *Electrons and Democratization in West Africa, 1990–2010* was published by Africa World Press in March 2011.

RICARDO REAL PEDROSA DE SOUSA is a doctoral candidate in development studies at the International Institute of Social Studies of the Erasmus University of Rotterdam in the Netherlands. He is also a researcher on conflict with the African Studies Center of ISCTE–Lisbon University Institute in Portugal. He holds an MS in development studies from the School of Oriental and African Studies (SOAS) of the University of London and a bachelor's (honors) degree in corporate organization and management from ISCTE–Lisbon University Institute. With a background in management for corporate transformation, he has had assignments in the private sector, public sector, and civil society as well as in multilateral institutions as a development practitioner. More recently, he has been involved in research projects regarding the dynamics of the political economy of conflict in Angola and in the Horn of Africa. His PhD research focuses on the relationship between external interventions and peace in Africa.

MARTIN SPECHLER is professor of economics at Indiana University–Purdue University Indianapolis and a faculty member of the Uralic and Altaic National Resource Center, Indiana University. A graduate of Harvard University, he has worked in Central Asia since 1997 as a consultant for the World Bank, Asian Development Bank, Global Development Network, and USAID. He is the author of more than one hundred articles and book reviews related to Eurasia. His most recent book is *The Political Economy of Reform in Central Asia: Uzbekistan under Authoritarianism*, published by Routledge in 2009 in their Central Asia Research Forum series, edited by Shirin Akiner. He has just completed a paper on human rights in Central Eurasia.

KOLA SUBAIR teaches at Kwara State University, Malete. He is presently the director of the Kwara State University Foundation Scheme and editor-in-chief of the *Journal of Economics and Allied Studies*, while also serving as an editorial board member of the *Journal of Economics and International Finance*. He has published articles in books and scholarly journals and is currently working on a new book titled *Entrepreneurship and Economic Development in Nigeria: Challenges and Opportunities*. He is a member of various professional associations and networks, including the American Economic Association, the Midwest Economics Association, the Nigerian Economic Society, International Development Economics Associates, and Social Science Research Network.

CHRISTOPHER E. S. WARBURTON is a member of the Economics Department at the John Jay College of Criminal Justice. He teaches international economics, corporate white-collar crime, and finance for forensic economics at the undergraduate level, and principles of economics and research methods at the graduate level. He obtained his PhD in economics from Fordham University in New York (2003) after specializing in international economics. His research interests include stabilization policies in Africa and Latin America, sustainable development, exchange rate valuation, corporate crime, and international economic law. His recent publications include "War and Exchange Rate Valuation," in *The Economics of Peace and Security Journal* (2009); "Corporate Crime and Macroeconomic Performance," in *The International Journal of Interdisciplinary Social Sciences* (2009); and "International Trade Law and Trade Theory," in the *Journal of International Trade Law and Policy* (2010).

BENAIAH YONGO-BURE is associate professor of social science at Kettering University, Flint, Michigan, where he teaches economics and social science. Yongo-Bure obtained his PhD and MA from Dalhousie University, Canada, after graduating with a BA (honors) from Makerere University, Uganda. Yongo-Bure has published numerous articles in journals and edited books. His main book publications are *Economic Development of Southern Sudan* (2007) and *North-South Relations in Sudan since the Addis Ababa Agreement* (coedited, 1988). His latest article is "Marginalization and War: From the South to Darfur" (2009). His areas of research interest include regional integration and economic development in Africa as well as issues of conflict and peace.

Index

Rochester Studies in
African History and the Diaspora

Toyin Falola, Senior Editor
The Frances Higginbotham Nalle Centennial Professor in History
University of Texas at Austin

(ISSN: 1092-5228)

*Power Relations in Nigeria: Ilorin Slaves
and their Successors*
Ann O'Hear

Dilemmas of Democracy in Nigeria
Edited by Paul Beckett and
Crawford Young

Science and Power in Colonial Mauritius
William Kelleher Storey

*Namibia's Post-Apartheid Regional
Institutions: The Founding Year*
Joshua B. Forrest

*A Saro Community in the Niger Delta,
1912–1984: The Potts-Johnsons of Port
Harcourt and Their Heirs*
Mac Dixon-Fyle

*Contested Power in Angola,
1840s to the Present*
Linda Heywood

*Nigerian Chiefs: Traditional Power in
Modern Politics, 1890s–1990s*
Olufemi Vaughan

*West Indians in West Africa, 1808–1880:
The African Diaspora in Reverse*
Nemata Blyden

*The United States and Decolonization in
West Africa, 1950–1960*
Ebere Nwaubani

Health, State, and Society in Kenya
George Oduor Ndege

Black Business and Economic Power
Edited by Alusine Jalloh and
Toyin Falola

Voices of the Poor in Africa
Elizabeth Isichei

*Colonial Rule and Crisis in Equatorial
Africa: Southern Gabon ca. 1850–1940*
Christopher J. Gray

*The Politics of Frenchness in
Colonial Algeria, 1930–1954*
Jonathan K. Gosnell

*Sources and Methods in African History:
Spoken, Written, Unearthed*
Edited by Toyin Falola and
Christian Jennings

*Sudan's Blood Memory:
The Legacy of War, Ethnicity, and
Slavery in Early South Sudan*
Stephanie Beswick

Few studies of globalization have analyzed its impact on African societies from the viewpoint of sustainable development. This volume answers that need. The essays here contribute to the store of knowledge about globalization in sub-Saharan Africa by documenting the affect of this global force on the continent's economic, political, and cultural development. This interdisciplinary collection provides comprehensive analyses—at the international, national, and local levels—of the theoretical issues revolving around the complex process of globalization, while offering detailed examinations of new models of economic development that can be implemented in sub-Saharan Africa to enhance economic growth, self-sufficiency, and sustainable development. These models are accessible to politicians, public policy analysts, scholars, students, international organizations, nongovernmental actors, and members of the public at large. Finally, the essays here provide insightful case studies of African countries that already demonstrate creative, indigenous-based models of entrepreneurship and discuss efforts to achieve sustainable development and economic independence at the grassroots level. Contributors represent the disciplines of law, history, political science, economics, sociology, anthropology, business and management, African studies and art history, and education.

Dr. Bessie House-Soremekun is an award-winning author and internationally recognized scholar, expert, and advocate on entrepreneurship and economic development. She is the director of Africana studies; Public Scholar in African American Studies, Civic Engagement, and Entrepreneurship; professor of political science and Africana studies; and the founding executive director of the Center for Global Entrepreneurship and Sustainable Development at Indiana University–Purdue University, Indianapolis.

Dr. Toyin Falola, Fellow of the Nigerian Academy of Letters and Fellow of the Historical Society of Nigeria, is the Frances Higginbotham Nalle Centennial Professor in History and Distinguished Teaching Professor at the University of Texas at Austin. He is also the Nelson Mandela Professor of African Studies at Large, the Julius Nyerere Chair in Modern African Studies at Benue State University in Nigeria, and the Ibn Khaldun Distinguished Research Professor.

Contributors: Aderonke Adesola Adesanya, Baiyee-Mbi Agbor-Baiyee, Iyiola Alade Ajayi, Adeyemi Babalola, Karen E. Bravo, Gracia Clark, Toyin Falola, Bessie House-Soremekun, Stephen D. Kpinpuo, Charles J. Mambula, John Babatunde Bamidele Ojo, Mary J. Osirim, Rubin Patterson, Ulf Richter, Abdoulaye Saine, Ricardo Real Pedrosa de Sousa, Martin Spechler, Kola Subair, Christopher E. S. Warburton, Benaiah Yongo-Bure

"Utilizing all of the social sciences, these essays approach the question of globalization with breadth and fresh thinking, and suggest avenues for further development in Africa with ingenuity. The result is a collection that will be of value to historians, economists, and political scientists on one side, and government policy planners on the other."

—Andrew Barnes, associate professor of history,
Arizona State University

"Bessie House-Soremekun and Toyin Falola have assembled here relevant, far-reaching, and carefully written essays on Africa's development in a global age. The volume is a timely response to the economic and political issues challenging Africa's growth at this crucial period in world history. A must read for those interested in contemporary Africa."

—Tanure Ojaide, Frank Porter Graham
Professor of Africana Studies, The University of
North Carolina at Charlotte

Lightning Source UK Ltd.
Milton Keynes UK
UKHW011948111119
353331UK00001B/3/P